W9-BER-497

STUDY GUIDE

for Stiglitz's

Economics

Second Edition

This single-user password is valid for 12 months
from first use of the StigWeb website:

www.wwnorton.com/stigweb

Password : 3L3C5MI

STUDY GUIDE

for Stiglitz's

Economics

Second Edition

LAWRENCE W. MARTIN
Michigan State University

W · W · NORTON & COMPANY · NEW YORK · LONDON

Copyright © 1997, 1993 by W. W. Norton & Company, Inc.

All rights reserved

Second edition

Printed in the United States of America

ISBN 0-393-96896-0 (pbk.)

W. W. Norton & Company, Inc., 500 Fifth Avenue, New York, N.Y. 10110
http://www.wwnorton.com

W. W. Norton & Company, Ltd., 10 Coptic Street, London WC1A 1PU

1 2 3 4 5 6 7 8 9 0

CONTENTS

PREFACE

This Study Guide is designed to aid in your understanding, assimilation, and the use of the material in Joseph Stiglitz's *Economics, Second Edition*. The chapters in this volume correspond those in the main text, and each one is divided into three parts. The first part contains a *Chapter Review,* an *Essential Concepts* section, and a *Behind the Essential Concepts* section. The *Chapter Review* begins with a brief paragraph explaining how each chapter in Stiglitz fits into the overall structure of the text. the *Essential Concepts* section is a summary of the chapter, bringing out the main points covered. a *Behind the Essential Concepts* offers suggestions about how to avoid common mistakes and provides some intuitive explanations for difficult concepts. This section also brings out the similarities among related ideas and the common structure of many economic theories and concepts.

The second part of each chapter provides a "Self-Test" with true-or-false, multiple-choice, and completion ques-
tions. After reading the chapter in the text and going over the first part of the Study Guide chapter, you should take the self-test. It will help you determine those areas that need further study.

The final part of each chapter is called "Doing Economics: Tools and Practice Problems." This part is designed to teach you the basic skills of economics. The only way to do this is to sharpen up your pencil and try some exercises. If you're willing (or your teacher has assigned this material), I think you'll find the program useful. For each type of problem, there is a Tool Kit box that gives step-by-step instructions about how to use the appropriate tool, a worked problem with a step-by-step solution that follows the procedure outlined in the Tool Kit box, and several practice problems for you to do. Answers are provided at the end of each chapter.

Best of success with your course!

Part One

Introduction

Chapter 1

THE AUTOMOBILE AND ECONOMICS

Chapter Review

The story of the automobile in the United States is a rich one, introducing as it does the principal ideas of economics. The dominant idea is that economics is about the choices made by the three major groups of participants: individuals or households, firms, and the government. These choices control the allocation of resources, another central concern of economics. The automobile story also highlights the three markets on which this book focuses: product, labor, and capital. The chapter closes with a discussion of how economists use models and theories to describe the economy and why they sometimes disagree. This chapter sets the stage for the introduction of the basic economic model in Chapter 2.

ESSENTIAL CONCEPTS

1   The brief history of the automobile given here illustrates the broad and varied subject matter of economics and many of the important themes of this book. We see the importance of investors and entrepreneurs and the risks they face, and the central roles of research, technological advance, and patents. The problem of incentives appears both in the conflicting interests of Henry Ford and his investors and in the effect of high wages on his workers.

The upheavals caused by oil price increases in the 1970s and the influx of competition from foreign producers show us how the U.S. economy now functions in the world economy. Finally, a large and growing government presence has mandated environmental and safety regulations, supplied money to bail out a major producer, and provided protection against foreign competition.

2   Economics studies how **choices** are made by individuals, firms, governments, and other organizations and how those choices determine the allocation of resources. **Scarcity,** the fact that there are not enough resources to satisfy all wants, requires that choices must be made by individuals and by the economy as a whole. The fundamental questions that an economy must answer are the following:

a   What is produced, and in what quantities?
b   How are these goods produced?
c   For whom are these goods produced?
d   Who makes economic decisions, and by what process?

3   The U.S. economy is a mixed one that relies primarily on private decisions to answer the basic economic questions. **Markets,** which exist wherever and whenever exchanges occur, influence the choices of individuals and firms, but government also plays a prominent role. For

starters, the government sets the legal structure within which market forces operate. It also regulates private activity, collects taxes, produces some goods and services, and provides support for the elderly, poor, and others.

4   Trade takes place between individuals and firms in three major markets: the **product market,** the **labor market,** and the **capital market.** Figure 1.1 sketches the interactions. Notice that in general, individuals buy goods and services from firms; they also supply labor and funds for investment to firms.

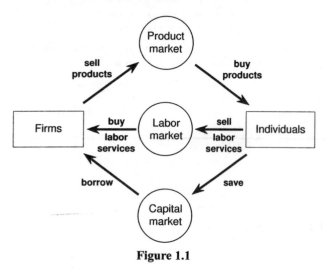

Figure 1.1

5   There are two broad branches in economics. **Microeconomics** studies the product, labor, and capital markets, focusing on the behaviour of individuals, households, firms, and other organizations that make up the economy. **Macroeconomics** looks at the performance of the economy as a whole and at such aggregate measures as unemployment, inflation, growth, and the balance of trade.

6   Economics uses models and theories, which are sets of assumptions and conclusions, to understand and predict the behaviour of the economy. Economists want to discover and interpret relationships among economic variables and especially to distinguish where there is causation and where there is only correlation.

7   Economists are frequently asked to give advice regarding public policy, and often they disagree, for two major reasons: they disagree about what is the appropriate theoretical model of the economy, and about the effects a policy will have.

BEHIND THE ESSENTIAL CONCEPTS

1   In this book you will learn many economic theories and models. Models and theories are simplified representations of the vast and complex economic world. The way that a model is made simple and workable is through assumptions. We assume that only certain factors are relevant to the problem at hand. Then we derive conclusions

from the assumptions and test the model by comparing its predictions with what we know of the world.

You need to do two different things with the models that you will come across in your study of economics. First, you must understand how the model works—specifically, what is assumed and how the conclusions follow. The second task is to evaluate how well the model explains what it is supposed to explain. As you read the many arguments and pieces of evidence, keep in mind how they fit with the model's basic assumptions and conclusions.

2   Economic **variables** are measurable, and they change. The price of potatoes is an economic variable; so is the rate of unemployment. We look for two types of relationships among these variables. First, we are interested in whether certain economic variables move together. For example, during the 1980s, the U.S. government ran up unprecedented peacetime budget deficits and also very high trade deficits. These two deficit variables were **correlated.** But we are also interested in whether a change in one variable **causes** a change in another variable. Specifically, did the high government budget deficits of the 1980s cause the large trade deficits? Before economists make conclusions, they require a sound model that shows how a change in an economic variable was caused and also some evidence that the model's assumptions are appropriate and that its predictions have actually occurred.

3   **Positive economics** focuses on questions about how the economy works. What does it do, and why does it do it? For example, how were the budget and trade deficits of the 1980s related? **Normative economics,** on the other hand, typically asks what should be done. Should we reduce the federal budget deficit? Keep in mind, however, that normative economics cannot prescribe which value to hold; it describes the appropriate policy given the value.

4   Microeconomics and macroeconomics are two ways of looking at the economy. Microeconomics looks from the bottom up; it starts with the behavior of individuals and firms and builds up to an understanding of markets and the economy as a whole. Macroeconomics, on the other hand, is a top-down look, beginning with a description of the performance of aggregate economic variables and then constructing explanations. Micro- and macroeconomics must fit together. The models that explain how individuals, firms, and markets work must be consistent with the models that we use to describe the economy as a whole. An important theme of this book is that the microeconomics in Parts One, Two, and Three provides a firm foundation for the macroeconomics to follow in Parts Four, Five, and Six.

SELF-TEST

True or False

1   Henry Ford patented the internal combustion engine.

2   Henry Ford paid his workers especially high wages because he wanted them to earn enough to buy his cars.

3 By and large, government has kept out of the automobile business.

4 Patents give exclusive rights to market an innovation for a limited period of time.

5 The U.S. government imposed a tariff on Japanese car imports in the early 1980s.

6 Economics studies how individuals, firms, governments, and other organizations make choices and how those choices determine the allocation of the economy's resources.

7 The four basic questions concerning how economies function are what is produced and in what quantities, how are the goods produced, for whom are they produced, and who makes the decisions?

8 Most resource allocation decisions are made by governments in the U.S. economy.

9 In centrally planned economies, most decisions are made by the government.

10 The three major markets are the product, labor, and insurance markets.

11 Microeconomics focuses on the behavior of the economy as a whole.

12 Macroeconomics studies the behavior of firms, households, and individuals.

13 Two economic variables are correlated if there is a systematic relationship between them.

14 When two variables are correlated, it is because changes in one cause changes in the other.

15 Normative economics deals with questions concerning how the economy actually works.

Multiple Choice

1 Henry Ford paid his workers more than the going rate chiefly because

a he feared that the government would set minimum wages if he paid low wages;

b he could thereby obtain a hard-working, productive labor force;

c he did not care about profits, only the well-being of his workers;

d his highly paid workers would buy more of his cars;

e his highly paid workers would pay more taxes.

2 Patents

a give inventors exclusive rights to produce and market their inventions for a limited time;

b allow inventors to charge high prices without fear of competition.

c provide incentives to encourage new inventions;

d are awarded for innovations, not ideas;

e all of the above.

3 In the 1980s, the U.S. government negotiated limitations on exports of Japanese automobiles to the United States. As a result,

a the U.S. automobile industry recaptured its lost market share;

b automobile prices increased;

c Japanese firms set up plants in the United States;

d the Japanese government retaliated with restrictions on exports of U.S. automobiles to Japan;

e b and c.

4 Because resources are scarce,

a questions must be answered;

b choices must be made;

c all except the rich must make choices;

d governments must allocate resources;

e some individuals must be poor.

5 Which of the following is not a fundamental question concerning how economies funtion?

a What is produced, and in what quantities?

b How are the goods produced?

c For whom are they produced?

d Who makes the decisions?

e All of the above are fundamental questions.

6 In market economies, the four basic questions are answered

a by elected representatives;

b in such a way as to ensure that everyone has enough to live well;

c by private individuals and firms, interacting in markets;

d according to the traditional way of doing things;

e by popular vote.

7 In market economies, goods are consumed by

a those who are most deserving;

b those who work the hardest;

c those who are politically well connected;

d those who are willing and able to pay the most;

e those who produce them.

8 Which of the following is one of the three major markets?

a goods market;

b labor market;

c capital market;

d Common Market;

e all of the above.

9 The detailed study of firms, households, individuals, and the markets where they transact is called

a macroeconomics;

b microeconomics;

c normative economics;

d positive economics;

e aggregate economics.

10 The study of the behavior of the economy as a whole, especially such factors as unemployment and inflation, is called

a macroeconomics.

b microeconomics.

c normative economics.

d   positive economics.
e   market economics.

11   An economic theory or model is a

a   mathematical equation;
b   prediction about the future of the economy;
c   recommended reform in government policy that pays attention to the laws of economics;
d   set of assumptions and conclusions derived from those assumptions;
e   small-scale economic community set up to test the effectiveness of a proposed government program.

12   Which of the following is an example of causation?

a   Taxes are too high.
b   The trade deficits of the 1980s were the direct result of the decade's budget deficits.
c   During the 1980s the United States experienced high trade and budget deficits.
d   In mixed economies there is a role for government and a role for markets.
e   U.S. interest rates fell during the early 1990s.

13   Which of the following is an example of correlation?

a   The high budget deficits of the 1980s caused the trade deficits.
b   Taxes are too high.
c   During recessions, output falls and unemployment increases.
d   In mixed economies, there is a role for markets and a role for government.
e   Economics studies choices and how choices determine the allocation of resources.

14   Which of the following is an example of normative economics?

a   The high budget deficits of the 1980s caused the trade deficits.
b   During recessions, output falls and unemployment increases.
c   Lower interest rates would encourage investment.
d   Interest rates should be reduced to encourage investment.
e   Expansionary monetary policy will reduce interest rates.

15   Which of the following is an example of positive economics?

a   Taxes are too high.
b   U.S. savings rates are too low.
c   Lower interest rates would encourage investment.
d   Interest rates should be reduced to encourage investment.
e   There is too much economic inequality in the United States.

16   In the United States, the question of what is produced and in what quantities is answered

a   primarily by private decisions influenced by prices;
b   by producing what was produced the previous year;
c   primarily by government planning;
d   randomly;
e   according to majority vote.

17   In which of the following does the government determine what is produced, how, and for whom?

a   market economies;
b   mixed economies;
c   centrally planned economies;
d   tradition-bound economies;
e   all of the above

18   Choices must be made because

a   resources are scarce;
b   human beings are choice-making animals;
c   government regulations require choices to be made;
d   economic variables are correlated;
e   without choices, there would be no economics as we know it.

19   Anything that can be measured and that changes is

a   a correlation;
b   a causation;
c   a variable;
d   a value;
e   an experiment.

20   In the labor market,

a   households purchase products from firms;
b   firms purchase the labor services of individuals;
c   firms raise money to finance new investment;
d   households purchase labor services from firms;
e   borrowing and lending are coordinated.

Completion

1   Exchanges take place in _____.

2   In a _____ economy, some decisions are made chiefly by government and others by markets.

3   All the institutions involved in borrowing and lending money make up the _____ market.

4   The behavior of the economy as a whole, and especially of certain aggregate measures such as unemployment and inflation, is called _____.

5   The branch of economics that focuses on firms, households, and individuals and studies product, labor, and capital markets is called _____.

6   The statement that crime rates are higher in low-income areas is an example of _____.

7   The statement that poverty leads to crime is an example of _____.

8   Economists use _____, which are sets of assumptions, conclusions, and data, to study the economy and evaluate the consequences of various policies.

9   _____ economics rests on value judgments; _____ economics describes how the economy behaves.

10   The four basic questions that economists ask about the economy are (1) what is produced and in what quantities, (2) _____, (3) for whom are they produced, and (4) who makes the decisions?

Answers to Self-Test

True or False

1	f	6	t	11	f
2	f	7	t	12	f
3	f	8	f	13	t
4	t	9	t	14	f
5	f	10	f	15	f

Multiple Choice

1	b	6	c	11	d	16	a
2	e	7	d	12	b	17	c
3	e	8	d	13	c	18	a
4	b	9	b	14	d	19	c
5	e	10	a	15	c	20	b

Completion

1 markets
2 mixed
3 capital
4 macroeconomics
5 microeconomics
6 correlation
7 causation
8 theories or models
9 Normative, positive
10 how are these goods produced

Chapter 2

THINKING LIKE AN ECONOMIST

Chapter Review

The concept of scarcity discussed in Chapter 1 implies that choices must be made. This chapter begins to explain how economists think about choice, and how choices are influenced and coordinated by markets. A basic economic assumption is that of rational choice, which simply says that people select the alternative they prefer most from among all those that are available. The alternatives available to any particular firm or individual, of course, depend upon the choices made by other firms and individuals. All of these rational choices must somehow fit together, and markets serve the function of coordinating them. How they do so is the subject of Chapters 3 through 5.

ESSENTIAL CONCEPTS

1   The **basic economic model** includes three elements: individuals, firms, and markets. Economic decisions such as what and how much of each type of good to produce, how to produce them, what kind of career to pursue, and how to spend one's earnings are made by **rational, self-interested individuals** and **rational,** **profit-maximizing firms. Markets** serve the economic role of coordinating these decisions.

2   The basic economic model assumes that markets are **perfectly competitive.** In perfectly competitive markets, there are many consumers and firms, and each is small relative to the size of the overall market. One key feature of perfect competition is that any firm charging more than the going price will lose all its customers. Without any ability to influence the market price, the firm is a **price taker.** (Later in this book, we will encounter monopolists and others known as **price makers,** who have the power to charge higher prices without losing all their customers.)

3   Private **property rights** play an important role in the basic model. They include the right to use resources in certain ways and the right to sell them in markets. These two aspects of property rights provide incentives to use resources efficiently and to transfer resources to their most valuable use. Inefficiencies can arise when property rights are ill-defined or restricted.

4   When compensation is tied to performance, people have strong incentives to work hard and be productive, but those who are more fortunate and successful also will earn higher incomes. On the other hand, distribut-

ing the output more equally undermines incentives. This **incentive-equality trade-off** is one of the basic questions facing societies: how should the tax and welfare system be constructed to balance the competing ends of providing strong incentives and promoting equality?

5   **Scarcity** implies that not everyone who desires a good or resource can have it: there is an allocation problem. In market economies, goods are allocated to the highest bidder. Another solution to the allocation problem is to **ration**. Rationing schemes include queues, first-come-first-served, lotteries, and coupons. Unless supplemented by markets, rationing schemes will likely lead to inefficiencies.

6   The basic economic model assumes that decisions are made rationally, which simply means that individuals and firms balance the benefits and costs of their decisions. Economists see rational decision making as a two-step process. First, find what alternatives are available. This step is the construction of the **opportunity set**. Next, select the best alternative from those within the opportunity set.

7   The chapter presents three types of opportunity sets. The **budget constraint** shows what combinations of goods can be consumed with a limtied amount of money. The **time constraint** indicates to what uses limited time can be put. Finally, the **production possibilities curve** depicts the combinations of goods that a firm or an entire economy can produce given its limited resources and the quality of the available technology.

8   The best alternatives in an opportunity set will lie along the outer edge. This is because people prefer more goods to less. Operating on the outer edge also implies that there will be a **trade-off**: more of one option means less of another. For example, on the budget constraint, consuming more of one good means that less money is available to spend on another good. On the time constraint, if an individual devotes more time to one activity, there is less time available for other endeavors. A society that chooses to produce more of one good must settle for less production of other goods.

9   The **opportunity cost** of a good or activity is the option forgone. The opportunity cost of consuming more of one good is consuming less of some alternative good. The opportunity cost of an activity is the other endeavor that would have been, but now cannot be, undertaken. The opportunity cost of producing one good is the necessarily lower production of another.

10 The opportunity cost, not the price, is the proper measure of the economic cost of any choice. For example, in addition to the ultimate purchase price, the opportunity cost of buying an automobile includes the time and expense devoted to investigating alternatives, searching for the best deal, and negotiating the terms.

11 Opportunity costs are measured in total and at the margin. When a firm is deciding where to locate its plant,

it compares the **total costs** at each location. When a firm is considering how large a plant to build, it looks at the costs of increasing or decreasing the size. These are the **marginal costs**, the costs of a little bit more or a little bit less.

BEHIND THE ESSENTIAL CONCEPTS

1   The basic competitive model introduced in this chapter is critical to your understanding of economics. It will be expanded and applied in all the chapters that follow, but you should master the concepts given in this chapter: rational individuals choose the best combinations of goods along their budget constraints, firms maximize profits, and trading takes place in competitive markets, where each individual and firm is a price taker.

2   The opportunity set itself shows all of the alternatives that are available. Because more is generally preferred to less, however, economists focus on the outer boundary of the opportunity set. For example, Figure 2.1 shows an opportunity set for a firm that must divide its resources between the production of canned and frozen vegetables. The entire shaded area shows all of the combinations that are possible. The economist's attention is drawn to the outer edge, the production possibilities curve, because to choose a combination inside (such as point *A*) would be inefficient.

3   The terms "opportunity set," "budget constraint," "trade-off," and "opportunity cost" are related, but they are distinct, and you should take care to understand each one. Figure 2.2 shows the opportunity set for a student who consumes hamburgers and pizzas. The **opportunity set** shows all of the combinations of hamburgers and pizzas that are affordable. Points *A* and *B* are affordable; they lie within the opportunity set, but have the critical characteristic of lying along its outer edge, which is the budget constraint. The trade-off is that more hamburgers mean fewer pizzas. If Joe chooses *B* rather than *A*, he eats another pizza and exactly two fewer hamburgers. The trade-off be-

Figure 2.1

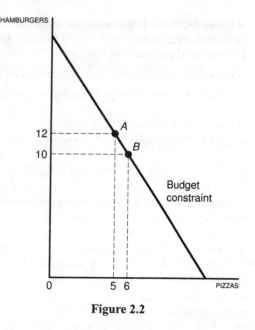

Figure 2.2

tween any two points measures the opportunity cost. In this case, the opportunity cost of this extra pizza is the two forgone burgers. When the outer edge of the opportunity set is a straight line, the trade-offs will be the same all along the line; when it is a curve, the trade-offs will change.

4   Opportunity costs are forgone alternatives—not money, not time, and not resources. For example, if you spend one hour in class tomorrow, the opportunity cost of attending that class is not the hour itself. That hour will pass whether you go to the class or not. The opportunity cost is what you would have done with that hour. It is the activity you give up. Strictly speaking, the opportunity cost of buying a book for $20 is not the money, but what would have been purchased with the $20 if it had not been spent on the book.

5   **Sunk costs,** outlays that cannot be recovered, are not opportunity costs. Because these expenditures are not affected by the choice of any alternative, they do not represent the opportunity cost of any alternative. For example, suppose that you sign a one-year lease on an apartment and are forbidden to sublet it. When you consider whether to stay in town for the summer or travel abroad, the rent owed your landlord is irrelevant. You cannot do anything about it. Regardless of which alternative you choose, you must pay the rent. The rent is a sunk cost, not an opportunity cost.

6   Be clear about the difference between total costs and marginal costs. Marginal costs are the costs of a little more or a little less of some activity. Before considering going into business, you evaluate that total opportunity costs of the enterprise—all of the costs of setting up the plant, designing and producing the product, and locating the market. When you are considering whether to produce another unit of output, however, it is the marginl opportunity cost that is important. The marginal cost of producing a little bit more is just the added cost

incurred when producing more with the plant already set up, the product designed, and the market found. These latter costs are not marginal.

7   **Diminishing returns** can be confusing at first. What the term means is that as more inputs are used in a production process, output increases at a diminishing rate. For example, suppose more migrant workers are hired to pick apples. Each additional worker results in more apples being picked in total, but the marginal contribution of the newest worker, how many extra apples are picked when he is hired, is not as great as that of the previously hired new workers. We can also say that the opportunity cost of increasing output—the marginal cost—is higher as output increases.

8   Another way to approach diminishing returns is to think about why the output of the marginal input is declining. The extra inputs are just as good at producing; however, as more are used, the production process becomes crowded. For example, when more workers are hired to pick apples, there are fewer apple trees per workers, and it is more difficult to pick apples.

SELF-TEST

True or False

1   The basic model of economics seeks to explain why people want what they want.

2   According to the basic competitive model, firms maximize profits (or stock market value).

3   Generally, inequality will be greater when society is organized to provide stronger incentives to perform efficiently.

4   A firm selling in a perfectly competitive market is a price taker because it cannot raise its price without losing all of its customers.

5   Both the right to use a resource in certain ways and the right to transfer that resource are important aspects of private property rights.

6   Commonly owned property is the reason for diminishing returns.

7   A legal entitlement—that is, the right to use a resource in certain ways but not to sell or trade it—probably prevents the resource from going to its highest valued use.

8   Lotteries are an inefficient means of allocating resources because they do not allocate goods to the highest bidder.

9   Rationing by queues wastes the time spent waiting in line.

10   The opportunity set includes only the best available alternative.

11   The production possibilities curve shows the boundary of the opportunity set.

12 The principle of diminishing returns says that as more units of any input are added to a production process, total output eventually falls.

13 If an economy is not using its resources in the most productive way, economists say that there is inefficiency.

14 Sunk expenditures do not represent opportunity costs.

15 If one pizza sells for $8 but two pizzas can be purchased for $12, the marginal cost of the second pizza is $6.

Multiple Choice

1 Which of the following is not a building block of the basic economic model?

   a   assumptions about how firms behave;
   b   assumptions about how consumers behave;
   c   assumptions about markets;
   d   assumptions about the behavior of government.
   e   All of the above are building blocks of the basic economic model.

2 Individuals and firms in the economy must make choices because of

   a   diminishing returns;
   b   rationality;
   c   scarcity;
   d   all of the above;
   e   none of the above.

3 The concept of rationality refers to

   a   the fact of scarcity;
   b   the principle of diminishing returns;
   c   the assumption that individuals have sensible goals;
   d   the assumption that individuals and firms weigh the costs and benefits of their choices;
   e   the assumption that individuals and firms are certain of the consequences of their choices.

4 A firm that cannot influence the price it sells its product for is called a

   a   price maker;
   b   price taker;
   c   rational decision maker;
   d   none of the above;
   e   all of the above.

5 In a pure market economy, incentives to work hard and produce efficiently are provided by

   a   the profit motive;
   b   government regulations;
   c   private property rights;
   d   both the profit motive and private property rights;
   e   all of the above.

6 When property is commonly owned, users

   a   do not maximize profits;
   b   violate the principle of rationality;
   c   ignore the principle of diminishing returns;
   d   have little incentive to maintain and preserve the value of the property;
   e   none of the above.

7 If owners are not allowed to sell their resources, then

   a   the resources will not go to the highest value users;
   b   the owners will not act rationally;
   c   their choices will not be limited to their opportunity sets;
   d   the market will be perfectly competitive;
   e   none of the above.

8 Allocating goods by lotteries, queues, and coupons are examples of

   a   rationing;
   b   not selling to the highest bidder;
   c   efficient ways of allocating resources;
   d   the profit motive;
   e   a and b.

9 Rationing by queues

   a   leads to an efficient allocation of resources;
   b   allocates goods to those willing to pay the most money;
   c   wastes the time spent waiting in line;
   d   is an efficient way of allocating scarce goods;
   e   a and c.

10 When goods are rationed by coupons and the coupons are not tradable,

   a   the goods do not go to the individuals who value them most;
   b   a black market may be established;
   c   individuals will not act rationally;
   d   a and b;
   e   none of the above.

11 Choices of individuals and firms are limited by

   a   time constraints;
   b   production possibilities;
   c   budget constraints;
   d   all of the above;
   e   none of the above.

12 Fred has $10 to spend on baseball cards and hamburgers. The price of baseball cards is $.50 per pack. Hamburgers sell at a price of $1.00 each. Which of the following possibilities is not in Fred's opportunity set?

   a   10 hamburgers and zero packs of baseball cards;
   b   5 hamburgers and 10 packs of baseball cards;
   c   2 hamburgers and 16 packs of baseball cards;
   d   1 hamburger and 18 packs of baseball cards.
   e   All of the above are in Fred's opportunity set.

13 The production possibilities curve

   a   shows the amounts of goods a firm or society might produce;
   b   is not a straight line because of the principle of diminishing returns;
   c   illustrates the trade-offs between goods;
   d   all of the above;
   e   none of the above.

14   Henry spends an hour shopping and buys one sweater for $30. The opportunity cost of the sweater is

   a   one hour;
   b $30;
   c   one hour plus $30;
   d   the next-best alternative uses of the hour and the $30;
   e   none of the above.

15   Renting an apartment, Jorge signs a lease promising to pay $400 each month for one year. He always keeps his word, and therefore he will pay the $400 each month whether he lives in the apartment or not. The $400 each month represents

   a   an opportunity cost;
   b   a sunk cost;
   c   a trade-off;
   d   a budget constraint;
   e   diminishing returns.

16   One box of Nature's Crunch Cereal sells for $2.55. Each box comes with a coupon worth $.50 off the purchase price of another box of Nature's Crunch Cereal. The marginal cost of the second box of this product is

   a $2.55;
   b $3.05;
   c $2.05;
   d $1.55;
   e   none of the above.

17   Making a rational choice involves

   a   identifying the opportunity set;
   b   defining the trade-off;
   c   calculating the opportunity costs;
   d   all of the above;
   e   none of the above.

18   Fred is considering renting an apartment. A one-bedroom apartment rents for $400, and a nice two-bedroom apartment can be had for $500. The $100 difference is

   a   the opportunity cost of the two-bedroom apartment;
   b   the marginal cost of the second bedroom;
   c   a sunk cost;
   d   the marginal cost of an apartment;
   e   none of the above.

19   If a firm changes from paying commissions on total sales to paying each member of its sales force a fixed salary, it will likely

   a   experience lower total sales;
   b   have greater equality in earnings of its sales representatives;
   c   see no difference because compensation is a sunk cost;
   d   a and b;
   e   none of the above.

20   Reducing taxes

   a   makes no difference because incentives do not matter;
   b   will likely increase inequality because those who work harder can keep more of their higher earnings;
   c   will likely increase inequality because those who are luckier can keep more of their higher earnings;
   d   b and c;
   e   none of the above.

Completion

1   Economists assume that people make choices _____, taking into consideration the costs and benefits of their alternatives.

2   A market with large numbers of buyers and sellers, each of whom cannot influence the price, is an example of _____.

3   The right of an owner of a resource to use it in certain ways and to sell it is called a _____.

4   Allocating goods and services by some means other than selling to the highest bidder is called _____.

5   The collection of all available opportunities is called the _____.

6   _____ limit choices.

7   The amount of goods that a business firm is able to produce is called its _____.

8   The idea that as more inputs are used in a production process each successive input eventually adds less to output is an example of the principle of _____.

9   The fact that more time spent studying means less time available for other activities illustrates a _____.

10   An expenditure that cannot be recovered is a _____ cost.

Answers to Self-Test

True or False

1	f	4	t	7	t	10	f	13	t
2	t	5	t	8	t	11	t	14	t
3	t	6	f	9	t	12	f	15	f

Multiple Choice

1	d	6	d	11	d	16	c
2	c	7	a	12	e	17	d
3	d	8	e	13	d	18	b
4	b	9	c	14	d	19	d
5	d	10	d	15	b	20	d

Completion

1   rationally
2   perfect competition
3   property right
4   rationing
5   opportunity set
6   Constraints
7   production possibilities
8   diminishing returns
9   trade-off
10   sunk

Doing Economics: Tools and Practice Problems

For the problem sets in this section, we reach into the economist's tool box for five important techniques, each of which will reappear throughout the remainder of the book. Three relate to the opportunity set: budget and time constraints, for which the outer edge of the opportunity set is a straight line; multiple constraints involving, for example, limits on both time and money; and production possibilities curves, which can be straight lines but more often exhibit diminishing returns and are curved. The remaining two techniques relate to costs: the distinction between sunk and opportunity costs, and the use of marginal analysis to balance costs and benefits.

STRAIGHT-LINE OPPORTUNITY SETS

The simplest type of opportunity set has an outer boundary that is a straight line. Examples include budget constraints, time constraints, and production possibilities, when there are constant returns. The budget constraint indicates what combinations of goods can be purchased with a limited amount of money. The time constraint indicates what combinations of time-consuming activities can be undertaken with a limited amount of time. The production possibilities curve (in this case it is a straight line) indicates what combinations of goods can be produced. Tool Kit 2.1 shows how to construct these opportunity sets.

Tool Kit 2.1: Plotting the Straight-Line Opportunity Set

Budget constraints, time constraints, and production possibilities are examples of straight-line opportunity sets. To draw the budget constraint you must know the size of the budget and the prices of the goods. The time constraint can be drawn given the total time available and the time requirements for each activity. To plot the production possibilities curve you need to know the resources and the technology. Follow this procedure to plot these straight-line opportunity sets.

Step one: Draw a set of coordinate axes. Label the horizontal axis as the quantity of one good or activity and the vertical axis as the quantity of the other good or activity.

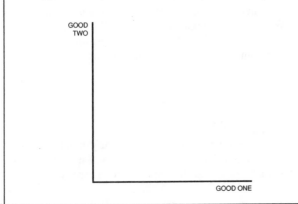

Step two: Calculate the maximum quantity of the good or activity measured on the horizontal axis. Plot this quantity along the horizontal axis.

Step three: Calculate the maximum quantity of the good or activity measured on the vertical axis. Plot this quantity along the vertical axis.

Step four: Draw a line segment connecting the two points. This line segment is the relevant part of the opportunity set.

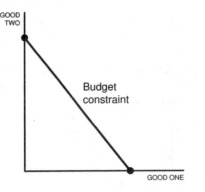

Step five: The slope is the opportunity cost of the good or activity measured on the horizontal axis. In the case of the budget constraint, it is called the relative price, the ratio of the price of the good measured on the horizontal axis divided by the price of the good measured on the vertical axis.

1   (Worked problem: budget constraint) Diana has an entertainment budget of $200 each month. She enjoys lunches with friends and going to the movies. The price of a typical lunch is $10. Movie tickets are $5 each. Construct her opportunity set.

Step-by-step solution

Step one: Draw coordinate axes and label the horizontal one "Lunches" and the vertical one "Movies." (There is no rule as to which good goes where. It would be fine if lunches were measured on the vertical axis and movies on the horizontal.)

Step two: Calculate the maximum quantity of lunches. This number is $200/$10 = 20 lunches. Plot this quantity along the horizontal axis.

Step three: Calculate the maximum quantity of movies. This number is $200/$5 = 40 movie tickets. Plot this quantity along the vertical axis.

Step four: Draw a line segment connecting these two points. This line segment is the budget constraint.

Step five: The slope of the budget constraint is 40/20 = 2. The price ratio is $10/$5 = 2. (Strictly speaking, these slopes are negative, but we follow the practice of dropping the negative sign as long as there is no confusion.)

2   (Practice problem: budget constraint) Velma Thomas must pay for both prescription medicine and nursing care for her elderly father. Each bottle of pills costs her $40, and the price of nursing care is $100 per day. She has been able to scrape together $1,000 each month for these expenses. Construct her opportunity set, going through all five steps.

3   (Practice problem: budget constraint) Construct the following opportunity sets.

   a   Clothing budget per year = $900; price of suits = $300; price of shoes = $90.
   b   Food budget = $200 per week; price of restaurant meals = $20; price of in-home meals = $5.
   c   School expense budget = $1,200 per semester; price of books = $50; price of courses = $200.
   d   Annual state transportation department budget = $100,000; cost of fixing potholes = $200; cost of replacing road signs = $500.

4   (Worked problem: time constraint) Ahmed likes to visit his invalid father across town. Each visit, including transportation and time with Dad, takes 3 hours. Another of Ahmed's favorite activities is his tango lessons. These are given downstairs in his apartment building and take only an hour each. With work and night school, Ahmed has only 15 hours each week to divide between visiting his father and tango lessons. Construct his opportunity set.

Step-by-step solution

Step one: The time constraint works very much like the budget constraint. Plot coordinate axes and label the horizontal one "Visits" and the vertical one "Lessons."

Step two: Calculate the maximum number of visits to his father. This number is 15/3 = 5 visits. Plot this quantity along the horizontal axis.

Step three: Calculate the maximum number of tango lessons. This number is 15/1 = 15 lessons. Plot this quantity along the vertical axis.

Step four: Draw a line segment connecting these two points. This line segment is the time constraint.

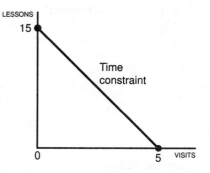

Step five: The slope of the time constraint is 15/5 = 3. The time-requirement ratio is 3/1 = 3.

5   (Practice problem: time constraint) Michael Terranova has 2 hours to make his house as clean as possible.

The place needs vacuuming and dusting. He can dust one piece of furniture in 10 minutes. Each room takes 20 minutes to vacuum. Plot his time constraint.

6   (Practice problem: time constraint) Construct the following opportunity sets.

   a   Total time available = 6 hours; time required to iron each shirt = 15 minutes; time required to iron each dress = 30 minutes.

   b   Total time available = 20 days; time required to study each chapter = 1/2 day; time required to write book reports = 2 days.

   c   Total time available = 40 hours; time required to counsel each disturbed teenager = 2 hours; time required to attend each meeting = 1 hour.

   d   Total time available = 8 hours; time required to visit each client = 4 hours; time required to telephone each client = 10 minutes.

7   (Worked problem: production possibilities curve) First, assume that there is one resource, which can be used in the production of either of two goods, and that there are no diminishing returns. In this case, the production possibilities curve is a straight line, and we treat it just as we did the budget and time constraints.

   There are 25 migrant farm workers employed at San Pueblo vegetable farm. Each worker can pick 4 bushels of cucumbers an hour. Alternatively, each worker can pick 1 bushel of peppers each hour. Each worker can work 8 hours a day. Plot the daily production possibilities curve.

Step-by-step solution

Step one: Plot coordinate axes and label the horizontal one "Cucumbers" (measured in bushels) and the vertical one "Peppers."

Step two: Calculate the maximum number of cucumbers that can be picked each day. This number is 25 (workers) × 8 (hours) × 4 (bushels an hour) = 800 bushels of cucumbers. Plot this number along the horizontal axis.

Step three: Calculate the maximum number of peppers that can be picked each day. This number is 25 (workers) × 8 (hours) × 1 (bushel an hour) = 200 bushels of peppers. Plot this number along the vertical axis.

Step four: Draw a line segment connecting these two points. This line segment is the production possibilities curve.

Step five: The slope is 200/800 = 1/4, which means that the opportunity cost of 1 bushel of cucumbers is 1/4 bushel of peppers.

8 (Practice problem: production possibilities curve) Coach Hun has four assistant coaches. They make recruiting visits and also run clinics for local youth. Each can make 32 recruiting visits a week. Alternatively, each can run 8 clinics in a week. Plot the production possibilities curve.

9 (Practice problem: production possibilities curve) Construct the following opportunity sets.

   a Total amount of land available = 10 acres of land; output of corn per acre = 2,000 bushels; output of wheat per acre = 1,000 bushels.

   b Total amount of labor available = 40 hours; output of donuts per hour = 150; output of sweet rolls per hour = 50.

   c Total amount of floor space available = 1,000 square feet; sales of women's sportswear per square foot = $500; sales of housewares per square foot = $200.

   d Total amount of fuel available = 5,000 gallons; miles per gallon for tank travel = 3; miles per gallon for armored personnel carriers = 9.

MULTIPLE CONSTRAINTS

Individuals often face more than one constraint. For example, many activities cost money and take up time. This means that the opportunity set includes only those alternatives that do not exceed both the budget and time constraints. Tool Kit 2.2 shows how to combine multiple constraints into a single opportunity set. Notice how the resulting opportunity set is convex.

Tool Kit 2.2: Plotting Multiple Constraints

When activities take both time and money, opportunities will be limited by two constraints. This is one example of the problem of multiple constraints. To plot the opportunity set when more than one constraint applies, follow this three-step procedure.

Step one: Plot the first constraint. (For example, this might be the budget constraint.)

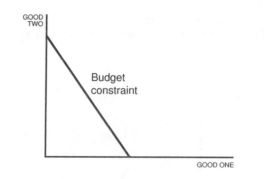

Step two: Plot the second constraint. (For example, this might be the time constraint.)

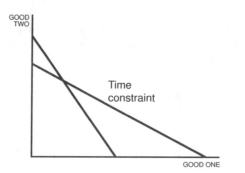

Step three: Darken the section of each constraint that lies under the other constraint. This is the outer edge of the opportunity set.

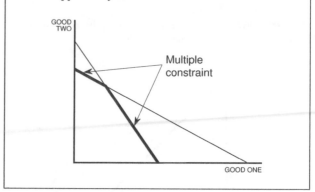

---

10 (Worked problem: multiple constraints) Out of work for six months, Donna feels that it is time to start looking for a job. Her father (gently) suggests that she apply in person to several of the retail stores on the west side of town. Each store application would require $5 in out-of-pocket expenses for transportation and dry

cleaning. (She realizes that only those who wear clean clothes stand any chance of receiving an offer.) Each trip would require 5 hours.

Donna's mother (not so gently) says that she should mail letters of application to a wide variety of potential employers. Each letter of application would require only $1 in mailing and copying costs and 1/2 hour of time.

Donna can devote 30 hours and $50 dollars each week to her job search campaign. Plot her opportunity set.

Step-by-step solution

Step one: Follow the procedure for plotting her budget constraint. Label the horizontal axis "Personal applications" and the vertical one "Mail applications." Your answer should look like this.

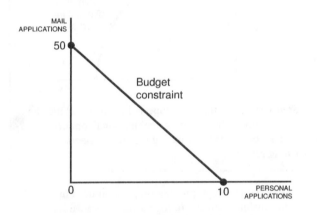

Step two: Follow the procedure for plotting her time constraint. Your answer should look like this.

Step three: Darken the section of each constraint that lies under the other constraint. Notice that between points *A* and *B* on the diagram, it is the budget constraint that is binding, but between *B* and *C*, the time constraint is the limiting one.

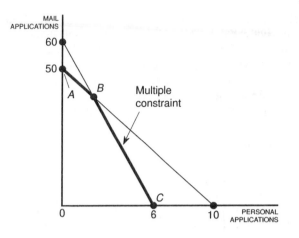

11 (Practice problem: multiple constraints) Harold's leaf-raking business is taking off. He has so many jobs to do that he is thinking of renting a leaf blower. This would cost him $20 per day. With a leaf blower, he could clean 10 lawns each day. He can only do 4 each day with his trusty rake, which costs nothing. Harold works 7 days each week, but has only $100 to spend. Plot his opportunity set for the week. (Hint: The axes should be labeled "Lawns cleaned with a leaf blower" and "Lawns raked by hand.")

12 (Practice problem: multiple constraints) The maintenance department at Alberti Van and Storage has 8 mechanic-hours to tune truck engines and replace the mufflers. It takes 1 hour to tune an engine and 1/2 hour to replace the muffler. In addition, the parts budget is only $100, the parts required to tune an engine cost $10, and each muffler costs $20. Construct the department's opportunity set.

13 (Practice problem: multiple constraints) Lamont tests swimming pools and cleans locker rooms for local country clubs. He has 20 hours available, and it takes him 1 hour to test each pool and 1/2 hour to clean each locker room. He has a budget of $50 to spend. It costs him $10 to test each pool and $1 to clean each locker room. Construct his opportunity set.

PRODUCTION POSSIBILITIES WITH DIMINISHING RETURNS

Usually, production is subject to diminishing returns. This means that as more of a resource is used in production, the extra (or marginal) output is less. In other words, although output increases, it does so at a diminishing rate. With diminishing returns the production possibilities curve acquires a convex shape. Tool Kit 2.3 shows how to plot the production possibilities curves when there are diminishing returns.

Tool Kit 2.3: Plotting the Production Possibilities Curve with Diminishing Returns

Diminishing returns mean that as more of some resource is used in production, the extra (or marginal) output declines. Follow this five-step procedure to plot the production possibilities curve with diminishing returns.

Step one: Draw and label a set of coordinate axes.

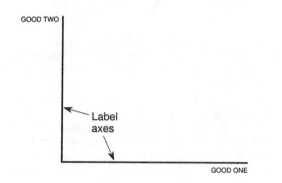

Step two: Calculate the total amount of the good measured on the horizontal axis that can be produced if all the resource is used. Plot this quantity along the horizontal axis.

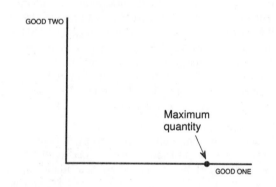

Step three: Calculate the total amount of the good measured on the vertical axis that can be produced if all the resource is used. Plot this quantity along the vertical axis.

Step four: Calculate and plot several other feasible combinations.

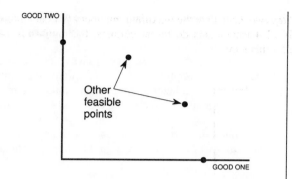

Step five: Draw a smooth curve connecting these points. This curve is the production possibilities curve.

Step six: Verify that the slope is increasing along the curve. Since the slope is the marginal opportunity cost of the horizontal axis good, this reflects diminishing returns.

14   (Worked problem: production possibilities curve with diminishing returns) Iatrogenesis, a medical laboratory, employs 4 lab technicians. Each is equally adept at analyzing throat cultures and distilling vaccines. The table below shows output per day for various numbers of lab technicians.

Technicians doing cultures	Throat cultures	Technicians doing vaccines	Vaccines
1	50	1	20
2	90	2	35
3	120	3	45
4	140	4	50

Plot the production possibilities curve for Iatrogenesis.

Step-by-step solution

Step one: Draw coordinate axes. Label the horizontal one "Throat cultures" and the vertical one "Vaccines."

Step two: Calculate the maximum number of throat cultures. If all 4 technicians do throat cultures, the number is 140. Plot this number.

Step three: Calculate the maximum number of vaccines. If all 4 technicians do vaccines, the number is 50. Plot this number.

Step four: Calculate several other feasible points. For example, if 1 technician does throat cultures, then 3 can do vaccines. Reading off the table, we see that the combination produced is 50 throat cultures and 45 vaccines. Similarly, if 2 do throat cultures and 2 do vaccines, the outputs are 90 throat cultures and 35 vaccines. Another feasible combination is 120 cultures and 20 vaccines. Plot these points.

Step five: Draw the production possibilities curve through the points that have been plotted.

Step six: Observe that, as expected, the slope gets steeper as the number of throat cultures is increased. This indicates diminishing returns.

15 (Practice problem: production possibilities curve with diminishing returns) Enormous State University has a crime problem. Members of the criminal element have stolen many bicycles and a great deal of stereo equipment. To address this crime wave, the campus police has hired 5 new officers. The following table gives the expected number of thefts for various assignments for these new officers.

New police officers assigned to bicycle duty	Reduction in bicycle thefts	New police officers assigned to dorm patrol	Reduction in thefts of stereo equipment
1	25	1	10
2	45	2	18
3	60	3	25
4	70	4	31
5	75	5	36

Plot the production possibilities curve.

16 (Practice problem: production possibilities curve with diminishing returns) Movaway Company has employed 4 maintenance inspectors for their fleet of trucks and forklifts. The following table shows how assigning inspectors leads to fewer breakdowns.

Inspectors assigned to check trucks	Reduced number of truck breakdowns	Inspectors assigned to check forklifts	Reduced number of forklift breakdowns
1	5	1	3
2	9	2	5
3	12	3	6
4	14	4	6

Plot Movaway's production possibilities curve, and verify that it shows diminishing returns.

17 (Practice problem: production possibilities curve with diminishing returns) The Dukakis vegetable farm (located on erstwhile corn-growing land in Iowa) has 800 tons of fertilizer. The following table shows how output of endive and bib lettuce is expected to respond to different amounts of fertilizer.

Fertilizer used on endive crop (tons)	Output of endive (bushels)	Fertilizer used on lettuce crop (tons)	Output of bib lettuce (bushels)
0	1,400	0	2,000
200	2,400	200	3,400
400	3,200	400	4,200
600	3,600	600	4,700
800	4,000	800	5,000

Plot the farm's production possibilities curve, and verify that it exhibits diminishing returns.

SUNK COSTS

Rational individuals make choices by carefully weighing the benefits and costs of their alternatives. Doing this requires a clear understanding of exactly what an opportunity cost is. Expenditures that cannot be recovered are not true opportunity costs. They are sunk costs and should be ignored when making decisions. Opportunity costs are foregone alternatives, and they are the only costs to consider. Tool Kit 2.4 shows how to distinguish true opportunity costs from sunk costs.

Tool Kit 2.4: Distinguishing Opportunity Costs and Sunk Costs

When an expenditure must be made regardless of what action is chosen, that expenditure is not an opportunity cost, it is a sunk cost. To find the opportunity cost of an action, it is necessary to see what is changed by undertaking that action rather than its alternative. Follow this four-step procedure.

Step one: To find the opportunity cost of an action, first specify the next-best alternative. This is what would be done if the action in question were not chosen.

Step two: Calculate the total cost for the action and its alternative.

Step three: Calculate the opportunity cost. Subtract the cost for the alternative from the cost for the action. This difference is the opportunity cost of the action.

Step four: Calculate the sunk costs. Any costs that are the same for both the chosen action and its alternative are sunk costs.

---

18   (Worked problem: opportunity costs and sunk costs) Upper Peninsula Airlines is studying the question of when to cancel flights for its Marquette to Detroit route. Flying nearly empty planes seems like bad business. The company wants to know the opportunity cost of going ahead with a scheduled round-trip flight. There are two scheduled flights each day. Here are some relevant cost data.

Salaries of crew	$ 1,000 per day
Fuel	$ 400 per round trip
Mortgage on plane	$ 100 per day
Landing fees	$ 50 in Marquette
	$ 100 in Detroit
Other in-flight costs	$ 100 per round trip

Calculate the opportunity cost of each round trip.

Step-by-step solution

Step one: The next-best alternative to going ahead with the scheduled round-trip flight is not flying.

Step two: Calculate the total cost for going ahead with the flight and canceling it. If the flight is made, the expenditures are all of those listed above. If the flight is canceled, the company saves on fuel, landing fees, and other in-flight costs. The salaries of the crew and the mortage must be paid whether the flight happens or not.

Expenditures if flight is not canceled =

$1,000 + $400 + $100 + $150 + $100 = $1,750.

Expenditures if flight is canceled = $1,000 + $100 = $1,100.

Step three: Calculate the opportunity costs: $1,750 − $1,100 = $650. This is the opportunity cost of the flight.

Step four: Calculate the sunk costs. The remaining $1,100 for salaries and mortgage are sunk costs. Whether or not the flight is canceled, these cannot be recovered.

19   (Practice problem: opportunity costs and sunk costs) Often during the summer term, courses are scheduled but canceled at Enormous State University's downtown education building. In order to see whether this is a good policy, the administration needs to know the opportunity cost of going ahead with a scheduled course offering. Here are some cost data.

Compensation for instructor	$4,000
Air conditioning and lighting	$1,000
Custodial services	$2,000
Property taxes	$2,500

Each course requires one room. Any rooms not used for summer courses can be rented to local groups for $1,200 for the summer term.

a   Find the opportunity cost of offering a course.
b   How much are sunk costs?

20   (Practice problem: opportunity cost and sunk costs) The Commerce Department is downsizing under Governor Scissorhands. It is considering offering early retirement to 8 bureaucrats in its strategic investment division. Each is 2 years from regular retirement age. (For simplicity, you may ignore discounting the second year's dollars in this problem.)

Salaries	$50,000 each (per year)
Fringe benefits	$20,000 each (per year)
Office space for all 8	$10,000 annually (lease signed for 1 more year)
Pension benefit	$20,000 each if retired (per year)

a If the 8 do receive early retirement, what is the opportunity cost?

b How much are sunk costs?

MARGINAL BENEFITS AND MARGINAL COSTS

The rational individual always considers the benefits and costs of any action. Once you decide to do something, however, there is the question of how much of it to do. Answering this question involves looking at the benefits and costs of a little more or a little less, the marginal benefits and marginal costs. Tool Kit 2.5 shows how to calculate and balance the marginal benefits and marginal costs of economic decisions.

Tool Kit 2.5: Using Marginal Benefits and Marginal Costs

The marginal benefit of an activity is the extra gain brought about by increasing that activity a little. The marginal cost is the corresponding cost. Rational individuals make efficient decisions by carefully balancing benefits and costs "at the margin." Follow this four-step procedure.

Step one: Identify the objective of the activity and the benefits and costs of various levels of the activity.

Step two: Calculate marginal benefits. These are the extra gains from a little bit more of the activity.

Step three: Calculate the marginal costs. These are the extra costs from a little bit more of the activity.

Step four: Choose the level of the activity for which the marginal benefits equal the marginal costs.

---

21 (Worked problem: marginal costs and marginal benefits) A new inoculation against Honduran flu has just been discovered. Presently, 55 people die from the disease each year. The new inoculation will save lives, but unfortunately, it is not completely safe. Some of the recipients of the shots will die from adverse reactions. The projected effects of the inoculation are given in Table 2.1.

Table 2.1

Percent of population inoculated	Deaths due to the disease	Deaths due to the inoculations
0	55	0
10	45	0
20	36	1
30	28	2
40	21	3
50	15	5
60	10	8
70	6	12
80	3	17
90	1	23
100	0	30

How much of the population should be inoculated?

Step-by-step solution

Step one: Identify the objective, benefits, and costs. The objective is to minimize total deaths from the disease and the inoculations, and the problem is to choose the percentage of the population to inoculate. The benefits are reduced deaths caused by the disease, and the costs are the deaths caused by the shots.

Step two: Calculate the marginal benefits. The first 10 percent of the population inoculated reduces deaths caused by the disease from 55 to 45. The marginal benefit of the first 10 percent is 10. From the second 10 percent (increasing the percentage from 10 to 20), the marginal benefit is 45 − 36 = 9. The schedule of the marginal benefit is given in Table 2.2.

Table 2.2

Percent of population	Marginal benefits
10	10
20	9
30	8
40	7
50	6
60	5
70	4
80	3
90	2
100	1

Step three: Calculate the marginal costs. Inoculating the first 10 percent causes no deaths. The second 10 percent (increasing the percent of the population getting the shots from 10 to 20 percent) causes 1 death. The schedule for the marginal costs is shown in Table 2.3.

Table 2.3

Percent of population	Marginal costs
0	0
10	1
20	1
30	1
40	1
50	2
60	3
70	4
80	5
90	6
100	7

Step four: Choose the level of inoculation percentage for which marginal benefits equal marginal costs. The percentage of the population to inoculate is 70. To see why this is correct, notice that inoculating 10 percent of the population saves 10 lives (marginal benefits = 10) and causes no deaths (marginal costs = 0). The net savings in lives is 10. Increasing the percentage to 20 percent saves 9 lives at a cost of 1 death. The net savings is 9 lives. Continuing as long as deaths do not rise gives 70 percent. Notice that increasing the percentage to 80 percent saves fewer people (marginal benefits = 2) than it kills (marginal costs = 4). This is a bad idea. We should stop at 70 percent.

22   (Practice problem: marginal costs and marginal benefits) The transportation department has 10 workers fixing potholes. It is considering allocating some of these workers to reprogram traffic lights. Each activity saves travel time for commuters, and this is the objective of the transportation department. Table 2.4 gives time savings of each activity as the number of workers assigned to it varies. Remember that if a worker is assigned to reprogram lights, he cannot fix potholes.

Table 2.4

Workers assigned to reprogramming	Total time saved	Workers assigned to fix potholes	Total time saved
1	100	1	125
2	190	2	225
3	270	3	305
4	340	4	365
5	400	5	415
6	450	6	455
7	490	7	485
8	520	8	510
9	540	9	530
10	550	10	540

How should the workers be assigned? (Hint: Let the number of workers assigned to reprogramming be the activity. What are the costs of assigning these workers?)

23   (Practice problem: marginal costs and marginal benefits) Bugout pesticide kills insects that eat lettuce leaves. Currently 11 leaves per head are eaten by the insects. In the right concentrations, Bugout can be effective. On the other hand, there are side effects. When the concentration is too great, leaves fall off the lettuce head. Table 2.5 shows the relationship between concentrations of Bugout, leaves eaten, and leaves fallen. What concentration should the manufacturer recommend?

Table 2.5

Concentration (parts per million)	Leaves eaten per head	Leaves fallen per head
1	7	0
2	4	1
3	2	3
4	1	6
5	0	10
6	0	15

Answers to Problems

2

3

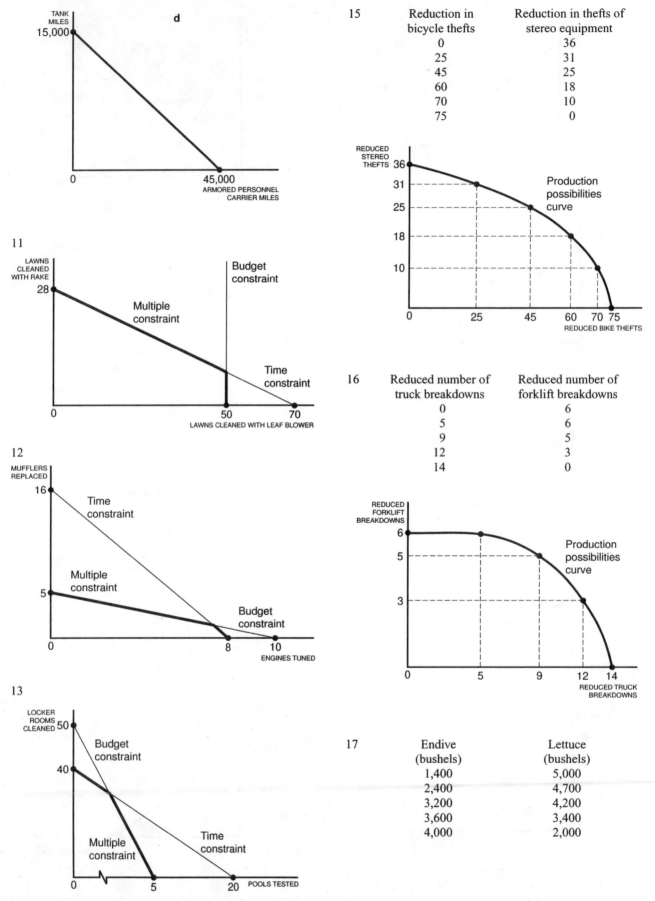

d

11

12

13

15

Reduction in bicycle thefts	Reduction in thefts of stereo equipment
0	36
25	31
45	25
60	18
70	10
75	0

16

Reduced number of truck breakdowns	Reduced number of forklift breakdowns
0	6
5	6
9	5
12	3
14	0

17

Endive (bushels)	Lettuce (bushels)
1,400	5,000
2,400	4,700
3,200	4,200
3,600	3,400
4,000	2,000

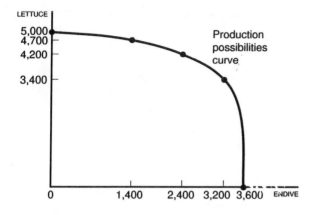

19

	Costs of holding class	Costs of canceling class
Compensation for instructor	$4,000	0
Air conditioning and lighting	$1,000	$1,000
Custodial services	$2,000	$2,000
Property taxes	$2,500	$2,500
Rent	0	− $1,200
Total	**$9,500**	**$4,300**

a   Opportunity cost = $9,500 – $4,300 = $5,200.
b   Sunk cost = $4,300.

20

	Cost of early retirements	Cost of retaining bureaucrats
Salaries	0	$50,000 × 8 × 2
Fringe benefits	0	$20,000 × 8 × 2
Office space for all 8	$ 10,000	$20,000
Pension benefit	$ 20,000 × 8 × 2	0
Total	$330,000	$1,140,000

a   Opportunity cost = $1,140,000 – $330,000 = $810,000.
b   Sunk cost = $330,000.

22   The marginal benefit of assigning a worker to reprogram the lights is the time saved; the marginal cost is the time lost because the worker was not assigned to fix potholes.

Workers assigned to reprogramming	Marginal benefits	Marginal costs
1	100	10
2	90	20
3	80	25
4	70	30
5	60	40
6	50	50
7	40	60
8	30	80
9	20	100
10	10	125

Assign 6 to reprogramming and 4 to fixing potholes.

23   The benefit of recommending higher concentrations of pesticides are the fewer leaves eaten; the costs are the leaves that fall off.

Concentration of pesticide	Marginal benefits	Marginal costs
1	4	0
2	3	1
3	2	2
4	1	3
5	1	4
6	0	5

The manufacturer should recommend a concentration of 3 ppm.

TRADE

Chapter Review

Chapter 3 takes up the key feature of markets: exchange. The fundamental aspect of market-based economies is voluntary trade. By definition, voluntary trade is mutually beneficial; it creates a surplus for both buyer and seller. If this were not true, the trade would not take place! An important insight of trade theory is the principle of comparative advantage, which shows how individuals and countries can specialize in production and thereby increase the gains they receive from trade. Economists emphasize these gains from trade and see little sense in protectionist arguments that trade between countries should be limited. The next two chapters will show how markets help realize some of the potential gains from trade.

ESSENTIAL CONCEPTS

1   Voluntary trade between rational individuals is **mutually beneficial;** it is good for both buyer and seller. Naturally, the buyer would like a lower price, and the seller prefers a higher price. Both might also benefit from better information. Nevertheless, the fact that the exchange takes place implies that given the information each has at the time of the transaction, both judge that they are better off trading than not trading.

2   Trade between individuals within a country and trade between individuals in different countries take place in markets. The three broad classes of markets are the product, labor, and capital markets. These three markets are all integrated internationally; this has led to a high degree of economic interdependence among nations.

3   Trade is many-sided, or multilateral. A typical person sells labor to an employer and uses the wages she earns both to purchase goods and services from many other firms and to save for future consumption. Similarly, a country may import more from some trading partners and export very little to those countries. With other trading partners, the country may export more than it imports. A country may also buy more goods and services than it sells abroad, and make up the difference by borrowing in capital markets or sending its workers to foreign labor markets.

4   The principle of **comparative advantage** says that individuals and countries will specialize in those goods that they are relatively more efficient in producing. To be relatively efficient means to have a lower opportunity

cost. Countries will have a comparative advantage in different goods. Each can import certain goods from abroad for a lower opportunity cost than it would incur producing them at home. Similarly, each can export to foreign countries those goods for which it has a comparative advantage.

5   Comparative advantage leads to **specialization** in trade, but specialization itself increases productivity and further lowers opportunity costs. First, individuals and countries grow more efficient at their specialties through practice. Second, producing for others allows a larger scale of operations, more **division of labor** into separate tasks, and more specialization. Finally, specialization creates conditions in which invention and innovation flourish.

6   Different countries and individuals have comparative advantages in different activities. Reasons for a comparative advantage can include natural endowments such as climate (for a country) or manual dexterity (for a tailor), human or physical capital, knowledge, and experience. These factors may be gifts of nature, or they may be the result of investment, experience, education, training, or other past actions.

7   **Protectionism** is the idea that the economy needs safeguarding against the perceived harmful effects of trade. Proponents of protectionism use many arguments; chief among them are the loss of domestic jobs, the vulnerability to foreign influences, the unfair trade practices of foreign governments, trade imbalances, and the potential damage to weak economies. To economists, none of these arguments is convincing.

BEHIND THE ESSENTIAL CONCEPTS

1   An exchange creates and divides a surplus. The surplus is the difference between the value to the seller of what is traded and its value to the buyer. If there is no surplus, the exchange does not take place; the seller simply refuses to trade if he thinks the good is worth more than the buyer is willing to pay. The division of the surplus is another matter. Both the buyer and seller will receive some of the surplus. This is what economists mean when they say that trade is mutually beneficial: each party receives some of the surplus. The buyer pays somewhat less than the maximum she is willing to pay, and the seller receives somewhat more than the minimum he is willing to accept. Of course, whatever the division of the surplus, each would prefer to receive more.

2   When individuals trade, both buyer and seller gain. Each is better off with the trade than he or she would be if the trade did not take place. Likewise, countries also gain from trade. Trade allows specialization on the basis of comparative advantage, and countries benefit from more goods and services. But although each country as a whole gains from trade, not every individual in each country is better off. Some businesses lose out to foreign competition, and some workers lose jobs. Other

businesses gain new markets, and new jobs are created. Thus, international trade creates both gains and losses, but overall, the gains outweigh the losses.

3   The problem with protectionism is that it looks only at the losers from international trade. Tariffs, quotas, and other protectionist policies can, at least temporarily, protect the losers, but only by limiting the trade. Limiting the trade means limiting the gains as well as the losses. Because the gains from trade exceed the losses, protectionism can only make matters worse for the economy as a whole.

4   To better understand comparative advantage, it helps to distinguish it from **absolute advantage.** A country has an absolute advantage in the production of a good or service if it requires fewer inputs to produce the good than another country. Comparative advantage, on the other hand, pertains to opportunity costs. As we have seen, the opportunity cost is not the inputs used in production; rather, it is the alternative use of those inputs. Thus, a country (or individual) has the comparative advantage in the production of a good or service if it has the lower opportunity cost.

For instance, assume that only labor is required to produce tomatoes or bookcases. Workers in country A can produce a carload of tomatoes in 40 hours, while workers in country B require 80 hours. Country A has an absolute advantage in producing tomatoes. To determine comparative advantage, however, we must look at how productive those workers are elsewhere in the economy. If the 40 hours of labor in country A produce 2 bookcases, but 80 hours in country B produce only 1, then country B has a comparative advantage in tomatoes. Why? Because a carload of tomatoes has an opportunity cost of 1 fewer bookcase in country B.

SELF-TEST

True or False

1   Unless the gain from trade is divided equally between buyer and seller, an exchange cannot be mutually beneficial.

2   While United States imports as a percentage of gross domestic product (GDP) have grown over the past three decades, the percentage of GDP devoted to exports has fallen.

3   Because of problems of information, problems of estimating risks, and difficulties in forming expectations about the future, many exchanges are not mutually beneficial.

4   With multilateral trade, imports from a particular country may not equal exports to that country.

5   The country that can produce a good with the least amount of labor is said to have a comparative advantage in the production of that good.

6   Trade on the basis of comparative advantage leads to complete specialization.

7 The extent of the division of labor is limited by the size of the market.

8 Comparative advantage is determined by the endowment of natural resources, human and physical capital, knowledge, and the experience that comes from specialization.

9 The marginal rate of transformation measures the trade-off between two commodities, indicating how much more of one commodity can be produced at the sacrifice of a given amount of another commodity.

10 Opposition to trade between nations is called protectionism.

11 A country that exports more than it imports will run a trade deficit.

12 Although trade benefits the country as a whole, many individuals may lose from trade in a particular product.

13 A country that runs a trade deficit must borrow from abroad.

14 The United States has comparative advantage in high-technology manufactured products, such as airplanes and computers, but must import wheat.

15 The North American Free Trade Agreement will eliminate all trade barriers between the United States, Canada, and Mexico within fifteen years.

Multiple Choice

1 Voluntary trade between two rational individuals

a benefits the buyer only;
b benefits the seller only;
c benefits the buyer or the seller but not both;
d benefits both the buyer and the seller;
e none of the above.

2 The gain from trade, that is, the difference between the value of a good to the buyer and its value to the seller,

a accrues entirely to the seller;
b accrues entirely to the buyer;
c is always divided equally;
d accrues to the government;
e none of the above.

3 When economists argue that both parties benefit from voluntary trade, they are assuming

a that both parties are well-informed;
b that both parties place the same value on the traded good;
c that both parties desire the same price;
d that the surplus is divided evenly between buyer and seller;
e none of the above.

4 Goods produced in the United States and sold in foreign countries are called

a imports;
b exports;

c either imports or exports;
d capital flows;
e none of the above.

5 For decades, Japan has imported raw materials from Australia, while Australia has purchased heavy equipment from the United States. Furthermore, Japan has exported consumer goods to the United States. This is an example of

a multilateral trade;
b bilateral trade;
c absolute advantage;
d protectionism;
e trade deficit.

6 If the United States has a comparative advantage in the production of a good, then

a fewer resources are required to produce the good in the United States;
b the United States also has an absolute advantage in the production of the good;
c the relative cost of producing the good is lower in the United States;
d the United States will import the good;
e all of the above.

7 If the United States has absolute advantage in the production of a good,

a production of the good in the United States is more efficient and requires fewer resources;
b the United States also has comparative advantage in the production of the good;
c the relative cost of producing the good is lower in the United States;
d the United States will import the good;
e the United States will export the good.

8 The trade-off between two commodities is called the

a comparative advantage;
b specialization;
c absolute advantage;
d marginal rate of transformation;
e none of the above.

9 Suppose that in the United States increasing wheat output by 1,000 tons would require a reduction in steel output of 500 tons, but in Canada increasing wheat output by 1,000 tons would require reducing steel output by 1,000 tons. Then we can infer that

a Canada has absolute advantage in wheat;
b the United States has absolute advantage in wheat;
c the United States will export steel;
d the United States has comparative advantage in steel;
e the United States has comparative advantage in wheat.

10 The slope of the production possibilities curve is called the

a marginal rate of transformation;
b comparative advantage;
c trade deficit;

d   marginal benefit;

e   marginal rate of production.

11   The principle of comparative advantage

    a   applies only to international trade;

    b   always leads to complete specialization;

    c   forms the basis for the division of labor;

    d   is relevant only in the absence of protection;

    e   all of the above.

12   Which of the following is not a reason why specialization increases productivity?

    a   Workers and countries grow more efficient by repeating the same tasks.

    b   Specialization saves time needed to switch from one task to another.

    c   Specialization allows larger-scale production with greater efficiency.

    d   Specialization allows the assignment of tasks to those who have a comparative advantage.

    e   All of the above, are reasons.

13   Important sources of comparative advantage include

    a   natural endowments;

    b   human and physical capital;

    c   superior knowledge;

    d   experience;

    e   all of the above.

14   If two countries have identical relative opportunity costs,

    a   there will never be any basis for trade;

    b   they might specialize in the production of certain goods and acquire a comparative advantage in those goods over time;

    c   each will gain from protectionist policies;

    d   the country with an absolute advantage will reap all of the gains from trade;

    e   none of the above.

15   When two countries trade,

    a   each individual and firm in both countries benefits;

    b   any individual benefits from the trades that she engages in;

    c   particular groups in each country may be hurt by trade in some goods;

    d   b and c;

    e   none of the above.

16   Increased immigration of unskilled workers into the United States will likely

    a   lower consumer goods prices;

    b   make American firms more competitive in international markets;

    c   lower wages of unskilled workers already in the United States;

    d   all of the above;

    e   a and b.

17   If a country runs a trade deficit for several years,

    a   it is importing more goods and services than it exports;

    b   it is exporting more goods and services than it imports;

    c   it must borrow from abroad;

    d   b and c;

    e   a and c.

18   Which of the following is not a basis of comparative advantage?

    a   natural endowments;

    b   acquired endowments;

    c   superior knowledge;

    d   protectionism;

    e   specialization.

19   With voluntary trade between countries,

    a   all individuals are made better off;

    b   all individuals in the larger country are made better off;

    c   some individuals are made worse off, but the gainers could more than compensate the losers;

    d   businesses gain but consumers lose;

    e   workers lose but consumers gain.

20   The North American Free Trade Agreement will lower trade barriers between which of the following countries?

    a   all countries in North America;

    b   all countries in North America and the Caribbean;

    c   all countries in North and South America;

    d   the United States, Canada, and Mexico;

    e   the United States and Canada.

Completion

1   The difference between what a person is willing to pay for an item and what she has to pay is a gain from trade, or _____.

2   If a country is relatively more efficient at producing a good than its trading partners, then that country is said to have the _____ in the production of that good.

3   _____ refers to having superior production skills or lower resource costs.

4   Because of trade possibilities, individuals and countries can produce more of what each has a comparative advantage in. This specialization or division of labor is limited by the _____ of the market.

5   _____, such as location, natural resources, and climate, are bases of comparative advantage.

6   Acquired endowments, such as physical and human _____, represent other sources of comparative advantage.

7   The doctrine that the economy of a country is injured by trade is called _____.

8   The marginal rate of transformation is the _____ of the production possibilities frontier.

9   The trade-off in producing two commodities is called the _____.

10   The _____ will reduce trade barriers among the United States, Canada, and Mexico over the next fifteen years.

Answers to Self-Test

True or False

1	f	4	t	7	t	10	t	13	t
2	f	5	f	8	t	11	f	14	f
3	f	6	f	9	t	12	t	15	t

Multiple Choice

1	d	6	c	11	c	16	d
2	e	7	a	12	e	17	e
3	e	8	d	13	e	18	d
4	b	9	e	14	b	19	c
5	a	10	a	15	d	20	d

Completion

1   surplus
2   comparative advantage
3   Absolute advantage
4   size
5   Natural endowments
6   capital
7   protectionism
8   slope
9   marginal rate of transformation
10   North American Free Trade Agreement

Doing Economics: Tools and Practice Problems

This chapter introduces comparative advantage, a very important concept. The principle of comparative advantage illustrates how individuals, firms, and countries can benefit by specializing in performing tasks or producing goods and trading with each other. This problem set will help you to identify comparative advantage and to see why comparative advantage determines the division of labor and the pattern of trade. You will also study the gains from trade when they proceed according to comparative advantage. Finally, you will use the idea of comparative advantage to construct the production possibilities curve for the case in which resources differ.

COMPARATIVE ADVANTAGE

The most important concept in exchange and production is comparative advantage. Countries have comparative advantage when their opportunity cost is lower. They will export the goods in which they have comparative advantage. Tool Kit 3.1 shows how to use production possibilities curve to

---

Tool Kit 3.1: Identifying Comparative Advantage

When a country or individual has a comparative advantage in performing some task or producing some good, that country or individual is relatively more efficient, which means that the country or individual has the lower opportunity cost. The following procedure shows how to identify comparative advantage and predict the pattern of trade. It is written for the case of two-country trade.

Step one: Plot the production possibilities curves for each country. Be sure to be consistent and measure units of the same good along the horizontal axis in each case.

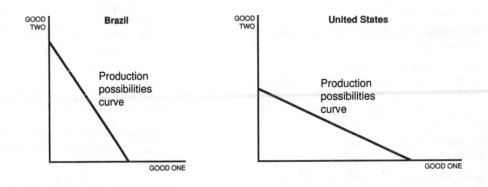

Step two: The slope of the production possibilities curve is the opportunity cost of the good on the horizontal axis, and it indicates the trade-off. The flatter slope implies comparative advantage for producing the good on the horizontal axis.

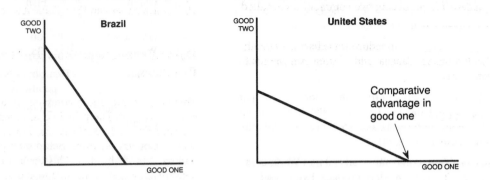

Step three: The steeper slope indicates comparative advantage for the good on the vertical axis.

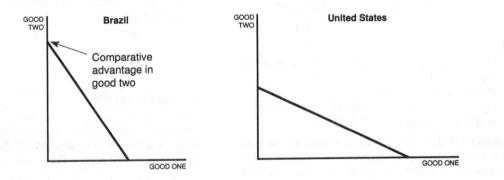

Step four: In a system of free trade, each country will produce more of the good in which it has a comparative advantage, and the relative price will lie somewhere between the opportunity costs of the two countries.

identify comparative advantage and determine the pattern or production and trade.

1   (Worked problem: comparative advantage) Workers in the United States and Brazil can produce shoes and computers. The annual productivity of a worker in each country is given in the table below.

Country	Computers	Shoes
United States	5,000	10,000
Brazil	200	5,000

a   Which country has a comparative advantage in computers? in shoes?

b   Predict the pattern of trade.

c   Indicate the range of possible relative prices that would bring about this pattern of trade.

Step-by-step solution

Step one (a): Plot the production possibilities curves. In this problem, the production possibilities curve for one worker

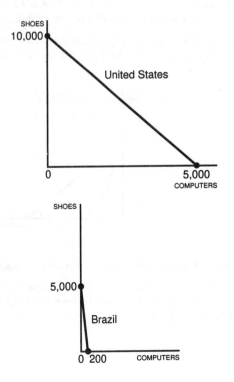

in each country will suffice. Measure computers on the horizontal axis.

Step two: The production possibilities curve for the United States has the flatter slope; therefore, the U.S. worker has a comparative advantage in the production of computers.

Step three: The production possibilities curve for Brazil is steeper, and the Brazilian worker has a comparative advantage in shoes.

Step four (b and c): Brazil will trade shoes for U.S. computers. The relative price must lie between 2 shoes per computer (the U.S. opportunity cost) and 25 shoes per computer (the Brazilian opportunity cost).

2   (Practice problem: comparative advantage) Workers in Nigeria and neighboring Niger produce textiles and sorghum. The productivities of each are given in the table below.

Country	Textiles (bales)	Sorghum (bushels)
Nigeria	100	500
Niger	50	400

  a   Which country has a comparative advantage in textiles? in sorghum?
  b   Predict the pattern of trade.
  c   Indicate the range of possible relative prices that would bring about this pattern of trade.

3   (Practice problem: comparative advantage) For each of the following, determine which country has a comparative advantage in each good, predict the pattern of trade, and indicate the range of possible relative prices consistent with this pattern of trade.

a	Country	Fish	Wheat (bushels)
	Greece	60	80
	Poland	35	70

b	Country	Heart bypass operations	Auto parts (containers)
	United States	5,000	10,000
	Canada	3,000	9,000

c	Country	Scrap steel (tons)	Finished steel (tons)
	Thailand	20	20
	Laos	10	2

d	Country	Wine (barrels)	Wool (bales)
	Portugal	2	2
	Great Britain	4	8

GAINS FROM TRADE

When countries trade there is mutual gain, in the sense that their opportunity sets expand beyond their production possibilities curves. To exploit the potential of trade, production

---

Tool Kit 3.2: Showing the Gains from Trade

When the pattern of trade is based upon comparative advantage, both countries can gain. Specifically, they each can consume a bundle of goods that lies beyond their own production possibilities curve. Follow these five steps.

Step one: Draw the production possibilities curve for each country, identify the country with a comparative advantage in each good, and identify the trade-offs for each country.

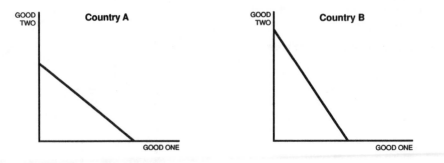

Step two: Choose a relative price between the trade-offs.

Step three: For the country with the comparative advantage in the horizontal-axis good, label the horizontal intercept *A* and draw a line segment from *A* with a slope equal to (–) the relative price. This line segment shows the bundles of goods that the country can consume by trading at the given relative price.

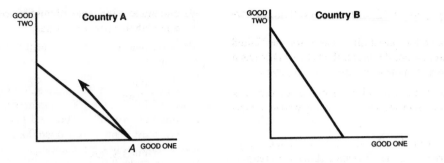

Step four: For the country with the comparative advantage in the vertical-axis good, label the vertical intercept *A* and draw a line segment from *A* with a slope equal to (–) the relative price. This line segment shows the bundles of goods that the country can consume by trading at the given relative price.

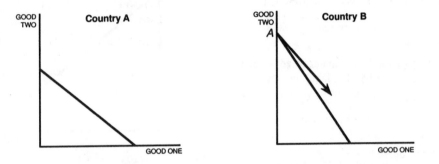

Step five: Pick a pair of consistent points, where A's exports equal B's imports, one on each line segment, and show how each country can benefit from trade.

and trade must be organized according to comparative advantage. Tool Kit 3.2 shows how both trading partners can gain from trade.

4   (Worked problem: gains from trade) This problem builds upon problem #1. Show that a worker in Brazil and a worker in the United States can benefit by trading on the basis of comparative advantage.

Step-by-step solution

Step one: Identify the country with a comparative advantage in each good and the trade-offs for each country. The U.S. worker has the comparative advantage in computers, and the trade-off is 2 shoes per computer. The Brazilian worker has the comparative advantage in shoes, and the trade-off is 25 shoes per computer.

Step two: Choose a relative price between the trade-offs. Let's choose 20 shoes per computer.

Step three: For the country with the comparative advantage in computers, which is the United States, label the horizontal intercept *A* and draw a line segment from *A* with a slope

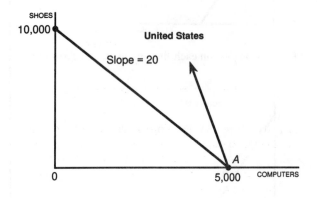

equal to –20. This line segment shows the bundles of goods that the United States can consume by trading at the given relative price.

Step four: For the country with the comparative advantage in shoes, label the vertical intercept *A* and draw a line segment

from *A* with a slope equal to –20. This line segment shows

the bundles of goods that Brazil can consume by trading at the given relative price.

Step five: Pick a pair of consistent points, one on each line segment, and show how each country can benefit from trade. Let the U.S. worker produce 4,800 computers for domestic consumption. This leaves 200 for trade. At a relative price of 20 shoes, the 200 computers trade for 4,000 shoes. Plot the point (4,000, 4,800) and label it *B*. The Brazilian worker must then produce 4,000 shoes for trade. This leaves 1,000 shoes for domestic consumption. The 4,000 shoes for trade 200 computers. Plot the point (200, 1,000) and label it *B*. At this point, the United States exports 200

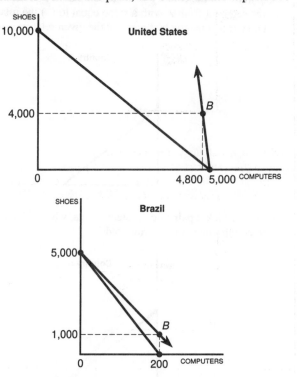

computers and imports 4,000 shoes, while Brazil imports 200 computers and exports 4,000 shoes. Trade is balanced, and each country consumes beyond its production possibilities curve.

5   (Practice problem: gains from trade) This problem builds upon problem #2. Show that workers in Nigeria and Niger can benefit by trading according to comparative advantage.

Production Possibilities with Different Resources

Free trade assigns to each country the task of producing those goods in which it has a comparative advantage. The same is true for trade between individuals. To see why this is efficient we consider the joint production possibilities curve in the case where there are two or more different types of resources that can be used in the production of two goods. To do this efficiently it is necessary to assign resources to produce the good in which they have comparative advantage.

Tool Kit 3.3: Plotting the Production Possibilities
Curve When Resources Are Different

When resources differ in their productivity, plotting
the production possibilities curve requires that they be
assigned to produce goods according to the principle
of comparative advantage. Follow these six steps.

Step one: Draw a set of coordinate axes. Label the horizontal axis as the quantity of one good and the vertical axis as the quantity of the other good.

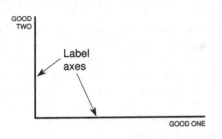

Step two: Calculate the maximum quantities of each
good that can be produced. Plot the quantity along the
vertical axis and label the point B. Plot the quantity
along the horizontal axis and label this point A.

Step three: Identify the resource with the comparative
advantage for each good.

Step four: Choose the resource with the comparative
advantage in the horizontal-axis good and assign it to
produce this good, while keeping the other resource
producing the vertical-axis good. Calculate the total
quantities produced, and plot this point. Label it *C*.

Step five: Connect the points *BCA* with line segments.
This is the production possibilities curve.

Step six: Verify that the slope is increasing. Because
the slope measures the opportunity cost of the horizontal-axis good, this means that the opportunity cost
is increasing, which is an implication of the principle
of diminishing returns.

Tool Kit 3.3 shows how. Compare its shape with Chapter 2's
opportunity sets for multiple constraints and diminishing returns.

6 (Worked problem: production possibilities curve) Harrigan and her daughter have formed a two-person firm to
handle business incorporations and real estate transactions. The hours required for each type of task are given
below. Each works 48 hours every week.

Lawyer	Hours required to perform each incorporation	Hours required to complete each transaction
Harrigan	4	8
Daughter	8	24

Plot their weekly production possibilities curve.

Step-by-step solution

Step one: Draw and label a set of coordinate axes. Put real
estate transactions on the horizontal axis and incorporations
on the vertical.

Step two: Calculate the maximum number of incorporations
they can do in a week. For Harrigan, this number is 48/4 =
12; for her daughter, it is 48/8 = 6. The pair can complete 18
incorporations. Plot this point along the vertical axis, and la-

bel it *A*. Concerning real estate transactions, Harrigan can do 48/8 = 6; her daughter, 48/24 = 2. The pair can do 8. Plot this point along the horizontal axis, and label it *B*.

Step three: Identify the resource with the comparative advantage for each good. Since it takes Harrigan 8 hours to complete each real estate transaction but only 4 to do an incorporation, each real estate transaction requires enough time to do 2 incorporations. The opportunity cost of a real estate transaction for Harrigan is, then, 2 incorporations. By the same argument, the opportunity cost for her daughter is 24/8 = 3 incorporations; thus, Harrigan has the comparative advantage in real estate transactions, while her daughter has the comparative advantage in incorporations.

Step four: We assign to Harrigan the task of real estate transactions, leaving her daughter to do the incorporations. With

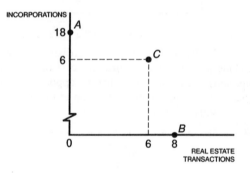

this assignment, they can do 6 incorporations and 6 real estate transactions (see step two). Plot this point, and label it *C*.

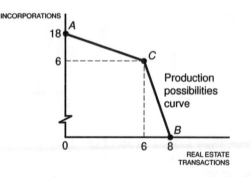

Step five: Draw line segments connecting the points. This is the production possibilities curve.

Step six: Note that between *A* and *C* the slope is 2, but be-

tween *C* and *B* the slope increases to 3. The shape of the production possibilities curve thus indicates diminishing returns.

7   (Practice problem: production possibilities curve) A farmer has 3 acres of land. Owing to various characteristics of the land, his ability to produce his two cash crops (corn and soybeans) differs on each acre. The technology of production is given in the table below.

Maximum outputs of each crop per acre (bushels)

	Acre #1	Acre #2	Acre #3
Corn	200	200	100
Soybeans	400	200	50

These figures represent the maximum output of each crop, assuming that only one crop is grown on the acre. That is, acre #1 can produce either 200 bushels of corn or 400 bushels of soybeans. Of course, the farmer can also divide the acre into one part corn and one part soybeans. For example, he can grow 100 bushels of corn and 200 bushels of soybeans on acre #1. Plot the production possibilities curve.

8   (Practice problem: production possibilities curve) Plot the following production possibilities curves.

a   Maximum harvest of each type of fish per trawler (tons)

	Trawler #1	Trawler #2	Trawler #3
Salmon	2	3	4
Tuna	2	6	6

b   Maximum amounts of pollutants removed (tons)

	Smokestack scrubbers	Coal treatment
Sulphur	100	50
Particulates	500	100

Answers to Problems

2   a   Nigeria has a comparative advantage in textiles. Niger has a comparative advantage in sorghum.
    b   Nigeria will trade its textiles for sorghum from Niger.
    c   The relative price will lie between 8 bushels of sorghum per bale of textiles and 5 bushels of sorghum per bale of textiles.

3   a   Greece has a comparative advantage in fish. Poland has a comparative advantage in wheat. Greece will trade its fish for Polish wheat. The relative price will lie between 4/3 bushels of wheat per fish and 2 bushels of wheat per fish.
    b   The United States has a comparative advantage in heart bypass operations, and Canada in auto parts. The United States will trade heart bypass operations for Canadian auto parts. The relative price will lie between 2 containers of auto parts per operation and 3 containers of auto parts per operation.
    c   Thailand has a comparative advantage in finished steel, Laos in scrap steel. Thailand will trade its finished steel for Laotian scrap steel. The relative price

will lie between 5 tons of scrap steel per ton of finished steel and 1 ton of scrap steel per ton of finished steel.

d Portugal has a comparative advantage in wine, Great Britain in wool. British wool will be traded for Portuguese wine. The relative price will lie between 1 and 2 bales per barrel of wine.

5   Choose, for example, 6 bushels of sorghum per bale of textiles as the relative price. Nigeria can produce 100 bales of textiles and trade 20 to Niger for 120 bushels of sorghum. The point (80, 120) lies outside its production possibilities curve. Niger can produce 400 bushels of sorghum and trade 120 bushels to Nigeria for 20 bales of textiles. The point (20, 280) lies outside its production possibilities curve.

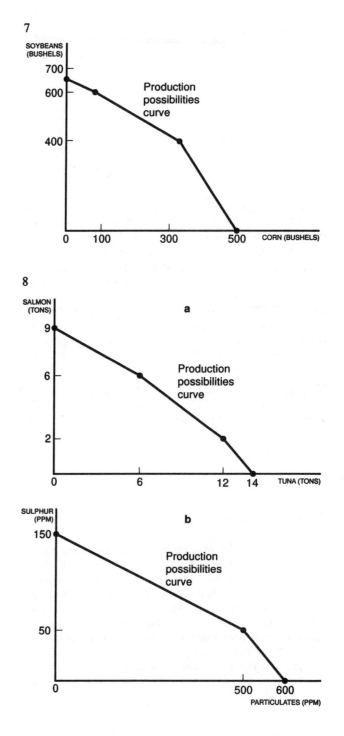

DEMAND, SUPPLY, AND PRICE

Chapter Review

Trade, the markets in which it occurs, and the gains it provides for both buyers and sellers are all important ideas from Chapter 3. Chapter 4 builds the basic model of markets, which is the supply and demand model. The focus is on prices and quantities—how they are determined and how they change when other factors change. Chapter 5 then applies the supply and demand model to major areas of concern to economists: what happens to the quantity demanded or supplied when prices change, and what happens when prices do not adjust, as when the government sets price floors or ceilings.

ESSENTIAL CONCEPTS

1 Consumers **demand** goods and services. They are willing and able to pay, and given a price, they will buy a certain quantity. Several factors influence demand, but the most important is **price.** As the price falls, people buy more of the good or service; as the price rises, they purchase less. The entire relationship between the price and the quantity that a person buys is called the individual **demand curve.**

2 Adding all the individual demand curves gives the **market demand curve.** For every price, ask how much each individual will buy. Add these quantities. The result is the market demand curve, which shows the total amount of the good that will be purchased by all individuals at each price.

3 Firms **supply** goods and services. They are willing and able to produce and sell the good, and at a given price, they will sell a certain quantity. Several factors influence the supply, but the most important is price. As the price rises, producers will supply more; as the price falls, producers will supply less. The entire relationship between the price and the quantity that the producer will sell is called the individual **supply curve.**

4 Adding up all of the individual supply curves gives the **market supply curve.** For every price, ask how much each producer will sell. Add these quantities. The result is the market supply curve, which shows how much of the good will be sold by all producers at each price.

5 The price at which consumers want to buy exactly the quantity that firms want to sell is the **equilibrium price.** This quantity, which is the same for demand and

supply, is the **equilibrium quantity.** It is an equilibrium because there are no forces that would cause it to change.

6 If the price were higher than the equilibrium price, firms would want to sell more than consumers would buy. Unable to sell all of their goods, many firms would compete, by lowering prices, to attract the relatively few consumers. Because this higher price would change, it is not an equilibrium. Similarly, if the price were lower than the equilibrium price, consumers would want to buy more than firms would sell. Seeing the glut of consumers, firms would raise their prices. In sum, if the price is above equilibrium, it falls; if it is below equilibrium, it rises. When price equals the equilibrium price, it does not change.

7 Many factors affect the demand and supply. For demand, these factors include changes in income, prices of substitutes and complements, the composition of the population, and people's tastes. This is only a partial list. When one of these factors—or anything else that affects the willingness to pay for the good—changes, the entire demand curve **shifts,** and a new equilibrium must be found.

Supply is affected by changes in technology and input price—more generally, anything that causes costs to change. Again, changes in these factors **shift** the supply curve and lead to a new equilibrium.

BEHIND THE ESSENTIAL CONCEPTS

1 The demand curve is the entire range, or schedule, that indicates how many goods will be purchased at each price. At a given price, this number is called the quantity demanded. In diagrams of demand curves, the quantity demanded is measured along the horizontal axis. To find the quantity demanded, simply read it off the demand curve at the current price. Economists, students, and sometimes professors are sloppy and say "change in demand" without being clear whether they mean a shift in the demand curve or a change in the quantity demanded. The latter is brought about by a change in price, and it involves only a movement along the same demand curve. To guard against confusion in stressful situations (like tests!), say "demand curve" when you refer to the entire schedule of prices and quantities and "quantity demanded" when you want to indicate the number of goods purchased.

2 It is very important to understand why the market demand curve is drawn as it is. When the price rises, the market quantity demanded falls for two reasons. First, each individual buys less. The principle of substitution says that other available goods and services can serve as alternatives, and at higher prices, people switch to consume these substitutes. Second, some individuals find the price to be too high altogether, and they leave the market completely. When the price falls, the opposite happens. People substitute away from other goods and buy more of the one with the lower price. Furthermore, the lower price attracts new consumers to the market.

3 The market supply curve slopes upward. This means that as the price rises, more is offered for sale. Again, there are two reasons. First, firms are willing to sell more at higher prices. Second, higher prices attract new products to the market.

4 Other factors that shift the demand curve include consumer income, tastes, prices of substitutes and complements, and the composition of the population. The supply curve shifts with changes in technology or input prices. While these factors are the most common causes of shifts, they do not comprise a complete list. Anything that affects the willingness and ability to pay for goods shifts the demand curve, and anything that affects costs shifts the supply curve. For example, if it rains in April, the supply of crops may increase, and the demand for umbrellas may also increase.

5 Successful supply and demand analysis proceeds in four steps:

a Start with an equilibrium.
b Figure out which curve shifts.
c Shift the curve and find the new equilibrium.
d Compare the price and quantity at the original and new equilibria.

Be careful to avoid a common pitfall. Suppose you are asked to show the effect of a change in tastes that shifts demand to the right. The failing student's analysis goes like this: "Demand shifts to the right, which increases quantity and price, but the increase in price leads producers to want to supply more, so the supply also shifts to the right." What is wrong with this answer? Stop before the "but." True, the demand shift does raise price and quantity, but that is the end of the story. The increase in price does lead producers to want to supply more. As they supply more, there is a movement along the supply curve, but not a shift. Changes in the price of a good *never shift* the demand curve for that good or the supply curve for that good; rather, changes in the price of a good cause a *movement* along the demand curve or supply curve. There is more discussion on this point and lots of practice problems in the "Doing Economics" section of this chapter.

SELF-TEST

True or False

1 Prices provide incentives to help the economy use resources efficiently.

2 As the price falls, the quantity demanded decreases.

3 The market demand curve is the sum of the quantities and prices of each individual demand.

4   The individual demand curve is an example of an equilibrium relationship.

5   One reason why the supply curve slopes upward is that at higher prices, more producers enter the market.

6   In equilibrium, there is neither excess demand nor excess supply.

7   If the price is above the equilibrium price, consumers can buy as much as they are willing.

8   If the price is below the equilibrium price, sellers cannot sell as much as they are willing.

9   The law of supply and demand says that the equilibrium price will be that price at which the quantity demanded equals the quantity supplied.

10   The individual supply curve is an example of an identity.

11   The price of diamonds is higher than the price of water because diamonds have a higher value in use.

12   A change in a consumer's income will shift her demand curve.

13   A change in the price of a good will shift its market demand curve to the right.

14   An increase in the price of a substitute will shift the demand curve for the good in question to the right.

15   A decrease in the price of a complement will shift the demand curve for the good in question to the left.

Multiple Choice

1   Market prices

   a   measure scarcity;
   b   communicate information;
   c   provide incentives;
   d   all of the above;
   e   a and b.

2   The individual demand curve for a good or service

   a   gives the quantity of the good or service the individual would purchase at each price;
   b   gives the equilibrium price in the market;
   c   shows which other goods or services will be substituted according to the principle of substitution;
   d   all of the above;
   e   a and c.

3   The idea that there are other goods or services that can serve as reasonably good alternatives to a particular good or service is called the

   a   law of demand;
   b   principle of substitution;
   c   market demand curve;
   d   principle of scarcity;
   e   none of the above.

4   If you knew the individual demand curves of each consumer, you could find the market demand curve by

   a   taking the average quantity demanded at each price;
   b   adding all of the prices;
   c   adding up, at each price, the quantities purchased by each individual;
   d   taking the average of all prices;
   e   none of the above.

5   As the price rises, the quantity demanded decreases along an individual demand curve because

   a   individuals substitute other goods and services;
   b   some individuals exit the market;
   c   some individuals enter the market;
   d   the quantity supplied increases;
   e   a and b.

6   As the price rises, the quantity demanded decreases along the market demand curve because

   a   individuals substitute other goods and services;
   b   some individuals exit the market;
   c   some individuals enter the market;
   d   the quantity supplied increases;
   e   a and b.

7   As the price rises, the quantity supplied increases along an individual supply curve because

   a   higher prices give firms incentives to sell more;
   b   the principle of substitution leads firms to substitute other goods and services;
   c   the market supply curve is the sum of all the quantities produced by individual firms at each price;
   d   b and c;
   e   none of the above.

8   As the price rises, the quantity supplied increases along the market supply curve because

   a   at higher prices, more firms are willing to enter the market to produce the good;
   b   each firm in the market is willing to produce more;
   c   the market supply curve is the sum of all the quantities produced by individual firms at each price;
   d   at higher prices, more firms substitute other goods and services;
   e   a and b.

9   If the market price is below equilibrium, then

   a   there is excess demand;
   b   there is excess supply;
   c   consumers will want to raise the price;
   d   firms will want to lower the price;
   e   all of the above.

10   If the market price is at equilibrium, then

   a   the quantity that consumers are willing to buy equals the quantity that producers are willing to sell;
   b   there is excess demand;
   c   there is excess supply;

d there are no forces that will change the price;

e a and d.

11 If the market price is above equilibrium, then

a there is excess supply;

b there is excess demand;

c firms will not be able to sell all that they would like;

d consumers will not be able to buy all that they would like;

e a and c.

12 The law of supply and demand is an example of

a an identity;

b an equilibrium relationship;

c a behavioral relationship;

d none of the above;

e all of the above.

13 The statement that market supply is equal to the sum of individual firms' supplies is an example of

a an identity;

b an equilibrium relationship;

c a behavioral relationship;

d none of the above;

e all of the above.

14 A diamond sells for a higher price than a gallon of water because

a luxuries always have higher prices than necessities;

b only a few people demand diamonds, but everyone needs water;

c the total use value of diamonds exceeds the total value of water;

d the total cost of diamond production exceeds the total cost of water production;

e none of the above.

15 Stationary exercise bicycles and stair-stepper machines are substitutes, according to the aerobically correct. An increase in the price of exercise bicycles will

a shift the demand for stair-stepper machines to the right;

b increase the price of stair-stepper machines;

c increase the quantity of stair-stepper machine sales;

d all of the above;

e none of the above.

16 As people have grown more concerned about saturated fat in their diets, the demand for beef has shifted to the left. The quantity of beef sold has also fallen. This change is a

a movement along the demand curve for beef;

b shift in the supply curve for beef;

c movement along the supply curve for beef;

d a and b;

e none of the above.

17 Which of the following is not a source of shifts in market demand?

a an increase in consumer income;

b a change in tastes;

c an increase in the population;

d a technological advance.

e All are sources of shifts.

18 If the price of an input falls,

a supply shifts to the left;

b demand shifts to the right;

c demand shifts to the left;

d supply shifts to the right;

e none of the above.

19 If ski-lift tickets and skiing lessons are complements, then an increase in the price of lift tickets

a shifts demand for skiing lessons to the left;

b shifts demand for skiing lessons to the right;

c shifts supply of skiing lessons to the left;

d shifts supply of skiing lessons to the right;

e a and d.

20 A recent regulation requires tuna fishing companies to use nets that allow dolphins to escape. These nets also allow some tuna to escape. This regulation causes

a the supply of tuna to shift to the left;

b the demand for tunas to shift to the right;

c the demand for tunas to shift to the left;

d the supply of tunas to shift to the right;

e none of the above.

Completion

1 _____ is defined as what is given in exchange for a good or service.

2 If the price of a good or service falls, the quantity demanded _____.

3 The quantity of the good or service purchased at each price is given by the _____.

4 The quantity of the good or service offered for sale at each price is given by the _____.

5 In an economic equilibrium, there are no forces for _____.

6 The law of supply and demand says that at the equilibrium price, the _____ equals the _____.

7 The statement that market supply equals market demand is an example of an _____.

8 The statement that market supply is the total of all individual supplies is an example of an _____.

9 An increase in the price of a good leads to a _____ its demand curve.

10 A change in technology leads to a _____ the supply curve.

Answers to Self-Test

True or False

1	t	4	f	7	t	10	f	13	f
2	f	5	t	8	f	11	f	14	t
3	f	6	t	9	t	12	t	15	f

Multiple Choice

1	d	6	e	11	e	16	c
2	a	7	a	12	b	17	d
3	b	8	e	13	a	18	d
4	c	9	a	14	e	19	a
5	a	10	e	15	d	20	a

Completion

1 Price
2 increases
3 demand curve
4 supply curve
5 change
6 quantity demanded, quantity supplied
7 equilibrium relationship
8 identity
9 movement along
10 shift in

Doing Economics: Tools and Practice Problems

Three techniques receive attention in this section. The first technique shows how to add individual demand and individual supply curves to get market demand and market supply curves. The next technique involves finding the equilibrium price and quantity, where the market clears. Finally, some general instructions about supply and demand analysis are given and developed in several problems. Each of these techniques is fundamental and will appear repeatedly throughout this book.

MARKET DEMAND AND MARKET SUPPLY

When the price falls, individual demanders want to buy more, and individual suppliers want to sell less. These individual demand and supply curves are behavioral relationships. The market demand and market supply curves are found by adding up all of these individual demands and supplies. Tool Kit 4.1 shows how to do this.

> **Tool Kit 4.1**: Calculating Market Demand and Supply
>
> The market demand is the sum of the individual demands. The market supply is the sum of the individual supplies. This tool kit shows how to add the individual demands and supplies.
>
> *Step one*: Make two columns. Label the left-hand column "Price" and the right-hand column "Quantity."
>
> Price   Quantity
>
> *Step two*: Choose the highest price at which goods are demanded. Enter this in the first row of the price column.

> Price   Quantity
> p1
>
> *Step three*: Find how many goods each individual will purchase. Add these quantities. Enter the total in the first row of the quantity column.
>
> Price   Quantity
> p1 $Q_1 = Q_a + Q_b + Q_c + \cdots$
>
> *Step four*: Choose the second highest price, and continue the process.

1 (Worked problem: market demand) The individual demands of Jason and Kyle for economics tutoring are given in Table 4.1. Calculate the market demand. (Jason and Kyle are the only two individuals in this market.)

Table 4.1

Jason		Kyle	
Price	Quantity	Price	Quantity
$10	6	$10	4
$ 8	8	$ 8	5
$ 6	10	$ 6	6
$ 4	12	$ 4	7

Step-by-step solution

Step one: Make and label two columns.

Price   Quantity

Step two: Choose the highest price. This is $10. Enter this in the first row under price.

Price   Quantity
$10

Step three: Find the market quantity. Jason would buy 6; Kyle would buy 4. The total is 6 + 4 = 10. Enter 10 in the corresponding quantity column.

Price   Quantity
$10   10

Step four: Repeat the process. The next lower price is $8. Jason would buy 8; Kyle would buy 5. The total is 8 + 5 = 13. Enter $8 and 13 in the appropriate columns.

Price   Quantity
$10   10
$ 8   13

Continue. The entire market demand is given below.

Price   Quantity
$10   10
$ 8   13
$ 6   16
$ 4   19

2 (Practice problem: market demand) Gorman's tomatoes are purchased by pizza sauce makers, by submarine sandwich shops, and by vegetable canners. The demands for each are given in Table 4.2. Find the market demand.

Table 4.2

Pizza sauce		Submarine shops		Vegetable canners	
Price	Quantity (bushels)	Price	Quantity (bushels)	Price	Quantity (bushels)
$5	25	$5	5	$5	55
$4	35	$4	6	$4	75
$3	40	$3	7	$3	100
$2	50	$2	7	$2	150
$1	80	$1	7	$1	250

3 (Practice problem: market supply) The technique for finding the market supply curve is the same as for the market demand. Simply sum the quantities supplied at each price. There are three law firms that will draw up partnership contracts in the town of Pullman. Their individual supply curves are given in Table 4.3. Find the market supply curve.

Table 4.3

Jones		Jones and Jones		Jones, Jones, and Jones	
Price	Quantity	Price	Quantity	Price	Quantity
$200	0	$200	6	$200	4
$220	0	$220	8	$220	8
$240	0	$240	12	$240	10
$260	8	$260	24	$260	11

EQUILIBRIUM

In equilibrium, markets clear. The market price will settle where the quantity that demanders would like to purchase exactly equals the quantity that suppliers choose to sell. Tool Kit 4.2 shows how to find the equilibrium.

Tool Kit 4.2: Finding the Equilibrium Price and Quantity

The equilibrium price in the demand and supply model is the price at which the buyers want to buy exactly the quantity that sellers want to sell. In other words, the quantity demanded equals the quantity supplied. The equilibrium quantity in the market is just this quantity. Here is how to find the equilibrium in a market.

Step one: Choose a price. Find the quantity demanded at that price and the quantity supplied.

Step two: If the quantity demanded equals the quantity supplied, the price is the equilibrium. Stop.

Step three: If the quantity demanded exceeds the quantity supplied, there is a shortage. Choose a higher price and repeat step one. If the quantity demanded is less than the quantity supplied, there is a surplus. Choose a lower price and repeat step one.

Step four: Continue until the equilibrium price is found.

---

4 (Worked problem: equilibrium price and quantity) The supply curve and demand curve for cinder blocks are given in Table 4.4. The quantity column indicates the number of blocks sold in one year.

Table 4.4

Demand		Supply	
Price	Quantity	Price	Quantity
$2.00	50,000	$2.00	200,000
$1.50	70,000	$1.50	160,000
$1.00	100,000	$1.00	100,000
$0.75	150,000	$0.75	50,000
$0.50	250,000	$0.50	0

a Find the equilibrium price and quantity.
b If the price is $1.50, is the market in equilibrium? Will there be a surplus or a shortage? If so, what is the size of the surplus or shortage? What will happen to the price? Why?
c If the price is $0.75, is the market in equilibrium? Will there be a surplus or a shortage? If so, what is the size of the surplus or shortage? What will happen to the price? Why?

Step-by-step solution

Step one (a): Choose a price. At a price of, say, $2.00, the quantity demanded is 50,000 and the quantity supplied is 200,000.

Step two: The quantities are not equal.

Step three: There is a surplus. The equilibrium price will be lower.

Step four: Continue. Try other prices until the quantity supplied equals the quantity demanded. The equilibrium price is $1.00, where the quantity equals 100,000. We can now see the answers to parts b and c.

Step five (b): If the price is $1.50, the quantity demanded is 70,000, and it is less than the quantity supplied, which is 160,000. There is a surplus of 90,000 (160,000 − 70,000). The price will fall because producers will be unable to sell all that they want.

Step six (c): If the price is $0.75, the quantity demanded is 150,000, and it is greater than the quantity supplied, which is 50,000. There is a shortage of 100,000 (150,000 − 50,000). The price will rise because producers will see that buyers are unable to buy all that they want.

5 (Practice problem: equilibrium price and quantity) The demand curve and supply curve in the market for billboard space space along Interstate 6 are given in Table 4.5. The price is the monthly rental price. The quantity column shows numbers of billboards.

Table 4.5

Demand		Supply	
Price	Quantity	Price	Quantity
$100	5	$100	25
$ 80	8	$ 80	21
$ 60	11	$ 60	16
$ 40	14	$ 40	14
$ 20	22	$ 20	3

a   Find the equilibrium price and quantity.

b   If the price is $20, is the market in equilibrium? Will there be a surplus or a shortage? If so, what is the size of the surplus or shortage? What will happen to the price? Why?

c   If the price is $80, is the market in equilibrium? Will there be a surplus or a shortage? If so, what is the size of the surplus or shortage? What will happen to the price? Why?

6   (Practice problem: equilibrium price and quantity) Find the equilibrium price and quantity in each of the following markets.

a   The supply and demand curves for new soles (shoe repair) are given in Table 4.6.

Table 4.6

Demand		Supply	
Price	Quantity	Price	Quantity
$35	17	$35	53
$30	21	$30	37
$25	25	$25	25
$20	30	$20	15
$15	35	$15	0

b   The supply and demand curves for seat cushions are given in Table 4.7.

Table 4.7

Demand		Supply	
$8	4	$8	32
$7	8	$7	28
$6	12	$6	22
$5	16	$5	19
$4	17	$4	17

SUPPLY AND DEMAND

Supply and demand is probably the most useful technique in microeconomics. Economists use it to study how markets are affected by changes, such as tastes, technology, government programs, and many others. Supply and demand offers a wealth of insights into the workings of the economy. It is very important to master the procedure spelled out in Tool Kit 4.3.

Tool Kit 4.3: Using Supply and Demand

Supply and demand analysis provides excellent answers to questions of the following form: "What is the effect of a change in _____ on the market for _____?" You are well on your way to success as a student of economics if you stick closely to this procedure in answering such questions.

Step one: Begin with an equilibrium in the relevant market. Label the horizontal axis as the quantity of the good or service and the vertical axis as the price. Draw a demand and a supply curve and label them *D* and *S*, respectively.

Step two: Figure out whether the change shifts the supply curve, the demand curve, or neither.

Step three: Shift the appropriate curve.

Step four: Find the new equilibrium, and compare it with the original one.

7   (Worked problem: using supply and demand) In response to concern about the fumes emitted by dry cleaning establishments, the Environmental Protection Agency has issued regulations requiring expensive filtering systems. How will this regulation affect the dry cleaning market?

Step-by-step solution

Step one: Start with an equilibrium.

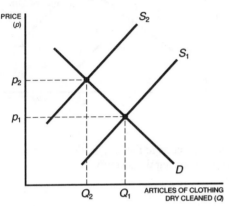

Step two: Figure out which curve shifts. The mandated filtering systems increase the dry cleaning firm's costs, shifting supply to the left.

Step three: Shift the curve.

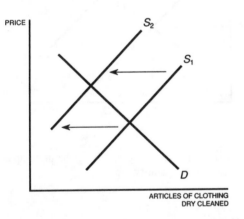

Step four: Find the new equilibrium and compare. The effect of the regulation is to raise the price and lower the quantity of clothes dry cleaned.

8   (Practice problem: using supply and demand) As the oil market comes to the realization that Kuwait's production will not return to prewar levels, the price of oil has increased by $4 per barrel. Explain the effect of this oil price increase on the market for natural gas.

9   (Practice problem: using supply and demand) For each of the following, show the effects on price and quantity. Draw the diagrams and follow the procedure.

a   an increase in income in the market for a normal good
b   a decrease in income in the market for a normal good
c   an increase in the price of a substitute
d   a decrease in the price of a substitute
e   an increase in the price of a complement
f   a decrease in the price of a complement
g   an increase in the price of an input
h   a decrease in the price of an input
i   an improvement in technology

Answers to Problems

2 | Price | Quantity (bushels) |
|---|---|
| $5 | 85 |
| $4 | 116 |
| $3 | 147 |
| $2 | 207 |
| $1 | 337 |

3 | Price | Quantity |
|---|---|
| $200 | 10 |
| $220 | 16 |
| $240 | 22 |
| $260 | 43 |

5   *a*   Equilibrium price = $40; quantity = 14.
    b   If the price is $20, there is a shortage of $22 - 3 = 19$. The price will be driven up.
    c   If the price is $80, there is a surplus of $21 - 8 = 13$. The price will be driven down.

6   *a*   Price = $25; quantity = 25.
    b   Price = $4; quantity = 17.

8   Oil and natural gas are substitutes, and therefore the demand curve shifts to the right, the price increases, and the quantity increases.

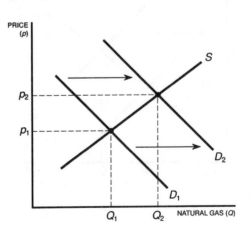

9   *a*   Demand shifts to the right, driving the price up and increasing the quantity.

b   Demand shifts to the left, driving the price down and decreasing the quantity.

c   Demand shifts to the right, driving the price up and increasing the quantity.

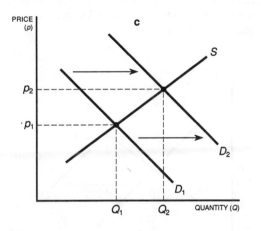

d   Demand shifts to the left, driving the price down and decreasing the quantity.

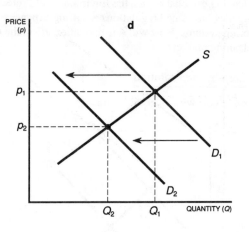

e   Demand shifts to the left, driving the price down and decreasing the quantity.

f   Demand shifts to the right, driving the price up and increasing the quantity.

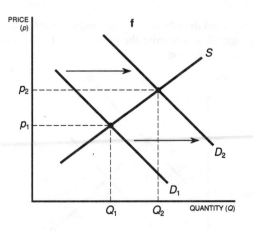

g   Supply shifts up (vertically), increasing the price but decreasing the quantity.

i   Supply shifts down (vertically), decreasing the price but increasing the quantity.

Supply shifts down (vertically), decreasing the price but increasing the quantity.

Chapter 5

USING DEMAND AND SUPPLY

Chapter Review

The model of demand and supply introduced in Chapter 4 is one of the most useful in all of the social sciences. The ideas of demand and supply form the basis of all economic study, and will be used throughout this text. This chapter develops the model in more detail and introduces the concept of elasticity. Elasticity is best thought of as "sensitivity." The price elasticity of demand, for instance, measures how sensitive the quantity demanded is to a change in price. The chapter then applies the model to the study of the effects of taxes and price controls. Chapter 6 extends the supply and demand framework to markets in which future goods and risk are exchanged.

ESSENTIAL CONCEPTS

1   When price falls, quantity demanded increases. If the demand curve is steep, the increase in quantity is smaller than it would be if the curve were flat. Although it might seem natural to measure how the quantity responds to price changes by the slope of the demand curve, economists employ the concept of **elasticity.** They do so because elasticity will produce the same measure no matter what units are used. The **price elasticity of demand**

is the percentage change in the quantity demanded brought about by a 1 percent change in price.

2   The **price elasticity of supply** is the percentage change in the quantity supplied brought about by a 1 percent change in price. It is the basic measure of how sensitive the quantity supplied is to changes in price.

3   The price elasticity of demand is greater when there are good, close substitutes available. Usually it is greater when the price is higher, because at higher prices, only those who consider the good essential remain in the market. Both the price elasticity of demand and the price elasticity of supply are greater in the long run because individuals and firms have more time to find substitutes and make adjustments.

4   When demand shifts, both the equilibrium price and quantity change. The price elasticity of supply determines which change is larger. If supply is more elastic, quantity changes by a greater percentage than price; if supply is less elastic, price changes more. Similarly, it is the price elasticity of demand that determines the relative changes in price and quantity when supply shifts. The more elastic the demand, the more quantity changes and the smaller is the change in price.

5   The economic effects of a tax are seen by focusing on the market affected by the tax. For example, a tax on the

sale of gasoline shifts the supply curve up (vertically) by the amount of the tax, raises consumer prices, and reduces the quantity of gasoline sold. Except in a case where supply or demand is perfectly inelastic or perfectly elastic, the increase in consumer price is less than the amount of the tax. This means that producers are able to pass on only part of the tax to their customers and must bear some of the burden themselves.

6   **Price ceilings,** when set below the market-clearing price, lead to shortages, which means that the quantity demanded exceeds the quantity supplied. **Price floors,** when set above the market-clearing price, result in surpluses; in this case, the quantity demanded is less than the quantity supplied. In each case, the quantity actually exchanged is less than it is at the market-clearing price.

BEHIND THE ESSENTIAL CONCEPTS

1   The concept of elasticity appears many times throughout the text, and is worth mastering. Suppose that price falls by 1 percent. We know that quantity will increase as consumers substitute toward the lower price, but by how much? The price elasticity provides the answer. It is the percent change in quantity brought on by a 1 percent change in price.

2   The relationship between elasticity and total revenue is very important. Total revenue is just price multiplied by quantity. If the price of a bicycle is $200 and there are 20 sold, then total revenue is $200 × 2 = $4,000. When price falls, total revenue is pushed down because each unit sells for less money; however, total revenue is pushed up because more units are sold. Whether on balance total revenue rises or falls depends on the elasticity. Table 5.1 helps to keep the relationship between elasticity and total revenue straight.

Table 5.1

If price rises,
   total revenue *falls* if the price elasticity of demand is greater than one (elastic).
   total revenue *rises* if the price elasticity of demand is less than one (inelastic).
   total revenue *does not change* if the price elasticity of demand equals one (unitary elasticity).

If price falls,
   total revenue *rises* if the price elasticity of demand is greater than one (elastic).
   total revenue *falls* if the price elasticity of demand is less than one (inelastic).
   total revenue *does not change* if the price elasticity of demand equals one (unitary elasticity).

3   What makes the demand for some goods (like motor boats) elastic, while the demand for others (like milk) is inelastic? The most important factor is the availability of substitutes. The **principle of substitution** says that consumers will look for substitutes when the price rises. If there are good, close substitutes available, then finding substitutes will be easy and consumers will switch. If good, close substitutes are not available, the consumers are more likely to swallow the price increase and continue purchasing the good.

4   Suppose that the government levies a tax on the supply of hotel rooms. Who pays the tax? While it is natural to think that the hotel pays the tax because it actually writes the check to the government, when you look at the issue through the lens of supply and demand, you see the value of economics. The tax increases the hotel's costs, and therefore it shifts the supply curve up and raises the price. Because they must pay higher prices for hotel rooms, consumers pay some of the tax.

5   The key to tax analysis is to find the market or markets in which the burden of the tax falls. Sometimes this is easy. A hotel room tax falls on the market for hotel rooms. In other cases, its not so clear. For example, an income tax affects the labor market, because workers must give up some of the earnings. It also affects the capital market because some of the interest earnings must be paid to the government. Once you find the relevant market, simply apply the basic method of supply and demand: start with an equilibrium, figure out which curve shifts (which side of the market is taxed), shift the curve, find the new equilibrium, and compare.

6   Price ceilings only make a difference if they are set below the market-clearing price (where the supply and demand curves intersect). A price ceiling set above the market-clearing price has no effect. Similarly, a price floor set below the market-clearing price does not do anything.

7   Price floors and ceilings also affect the quantity traded in the market. If there is a price ceiling, then the quantity demanded exceeds the quantity supplied. The supply is the short side of the market, and although consumers would like to buy more of the good, the quantity traded is what producers are willing to sell. This is shown in Figure 5.1A. With price floors, the opposite is true. The demand is the short side of the market, and the quantity traded equals the amount that consumers are willing to buy, as shown in panel B. In each case, we say that the short side of the market determines the actual quantity traded, and the actual quantity trade is less than the market-clearing quantity.

Figure 5.1

Figure 5.1

SELF-TEST

True or False

1 The price elasticity of demand is greater for goods and services that have better close substitutes.

2 The price elasticity of demand is always constant along the demand curve.

3 Total revenue increases as price falls when the demand is elastic.

4 A horizontal demand curve is perfectly elastic.

5 A vertical supply curve is perfectly inelastic.

6 If the supply curve is unitary elastic, then total revenue is constant as price changes.

7 If the supply curve is upward sloping, a rightward shift in the demand curve increases the equilibrium price and the equilibrium quantity.

8 If the demand curve is downward sloping, a rightward shift in the supply curve increases the equilibrium price and the equilibrium quantity.

9 When the demand curve is very elastic, relatively more of a tax on the production of some good or service will be borne by producers.

10 A tax on the sale of beer shifts the supply curve vertically by the amount of the tax.

11 When prices are sticky, shortages and surpluses can result in the short run.

12 A price ceiling set above the equilibrium price will have no effect on the market.

13 A price ceiling set below the equilibrium price will have no effect on the market.

14 A price floor set above the equilibrium price in the milk market will lead to a surplus of milk.

15 When demand and supply are more elastic, minimum wages set above the equilibrium wage lead to relatively more unemployment.

Multiple Choice

1 The quantity demanded is more sensitive to price changes when

 a supply is relatively inelastic;
 b close substitutes are available;
 c consumers are rational;
 d consumers are relatively more informed about quality for some goods;
 e all of the above.

2 Suppose that price falls by 10 percent and the quantity demanded rises by 20 percent. The price elasticity of demand is

 a 2;
 b 1;
 c 0;
 d 1/2;
 e none of the above.

3 Suppose that the price elasticity of demand is 1/3. If price rises by 30 percent, how does the quantity demanded change?

 a Quantity demanded rises by 10 percent.
 b Quantity demanded falls by 10 percent.
 c Quantity demanded rises by 90 percent.
 d Quantity demanded falls by 90 percent.
 e Quantity demanded does not change.

4 Suppose that the price elasticity of demand is 1.5. If price falls, total revenue will

 a remain the same;
 b fall;
 c rise;
 d double;
 e c and d.

5 Suppose that the price elasticity of demand is 0.7. The demand for this good is

 a perfectly inelastic;
 b inelastic;
 c unitary elastic;
 d elastic;
 e perfectly elastic.

6 Which of the following are true statements concerning the price elasticity of demand?

 a The price elasticity is constant for any demand curve.
 b Demand is more price elastic in the short run than in the long run.
 c If total revenue falls as price increases, the demand is relatively inelastic.
 d a and c.
 e None of the above.

7 If the supply curve is vertical, then the price elasticity of supply is

 a 0;
 b inelastic.
 c 1;

d elastic;

e infinite.

8 The long-run elasticity of supply is greater than the short-run elasticity of supply because

  a in the long run, the stock of machines and buildings can adjust;

  b in the long run, new firms can enter and existing firms can exit the industry;

  c in the long run, customers can discover substitutes;

  d a and b;

  e all of the above.

9 Suppose that supply is perfectly elastic. If the demand curve shifts to the right, then

  a price and quantity will increase;

  b quantity will increase, but price will remain constant;

  c price will increase, but quantity will remain constant;

  d neither price nor quantity will increase;

  e price will increase, but quantity will decrease.

10 Suppose that demand is perfectly inelastic, and the supply curve shifts to the left. Then

  a price and quantity will increase;

  b quantity will increase, but price will remain constant;

  c price will increase, but quantity will remain constant;

  d neither price nor quantity will increase;

  e price will increase, but quantity will decrease.

11 The price elasticity of demand for tires is 1.3, and the supply curve is upward sloping. If a $1-per-tire tax is placed on the production of tires, then the equilibrium price will

  a not change because the tax is on production and not on consumption;

  b increase by $1;

  c increase by less than $1;

  d fall by less than $1;

  e fall by $1.

12 In general, consumers bear more of a tax when the demand is

  a relatively inelastic;

  b unitary elastic;

  c relatively elastic;

  d such that consumers always bear the entire burden;

  e none of the above.

13 Suppose that the supply of a good is perfectly elastic. A tax of $1 on that good will raise the price by

  a less than $1;

  b $1;

  c more than $1;

  d $.50;

  e none of the above.

14 A price ceiling set below the equilibrium price will

  a create a shortage;

  b increase the price;

  c create a surplus;

  d a and b;

  e have no effect.

15 A price ceiling set above the equilibrium price will

  a create a shortage;

  b increase the price;

  c create a surplus;

  d a and b;

  e have no effect.

16 A price ceiling set below the equilibrium price will

  a increase the quantity demanded;

  b increase the quantity supplied;

  c decrease the quantity supplied;

  d a and c;

  e have no effect.

17 Rent control

  a creates a shortage of rental housing;

  b leads to a larger shortage in the long run;

  c lowers rents for renters who have apartments;

  d all of the above;

  e none of the above.

18 A price ceiling on insurance rates will

  a shift demand to the left;

  b shift demand to the right;

  c shift supply to the left;

  d shift supply to the right;

  e none of the above.

19 Which of the following is not a cause of surpluses or shortages?

  a price ceilings;

  b price floors;

  c taxes;

  d sticky prices;

  e All of the above cause surpluses or shortages.

20 Recently, the demand for housing has fallen in the northeast United States. Housing prices are sticky, and therefore

  a temporary shortages of housing have appeared;

  b temporary surpluses of housing have appeared;

  c the housing market has cleared;

  d supply has also shifted to the left;

  e none of the above.

Completion

1 The percentage change in the quantity demanded as a result of a 1 percent price change is called the _____.

2 Price changes have no effect on revenue if the price elasticity of demand is _____.

3 If the price elasticity of demand lies between 0 and 1, then we say that demand is relatively _____.

4   A horizontal demand curve indicates that demand is
    _____.

5   If the supply curve is vertical, then the price elasticity
    of supply equals _____.

6   A $.50-per-gallon tax on the production of gasoline
    can be expected to shift the supply curve _____
    by _____.

7   If demand is relatively inelastic, most of the tax is
    borne by _____.

8   A price ceiling set below the equilibrium price will
    create a _____.

9   A price floor set above the equilibrium price will cre-
    ate a _____.

10 The minimum wage is an example of a _____.

Answers to Self-Test

True or False

1	t	4	t	7	t	10	t	13	f
2	f	5	t	8	f	11	t	14	t
3	t	6	f	9	t	12	t	15	t

Multiple Choice

1	b	6	e	11	c	16	d		
2	a	7	a	12	a	17	d		
3	b	8	d	13	b	18	e		
4	c	9	b	14	a	19	c		
5	b	10	c	15	e	20	b		

Completion

1   price elasticity of demand
2   1
3   inelastic
4   perfectly elastic
5   zero
6   vertically, $.50
7   consumers
8   shortage
9   surplus
10 price floor

Doing Economics: Tools and Practice Problems

Three techniques receive attention in this section. You'll
first learn how to calculate elasticity, then how to measure
the effects of taxes, and finally how to analyze the effects of
price controls.

ELASTICITY

When price changes, how much does quantity change? Economists answer this question with the concept of elasticity. The
price elasticity of demand measures how responsive quantity
demand is to changes in the price. Similarly, the elasticity of
supply measures the responsiveness of quantity supplied to

price changes. Tool Kit 5.1 shows how to calculate elasticity.
The problems focus on elasticity of demand and illustrate the
relationship between elasticity and total revenue.

Tool Kit 5.1: Calculating Elasticity

Elasticity measures how sensitive the quantity is to
changes in price. Follow these steps to calculate elasticity.

Step one: To find the elasticity between two points on
the demand or supply curve, let p_1 and Q_1 be the price
and quantity at the first point and p_2 and Q_2 be the
price and quantity at the second point.

Step two: Substitute the prices and quantities into the
formula

elasticity $= (Q_1 - Q_2)(p_1 + p_2)/(Q_1 + Q_2)(p_1 - p_2)$.

---

1   (Worked problem: calculating elasticity) The demand
    curve for bulletin boards is given below.

Price	Quantity
$35	800
$30	1,000
$25	1,200
$20	1,300

a   Calculate total revenue for each price.
b   Calculate the price elasticity of demand between
    $35 and $30, between $30 and $25, and between $25
    and $20. Does elasticity change along this demand?
c   Verify the relationship between elasticity and total
    revenue.

Step-by-step solution

Step one (a): Total revenue at $35 is 800 × $35 = $28,000.
Total revenue at $30 is 1,000 × $30 = $30,000. Continue,
and enter the numbers in the table.

Price	Quantity	Total revenue
$35	800	$28,000
$30	1,000	$30,000
$25	1,200	$30,000
$20	1,300	$26,000

Step two (b): Let $35 = p_1, 800 = Q_1, $30 = p_2, and 1,000 =
Q_2. Substituting into the formula gives

elasticity $= (35 + 30)(1,000 - 800)/(800 + 1,000)(35 - 30)$
$= 1.44$, which is elastic.

Step three: Between $30 and $25,

elasticity $= (30 + 25)(1,200 - 1,000)/(1,000 + 1,200)(30 - 25)$
$= 1$, which is unitary elastic.

Step four: Between $25 and $20,

elasticity $= (25 + 20)(1,300 - 1,200)/(1,200 + 1,300)(25 - 20)$
$= 0.36$, which is inelastic.

Clearly, the elasticity is not constant. The demand curve is
less elastic at lower prices.

Step five (c): Between $35 and $30, where the demand is elastic, total revenue rises from $28,000 to $30,000 as price falls. Between $30 and $25, where the demand is unitary elastic, total revenue is constant at $30,000 as the price falls. Between $25 and $20, where the demand is inelastic, total revenue falls from $30,000 to $26,000 as the price falls. Check Table 5.1 to verify that these numbers are consistent with the general relationship between price elasticity of demand and total revenue.

2   (Practice problem: calculating elasticity) The demand curve for bookends is given below.

Price	Quantity
$10	70
$ 8	90
$ 6	120
$ 4	130

a   Calculate total revenue for each price.
b   Calculate the price elasticity of demand between each of the adjacent prices. Does elasticity change along this demand?
c   Verify the relationship between elasticity and total revenue.

3   (Practice problem: calculating elasticity) For each of the following, calculate the total revenue for each price and the price elasticity for each price change, and verify the relationship between elasticity and total revenue.

a   Price   Quantity

Price	Quantity
$12	6
$10	8
$ 8	10
$ 6	12

b   Price   Quantity

Price	Quantity
$100	80
$ 80	85
$ 60	90
$ 40	95

c   Price   Quantity

Price	Quantity
$9	10
$8	8
$7	6
$6	4

TAX INCIDENCE

The economic effects of taxes can be analyzed using the method of supply and demand introduced in Chapter 4. The key idea is that the burden of a tax—its incidence—does not necessarily fall on the person or firm that must deliver the money to the government. Taxes affect exchanges, and their impact must be analyzed by looking at the markets where the affected exchanges occur. The basic conclusions of this analysis are that, except when demand or supply is perfectly elastic or perfectly inelastic, consumers and producers share the burden of the tax, taxes reduce the level of economic activity, and, perhaps surprisingly, the effects of the tax are the same whether the supplier or the demander pays. Tool Kit 5.2 shows how to use supply and demand to do tax incidence.

Tool Kit 5.2: Using Supply and Demand for Tax Incidence

Supply and demand analysis shows how markets are affected by taxes and how the burden of taxes is allocated between suppliers and demanders. Follow this five-step procedure.

Step one: Start with an equilibrium in the relevant market.

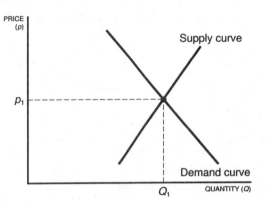

Step two: Identify whether the demander or supplier must pay the tax.

Step three: If the supplier must pay the tax, shift the supply curve up (vertically) by exactly the amount of the tax. If the demander must pay the tax, shift the demand curve down by exactly the amount of the tax.

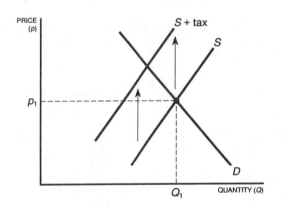

Step four: Find the new equilibrium.

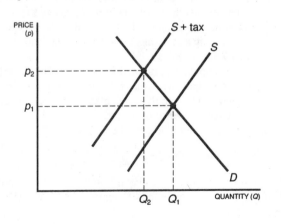

Step five: Determine the economic incidence of the tax. If the supplier must pay the tax, then use the following formulas to calculate economic incidence.

Demander's burden = new equilibrium price – original equilibrium price;

supplier's burden = original equilibrium price – new equilibrium price + tax.

If the demander must pay the tax, use the following formulas to calculate tax incidence.

Demander's burden = new equilibrium price + tax – original equilibrium price;

supplier's burden = original equilibrium price – new equilibrium price.

4   (Worked problem: tax incidence) The demand curve and supply curve for two-bedroom apartments in Takoma Park are given in Table 5.2.

Table 5.2

Demand		Supply	
Price	Quantity	Price	Quantity
$800	100	$800	500
$750	200	$750	500
$700	300	$700	450
$650	400	$650	400
$600	500	$600	300

a   Find the equilibrium price and quantity.
b   Suppose that landlords are required to pay $100 per apartment in a renter's tax to the city government. Use supply and demand analysis to determine the incidence of the tax.
c   Now suppose that rather than being paid by the sellers of an apartment, the tax must be paid by the demanders. Use supply and demand analysis to determine the incidence of the tax.
d   Does it matter who pays the tax?

Step-by-step solution

Step one (a): Find the no-tax equilibrium. When the price is $650, the market clears with 400 apartments rented. This is the answer to part a.

Step two (b): Identify whether the demander or supplier must pay the tax. For part b, the supplier pays the tax.

Step three: Because the tax is paid by sellers, the supply curve shifts up by $100, the amount of the tax. The new supply curve is found by adding $100 to the price column, as in Table 5.3.

Table 5.3

Supply	
Price	Quantity
$900	500
$850	500
$800	450
$750	400
$700	300

Step four: Find the new equilibrium. The market clears at a price of $700 and a quantity of 300.

Step five: Determine the economic incidence of the tax.

Demander's burden = new equilibrium price – original equilibrium price
$$= \$700 - \$650 = \$50.$$
supplier's burden = original equilibrium price – new equilibrium price + tax
$$= \$650 - \$700 + \$100 = \$50.$$

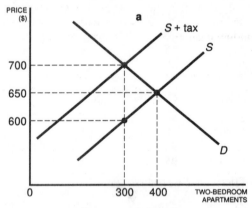

Step six (c): To answer part c, we repeat the procedure for the case where the demander must pay the tax.

Step seven (one): The original no-tax equilibrium is the same with the price equal to $650 and 400 apartments rented.

Step eight (two): In this case, the demanders pay the tax.

Step nine (three): We shift the demand curve down by $100. The new demand curve is given in Table 5.4.

Table 5.4

Demand	
Price	Quantity
$700	100
$650	200
$600	300
$550	400
$500	500

Step ten (four): The market clears at a price of $600 and a quantity of 300.

Step eleven (five): We determine the incidence as follows.

Demander's burden = new equilibrium price
+ tax − original equilibrium price.
$$= \$600 + \$100 - \$650 = \$50.$$
supplier's burden = original equilibrium price
− new equilibrium price
$$= \$650 - \$600 = \$50.$$

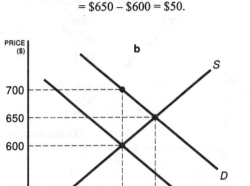

Step twelve (d): It does not matter who pays the tax! In either situation, the total amount that demanders pay is $700, the net amount that sellers receive is $600, and the equilibrium quantity is 300. The diagrams illustrate the solution.

5 (Practice problem: tax incidence) The demand curve and supply curve for unskilled labor are given in Table 5.5.

Table 5.5

Demand		Supply	
Wage	*Quantity*	*Wage*	*Quantity*
$6.50	1,000	$6.50	1,900
$6.00	1,200	$6.00	1,800
$5.50	1,400	$5.50	1,700
$5.00	1,600	$5.00	1,600
$4.50	1,800	$4.50	1,500
$4.00	2,000	$4.00	1,400

a Find the equilibrium wage and quantity hired.
b Consider the effect of the unemployment insurance tax. Suppose that it equals $1.50 per hour and is paid by the employers (they are the demanders in this market). Use supply and demand analysis to determine the incidence of this tax.
c Now suppose that rather than being paid by the employers, the tax must be paid by the workers. Use supply and demand analysis to determine the incidence of this tax.
d Does it matter who pays the tax?

PRICE CONTROLS

When the government interferes with the law of supply and demand and sets price controls, the effects can be analyzed with the basic method of supply and demand. To see the effects, start with an equilibrium.

The price control (if it is effective) will change the price without changing either the demand curve or the supply curve. The new equilibrium occurs at the price set by the government, but the quantity demanded is read off the demand curve, and the quantity supplied is read off the supply curve. The actual quantity transacted is always the short side of the market (the smaller of the quantity demanded and the quantity supplied).

The basic results of this analysis are that price ceilings, when set below the market-clearing price, lower the price, cause shortages, and reduce the quantity transacted. Price floors, when set above the market-clearing price, raise the price, cause surpluses, and reduce the quantity transacted. Tool Kit 5.3 shows how to use supply and demand to analyze price controls.

Tool Kit 5.3: Using Supply and Demand for Price Controls

The impact of price controls is made clear through the use of supply and demand. This four-step procedure shows how to analyze price controls.

Step one: Start with a market-clearing equilibrium.

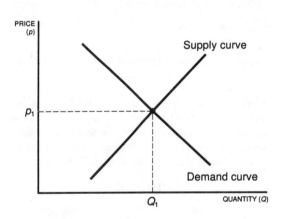

Step two: Identify the controlled price, and decide whether it is a floor or a ceiling.

Step three: Find the new equilibrium price. If it is a price floor set below the market-clearing price or a price ceiling set above the market-clearing price, then the equilibrium is the market-clearing one found in step one. If it is a price floor set above the market-clearing price or a price ceiling set below market clearing, then the controlled price is the equilibrium price.

Step four: Determine the shortage or surplus. For a price floor set above the market-clearing price, there is a surplus:

shortage = quantity supplied – quantity demanded.

For a price ceiling set below the market-clearing price, there is a shortage:

surplus = quantity demanded – quantity supplied.

6   (Worked problem: price controls) Dental bills in Yellowville rose again last year. The City Council is considering a bill to place a ceiling on fees that dentists can charge for teeth cleaning. The supply curve and demand curve for teeth cleanings are given in Table 5.6.

Table 5.6

Demand		Supply	
Price	Quantity	Price	Quantity
$65	100	$65	190
$60	120	$60	180
$55	140	$55	170
$50	160	$50	160
$45	180	$45	150
$40	200	$40	140

a   Find the equilibrium price and quantity for teeth cleanings in Yellowville.

b   The City Council passes a price ceiling ordinance, setting the maximum price at $40 per cleaning. Use supply and demand analysis to determine the effects of the price control.

Step-by-step solution

Step one (a): Find the equilibrium price and quantity. The market clears at a price of $50 and quantity equal to 160.

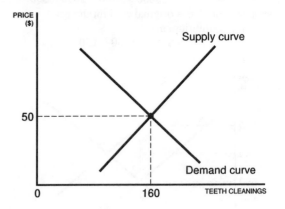

Step two (b): Identify the controlled price and whether it is a floor or a ceiling. The price control is a price ceiling set at $40.

Step three: Determine the new equilibrium price. The ceiling is below the market-clearing price; therefore, the new price is equal to the ceiling price of $40.

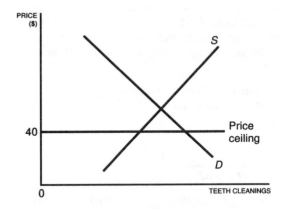

Step four: Determine the shortage or surplus. When the price is $40, the quantity demanded is 200 and the quantity supplied is 140. Although consumers would like more, there are only 140 cleanings actually performed. This results in a shortage of 200 − 140 = 60 teeth cleanings. The diagram illustrates the solution.

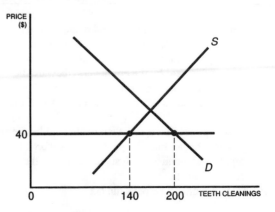

7 (Practice problem: price controls) Many states are considering price ceilings on automobile insurance premiums. In West Dakota, the supply curve and demand curve for automobile insurance policies ($250 deductible on liability, no collision) are given in Table 5.7.

Table 5.7

Demand		Supply	
Price	Quantity	Price	Quantity
$800	1,000	$800	1,800
$750	1,100	$750	1,500
$700	1,200	$700	1,200
$650	1,400	$650	900
$600	1,600	$600	600

a Find the equilibrium price and quantity.
b Suppose that a price ceiling of $650 is imposed. Use supply and demand analysis to determine the effects of the price control.

8 (Practice problem: price controls) Fearful of a restless urban population, Corporal Thug, the new supreme ruler of Costa Guano, attempts to mollify the masses with a wage increase. He mandates that employers must pay at least $8 per day. The supply and demand curves for urban labor are given in Table 5.8.

Table 5.8

Demand		Supply	
Wage	Quantity	Wage	Quantity
$8.50	400	$8.50	4,000
$8.00	600	$8.00	3,200
$7.50	700	$7.50	2,600
$7.00	800	$7.00	2,200
$6.50	900	$6.50	1,800
$6.00	1,000	$6.00	1,000

a Find the quantity demanded, the quantity supplied, and the size of the surplus or shortage, if any.
b Democracy comes to Costa Guano! Corporal Thug is overthrown and the minimum wage repealed. Use supply and demand analysis to determine the effects of the price control.

Answers to Problems

2 a

Price	Quantity	Revenue
$10	70	$700
$ 8	90	$720
$ 6	120	$720
$ 4	130	$520

b Between $10 and $8,
elasticity $= (10 + 8)(90 - 70)/(10 - 8)(90 + 70)$
$= 1.125.$

Between $8 and $6,
elasticity $= (8 + 6)(120 - 90)/(8 - 6)(120 + 90)$
$= 1.$
Between $6 and $4,
elasticity $= (6 + 4)(130 - 120)/(6 - 4)(130 + 120)$
$= 0.2.$

c When elasticity is 1.125, the demand curve is elastic, and total revenue rises from $700 to $720 as price falls. When elasticity is 1, the demand curve is unitary elastic, and total revenue remains constant at $720 as price falls. Finally, when elasticity is 0.2, the demand curve is inelastic, and total revenue falls from $720 to $520 as price falls.

3 In the following tables, the number in the elasticity column corresponding to each price refers to the elasticity over the interval between that price and the next highest price.

a

Price	Quantity	Total revenue	Elasticity
$12	6	$72	
$10	8	$80	1.57
$ 8	10	$80	1.00
$ 6	12	$72	0.64

b

Price	Quantity	Total revenue	Elasticity
$100	80	$8,000	
$ 80	85	$6,800	0.26
$ 60	90	$5,400	0.20
$ 40	95	$3,800	0.14

c

Price	Quantity	Total revenue	Elasticity
$9	10	$ 90	
$8	14	$112	2.430
$7	18	$126	1.875
$6	22	$132	1.300

5 a Wage = $5.00; quantity = 1,600.
b The new supply is given in Table 5.9.

Table 5.9

Supply	
Wage	Quantity
$8.00	1,900
$7.50	1,800
$7.00	1,700
$6.50	1,600
$6.00	1,500
$5.50	1,400

The new equilibrium wage = $5.50; quantity = 1,400. Demander's burden = $5.50 − $5.00 = $0.50; supplier's burden = $5.00 + $1.50 − $5.50 = $1.00.
c The new demand curve is given in Table 5.10.

Table 5.10

Demand	
Wage	Quantity
$5.00	1,000
$4.50	1,200
$4.00	1,400
$3.50	1,600
$3.00	1,800
$2.50	2,000

The new equilibrium wage = $4.00; quantity = 1,400. Demander's burden = $4.00 + $1.50 − $5.00 = $0.50; supplier's burden = $5.00 − $4.00 = $1.00.

d   No. The demander's burden, supplier's burden, and equilibrium quantity are the same in each case.

7   a   Price = $700; quantity = 1,200.

b   Price = $650; quantity demanded = 1,400; quantity supplied = 900; shortage = 1,400 − 900 = 500.

8   a   Wage = $8.00; quantity demanded = 600; quantity supplied = 3,200; surplus = 3,200 − 600 = 2,600.

b   Price = $600; quantity = 1,000.

Chapter 6

TIME AND RISK

Chapter Review

When trades involve the future, as they do when individuals save, borrow money, or buy a house, people must be concerned with the time value of money and with the risk that the trade will not proceed as stipulated. Time and risk therefore affect today's demand and supply curves. This chapter explores markets for risk and insurance along with the broad class of capital markets (stock markets, foreign exchange markets, and so on) where firms raise funds to finance investment and where people transfer risks. Chapter 7 closes the introductory part of the book, with a look at the public sector and the large role government plays in the economy.

ESSENTIAL CONCEPTS

1   The value of a dollar today is greater than the value of a dollar to be received in the future. In other words, money has a time value. Any decision that involves present and future dollars must account for the time value of money. Economists calculate the present discounted value; they convert future dollars to their present equivalent. The formula for the present discounted value of $1.00 next year is $1.00/(1 + interest rate).

2   The market for loanable funds brings together all those who want to borrow and those who want to save. The price in this market is the **interest rate.** Figure 6.1 shows the demand curve for loanable funds sloping downward, which indicates that at lower interest rates, more borrowers would like to borrow more funds. The supply curve slopes upward because at higher interest rates, individuals will save more. The interest rate adjusts to clear the market, and the equilibrium quantity of savings equals the equilibrium quantity of borrowing.

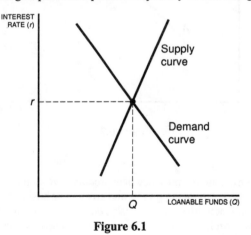

Figure 6.1

3 **Assets,** such as land, housing, stocks, and bonds, last a long time and can be bought today and sold in the future. The prices of assets are determined by supply and demand; however, supply and demand are affected by both today's conditions and what people expect future prices to be. Buyers and sellers of assets must form their **expectations** and make forecasts with care; nevertheless, they are likely to make mistakes, disagree, and revise their expectations. Changing expectations explain large changes in asset prices and make asset markets volatile and risky.

4 Most people are **risk averse** and would prefer to reduce the uncertainty about future economic conditions. The **market for risk** is a whole set of institutions and arrangements by which risk is transferred. People can manage risk by avoiding certain risk endeavors altogether, taking steps to keep options open, diversifying, and transferring risks through the **insurance market,** where individuals purchase policies that protect against the risk of specific events, such as disability or accidents.

5 There are important risks, however, for which insurance markets do not offer such protection. One reason is **adverse selection,** which means that the riskiest customers are the most likely to buy insurance. Another problem, **moral hazard,** arises because people who have bought insurance have less incentive to protect themselves against loss.

6 One of the most fundamental **trade-offs** in the economy involves **risk and incentives.** In markets for both risk and capital, when risks are reduced, so are incentives. Figure 6.2 shows the trade-off. At point *A,* there is low risk and limited incentives. Both risk and incentives increase by moving from *A* to *B.*

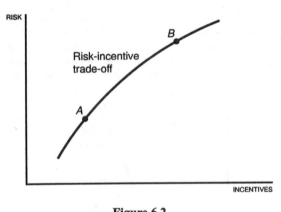

Figure 6.2

7 Entrepreneurs introduce new products, develop new ways of producing goods, and create new businesses. These activities are very risky, but they are not insurable. An important function for entrepreneurs is bearing the risks of these necessary endeavors.

BEHIND THE ESSENTIAL CONCEPTS

1 The distinction between real and nominal interest rates is very important, especially in macroeconomics. When you deposit money in your bank account, the bank pays you the nominal interest rate. Say it is 5 percent. Your money grows at 5 percent each year, but your purchasing power may not, because each year prices may also be changing. Suppose that the inflation rate (the rate of increase in the general price level) is 4 percent. This means that each year goods become 4 percent more expensive, and you can buy only 5 percent − 4 percent = 1 percent more goods. The 1 percent is the real interest rate, and also the rate of increase in your purchasing power.

2 Many economic activities, from purchasing an asset to making an investment, are oriented toward the future. Households and firms must form expectations about the future. Economists distinguish three ways of forming expectations. If you think that tomorrow will be like today, then your expectations are **myopic.** You have **adaptive expectations** if you think that current trends will continue. Finally, you have **rational expectations** (and are well on your way to becoming an economist) if you use all available information, including what you learn in economics.

3 Because people are risk averse, they are willing to pay something to reduce risk. The extra payment is called the risk premium. Here is how it works. Suppose that you have a $5,000 car, and its chance of being stolen is 1 percent. Your expected payment (if uninsured) is 1 percent of $5,000, or $50. If you buy a theft insurance policy for $55, then the risk premium is $55 − $50 = $5.00. In other words, it is the amount (beyond the expected payment) received by the insurance company to bear the risk of theft.

4 **Adverse selection** and **moral hazard** are important problems, and you should be clear about the difference. Adverse selection occurs when the mix of customers is affected by the insurance contract. For example, an insurance company may find that its policyholders have more accidents than the population at large. The company reasons that high-risk people buy more insurance. **Moral hazard,** on the other hand, involves the behavior of the insured. People who have insurance may not take the same precautions as those without insurance. They may fail to buckle up or may even drive recklessly.

5 Adverse selection, moral hazard, and the risk-incentive trade-off are not limited to the insurance industry. They are pervasive in the economy. If you are a banker and charge higher interest rates, then you may find that only risky borrowers apply for loans. We say that the pool of applicants for your loans is adversely selected. It may be wise for you to move along the risk-incentive trade-off. You can do this by requiring collateral. This increases the borrower's risk—the collateral will be forfeited if she defaults—but it gives better incentives to repay the loan.

Here is another example. Suppose that you own a business and you pay your sales force a fixed salary. You may find that they do not work as hard as you would like, and sales decline. Because it is the behavior of your sales force that changes, it is called moral hazard. Again, you can move along the risk-incentive trade-off by replacing the fixed salary with a commission pay based on how much each employee sells. This policy exposes your sales force to more risk, but gives them incentives to work hard.

SELF-TEST

True or False

1   The present discounted value of a future dollar is what one would pay today for that future dollar.

2   The interest rate is the price in the market for loanable funds.

3   The nominal interest rate is the real interest rate minus the inflation rate.

4   Current prices of assets are based upon expectations about their future prices.

5   Someone who always expects that what is true today will be true tomorrow has myopic expectations.

6   Someone who expects current trends to continue has adaptive expectations.

7   People with rational expectations do not make mistakes.

8   Keeping options open only exacerbates risk.

9   The risk premium equals the expected payment.

10   Individuals demand insurance because they are risk averse.

11   The adverse selection problem arises because insurance companies are not sure about the riskiness of their customers.

12   The moral hazard problem arises because insured individuals have less incentive to protect against loss.

13   When risks are higher, so are incentives to protect against losses.

14   The individuals who are responsible for creating new businesses, new products, and new production processes are called entrepreneurs.

15   Most of the risks faced by entrepreneurs, such as the risk that the business will not succeed, cannot be insured against.

Multiple Choice

1   If you deposit $1,100 in the bank today and the interest rate on your deposit is 10 percent, how much money will be in your account at the end of one year?

a $1,200;
b $1,210;
c $121;
d $1,000;
e   none of the above.

2   If you are to receive $1,100 from a client one year from today, and the interest rate is 10 percent, what is the present discounted value of that future receipt?

a $1,100;
b $1,000;
c $1,200;
d $979;
e   none of the above.

3   If the interest rate increases, the present discounted value of the future returns from investment projects

a   increases;
b   remains unchanged;
c   decreases;
d   either a or b;
e   none of the above.

4   If you borrow $4,000 for a used car purchase at 11 percent interest, the 11 percent is the

a   real rate of interest;
b   rate of inflation;
c   nominal rate of interest;
d   real rate of interest – nominal rate of interest;
e   nominal rate of interest – rate of inflation.

5   Suppose that the interest rate offered for certificates of deposit is 8 percent. The inflation rate is expected to be 5 percent. What is the real rate of interest?

a   8 percent;
b   5 percent;
c   13 percent;
d   3 percent;
e   none of the above.

6   When market prices for assets change dramatically, it is usually because of

a   changes in the supply of assets;
b   government price floors;
c   changes in expectations about future prices;
d   changes in tastes;
e   changes in income.

7   People who use all available information to form expectations about the future are said to have

a   myopic expectations;
b   adaptive expectations;
c   rational expectations;
d   insider expectations;
e   random walk expectations.

8   Most people are risk averse. This means they

a   try to avoid or minimize serious risks;
b   have myopic expectations;
c   never take risks;
d   focus on the nominal rate of interest;
e   a and b.

9   An important market for risk is the insurance market. Which of the following is true about insurance markets?

  a   Buyers are risk averse.
  b   Insurance companies spread risks among its many owners.
  c   Insurance companies can forecast accurately the annual amount of claims.
  d   All of the above.
  e   a and b.

10 For insurance companies, the selection problem refers to

  a   selecting the best employees to hire;
  b   selecting the right premium to charge;
  c   selecting the best risks to insure;
  d   selecting the best corporate logo;
  e   none of the above.

11 Adverse selection

  a   is a consequence of the fact that the insurance company has limited information about the riskiness of individual customers;
  b   implies that those more likely to buy insurance tend to be the higher risks;
  c   causes those customers with lower risk to avoid insurance at high rates;
  d   makes the fraction of customers who will have an accident larger when premiums are higher;
  e   all of the above.

12 Moral hazard means that

  a   insurance buyers are risk averse;
  b   insurance companies can predict losses accurately;
  c   higher-risk individuals demand more insurance at higher prices;
  d   insured individuals have less incentive to avoid accidents;
  e   the premium must include an allowance for false claims.

13 An individual who sometimes drives under the influence of alcohol has a great demand for automobile insurance. This is an example of

  a   adverse selection;
  b   moral hazard;
  c   risk aversion;
  d   adaptive expectations;
  e   none of the above.

14 After buying more malpractice insurance, a doctor spends less time with each patient. This is an example of

  a   adverse selection;
  b   moral hazard;
  c   risk aversion;
  d   adaptive expectations;
  e   none of the above.

15 Individuals respond to risk by

  a   avoiding or mitigating risks;
  b   keeping options open;
  c   diversifying;
  d   transferring risk to others;
  e   all of the above.

16 Investing in a wide variety of stocks or in mutual funds, rather than owning a single asset, is an example of

  a   avoiding or mitigating risks;
  b   keeping options open;
  c   diversifying;
  d   transferring risk to others;
  e   none of the above

17 Suppose that a certain business is losing money on a certain product line. If it delays abandoning production for a while in the hopes that demand will pick up, it is

  a   avoiding or mitigaing risks;
  b   keeping options open;
  c   diversifying;
  d   transferring risk to others;
  e   none of the above.

18 The risk-incentive trade-off shows that

  a   insurance buyers have adaptive expectations;
  b   bonds are riskier than stocks;
  c   fully insured individuals have less incentive to protect against risk;
  d   as risk is decreased, the moral hazard problem becomes less severe;
  e   c and d.

19 For the most part, the risk of business failure is borne by

  a   insurance companies;
  b   corporate lawyers;
  c   accounting firms;
  d   entrepreneurs;
  e   the loanable funds market.

20 Those who provide new businesses with capital earn higher rates of returns. This extra return is

  a   a risk premium;
  b   adverse selection;
  c   a moral hazard;
  d   diversification;
  e   insurance.

Completion

1   The return received for giving up current consumption in exchange for increased future consumption is called the _____.

2   The _____ of a dollar to be received in the future shows how much that future dollar is worth today.

3   The formula used to calculate the present value of $1 next year is _____.

4   When the interest rate rises, the present discounted value of future income _____.

5   The interest rate is the price in the market for _____.

6 A savings account that pays 10 percent compounded daily will return _____ to the saver than another savings account that pays 10 percent compounded monthly.

7 The interest rate that indicates how much consumption tomorrow must be forgone for extra consumption today is the _____ interest rate.

8 The real interest rate is the nominal interest rate minus the _____.

9 Current prices of assets, such as land, depend upon _____ about their future prices.

10 The fact that insured individuals have less incentive to take precaution against accident is called _____.

Answers to Self-Test

True or False

1	t	6	t	11	t
2	t	7	f	12	t
3	f	8	f	13	t
4	t	9	f	14	t
5	t	10	t	15	t

Multiple Choice

1	b	11	e
2	b	12	d
3	c	13	a
4	c	14	b
5	d	15	e
6	c	16	c
7	c	17	b
8	a	18	c
9	d	19	d
10	c	20	a

Completion

1 interest rate
2 present value
3 $1/(1 + \text{interest rate})$
4 falls
5 loanable funds
6 more
7 real
8 inflation rate
9 expectations
10 moral hazard

Doing Economics: Tools and Practice Problems

Payments to be received in the future are not worth as much as payments received today. This statement reflects the time value of money. Decisions involving present and future costs and returns require a consistent standard for comparison. This standard is present discounted value, and it is illustrated in Tool Kit 6.1.

Tool Kit 6.1: Calculating the Present Discounted Value

To compare the worth of present and future payments, it is necessary to compute the present discounted value, which is the current dollar equivalent of an amount to be rendered in the future. Follow the steps.

Step one: Make a table with four columns, and label them as shown.

Year	Amount	Discount factor	Present discounted value

Step two: For every payment or receipt, enter the year and the amount. Let Y_1 be the amount in the first year, Y_2 the amount the second year, and so on.

Year	Amount	Discount factor	Present discounted value
1	Y_1		
2	Y_2		

Step three: Calculate the discount factor for each year. The formula is $1/(1 + r)^n$, where r is the interest rate and n is the number of years until the payment or receipt. Enter these discount factors in the table.

Year	Amount	Discount factor	Present discounted value
1	Y_1	$1/(1 + r)$	
2	Y_2	$1/(1 + r)^2$	

Step four: Multiply the number in the amount column by the corresponding discount factor. Enter the product in the present discounted value column.

Year	Amount	Discount factor	Present discounted value
1	Y_1	$1/(1 + r)$	$Y_1 \times 1/(1 + r)$
2	Y_2	$1/(1 + r)^2$	$Y_2 \times 1/(1 + r)^2$

Step five: Add the numbers in the right-hand column. The sum is the present discounted value.

Year	Amount	Discount factor	Present discounted value
1	Y_1	$1/(1 + r)$	$Y_1 \times 1/(1 + r)$
2	Y_2	$1/(1 + r)^2$	$Y_2 \times 1/(1 + r)^2$

Present discounted value = $Y_1 \times 1/(1 + r) + Y_2 \times 1/(1 + r)^2$

---

1 (Worked problem: present discounted value) Ethel has two years before retirement from a career of teaching unruly high school delinquents. Her salary is $40,000, paid at the end of each year. The school board has offered her $70,000 now to retire early. The relevant interest rate is 7 percent. In monetary terms alone, is working worth more than retiring?

Step-by-step solution

First, calculate the present discounted value of continuing to work.

Step one: Make a table with four columns, and label them as shown.

Year	Amount	Discount factor	Present discounted value

Step two: For every payment or receipt, enter the year and the amount. Ethel receives $40,000 each year for two years.

Year	Amount	Discount factor	Present discounted value
1	$40,000		
2	$40,000		

Step three: Calculate the discount factor for each year. For the first year, the discount factor is $1/(1 + .07) = 0.93$, and for the second year it is $1/(1 + .07)^2 = 0.86$. Enter these discount factors in the table.

Year	Amount	Discount factor	Present discounted value
1	$40,000	0.93	
2	$40,000	0.86	

Step four: Multiply the number in the amount column by the corresponding discount factor. Enter the product in the present discounted value column.

Year	Amount	Discount factor	Present discounted value
1	$40,000	0.93	$37,380
2	$40,000	0.86	$34,400

Step five: Add the numbers in the right-hand column. The sum is the present discounted value.

Year	Amount	Discount factor	Present discounted value
1	$40,000	0.93	$37,380
2	$40,000	0.86	$34,400

Present discounted value = $71,780.

Next, compare the lump-sum payment with the present discounted value of continuing to work. Ethel can postpone retirement and increase the present discounted value of her earnings by only $1,780. The reason that the gain is so little is that earnings come in the future and must be discounted, while the retirement bonus is paid now.

2 (Practice problem: present discounted value) The Transportation Department is considering the bids of two paving companies for repaving South Street. The Do-It-Rite firm will do the job for $200,000, and they will guarantee that their new process will make the road free of potholes for 3 years. The Let-It-Go company only charges $100,000, but estimated pothole repair costs are $40,000 each year. The interest rate is 8 percent.

   a Calculate the present discounted value of the entire cost with the Let-It-Go firm.
   b Which is the least expensive bid?

3 (Practice problem: present discounted value) Calculate the present discounted value of each of the following.

   a Interest rate equals 10 percent.

Year	Amount	Discount factor	Present discounted value
1	$10,000		
2	$15,000		

   b Interest rate equals 5 percent.

Year	Amount	Discount factor	Present discounted value
1	$ 0		
2	$20,000		

   c Interest rate equals 15 percent.

Year	Amount	Discount factor	Present discounted value
1	$5,000		
2	$5,000		
3	$5,000		

   d Interest rate equals 5 percent.

Year	Amount	Discount factor	Present discounted value
1	$ 5,000		
2	$ 0		
3	$25,000		

EXPECTED VALUE AND THE RISK PREMIUM

Markets provide incentives to take or accept risks. These incentives include the risk premium, which is the extra payment offered to one who accepts a certain risk. The ultimate consequence of the risky alternative is unknown, of course, so it is measured using the concept of expected value. Risk premiums appear in many settings, including insurance, investment, and risky employment. Tool Kit 6.2 shows how to calculate the risk premium.

Tool Kit 6.2: Calculating Expected Value and the Risk Premium

The risk premium is the extra payment that markets offer for accepting risk. It is calculated using expected value. Follow these three steps.

Step one: Identify the safe and risky alternative and also the amounts and probabilities of gain or loss.

Step two: Calculate the expected value of the risky alternative. Use the formula for expected value.

Expected value = (probability of bad event)
(payments if bad event occurs)
+ (probability of good event)
(payments if good event occurs).

Step three: Subtract the value of the safe alternative from the expected value of the risky alternative (calculated in step two). The difference is the risk premium.

Expected value of the risky alternative
− value of the safe alternative =
risk premium.

---

4   (Worked problem: risk premium) Municipal Money Managers is a small firm that provides short-term money management to municipalities and depends upon the knowledge and personal reputation of its founder. Should he die or be forced to retire for health reasons, the value of the business would fall by $200,000. The probability of this happening is 0.01. An insurance policy is available for $2,500. This policy would compensate the business in the event of the loss of the founder.

a   Point out the safe and risky alternatives.
b   What is the expected loss?
c   How much is the risk premium?

Step-by-step solution

Step one: Identify the safe and risk alternatives. Buying the insurance is the safe alternative. Bearing the risk of the loss of the founder is the risky one.

Step two: Calculate the expected value (EV) of the risky alternative.

EV = 0.01(–$200,000) + 0.99(0) = –$2,000.

Step three: Subtract the value of the safe from the expected value of the risky alternative. The insurance policy costs $2,500.

Risk premium = –$2,000 – ($–2,500) = $500.

5   (Practice problem: risk premium) Barbara is considering leaving her safe job in state govenment to strike out on her own as a consultant. She currently earns $40,000 and estimates that the consultant business will pay $75,000 if she wins an important contract but nothing otherwise. Her best guess is that the probability of her winning the contract is 2/3.

a   Point out the safe and risky alternatives.
b   What is the expected value of the consulting business?
c   How much is the risk premium?

6   (Practice problem: risk premium) If Kim keeps her retirement savings in safe assets she expects to have $250,000 at retirement. Her brother-in-law advises that she move into derivatives. Her financial advisor points out that following the advice of the brother-in-law might result in $600,000 at retirement. Losing it all is another possibility. The probability of each is 1/2.

a   Point out the safe and risky alternatives.
b   What is the expected loss?
c   How much is the risk premium?

Answers to Problems

2 a

Firm	Cost
Do-It-Rite	$200,000
Let-It-Go	$100,000 + $\frac{\$40,000}{1.08}$ +

$$\frac{\$40,000}{(1.08)^2} + \frac{\$40,000}{(1.08)^3} =$$

$203,083.

b   The Do-It-Rite bid.

3 a $21,488.
b $18,141.
c $12,447.
d $26,358.

5 a   Safe alternative = state government; risky alternative = consultant.
b $75,000 × 2/3 + $0 × 1/3 = $50,000.
c $50,000 – $40,000 = $10,000.

6 a   Safe alternative = safe assets; risky alternative = derivatives.
b $600,000 × 1/2 + $0 × 1/2 = $300,000.
c $300,000 – $250,000 = $50,000.

Chapter 7

THE PUBLIC SECTOR

Chapter Review

The text's focus so far has been on private markets. This is overly simple, as the history of the automobile given in Chapter 1 illustrates. While the American automobile industry consists of private firms, government has played a large role throughout the industry's history, from issuing patents and regulating safety and environmental standards to occasionally protecting domestic manufacturers from foreign competition and providing unemployment benefits to laid-off workers. This blend of the public and private sectors is called a mixed economy.

This chapter considers the economic role of the public sector and how it operates differently from the private sector. Important roles for the public sector include improving the market's allocation of resources, stabilizing the overall performance of the economy, and redistributing income. The chapter also discusses government policies and emphasizes that government action may not always succeed in correcting market failures.

ESSENTIAL CONCEPTS

1   For the most part, the economic system relies on private markets to allocate resources, but government has al-ways played a major role. The balance between public and private sectors has changed over the years as government has taken on new responsibilities to improve perceived failures in the private economy. Government differs from private institutions in that its decisions are made by elected representatives or their appointed officers, and government has the power to force compliance with some of its orders.

2   Economists see roles for government in redistributing income and correcting market failures. These include stabilizing the economy's fluctuations, enhancing competition, and improving the performance of the economy where there are externalities, public goods, missing markets, or information problems. Government also intervenes to discourage or prohibit certain actions, overriding the principle of consumer sovereignty.

3   The **public sector** has a variety of instruments with which to accomplish its goals. It can take direct action, either producing the good or service itself or purchasing it from private firms. It can mandate private sector action, regulate private activity, or ban certain behaviors altogether. Finally, with a somewhat lighter hand, the government can provide incentives to increase or decrease certain types of actions through the use of its tax and subsidy powers.

4   While market failures imply that there is potential for improvement, government programs carry with them additional problems. Imperfect information, poor incentives for government administrators, waste, and the failure to foresee all of the consequences of government actions can cause public failures.

BEHIND THE ESSENTIAL CONCEPTS

1   **Externalities** exist whenever individuals or firms do not face the full costs and benefits of their decisions, and left alone, externalities create incentive problems. Negative externalities are costs borne by others, such as pollution, congestion, and noise. Positive externalities are benefits received by others, such as contributions for medical and other research, innovation, public parks, and endangered species preservation. Because decision makers can ignore the costs that spill over onto others, private firms overproduce negative externalities. Similarly, because they are not compensated, producers of positive externalities do not create enough. Governments can improve the allocation of resources by inducing individuals to produce fewer negative and more positive externalities.

2   **Public goods** have two important characteristics. Once they are provided, the marginal cost of another consumer's enjoying the good is zero. For example, a second, third, or fourth person can view a public statue without affecting the first person's enjoyment. The second characteristic is that it is costly to exclude individuals from enjoying the public good. Placing the statue in a private viewing area and charging admission misses the point of a monument. This feature makes it difficult for private individuals to collect enough funds to provide public goods. The fact that people can choose to enjoy public goods without paying for them is called the **free-rider** problem, and it is one reason economists often recommend that the public sector take a role in providing public goods.

3   When the private market fails to allocate resources efficiently, there is a potential role for government action. For example, when a public good such as a traffic light is needed, the government is the natural choice to provide it. When negative externalities are present, such as pollution, the government may be able to discourage them. The income distribution produced by private markets may be unacceptable, and the government may be able to redistribute it. Governments are large organizations, however, and policies do not always work as intended.

4   The existence of market failures prompts the call for more government intervention. **Government failures** justify calls for less intervention. Often what is needed is different, better government action, which harnesses market incentives to bring about a better allocation of resources.

SELF-TEST

True or False

1   The American economic system relies primarily on private markets.

2   Government's role in the economy has remained essentially unchanged since the early 1900s.

3   Services, such as police and fire protection, education, and parks, are provided mostly by state and local governments.

4   Adam Smith's "invisible hand" refers to the role of government in correcting market failures.

5   Government action is distinguished from private sector action in that government always has better information.

6   While markets often are efficient producers of wealth, they do not necessarily distribute that wealth equally.

7   Externalities are present whenever an individual or a firm can take an action without bearing all the costs and benefits.

8   The marginal cost of an additional consumer is zero for a public good.

9   The marginal cost of production is zero for a public good.

10   It is very costly to exclude those who do not pay from consuming private goods.

11   Markets for new inventions fail if those who benefit from new inventions do not pay the inventor.

12   The free-rider problem implies that private markets may not provide public goods efficiently.

13   If the private market provides too little of some good or service, then government can increase the quantity provided by subsidizing the good or service.

14   Even though markets may fail to allocate resources efficiently, government action may make matters worse.

15   Civil service rules and political pressures create incentive problems that may lead to public failures.

Multiple Choice

1   Which of the following is not one of the four basic questions an economy must answer?

   a   What is produced, and in what quantities?
   b   How are goods and services produced?
   c   For whom are the goods and services produced?
   d   Who makes the decisions?
   e   All of the above are basic questions.

2   Private institutions, such as business firms and not-for-profit organizations, are distinguished from government in that

   a   private decision makers are rational;
   b   government decision makers have adaptive expectations;

c   government decision makers are elected or appointed by someone who is elected;

d   government has certain powers of coercion;

e   c and d.

3   In his book *The Wealth of Nations,* Adam Smith argued that the public interest is best promoted by

a   government control of the economy;

b   the benevolence of well-meaning citizens;

c   individuals pursuing their own self-interest;

d   adherence to time-honored traditions;

e   all of the above.

4   Which of the following is not a legitimate role of government?

a   solving the problem of scarcity;

b   redistributing income;

c   stabilizing the level of economic activity;

d   correcting market failures.

e   All of the above are legitimate roles.

5   Which of the following is an example of market failure?

a   Housing is expensive.

b   The poor often cannot afford adequate health care.

c   The ostentatious displays of wealth by the rich and famous are offensive.

d   Periodic episodes of high unemployment trouble market economies.

e   All of the above.

6   The right to seize private property (with proper compensation) for public use is called

a   diminishing returns;

b   taxation;

c   deregulation;

d   nationalization;

e   eminent domain.

7   Which of the following is not an example of an externality?

a   environmental pollution;

b   research and development;

c   restoring buildings in decaying areas;

d   contributions to philanthropic organizations.

e   All of the above are examples of externalities.

8   When farmers irrigate their crops with water provided by the government at subsidized prices, there is

a   an externality;

b   a public good;

c   a market;

d   a patent;

e   none of the above.

9   Which of the following is (are) true of pure public goods?

a   The marginal cost of an additional individual using the good is zero.

b   It is impossible to exclude people from receiving the good.

c   They are efficiently provided through the interaction of supply and demand.

d   a and b.

e   All of the above.

10   Private markets have difficulty supplying public goods because

a   of the free-rider problem;

b   of the federal system of government;

c   the level of private activity fluctuates;

d   the income distribution is inequitable;

e   all markets are efficient.

11   One advantage that government has in the provision of public goods is that it

a   is not subject to scarcity;

b   does not face uncertainty about the demand for public goods;

c   can coerce citizens to pay for them;

d   need not always be rational;

e   none of the above.

12   The free-rider problem refers to

a   the idea that public transportation always runs large deficits;

b   the idea that when people can enjoy a public good without paying for it, they often do not contribute;

c   the idea that markets fail to allocate resources efficiently when there are externalities;

d   the idea that the marginal cost of an additional consumer enjoying a pure public good is zero;

e   none of the above.

13   Which of the following is not an example of direct government action to correct market failure?

a   A country nationalizes its banking system.

b   Tax breaks are offered for exploring for new deposits of oil.

c   A large city builds shelters for the homeless.

d   The army purchases tanks from a private firm.

e   All of the above are examples of direct action.

14   Which of the following is not an example of mandating private sector action?

a   Tuna fishers are required to use nets with larger openings so that captured dolphins may escape.

b   Electric utilities are required to install scrubbing devices in smokestacks.

c   Trucking firms are required to pay vehicle use fees.

d   a and b.

e   All of the above.

15   Consumer sovereignty means that

a   individuals are the best judges of what is in their own interest;

b   there is no role for government in product-safety regulations;

c   consumers always have good information;

d   consumers are rational decision makers;

e   a and c.

16   Which of the following is not a reason for government failure?

a imperfect information;

b government waste;

c incentives of public administrators;

d missing markets.

e All of the above are reasons for government failure.

17 Which of the following is not a reason for market failure?

a externalities;

b public goods;

c missing markets;

d lack of competition.

e All of the above are reasons for market failure.

18 Private markets may not provide information efficiently because

a information is scarce;

b information is costly to produce;

c certain types of information are public goods;

d the principle of consumer sovereignty does not apply to information;.

e private markets cannot exercise eminent domain.

19 Market failure occurs when

a there are positive externalities;

b there are negative externalities;

c there are positive or negative externalities;

d there are no externalities;.

e none of the above.

20 Government can provide incentives to produce more of some good by

a taxing it;

b subsidizing it;

c banning its production;

d redistributing it;

e using the "invisible hand."

Completion

1 The failure of private markets to produce economic efficiency is called _____.

2 When an individual or firm can take an action without bearing the full costs and benefits, there is said to be an _____.

3 Goods for which it costs nothing extra to have an additional individual enjoy are called _____.

4 Because it is difficult to exclude those who do not pay from benefiting from public goods, the private markets do a poor job of providing public goods. This is the _____ problem.

5 If the government seeks to encourage some activity, such as recycling, it can _____ the activity.

6 Government's ability to seize private property for legitimate public purpose is called _____.

7 When resources are idle, the economy is operating _____ its production possibilities curve.

8 Three legitimate economic roles of government are to redistribute income, stabilize the economy, and _____.

9 During the late 1970s and early 1980s, many regulations were reduced or eliminated in transportation, telecommunications, and banking. This process is an example of _____.

10 Three instruments of government for economic purposes are taking direct action, mandating private action, and providing _____ to the private sector through taxes and subsidies.

Answers to Self-Test

True or False

1	t	4	f	7	t	10	f	13	t
2	f	5	f	8	t	11	t	14	t
3	t	6	t	9	f	12	t	15	t

Multiple Choice

1	e	6	e	11	c	16	d
2	e	7	e	12	b	17	e
3	c	8	a	13	b	18	c
4	a	9	d	14	c	19	c
5	d	10	a	15	a	20	b

Completion

1 market failure

2 externality

3 public goods

4 free-rider

5 subsidize

6 eminent domain

7 inside

8 reallocate resources

9 deregulation

10 incentives

Doing Economics: Tools and Practice Problems

When an activity causes positive externalities, or external benefits, the government can often improve matters through subsidies. This section explores two questions. First, how do subsidies encourage more of the subsidized activity? Our analysis will be very much like the treatment of the economic effects of taxation in Chapter 5. The other issue is why decisions are likely to be inefficient when there are externalities. This is an application of the technique of balancing marginal benefits and marginal costs introduced in Chapter 2.

SUBSIDIES

Many goods and services receive subsidies from various levels of government. Sometimes, as in the case of home ownership, the demanders benefit directly. In other cases, as with federal water projects, the subsidies are paid directly to the suppliers. Subsidies have their effects by shifting supply or demand curves, bringing about new equilibrium quantities. Tool Kit 7.1 shows how to analyze the impacts of subsidies.

Tool Kit 7.1: Using Supply and Demand to Determine the Effects of Subsidies

If subsidies are paid directly to demanders, the demand curve shifts. If paid directly to suppliers, subsidies shift the supply curve. The remainder of the analysis parallels the basic method of supply and demand. Follow these steps.

Step one: Start with a no-subsidy equilibrium in the appropriate market.

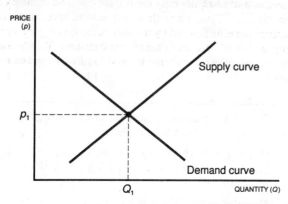

Step two: Identify the magnitude of the subsidy and whether it is paid directly to the demanders or suppliers.

Step three: If the subsidy is paid to demanders, shift the demand curve up (vertically) by exactly the amount of the subsidy. If the subsidy is paid to suppliers, shift the supply curve down by exactly the amount of the subsidy.

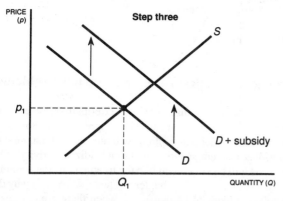

Step four: Find the new equilibrium and compare it with the original equilibrium.

1   (Worked problem: effects of subsidies) Home ownership is treated very favorably by the U.S. tax system. The interest paid on mortgages is tax deductible, and the taxes on capital gains earned by selling at more than the purchase price can be deferred and even avoided altogether. To see how the subsidy affects the housing market, consider the market for three-bedroom bungalows in Little Spoon. The market demand and supply curves without the subsidy are given in Table 7.1.

Table 7.1

Demand		Supply	
Price	Quantity	Price	Quantity
$125,000	10	$125,000	50
$100,000	14	$100,000	42
$ 90,000	25	$ 90,000	31
$ 80,000	28	$ 80,000	28
$ 70,000	31	$ 70,000	20

a   Find the equilibrium price and quantity.
b   The tax advantages accruing to the home owner amount to $20,000 over the life of the occupancy. Calculate the demand curve with the subsidy included.
c   Find the equilibrium price and quantity with the subsidy in place. How does the subsidy change the number of bungalows sold in Little Spoon?

Step-by-step solution

Step one (a): Start with a no-subsidy equilibrium in the appropriate market. The price is $80,000; the market clears with 28 houses sold. This is the answer to part a.

Step two (b): Identify the magnitude of the subsidy and whether it is paid directly to the demanders or suppliers. The subsidy is $20,000, paid to demanders.

Step three: Because it is paid to demanders, the subsidy causes the demand curve to shift vertically by $20,000. To calculate this, add $20,000 to each entry in the price column of the demand curve. The new demand curve is given in Table 7.2, which is the answer to part b.

Table 7.2

Demand	
Price	Quantity
$145,000	10
$120,000	14
$110,000	25
$100,000	28
$ 90,000	31

Step four (c): Find the new equilibrium and compare it with the original equilibrium. The new equilibrium price is $90,000, and the market clears at 31 houses sold. The subsidy has increased the number of home owners in Little Spoon from 28 to 31. The price is $10,000 higher, so the $20,000 subsidy makes home owners only $10,000 better off. Producers share in the benefits with a $10,000 higher price. The solution is illustrated in the diagram.

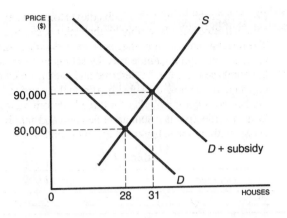

2   (Practice problem: effects of subsidies) Her eyes brightening at the thought of thousands of stressed, child-raising voters, Senator Shill has proposed child care grants of $10,000 per family. The demand and supply curves for child care services (measured in days) are given in Table 7.3.

Table 7.3

Demand		Supply	
Price (thousands)	Quantity (days)	Price (thousands)	Quantity (days)
$50	50,000	$50	100,000
$45	60,000	$45	80,000
$40	70,000	$40	70,000
$35	80,000	$35	60,000
$30	100,000	$30	50,000

a   Find the equilibrium price and quantity without the subsidy.
b   Calculate the demand with the subsidy.
c   Find the equilibrium price and quantity with the subsidy. Compare the equilibria, and explain the effects of the subsidy.

3   (Practice problem: effects of subsidies) To promote conversion to renewable sources of energy, the government has offered various tax deductions and credits for the purchase and installation of solar water heaters. The value to a typical taxpayer of the tax provisions is $3,000. The supply and demand curves for solar water heaters are given in Table 7.4.

Table 7.4

Demand		Supply	
Price	Quantity	Price	Quantity
$8,000	1,000	$8,000	10,000
$7,000	3,000	$7,000	9,000
$6,000	5,000	$6,000	8,000
$5,000	7,000	$5,000	7,000
$4,000	9,000	$4,000	6,000
$3,000	11,000	$3,000	5,000

a   Find the equilibrium price and quantity without the subsidy.

b   Calculate the demand with the subsidy.
c   Find the equilibrium price and quantity with the subsidy. Compare the equilibria, and explain the effects of the subsidy.

POSITIVE EXTERNALITIES

Individuals make decisions by balancing their private benefits and costs at the margin, but efficiency requires that all benefits and costs, not only the private ones, be included in the decision. Thus, when there are externalities, there are costs or benefits ignored by the individual making the decision, and this fact leads to inefficient decisions. This tool kit focuses on positive externalities and the inefficiencies that result.

Tool Kit 7.2: Showing How Positive Externalities Lead to Inefficiencies

Positive externalities occur when decision makers ignore some benefits of their actions. Follow these steps to see how this leads to inefficient decisions.

Step one: Find the private marginal benefits and costs of the relevant activity.

Step two: Find the equilibrium level of the activity, which is the level at which private marginal benefits equal marginal cost.

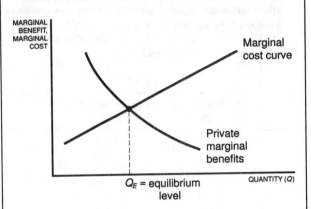

Step three: Calculate the social marginal benefits by adding the external benefit to the private marginal benefit at each level of the activity.

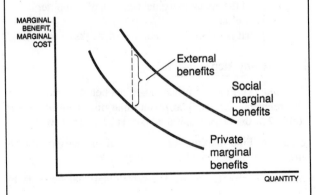

Step four: Find the efficient level of the activity, which is the level at which social marginal benefits equal marginal cost.

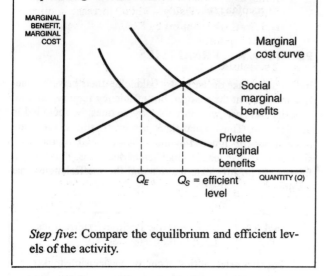

Step five: Compare the equilibrium and efficient levels of the activity.

4   (Worked problem: positive externalities) An important example of an activity that generates positive externalities is worker training. When firms train their employees, the employees not only become more productive in the job, they can also earn higher wages elsewhere. This increase in earning power is a positive externality. The QXV Corporation is considering sending some of its white-collar employees to computer school. The cost is $1,000 per week, and the private marginal benefits to QXV are given in Table 7.5. Also, the value of the external benefit is $500 per week.

Table 7.5

Weeks at school	Private marginal benefits
1	$1,500
2	$1,250
3	$1,000
4	$ 750
5	$ 500
6	$ 250

a   How many weeks of computer schooling will the company provide?
b   Find the social marginal benefits of computer schooling.
c   What is the efficient number of weeks of schooling?

Step-by-step solution

Step one (a): Find the private marginal benefits and costs of the relevant activity. The private marginal benefits are in Table 7.5; the private marginal cost is $1,000 per week.

Step two: Find the equilibrium level of the activity. Private marginal benefits equal $1,000 at 3 weeks.

Step three (b): Calculate the social marginal benefits by

adding the external benefit to the private marginal benefit at each level of the activity. The answer is in Table 7.6.

Table 7.6

Weeks at school	Private marginal benefits	Social marginal benefits
1	$1,500	$2,000
2	$1,250	$1,750
3	$1,000	$1,500
4	$ 750	$1,250
5	$ 500	$1,000
6	$ 250	$ 750

Step four (c): Find the efficient level of the activity. Social marginal benefits equal marginal cost at 5 weeks.

Step five: Compare the equilibrium and efficient levels of the activity. The equilibrium number of weeks is 3, which is less than the efficient number, which is 5. The number of weeks provided is too low because the firm ignores the externality.

5   (Practice problem: positive externalities) ZZZX Pharmaceuticals is considering how many scientists to put to work researching a new drug for Angolan flu. Each scientist, complete with equipment and assistance, costs $200,000. The research will bring profits to ZZZX, but it will also bring about advances in viral research that other companies may build on in their own research. The private benefits are given in Table 7.7. The external marginal benefits are $150,000.

Table 7.7

Scientists	Private benefits
1	$400,000
2	$600,000
3	$700,000
4	$750,000
5	$750,000

a   How many scientists will the company use? (Hint: First find the private marginal benefits.)
b   Find the social marginal benefits of research scientists.
c   What is the efficient number of scientists?

6   (Practice problem: positive externalities) Hillside County farmers have been advised to erect earthen dikes for erosion control. Each dike costs $2,000. The private marginal benefits are given in the second column of Table 7.8, but they do not include the external benefit that one farmer's erosion control efforts provide to her neighbors. The external benefits appear in the third column of the table.

Table 7.8

Dikes	Private marginal benefits	External marginal benefits
1	$3,000	$8,000
2	$2,000	$7,000
3	$1,500	$6,000
4	$1,000	$5,000
5	$ 500	$4,000
6	$ 0	$3,000
7	$ 0	$2,000

a   How many dikes will each farmer erect?
b   Find the social marginal benefits of a farmer's dikes.
c   What is the efficient number of dikes?

Answers to Problems

2   a   Price = $40; quantity = 70,000.
    b   The new demand curve is given in Table 7.9.

Table 7.9

Demand	
Price	Quantity
$60	50,000
$55	60,000
$50	70,000
$45	80,000
$40	100,000

c   The new equilibrium price is $45,000, and the quantity is 80,000. The subsidy increases the quantity from 70,000 to 80,000. Consumers are better off by $5,000 ($10,000 subsidy – $5,000 increase in price), and firms are better off by $5,000, which is the increase in price.

3   a   Price = $5,000; quantity = 7,000.
    b   The new demand curve is given in Table 7.10.

Table 7.10

Demand	
Price	Quantity
$11,000	1,000
$10,000	3,000
$ 9,000	5,000
$ 8,000	7,000
$ 7,000	9,000
$ 6,000	11,000

c   The new equilibrium price is $7,000, and the quantity is 9,000. The subsidy increases the quantity from 7,000 to 9,000. Consumers are better off by $1,000 ($3,000 subsidy – $2,000 increase in price), and firms are better off by $2,000, which is the increase in price.

5   a   2 scientists.
    b   The social marginal benefits are given in Table 7.11.

Table 7.11

Scientists	Private benefits	Private marginal benefits	Social marginal benefits
1	$400,000	$400,000	$550,000
2	$600,000	$200,000	$350,000
3	$700,000	$100,000	$250,000
4	$750,000	$ 50,000	$200,000
5	$750,000	$ 0	$150,000

c   The efficient number is 4 scientists. The company chooses only 2 because it ignores the externality.

6   a   2 dikes.
    b   The social marginal benefits are given in Table 7.12.

Table 7.12

Dikes	Private marginal benefits	External marginal benefits	Social marginal benefits
1	$3,000	$8,000	$11,000
2	$2,000	$7,000	$ 9,000
3	$1,500	$6,000	$ 7,500
4	$1,000	$5,000	$ 6,000
5	$ 500	$4,000	$ 4,500
6	$ 0	$3,000	$ 3,000
7	$ 0	$2,000	$ 2,000

c   The efficient number of dikes is 7. Farmers only erect 2 because they ignore the external benefits.

Part Two

Perfect Markets

Chapter 8

THE CONSUMPTION DECISION

Chapter Review

The detailed study of microeconomics, the branch that focuses on the behavior of individuals and firms and builds up to an understanding of markets, begins in this chapter and continues throughout Parts Two and Three of the text. The basic competitive model of the private economy developed here is one you'll use throughout this course. Chapters 8–13 build on this model; exploring first the decisions individuals make—how much to consume, save, invest, and work—and then the decisions firms take—what and how much to produce and by what method. The entire model is put together in Chapter 13.

ESSENTIAL CONCEPTS

1   The consumer's decisions about how much of each good to purchase—that is, the demand for each—are made in a two-step procedure. First, the consumer finds how much can be consumed given the amount of money available. This step is the construction of the **opportunity set,** the outer edge of which is the **budget constraint.** Second, he chooses the best alternative along

the budget constraint. Figure 8.1 depicts a budget constraint.

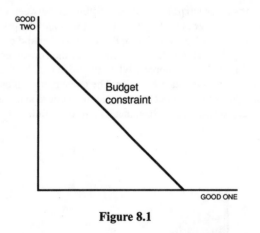

Figure 8.1

2   The budget constraint shows how much of each good can be purchased with the money available. The **slope** of the budget constraint is the **relative price** of the good measured on the horizontal axis. This relative price indicates the **trade-off**: how much of one good must be forgone to consume one more unit of the other.

3   The benefit or utility that a consumer derives from a good is measured by how much she is willing to pay. Consumers focus on the margin (the next unit) and continue to purchase more of the good until the *marginal benefit equals the price.*

4   When income increases, the budget constraint shifts out, but its slope does not change. Consumers buy more normal goods. Goods that people buy less of as income increases are called inferior goods, but these are the exceptions. The **income elasticity of demand** measures how much the quantity demanded changes as income changes. It is positive for **normal goods** and negative for **inferior goods.**

5   When price changes, the budget constraint rotates, becoming steeper if the price of the good on the horizontal axis rises and flatter if it falls. Introduced in Chapter 5, the **price elasticity of demand** measures how much the quantity demanded changes as price changes.

6   Price changes cause substitution and income effects. Suppose the price of a good rises. Because the good is relatively more expensive, the principle of substitution says that consumers will shift some of their consumption to other goods. This change is the **substitution effect.** At the same time, when the price is higher, the consumer is worse off and tends to buy less if the good is normal but more if the good is inferior. This change is the **income effect.**

7   **Utility** is the term economists use for the benefits that individuals receive for consuming goods. As people consume more of a particular good, they get smaller increments of utility. In other words, there is **diminishing marginal utility.** When the consumer has chosen the best bundle of goods, her utility is maximized and the marginal utility of each good equals its price.

8   **Consumer surplus** equals the difference between what the consumer is willing to pay for goods and the price (what he has to pay). Figure 8.2 shows a demand curve for apples, which also represents what the consumer is willing to pay for apples. When the price is $.25, the consumer purchases 8 apples. The consumer surplus, shown as the area between the demand curve and the price, measures the consumer's gain from trade.

Figure 8.2

BEHIND THE ESSENTIAL CONCEPTS

1   The budget constraint shows what quantities of goods are affordable. If you know the prices of goods and an individual's income, you can draw her budget constraint. As you might expect, people who have the same income and must pay the same prices have the same budget constraint. As price changes, each individual's budget constraint changes in the same way. The budget constraint indicates opportunities; it says nothing about the value that the consumer places on the goods. Individual tastes only come into the picture when the actual choices are made.

2   The slope of the budget line depends only on prices, not on income. Therefore, changes in income cannot change the slope of the budget line. Changes in income bring about a parallel shift in the budget constraint. Price changes, on the other hand, do change the slope. The budget constraint rotates when price changes.

3   Economists measure the responsiveness of quantity to income or price changes by using elasticities. In this chapter, there are two elasticities: the income elasticity of demand and the price elasticity of demand. Elasticities are relative percentage changes. The income elasticity equals the percentage that the quantity demanded changes when income changes by 1 percent. The price elasticity tells the percentage change in quantity demanded as the result of a 1 percent change in price.

4   The distinction between substitution and income effects is important, and it will reappear in the next chapter and throughout the course. Two points are key here. First, income effects are small in the consumption decision. Suppose that the price of milk rises by 10 percent. If I were spending $10 per month on milk, now I must spend $1 more to buy the same amount of milk. This makes me worse off by approximately $1, not a very important change in my well-being. The income effect captures how much extra milk can be bought with $1 of extra income. The second point is that the relatively more important substitution effect governs many important issues concerning the response to price changes, such as how elastic are demand curves, whether goods are substitutes or complements, and why taxes lead to inefficiencies.

5   The basic economic model says that individuals balance the benefits and costs of their decisions. It emphasizes choice at the margin, for the next unit of a good or service. Individuals continue buying until the marginal benefit equals the marginal cost. For the consumer, the marginal benefit (called the marginal utility) is just how much she is willing to pay for another unit. The marginal cost is the price. When marginal utility equals price, the consumer has realized all the possible gains from the purchase of the good.

6   There are two important diagrams in this chapter: the budget constraint and the demand curve. Although each is downward sloping, they should not be confused. The budget constraint drawn in Figure 8.1 shows the combinations of goods that a person can afford. Quantities of

goods are measured on each axis. The demand curve drawn in Figure 8.2 shows how much of *one* good will be purchased at each price. The quantity of the good is measured on the horizontal axis, and the price is measured on the vertical.

SELF-TEST

True or False

1 The budget constraint indicates that the amount spent on goods cannot exceed after tax income.

2 The slope of the budget constraint shows the trade-off between two goods.

3 Income determines the slope of the budget constraint.

4 The amount that an individual is willing to pay for coffee is called the marginal utility of coffee.

5 The amount that an individual is willing to pay for an extra cup of coffee is called the marginal utility of coffee.

6 A rational individual will increase her consumption of a good until the marginal utility equals the price.

7 When income increases, the budget constraint rotates, becoming flatter.

8 When income increases, the consumer demands more of inferior goods.

9 If an individual demands more of a good when income falls, the good is a complement.

10 If the income elasticity is less than zero, then the good is an inferior good.

11 The long-run income elasticity of demand is greater than the short-run income elasticity of demand.

12 If when the price of one good rises the demand for another also rises, the goods are substitutes.

13 If when the price of one good falls the demand for another also falls, the goods are complements.

14 When the price of a good falls, the substitution effect encourages more consumption of that good.

15 When the price of a normal good falls, the income effect encourages more consumption of that good.

Multiple Choice

1 Assuming that there is no saving or borrowing and a consumer's income is fixed, his budget constraint

a defines his opportunity set;
b indicates that total expenditures cannot be greater than total income;
c shows that marginal utility is decreasing;
d all of the above.
e a and b.

2 Suppose that the price of a movie ticket is $5 and the price of a pizza is $10. The trade-off between the two goods is

a one pizza for one movie ticket;
b two movie tickets for one pizza;
c two pizzas for one movie ticket;
d $2 per movie ticket;
e none of the above.

3 The marginal utility of a good indicates

a that the usefulness of the good is limited;
b the willingness to pay for an extra unit;
c that the good is scarce;
d that the slope of the budget constraint is the relative price;
e none of the above.

4 Diminishing marginal utility means that

a the usefulness of the good is limited;
b the willingness to pay for an extra unit decreases as more of that good is consumed;
c the good is less scarce;
d the slope of the budget constraint is flatter as more of that good is consumed;
e none of the above.

5 If Fred is willing to pay $100 for one espresso maker and $120 for two, then the marginal utility of the second espresso maker is

a $20;
b $120;
c $100;
d $60;
e $50.

6 When the income of a consumer increases, her budget constraint

a shifts outward parallel to the original budget constraint;
b rotates and becomes steeper;
c rotates and becomes flatter;
d shifts inward parallel to the original budget constraint;
e none of the above.

7 The percentage change in quantity demanded brought about by a 1 percent increase in income is

a 1;
b greater than zero;
c the income elasticity of demand;
d the price elasticity of demand;
e none of the above.

8 If the share of income that an individual spends on a good decreases as her income increases, then the income elasticity of demand is

a greater than 1;
b between zero and 1;
c zero;
d less than 1;
e less than zero.

9 In the long run,

a the price elasticity of demand is greater than in the short run;

b   the income elasticity of demand is greater than in the short run;

c   the price elasticity of demand is less than in the short run;

d   the income elasticity of demand is less than in the short run;

e   a and b.

10   When the price of a good (measured along the horizontal axis) falls, the budget constraint

a   rotate, and becoming flatter;

b   rotate, and becoming steeper;

c   shifts out parallel to the original budget constraint;

d   shifts in parallel to the original budget constraint;

e   none of the above.

11   If demand for a good falls as income rises, then

a   the good is a normal good;

b   the good is an inferior good;

c   the income elasticity is less than zero;

d   the income elasticity is between zero and 1;

e   b and c.

12   When the price of a good falls, the substitution effect

a   encourages the individual to consume more of the good;

b   encourages the individual to consume less of the good;

c   leads to more consumption if the good is an inferior good, but less if the good is a normal good;

d   leads to less consumption if the good is an inferior good, but more if the good is a normal good;

e   a and c.

13   When the price of a good falls, the income effect

a   encourages the individual to consume more of the good;

b   encourages the individual to consume less of the good;

c   leads to more consumption if the good is an inferior good, but less if the good is a normal good;

d   leads to less consumption if the good is an inferior good, but more if the good is a normal good;

e   a and c.

14   The rational consumer chooses her purchases for each good so that the

a   utility equals total expenditure;

b   marginal utility equals price;

c   consumer surplus equals zero;

d   marginal utility is diminishing;

e   income elasticity equals 1.

15   The difference between what the consumer is willing to pay for an item and what she has to pay is called

a   marginal utility;

b   the substitution effect;

c   consumer surplus;

d   the income effect;

e   the price elasticity of demand.

16   In general, the price elasticity of demand is greater when

a   the good is an inferior good;

b   there are good, close substitutes available;

c   there are good, close complements available;

d   the income elasticity of demand is less;

e   none of the above.

17   For normal goods, when income rises,

a   the budget constraint shifts out, parallel;

b   the demand curve shifts to the right;

c   quantity demanded increases;

d   more money is spent on the good;

e   all of the above.

18   For normal goods, as price rises,

a   the substitution effect encourages less consumption;

b   the income effect encourages less consumption;

c   the quantity demanded falls;

d   the demand for substitute goods increases;

e   all of the above.

19   For inferior goods, as price rises,

a   the substitution effect encourages less consumption;

b   the income effect encourages less consumption;

c   the income effect encourages more consumption;

d   the quantity demanded rises;

e   a and c.

20   The slope of the budget constraint depends on

a   the relative price of the goods;

b   the income of the consumer;

c   the availability of substitute goods;

d   whether the good is normal or inferior;

e   a and b.

Completion

1   The opportunity set for the consumer is defined by the _____, which says that expenditures cannot exceed income.

2   The slope of the budget line equals the _____ of the two goods.

3   The benefits of consumption are called _____.

4   The willingness to pay for an extra unit of some good is its _____.

5   When income increases, the budget constraint shifts outward in a _____ way.

6   The _____ of demand measures how consumption of a good changes in response to a change in income.

7   When the price of a good changes, the budget constraint _____.

8   The _____ of demand measures how consumption of a good changes in response to a change in price.

9 When the price of a good falls, the _____ effect always encourages more consumption of the good.

10 The difference between what the consumer is willing to pay for an item and what she has to pay is called _____.

Answers to Self-Test

True or False

1 t	4 f	7 f	10 t	13 f
2 t	5 t	8 f	11 t	14 t
3 f	6 t	9 f	12 t	15 t

Multiple Choice

1 e	6 a	11 e	16 b
2 b	7 c	12 a	17 e
3 b	8 d	13 d	18 e
4 b	9 e	14 b	19 e
5 a	10 a	15 c	20 a

Completion

1 budget constraint
2 relative price
3 utility
4 marginal utility
5 parallel
6 income elasticity
7 rotates
8 price elasticity
9 substitution
10 consumer surplus

Doing Economics: Tools and Practice Problems

The most important model in this chapter is the opportunity set for the consumer: the budget constraint. This section will first review how to construct the budget constraint and then explain how the budget constraint changes when price and income change. A somewhat more advanced topic follows, as we explore how to illustrate the substitution and income effects of price changes. Next, there are some applications: in-kind transfers and tax-subsidy schemes. Finally, we turn to marginal utility.

THE BUDGET CONSTRAINT

Because we have limited income, we must limit our purchases. The budget constraint shows what combinations of goods are affordable. Tool Kit 8.1 shows how to plot the budget constraint. After some practice problems, we study the effects of income and price changes. The basic technique is to first draw the budget constraint using the original income and price, then draw a new budget constraint using the new income and prices. Finally, we compare the old and new budget constraints.

Tool Kit 8.1: Plotting the Budget Constraint

The budget constraint shows what combinations of goods can be purchased with a limited amount of money. Constructing the budget constraint is one of the essential techniques needed in Part Two. Follow these four steps.

Step one: Draw a set of coordinate axes. Label the horizontal axis as the quantity of one good consumed and the vertical axis as the quantity of a second good consumed.

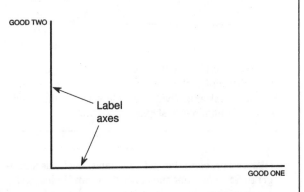

Step two: Calculate the quantity of the good measured on the horizontal axis that can be purchased if all the consumer's money is spent on it. Plot this quantity along the horizontal axis.

Step three: Calculate the quantity of the good measured on the vertical axis that can be purchased if all the consumer's money is spent on it. Plot this quantity along the vertical axis.

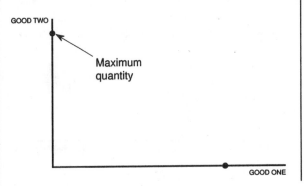

Step four: Draw a line segment connecting the two points. This line segment is the budget constraint.

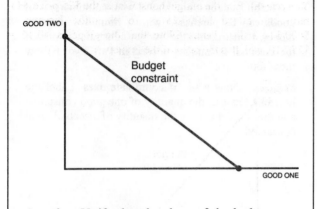

Step five: Verify that the slope of the budget constraint is (minus) the price of the good measured on the horizontal axis divided by the price of the good measured on the vertical axis.

1   (Worked problem: budget constraint) Dick has a budget of $500 to paint and paper the rooms in his new condominium. The price of enough paint for 1 room is $25; the price of wallpaper is $50 per room. Draw Dick's budget constraint.

Step-by-step solution

Step one: Draw a set of coordinate axes, and label the horizontal one "Rooms painted" and the vertical one "Rooms papered." (There is no rule as to which good goes on which axis. It is fine either way.)

Step two: Calculate how many rooms can be painted with the entire $500. This number is $500/$25 = 20 rooms. Plot this quantity along the horizontal axis.

Step three: Calculate how many rooms can be papered with the entire $500. This number is $500/$50 = 10 rooms. Plot this quantity along the vertical axis.

Step four: Draw a line segment connecting these two points. This line segment is the budget constraint.

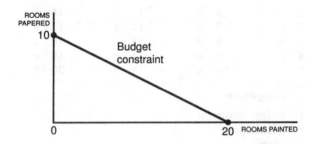

Step five: Verify the slope. The slope of the budget constraint is 10/20 = 1/2. The price ratio is $25/$50 = 1/2.

2   (Practice problem: budget constraint) Dean Lewis would like to have some of the practice pianos tuned in the charming but decaying music building. She could use some of the $1,000 in the supplies and services budget, but that money must pay for repairing broken lockers. The piano tuner charges $50 per piano, and the carpenter charges $40 per locker. Plot her budget constraint and verify that the slope is the relative price.

3   (Practice problem: budget constraint). Draw the following budget constraints.

   a Budget for hiring groundskeepers = $100,000; price of a full-time employee = $20,000; price of a part-time employee = $8,000.

   b Budget for food = $250; price of microwave snacks = $2.00. (Plot expenditures on all other food on the vertical axis.)

   c Budget for landscaping = $2,000; price of lilac bushes = $50; price of cherry trees = $80.

   d Budget for library acquisitions = $50,000; price of books = $40; price of journal subscriptions = $100.

4   (Worked problem: budget constraint with income and price changes) Bill Kutt, a somewhat diminutive and lazy student, has decided to take a course on the nineteenth-century American novel. Many books are assigned, and all are available in the abridged "Fred's Notes" versions at $8 each. The unabridged versions are $3 each. Bill has $72 to spend.

   a Plot his budget constraint.

   b Show how it changes when Bill finds that he has another $24 (for a total of $96).

Step-by-step solution

Step one (a): Plot Bill's budget constraint using the procedure outlined above. He can afford $72/$8 = 9 abridged and $72/$3 = 24 unabridged notes. Note that the slope is 9/24 = $3/$8, which is the ratio of the prices.

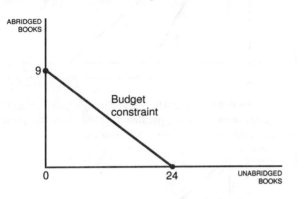

Step two (b): Plot Bill's budget constraint with $96 to spend. He can now afford $96/$8 = 12 abridged and $96/$3 = 32 unabridged notes.

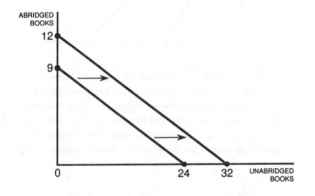

Step three: Verify that the shift in the budget constraint is parallel. The slope is 12/32 = $3/$8, which is the ratio of the prices. Because the prices have not changed, the slope has not changed. The income increase causes a parallel shift.

5 (Practice problem: budget constraint with income and price changes) Helen is nervous about graduate school. She is considering hiring a tutor for her economics course at $10 per hour. Another possibility is to attend sessions on how to improve the score of her GMAT test. These cost $30 each. She has $90.

   a Plot her budget constraint.
   b Oops! Unexpectedly stuck with the tab at Ernie's Ice House, Helen now has only $60 to spend. Plot her new budget constraint.

6 (Worked problem: budget constraint with income and price changes) Dissatisfied with his social life, Horatio has budgeted $400 for self-improvement. He is considering elocution lessons at $25 per hour and ballroom dancing classes at $10 each.

   a Plot Horatio's budget constraint.
   b Good news! A new elocution studio offers lessons at the introductory price of $20. Plot the new budget constraint.

Step-by-step solution

Step one (a): Plot the budget constraint at the $25 price. Horatio can afford $400/$25 = 16 elocution lessons or $400/$10 = 40 classes. Note that the slope is 40/16 = $25/$10, which is the ratio of the prices.

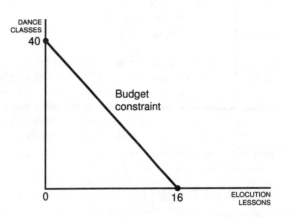

Step two (b): Plot the budget constraint at the $20 price. Horatio can now afford $400/$20 = 20 elocution lessons, which is 4 more, but he still can only buy 40 dance lessons.

Step three: Verify that the budget constraint rotates. The slope is now 40/20 = $20/$10, which is the ratio of the new prices and is flatter. The price decrease rotated the budget constraint. The point at 0 elocution lessons and 40 dance classes does not change, because when no elocution lessons are purchased, the price change makes no difference.

7 (Practice problem: budget constraint with income and price changes) With some of her extra cash ($100 each month), Sho-Yen buys meals and blankets and donates them to the nearby shelter for the homeless. The meals cost $2 each, and she buys the blankets for $5 each.

   a Plot her budget constraint.
   b The supplier of meals cuts the price to $1. Plot the new budget constraint.

8 (Practice problem: budget constraint with income and price changes) For each of these problems, draw the budget constraints before and after the change. Plot "Expenditures on other goods" on the vertical axis.

   a Income = $400; price of potatoes = $1 per sack; price of potatoes rises to $2 per sack.

b   Income = $5,000; price of therapy sessions = $100 per hour; income rises to $6,000.

c   Income = $450; price of housecleaning = $45; income falls to $225.

d   Income = $100; price of pizzas = $5; price increases to $10.

Substitution and Income Effects

Price changes rotate the budget constraint and bring about two effects, substitution and income. The substitution effect indicates that consumers buy more when the price falls and less when it rises. The income effect, on the other hand, is not necessarily in the opposite direction of the price change. Tool Kit 8.2 uses the budget constraint to distinguish substitution and income effects.

Tool Kit 8.2: Distinguishing Between Substitution and Income Effects

When the price of a good changes, there are two effects: substitution and income. These can be illustrated using the budget constraint. This technique clarifies the point that while the substitution effect is always in the opposite direction to the price change, the income effect may go either way. Follow these steps.

Step one: Draw the budget line with the original price.

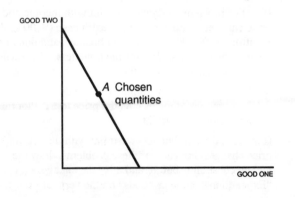

Step two: Find the chosen quantities along the budget line. Label this point *A*.

Step three: Draw the budget line with the new price.

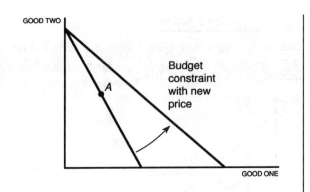

Step four: Draw a dashed line through point *A* and parallel to the *new* budget line.

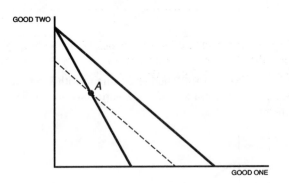

Step five: Darken the portion of the dotted-line segment that lies above the original budget line. The points along this darkened segment represent the quantities made possible by the substitution effect of the price change. The income effect shifts this line parallel out to the new budget line drawn in step three.

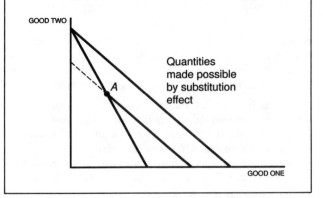

---

9   (Worked problem: substitution and income effects) Always diligent in keeping up with out-of-town friends and acquaintances, Lurleen budgets $30 per month for postage and phone calls. A long-distance call costs her $2 on average, and the price of a stamped envelope is $.30. She makes 6 calls and mails 60 letters each month.

a   Plot her budget constraint, and label the point that she has chosen.

b   Headline news! The price of a stamped envelope falls to $.20. Illustrate the substitution and income effects of the price change.

Step-by-step solution

Step one (a): Draw the original budget constraint. The maximum quantity of calls is $30/$2 = 15, and the maximum quantity of letters is $30/$.30 = 100.

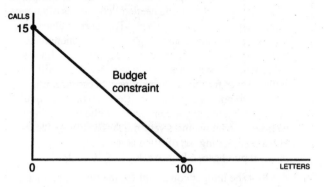

Step two: Plot and label the chosen point (6 calls, 60 letters). Note that this is on the budget constraint because (6 × $2) + (60 × $.30) = $30. Label this point *A*.

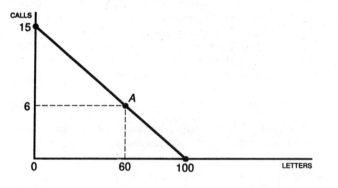

Step three (b): Draw the new budget constraint. The maximum quantities are 15 calls and 30/$.20 = 150 letters.

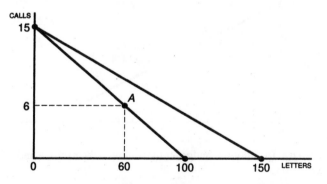

Step four: Draw a dashed line segment through *A* parallel to the new budget constraint.

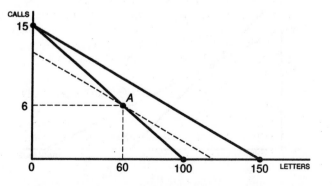

Step five: Darken the portion of the dashed line segment that lies above the original budget constraint. Notice that the substitution effect would lead Lurleen to choose a point like *B* along this segment, where the quantity of letters is greater. We say that the substitution effect of a price decrease is always to increase the quantity demanded. The income effect moves this darkened segment out to the new budget constraint. Lurleen would write more letters if letters were a normal good, but she would write fewer if letters were inferior. The income effect can go either way in principle, although most goods are normal.

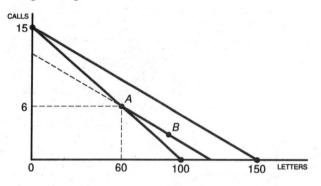

10 (Practice problem: substitution and income effects) Yves loves to wear whites for tennis. He sends his outfits to the cleaners at a price of $3.60 each. Playing tennis also requires new balls, which cost $2. Yves' tennis budget is $36 per week, which allows him his current consumption levels of 8 cans of balls and 5 clean outfits.

    a   Plot his budget constraint, and show his current consumption choice.

    b   The price of tennis balls has risen to $4.50. Illustrate the substitution and income effects of this price increase.

11 (Practice problem: substitution and income effects) For each of the following, illustrate the substitution and income effects of the price change. Plot "Expenditures on other goods" on the vertical axis, and pick any point on the original budget line as the quantities consumed before the price change.

    a   Income = $100; price of bricks = $.10 each; price changes to $.20.

    b   Income = $1,000; price of haircuts = $20; price changes to $25.

    c   Income = $500; price of pies = $5; price changes to $4.

    d   Income = $10; price of baseball cards = $.50; price changes to $.25

APPLICATIONS

Now that you have mastered plotting the budget constraint and analyzing how it changes when price or income changes, you are ready for some applications. The following problems look at how the budget constraint is affected by in-kind transfers, such as food stamps and tax changes. These latter problems illustrate the relationship between the substitution effect and tax distortions.

12   (Worked problem: applications) Many government programs deliver benefits in kind to people. For example, food stamps can only be used to buy food. Economists often argue that cash transfers are better. The typical food stamp recipient has $200 per week in income in addition to $80 per week in food stamps.

   a   Draw the budget constraint.
   b   One proposal is to substitute $80 in cash for the stamps. Draw the budget constraint that results from this proposal.
   c   Which would the recipient prefer? Why?

Step-by-step solution

Step one (a): Draw the budget constraint with the food stamps. Label the axes "Food consumption in dollars" and "Expenditures on other goods." The slope is 1 because $1 less spent on other goods means $1 spent on food. Note that no more than $200 may be spent on other goods.

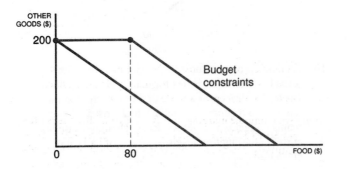

Step two (b): Draw the budget constraint with the cash grants replacing the food stamps.

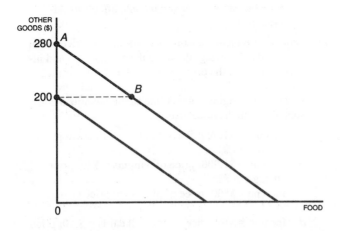

Step three (c): Compare. The difference is that the cash grant allows the recipient to choose the points between *A* and *B*. Many recipients would not choose these low levels of food consumption anyway; so there would be no difference. Some might, however, and these people would prefer the cash.

13   (Practice problem: applications) The city of Lansing, Michigan, recently planted 2 trees (worth $20 each) in every yard. The typical Lansing resident has $4,000 in disposable income this summer.

   a   Plot the budget constraint with the in-kind transfer of 2 trees.

   b   Plot the budget constraint with the $40 refunded through the tax system.
   c   Which opportunity set is preferred? How could the tree planting be justified?

15   (Worked problem: applications) When less consumption of some good or service is needed, economists often recommend putting a tax on the good or service. One objection is that the taxes lead to higher prices, which make people worse off. If the tax revenue is refunded, however, people can be approximately as well off, yet still face higher prices for the good or service. In essence, it is possible to put the substitution effect to work and reduce consumption of the good or service without reducing the well-being of consumers very much. The city of Pleasantville is running out of room at the dump. The typical resident purchases 6 bags weekly at $.10 each.

   a   Plot the budget constraint for the typical resident, and show the current consumption choice.
   b   In an effort to encourage recycling and discourage disposal, the city institutes a user fee of $1.90 per trash bag. (Trash bags now cost $2.) Keeping to their "No new taxes" pledge, the city council members vote to combine the user fee with a tax refund. Each citizen receives a tax refund of $1.90 × 6 = $11.40. Plot the new budget constraint.
   c   Discuss the user fee–tax refund plan.

Step-by-step solution

Step one (a): Plot the budget constraint with neither a user fee nor a tax refund. Label the resident's chosen point *A*.

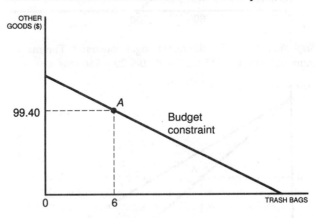

Step two (b): Plot the budget constraint with the user fee and tax refund.

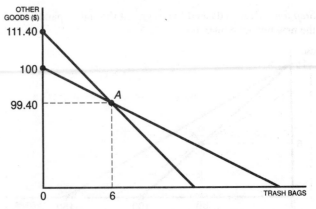

Step three (c): We see that the net effect of the entire user fee–tax refund scheme is only the substitution of the increase in the price of bags to $2. The resident is no worse off (because he can still consume as he did before the user fee), but he will be motivated to use fewer bags. (One minor flaw in the program is that as people substitute away from trash bags, they will pay less in user fees than is needed to finance the tax relief.)

16 (Practice problem: applications) Since the Gulf War, gasoline consumption has been on the mind of Senator Adam Smith. He proposes a $1-per-gallon tax on gasoline, which currently sells for $1. Assume that this tax will increase the price of gas to $2. The senator also proposes refunding the gas-tax revenues through an income tax cut large anough to allow consumers to buy the same amount of gas as before the tax.

   a Plot the budget constraint with no added gas tax.
   b Plot the budget constraint with the gas tax and the refund.
   c Columnist Kirk Jimpatrick writes, "This plan will have no effect. The government takes money away with one hand and gives it back with the other." Is he right? Why or why not?

UTILITY AND PREFERENCES

The first step in the consumption decision is to determine what is affordable—to plot the budget constraint. The second step is to choose the best bundle of goods from all those that lie along the budget constraint. Economists say that the best bundle gives the greatest utility. When the consumer has chosen the best bundle, the marginal utility (what she would be willing to pay for another unit) equals the price. Tool Kit 8.3 shows how to use marginal utility to interpret the consumption decision and also calculate consumer surplus.

Tool Kit 8.3: Using Marginal Utility to Choose the Best Bundle of Goods

The rational consumer demands the quantity of a good for which marginal equals price. The difference between what she is willing to pay and her expenditure is consumer surplus. Follow these steps to see how it works.

Step one: Identify the product price and utility (willingness to pay) for each quantity of the good.

Step two: Compute marginal utility for each quantity of the good.

Marginal utility = change in utility
= utility of one fewer unit – utility.

Step three: Choose the quantity for which marginal utility equals price.

Step four: Compute her expenditure.

Expenditure = price × quantity.

Step five: Calculate consumer surplus.

Consumer surplus = utility – expenditure.

---

17 (Worked problem: marginal utility) Table 8.1 gives Ching-Fan's willingness to pay (utility) for various hours of on-line access per week. On-line time is priced at $12 per hour.

   a Compute marginal utility for each hour.
   b How many hours will Ching-Fan purchase?
   c Compute his consumer surplus for this good.

Table 8.1

Number of on-line hours	Utility (willingness to pay)
0	0
1	$ 20
2	$ 38
3	$ 54
4	$ 68
5	$ 80
6	$ 90
7	$ 98
8	$104

Step-by-step solution

Step one: Identify utility for each quantity and the price. The price is $12 and utility is given in Table 8.1.

Step two: Compute marginal utility. The first unit raises utility from $0 to $20. The marginal utility is then $20 – $0 = $20. Similarly, marginal utility for the second unity equals $38 – $20 = $18. Continuing, we have the following table. Notice that marginal utility diminishes as quantity increases.

Table 8.1A

Number of on-line hours	Utility (willingness to pay)	Marginal Utility
0	0	
1	$ 20	$20
2	$ 38	$18
3	$ 54	$16
4	$ 68	$14
5	$ 80	$12
6	$ 90	$10
7	$ 98	$ 8
8	$104	$ 6

Step three: Choose the quantity for which marginal utility equals price. The price ($12) equals marginal utility when 5 hours are purchased.

Step four: Calculate expenditure. Expenditure is $12 × 5 = $60.

Step five: Calculate consumer surplus. His utility is $80 when he buys 5 hours. Consumer surplus is $80 – $60 = $20.

18 Table 8.2 gives Marneta's willingness to pay for concert tickets. The price of concerts is $20 each.

   a Compute marginal utility for ticket.
   b How many hours will Marneta purchase?
   c Compute her consumer surplus.

Table 8.2

Number of tickets	Utility (willingness to pay)
0	$ 0
1	$ 35
2	$ 65
3	$ 90
4	$110
5	$125
6	$135
7	$140

19   Table 8.3 gives Charlie's consumer surplus for tennis balls, which sell for $2 each.

   a   Compute marginal utility for each can.

   b   How many hours will Charlie purchase?

   c   Compute his consumer surplus for this good.

Table 8.3

Number of cans of tennis balls	Utility (willingness to pay)
0	$ 0
1	$10
2	$16
3	$20
4	$22
5	$23
6	$23.50
7	$23.75

Answers to Problems

2

3

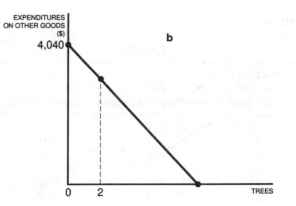

c   The budget constraint with the tax refund, which is shown in part b, is preferred because it allows more choices. If desired, the resident can spend as much as $4,040 on other goods, and with the in-kind transfer of trees, she can spend a maximum of $4,000 on other goods.

16

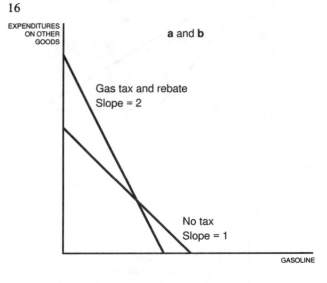

c   He is wrong. The gas tax and rebate program results in a budget constraint with more alternatives that involve less gasoline consumption. It motivates individuals to substitute other goods for gasoline.

18   *a*

Table 8.2

Number of tickets	Utility (willingness to pay)	Marginal Utility
0	0	
1	$ 35	$35
2	$ 65	$30
3	$ 90	$25
4	$110	$20
5	$125	$15
6	$135	$10
7	$140	$ 5

b   4.

c $110 − ($20 × 4) = $30.

13

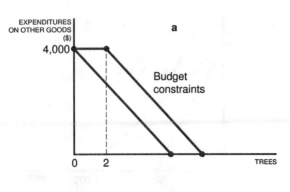

19   *a*

Table 8.3

Number of cans of tennis balls	Utility (willingness to pay)	Marginal Utility
0	$ 0	
1	$10	$10
2	$16	$ 6
3	$20	$ 4
4	$22	$ 2
5	$23	$ 1
6	$23.50	$ 0.50
7	$23.75	$ 0.25

b. 4.

c. $22 − ($2 × 4) = $14.

Chapter 9

LABOR SUPPLY AND SAVINGS

Chapter Review

Chapter 8 explored the individual's decision to spend her income. This chapter continues the discussion of household decision-making. First, it examines the labor supply decision, the choice between leisure and the income needed for consumption. As with the consumption decision in Chapter 8, the individual chooses the best alternative along the budget constraint. The chapter examines how much labor time to offer, what level of education to pursue, and when to retire. Next comes the savings decision, where the trade-off pits current versus future consumption.

ESSENTIAL CONCEPTS

1   The decision to supply labor is primarily a time-allocation problem. Individuals have only so much time available, and they must divide their time between working and other activities. Any time not devoted to working and earning money, whether it is spent in recreation, sleep, chores, or errands, is called leisure. The income earned while working is available for consumption; therefore, the *trade-off* is between **leisure** and **con-**

sumption, between consuming time and consuming goods.

2   The chapter focuses on the budget constraint between leisure and consumption, shown here in Figure 9.1. The slope is the wage rate, and changes in the wage rate rotate the budget constraint, causing income and substitution effects. When an individual's wage increases, leisure becomes more expensive; thus, the *substitution*

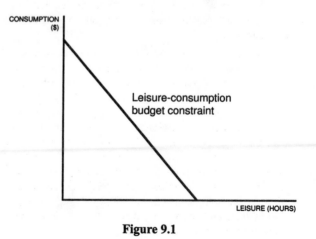

Figure 9.1

effect encourages less leisure and more work. On the other hand, the *income effect* leads the individual to want to consume more leisure, which results in less work. Because the income and substitution effects work in opposite directions, the supply curve for labor may slope upward or even bend backward.

3   There are more dimensions to labor supply than hours worked. Individuals choose whether or not to participate in the work force. They must also decide how much education and training to acquire, and when to retire. Each of these decisions can be understood as the choice of the best alternative within an appropriately specified budget constraint.

4   Government policy also affects labor supply. Taxation reduces the consumption that a given amount of labor will yield. The Social Security system affects the decision to retire through the earnings limit, by discouraging the elderly from participating in the labor force. Both the substitution and income effects of the welfare system encourage recipients to work less or not at all. Each of these policies is analyzed in terms of how it alters the leisure-consumption budget constraint.

5   According to **human capital** theory, individuals invest in education and training to acquire human capital, or skills that increase their productivity and wages. Another view is that education signals to employers which potential workers are innately more productive. This signal leads to credentials competition, the process by which people gather degrees not for any learning that takes place, but rather to show that they will be productive if hired.

6   The **savings decision** is basically a decision about *when* to consume; households choose whether to spend all of their income now, or to save it for future consumption. The **two-period budget constraint** employs the techniques we learned in Chapter 8 to show what combinations of consumption in the present and consumption in the future are affordable, given present and future incomes and the interest rate. As in Chapter 8, the slope of the budget constraint indicates the *trade-off,* and it equals the relative price. Since current consumption is measured on the horizontal axis, the slope is the **relative price of current consumption,** which is **1 plus the interest rate.**

7   When the interest rate changes, the budget constraint rotates, becoming steeper if the interest rate increases and flatter if it decreases. In exactly the same manner as Chapter 8's analysis of the consumption decision, the change in the budget constraint causes income and substitution effects. Higher interest rates make savers better off, and because current consumption is a normal good, the *income effect* makes them want to consume more today, thus reducing savings. On the other hand, higher interest rates lower the relative price of future consumption. The resulting *substitution effect* increases savings. In the decision to save, the substitution and income effects work in opposite directions.

8   There are several motives for saving. People save during their working lives to provide for retirement. This is called **life-cycle savings.** People set aside **precautionary savings** to guard against the chance of accident or illness. The **bequest motive** leads people to save for their heirs. People save to meet a particular goal, such as buying a house or starting a business. We call this motive **target savings.** Furthermore, government policies affect savings; some encourage saving, others do not. For example, Social Security benefits tend to reduce life-cycle savings because people do not feel as compelled to save for retirement. Taxes on interest lower the after-tax rate of interest and thus provide less incentive to save.

BEHIND THE ESSENTIAL CONCEPTS

1   The basic diagram for the first part of the chapter is the budget constraint for leisure and consumption. It is important to understand that this diagram is very much like the consumer's budget constraint in Chapter 8. Each shows which combinations are affordable. The slopes are the relative prices; in this case, the relative price of leisure is the wage rate. If the individual wants to consume another hour of leisure, the opportunity cost is the money that could be earned in that hour. Changes in nonwage income, such as investment returns, bring about a parallel shift in the budget constraint, but changes in the wage rate rotate it. Again, this is very similar to the Chapter 8 budget constraint.

2   Changes in the wage rate rotate the budget constraint and cause substitution and income effects. The income effect leads to more leisure (less work) when the wage rate increases. The substitution effect, on the other hand, causes less leisure (more work) when the wage rate increases. As with the savings decision, the substitution and income effects of wage changes work in opposite directions. For consumption, however, they work in the same direction. Thus, while the demand curves for goods and services are downward sloping the supply curves for savings and labor may be upward sloping or bend backward.

3   Table 9.1 may help you keep straight the substitution and income effects.

Table 9.1

If the wage rate rises,
the *substitution* effect leads to more work because leisure is more expensive.
the *income* effect leads to less work because the worker is better off and demands more leisure.
If the wage rate falls,
the *substitution* effect leads to less work because leisure is less expensive.
the *income* effect leads to more work because the worker is worse off and demands less leisure.

4   Be sure not to confuse the budget constraint with the labor supply curve. The budget constraint shows the

combinations of leisure and consumption the individual can afford given the wage rate and any nonwage income. The labor supply curve shows the quantity of labor she supplies at each wage rate. As usual, it is important to pay attention to what is measured along each axis.

5   The basic diagram in the second part of this chapter is the two-period budget constraint shown in Figure 9.2. It is important to see how similar this diagram is to the consumer's budget constraint of Chapter 8. There, the trade-off was between consuming different goods. Here, the trade-off involves consuming at different time periods. In each case, the slope is the relative price. When the relative price changes, there are substitution and income effects. Price changes rotate the budget constraint, but income changes bring about a parallel shift. This basic approach will also be used later for the labor supply decision and for other issues throughout the course.

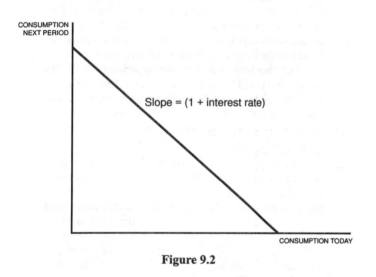

Figure 9.2

6   Think about the slope of the two-period budget constraint. If an individual desires to consume more in the future, he can save today. One dollar saved today results in (1 plus the interest rate) dollars of consumption in the future. That is, he can buy $(1 + r)$ dollars of future consumption at an opportunity cost of only 1 dollar today. Conversely, when he buys 1 more dollar of current consumption, he must give up $(1 + r)$ dollars of future consumption. The relative price of current consumption is, then, 1 plus the interest rate.

7   One plus the interest rate is also the slope of the budget constraint; therefore, only changes in the interest rate can change the slope. If the interest rate rises, the budget constraint becomes steeper. If the interest rate falls, the budget constraint becomes flatter. Income changes, either now or in the future, only shift the budget constraint in a parallel way.

8   Table 9.2 may help you keep the substitution and income effects straight.

Table 9.2

If the interest rate rises,
   the *substitution* effect leads to more savings because current consumption is relatively more expensive.
   the *income* effect leads to less savings because the saver is better off and desires to consume more today.
If the interest rate falls,
   the *substitution* effect leads to less savings because current consumption is relatively less expensive.
   the *income* effect leads to more savings because the saver is worse off and desires to consume less today

SELF-TEST

True or False

1   The percentage change in hours worked resulting from a 1 percent change in the real wage is the elasticity of supply of labor.

2   The income effect of a decrease in wages is to increase the quantity of labor supplied.

3   The substitution effect of a decrease in wages is to increase the quantity of labor supplied.

4   Investment in education is an example of human capital.

5   An increase in nonwage income rotates the budget constraint.

6   An increase in Social Security benefits will lead people, on average, to retire later.

7   The labor force participation of women has increased since World War II.

8   According to human capital theory, education increases the productivity of students, enabling them to earn more in the labor market.

9   The slope of the budget constraint equals the rate of interest.

10   As the interest rate increases, the income effect leads individuals with savings to save less.

11   As the interest rate increases, the substitution effect leads people to save less.

12   As the interest rate increases, the budget constraint shifts out in a parallel way.

13   An increase in Social Security benefits will increase national savings.

14   When the interest rate changes, the income and substitution effects work in the same direction.

15   A cut in interest taxes matters because people are concerned with the after-tax rate of interest.

Multiple Choice

1   If a person can earn $10 per hour, then the slope of the leisure-consumption budget constraint is

    a   1/10;

    b   10;

    c   .01;

    d   .10;

    e   none of the above.

2   If nonwage income increases, then the budget constraint

    a   rotates, becoming steeper;

    b   rotates, becoming flatter;

    c   shifts out parallel;

    d   shifts in parallel;

    e   none of the above.

3   If the wage increases, then the budget constraint

    a   rotates, becoming steeper;

    b   rotates, becoming flatter;

    c   shifts out parallel;

    d   shifts in parallel;

    e   none of the above.

4   An increase in nonwage income will usually lead to

    a   a decrease in the quantity of labor supplied through the substitution effect;

    b   a decrease in the quantity of labor supplied through the income effect;

    c   an increase in the quantity of labor supplied through the substitution effect;

    d   an increase in the quantity of labor supplied through the income effect;

    e   none of the above.

5   The substitution effect of a wage increase leads to

    a   a decrease in the quantity of labor supply;

    b   an increase in the quantity of labor supply;

    c   a decrease in leisure;

    d   a parallel shift in the budget constraint;

    e   b and c.

6   A decrease in the marginal income tax rate will

    a   cause a big increase in the quantity of labor supplied because the income effect is weaker than the substitution effect;

    b   cause a big decrease in the quantity of labor supplied because the substitution effect is weaker than the income effect;

    c   lead to little change in the quantity of labor supplied;

    d   have no effect on the quantity of labor supplied because taxes do not affect the budget constraint;

    e   none of the above.

7   Currently in the United States, the elasticity of female labor supply is

    a   higher than the elasticity of male labor supply;

    b   lower than the elasticity of male labor supply;

    c   equal to the elasticity of male labor supply;

    d   perfectly elastic;

    e   irrelevant, because few women work.

8   The effective tax rate for the secondary earner in a marriage is

    a   higher than for the primary earner;

    b   the same as for the primary earner;

    c   lower than for the primary earner;

    d   irrelevant, because only one spouse works;

    e   none of the above.

9   Increased lifetime wealth leads to

    a   earlier retirement through the income effect;

    b   later retirement through the substitution effect;

    c   earlier retirement through the substitution effect;

    d   later retirement through the income effect;

    e   a and c.

10   Which of the following is not an example of investment in human capital?

    a   formal schooling;

    b   on-the-job learning;

    c   technical training;

    d   plant and equipment.

    e   All of the above are examples.

11   The opportunity costs of attending college do not include

    a   tuition expenses;

    b   costs of materials and books;

    c   room and board;

    d   foregone earnings while attending class and studying.

    e   All of the above are opportunity costs of attending college.

12   Most capital in the United States is

    a   human capital;

    b   credentials;

    c   capital goods;

    d   compensating differentials.

    e   About 50 percent of the capital are goods and 50 percent human.

13   Using the budget constraint to analyze the savings decision underscores the fact that the individual is really deciding

    a   when to consume;

    b   what the slope of the budget constraint should be;

    c   without knowing what the future will bring;

    d   what the interest rate should be;

    e   none of the above.

14   The slope of the intertemporal budget constraint

    a   equals 1 plus the interest rate;

    b   shows the trade-off between consuming now and waiting to consume;

    c   indicates the relative price of current and future consumption;

    d   all of the above;

    e   a and b.

15   If the interest rate falls, the budget constraint

    a   shifts to the left in a parallel way;

    b   shifts to the right in a parallel way;

    c   rotates, becoming steeper;

    d   rotates, becoming flatter;

    e   none of the above.

16 If the interest rate falls, the substitution effect

    a encourages people to consume more in the future, because the relative price of future consumption is less;

    b increases savings;

    c decreases savings;

    d encourages people to consume less in the future, because the relative price of current consumption is lower;

    e c and d.

17 If the interest rate rises, the income effect for people who are saving

    a encourages people to consume more in the future, because the relative price of future consumption is less;

    b leads people to want to consume more both now and in the future;

    c increases savings;

    d decreases savings;

    e b and d.

18 If the interest rate rises, the substitution effect increases life-cycle savings because

    a the relative price of future consumption is higher;

    b people are better off and want to consume more today;

    c the budget constraint rotates, becoming flatter;

    d people are worse off and want to consume more today;

    e none of the above.

19 Social Security benefits are paid to retired persons

    a from an endowment created by investing the taxes paid during their working years;

    b out of general fund tax revenues;

    c from Social Security taxes paid by those currently working;

    d from revenues raised through taxing corporations;

    e all of the above.

20 An increase in Social Security benefits will

    a reduce national savings;

    b increase national savings;

    c have no effect on the national savings rate;

    d raise savings through the income effect, but reduce savings through the substitution effect;

    e reduce savings through the income effect, but increase savings through the substitution effect.

Completion

1 The decision concerning how much labor to supply is a choice between _____ and _____.

2 The slope of the budget line is equal to (minus) the _____.

3 When the nonwage income of an individual decreases, his labor supply _____.

4 The _____ effect of a wage decrease leads individuals to decrease their labor supply.

5 If an individual's labor supply is backward bending, then the _____ effect is stronger.

6 The labor supply of women is usually _____ elastic than the labor supply of men.

7 The relative price of consumption today and consumption tomorrow is 1 plus the _____.

8 If the interest rate increases, the budget constraint for the savings decision becomes _____.

9 The income effect of higher interest rates _____ savings.

10 The Social Security system is funded on a _____ basis, which means that benefits received by older retirees are financed through taxes paid by younger workers.

True or False

1	t	4	t	7	t	10	t	13	f
2	t	5	f	8	t	11	f	14	f
3	f	6	f	9	f	12	f	15	t

Multiple Choice

1	b		6	c		11	c		16	e
2	c		7	a		12	a		17	e
3	a		8	a		13	a		18	e
4	b		9	a		14	d		19	c
5	e		10	d		15	d		20	a

Completion

1 leisure, consumption
2 wage
3 increases
4 substitution
5 income
6 more
7 interest rate
8 steeper
9 reduces
10 pay as you go

Doing Economics: Tools and Practice Problems

LABOR SUPPLY

The most important model in the first part of this chapter is the opportunity set for the labor supply decision: the leisure-consumption budget constraint. In this section, we first review how to construct the budget constraint. We then see how the budget constraint changes when the wage rate or nonwage income changes. As in Chapter 8, the substitution and income effects of wage changes can be illustrated using the budget constraint. Finally, there are some applications.

THE LEISURE-CONSUMPTION BUDGET CONSTRAINT

We work in order to earn money for consumption, but we give up time that could be used for leisure. Economists see the labor supply decision as involving a trade-off between leisure and consumption. The basic tool for analyzing labor supply is the budget constraint. Tool Kit 9.1 shows how to construct the leisure-consumption budget constraint.

Tool Kit 9.1: Plotting the Leisure-Consumption Budget Constraint

The budget constraint shows what combinations of leisure and consumption can be afforded given the wage rate and the amount of nonwage income. To plot the budget constraint, follow this five-step procedure.

Step one: Draw a set of coordinate axes. Label the horizontal axis as the quantity of leisure consumed and the vertical axis as the consumption level.

Step two: If an individual chooses to do no work, leisure equals the total time available, and consumption is equal to the nonwage income. Plot this point.

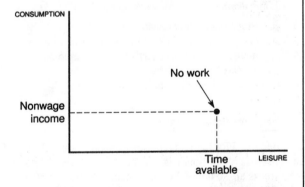

Step three: Calculate the maximum earnings if the individual consumes no leisure. Add this amount to the nonwage income, and plot this quantity along the vertical axis.

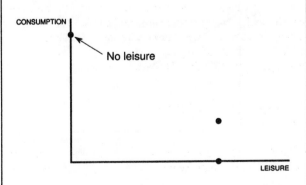

Step four: Draw a line segment connecting the two points. This line segment is the leisure-consumption budget constraint.

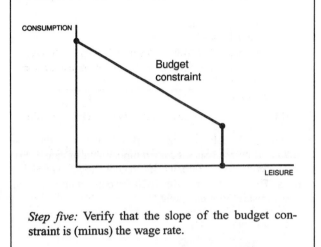

Step five: Verify that the slope of the budget constraint is (minus) the wage rate.

---

1 (Worked problem: leisure-consumption budget constraint) In his spare time, Mike, a student at Enormous State University, referees intramural basketball games. Each game pays $7, and if he could stand the abuse, Mike could referee as many as 60 each month. On average, each game takes 1 hour. This is not Mike's only source of income; each month his parents send him $200 for expenses.

a Construct Mike's budget constraint.
b Suppose that Mike chooses to referee 20 games. Label his chosen alternative, and indicate his total income, income from refereeing, hours worked, and leisure.

Step-by-step solution

Step one (a): Draw the two axes, and label the vertical one "Consumption" and the horizontal one "Leisure."

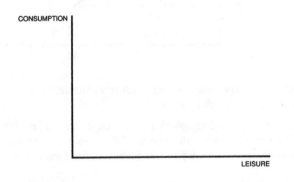

Step two: Plot the no-work consumption point. If Mike referees no games, he consumes all 60 hours as leisure. This leaves him $200 (from his parents) for consumption. Plot this point.

Step three: Calculate total income if Mike works all the time available. If he referees the maximum number of games, 60, he earns $420 from refereeing and retains the $200 from his parents. This leaves him with $620 for consumption but no time for leisure. Plot this point.

Step four: Draw a line segment between the two plotted points. This is the budget constraint.

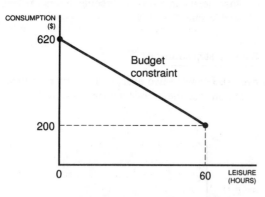

Step five: The slope of the budget constraint is (620 − 200)/60 = 7, which is the wage.

Step six (b): If Mike referees 20 games, then he is left with 40 hours of leisure, and he earns $140 in wage income for a total of $340. Plot the point, and label appropriately.

2   (Practice problem: leisure-consumption budget constraint) College professors can earn extra cash by reviewing papers for journals. Editors pay around $50 per paper for an academic opinion about whether it should be accepted for publication. Reviewing a paper takes 1 hour. Professor Cavendish has 15 hours available each month for outside work such as reviewing.

He draws $3,000 monthly from McCavendish College, and that is his only other source of income.

a   Plot Cavendish's budget constraint.
b   Suppose that the professor reviews 6 papers in March. Plot and label his chosen alternative.

3   (Practice problem: leisure-consumption budget constraint) For each of the following, draw a budget constraint. Also, choose a point along the budget constraint, and show the corresponding amount of leisure, work, nonwage income, and wage income.

	Wage	Total time	Nonwage income
a.	$25/hour	80 hours	$ 1,000
b.	$200/day	30 days	$ 0
c.	$1,000/week	50 weeks	$15,000
d.	$5/hour	100 hours	$ 0

4   (Worked problem: leisure-consumption budget constraint) When either nonwage income or the wage rate changes, the budget constraint moves. The basic technique here is to draw the budget constraint using the original nonwage income and wage rate, following the procedure shown above. Then draw a new budget constraint using the new nonwage income and wage rate. Compare the two budget constraints, and verify that the shift is parallel when nonwage income changes, but the budget constraint rotates when the wage rate changes. Art supplements his pension by repairing automatic teller machines. Each service call takes an hour, and he receives $50 per call. His pension and other nonwage income is $200 per week. Art has 30 hours available and can work as much as he likes.

a   Plot Art's budget constraint.
b   His pension fund has done well with its investments and increases Art's nonwage income to $300. Plot his new budget constraint.
c   How will Art change his work effort?

Step-by-step solution

Step one (a): Plot his budget constraint in the usual way. If he consumes all 30 hours as leisure, Art can consume $200. If he works all 30 hours, he can consume $200 + ($50 × 30) = $1,700. Note that the slope is (1,700 − 200)/30 = 50, which is the wage.

Step two (b): Plot his budget constraint with nonwage income equal to $300. His no-work consumption is now $300 + (30 × $50) = $1,800, if he works all of the available time. Note that the nonwage income increase brings about a parallel shift.

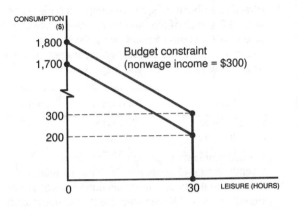

Step three (c): The change in the budget constraint is an income effect. The income effect reduces work effort when income rises. Art will work less.

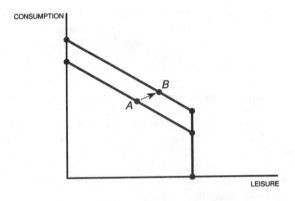

5 (Practice problem: leisure-consumption budget constraint) Liza's job as a broker requires making unsolicited, or "cold," calls to potential clients in an attempt to persuade them to put their portfolio in her hands. On average, cold calls earn Liza $10 each. She can make 4 per hour, and she can work as much as 80 hours per week. Her base salary (nonwage income) is $100 per week.

   a Plot her budget constraint.
   b Suppose that the firm offers her an increase in the base salary to $150 per week. Plot her new budget constraint.
   c Will Liza make more or fewer cold calls? Why?

6 (Practice problem: leisure-consumption budget constraint) Sara is offered a position as tour guide for a local museum. She can conduct 2 tours per hour and earn $10 each. She has no nonwage income, but she must pay 25 percent of her salary in taxes. The museum will allow her to work as much as 20 hours each week.

   a Plot her budget constraint.
   b Taxes are reduced to 20 percent. Plot her budget constraint.

7 (Practice problem: leisure-consumption budget constraint) Theodore tutors some of his fellow students in economics for $10 per hour. He also receives $2,000 in expense money per semester from his scholarship. He can work as much as 100 hours per semester.

   a Plot his budget constraint.
   b Students realize that there is a plethora of semi-intelligent grad students who will take less pay. Theodore now only receives $8 per hour. Plot his new budget constraint.

8 (Practice problem: leisure-consumption budget constraint) For each of the following, plot the budget constraint before and after the change.

   a Nonwage income = $100; wage = $20 hour; total time available = 40 hours; nonwage income changes to $0.
   b Nonwage income = $0; wage = $500/week; total time available = 52 weeks; wage changes to $300/week.
   c Nonwage income = $10,000; wage = $40/hour; total time available = 50 hours; available time increases to 60 hours.
   d Nonwage income = $500; wage = $200/week; total time available = 52 weeks; wage changes to $400/week.

SUBSTITUTION AND INCOME EFFECTS

As in the case of Chapter 8's budget constraint, price changes cause two kinds of effects: substitution and income. When the wage increases, the substitution effects motivate household to supply more labor, but the income effects indicate that they supply less labor. These concepts show how the labor supply curve can bend backward. Tool Kit 9.2 uses the budget constraint to distinguish between substitution and income effects.

Tool Kit 9.2: Distinguishing Between Substitution and Income Effects of Wage Changes

When the wage rate changes, there are two effects: substitution and income. These can be illustrated using the leisure-consumption budget constraint. This technique clarifies the fact that, as in the case of savings, the substitution and income effects work in opposite directions.

Step one: Draw the budget line with the original wage.

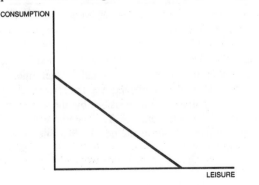

Step two: Find the chosen point along this budget line. Label this point *A*.

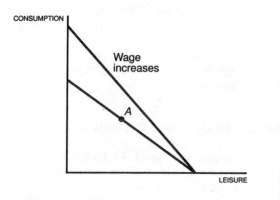

Step three: Draw the budget line with the new wage.

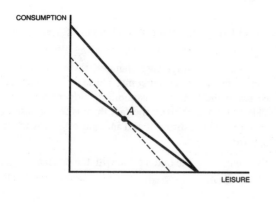

Step four: Draw a dotted line segment through point *A* and parallel to the *new* budget line.

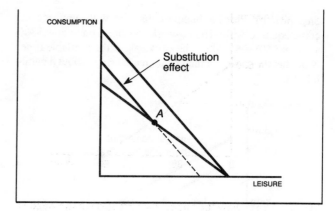

Step five: Darken the portion of the dotted line segment that lies above the original budget line. The points along this darkened segment represent the new alternatives made possible by the substitution effect of the wage change. The income effect shifts this line parallel out to the new budget line drawn in step three.

9   (Worked problem: wage changes/applications) John currently works 45 hours per week tuning pianos at a wage of $20 per hour. This is his only income. He is offered a raise to $30 per hour. He has 80 hours available for work each week.

 a Draw the budget constraint at $20 per hour. Label his chosen alternative along this budget line.
 b Draw the budget constraint at $30 per hour.
 c Show the substitution effect of the wage increase. Why must the substitution effect lead John to work no less at the new, higher wage?

Step-by-step solution

Step one (a): Draw the budget constraint at the original wage. We label the horizontal axis "Leisure" and the vertical one "Consumption." If John does not work, he has 80 hours of leisure and no consumption. If he works all 80 hours (leisure = 0), he consumes $1,600. Draw John's budget constraint connecting the two points.

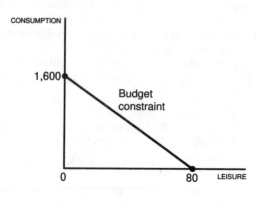

Step two: Find the chosen point along this budget line. John chooses 80 − 45 = 35 hours of leisure, which give him 45 × $20 = $900. Label this point *A*, and note that it does lie along the budget constraint.

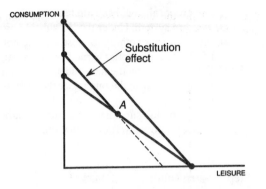

Step three (b): Draw the budget constraint when the wage is $30. The no-work alternative still offers consumption equal to $0, but now if John works the 80 hours available, he consumes $30 × 80 = $2,400. Plot and connect the two end points.

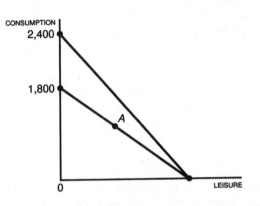

Step four (c): Draw a dotted line parallel to the $30 budget constraint through point *A*.

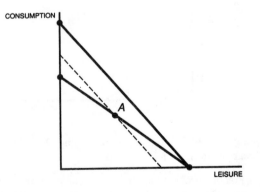

Step five: Darken the portion that lies above the budget constraint drawn in step one. These are the alternatives made possible by the substitution effect of the wage increase. All of these points involve more work than at point *A*, the alternative chosen when the wage is $20.

10 (Practice problem: applications) Arna loves her job as a design consultant. She can earn $60 per hour and has been able to work as much as she likes up to 50 hours per week. She has no nonwage income. She is currently working 15 hours per week.

  a Plot her budget constraint. Find her chosen alternative, and label the point *A*.
  b A new city income tax of 10 percent is passed. Arna now takes home only $54 per hour. Plot her new budget constraint.
  c Show the substitution effect of the wage decrease.

11 (Practice problem: substitution and income effects) For each of the following, draw the budget constraint with the wage in the first column and a new budget line with the wage in the second column. Pick an alternative along the first budget constraint, and show the substitution effect. There is no nonwage income.

	Old wage	New wage	Total time
a	$25/hour	$ 50/hour	80 hours
b	$200/day	$ 100/day	30 days
c	$1,000/week	$1,500/week	50 weeks
d	$5/hour	$ 4/hour	100 hours

APPLICATIONS OF THE LEISURE-CONSUMPTION BUDGET CONSTRAINT

The following applications use the leisure-consumption budget constraint. We analyze welfare programs, overtime pay, and even divorce arrangements. The basic technique is to draw the budget constraint without the policy in question, draw another budget constraint with the policy in place, and compare the two using substitution and income effects.

12 (Worked problem: application) In Smithsville, the welfare system pays $100 per week. Anyone in Smithsville can earn the minimum wage of $4.00 per hour at the local pickle plant, but welfare recipients cannot receive more than $100 per week. This means that any earnings are subtracted from welfare benefits. There are 80 hours available for work.

  a Draw the budget constraint for a Smithsville welfare recipient.

b   A new proposal would substitute a job subsidy for the welfare system. Under the job subsidy proposal, the town pays nothing to those who do not work and $.50 for every dollar earned, up to a total payment of $100. Draw the new budget constraint, and compare it with the one under the welfare system.

c   Do you think job subsidies are a better program than unconditional welfare? What other factors are involved?

Step-by-step solution

Step one (a): Draw a set of axes labeled "Leisure" and "Consumption." If the recipient does no work, she consumes $100. Plot this point, and label it *A*.

Step two: If the recipient earns $100, she loses all of her benefits and still consumes $100. At $4 per hour, $100 is earned in $100/$4 = 25 hours, which leaves 80 − 25 = 55 hours of leisure. Plot the point (100, 55). Label this point *B*.

Step three: If the recipient works all 80 hours, she consumes $4 × 80 = $320. Plot this point, and label it *C*.

Step four: Draw line segments connecting points *A* and *B* and points *B* and *C*. This is the budget constraint under the welfare system.

Step five (b): Under the job subsidy program, if the person works no hours, he consumes nothing. Plot the point (0.80). Label it *D*.

Step six: If the person earns $200, he receives the maximum subsidy, which is $100. The total consumption is then $300. To earn $200 (and consume $300) takes $200/$4 = 50 hours of work, leaving 80 − 50 = 30 hours of leisure. Plot the point (300, 30), and label it *E*.

Step seven: If the person works all 80 hours, he consumes $100 + (80 × $4) = $420. Plot the point (420, 0), and label if *F*.

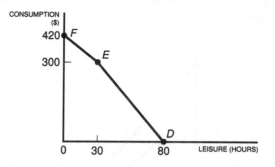

Step eight: Draw line segments connecting *DEF*. This is the budget constraint for job subsidies.

13 (Practice problem: applications) The management at Acme Manufacturing is disturbed that although the typical factory worker is required to work 250 days each year, most only work 230. It proposes a $100 bonus for any employee who works more than 240 days each year. The wage of the typical factory worker is $120 per day.

a   Draw the budget constraint without the attendance bonus.

b   Draw the budget constraint with the attendance

bonus. How is attendance likely to change for the typical factory worker?

c   Suppose that the company simply gives each worker $100. How is the opportunity set different from the one with the attendance bonus?

d   Under which scheme will the typical worker work more? Why?

14 (Practice problem: applications) The Quantity Bakery Company has paid its workers $6 per hour to make donuts, cakes, and pies. There are always sweets to make, and the workers can work as many hours as they choose, up to 80 hours per week. Recently, the company union won a new contract that, although it keeps the wage at the same level, now allows for overtime pay of "time and a half" for any hours worked in excess of 40 per week.

a   Draw the budget constraint under the old contract with no provision for overtime pay.

b   Draw the budget constraint with the overtime pay.

c   What is likely to happen to the number of hours that Quantity Bakery workers work under the new contract? Explain.

15 (Practice problem: applications) Under the U.S. tax code, earnings below $20,000 or so are taxed at 15 percent. Any earnings above $20,000 incur a 28 percent tax rate. Lucinda Gamez, a private investigator, earns $800 per week, and she has 50 weeks per year available for work.

a   Draw her budget constraint if she pays no taxes.

b   Draw her budget constraint under the schedule described above. How do progressive income taxes shape the budget constraint.

16 (Practice problem: applications) Harry Gold makes $5,000 by working 20 days each month as a plumber. His wage is $250 per day, and he can work as many as 30 days each month (except February, of course). The income tax rate for Harry is 20 percent. Also, he pays $1,000 monthly in property taxes on a very nice condo down by the river. His nonwage income is $4,000 per month. (Hint: Review the solutions to problems 15 and 16 of Chapter 8.)

a   What is Harry's net wage after taxes?

b   Draw his budget constraint.

c   The new governor proposes eliminating the income tax and increasing property taxes. Harry figures that his property tax bill will rise to $2,000. Draw his budget constraint under the governor's proposed tax changes.

d   Will Harry work more or less under the new tax plan? Why?

e   Is Harry better off under the new tax plan? Why or why not?

17 (Practice problem: applications) After 10 miserable years, Al and Norma Bennet are getting a divorce. They have agreed that Norma will remain custody of their two children. Al makes $50 per hour from his job as a marriage counselor, and this is his only income. Although he could work as much as 40 hours, Al is only working 20 hours currently. The court has ruled that Al must pay $250 per week in child support regardless of his earnings. (Hint: Review the solutions to problems 15 and 16 of Chapter 8.)

a   Draw Al's (postdivorce) leisure-consumption budget constraint.

b   Many states (for example, Wisconsin and Michigan) have established fixed guidelines for child support payments. Suppose the guideline requires that noncustodial parents pay 25 percent of their income per child. Draw Al's budget line for this child care payment.

c   Under which plan will Al work more? Why?

SAVINGS

Now we turn to the saver's opportunity set: the two-period budget constraint. Given the wealth or income of the household and the interest rate, we can construct the two-period budget constraint. We see how the budget constraint is altered when income (either present or future) and interest rates change. We show the substitution and income effects by using the rotation and shift technique introduced in the last chapter. Finally, we learn some applications: different borrowing and lending interest rates, individual retirement, college and housing accounts, and how Social Security benefits affect savings.

The Two-Period Budget Constraint

When we save money, we forgo current consumption in order to increase consumption at some later date. The trade-off involves current and future consumption. Tool Kit 9.3 shows how to plot the two-period budget constraint, which is the economist's basic tool for analyzing savings.

Tool Kit 9.3: Plotting the Two-Period Budget Constraint

The two-period budget constraint shows what combinations of consumption in each period are possible, given the income and interest rate. Follow the steps.

Step one: Draw a set of coordinate axes. Label the horizontal axis consumption in period one and the vertical axis consumption in period two.

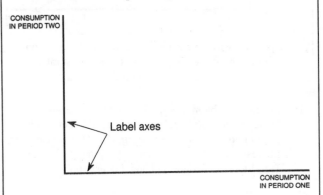

Step two: Calculate the maximum possible consumption in period one. (This quantity is the present discounted value of income.) Plot this quantity along the horizontal axis.

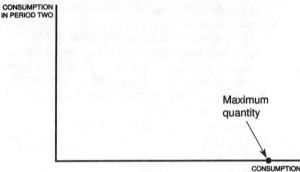

Step three: Calculate the maximum possible consumption in period two. (This quantity is the future value of income.) Plot this quantity along the vertical axis.

Step four: Draw a line segment connecting the two points. This line segment is the two-period budget constraint.

Step five: Verify that the slope of the budget constraint is (minus) $1 + r$, where r is the interest rate.

18 (Worked problem: two-period budget constraint) Nancy won the lottery! It is only $5,000, but that looks pretty good to someone making $18,000 per year. Her interest rate is 6 percent, and the capital market is perfect. Plot her two-period budget constraint.

Step-by-step solution

Step one: Draw coordinate axes, labeling the horizontal axis "Consumption now" and the vertical axis "Consumption next year."

Step two: The maximum consumption today is the present discounted value of all income. Make the following table, and compute and plot the amount along the horizontal axis.

Year	Income	Discount factor	Present discounted value
Now	$23,000	1	$23,000
Next year	$18,000	1/(1.06)	$16,980

Present discounted value = $39,980.

Step three: The maximum consumption next year is

$$\$23,000 \, (1 + .06) + \$18,000 = \$42,380.$$

Plot this point.

Step four: Draw a line segment connecting the two points.

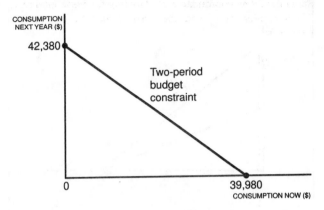

Step five: Verify that the slope equals 1 plus the interest rate. It is 42,380/39,980 = 1.06 = 1 + r.

19 (Practice problem: two-period budget constraint) Current income is $40,000. Retirement income is $15,000. The interest rate for the period between now and retirement is 150 percent. Plot the two-period budget constraint.

20 (Practice problem: two-period budget constraint) Plot the two-period budget constraints for the following.

	Interest rate	Present income	Future income
a	100%	$100,000	$ 25,000
b	50%	$ 40,000	$ 10,000
c	250%	$ 20,000	$ 0
d	80%	$ 0	$150,000

21 (Worked problem: two-period budget constraint) When the interest rate, current income, or future income changes, the two-period budget constraint moves. The basic technique here is to draw the two-period budget constraint using the original income and interest rate, and then draw a new two-period budget constraint using the new incomes and interest rate. Compare the two budget constraints and verify that the shift is parallel when either current or future income changes, but the budget constraint rotates when the interest rate changes. Michael is earning $25,000 as a secretary and expects to earn the same in the future. His interest rate is 5 percent.

a Plot his two-period budget constraint.
b He receives word that his aunt is sick and has one year to live. She plans to leave him $50,000. Plot his two-period budget constraint.

Step-by-step solution

Step one (a): Follow the procedure to plot the two-period budget constraint. The slope is 1 + r = 1.05, and it passes through the point $25,000 now and $25,000 next year.

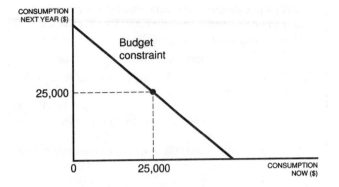

Step two (b): Plot the new budget constraint. Because the interest rate is the same, the slope does not change. The new budget constraint passes through the point $25,000 now and $75,000 next year.

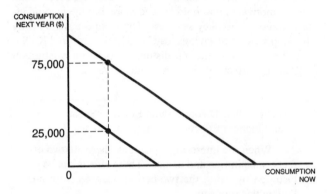

22 (Practice problem: two-period budget constraint) Boris currently takes home $45,000 as a skilled lathe operator. His union contract guarantees him the same salary next year. The credit union at the plant pays 8 percent interest.

a Plot his two-period budget constraint.
b Boris' employer is experiencing low profits this year. He proposes that Boris accept $35,000 this year and $55,000 next year. Plot his two-period budget constraint. Does the offer shift the budget constraint? How?

23 (Practice problem: two-period budget constraint) Monica plans to retire in 20 years. She now takes home $40,000 and expects $20,000 in retirement income. The interest rate for the 20 years is 180 percent.

a Plot her budget constraint.
b A new broker promises her a 20-year return of 250 percent. She believes him. Plot her new budget constraint.

24 (Practice problem: two-period budget constraint) The Coddingtons now take home $375,000 per year, but they have no retirement income planned. Their portfolio will earn them 100 percent over the 12 years left until retirement.

a Plot their budget constraint.
b Tax increases reduce their after-tax return to 60 percent. Plot their new budget constraint.

25   (Practice problem: two-period budget constraint) Plot the budget constraints before and after the change.

	Current income	Future income	Interest rate	Change
a	$100,000	$ 0	40%	interest rate = 60%
b	$100,000	$ 0	40%	future income = $100,000
c	$ 0	$50,000	10%	current income = $25,000
d	$ 60,000	$80,000	50%	interest rate = 20%

SUBSTITUTION AND INCOME EFFECTS

As in the case of the other budget constraints that you have studied, price changes cause two kinds of effects: substitution and income. When the interest rate increases, the substitution effects motivate household to save more, but the income effects indicate that they save less. These concepts show why the supply curve of savings may bend backward. Tool Kit 9.4 uses the budget constraint to distinguish between substitution and income effects of changes in interest rates.

Tool Kit 9.4: Distinguishing Between Substitution and Income Effects of Changes in Interest Rates

When the interest rate changes, there are two effects: substitution and income. These effects can be illustrated by using the two-period budget constraint. Follow this procedure.

Step one: Draw the two-period budget line with the original interest rate.

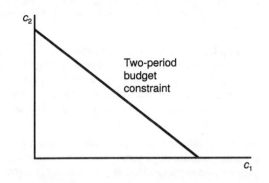

Step two: Find the chosen current and future consumption level along this budget line. Label this point A.

Step three: Draw the two-period budget line with the new interest rate.

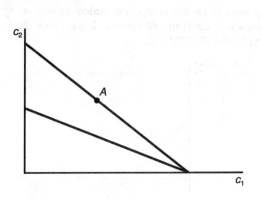

Step four: Draw a dotted line segment through point A and parallel to the *new* budget line.

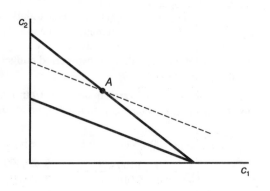

Step five: Darken the portion of the dotted line segment that lies above the original budget line. The points along this darkened segment represent the quantities made possible by the substitution effect of the interest rate change. The income effect shifts this line out in a parallel way to the new budget line drawn in step three.

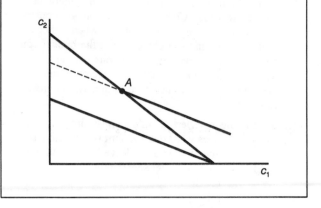

26   (Worked problem: substitution and income effects) Show the substitution and income effects of the change n the rate of return for Monica's portfolio in problem 23. She is currently saving $5,000 per year.

Step-by-step solution

Step one: Draw the two-period budget constraint with the interest rate equal to 180 percent. It must pass through the point ($40,000, $20,000).

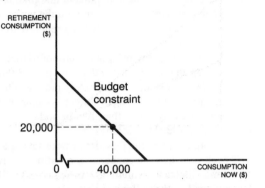

Step two: Label Monica's current consumption ($40,000 − $5,000 = $35,000) point *A*.

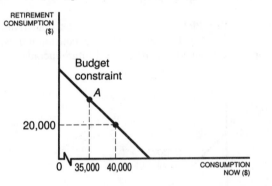

Step three: Draw the two-period budget constraint with the interest rate equal to 250 percent. It also must pass through the point ($40,000, $20,000).

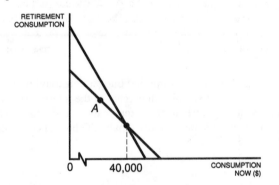

Step four: Draw a dotted line with a slope of 1 + 2.50 = 3.50 through *A*.

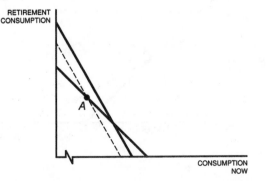

Step five: Darken the portion of the dotted line that lies above the original budget constraint drawn in step one. These are the alternatives made possible by the substitution effect of the interest rate change. All of these involve more savings; thus, the substitution effect of an increase in the interest rate is an increase in savings. The income effect shifts this darkened line segment out parallel to the budget constraint drawn in step two and reduces savings.

27 (Practice problem: substitution and income effects) Show the substitution and income effects for the change in the Coddingtons' after-tax interest rate in problem 24. Currently they have no savings.

28 (Practice problem: substitution and income effects) Show the substitution and income effects for parts a through d in problem 25. In each case, savings equal $10,000 before the interest rate changes.

APPLICATION OF THE TWO-PERIOD BUDGET CONSTRAINT

The following applications show how the two-period budget constraint can be used to analyze imperfect capital markets, Social Security, and government programs that affect savings incentives. Again, the procedure is to draw budget constraints with and without the feature of interest and compare using substitution and income effects.

29 (Worked problem: applications) If the capital market were perfect, then the interest rates for borrowing and lending would be the same. The rates for borrowing, however, are higher. Haywood and Myrna take home $40,000 each year. They can earn 4 percent on any savings, but they must borrow at 14 percent. Plot their two-period budget constraint.

Step-by-step solution

This is an application of the opportunity set with multiple constraints introduced in Chapter 2.

Step one: Plot the budget constraint with the 4 percent interest rate. The slope is 1.04, and it passes through the point $40,000 now and $40,000 next year.

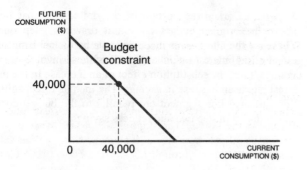

Step two: Plot the budget constraint with the 14 percent interest rate. The slope is 1.04, and it passes through the point $40,000 now and $40,000 next year.

Step three: Darken the portion of each budget constraint that lies under the other constraint.

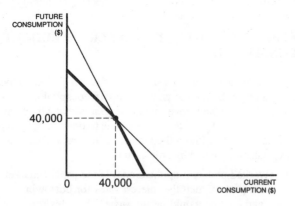

30   (Practice problem: applications) Bob takes home $20,000 this year, but he anticipates taking home $30,000 next year. He can earn 8 percent on savings, but he has a poor credit rating and must pay 19 percent to borrow. Plot his two-period budget constraint.

31   (Worked problem: applications) Concern about low U.S. savings rates, among other motivations, has prompted a number of proposals for tax-exempt savings accounts. They range from the Bush administration's family savings accounts to special tax-exempt accounts for college expenses or down payments on a first home. The Davidsons take home $100,000 per year after taxes. If he gets his grades up, David, their

son, will enter college in 3 years. The Davidsons can earn a 25 percent real rate of return before taxes over the three-year period.

a   Draw their two-period budget constraint.
b   The Davidsons face a 40 percent marginal tax rate. Draw their budget constraint with the tax on interest. (Hint: What is their after-tax real rate of return on savings?)
c   A new college savings plan is proposed that offers parents an opportunity to deposit up to $3,000 in a special tax-exempt account. Any money withdrawn and not used for college tuition payments is subject to penalty. Draw their two-period budget constraint if the plan becomes law.
d   Before the plan, the Davidsons were saving $3,500 each year. Use the concepts of substitution and income effects to explain how their savings will be affected by the college savings plan.

Step-by-step solution

Step one (a): Plot the two-period budget constraint. The slope is $1 + 0.25 = 1.25$, and the budget constraint must pass through the point where current and future income are each $100,000.

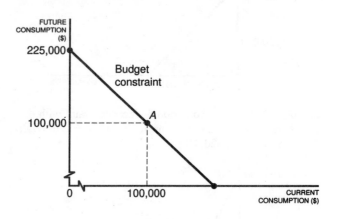

Step two (b): Plot the two-period budget constraint with the tax on interest. Taxes take 40 percent of the interest, so their after-tax interest rate for the three years is 15 percent. The slope is now 1.15. Interest taxes make the budget constraint flatter.

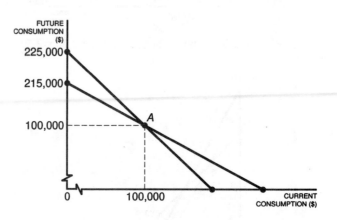

Step three (c): The college savings plan allows the Davidsons to save along the tax-free budget constraint, where the slope is 1.25 until their savings reach $3,000. At that point (*B*), there is a kink, and the slope of the budget constraint returns to the flatter after-tax slope of 1.15.

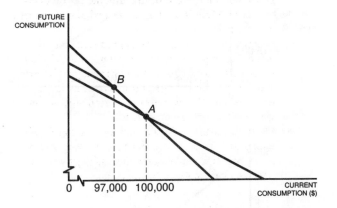

Step four (d): Since the Davidsons save more than $3,000, the program will have only an income effect. The program will not change their after-tax marginal rate of return, because only the first $3,000 of savings is tax exempt.

32 (Practice problem: applications) The Shades do not know where they will find the money to send their four bright but impecunious children to college in 5 years. They make $26,000 per year and have been unable to save a nickel. Their marginal tax rate is 20 percent, and they could earn 40 percent interest on savings over the 5-year period.

 a Plot the Shades' two-period budget constraint ignoring the tax on interest.
 b Plot their two-period budget constraint including the tax on interest.
 c Plot their two-period budget constraint under the college savings plan spelled out in problem 31.
 d Use the concepts of substitution and income effects to explain how their savings will be affected by the college savings plan.

33 (Worked problem: applications) Social Security reduces the incentives that individuals have to save for retirement, and because it is financed on a pay-as-you-go basis, it reduces national savings. Melissa is already fantasizing about retirement, even though it is 40 years away. She estimates that a dollar deposited today will return $3.50 in interest when she retires. She currently takes home $25,000 after paying taxes, including $3,250 annually in Social Security taxes, and expects to draw $14,625 in Social Security benefits. Although she is thinking about retirement, Melissa has no savings.

 a Calculate the present discounted value of Melissa's Social Security benefits.
 b Draw her two-period budget constraint, and label her levels of consumption now and in the future.
 c Suppose that the entire Social Security system (taxes and benefits) is eliminated. Draw her two-period budget constraint.
 d How much does Melissa save?

Step-by-step solution

Step one (a): The present discounted value of her benefit payment is $14,625/(1 + r) = $3,250, which is exactly her taxes.

Step two (b): Draw Melissa's two-period budget constraint. Label the axes "Current consumption" and "Consumption 40 years in the future." The slope is 1 + r, and the interest rate for the 40-year period is 350 percent. Also, the budget constraint must pass through her current choice: $25,000 now and $14,625 in 40 years.

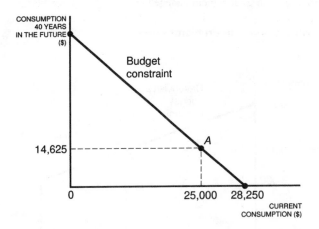

Step three (c): Eliminating Social Security reduces her future income to $0, but because she no longer pays Social Security taxes, her current after-tax income rises to $28,250. Because the present discounted value of her two-period income does not change, the budget constraint does not change. (In general, the Social Security system shifts out the budget constraint for low-income people and shifts it in for high-income people.)

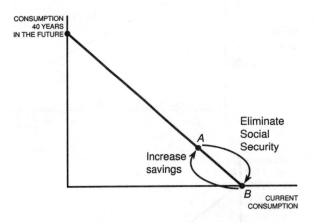

Step four (d): Because Melissa has the same budget constraint, she chooses the same point. This means that she must save $3,250 (which returns $14,625 in 40 years), which is exactly the amount she now pays in taxes. Eliminating Social Security would (for Melissa) lead to the same consumption, but greater national savings.

34 (Practice problem: applications) Melissa's uncle is only 10 years from retirement. He can expect to re-

ceive $1 in interest for every $1 saved for retirement. He takes home $50,000 annually, saves $10,000, and expects Social Security benefits of $20,000 when he retires.

a   Plot his two-period budget constraint.
b   Suppose that the American Association of Retired Persons has a banner year lobbying Congress and wins a 50 percent increase in benefits. Taxes also rise, so that the budget constraint of Melissa's uncle does not change. How will his earnings change? How will his consumption now and during retirement change?

Answers to Problems

2

3

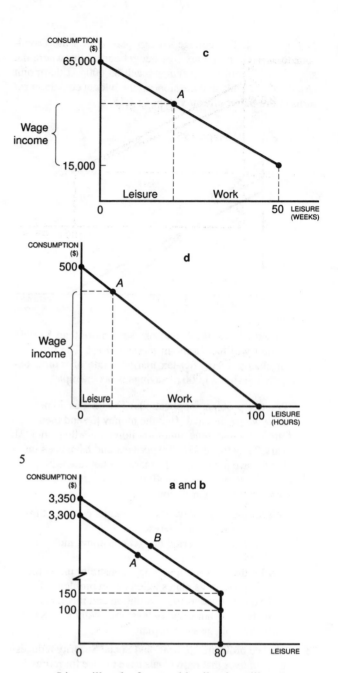

5

c   Liza will make fewer cold calls, she will consume more leisure when her income increases, as shown by the movement from point *A* to point *B*.

6

7

8

a

b

c

d

10

11

a

b

13

14

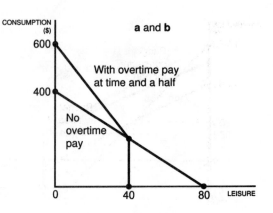

c   All the new alternatives made possible by the overtime provision involve working more than 40
hours. Work time probably will increase.

15

16

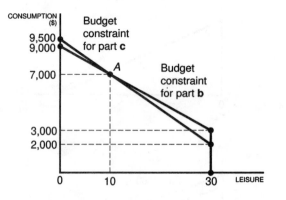

d   An unconditional bonus of $100 simply shifts the
budget constraint up in a parallel way, causing an
income effect. The typical worker consumes more
leisure at point C. The attendance bonus does not
offer the points along the dashed budget constraint. Point B or another point involving even
more work will be chosen. Clearly, there is a
greater incentive to work with the attendance
bonus.

a $200/day.
d   He will work more because the tax change offers
him new alternative with more work. In effect it
leaves him with the substitution effect of a wage
increase, with the income effect being canceled
by the property tax increase.
e   He is better off because he can continue to
choose point A, but he also has some new alternatives.

17

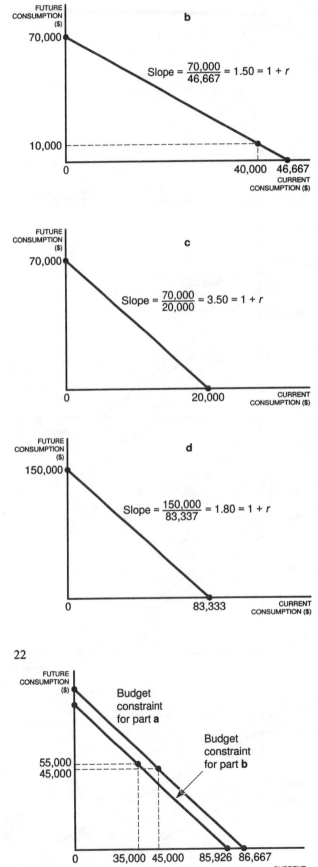

c Al will likely work more under the lump-sum child care requirement. The other system leaves him with the substitution effect of a wage decrease.

19

20

23

RETIREMENT CONSUMPTION ($)

Budget constraint for part **b**

20,000

Budget constraint for part **a**

0   40,000   CURRENT CONSUMPTION ($)

24

FUTURE CONSUMPTION ($)

750,000

Budget constraint for part **a**

600,000

Budget constraint for part **b**

0   375,000   CURRENT CONSUMPTION ($)

25

FUTURE CONSUMPTION ($)

a

160,000

140,000

Budget constraints

0   100,000   CURRENT CONSUMPTION ($)

FUTURE CONSUMPTION ($)

b

240,000

140,000

100,000

0   100,000   CURRENT CONSUMPTION ($)

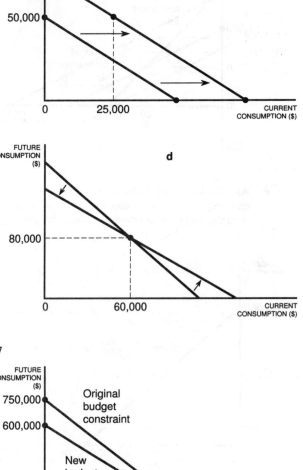

FUTURE CONSUMPTION ($)

c

77,500

50,000

0   25,000   CURRENT CONSUMPTION ($)

FUTURE CONSUMPTION ($)

d

80,000

0   60,000   CURRENT CONSUMPTION ($)

27

FUTURE CONSUMPTION ($)

750,000

Original budget constraint

600,000

New budget constraint

0   375,000   CURRENT CONSUMPTION ($)

28

FUTURE CONSUMPTION ($)

a

160,000

140,000

Budget constraints

A

0   90,000   100,000   CURRENT CONSUMPTION ($)

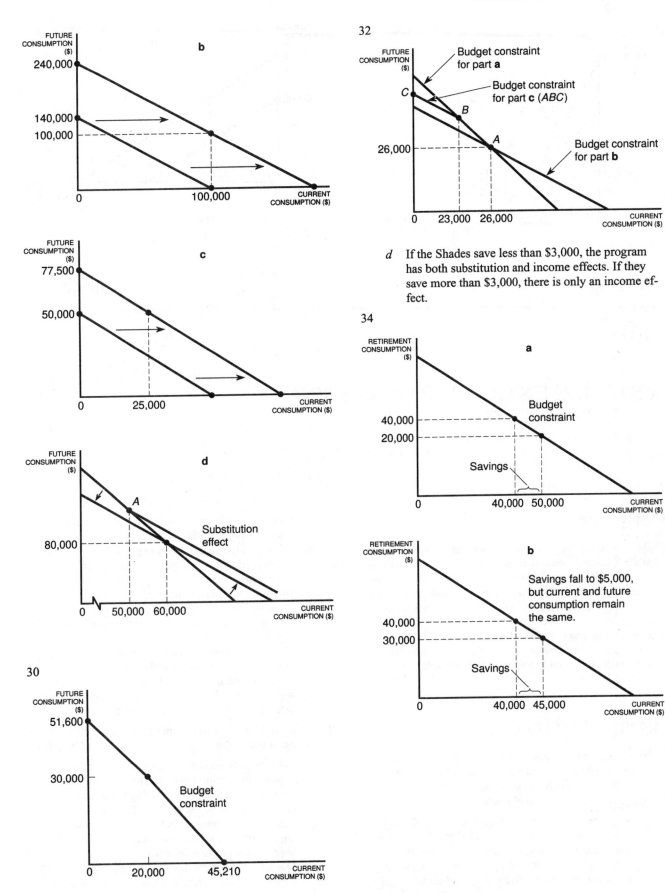

32

d   If the Shades save less than $3,000, the program has both substitution and income effects. If they save more than $3,000, there is only an income effect.

34

A STUDENT'S GUIDE TO INVESTING

Chapter Review

Chapter 10 moves on from the budget constraint to explore what the household does with its savings. This is the investment decision. Financial markets offer a wide array of investment opportunities, from savings accounts to Treasury bills to corporate stock, all with different characteristics. Why investors value certain characteristics of assets and how returns to assets reflect these characteristics form the central focus of this chapter. Chapter 10 completes the discussion of the household's role in capital markets.

ESSENTIAL CONCEPTS

1   **Financial investments** are purchases of financial assets in the expectation of receiving a return. Among the most important are bank deposits, housing, bonds, shares of stock, and mutual funds.

   a   Bank deposits include savings accounts and certificates of deposit. Insured by the Federal Deposit Insurance Corporation, they are safe and liquid.

   b   Housing is a tax favored investment in that property taxes and interest are deductable, and capital gains

taxation usually can be avoided. Housing investment is risky and illiquid, however.

   c   Bonds, which are promises to pay a fixed amount in a specified number of years, are a way for businesses and government to borrow. Bondholders bear the risk of default and/or inflation.

   d   Shares of stock represent ownership rights in corporations. Investors hold stock in the hopes of receiving dividends and capital gains.

   e   Mutual funds combine money from many different investors and purchase a wide variety of assets. This is called diversification. Although they are not insured by the federal government, mutual funds are safer than individual stocks or bonds.

2   There are four important properties of financial investments: expected return, risk, tax treatment, and liquidity.

   a   Since returns are uncertain, the investor must balance the high returns with the low. The **expected return** is calculated by multiplying the possible returns by the probability each will occur.

   b   Assets with a greater chance of very low and very high returns are **risky**. Most individuals are **risk averse**; they prefer safer assets.

   c   The returns from some assets, such as housing and municipal bonds, are taxed less than the returns from other assets. The **tax advantages** make these assets more appealing to investors.

d The ease with which an investment can be converted to cash is called **liquidity.** Bank accounts are very liquid; housing is illiquid. Most investors prefer liquidity.

3 The **efficient market theory** says that market prices reflect the characteristics of assets, incorporate all currently available information, and change unpredictably. An important implication of this theory is that without inside information, investors cannot continue to earn more than average returns.

4 The chapter closes with some investment advice. Although unlikely to appear on a test, this advice is immensely valuable.

a Carefully evaluate the characteristics of each asset you own as it relates to your personal situation.
b Diversify. Give your portfolio a broad base.
c Consider all your risks, not just those in your financial investment portfolio.
d Think again before you imagine that you can beat the market.

BEHIND THE ESSENTIAL CONCEPTS

1 What do investors want from their financial assets? In addition to high expected returns, individuals value the characteristics of investments with low risk, favorable tax treatment, and liquidity. The demand for investments with these characteristics is higher; therefore, their price is higher. The fact that market prices are higher for assets with desirable characteristics—in other words, that asset prices reflect these characteristics—is one of the central ideas of efficient market theory.

2 Assets that pay higher returns in bad times are especially valuable. When the economy is in recession, the typical individual loses money on investments. People do not like to see their wealth fluctuate and are willing to pay something to smooth out these ups and downs. Assets that pay higher returns when the economy is weak help to stabilize the overall portfolio. Again, efficient market theory predicts that the prices of these assets will be higher.

3 Efficient market theory says that prices also reflect all available information. For example, when Iraq invaded Kuwait in August 1990, the prices of oil and oil stocks shot up immediately. The new information that oil would be in short supply in the future made firms that owned large oil reserves worth more, and their stock prices immediately reflected this additional worth.

4 Many people are mystified by the notion that in an efficient market, asset prices change randomly. Once you understand the logic, however, you can see why this must be true. Since market prices reflect available information, you can only beat the market if you have information others do not. Anyone who had known in April 1990 that Iraq would invade Kuwait could have bought oil stocks before their prices rose. Once the invasion

happened, however, it was too late. Prices had already risen. Since the invasion was a surprise, the sudden changes in the prices of oil stocks were also surprises. This is what is meant by random movements in prices: the changes are unpredictable, though they are not without rational cause.

SELF-TEST

True or False

1 The ease with which an asset can be converted to cash is called its liquidity.

2 To find the expected return, simply take the average of the possible returns.

3 Housing is a tax-favored investment because interest is tax deductible and capital gains taxes may be postponed.

4 If the interest rate rises, bond prices fall.

5 Bondholders bear no risk from inflation.

6 If a company goes bankrupt, bondholders are paid before stockholders.

7 The portion of a company income not paid to stockholders in dividends is called retained earnings.

8 Risky assets pay higher rates of return on average.

9 Illiquid assets pay lower rates of return on average.

10 An increase in the price of a share of stock is called a capital gain.

11 If stock prices vary randomly, then the market cannot be efficient.

12 Owing to the quality of their research staffs, most mutual funds continue to earn more than the market rate of return year after year.

13 Because most people prefer safe, tax-favored, liquid assets, those assets yield higher returns.

14 A fund that gathers money from many investors and purchases a range of assets is called a mutual fund.

15 If stock prices reflect all available information, then changes in price must result from unanticipated events and must be random.

Multiple Choice

1 Which of the following are financial investments?
a stocks;
b bonds;
c money market accounts;
d certificates of deposit;
e all of the above.

2   Which of the following are real investments?

a   preferred stock;
b   mutual funds;
c   purchases of new factories;
d   bank accounts;
e   none of the above.

3   Liquidity refers to

a   the correlation of the return on an asset and the market return;
b   the term to maturity of a bond;
c   the ease with which an asset can be converted into cash;
d   the likelihood that an investor will be repaid if a corporation goes bankrupt;
e   a and d.

4   Which of the following is not a risk borne by bond-holders?

a   The market interest rate may rise, causing the price of the bond to fall.
b   Inflation may lower the real value of the fixed return.
c   A corporation may go bankrupt and default on the bond.
d   At the end of the term, even if it does not default, a company may not pay a bondholder what she expected to receive.
e   All of the above are risks of holding bonds.

5   Junk bonds are

a   highly risky bonds usually issued by firms with high debt levels;
b   bonds that must be held by the original purchaser and cannot be sold;
c   bonds that have procyclical returns;
d   bonds that are not convertible into stock;
e   bonds issued by firms in the used vehicle industry.

6   The amount of a firm's earnings not paid out to stockholders as dividends is called

a   economic profits;
b   the average return;
c   retained earnings;
d   liquidity;
e   accounting profits.

7   If an investor sells a share of stock for more than he paid for it, he earns a

a   liquidity premium;
b   capital gain;
c   retained earning;
d   risk premium;
e   procyclical return.

8   Who must be repaid before owners of common stock when the firm goes bankrupt?

a   bondholders;
b   owners of preferred stocks;
c   creditors;
d   the Internal Revenue Service;
e   all of the above

9   Suppose that an antique automobile purchased for $25,000 is to be sold next year. The investor thinks that the sales price may be $20,000 or $40,000, and the probability of each price is one-half. What is its expected return?

a $5,000;
b $30,000;
c $35,000;
d   –$5,000;
e   none of the above

10   If there were no differences between assets other than the ways in which they produced returns, then

a   the expected returns to all assets would be the same;
b   the returns to stock ownership would exceed the returns to bond holding;
c   assets that paid returns through capital gains would pay more than assets that paid returns through interest or dividends;
d   no investor would hold bonds;
e   none of the above.

11   Why are stocks risky financial investments?

a   The price of the stock may go up or down.
b   The amount of the dividend payment may go up or down.
c   The firm may go bankrupt.
d   All of the above.
e   a and c.

12   Most investors are risk averse. This means that they will

a   never purchase risky assets;
b   look only at the risk of an investment, not the expected return;
c   always prefer bonds to stocks;
d   always prefer bank accounts to bonds because bank accounts are insured by the Federal Deposit Insurance Corporation;
e   prefer safe to risky assets of equal expected return.

13   Suppose that an asset has a one-half probability of earning 30% and a one-half probability of earning nothing. Its expected return equals

a   0;
b   15 percent;
c   25 percent;
d   30 percent;
e   100 percent.

14   When investors, seeking the highest rate of return, bid up the prices of profitable assets, they are engaging in

a   diversification;
b   liquidity;
c   insurance;
d   capital gains;
e   arbitrage.

15   State and municipal bonds yield

a   lower returns than corporate bonds chiefly because they are less risky;

b   higher returns than corporate bonds chiefly be-
    cause they are more liquid;

c   lower returns than corporate bonds of equivalent
    risks and liquidity because interest on them is tax-
    exempt;

d   higher returns than corporate bonds of equivalent
    risk and liquidity because interest on them is tax-
    exempt;

e   returns equal to those paid by corporate bonds of
    equivalent risk and liquidity because interest on
    them is tax-exempt.

16 Housing is a tax-favored investment in that

a   mortgage interest is tax deductible;
b   housing is liquid;
c   it is possible to avoid capital gains taxes on hous-
    ing;
d   housing is financed by municipal bonds;
e   a and c.

17 Which of the following assets is most liquid?

a   stocks;
b   bonds;
c   bank accounts;
d   housing;
e   mutual funds.

18 The demand for an asset depends on its

a   liquidity;
b   average returns;
c   risk;
d   tax treatment;
e   all of the above.

19 Efficient market theory says that

a   all assets are perfectly liquid;
b   all assets are treated the same by the tax system;
c   asset characteristics are perfectly reflected in their
    prices;
d   average returns are equal for all assets;
e   a, b, and d.

20 The advice to diversify your portfolio means

a   own a wide variety of assets with different risks;
b   stay away from risky assets;
c   choose only assets with procyclical returns;
d   follow a random walk strategy;
e   none of the above.

Completion

1   Purchases of new factories and machinery are exam-
    ples of _____ investment.

2   Purchases of stocks and bonds and deposits in money
    market accounts are examples of _____ invest-
    ment.

3   _____ refers to the ease with which an invest-
    ment can be turned into cash.

4   An unexpected decline in the rate of interest causes the
    prices of bonds to _____.

5   Because most individuals are _____, risky assets
    must offer a higher average return than safe assets.

6   In general, stocks that go up in value when the econo-
    my is weak are worth _____ than stocks that go
    up in value during good economic times.

7   Because municipal bonds are exempt from taxes, their
    prices are _____ than prices for comparable tax-
    able bonds.

8   The demand for an asset depends upon its average re-
    turn, _____, tax treatment, and liquidity.

9   To find the expected return on an asset, multiply the
    possible returns by the corresponding _____.

10 The theory that market prices perfectly reflect the
    characteristics of assets is called the _____
    theory.

Answers to Self-Test

True or False

1	t	6	t	11	f
2	f	7	t	12	f
3	t	8	t	13	f
4	t	9	f	14	t
5	f	10	t	15	t

Multiple Choice

1	e	2	c	3	c	4	d
5	a	6	c	7	b	8	e
9	a	10	a	11	d	12	e
13	b	14	e	15	c	16	e
17	c	18	e	19	c	20	a

Completion

1   real
2   financial
3   Liquidity
4   rise
5   risk averse
6   more
7   higher
8   risk
9   probabilities
10 efficient market

Doing Economics: Tools and Practice Problems

The concept of expected returns appears for the first time in
this chapter. We study how to calculate the expected return
on an investment and what it means. We go on to consider
the opportunity set for the investor and learn how he perceives trade-offs of risk and expected return, and also liquidity and returns. The last issue we take up is the relationship
between bond prices and interest rates. A few problems use
the concept of present value (introduced in Chapter 6) to
show why an increase in interest rates leads to a decrease in
bond prices.

EXPECTED RETURNS

When we purchase an asset, we do not know exactly what it will earn in the future. Investors calculate the expected return, which is the average of all the possible returns. The expected return is one of the important desirable properties of financial investments. Tool Kit 10.1 shows how to calculate expected returns.

Tool Kit 10.1: Calculating Expected Returns

Because the returns on financial investments come in the future, at the time the decision is made an investor is uncertain about what the returns will actually be. Good investors think carefully about all the possibilities and calculate the expected returns.

Step one: Make a three-column table showing all the possible returns in the left-hand column and the corresponding probabilities in the middle column.

Returns	Probability	Product
r_1	P_1	
r_2	P_2	

Step two: Multiply each possible return by its probability, and enter the product in the right-hand column.

Returns	Probability	Product
r_1	P_1	$r_1 \times P_1$
r_2	P_2	$r_2 \times P_2$

Step three: Add the numbers in the right-hand column. The sum is the expected return.

Returns	Probability	Product
r_1	P_1	$r_1 \times P_1$
r_2	P_2	$r_2 \times P_2$

Average returns = $(r_1 \times P_1) + (r_2 \times P_2)$.

---

1 (Worked problem: expected returns) Envious of his brother's life-style, Dr. Mendez is considering investing in one of his brother's real estate ventures. His brother promises a return of 100 percent in one year, but Dr. Mendez thinks the probability that this will happen is only 1/4. More likely (probability = 1/2) is a return of 8 percent. Finally, there is another 1/4 probability that the project will go under and the doctor will lose all his money (return = −100 percent). Calculate the expected return.

Step-by-step solution

Step one: Make a table, and enter the possible returns and the corresponding probabilities.

Returns	Probability	Product
100%	1/4	
8%	1/2	
−100%	1/4	

Step two: Multiply each return by its probability, and enter the result.

Returns	Probability	Product
100%	1/4	25%
8%	1/2	4%
−100%	1/4	−25%

Step three: Add the numbers in the right-hand column.

Returns	Probability	Product
100%	1/4	25%
8%	1/2	4%
−100%	1/4	−25%

Expected returns = 4%.

Thus, in spite of the considerable risk, the investment pays an average of only 4 percent. The good doctor should stick to medicine and put his money in a safe investment.

2 (Practice problem: expected returns) Black Dust, Montana, flush with a consultant's prediction of its future as a high-technology center, is issuing bonds for a new city government building. The bonds pay 20 percent. Most financial analysts think the probability of default is 1/10. In case of default, the bondholders lose their investments (returns = −100 percent). Calculate the expected return on the Black Dust bond.

3 (Practice problem: expected returns) Calculate the expected return on each of the following.

	Returns	Probability	Product
a	50%	1/4	
	12%	5/8	
	−100%	1/8	
b	10%	1/4	
	20%	3/4	
c	200%	1/3	
	40%	1/3	
	−100%	1/3	
d	50%	1/3	
	12%	2/3	

RISK AND RETURNS

There are four desirable characteristics of financial investments: expected returns, risk, tax treatment, and liquidity. Seeking the best combination of these characteristics, an investor faces trade-offs. Some problems show how this trade-off looks to a potential investor.

4 (Worked problem: risk and returns) The table below gives the returns on six bond issues if there is no default, and also the probabilities of default for each. If there is a default, the investor loses all of her money (returns = −100 percent). Also, note that if the probability

of default is 0.1, then the probability of not experiencing a default must be 0.9.

a   Compute the expected return for each bond.
b   Measure risk as the probability of default. Construct the opportunity set, and interpret its outer edge as the risk-return trade-off.
c   Are there any bonds a rational investor would never buy? Why or why not?

Company	Returns (if no default)	Probability of default
Do Music Co.	5%	0
Re Music Co.	19%	0.1
Mi Music Co.	30%	0.2
Fa Music Co.	12%	0.05
Sol Music Co.	8%	0.02
Fred's Music Co.	15%	0.07

Step-by-step solution

Step one (a): Calculate the expected returns for each bond. Follow the procedure for calculating expected returns.

Do Music Co.	$(5\% \times 1) - (100\% \times 0) = 5\%$
Re Music Co.	$(19\% \times .9) - (100\% \times .1) = 7.1\%$
Mi Music Co.	$(30\% \times .8) - (100\% \times .2) = 4\%$
Fa Music Co.	$(12\% \times .95) - (100 \times .05) = 6.4\%$
Sol Music Co.	$(8\% \times .98) - (100\% \times .02) = 5.84\%$
Fred's Music Co.	$(15\% \times .93) - (100\% \times .07) = 6.95\%$

Step two (b): Plot the expected returns on the vertical axis and risk (measured as the probability of default) on the horizontal. This is the risk-return trade-off.

Step three (c): Since Mi Music Co.'s bonds do not lie on the outer edge, no one will buy them. All of the other issues offer higher average returns and lower risk, as shown in the figure.

5   (Practice problem: risk and returns) The four hospitals in Greenville are racing to install the latest medical technologies. Each is trying to raise money in the bond market, and their returns and default risks are given below. If there is a default, the return is −100 percent.

a   Calculate the expected returns for each.

b   Plot the risk-return trade-off.

Hospital	Returns (if no default)	Probability of default
Northside	6%	0
Southside	18%	0.09
Eastside	22%	0.1
Westside	12%	0.05

6   (Practice problem: risk and returns) The Kannapans have set aside some money in case of emergency. They are considering where to invest it, but they are concerned about how quickly they will have access to the money when it is needed. The four possible assets, their returns, and the times needed to withdraw the principal (or sell the asset) are given below. Construct the liquidity-return trade-off.

Asset	Returns	Waiting period
Bank account	5%	none
Bond	7%	2 days
Diamonds	4%	1 week
Rental housing	9%	1 month

BOND PRINCES AND INTEREST RATES

When interest rates rise, bond prices fall. This fact of financial markets follows from the concept of present discounted value, introduced in Chapter 6. The market price for a bond is the present discounted value of the promised repayments.

7   (Worked problem: present value) Bonds issued by Hitek, Inc., promise to pay $100 at the end of the year for 2 years. In addition, the face value equal to $1,000 is repaid at the end of 3 years. The market interest rate is 8 percent.

a   Calculate the present discounted value of the bond.
b   The interest rate rises to 10 percent. Recalculate the bond value.

Step-by-step solution

Step one (a): Make a table, and enter the years and the payments.

Year	Amount	Discount factor	Present discounted value
1	$ 100		
2	$ 100		
3	$1,000		

Step two: Calculate and enter the discount factors for each year. For the first year, the discount factor is $1/(1 + .08) = 0.92$. For the second year, it is $1/(1 + .08)^2 = 0.85$, and for the third, it is $1/(1 + .08)^3 = 0.78$.

Step three: Multiply the amounts by the corresponding discount factor. Enter the product in the right-hand column.

Step four: Add the numbers in the right-hand column.

Year	Amount	Discount factor	Present discounted value
1	$ 100	0.92	$ 92
2	$ 100	0.85	$ 85
3	$1,000	0.78	$780

Present discounted value = $957.

Step five (b): Repeat the procedure for a 10 percent interest rate. The table looks like this.

Year	Amount	Discount factor	Present discounted value
1	$ 100	0.90	$ 90
2	$ 100	0.81	$ 81
3	$1,000	0.73	$730

Present discounted value = $901.

The rise in the interest rate from 8 percent to 10 percent causes the bond price to fall by $56 ($957 – $901). It should be clear why ripples in interest rates cause waves in the bond market.

8 (Practice problem: present value) Deuce Hardwear, a franchiser of motorcycle clothing, has issued a bond that promises to pay $800 at the end of each of the next two years and $12,000 at the end of the third year. The interest rate is 7 percent.

a   Calculate the present discounted value of the bond.
b   The interest rate falls to 6 percent. How much does the price of the bond change?

9 (Practice problem: present value) For each of the following, calculate the change in the price of the bond.

a   The interest rate falls from 10 percent to 8 percent.

Year	Amount	Discount factor	Present discounted value
1	$ 88		
2	$ 88		
3	$1,000		

Present discounted value = $

b   The interest rate rises from 10 percent to 13 percent.

Year	Amount	Discount factor	Present discounted value
1	$ 800		
2	$ 700		
3	$13,000		

Present discounted value = $

Answers to Problems

2   Expected return = $(9 \times 20) - (.1 \times 100) = 8\%$.

3   a   7.5%.
    b   17.5%.
    c   46.7%.
    d   24.7%.

5   a   The expected returns for each bond are given in the table.

Hospital	Returns (if no default)	Probability of default	Expected returns
Northside	6%	0	6%
Southside	18%	0.09	7.38%
Eastside	22%	0.1	9.8%
Westside	12%	0.05	6.4%

6

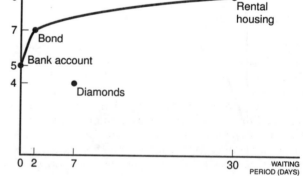

8   a   Present discounted value = $800/(1.07) + $800/(1.07)² + $12,000/(1.07)³ = $11,243.
    b   Present discounted value = $11,542.

9   a   Price of the bond rises from $904 to $950.
    b   Price of the bond falls from $11,073 to $10,263.

Chapter 11

THE FIRM'S COSTS

Chapter Review

One side of the competitive model, the household's, is complete. Business enterprises—firms—occupy the other side. This chapter begins the discussion of the role of firms in a market-based economy. We learn about the production function, which summarizes the relationship between the inputs that the firm demands (especially in the labor market) and the outputs that it supplies in the product market. Payments to purchase inputs make up most of the firm's costs, and this chapter treats these costs in depth. How the costs are balanced against revenues is the subject of Chapter 12.

ESSENTIAL CONCEPTS

1   In the basic competitive model, the firm's objective is to maximize its market value. Because the value of the firm depends on its profit-making potential, another way to put this is to say the firm's objective is to maximize its (long-term) profits. **Profits** equal revenues minus costs, and revenues are simply price times quantity.

2   The **production function** shows the relationship between inputs and outputs. The increase in output resulting from a small increase in the use of an input is called the **marginal product.** The **principle of diminishing returns** states that as more of one input is used, holding other inputs fixed, the marginal product declines. While diminishing returns represent the usual case, some production functions exhibit **increasing returns,** where the marginal product increases as more of an input is used. If doubling the input doubles the output, then there are **constant returns.** Inputs that do not change as output changes are called **fixed inputs**; inputs that do change with output are called **variable inputs.**

3   There are costs associated with each type of input: either **fixed costs,** which do not change when output changes, or **variable costs,** which do. The important concept to grasp is how the various measures of costs change as output changes. The **average cost** curve is typically U-shaped; the **marginal cost** curve lies below it when average cost falls, equals average cost at the minimum, and lies above it when average cost increases.

4   The **principle of substitution** says that as the price of an input increases, firms substitute other inputs. The firm always chooses the least-cost production technique. In the long run, all inputs are variable; the firm has more choices. The **long-run average cost curve** is the lower boundary of all possible short-run average cost curves.

5   In the long run, firms can increase in the same proportion, there are **constant returns to scale** if output increases in the same proportion. If output increases by less, there are **diminishing returns to scale**. **Increasing returns to scale** imply that output increases by a greater proportion than do inputs. **Economies of scope** refer to the cost savings from producing several goods together rather than separately.

BEHIND THE ESSENTIAL CONCEPTS

1   Of the many diagrams in this chapter, there are four that you should master. Each is explained below. Notice how the economic idea (such as diminishing returns or increasing returns to scale) determines the shape of the curves.

    a   The first diagram to master is the production function (Figure 11.1, which is similar to Figure 11.4 in the text). The production function indicates how output (measured on the vertical axis) changes as the quantity of the variable input (measured on the horizontal axis) changes. There are two important facts to know. The first is that the shape indicates whether the production function has diminishing, constant, or increasing returns. Figure 11.1 shows diminishing returns. Also, the slope of the line from the origin to the curve is equal to the average product.

difference between the parallel variable and total cost curves equals fixed cost. The second feature is that the total cost curve inherits its shape from the production function. This will be explored in the analysis part of this chapter.

Figure 11.2

    c   Third, there is the average cost–marginal cost diagram, shown in Figure 11.3 (which duplicates Figure 11.6 in the text). The important concept here is the relationship between the marginal and average cost curves. The average cost curve is typically U-shaped. When marginal cost is below average cost, average cost is downward sloping. Marginal cost equals average cost at the minimum of average cost, and marginal cost is above average cost when average cost is upward sloping. Average cost falls as fixed costs are spread over more units. Average cost rises because diminishing returns drive the marginal cost curve above the average cost curve.

Figure 11.1

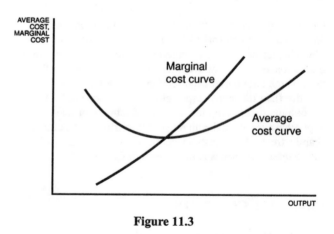

Figure 11.3

    b   The second diagram is the total cost curves, shown in Figure 11.2 (which summarizes Figure 11.5 A, B, and C of the text). Output is measured along the horizontal axis, and cost along the vertical one. Again, there are two important features to observe. First, total cost is the sum of fixed and variable costs. Because by definition fixed costs don't change, the

    d   Finally, there is the long-run average cost curve. For every production process, there are fixed inputs and an associated average cost curve. The long-run average cost curve is the lower boundary, as shown in Figure 11.4 (which duplicates Figure 11.14 in the text). The curve is drawn flat, which represents constant returns of scale.

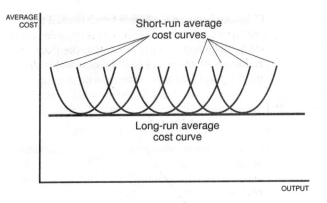

Figure 11.4

2 In reviewing these four diagrams, keep in mind three pointers.

    a Remember to note what is measured along each axis. It's easy to make the mistake of memorizing the shapes of the curves while forgetting how to label the axes.

    b Note the relationships among the curves, especially the marginal cost and average cost relationship.

    c The shape of the curves illustrate the economic properties. It's important to be able to recognize economic properties like diminishing returns and economies of scale in the diagrams of production functions and cost curves.

3 Diminishing returns refer to production processes in which some, but not all, inputs are variable. Diminishing returns imply that the marginal product decreases as more inputs are used. Economists add the words "to scale" when describing a production process in which all inputs are variable. Thus, decreasing returns to scale mean that as all inputs are increased in a certain proportion, output increases by less.

SELF-TEST

True or False

1 According to the basic competitive model, firms maximize profits.

2 Firms in competitive markets are price takers.

3 The marginal product is the last unit of output.

4 The principle of diminishing returns says that as more of one input is added, while other inputs remain unchanged, the marginal product of the added input diminishes.

5 With constant returns, if all inputs are increased by one-third, then output increases by one-third.

6 Costs associated with inputs that change as output changes are called variable costs.

7 Total costs are the sum of average and marginal costs.

8 If labor is the only variable input, then marginal cost equals the wage divided by the marginal product.

9 The average variable cost curve lies below the average total cost curve.

10 The marginal cost curve intersects the average cost curve at the minimum of the marginal cost curve.

11 If the price of an input rises, the firm will substitute other inputs to some extent, but its cost curves will still shift up.

12 Short-run average cost curves are typically U-shaped.

13 If there are economies of scale, the long-run average cost curve slopes downwards.

14 The long-run average cost curve is the lower boundary of all short-run average cost curves.

15 Economies of scope imply that producing a set of goods is cheaper than producing each of them singly.

Multiple Choice

1 In the basic competitive model, a firm that charges more than the going price

    a will lose some of its customers slowly over time;

    b will lose all its customers;

    c may keep its customers if its goods are of higher quality than those of its competitors;

    d will lose no customers if its price equals its marginal cost;

    e none of the above.

2 The statement that firm in competitive markets are price takers means that

    a firms accept the price set by the market;

    b firms maximize profits;

    c production has constant returns;

    d marginal cost is upward sloping;

    e average cost equals marginal cost at the minimum of average cost.

3 Profits equal

    a fixed costs minus average costs;

    b revenues minus fixed costs;

    c revenues minus variable costs;

    d price minus average cost;

    e revenues minus total cost.

4 The marginal product of an input is

    a the cost of producing one more unit of output;

    b the extra output that results from hiring one more unit of the input;

    c the cost required to hire one more unit of the input;

    d output divided by the number of inputs used in the production process;

    e a and c.

5 According to the principle of diminishing returns,

    a as more of one input is added, the marginal product of the added input diminishes;

    b as more of one input is added, holding other inputs unchanged, the marginal product of the added input diminishes;

c   as more of the output is produced, the cost of production diminishes;

d   as more of the output is produced, the marginal cost of production diminishes;

e   none of the above.

6   If the production function exhibits increasing returns,

a   the marginal product of input increases with the amount produced;

b   the marginal cost increases with output;

c   productivity is higher;

d   the production function is downward sloping;

e   a and d.

7   If, when the total quantity of all inputs is doubled, output exactly doubles, the production function exhibits

a   constant returns;

b   diminishing returns;

c   increasing returns;

d   economies of scale;

e   none of the above.

8   Fixed inputs are

a   inputs that cannot be moved;

b   inputs that can be purchased in only one fixed configuration;

c   inputs that can be purchased at a fixed price;

d   inputs that do not depend on the level of output;

e   none of the above.

9   Fixed costs

a   are the costs associated with fixed inputs.

b   do not change with the level of output;

c   include payment to some variable factors;

d   all of the above;

e   a and b.

10 The relationship between the marginal product of labor and the marginal cost of output is the following.

a   Marginal cost is the inverse of marginal product.

b   Marginal cost equals the wage divided by the marginal product.

c   Marginal cost is downward sloping when marginal product is downward sloping.

d   Marginal cost is constant, but marginal product is subject to diminishing returns.

e   b and d.

11 The principle of diminishing returns implies that

a   marginal product diminishes as more of the input is hired;

b   marginal cost increases with the level of output;

c   productivity is higher in large firms;

d   all of the above;

e   a and b.

12 Total cost equals

a   the sum of fixed and variable costs;

b   the product of fixed and variable costs;

c   the ratio of fixed and variable costs;

d   the sum of average costs and average variable costs;

e   none of the above.

13 When the marginal cost curve is above the average cost curve,

a   the average cost curve is at its minimum;

b   the marginal cost curve is at its maximum;

c   the marginal cost curve is downward sloping;

d   the average cost curve is downward sloping;

e   the average cost curve is upward sloping.

14 According to the principle of substitution,

a   marginal cost equals average cost at the minimum of average costs;

b   an increase in the price of an input will lead the firm to substitute other inputs;

c   a decrease in the price of an input will lead the firm to substitute other inputs;

d   if the firm does not know its marginal cost curve, it can substitute its average cost curve;

e   none of the above.

15 The difference between the long run and the short run is

a   that in the short run, there are constant returns, but not in the long run;

b   that in the long run, all inputs can be varied;

c   three months;

d   that in the short run, the average cost is decreasing, but it is increasing in the long run;

e   a and b.

16 In the short run, the typical average cost curve is

a   upward sloping;

b   downward sloping;

c   U-shaped;

d   horizontal;

e   none of the above.

17 The long-run average cost curve is

a   the sum of the short-run average cost curves;

b   the lower boundary of the short-run average cost curves;

c   the upper boundary of the short-run average cost curves;

d   horizontal;

e   none of the above.

18 The long-run average cost curve

a   may slope down because of overhead costs;

b   may eventually slope up because of managerial problems;

c   always exhibits increasing returns to scale;

d   a and c;

e   a and b.

19 The concept of increasing returns to scale means that

a   it is more expensive to produce a variety of goods together than to produce them separately;

b   it is more expensive to produce a large quantity than a small quantity;

c   the average cost of production is lower when a larger quantity is produced;

d   the marginal cost curve is downward sloping;

e   a and b.

20 The concept of economies of scope means that

    a it is less expensive to produce a variety of goods together than to produce them separately;

    b it is more expensive to produce a large quantity than a small quantity;

    c the average cost of production is lower when a larger quantity is produced;

    d the marginal cost curve is downward sloping;

    e a and b.

Completion

1 The relationship between the inputs used in production and the level of output is called the _____.

2 The increase in output that results from using one more unit of an input is the _____.

3 The principle of _____ says that as more and more of one input is added, while other inputs remain unchanged, the marginal product of the added input diminishes.

4 Costs that do not depend upon output are called _____ or overhead costs.

5 The _____ is the extra cost of producing one more unit of output.

6 The marginal cost curve intersects the average cost curve at the _____ of the _____ cost curve.

7 If marginal costs are above average costs, then producing an additional unit will _____ the average.

8 An increase in the price of one input will lead a firm to substitute other inputs. This is a statement of the _____ _____.

9 If the average cost is lower when the firm produces a larger quantity, then there are economies of _____.

10 If it is less expensive to produce a variety of goods together than to produce each good separately, then there are economies of _____.

Answers to Self-Test

True or False

1	t	6	t	11	t
2	t	7	f	12	t
3	f	8	t	13	t
4	t	9	t	14	t
5	t	10	f	15	t

Multiple Choice

1	b	6	a	11	e	16	c
2	e	7	a	12	a	17	b
3	e	8	d	13	e	18	e
4	b	9	e	14	b	19	c
5	b	10	b	15	b	20	a

Completion

1 production function
2 marginal product
3 diminishing returns
4 fixed
5 marginal cost
6 minimum, average
7 raise
8 principle of substitution
9 scale
10 scope

Doing Economics: Tools and Practice Problems

There is quite a bit of technical detail in this chapter, including production functions and a host of cost curves. First, we will explore the production function, calculating the marginal and average product and plotting the curves. It is important to understand how the shape of the production function exhibits diminishing, constant, or increasing returns. Next, we turn our attention to the cost curves; we calculate the various cost concepts and plot the curves. Again, it is important to understand the relationships between the curves and the economic meaning of the shapes of the curves.

THE PRODUCTION FUNCTION

The relationship between inputs and outputs is given by the production function. It shows how much output will result from the efficient use of each possible quantity of the inputs. Economists are interested also in the marginal product, the extra returns brought about by using one more input, and the average product, output per input. In order to understand the decisions of firms, you must understand the production function and its relationship to marginal and average product. Table 11.1 lists the key facts and Tool Kit 11.1 shows how to calculate and graph the key concepts.

Table 11.1
Production Function

The marginal product is the slope of the production function:

    marginal product = change in output/change in number of inputs.

The average product is the slope of a line from the origin to the production function:

    average product = output/input.

If returns are diminishing,

    the marginal product is decreasing.

    the slope of the production function is becoming flatter.

If returns are constant,

    the marginal product is constant.

    the slope of the production function is constant.

If returns are increasing,

    the marginal product is increasing.

    the slope of the production function is becoming steeper.

Tool Kit 11.1: Calculating and Graphing Marginal and Average Products

The production function summarizes the relationship between inputs and outputs. It is important to understand its relationship with the marginal and average product, which can be calculated from the information in the production function and also can be derived from the graph of the production function. Here is how it is done.

Step one: Identify and graph the production function.

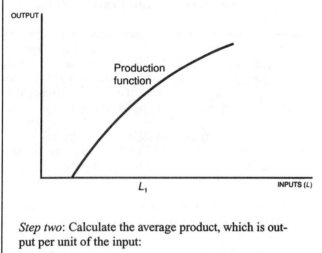

Step two: Calculate the average product, which is output per unit of the input:

average product = output/number of inputs.

The average product is the slope of a line from the origin to the production function.

Step three: Calculate the marginal product, which is the extra output resulting from the use of one more unit of the input:

marginal product = change in output/change in input.

The marginal product equals the slope of the production function.

1   (Worked problem: marginal and average products) Table 11.2 gives the production function for keyboards at Tek-Tek computer products.

Table 11.2

Number of workers	Output	Average product	Marginal product
1	80		
2	150		
3	210		
4	260		
5	300		

    a   Compute the average and marginal product, and fill in the table.

    b   Plot the production function. For each point, verify that the slope of the line from the origin to the production function equals the average product.

    c   Between each two adjacent points on the production function, verify that the slope equals the marginal product.

    d   Does the production function exhibit diminishing, constant, or increasing returns?

Step-by-step solution

Step one (a): Identify and graph the production function. This is given in Table 11.2.

Step two: Calculate and graph the average product. The average product is output divided by the number of workers. If output is 80, the average product is 80/1 = 80. Enter this number. If output is 150, the average product is 150/2 = 75. Complete the average product column. The result is given in Table 11.3.

Table 11.3

Number of workers	Output	Average product	Marginal product
1	80	80	80
2	150	75	70
3	210	70	60
4	260	65	50
5	300	60	40

Step three: Calculate the marginal product. The marginal product is the extra output resulting from using one more input. The marginal product of the first worker is 80. Enter this number. When the second worker is used, output rises to 150. The marginal product of this worker is 150 − 80 = 70. Enter this number. Complete the marginal product column. Table 11.3 gives the result.

Step four (b): Plot the production function.

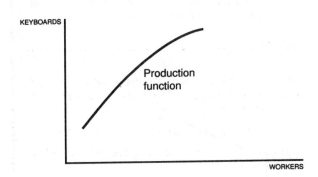

Step five: Choose a point on the production function, and verify that the slope of a line from the origin to that point is equal to the average product. Choose the point labelled *A*, where output is 210 and the number of workers is 3. Draw a line from the origin to point *A*. The slope is rise/run = 210/3 = 70, which is the average product.

Step six (c): Verify that the slope of the production function is the marginal product. The slope of the production function between *A* and *B*, where output is 300 and the number of workers is 5, is (300 − 260)/(5 − 4) = 40, which is the marginal product of the fourth worker.

Step seven (d): The marginal product is decreasing; this indicates diminishing returns.

2 (Practice problem: marginal and average products) Table 11.4 gives the production function for the insect spray Nobeetle at Bugout Pesticide Company.

Table 11.4

Number of workers	Output	Average product	Marginal product
1	1,200		
2	2,200		
3	3,000		
4	3,600		
5	4,000		

a Compute the average and marginal products, and fill in the table.
b Plot the production function. For each point, verify that the slope of the line from the origin to the production function equals the average product.
c Between each two adjacent points on the production function, verify that the slope equals the marginal product.
d Does the production function exhibit diminishing, constant, or increasing returns?

3 (Practice problem: marginal and average products) For the following production functions, answer parts a through d in problem 2.

a Bedford Waterbeds

Number of workers	Output	Average product	Marginal product
1	24		
2	42		
3	57		
4	68		
5	75		

b Worry-Free Insurance

Number of sellers	Policies	Average product	Marginal product
10	200		
20	500		
30	700		
40	800		
50	850		

COST

A firm's costs are its payments to inputs. Some of these inputs are fixed and some are variable. We are interested in the total cost curves and also in average and marginal costs. Thus we have many cost curves. Table 11.5 summarizes the important information about cost curves and Tool Kit 11.2 shows how to calculate and graph the key concepts.

Tool Kit 11.2: Calculating and Graphing Cost Measures

There are two sets of cost curves: the total curves (total cost, fixed cost, and variable cost) and the average-marginal curves (average cost, marginal cost). It is important to be able to calculate each of the cost concepts and also to recognize their relationships on the graphs. Follow along.

Step one: Identify and graph the total cost curve.

Step two: Calculate and graph the variable cost curve:

$$\text{variable cost} = \text{total cost} - \text{fixed cost}.$$

The variable cost curve is parallel to the total cost curve, lying below it by the amount of fixed costs.

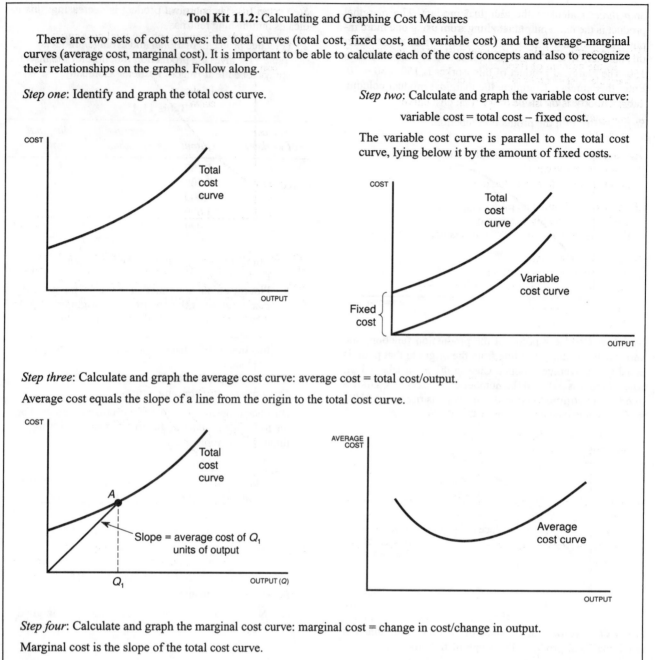

Step three: Calculate and graph the average cost curve: average cost = total cost/output.

Average cost equals the slope of a line from the origin to the total cost curve.

Step four: Calculate and graph the marginal cost curve: marginal cost = change in cost/change in output.

Marginal cost is the slope of the total cost curve.

Table 11.5 summarizes the key information about cost curves.

Table 11.5
Cost Curves

Variable cost is parallel to the total cost curve, and below it
  by the amount of fixed cost:
  variable cost = total cost − fixed cost.

Marginal cost is the slope of the total cost curve:
  marginal cost = change in total cost/change in
    output.

Average cost is the slope of the line from the origin to the
  total cost curve:
  average cost = total cost/output.

If returns are diminishing,
  the marginal cost is increasing.
  the slope of the total cost curve is becoming steeper.

If returns are constant,
  the marginal cost is constant.
  the slope of the total cost curve is constant.

If returns are increasing,
  the marginal cost is decreasing.
  the slope of the total cost curve is becoming flatter.

If marginal cost is below average cost,
  the average cost curve is decreasing.

If marginal cost equals average cost,
  the average cost curve is at its minimum.

If marginal cost is above average cost,
  the average cost curve is increasing.

4   (Worked problem: cost curves) The total fixed costs at
    Stay-Brite Cleaning Company are $100,000. Table
    11.6 gives their total costs for different levels of out-
    put measured in truckloads of Stay-Brite Cleaning So-
    lution.

Table 11.6

Output	Total cost	Variable cost	Average cost	Marginal cost
1,000	$180,000			
2,000	$280,000			
3,000	$420,000			
4,000	$600,000			
5,000	$800,000			

a   Compute variable, average, and marginal cost, and
    enter in the table.
b   Plot the total cost and variable cost curves on one
    diagram, and verify the relationships given in Table
    11.5.
c   Plot the average cost and marginal cost curves, and
    verify the marginal-average relationship.
d   Do the cost curves exhibit increasing, constant, or
    diminishing returns?

Step-by-step solution

Step one(a): Identify and graph the total cost curve.

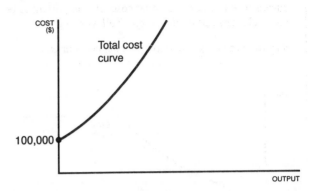

Step two: Calculate and graph the variable cost curve. Variable cost is just the difference between total cost and total
fixed cost. The variable cost of 1,000 units is $180,000 −
$100,000 = $80,000. Enter this number. Complete the variable cost column.

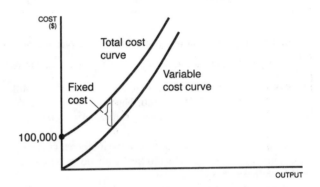

Step three: Calculate and graph the average cost curve. Average cost is total cost divided by output. The average cost
of 1,000 units is $180,000/1,000 = $180. Enter this number.
Complete the average cost column.

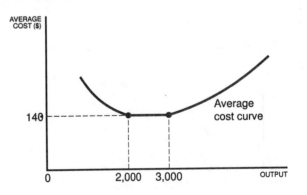

Step four: Calculate and graph the marginal cost curve. Marginal cost is the extra cost of producing one more unit. The
marginal cost per unit for the first 1,000 units is $80,000/
1,000 = $80. Enter this number, and continue to fill in the col-
umn. The complete information appears in Table 11.7.

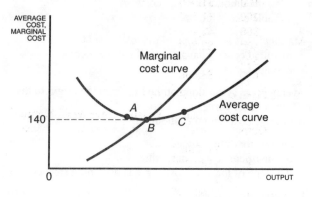

is rising; they are equal at *B*, which is the minimum of average cost; and marginal cost is above average cost at *C*, where average cost is rising.

Step seven: The cost curves exhibit diminishing returns. Marginal cost is increasing, and total cost is becoming steeper.

Table 11.7

Output	Total cost	Variable cost	Average cost	Marginal cost
1,000	$180,000	$ 80,000	$180	$ 80
2,000	$280,000	$180,000	$140	$100
3,000	$420,000	$320,000	$140	$140
4,000	$600,000	$500,000	$150	$180
5,000	$800,000	$700,000	$160	$200

Step five (b): Choose a point on the total cost curve, and verify the relationships.

Variable cost is parallel to total cost. For example, between *A* and *B*, the slope of the total cost curve is ($600,000 − $420,000)/(4,000 − 3,000) = 180. The slope of the variable cost curve for the same levels of output is ($500,000 − $320,000)/(4,000 − 3,000) = 180.

The variable cost curve lies below the total cost curve by the amount of fixed cost. The difference all along the curves is $100,000, which is fixed cost.

The slope of the total cost curve equals marginal cost. Between *A* and *B*, the slope is 180, which is the marginal cost at 4,000 workers.

The slope of a line from the origin to the total cost curve equals average cost. Between the origin and point *A*, the slope of the line is $420,000/3,000 = 140, which is average cost.

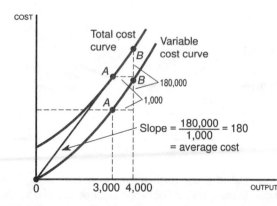

Step six (c): Plot the average and marginal cost curves, and verify the average-marginal relationship. As you can see, marginal cost is above average cost at *A*, where average cost

5   (Practice problem: cost curves). The fixed costs at Pestle Mortar Company are $50,000. Table 11.8 gives their costs for different levels of output measured in mortars.

Table 11.8

Output	Total cost	Variable cost	Average cost	Marginal cost
1,000	$ 250,000			
2,000	$ 500,000			
3,000	$ 800,000			
4,000	$1,200,000			
5,000	$1,800,000			

 a Compute variable, average, and marginal costs, and enter in the table.

 b Plot the total cost and variable cost curves on one diagram, and verify the relationships given in Table 11.5.

 c Plot the average cost and marginal cost curves, and verify the marginal-average relationship.

 d Do the cost curves exhibit increasing, constant, or diminishing returns?

6   (Practice problem: cost curves) For the following cost data, answer parts a through d in question 5.

 a Fixed costs are $1,000.

Output	Total cost	Variable cost	Average cost	Marginal cost
10	$1,500			
20	$2,200			
30	$3,000			
40	$4,000			
50	$6,000			

b Fixed costs are $0.

Output	Total cost	Variable cost	Average cost	Marginal cost
100	$1,000			
200	$1,800			
300	$2,400			
400	$2,800			
500	$3,200			
600	$3,600			

c Fixed costs are $80,000.

Output	Total cost	Variable cost	Average cost	Marginal cost
1	$140,000			
2	$180,000			
3	$220,000			
4	$260,000			
5	$300,000			
6	$340,000			

Answers to Problems

2 *a* The marginal and average products are given in Table 11.9.

Table11.9

Number of workers	Output	Average product	Marginal product
1	1,200	1,200	1,200
2	2,200	1,100	1,000
3	3,000	1,000	800
4	3,600	900	600
5	4,000	800	400

b The production function is drawn in the figure. The average product for 3 workers, which is 1,000, is shown as the slope of the line from the origin to point *B*.

c The marginal product of the 4th worker, which is 600, is shown as the slope between points *B* and *C*.

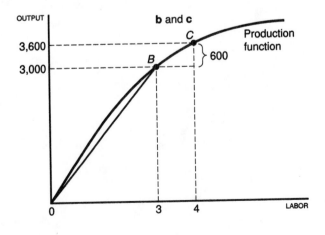

d The production function exhibits diminishing returns.

3 *a* Bedford Waterbeds—diminishing returns

Number of workers	Output	Average product	Marginal product
1	24	24	24
2	42	21	18
3	57	19	15
4	68	17	11
5	75	15	7

b Worry-Free Insurance—diminishing returns

Number of sellers	Policies	Average product	Marginal product
10	200	20.0	20
20	500	25.0	30
30	700	23.3	20
40	800	20.0	10
50	850	17.0	5

5 *a* The completed table is given in Table 11.10.

Table11.10

Output	Total cost	Variable cost	Average cost	Marginal cost
1,000	$ 250,000	$ 200,000	$250	$200
2,000	$ 500,000	$ 450,000	$250	$250
3,000	$ 800,000	$ 750,000	$267	$300
4,000	$1,200,000	$1,150,000	$300	$400
5,000	$1,800,000	$1,750,000	$360	$600

b The diagram shows the total cost and variable cost curves. The variable cost curve is parallel and lies below the total cost curve by $50,000, which is the amount of fixed cost.

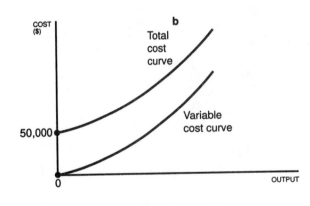

c The diagram shows the average and marginal cost curves. Average and marginal costs are equal at $250, which is the minimum of the average cost curve. Average cost rises after this point, while marginal cost hovers above.

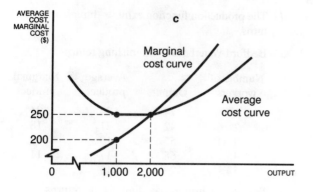

d   The cost curves exhibit diminishing returns.

6   The completed cost tables appear below.

a   These cost curves show diminishing returns.

Output	Total cost	Variable cost	Average cost	Marginal cost
10	$1,500	$ 500	$150	$ 50
20	$2,200	$1,200	$110	$ 70
30	$3,000	$2,000	$100	$ 80
40	$4,000	$3,000	$100	$100
50	$6,000	$5,000	$120	$200

b   These cost curves show increasing returns.

Output	Total cost	Variable cost	Average cost	Marginal cost
100	$1,000	$1,000	$10.00	$10
200	$1,800	$1,800	$ 9.00	$ 8
300	$2,400	$2,400	$ 8.00	$ 6
400	$2,800	$2,800	$ 7.00	$ 4
500	$3,200	$3,200	$ 6.50	$ 4
600	$3,600	$3,600	$ 6.00	$ 4

c   These cost curves show increasing returns until output equals 2, and constant returns thereafter.

Output	Total cost	Variable cost	Average cost	Marginal cost
1	$140,000	$ 60,000	$140,000	$60,000
2	$180,000	$100,000	$ 90,000	$40,000
3	$220,000	$140,000	$ 73,333	$40,000
4	$260,000	$180,000	$ 65,000	$40,000
5	$300,000	$220,000	$ 60,000	$40,000
6	$340,000	$260,000	$ 56,667	$40,000

Chapter 12

PRODUCTION

Chapter Review

This chapter moves the discussion from the firm's costs to decisions firms must make regarding production. In the process, it shows the role of the firm in the competitive model. The firm is a supplier in product markets and a demander in input markets, especially in labor markets. The chapter also explains why and when new firms will enter an industry and why and when existing firms will shut down. Each of these issues requires carefully distinguishing opportunity costs from sunk costs, and profits from rents. This close examination of the firm's production decision completes the discussion of all the individual parts of the basic competitive model that began in Chapter 8. What remains is to put them together and evaluate how the model works. This is done in Chapter 13.

ESSENTIAL CONCEPTS

1 Firms choose output to **maximize profits.** Profit is the difference between total revenue and total costs. The output decision can be illustrated in two ways. One way, shown in Figure 12.1A, is to draw the total revenue and total cost curves and find the quantity where the total revenue curve is above the total cost curve by the greatest amount. At this point, the curves are parallel and their slopes are equal. The second way, shown in panel B, uses the marginal revenue curve. The slope of the total revenue curve is marginal revenue, which for the competitive firm equals the price of its product. The slope of the total cost curve is marginal cost. Therefore, at this point, marginal revenue (price) equals marginal cost, and profit maximization can be shown by the intersection of these two curves.

2 If the market price for a good or service exceeds the minimum average cost, then it pays new firms to enter the market. In deciding whether to *exit* the market, however, a firm must pay attention to those costs it cannot recover. Costs that the firm must pay whether or not it leaves the market are called **sunk costs.** The firm should stay in the market whenever it can earn revenues greater than all the costs not sunk. If all the fixed costs are nonrecoverable sunk costs, then the firm will exit when price falls below the minimum of the average variable cost curve.

3 The *supply curve of the firm* is the marginal cost curve above the minimum price needed to keep the firm from exiting. The *market supply curve* is the sum of the quantities supplied of all firms in the market, and it takes

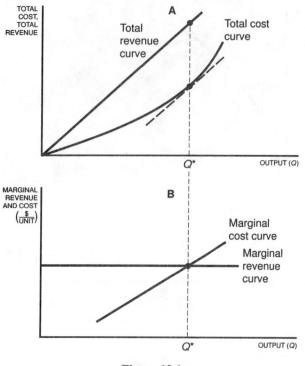

Figure 12.1

into account both the adjustments made by existing firms and the new entrants attracted to the market as the price rises. This curve is more elastic in the long run than in the short run, because existing firms have time to adjust to the lowest-cost production techniques and new firms have time to enter the market and produce.

4   When the going price in a competitive industry exceeds the minimum of the average cost, new firms will enter. The reason is that they will be able to earn higher profits in this industry than elsewhere in the economy. (Recall that the normal rate of return to captial is included in average cost.) Competition thus forces all firms to produce at minimum cost and drives any inefficient firms out of the market. In a similar vein, the theory of **contestable markets** argues that the threat of entry alone will compel a firm to earn zero profits even if it is the only one in the industry.

5   Firms exit an industry when they can no longer earn enough revenues to cover their costs, but the focus is on recoverable costs. Sunk costs are ignored in making the exit decision. The existence of significant sunk costs breaks down the theory of contestible market. The threat of entry is not so strong if the entrant risks losing its investment.

6   The firm's demand for inputs follows from its decision about how much to produce. More formally, the demand for an input is the **value of its marginal product,** which equals its marginal product (how much extra output the marginal input produces) times the product price (how much revenue the firm receives in selling the output). Again, the market demand is just the sum of the quantities demanded by all firms in the market. Because labor is by far the most important input in production, it is

used as the main example of an input in the text. Nevertheless, the demand for any input is the value of its marginal product.

BEHIND THE ESSENTIAL CONCEPTS

1   It is important that cost include all opportunity costs of production borne by the firm. Not only are such explicit costs as wages, energy, raw materials, and interest included, but also more subtle *opportunity costs* are taken into account, such as the value of the entrepreneur's time or the alternative earnings on the equity invested by the owners of the firm. These are considered opportunity costs because if the firm did not produce, the entrepreneur would devote time to some other activity, and the owners would take their investment capital elsewhere.

When a firm is making zero *economic* profits, its revenues are sufficient to cover all costs, including normal returns on the invested financial capital. An economist would say that the firm is only making enough to compensate the owners for the opportunity cost of putting their money into the firm. An accountant would view the situation differently, saying that a firm earning normal returns was actually making positive accounting profits.

2   Another difference between the way economists and accountants view profits concerns rent. **Rent** is the return to anything that is supplied inelastically. For example, suppose a firm's superior location enables it to earn 50 percent more than its competitors. An accountant would say that this firm's profits are 50 percent higher. An economist would call this extra return a rent, because the firm's earnings are higher than the minimum necessary to induce it to stay in its location. Although land is a good example, the concept of rent applies to any payment to a factor of production above the minimum necessary to bring the factor on to the market.

3   Sunk costs and fixed costs are distinct ideas. *Sunk costs* cannot be recovered no matter what the firm does. The firm can shut down production, sell off all its assets, and even go out of business, but it cannot recover its sunk costs. *Fixed costs* do not change as output changes, but they may be recoverable if the firm exits the industry. For example, the firm may own a plant, and the alternative earnings (the opportunity cost) of its plant do not depend on whether the firm produces a little or a great deal of output. If the firm can sell the factory when it exits the industry, then the costs of the plant are fixed but not sunk.

4   There is only one way to maximize profits. If the firm produces goods for the least cost and sets price equal to marginal cost, then it must set the input price equal to the value of the marginal product of that input. Thus, the profit-maximizing demand for labor is just the other side of the coin of the profit-maximizing supply of output. This fact is illustrated in Figure 12.2, where in panel A the firm sets the product price equal to marginal cost and produces Q^* units of output. (Note that this is

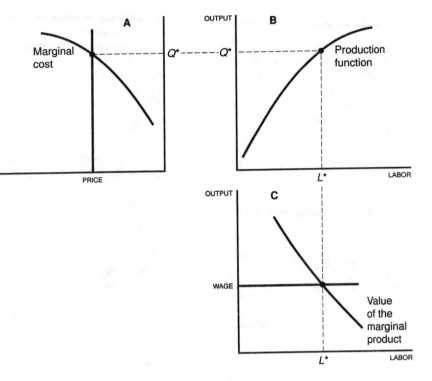

Figure 12.2

the usual diagram turned on its side.) The production function, drawn in panel B, shows that this level of output requires L^* hours of labor. Finally, panel C shows that when the firm sets the wage equal to the value of the marginal product of labor, it chooses exactly L^* hours of labor.

5   The competitive firm has four basic decisions to make: when to enter, when to exit, how much to produce, and how many inputs to hire. Table 12.1 summarizes the decision rules.

Table 12.1

Entry	Enter when price > minimum average cost.
Exit	Exit when revenues < nonrecoverable costs.
Supply	Produce the quantity of output for which price equals marginal cost.
Demand	Hire the quantity of inputs for which the input price equals the value of the marginal product.

SELF-TEST

True or False

1   The firm is choosing the profit-maximizing level of output when price equals marginal cost.

2   The firm is choosing the profit-maximizing level of any input when the input price equals the value of the marginal product.

3   The value of the marginal product equals the marginal product divided by the wage.

4   In the competitive model, marginal revenue is less than price because increasing output leads to a fall in price.

5   All fixed costs are sunk, but not all sunk costs are fixed.

6   Accounting profits are always less than economic profits.

7   In the long run in a competitive industry, economic profits are zero for any potential entrant.

8   Firms exit the industry when price falls below the minimum of the average cost.

9   A firm will enter an industry if the price is above the minimum of the average variable cost curve.

10   Economic rent is any payment to an input in excess of that needed to keep the input in its current use.

11   Land is the only input that can earn economic rent.

12   The long-run supply is more elastic than the short-run supply for the industry but not for the individual firm.

13   The long-run supply curve is the sum of the supply curves of individual firms, including those that enter at high prices.

14   Even if a firm's supply curve is upward sloping in the short run, it may be perfectly elastic in the long run.

15   Correctly measured, total cost should include all opportunity costs of operating.

Multiple Choice

1 Marginal revenue

 a is less than price for the competitive firm be-
    cause as it sells more output, it must lower the
    price;
 b equals price for the competitive firm;
 c is the revenue that the firm receives for selling an-
    other unit of output;
 d is the extra profit that the firm receives from sell-
    ing another unit of output, after accounting for all
    opportunity costs;
 e b and c.

2 The firm supplies the profit-maximizing level of output when

 a marginal revenue equals price;
 b marginal revenue equals marginal cost;
 c economic profits are zero;
 d accounting profits are zero;
 e sunk costs equal fixed costs.

3 The extra cost of producing an additional unit of output is called

 a marginal cost;
 b fixed cost;
 c overhead cost;
 d sunk cost;
 e marginal revenue.

4 It pays a firm to enter a market whenever

 a the market price is greater than the minimum aver-
    age cost at which the firm can produce;
 b the firm can earn revenues greater than any nonre-
    coverable costs;
 c price is greater than the minimum of the average
    variable cost curve;
 d price equals marginal cost;
 e marginal revenue equals marginal cost.

5 The firm should exit the market whenever

 a it cannot earn revenues equal to at least its nonre-
    coverable costs;
 b price is less than marginal cost;
 c price is less than the minimum of the average cost
    curve;
 d price is less than the minimum of the average vari-
    able cost curve;
 e all of the above.

6 Sunk costs are

 a costs that do not change when output changes;
 b the costs of starting the business;
 c nonrecoverable costs;
 d variable costs;
 e opportunity costs.

7 Which of the following is true?

 a Accounting costs are always greater than econom-
    ic costs.
 b Economic costs are always greater than accounting
    costs.
 c Accounting profits are always greater than eco-
    nomic profits.
 d Economic profits are always greater than account-
    ing profits.
 e None of the above.

8 The firm's economic costs include

 a the opportunity cost of the time of the entrepre-
    neur;
 b the revenue that could be earned in alternative uses
    by the assets that the firm owns;
 c the return on the equity invested in the firm by the
    owners;
 d depreciation on company-owned buildings and
    machinery;
 e all of the above

9 The long-run supply curve for the industry is

 a perfectly elastic;
 b more elastic than the short-run supply curve;
 c less elastic than the short-run supply curve;
 d the lower boundary of the short-run supply
    curves;
 e the sum of the short-run supply curves.

10 Economic rent refers to

 a economic profit minus sunk cost;
 b any payment to an input above the minimum need-
    ed to keep the input in its present use;
 c payments from tenants to landlords;
 d the wages of especially skilled labor;
 e revenues received by efficient firms.

11 In the basic competitive model, profits are driven to
   zero. This means that

 a revenues are just enough to cover all nonrecover-
    able costs;
 b revenues are just enough to cover all costs, includ-
    ing the opportunity cost of invested financial capi-
    tal;
 c price equals the minimum of the average variable
    cost curve;
 d accounting profits are equal to zero;
 e b and d.

12 When price is greater than the minimum of the average variable cost curve, the firm

 a enters the market;
 b exits the market;
 c may continue or exit depending upon the magni-
    tude of sunk costs;
 d shuts down production but does not exit;
 e enters the market only if overhead costs are
    zero.

13 The market supply curve

 a is the sum of the quantities of the supply curves of
    all of the firms;
 b is less elastic than the supply curves of all of the
    firms;
 c is the marginal cost curve of the last firm to enter
    the market;

d is always horizontal;

e none of the above.

14 The value to the firm of hiring one more worker is

a equal to marginal cost;

b equal to marginal revenue;

c equal to the marginal product of labor;

d equal to the marginal product of labor multiplied by the product price;

e equal to the marginal product of labor multiplied by the wage.

15 The value of the marginal product is

a the revenue that the firm receives for the last unit of output;

b the revenue that the firm receives for entering the market;

c the marginal product multiplied by the wage;

d the marginal product multiplied by the product price;

e none of the above.

16 The market demand for labor equals

a the market supply of output;

b the sum of the demands for labor of all the firms;

c the wage;

d the marginal product of labor;

e none of the above.

17 If all of a firm's fixed costs are sunk, then it shuts down when

a price is less than marginal cost;

b price is less than the minimum of the average cost curve;

c price is less than the minimum of the average variable cost curve;

d accounting profits fall below zero;

e economic profits fall below zero.

18 If none of a firm's fixed costs are sunk, then it shuts down when

a price is less than marginal cost;

b price is less than the minimum of the average cost curve;

c price is less than the minimum of the average variable cost curve;

d economic profits fall below zero;

e b and d.

19 If a firm with a U-shaped short-run average cost curve doubles its output by doubling the number of plants and keeps its average cost the same, then the long-run supply is

a perfectly elastic;

b perfectly inelastic;

c upward sloping;

d downward sloping;

e none of the above.

20 The real product wage is equal to

a the value of the marginal product of labor;

b the marginal cost;

c the product price;

d the wage divided by the marginal product;

e the wage divided by the product price.

Completion

1 The extra revenue that a firm receives for selling another unit of output is the _____.

2 In the basic competitive model, the marginal revenue equals the _____.

3 The extra cost that the firm bears for producing another unit of output is the _____.

4 The level of output that maximizes profits is found by setting _____ equal to _____.

5 The supply curve of the competitive firm is the same as the _____ curve when price is high enough to keep the firm in the market.

6 Costs that are not recoverable are called _____ costs.

7 Economic profits equal revenues received in excess of all _____ costs of operating the firm.

8 The demand for inputs is the _____ of the _____.

9 New firms enter the industry whenever price is greater than the minimum of the _____ curve.

10 The value of the marginal product is found by multiplying the _____ by the _____.

Answers to Self-Test

True or False

1	t	4	f	7	t	10	t	13	t
2	t	5	f	8	f	11	f	14	t
3	f	6	f	9	f	12	f	15	t

Multiple Choice

1	e	6	c	11	b	16	b
2	b	7	e	12	c	17	c
3	a	8	e	13	a	18	e
4	a	9	b	14	d	19	a
5	a	10	b	15	d	20	e

Completion

1 marginal revenue

2 price

3 marginal cost

4 price, marginal cost

5 marginal cost

6 sunk

7 opportunity

8 value, marginal product

9 average cost

10 marginal product, product price

Doing Economics: Tools and Practice Problems

The firm's decision of how much output to supply requires marginal benefit and marginal cost reasoning. So does the firm's demand for labor or any other input. In this section, we will do problems involving the profit-maximizing quantity of output and corresponding quantities of inputs. Next, we will investigate the entry and exit decisions, reviewing opportunity and sunk costs. A good understanding of costs allows us to derive the entire supply curve of output. Finally, we will tackle a capstone problem that integrates the production function, cost curves, entry decision, exit decision, supply curve, and demand curve for the competitive firm.

SUPPLY OF OUTPUT

Firms must decide how much output to offer for sale. This supply decision involves balancing marginal revenue and marginal cost. Competitive firms are price takers, so marginal revenue equals price. All this implies that price must equal marginal cost, and this is the rule for profit maximization in the supply of output. Tool Kit 12.1 shows how to solve the problem of how much output to supply.

Tool Kit 12.1: Finding the Quantity of Output to Supply

The quantity of output that maximizes the firm's profits is found by setting marginal revenue equal to marginal cost. When the firm is a price taker, the marginal revenue equals the product price. The rule is then to find the quantity for which price equals marginal cost.

Step one: Calculate the marginal cost for each unit of output.

Step two: Identify the market price.

Step three: Find the greatest level of output for which price equals marginal cost. This is the quantity supplied.

---

1   (Worked problem: quantity supplied) Barbara's Carpet Cleaners has fixed costs of $100 per month and a total cost curve as given in Table 12.2. Output is the number of carpets cleaned.

Table 12.2

Output	Total cost
10	$ 200
20	$ 320
30	$ 460
40	$ 620
50	$ 800
60	$1,000

a   The current price for cleaning a carpet is $18. How many carpets must be cleaned to maximize profits? What will the profit be?
b   Suppose that the price falls to $14. Calculate the profit-maximizing output and the total profits.

Step-by-step solution

Step one (a): Marginal cost is the extra cost of cleaning another carpet. When output is increased from 0 to 10, total costs increase by $200 − $100 = $100; therefore, the marginal cost is $100/10 = $10. Derive the marginal cost curve shown in Table 12.3.

Table 12.3

Output	Total cost	Marginal cost
10	$ 200	10
20	$ 320	12
30	$ 460	14
40	$ 620	16
50	$ 800	18
60	$1,000	20

Step two: Identify the market price. It is $18.

Step three: Find the greatest level of output for which price equals marginal cost. The $18 price equals marginal cost when output is 50.

Step four: Calculate profits. Profits equal revenues minus costs. Revenues equal $900 (50 × $18); profits equal $900 − $800 = $100. So the firm makes profits equal to $100.

Step five (b): If the price falls to $14, then price equals marginal cost at 30 units. Profits = (30 × $14) − $460 = −$40, and the firm loses $40.

2   (Practice problem: quantity supplied) The fixed cost for Martin Block, Inc., is $10,000. The company's cost curve is given in Table 12.4.

Table 12.4

Output	Total cost	Marginal cost
10,000	$21,000	
20,000	$32,100	
30,000	$43,300	
40,000	$54,600	
50,000	$66,000	
60,000	$77,500	

a   The current price for blocks is $1.12. Find the profit-maximizing quantity of blocks to produce. What will the profit be?
b   Suppose that the price rises to $1.15. Calculate the profit-maximizing output and the total profits.

3   (Practice problem: quantity supplied) For each of the following, find the profit-maximizing output level, and calculate total profits.

a   Fixed costs = $40,000; price = $600.

Output	Total cost	Marginal cost
100	$ 80,000	
200	$120,000	
300	$170,000	
400	$230,000	
500	$300,000	
600	$380,000	
700	$470,000	

b   Fixed costs = $900; price = $3.00.

Output	Total cost	Marginal cost
1,000	$ 1,900	
2,000	$ 2,900	
3,000	$ 4,600	
4,000	$ 6,600	
5,000	$ 9,400	
6,000	$12,400	
7,000	$16,000	
8,000	$20,000	

c   Fixed costs = $0; price = $80.

Output	Total cost	Marginal cost
1	$ 40	
2	$ 90	
3	$150	
4	$210	
5	$280	
6	$360	
7	$450	
8	$550	

DEMAND FOR INPUTS

Profits are always maximized by setting marginal revenue equal to marginal cost. When the firm is a price taker in both product and input markets, the marginal revenue from hiring another input is the value of the marginal product, which is the marginal product of that input multiplied by the product price. The marginal cost of hiring another input is the input price. In the case of labor, the input price is the wage. Tool Kit 12.2 shows how to solve for the input demand.

Tool Kit 12.2: Finding the Quantity of an Input to Demand

The demand for an input is its value of the marginal product. This is found by multiplying the marginal product by the product price. Follow this five step procedure to determine the profit maximizing quantity of an input.

Step one: Calculate the marginal product for each level of the input.

Step two: Identify the product price.

Step three: Compute the value of the marginal product by multiplying the marginal product by the product price for each level of the input:

value of the marginal product = marginal product × product price.

Step four: Identify the input price. (In the case of labor, this is the wage.)

Step five: Find the level of the input for which the value of the marginal product equals the input price. This is the quantity demanded.

---

4   (Worked problem: quantity demanded) The new company The Hair Cuttery is ready to start hiring. The price of haircuts is $8, and the production function is given in Table 12.5.

Table 12.5

Stylists	Haircuts per day	Marginal product	Value of the marginal product
1	8		
2	16		
3	23		
4	29		
5	34		
6	38		

a   The wage paid to hair stylists is $40 per day. Find the profit-maximizing number of hair stylists to hire.

b   Suppose that the wage rises to $64 per day. Find the number of hair stylists that maximizes profits.

Step-by-step solution

Step one (a): The marginal product is the extra output that results from hiring one more input. When the first hair stylist is hired, output rises from 0 to 8. The marginal product is 8. Enter this number. When the second hair stylist is hired, output rises from 8 to 16. The marginal product is 16 − 8 = 8; enter this number and continue. The marginal product column is given in Table 12.6.

Table 12.6

Stylists	Haircuts per day	Marginal product	Value of the marginal product
1	8	8	
2	16	8	
3	23	7	
4	29	6	
5	34	5	
6	38	4	

Step two: The product price is $8.

Step three: The value of the marginal product equals the product price multiplied by the marginal product. The value of the marginal product of the first worker is 8 × $8 = $64. Continue to enter the results in the appropriate column. The completed information is given in Table 12.7.

Table 12.7

Stylists	Haircuts per day	Marginal product	Value of the marginal product
1	8	8	$64
2	16	8	$64
3	23	7	$56
4	29	6	$48
5	34	5	$40
6	38	4	$32

Step four: The wage is $40 per day.

Step five: Profits are maximized when the wage is set equal to the value of the marginal product. The wage is $40, which equals the value of the marginal product when 5 hair stylists are hired.

Step six (b): When the wage is $64, it equals the value of the marginal product if 2 stylists are hired.

5   (Practice problem: quantity demanded) Moe's Lawn Service mows lawns for $20 each. Moe's production function is given in Table 12.8. Output is measured as the number of lawns mowed.

Table 12.8

Workers	Output per day	Marginal product	Value of the marginal product
1	5.0		
2	9.0		
3	13.0		
4	16.5		
5	19.5		
6	22.0		
7	24.0		

Moe pays his lawn mowers $40 per day.

a   Find the profit-maximizing number of mowers to hire.

b   Suppose that the wage rises to $70 per day. Find the profit-maximizing number of mowers to hire.

6   (Practice problem: quantity demanded) For each of the following, complete the table and find the profit-maximizing number of inputs.

a   Product price = $10; wage = $100 per day.

Workers	Output per day	Marginal product	Value of the marginal product
10	200		
20	360		
30	500		
40	620		
50	720		
60	800		

b   Product price = $10,000; wage = $10,000 per month.

Workers	Output per day	Marginal product	Value of the marginal product
10	20		
20	40		
30	55		
40	65		
50	70		
60	70		

c   Product price = $5; input price = $40.

Workers	Output per day	Marginal product	Value of the marginal product
1,000	10,000		
2,000	18,000		
3,000	25,500		
4,000	31,500		
5,000	36,000		
6,000	40,000		

ENTRY AND EXIT

A firm should seize the opportunity and enter an industry whenever it can make positive (or at least zero) economic profits. This occurs when price is greater than the minimum of the average cost curve. A firm should give up and exit an industry whenever it can no longer earn revenues in excess of its nonrecoverable costs. If all fixed costs are recoverable, then the firm exits whenever price falls below the minimum of the average cost curve. If none of the fixed costs are recoverable, then the firm exits when price falls below the minimum of the average *variable* cost curve. If some costs are recoverable, the exit price lies somewhere in between. Tool Kit 12.3 explores this idea.

Tool Kit 12.3: Determining Entry and Exit Prices

Firms enter the market when the price rises above the minimum average cost. They exit when the price falls below the minimum average recoverable cost. Follow this procedure to find these prices.

Step one: Calculate the average cost for each level of output.

Step two: Find the minimum average cost; this is the entry price. When the price is greater than or equal to the minimum average cost, then the firm should enter the market.

Step three: Identify all costs that are not sunk (nonrecoverable).

Step four: Calculate the average of the costs that are not sunk.

Step five: Find the minimum average nonsunk cost; this is the exit price. When the price falls below this level, the firm should exit the market.

---

7   (Worked problem: entry and exit prices) Let's return to Barbara's Carpet Cleaners in problem 1. The total cost curve is given in Table 12.9.

Table 12.9

Output	Total cost
10	$ 200
20	$ 320
30	$ 460
40	$ 620
50	$ 800
60	$1,000

a Find the entry price, which is the minimum price that will induce the firm to enter the market.
b Assume that all the fixed costs are sunk. Find the exit price, which is the maximum price that will induce the firm to exit the market.
c Now assume that $50 of the fixed cost is recoverable. Find the exit price.

Step-by-step solution

Step one (a): Calculate the average cost for each level of output, and enter in the table. The average cost at 10 carpets is $200/10 = $20. Continue to fill in the column as in Table 12.10.

Table 12.10

Output	Total cost	Average cost
10	$ 200	$20.00
20	$ 320	$16.00
30	$ 460	$15.33
40	$ 620	$15.50
50	$ 800	$16.00
60	$1,000	$16.66

Step two: The minimum of the average cost curve is $15.33, and this is the entry price. This is the answer to part a.

Step three (b): Identify the costs that are not sunk. If all fixed costs are sunk, then only the variable costs can be recovered. In this case, the exit price is the minimum of the average variable cost curve. First, compute variable cost by subtracting fixed costs from total cost. The variable cost for 10 units of output is $200 – $100 = $100. Continue to fill in this column as in Table 12.11.

Table 12.11

Output	Total cost	Variable cost
10	$ 200	$100
20	$ 320	$220
30	$ 460	$360
40	$ 620	$520
50	$ 800	$700
60	$1,000	$900

Step four: Compute average variable cost. For 10 carpets, the average variable cost is $100/10 = $10. Enter the results as given in Table 12.12.

Table 12.12

Output	Total cost	Variable cost	Average variable cost
10	$ 200	$100	$10
20	$ 320	$220	$11
30	$ 460	$360	$12
40	$ 620	$520	$13
50	$ 800	$700	$14
60	$1,000	$900	$15

Step five: The minimum of the average variable cost curve is $10; therefore, the firm should exit when the price falls below $10. This is the answer to part b.

Step six (c): Only $50 is sunk; thus, the firm exits when revenues fall below variable costs plus $50. To find the recoverable costs, simply add $50 to the variable cost. Next, find the average of these numbers, and the minimum of these averages is the exit price. The results appear in Table 12.13.

Table 12.13

Output	Variable cost	Recoverable cost	Average recoverable cost
10	$100	$150	$15.00
20	$220	$270	$13.50
30	$360	$410	$13.66
40	$520	$570	$14.25
50	$700	$750	$15.00
60	$900	$950	$15.83

The minimum of the average recoverable cost column is $13.50, which is the exit price. When the price is $13.50, the firm loses $50, which means that revenues cover all but the nonrecoverable costs.

8 (Practice problem: entry and exit prices) Now let's return to Martin Block in problem 2. The total cost curve is reprinted in Table 12.14. Fixed costs equal $10,000.

Table 12.14

Output	Total cost
10,000	$21,000
20,000	$32,100
30,000	$43,300
40,000	$54,600
50,000	$66,000
60,000	$77,500

a Find the entry price, which is the minimum price that will induce the firm to enter the market.
b Assume that all of the fixed costs are sunk. Find the exit price, which is the maximum price that will induce the firm to exit the market.

9 (Practice problem: entry and exit prices) Find the entry price and the exit price for the firms in problem 3. Assume that all the fixed costs are sunk.

10 (Worked problem: applications) The competitive firm is a price taker in product and input markets. It has a production function and a level of fixed costs. Given this information, we can derive all the firm's cost curves, its supply curve, its demand curve, and the price at which it will enter or exit the industry. Remo's Repos recovers the automobiles of delinquent borrowers. Local banks pay him $50 per car recovered. Remo hires agents at $100 per night to repossess the cars. He

runs a low-budget operation with fixed costs of only $500. The production function is given in Table 12.15, where output is measured as the number of cars repossessed.

a Complete the table below, and calculate the profit-maximizing number of agents to hire.

Table 12.15

Agents	Output	Marginal product	Value of the marginal product
1	8		
2	15		
3	21		
4	26		
5	30		
6	33		
7	35		
8	36		
9	37		

b Complete the cost table below, and calculate the profit-maximizing number of automobiles to repossess.

Output	Total cost	Variable cost	Average cost	Average variable cost	Marginal cost

c Verify that the number of agents hired repossesses the quantity of output produced.
d Find the entry price.
e Assume that the fixed costs are sunk, and find the exit price.

Step-by-step solution

Step one (a): Follow along with the solution to problem 4, and complete the table given above. The results are given in Table 12.16.

Table 12.16

Agents	Output	Marginal product	Value of the marginal product
1	8	8	$400
2	15	7	$350
3	21	6	$300
4	26	5	$250
5	30	4	$200
6	33	3	$150
7	35	2	$100
8	36	1	$ 50
9	37	1	$ 50

Step two: Set the input price ($100) equal to the value of the marginal product, which is $100 when 7 agents are hired.

Step three (b): Compute the cost for each output level in the production function. For 8 cars repossessed, 1 agent is hired

at $100 and fixed costs are $500; therefore, total costs equal $100 + $500 = $600. Enter this number. For 15 cars, 2 agents at $100 each added to the $500 gives a total cost of $700. Continue and complete the total cost column. The result is given in Table 12.17.

Table 12.17

Output	Total cost
8	$ 600
15	$ 700
21	$ 800
26	$ 900
30	$1,000
33	$1,100
35	$1,200
36	$1,300
37	$1,400

Step four: Follow the solution to problems 1 and 7, and complete the table. Be careful with marginal cost. For example, the marginal cost at 8 cars is ($600 − $500)/8 = $12.50. The marginal cost at 15 cars is ($700 − $600)/(15 − 8) = $14.29. The complete information is given in Table 12.18.

Table 12.18

Output	Total cost	Variable cost	Average cost	Average variable cost	Marginal cost
8	$ 600	$100	$75.00	$12.50	$ 12.50
15	$ 700	$200	$46.66	$13.33	$ 14.29
21	$ 800	$300	$38.09	$14.28	$ 16.66
26	$ 900	$400	$34.61	$15.38	$ 20.00
30	$1,000	$500	$33.33	$16.66	$ 25.00
33	$1,100	$600	$33.33	$18.18	$ 33.33
35	$1,200	$700	$34.28	$20.00	$ 50.00
36	$1,300	$800	$36.11	$22.22	$100.00
37	$1,400	$900	$37.83	$24.32	$100.00

Step five: Set price equal to marginal cost. The price is $50, which equals marginal cost when 35 cars are repossessed.

Step six (c): Check the production function to make sure that when 7 agents are hired, 35 cars are repossessed.

Step seven (d): The entry price is the minimum of the average cost curve, which is $33.33. Note that marginal cost equals average cost at the minimum of the average cost curve.

Step eight (e): The exit price for the case in which all fixed costs are sunk is the minimum of the average variable cost, which is $12.50. Again, note that at the minimum of average variable cost, it is equal to marginal cost.

11 (Practice problem: applications) Perry's Perfect Pet Place hires people to bathe dogs. Perry pays the bather $20 per day and charges the dogs $10 per bath. His fixed costs are $50. The production function is given in Table 12.19.

a Complete the table below, and calculate the profit-maximizing number of bathers to hire.

Table 12.19

Bathers	Baths	Marginal product	Value of the marginal product
1	6		
2	11		
3	15		
4	18		
5	20		
6	21		

b Complete the cost table below, and calculate the profit-maximizing number of dogs to bathe.

Output	Total cost	Variable cost	Average cost	Average variable cost	Marginal cost

c Verify that the number of bathers hired does give the profit-maximizing number of baths.
d Find the entry price.
e Assume that the fixed costs are sunk, and find the exit price.

Answers to Problems

2 a The marginal cost is given in Table 12.20.

Table 12.20

Output	Total cost	Marginal cost
10,000	$21,000	—
20,000	$32,100	$1.11
30,000	$43,300	$1.12
40,000	$54,600	$1.13
50,000	$66,000	$1.14
60,000	$77,500	$1.15

When the price is $1.12, output is 30,000, and profits equal ($1.12 × 30,000) − $43,300 = −$9,400.

b When the price is $1.15, output is 60,000, and profits equal ($1.15 × 60,000) − $77,500 = −$8,500.

3 a The marginal cost is given in Table 12.21.

Table 12.21

Output	Total cost	Marginal cost
100	$ 80,000	$400
200	$120,000	$400
300	$170,000	$500
400	$230,000	$600
500	$300,000	$700
600	$380,000	$800
700	$470,000	$900

Output = 400; profits = ($600 × 400) − $230,000 = $10,000.

b The marginal cost is given in Table 12.22.

Table 12.22

Output	Total cost	Marginal cost
1,000	$ 1,900	$1.00
2,000	$ 2,900	$1.00
3,000	$ 4,600	$1.70
4,000	$ 6,600	$2.00
5,000	$ 9,400	$2.80
6,000	$12,400	$3.00
7,000	$16,000	$3.60
8,000	$20,000	$4.00

Output = 6,000; profits = ($3.00 × 6,000) − $12,400 = $5,600.

c The marginal cost is given in Table 12.23.

Table 12.23

Output	Total cost	Marginal cost
1	$ 40	$ 40
2	$ 90	$ 50
3	$150	$ 60
4	$210	$ 60
5	$280	$ 70
6	$360	$ 80
7	$450	$ 90
8	$550	$100

Output = 6; profits = (6 × $80) − $360 = $120.

5 The value of the marginal product is given in Table 12.24.

Table 12.24

Workers	Output per day	Marginal product	Value of the marginal product
1	5.0	5.0	$100
2	9.0	4.0	$ 80
3	13.0	4.0	$ 80
4	16.5	3.5	$ 70
5	19.5	3.0	$ 60
6	22.0	2.5	$ 50
7	24.0	2.0	$ 40

a When the wage is $40, it equals the vmp if 7 are hired.
b When the wage is $70, it equals the vmp if 4 are hired.

6 a The value of the marginal product is given in Table 12.25. The quantity demanded is 50 workers.

Table 12.25

Workers	Output per day	Marginal product	Value of the marginal product
10	200	20	$200
20	360	16	$160
30	500	14	$140
40	620	12	$120
50	720	10	$100
60	800	8	$ 80

b   The value of the marginal product is given in Table 12.26. The quantity demanded is 40 workers.

Table 12.26

Workers	Output per day	Marginal product	Value of the marginal product
10	20	2.0	$20,000
20	40	2.0	$20,000
30	55	1.5	$15,000
40	65	1.0	$10,000
50	70	0.5	$ 5,000
60	70	0	$ 0

c   The value of the marginal product is given in Table 12.27. The quantity demanded is 2,000 workers.

Table 12.27

Workers	Output per day	Marginal product	Value of the marginal product
1,000	10,000	10.0	$50.00
2,000	18,000	8.0	$40.00
3,000	25,500	7.5	$37.50
4,000	31,500	6.0	$30.00
5,000	36,000	4.5	$22.50
6,000	40,000	4.0	$20.00

8   The cost measures are given in Table 12.28.

Table 12.28

Output	Total cost	Average cost	Variable cost	Average variable cost
10,000	$21,000	$2.10	$11,000	$1.10
20,000	$32,100	$1.61	$22,100	$1.11
30,000	$43,300	$1.43	$33.300	$1.11
40,000	$54,600	$1.37	$44,600	$1.12
50,000	$66,000	$1.32	$56,000	$1.12
60,000	$77,500	$1.29	$67,500	$1.13

a   Entry price = $1.29.
b   Exit price = $1.10.

9   a   The cost measures appear in Table 12.29.

Table 12.29

Output	Total cost	Average cost	Variable cost	Average variable cost
100	$ 80,000	$800	$ 40,000	$400
200	$120,000	$600	$ 80,000	$400
300	$170,000	$567	$130,000	$433
400	$230,000	$575	$190,000	$475
500	$300,000	$600	$260,000	$520
600	$380,000	$633	$340,000	$567
700	$470,000	$671	$430,000	$614

Entry price = $567; exit price = $400.
b   The cost measures appear in Table 12.30.

Table 12.30

Output	Total cost	Average cost	Variable cost	Average variable cost
1,000	$ 1,900	$1.90	$ 1,000	$1.00
2,000	$ 2,900	$1.45	$ 2,000	$1.00
3,000	$ 4,600	$1.53	$ 3,700	$1.23
4,000	$ 6,600	$1.65	$ 5,700	$1.43
5,000	$ 9,400	$1.88	$ 8,500	$1.70
6,000	$12,400	$2.07	$11,500	$1.92
7,000	$16,000	$2.29	$15,100	$2.16
8,000	$20,000	$2.50	$19,100	$2.39

Entry price = $1.45; exit price = $1.00.
c   The cost measures appear in Table 12.31.

Table 12.31

Output	Total cost	Average cost	Variable cost	Average variable cost
1	$ 40	$40.00	$ 40	$40.00
2	$ 90	$45.00	$ 90	$45.00
3	$150	$50.00	$150	$50.00
4	$210	$52.50	$210	$52.50
5	$280	$56.00	$280	$56.00
6	$360	$60.00	$360	$60.00
7	$450	$64.29	$450	$64.29
8	$550	$68.75	$550	$68.75

Entry price = $40; exit price = $40.

11   a   The complete information is given in Table 12.32.

Table 12.32

Bathers	Baths	Marginal product	Value of the marginal product
1	6	6	$60
2	11	5	$50
3	15	4	$40
4	18	3	$30
5	20	2	$20
6	21	1	$10

    Perry should hire 5 bathers.

b The completed cost information appears in Table 12.33.

Table 12.33

Output	Total cost	Variable cost	Average cost	Average variable cost	Marginal cost
6	$ 70	$ 20	$11.67	$3.33	$ 3.33
11	$ 90	$ 40	$ 8.18	$3.64	$ 4.00
15	$110	$ 60	$ 7.33	$4.00	$ 5.00
18	$130	$ 80	$ 7.22	$4.44	$ 6.33
20	$150	$100	$ 7.50	$5.00	$10.00
21	$170	$120	$ 8.10	$5.71	$20.00

    Perry should sell 20 baths.

c 5 bathers complete 20 baths.

d Entry price = $7.22.

e Exit price = $3.33.

COMPETITIVE EQUILIBRIUM

Chapter Review

The elements of the basic competitive model have been presented over the last six chapters of the text. In Chapter 13, these elements—from individuals and their decisions regarding consumption, savings, investment, and work, to firms and their choices regarding production and costs—are brought together in the general equilibrium model. The focus of the model is on the interdependencies of the product, labor, and capital markets. Another major topic is a normative one: how well does the competitive economy perform? The notion of Pareto efficiency provides a tool with which economists can evaluate how well the market economy answers the basic economic questions. This chapter completes the presentation of the competitive model and closes Part Two. In Part Three, attention shifts to imperfect markets.

ESSENTIAL CONCEPTS

1   Partial equilibrium analysis looks at one market in isolation. This kind of analysis can be inappropriate if changes in the market under consideration cause disturbances in the rest of the economy, which then feed back in an important way to the original market. General equilibrium analysis takes into account the relationships among different markets and keeps track of the interactions.

2   The basic competitive three-market model is a relatively simple general equilibrium model, and is very good for analyzing the interactions among markets. The three markets are the labor, capital, and product markets. They are interdependent in that as the price changes in one market, demand and supply curves shift in the others. In general equilibrium, the three prices (wage, interest rate, and product price) are set so that each market clears.

   a   Demand equals supply in the labor market.
   b   Demand equals supply in the capital market.
   c   Demand equals supply in the goods market.

3   Another view of the general equilibrium of the economy is given by the circular flow model. The simple version given in Figure 13.1 shows that households supply labor and financial capital to firms and demand products. Firms demand labor and capital and supply products. The flows of funds balance. For example, the revenues that firms receive for the sale of their goods equal the payments to labor as wages and to capital as dividends and interest. The circular flow model can be expanded

Figure 13.1

to keep track of flows between one country and the rest of the world and between the private sector and the government.

4   The concept of efficiency used by economists is called **Pareto efficiency**. An allocation of resources is Pareto efficient if there is no way to reallocate resources to make anyone better off without hurting someone else. The equilibrium of the competitive economy is Pareto efficient. There is **exchange efficiency** because the goods and services produced by the economy are distributed efficiently among individuals, **production efficiency** because the economy is on its production possibilities curve, and **product-mix efficiency** because the mix of goods matches consumers' tastes.

5   Free-market economists take the view that the basic competitive model provides a good description of the world and they see a quite limited role for government. Imperfect-market economists, on the other hand, take the competitive model as an important base but move beyond its boundaries to investigate circumstances where the economy is inefficient. Although they see the role for government in market failures, all economists caution that this does not necessarily imply that any particular government intervention will improve matters. Effective government intervention requires careful consideration of the reasons for market inefficiencies and the design of the remedy.

BEHIND THE ESSENTIAL CONCEPTS

1   The interdependencies of markets demonstrate another facet of the principle of substitution. When the price of one good rises, the demand for its substitutes rises, while the demand for its complement falls. When the price of one input rises, firms substitute other inputs. A change in the capital market affects the wealth of con-

sumers and the costs of firms. The economy is a spider's web, and a movement in any one part reverberates throughout the whole.

2   Even though there are connections among all markets, in many cases the effects beyond a single market may be small. When this is true, it is sufficient to concentrate on the one market, that is, to employ partial equilibrium analysis, and ignore any general equilibrium repercussions. The art of economic analysis is to bring to light the important general equilibrium considerations and leave aside the portion of the economy that remains relatively unaffected.

3   If a firm produces several goods and there exists a way to rearrange its production and increase the output of one good without reducing the output of any other, an economist would say that this firm is inefficient. The firm is wasting inputs, because it is not getting the maximum output from the inputs. The output of the economy is the satisfaction (the utility) of its members. Therefore, if the economy is doing things one way, and there exists another way to do things that increases the utility of one individual (makes her better off) without reducing the utility of anyone else, then, just like the firm above, the economy is inefficient. Pareto efficiency is a natural definition of efficiency for the economy, the important output of which is ultimately not goods and services but human satisfaction.

SELF-TEST

True or False

1   A general equilibrium analysis takes into account all the important interactions among markets.

2   A partial equilibrium analysis focuses on one market only.

3   General equilibrium and partial equilibrium analyses always differ quite dramatically.

4   For the most part, in the capital market, firms are demanders and households are suppliers.

5   In the product market, firms are demanders and households are suppliers.

6   In the labor market, firms are demanders and households are suppliers.

7   The economy is in equilibrium when most of its markets clear.

8   In the circular flow model, the flows to households must equal the flows from households.

9   In the circular flow model, exports plus funds lent abroad must equal imports plus money borrowed from abroad.

10 The allocation of resources is Pareto efficient in competitive equilibrium.

11 The allocation of resources is equal in competitive equilibrium.

12 Pareto efficiency means that everyone can be made better off by some reallocation of resources.

13 Imperfect-market economists despair of the market's ability to produce efficient outcomes and advocate government control over the economy.

14 All points along the production possibilities curve are Pareto efficient.

15 Pareto efficiency requires exchange efficiency, production efficiency, and product-mix efficiency.

Multiple Choice

1 When an analysis focuses on the interactions between markets, it is called

a   partial equilibrium;
b   interactive equilibrium;
c   disequilibrium;
d   general equilibrium;
e   none of the above;

2 When an analysis looks only at the changes in one market, it is called

a   partial equilibrium;
b   interactive equilibrium;
c   disequilibrium;
d   general equilibrium;
e   none of the above;

3 In a general equilibrium model, the supply of labor depends upon

a   product prices;
b   the wage;
c   interest rates;
d   a and b;
e   all of the above.

4 In a general equilibrium model, the supply of products depends upon the wage and interest rates because

a   these input prices affect costs;
b   household income is affected by changes in the wage and interest rates;
c   households can substitute leisure or future consumption for current products;
d   the demand for capital depends upon the wage rate;
e   all of the above.

5 Which of the following is not necessarily true when the economy is in full, general equilibrium?

a   The supply of labor equals the demand.
b   The supply of products equals the demand.
c   The supply of capital equals the demand.
d   The distribution of income is fair.
e   All of the above are true when the economy is in equilibrium.

6 A increase in immigration will

a   shift the supply of labor to the left, decreasing wages;
b   shift the supply of labor to the right, decreasing wages;

c   shift the supply of products to the right, decreasing prices;
d   shift the supply of products to the left, increasing prices;
e   b and c.

7 In general equilibrium, a tax on business profits will be paid by individuals through

a   increases in product prices;
b   decreases in wages;
c   decreases in dividends;
d   capital losses on stock ownership;
e   all of the above.

8 An increase in the tax rate on commercial property will

a   have no effect on the returns to other forms of capital investment;
b   cause financial capital to flow from commercial property to other forms of capital investment, reducing the average return to capital;
c   have no effect on the allocation of financial capital;
d   have no effect on the returns to capital because all investments must be equally profitable in equilibrium;
e   a and c.

9 If the allocation of resources is Pareto efficient,

a   the distribution of income is fair;
b   there is a way to reallocate resources and make everyone better off;
c   there is a way to reallocate resources and make some people better off without hurting others;
d   there is no way to reallocate resources and make anyone better off without hurting some other person;
e   none of the above.

10 In the basic circular flow model,

a   households demand goods and services;
b   firms supply goods and services;
c   households supply labor and financial capital;
d   firms demand labor and financial capital;
e   all of the above.

11 The circular flow model shows that

a   some taxes are paid by businesses and some by households;
b   all taxes are paid by businesses through either lower product prices, higher wages, or higher costs of capital;
c   all taxes are paid by households through either higher product prices, lower wages, or lower returns to capital;
d   the government pays all taxes;
e   none of the above.

12 Which of the following probably does not require a general equilibrium analysis?

a   a corporate income tax;
b   a ban on foreign investment;

c   a national sales tax;

d   elimination of trade restrictions.

e   All of the above require general equilibrium analysis.

13   Which of the following probably requires only a partial equilibrium analysis?

a   an increase in the supply of green beans;

b   stricter antipollution regulations;

c   a reduction in the size of the military by one-half;

d   an end to agricultural price supports;

e   all of the above.

14   According to the circular flow model, if the personal income tax is cut, then

a   government borrowing must increase;

b   some other tax must be increased;

c   government spending must decrease;

d   either b or c;

e   either a, b, or c.

15   Free-market economists believe that

a   market outcomes are usually efficient;

b   the market's determination of the distribution of income is just;

c   markets cannot be relied upon to produce efficient outcome;

d   the market brings about production efficiency but not exchange efficiency;

e   the market brings about exchange efficiency but not production efficiency.

16   Imperfect-market economists believe that

a   market outcomes are usually efficient;

b   the market's determination of the distribution of income is just;

c   markets cannot be relied upon to produce efficient outcomes;

d   the market brings about production efficiency but not exchange efficiency;

e   the market brings about exchange efficiency but not production efficiency.

17   Exchange efficiency means that

a   the distribution of the goods and services that the economy produces is efficient;

b   the distribution of the goods and services that the economy produces is equitable;

c   the economy is operating along its production possibilities curve;

d   a and b;

e   all of the above.

18   Production efficiency means that

a   the mix of goods and services that the economy produces reflects the preferences of consumers;

b   the economy is operating along its production possibilities curve;

c   the distribution of what the economy produces is efficient;

d   the distribution of what the economy produces is equitable;

e - all of the above.

19   Which of the following is not implied by Pareto efficiency?

a   exchange efficiency;

b   production efficiency;

c   efficiency of the product mix.

d   All individuals share equally in the decisions that the economy makes.

e   All of the above are implied by Pareto efficiency.

20   If the competitive model is an accurate depiction of the economy, then

a   the allocation of resources is Pareto efficient;

b   the distribution of income may be quite unequal;

c   the economy is operating on the production possibilities curve;

d   the economy is operating on the utility possibilities curve;

e   all of the above.

Completion

1   Focusing on a single market while ignoring any spillover effects on other markets is called _____ analysis.

2   _____ analysis takes into account all the interactions and interdependencies between various parts of the economy.

3   In the simple circular flow model of the economy, households _____ labor and savings (financial capital) to firms and _____ goods and services.

4   In the simple circular flow model of the economy, firms _____ labor and financial capital from households and _____ goods and services.

5   When there is no way to make anyone better off without hurting someone else, the allocation of resources is _____.

6   _____ requires that the economy's output of goods and services be distributed efficiently among its consumers.

7   When the economy is productively efficient, it is operating on its _____ curve.

8   The view that the basic competitive model gives a good description of the world is held by _____.

9   _____ believe that there are many examples of market failure and that well-designed government intervention can improve matters.

10   Environmental degradation and unemployment are examples of _____.

Answers to Self-Test

True or False

1	t	4	t	7	f	10	t	13	f
2	t	5	f	8	t	11	f	14	f
3	f	6	t	9	f	12	f	15	t

Multiple Choice

1	d	6	e	11	c	16	c
2	a	7	e	12	e	17	a
3	e	8	b	13	a	18	b
4	a	9	d	14	e	19	d
5	d	10	e	15	a	20	e

Completion

1 partial equilibrium
2 General equilibrium
3 supply, demand
4 demand, supply
5 Pareto efficient
6 Exchange efficiency
7 production possibilities

8 free-market economists
9 Imperfect-market economists
10 market failure

Doing Economics: Tools and Practice Problems

The skill in general equilibrium analysis lies in choosing which interdependencies are important and which can be left aside. In this problem set, we first use the three-market model to analyze the effects of major changes in the economy: the introduction of a national sales tax, an important technological advance, and an increase in savings. Finally, there are a few problems that focus on the connections between two markets. We consider corporate taxation, compensating differentials, and natural resource prices.

Tool Kit 13.1: Using General Equilibrium Analysis

When doing general equilibrium analysis, keep the following procedure in mind.

Step one: Identify the relevant markets.

Step two: Start with an equilibrium in each market, as in the figure.

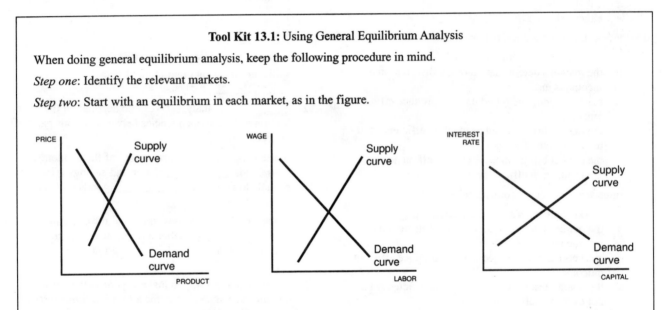

Step three: Identify a change, and determine which curves shift as a direct result of the change. In the second row of the figure, the demand for labor shifts outwards.

Step four: Shift the curves, and find the new equilibrium. In the general equilibrium model, this is only a temporary equilibrium because there are second-round effects to be accounted for. Observe which prices have changed. In the diagram, wages increase.

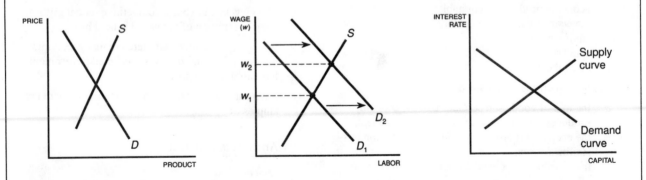

Step five: Determine which curves shift as a result of the price changes observed in step four.

Step six: Shift the curves, as shown here by lower supply in the product market and higher demand in the capital market, and find the new equilibrium.

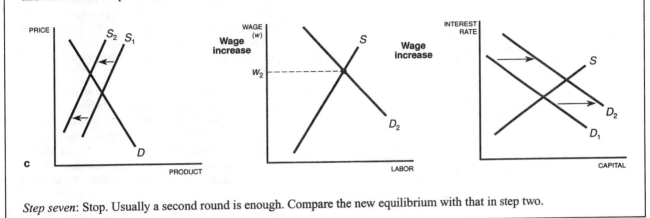

Step seven: Stop. Usually a second round is enough. Compare the new equilibrium with that in step two.

1 (Worked problem: general equilibrium analysis) There are three major markets: labor, capital, and product. They are interrelated in that the prices in other markets cause the demand curves and supply curves to shift. Because of this interdependence, there will be important second-round effects in the three-market model. Most European countries have value-added taxes, a type of national sales tax.

a Use the three-market model to evaluate the effects of a value-added tax.

b Who pays the value-added tax?

Step-by-step solution

Step one (a): Identify the relevant markets. We will use the labor, capital, and product markets.

Step two: Start with an equilibrium in each market.

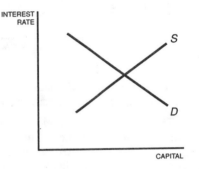

Step three: The value-added tax shifts the product market supply curve up by the amount of the tax. (This step is exactly like the analysis of the effects of taxes in Chapter 5.)

Step four: Find the new (temporary) equilibrium. Note that some of the tax is paid by consumers in the form of higher product prices. On the other hand, firms also receive less after the tax. This completes the first round.

Step five: Determine which curves shift as a result of the price changes observed in step four. The lower net of tax product prices observed in step four implies that the value of the marginal product of inputs is lower. This means that the demand curve for labor and the demand curve for capital must shift to the left.

Step six: Shift the curves, and find the new equilibrium.

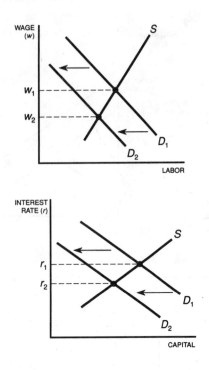

Step seven: Compare the new equilibrium with that in step two. We see that the wage and the interest rate are lower.

Step eight (b): The value-added tax is paid for in three ways. First, it is shifted forward to consumers in the form of higher product prices. Second, it is shifted backward to workers through lower wages. Third, it is shifted backward to savers in terms of lower interest rates. A vital lesson of the general equilibrium approach is that all taxes are ultimately paid by individuals. A partial equilibrium treatment in the product market alone would imply that firms pay some of the tax. The full general equilibrium analysis reveals that the producers' share of the tax is passed backward to workers and savers.

2   (Practice problem: general equilibrium analysis) A substantial share in the growth of developed countries is accounted for by technological advance, by improvements in how goods and services are produced, and by the introduction of new and better products. The hope for continued economic progress rests on technological advance in production. Use the three-market model to analyze the effects of a major technological advance.

a   Start with an equilibrium in the three markets.
b   Better technology increases the marginal products of labor and capital. Which curves are shifted? (Hint: Remember the formula for the value of the marginal product and the relationship between marginal product and marginal cost.)
c   In the second round, how does the equilibrium change?

3   (Practice problem: general equilibrium analysis) Many people are concerned about relatively low savings rate. One cause for optimism is that the aging of the relatively large baby boom generation will lead to more savings. Suppose that households decrease their consumption and increase their savings. Trace through the effects using the three-market model.

4   (Worked problem: general equilibrium analysis) Often when a change occurs in one market, there is another market closely linked to the first. In these cases, both markets must be included in the analysis. Investors seeking the highest possible returns can choose to buy stock in corporations or to invest their money in other noncorporate businesses. If the returns were higher in the corporate sector of the economy, then no one would invest in the noncorporate sector. If the returns were higher in the noncorporate sector, all money would flow out of the corporate sector. In equilibrium, then, the rate of return must be equal in the two sectors.

a   Illustrate an equilibrium in the markets for corporate and noncorporate investment.
b   In the United States, corporations must pay taxes on their income. The corporate income tax is in addition to the taxes paid by investors on their dividend income. Show how a tax on corporate income affects the market for corporate investment.
c   Show how the noncorporate investment market will adjust to restore both markets to equilibrium.
d   Who pays the corporate income tax?

Step-by-step solution

Step one (a): Start with an equilibrium. In this case, not only must supply and demand be equal in each market, but also each market must pay the same returns.

Step two (b): Determine which curve shifts. The corporate tax is paid by the demanders (corporations); therefore, the demand curve in the market for corporate investment shifts down.

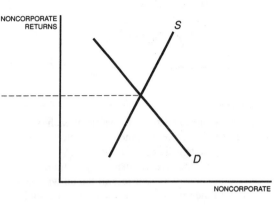

Step three: The (temporary) equilibrium in the market for corporate investment has a lower rate of return than in the market for noncorporate investment.

Step four (c): Determine the effects in the noncorporate investment market. Because they can earn higher after-tax returns in the noncorporate sector, corporate investors will move their money. The supply of corporate investment will shift left, and the supply of noncorporate investment will shift right, until the returns are equal.

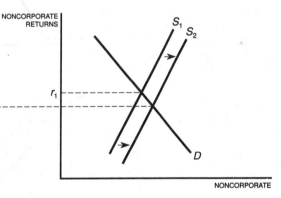

Step five (d): Find the new equilibrium and compare. In the new equilibrium, the returns are equal in each sector, but overall the returns are lower. We conclude that the corporate tax is paid by both noncorporate and corporate investors.

5   (Practice problem: general equilibrium analysis) Differences in wages that reflect differences in the characteristics of jobs are called compensating differentials. Truck drivers who haul freight over long distances are paid more than those who drive local routes. Suppose that the difference is $50 per week in equilibrium.

   a Start with an equilibrium in the markets for local truck drivers and long-haul drivers. Be sure that the difference in wages is $50 per week.

   b A new policy, agreed upon by both union and management, specifies that each driver must earn the same amount. Explain how the markets will adjust.

6   (Practice problem: general equilibrium analysis) Many people are concerned about the possible exhaustion of the limited supplies of natural resources, such as oil. To understand the economics of this issue, consider a two-period problem. Known reserves of oil equal 100,000 barrels. The oil can be sold now or be saved and sold in the future period. The discount rate is 50 percent over the time between the periods. The demand is the same now and in the future, and it is given in Table 13.1.

Table 13.1

Price	Quantity	Present discounted value of the future price
$50	20,000	
$45	30,000	
$40	40,000	
$35	55,000	
$30	70,000	
$25	80,000	
$20	90,000	
$10	100,000	

a   Calculate the present discounted value of each of the prices for the future demand. This is the current value of waiting to sell at the future price.

b   If the current price is greater than the present discounted value of the future price, all the oil will be sold today. If the reverse is true, the oil will be sold in the future. In equilibrium, current price must equal the present discounted value of the future price, and the total quantity sold in both periods must equal 100,000 barrels. Find the equilibrium price today, the price in the future, and the quantity sold in each period.

Answers to Problems

2 a   The initial equilibrium price is p_1, the wage is w_1, and the interest rate is r_1.

b   The technical advance shifts the demands for labor and capital to the right because both factors are made more productive, and it shifts the supply of products to the right because costs are lower. The product price falls to p_2, the wage rises to w_2, and the interest rate rises to r_2.

c   In the second round, the supply curve for products shifts left (mitigating the effects of the original shift) because wages and interest rates are higher. The demand curves for labor and capital shift back to the left (offsetting somewhat the effects of the original shift) because product prices are lower. (Recall that the demand for a factor of production is the value of the marginal product, which is price

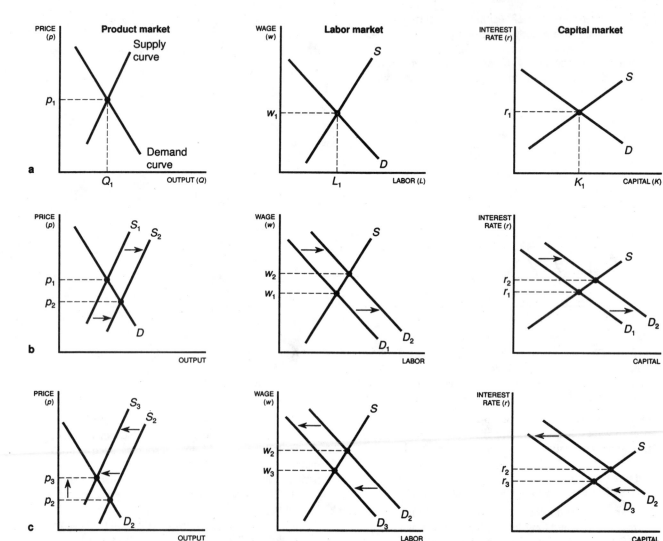

multiplied by marginal product.) The ultimate price is p_3, which is higher than p_1 but lower than p_2, because of the general equilibrium repercussions. Similarly, w_3 is greater than w_1 and r_3 is greater than r_1, but the changes are less great than a partial equilibrium analysis would imply.

3 a The initial equilibrium price is p_1, the wage is w_1, and the interest rate is r_1.
  b As people consume less, the demand for output falls. As they save more, the supply shifts to the

right in the capital market. Product prices and interest rates fall as a result.
  c In the second round, the fall in interest rates shifts the supply of output to the right and further reduces product prices. The fall in product prices, observed in part b, reduces the demand for capital and leads to a further decrease in the interest rate. In the labor market, demand shifts up because of lower interest rates, but shifts down because of lower product prices. The ultimate impact on the wage is not certain.

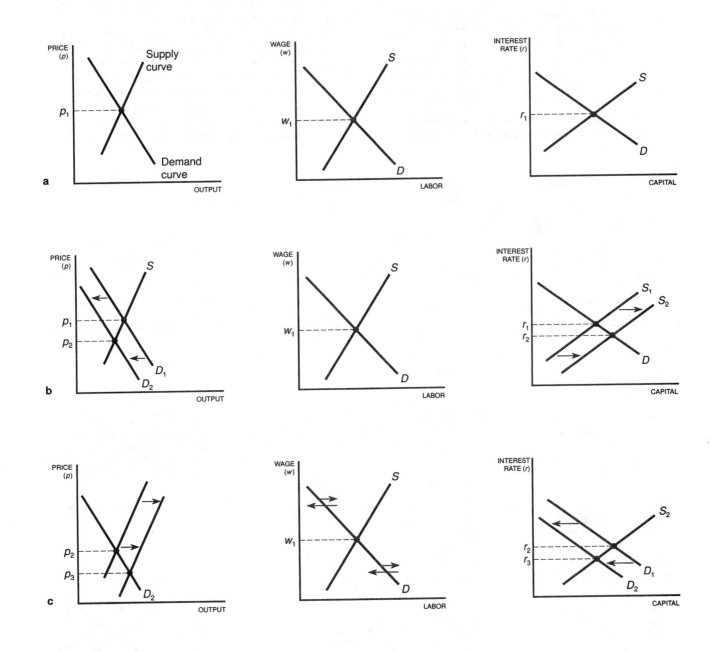

5 *a*   In the initial equilibrium, both markets clear, and
        the weekly wage is $50 higher in the long-haul mar-
        ket.

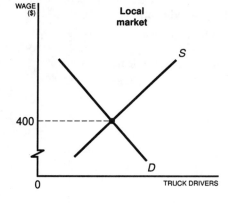

b   When the same wage is paid in the two markets,
        there is a shortage of long-haul drivers, and a sur-
        plus of drivers in the local market.

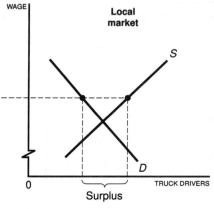

6 *a*   The present discounted value of the future price is
        given in Table 13.2.

b   The current price is $30, and 70,000 barrels are
        sold. The future price is $45, and 30,000 barrels are
        sold. The total is 70,000 + 30,000 = 100,000. The
        present discounted value of the future price is $30,
        which is the current price.

Table 13.2

Price	Quantity	Present discounted value of the future price
$50	20,000	$50/(1 + $.50) = $33.33
$45	30,000	$30.00
$40	40,000	$26.67
$35	55,000	$23.33
$30	70,000	$20.00
$25	80,000	$16.67
$20	90,000	$13.33
$10	100,000	$ 6.67

Part Three

Imperfect Markets

Chapter 14

MONOPOLIES AND IMPERFECT COMPETITION

Chapter Review

With the detailed study of perfect competition completed in Part Two, this chapter begins the study of imperfect competition. The real world differs from the basic competitive model in many important ways, and these differences shape the remainder of the text.

The first difference involves setting prices. While the competitive firm must accept the market price as a given fact, most firms in the real world have some control over their prices. How prices are set in monopolies, where there is only one seller, is the first topic taken up in the textbook chapter. The chapter then turns to a discussion of barriers to entry, which keep new firms from competing in an established industry, and competition among many firms producing similar but not identical products. Chapters 15, 16, 17, 18, and parts of Chapter 20 consider related problems and build on this chapter's techniques for analyzing imperfect competition.

ESSENTIAL CONCEPTS

1   There are four important types of **market structure: perfect competition, monopoly, monopolistic competition**, and **oligopoly**. A monopoly has a single seller.

Under monopolistic competition there are many firms, each selling a distinct product. Few firms dominate the industry in oligopolies. The essential differences are summarized in Table 14.1.

Table 14.1

Market structure	Firm's demand curve	Entry	Product differentiation	Examples
Perfect competition	Horizontal	Free entry	Homogenous products	Wheat, corn
Monopoly	Downward sloping	Barriers to entry	Only one firm	Major league baseball, holders of patents
Monopolistic competition	Downward sloping	Free entry	Differentiated products	Restaurants, designer clothing
Oligopoly	Downward sloping	Barriers to entry	Either homogenous or differentiated products	Aluminum manufacturers, automobiles

2   Like all firms, monopolies maximize profit by setting marginal cost equal to marginal revenue. Unlike for

competitive firms, for monopolies marginal revenue is less than price. This fact is shown by the following formula: Marginal revenue = Price (1 − 1/elasticity of demand). Barriers to entry allow monopolists to earn above-normal profits (also called monopoly rents). Finally, as price makers, monopolists can sometimes profitably charge different prices to different customers, a practice known as **price discrimination.**

3   Monopolistic competition and oligopoly are two special types of imperfect competition. In these industries firms have market power, which means that they can raise price without losing all of their sales. **Market power** is greater when the number of firms is lower and when there is more product differentiation. When products are more differentiated, they are more distant substitutes and firms' demands are less elastic. The characteristics of products, locations of the sellers, and the information and perceptions of buyers cause products to differ.

4   Factors that prevent entry into markets are called **barriers to entry.** Government policies such as licence requirements and patents create barriers to entry. The cost structure of the industry can also be a barrier, specifically the fraction of market demand accounted for by the output at the minimum of the firm's average cost curve. If one firm can produce the entire market demand for less than it could if it shared the market, the structure is called a **natural monopoly.** A monopoly can be sustained if a firm has control over an essential resource or if the firm has information advantages. Finally, strategies of existing firms can create barriers, if they can credibly convince potential competitors that entry would be met with fierce competition.

5   Monopolistic competition describes the market structure made up of many firms, each ignoring the reactions of the others. The demand curves facing the firms slope down (thus, price is above marginal cost), but new firms enter when there are profit opportunities (thus, in equilibrium, price equals average cost). New entrants produce close substitutes to the products of existing firms. Each entry shifts the demand curves facing existing firms to the left, reducing their profits.

BEHIND THE ESSENTIAL CONCEPTS

1   One important idea in the theory of imperfect competition is the relationship between marginal revenue and price. Marginal revenue is the extra revenue that the firm takes in when it sells another unit. In perfect competition, this amount is the price. But in imperfect competition, the price falls as more output is sold. Thus, there are two effects on revenue, shown in Figure 14.1. The firm is initially selling 10 units for $10 each. If it chooses to produce and sell 11 units, the price falls to $9.50. The first effect on revenue is that the firm sells more units at $9.50. This is shown as the area with pluses. If the demand curve facing the firm were horizontal, as under perfect competition, this would be the end of

Figure 14.1

the story: the extra revenue would be price times the extra quantity sold. However, the downward-sloping demand curve makes the price drop in order to sell one extra unit. This is the second effect. It means that the firm loses revenue on all its existing sales (because the price is lower for all units). This effect is shown as the area with minuses, and it makes marginal revenue less than the simple price times quantity calculation.

2   All imperfectly competitive firms face a downward-sloping demand curve. Thus, their profit-maximizing price is greater than marginal cost. In monopoly, there are barriers to entry, which allow monopolies to earn pure profits without attracting new competition. Monopoly prices are greater than average costs. In monopolistic competition, however, new entry drives economic profits to zero. When profits are zero, price equals average cost. To sum up,

a   downward-sloping demand implies that price is greater than marginal cost.
b   barriers to entry imply that price is greater than average cost.

3   Monopoly and monopolistic competition are similar in that each firm faces a downward-sloping demand curve and sets marginal revenue equal to marginal cost, which is less than price. The similarities stop here, however, because in a monopoly no new firm may enter even though a firm may earn pure profits. In monopolistically competitive industries, new firms enter, produce close substitutes, and capture customers. This entry shifts demand to the left until price equals average cost. The basic difference in the equilibria is that monopolies earn pure profits.

4   Monopolies are inefficient because price (which equals the marginal benefit of the good to consumers) is greater than marginal cost. Producing another unit would benefit customers more than it would cost. In monopolistic competition, things are not so simple. If all firms produce more goods, there are gains to both consumers and firms because price is greater than marginal cost and also because average cost falls. (Remember that the monopolistically competitive firm produces along the downward-sloping part of average cost.) On the other hand, the overall industry demand is only so

large, and if the firms become bigger, there will be room for fewer firms. Fewer firms mean fewer types of goods, so there is a trade-off between costs and variety.

SELF-TEST

True or False

1 The demand curve facing the firm is downward sloping in perfect competition.

2 The demand curve facing the firm is downward sloping in monopolistic competition.

3 When the demand curve facing the firm is downward sloping, marginal revenue is less than price.

4 Marginal revenue is less than price because price must fall for output to increase.

5 An industry with a single seller is a monopoly.

6 The demand curve facing a monopolist is the same as the industry demand curve.

7 Price is greater than marginal cost in monopoly.

8 Price is greater than marginal cost in monopolistic competition.

9 Compared to perfect competition, monopolies produce more but charge higher prices.

10 If there is a barrier to entry, firms may continue to earn pure profits.

11 Product differentiation is caused by barriers to entry.

12 In a natural monopoly, one firm can produce at a lower average cost than it could if it shared the market with other firms.

13 In equilibrium in monopolistic competition, price is greater than average cost.

14 The extent of a firm's market power is measured by how steeply the industry demand curve slopes downward.

15 The more elastic the demand, the more price exceeds marginal cost in monopolies.

Multiple Choice

1 In the competitive model,
a marginal revenue for the firm equals the market price;
b if the firm raises its price above that charged by its competitors, it will lose all its customers;
c the demand curve facing the firm is horizontal;
d the firm is a price taker;
e all of the above.

2 If a single firm supplies the entire market, the market structure is
a perfect competition;
b oligopoly;
c monopoly;
d monopolistic competition;
e none of the above.

3 If the market is dominated by several firms, its market structure is
a perfect competition;
b oligopoly;
c monopoly;
d monopolistic competition;
e none of the above.

4 Monopolistic competition is distinguished from oligopoly by the fact that
a in monopolistic competition, firms do not worry about the reactions of their rivals;
b there is no competition in oligopoly;
c oligopoly is a form of imperfect competition;
d the demand curve facing the firm is downward sloping in monopolistic competition;
e price is above marginal cost in an oligopoly.

5 When there is imperfect competition,
a the demand curve facing the firm equals the market demand curve;
b the demand curve facing the firm is horizontal;
c the demand curve facing the firm is downward sloping;
d the demand curve facing the firm is upward sloping;
e the demand curve facing the firm is vertical.

6 When the demand curve facing the firm is downward sloping, marginal revenue is less than price
a because of the principle of diminishing returns;
b in the short run, but not in the long run;
c because as output increases, the price must fall on all units;
d because taxes must be paid;
e none of the above.

7 "Marginal cost equals price" is the rule for maximizing profits for firms in which of the following market structures?
a perfect competition;
b monopolistic competition;
c monopoly;
d oligopoly;
e all of the above.

8 Compared with competition, a monopoly
a charges a higher price;
b sells more output;
c charges a lower price;
d sells less output;
e a and d.

9 The market demand curve is the same as the demand curve facing the firm when the market structure is
a perfect competition;
b monopoly;

  c oligopoly;
  d monopolistic competition;
  e all of the above.

10 A monopoly increases price above marginal cost by a
    greater amount when the demand is

  a more elastic;
  b more inelastic;
  c unitary elastic;
  d perfectly elastic;
  e none of the above.

11 Because they are single sellers, monopolies can earn

  a pure economic profits;
  b pure accounting profits;
  c zero profits;
  d the normal rate of return on invested capital;
  e c and d.

12 The measure of a firm's market power is

  a the number of employees it has;
  b the size of its capital stock;
  c the market price of its stock shares;
  d the extent to which the demand curve it faces is
     downward sloping;
  e all of the above.

13 How much the demand curve facing the firm slopes
    downwards is determined by

  a the number of firms in the industry;
  b the extent to which its product is differentiated
     from those of its competitors;
  c the size of its capital stock;
  d the minimum of its average cost curve.
  e a and b.

14 The four-firm concentration ratio measures

  a the number of firms in the industry;
  b the elasticity of industry demand;
  c the extent to which production is concentrated
     among a few firms;
  d the extent to which foreign firms dominate the in-
     dustry;
  e the average elasticity among the four largest
     firms.

15 Product differentiation is caused by

  a differences in characteristics of products produced
     by different firms;
  b differences in the location of firms;
  c perceived differences, often induced by advertis-
     ing;
  d imperfect information about price and availabili-
     ty;
  e all of the above.

16 When the products sold in one industry are differenti-
    ated, if one firm raises its price,

  a it will lose all of its customers;
  b it will lose none of its customers;
  c it will lose some but not all of its customers;
  d it will go out of business;
  e its profits will rise.

17 Barriers to entry

  a are factors that prevent new firms from entering
     the market;
  b are illegal;
  c allow firms in the industry to continue to earn eco-
     nomic profits;
  d imply that marginal revenue is greater than mar-
     ginal cost.
  e a and c.

18 In the equilibrium of monopolistic competition,

  a firms make zero economic profits;
  b price equals average cost;
  c marginal revenue equals marginal cost;
  d price is greater than marginal cost;
  e all of the above.

19 The practice of charging different prices to different
    customers is called

  a product differentiation;
  b price discrimination;
  c predatory pricing;
  d limit pricing;
  e natural monopoly.

20 Economies of scale refer to

  a lower average cost as output is increased;
  b charging different prices to different customers;
  c any factor that erects barriers to the entry of new
     competitors;
  d lower average cost as different goods are produced
     with the same plant and equipment;
  e charging low prices for a limited time in order to
     drive competitors from the market.

Completion

1 The way in which an industry is organized is called its
   _____.

2 A few firms dominate an industry in _____.

3 An industry with a single seller is called _____.

4 In monopolistic competition, there are enough
   firms that each firm _____ the reactions of
   rivals.

5 In industries where the characteristics of products are
   different, there is said to be _____.

6 In imperfect competition, marginal revenue is
   _____ than price.

7 Any factor that prevents new firms from coming into
   an industry is called a _____.

8 If the market demand curve intersects the average cost
   curve for the firm at a point where it is decreasing, the
   industry is a _____.

9 In monopolistic competition, there is a trade-off between lower prices and more _____.

10 In equilibrium in monopolistic competition, price
    _____ average cost.

Answers to Self-Test

True or False

1	f	6	t	11	f
2	t	7	t	12	t
3	t	8	t	13	f
4	t	9	f	14	f
5	t	10	t	15	f

Multiple Choice

1	e	6	c	11	a	16	c
2	c	7	a	12	d	17	e
3	b	8	e	13	e	18	e
4	a	9	b	14	c	19	b
5	c	10	b	15	e	20	a

Completion

1 market structure
2 oligopoly
3 monopoly
4 ignores
5 product differentiation
6 less
7 barrier to entry
8 natural monopoly
9 variety
10 equals

Doing Economics: Tools and Practice Problems

In this section, we start with two basic topics and several applications. First, we calculate marginal revenue and find the profit-maximizing price and quantity for the monopolist. The second topic is price discrimination, which is the practice of firms in imperfectly competitive markets charging different prices to different consumers in order to raise profits. The applications that follow include the effects of taxes and price controls in monopoly markets and a couple of puzzles. Artists, entertainers, and authors are often paid a percentage of revenues. Also, they generally prefer lower prices than their producers and publishers. Two problems toward the end of this problem set show why this is true. Other problems explore the effects of taxes and price ceilings in monopoly markets and show that the monopolist always produces along the elastic portion of the demand curve.

MARGINAL REVENUE

The key idea that distinguishes perfect from imperfect competition is that for the latter, marginal revenue is less than price. This is because price must be lowered on all units in order to sell more. Tool Kit 14.1 shows how to calculate marginal revenue from the demand schedule.

Tool Kit 14.1: Calculating Marginal Revenue

The first step in solving the monopolist's problem is to calculate marginal revenue.

Step one: Make a table with four column headings: Price, Quantity, Revenues, and Marginal revenue. Enter the demand curve in the first two columns.

Price   Quantity   Revenues   Marginal revenue

Step two: Calculate revenues for each point on the demand curve, and enter the result in the table. Revenues are price multiplied by quantity:

$$revenues = price \times quantity.$$

Step three: Calculate marginal revenue for each interval along the demand curve, and enter the result in the table. Marginal revenue is the change in total revenue divided by the change in quantity:

marginal revenue =
change in revenues/change in quantity.

After calculating marginal revenue, choose the price and quantity for which marginal revenue equals marginal cost.

---

1 (Worked problem: marginal revenue) As the only cement producer within 200 miles, Sam's Cement faces a downward-sloping demand curve, which is given in Table 14.2.

Table 14.2

Price	Quantity (tons)
$4.00	400
$3.50	800
$3.00	1,400
$2.50	2,800
$2.00	4,000

Sam's marginal cost is $2.00 per ton, and he has fixed costs of $1,000.

a Calculate revenues and marginal revenue, and add these two columns to the table.
b Find the profit-maximizing price and quantity.
c Compute Sam's costs and profits at this price.
d Suppose that Sam's fixed costs fall to $500. What is his profit-maximizing price and quantity, and how much does he earn in profits?
e Illustrate your answer with a diagram.

Step-by-step solution

Step one (a): Make a table.

Price   Quantity   Revenues   Marginal revenue

Step two: Calculate revenues for each point on the demand

curve. When the price is $4, revenues are $4 × 400 = $1,600. Continuing, we derive Table 14.3.

Table 14.3

Price	Quantity	Revenues	Marginal revenue
$4.00	400	$1,600	
$3.50	800	$2,800	
$3.00	1,400	$4,200	
$2.50	2,800	$7,000	
$2.00	4,000	$8,000	

Step three: Calculate marginal revenue for each interval along the demand curve. For the first 400 units, revenue rises from $0 to $1,600. Thus, marginal revenue is $1,600/400 = $4. As output is increased to 800, total revenue grows from $1,600 to $2,800. Marginal revenue is ($2,800 − $1,600)/(800 − 400) = $3. Complete the marginal revenue column as shown in Table 14.4.

Table 14.4

Price	Quantity	Revenues	Marginal revenue
$4.00	400	$1,600	$4.00
$3.50	800	$2,800	$3.00
$3.00	1,400	$4,200	$2.33
$2.50	2,800	$7,000	$2.00
$2.00	4,000	$8,000	$0.83

Step four (b): To find the monopoly output and price, set marginal revenue equal to marginal cost. This occurs when the price is $2.50 and output is 2,800.

Step five (c): To find total costs, add fixed costs, which are $1,000, plus total variable costs. Each unit costs $2, and 2,800 units are produced. Total costs equal $1,000 + ($2 × 2,800) = $6,600. Profits equal revenues minus costs. Revenues are $7,000, so profits equal $7,000 − $6,600 = $400.

Step six (d): If fixed costs fall, marginal cost does not change. The profit-maximizing price is still $2.50, but total profits now equal $7,000 − ($500 + $5,600) = $900. Unless the firm decides to shut down, fixed costs do not affect the output and pricing decisions.

Step seven (e): The solution is illustrated in the diagram.

2   (Practice problem: marginal revenue) The Mudville Nine is the only professional baseball team within several hundred miles. The marginal cost of admitting another fan is $1. Fixed costs, which include player salaries, are $100,000. The demand curve is given in Table 14.5. The quantity column gives the season's attendance.

Table 14.5

Price	Quantity	Revenues	Marginal revenue
$8	100,000		
$7	150,000		
$6	200,000		
$5	250,000		
$4	300,000		
$3	350,000		
$2	400,000		

a   Compute marginal revenue, and complete the column.

b   Find the profit-maximizing price and quantity.

c   Compute Mudville's costs and profits at this price.

d   Suppose that the players win the right to negotiate with any team, and the increase in salaries raises fixed costs to $150,000. What is Mudville's profit-maximizing price and quantity, and how much profit does the team earn?

e   Illustrate your answer with a diagram.

3   (Practice problem: marginal revenue) For each of the following firms, find the profit-maximizing price and quantity and total profits earned.

a   Fixed costs = $0; marginal cost = $8.

Price	Quantity	Revenues	Marginal revenue
$10	1		
$ 9	2		
$ 8	3		
$ 7	4		
$ 6	5		
$ 5	6		
$ 4	7		

b   Fixed costs = $50,000; marginal cost = $.10.

Price	Quantity	Revenues	Marginal revenue
$0.50	500,000		
$0.45	600,000		
$0.40	700,000		
$0.35	800,000		
$0.30	900,000		

c   Compute marginal cost from the table.

Price	Quantity	Revenues	Marginal revenue	Total costs	Marginal costs
$20	400			$ 5,000	
$18	800			$ 7,000	
$16	1,200			$ 9,400	
$14	1,600			$12,600	
$12	2,000			$16,200	
$10	2,400			$21,000	

d Compute marginal cost from the table.

Price	Quantity	Revenues	Marginal revenue	Total costs	Marginal costs
$1.00	1,000			$ 200	
$0.90	2,000			$ 300	
$0.80	3,500			$ 450	
$0.70	5,500			$ 650	
$0.60	8,000			$ 900	
$0.50	11,000			$1,230	
$0.40	15,000			$1,730	
$0.30	20,000			$2,355	

PRICE DISCRIMINATION

When it is possible to do so, an imperfectly competitive firm can improve profits by charging different prices to different consumers. This is called price discrimination. The idea is to segment the markets and set marginal revenue equal to marginal cost in each market and charge the corresponding price.

4 (Worked problem: price discrimination) Although the sale of the product is illegal, a drug enterprise operates according to sound business practices. It sells addictive designer drugs to two types of customers: nonaddicted experimenters and addicts (former experimenters). The demands for each type of customer are given in Table 14.6. The drug has no fixed costs and has marginal cost equal to $10 per dose.

Table 14.6

	Nonaddicts				Addicts		
Price	Quantity	Revenues	Marginal revenue	Price	Quantity	Revenues	Marginal revenue
$50	100			$50	500		
$40	300			$40	700		
$30	500			$30	1,050		
$20	1,000			$20	1,650		

a Calculate marginal revenue for each demand curve.
b Find the profit-maximizing price and quantity for each type of consumer.
c Calculate total profits.

Step-by-step solution

Step one (a): Follow the procedure outlined above to calculate marginal revenue. The result should look like Table 14.7.

Table 14.7

	Nonaddicts				Addicts		
Price	Quantity	Revenues	Marginal revenue	Price	Quantity	Revenues	Marginal revenue
$50	100	$ 5,000	$50	$50	500	$25,000	$50.00
$40	300	$12,000	$35	$40	700	$28,000	$15.00
$30	500	$15,000	$15	$30	1,050	$31,500	$10.00
$20	1,000	$20,000	$10	$20	1,650	$33,000	$ 2.50

Step two (b): Find the profit-maximizing price in each market. Marginal cost, which is $10, equals marginal revenue for nonaddicts at a price of $20 and a quantity of 1,000. For addicts, marginal revenue equals marginal cost at a price of $30 and a quantity of 1,050.

Step three (c): Calculate total profits. Revenues are $20,000 from the nonaddicts and $31,500 from the addicts. Costs are $10 × (1,000 + 1,050) = $20,500; so profits equal $51,500 − $20,500 = $31,000.

5 (Practice problem: price discrimination) A common instance of price discrimination is dumping, which occurs when a firm faces less competition in its home market than abroad. In these cases, it will pay the company to charge different prices in the two markets. Opus Company sells carpet fibres in the foreign and domestic markets. Its marginal cost is $1 per spool, and it has fixed costs of $5,000. The domestic and foreign demands are given in Table 14.8.

Table 14.8

	Home market				Foreign market		
Price	Quantity	Revenues	Marginal revenue	Price	Quantity	Revenues	Marginal revenue
$10	2,000			$10	2,000		
$ 9	2,500			$ 9	3,000		
$ 8	3,000			$ 8	4,000		
$ 7	3,500			$ 7	5,000		
$ 6	4,000			$ 6	6,000		
$ 5	4,500			$ 5	7,000		
$ 4	5,000			$ 4	8,000		

a Calculate marginal revenue for each demand curve.
b Find the profit-maximizing price and quantity for each type of consumer.
c Calculate total profits.

6 (Practice problem: price discrimination) Mark's Markets is one of the few chains that has not closed its inner-city stores. Mark's has expanded to the suburbs, but he faces more competition there. An example of a product he sells in both markets is hamburger, which has a marginal cost equal to $1. The space required to sell hamburger costs Mark's Markets about $100, and the demand curves in the suburbs and inner city are given in Table 14.9.

Table 14.9

	Suburbs				Inner city		
Price	Quantity	Revenues	Marginal revenue	Price	Quantity	Revenues	Marginal revenue
$4.00	200			$4.00	100		
$3.50	400			$3.50	120		
$3.00	600			$3.00	140		
$2.50	800			$2.50	160		
$2.00	1,000			$2.00	180		
$1.50	1,200			$1.50	200		

a Calculate marginal revenue for each demand curve.

b Find the profit-maximizing price and quantity for each type of consumer.

c Calculate total profits.

APPLICATIONS

The following problems apply the idea of marginal revenue and monopoly decision-making to percentage of gross revenue contracts, tax incidence, price controls, and elasticity. Simply follow the procedure outlined in Tool Kit 14.1.

8 (Worked problem: marginal revenue) After the surprising success of her first novel, Imelda has negotiated a deal in which she receives 20 percent of the revenues from the sale of her second novel. The demand curve is given in Table 14.10. The publisher has fixed costs of $20,000, and the marginal cost of printing and distributing each book printed is $20.

Table 14.10

Price	Quantity	Revenues	Marginal revenue	Imelda's revenue
$40	10,000			
$35	20,000			
$30	30,000			
$25	40,000			
$20	50,000			

a Calculate marginal revenue, and enter in the table.

b Find the profit-maximizing price and quantity.

c Compute Imelda's revenue for each price, and enter in the table.

d What price maximizes Imelda's revenues?

e Draw a diagram illustrating your answer.

Step-by-step solution

Step one (a): Calculate marginal revenue. Follow the usual procedure. The answer is in Table 14.11.

Table 14.11

Price	Quantity	Revenues	Marginal revenue	Imelda's revenue
$40	10,000	$ 400,000	$40	
$35	20,000	$ 700,000	$30	
$30	30,000	$ 900,000	$20	
$25	40,000	$1,000,000	$10	
$20	50,000	$1,000,000	$ 0	

Step two (b): Find the profit-maximizing price and quantity. Marginal cost equals marginal revenue for the publisher at a price of $30, where the quantity sold is 30,000.

Step three (c): Calculate Imelda's revenue. She receives 20 percent of the total. At a price of $40, she receives .20 × $400,000 = $80,000. Continue to calculate, and enter the results. They are given in Table 14.12.

Table 14.12

Price	Quantity	Revenues	Marginal revenue	Imelda's revenue
$40	10,000	$ 400,000	$40	$ 80,000
$35	20,000	$ 700,000	$30	$140,000
$30	30,000	$ 900,000	$20	$180,000
$25	40,000	$1,000,000	$10	$200,000
$20	50,000	$1,000,000	$ 0	$200,000

Step four (d): Imelda prefers a price of $25 or $20, which earns her $200,000, more than the $180,000 that she earns at the publisher's preferred price.

Step five (e): Draw a diagram. Note that the publisher sets marginal revenue equal to marginal cost. Imelda is only concerned with revenues, so she prefers the point where marginal revenue equals zero.

9 (Practice problem: marginal revenue) Magdalena, a budding female recording artist, has just completed her first album. She will receive 25 percent of the revenues. The record company reports that its demand curve is as given in Table 14.13, and its marginal costs are $6 per CD.

Table 14.13

Price	Quantity	Revenues	Marginal revenue	Magdalena's revenue
$20	20,000			
$18	25,000			
$16	30,000			
$14	35,000			
$12	40,000			
$10	48,000			

a Calculate marginal revenue, and enter in the table.

b Find the profit-maximizing price and quantity.

c Compute Magdalena's revenue for each price, and enter in the table.

d What price maximizes Magdalena's revenues?

e Draw a diagram illustrating your answer.

10 (Practice problem: marginal revenue) Like most cities, South Potato is a one-newspaper town. The *South Potato Truth* distributes its daily paper for a marginal cost of $0.10. The demand curve is given in Table 14.14.

Table 14.14

Price	Quantity	Revenues	Marginal revenue
$1.00	30,000		
$0.95	40,000		
$0.90	50,000		
$0.85	60,000		
$0.80	70,000		
$0.75	80,000		
$0.70	90,000		
$0.65	100,000		
$0.60	110,000		
$0.55	120,000		

a Calculate marginal revenue, and enter in the table.

b Find the profit-maximizing price and quantity.

c Suppose that a tax of $0.10 per paper is instituted. The tax will be paid by the newspaper company. Find the new profit-maximizing price and quantity.

d How much of the tax is paid by consumers?

e Draw a diagram illustrating your answer.

11 (Practice problem: marginal revenue) In competitive markets, price ceilings lower price and reduce the quantity sold. This is not true in monopoly markets. The demand for cable subscriptions in Motelville is given in Table 14.15. The marginal cost, including payments to cable programming providers, is $15.

Table 14.15

Price	Quantity	Revenues	Marginal revenue
$45	60,000		
$40	80,000		
$35	100,000		
$30	120,000		
$25	140,000		

a Calculate marginal revenue, and enter in the table.

b Find the profit-maximizing price and quantity of subscriptions.

c Now suppose that the town sets a price ceiling equal to $25. How much will the company charge, and how many subscriptions will be sold?

d Draw a diagram illustrating your answer.

12 (Practice problem: marginal revenue) Because a monopoly is a single seller of a good, it has no competition. Since price elasticity is generally lower when consumers have little opportunity to find substitutes, you might think that the demand for the monopolist's product is always inelastic. Nevertheless, it is true that the monopolist always produces on the elastic portion of its demand curve. To see this, compute elasticity along the demand curve given in question 3a. Show that at the chosen price and quantity, the price elasticity of demand is greater than 1.

Answers to Problems

2 *a* Marginal revenue appears in Table 14.15.

Table 14.16

Price	Quantity	Revenues	Marginal revenue
$8	100,000	$ 800,000	—
$7	150,000	$1,050,000	$5
$6	200,000	$1,200,000	$3
$5	250,000	$1,250,000	$1
$4	300,000	$1,200,000	–$1
$3	350,000	$1,050,000	–$3
$2	400,000	$ 800,000	–$5

b Profits are maximized when the price is $5 and the number of fans is 250,000.

c Costs = $100,000 + (250,000 × $1) = $350,000; profits = $1,250,000 – $350,000 = $900,000.

d The price and quantity remain as in part a, but profits fall to $1,250,000 – $400,000 = $850,000.

e The solution is illustrated in the diagram.

3 *a* Marginal revenue appears in Table 14.17.

Table 14.17

Price	Quantity	Revenues	Marginal revenue
$10	1	$10	—
$ 9	2	$18	$8
$ 8	3	$24	$6
$ 7	4	$28	$4
$ 6	5	$30	$2
$ 5	6	$30	$0
$ 4	7	$28	–$2

Price = $9; quantity = 2; profits = $18 – ($8 × 2) = $2.

b   Marginal revenue appears in Table 14.18.

Table 14.18

Price	Quantity	Revenues	Marginal revenue
$0.50	500,000	$250,000	—
$0.45	600,000	$270,000	$0.20
$0.40	700,000	$280,000	$0.10
$0.35	800,000	$280,000	$0
$0.30	900,000	$270,000	–$0.10

Price = $0.40; quantity = 700,000; profits = $280,000 – [$50,000 + (700,000 × $0.10)] = $160,000.

c   The complete table appears in Table 14.19.

Table 14.19

Price	Quantity	Revenues	Marginal revenue	Total costs	Marginal cost
$20	400	$ 8,000	—	$ 5,000	—
$18	800	$14,400	$16	$ 7,000	$ 5
$16	1,200	$19,200	$12	$ 9,400	$ 6
$14	1,600	$22,400	$ 8	$12,600	$ 8
$12	2,000	$24,000	$ 4	$16,200	$ 9
$10	2,400	$24,000	$ 0	$21,000	$12

Price = $14; quantity = 1,600; profits = $22,400 – $12,600 = $9,800.

d   The completed table appears in Table 14.20.

Table 14.20

Price	Quantity	Revenues	Marginal revenue	Total costs	Marginal cost
$1.00	1,000	$1,000	—	$ 200	—
$0.90	2,000	$1,800	$0.80	$ 300	$0.10
$0.80	3,500	$2,800	$0.67	$ 450	$0.10
$0.70	5,500	$3,850	$0.52	$ 650	$0.10
$0.60	8,000	$4,800	$0.38	$ 900	$0.10
$0.50	11,000	$5,500	$0.23	$1,230	$0.11
$0.40	15,000	$6,000	$0.12	$1,730	$0.12
$0.30	20,000	$6,000	$0	$2,355	$0.14

Price = $0.40; quantity = 15,000; profits = $4,270.

5   a   The marginal revenue figures appear in Table 14.21.

Table 14.21

	Home market				Foreign market		
Price	Quantity	Revenues	Marginal revenue	Price	Quantity	Revenues	Marginal revenue
$10	2,000	$20,000	—	$10	2,000	$20,000	—
$ 9	2,500	$22,500	$5	$ 9	3,000	$27,000	$7
$ 8	3,000	$24,000	$3	$ 8	4,000	$32,000	$5
$ 7	3,500	$24,500	$1	$ 7	5,000	$35,000	$3
$ 6	4,000	$24,000	–$1	$ 6	6,000	$36,000	$1
$ 5	4,500	$22,500	–$3	$ 5	7,000	$35,000	–$1
$ 4	5,000	$20,000	–$5	$ 4	8,000	$32,000	–$3

b   Home market price = $7; quantity = 3,500. Foreign market price = $6; quantity = 6,000.

c   Profits = $24,500 + $36,000 – [(3,500 + 6,000) × $1] – $5,000 = $46,000.

6   a   The completed table appears in Table 14.22.

Table 14.22

	Home market				Foreign market		
Price	Quantity	Revenues	Marginal revenue	Price	Quantity	Revenues	Marginal revenue
$4.00	200	$ 800	—	$4.00	100	$400	—
$3.50	400	$1,400	$3	$3.50	120	$420	$1
$3.00	600	$1,800	$2	$3.00	140	$420	$0
$2.50	800	$2,000	$1	$2.50	160	$400	–$1
$2.00	1,000	$2,000	$0	$2.00	180	$360	–$2
$1.50	1,200	$1,800	–$1	$1.50	200	$300	–$3

b   Suburbs price = $2.50; quantity = 800. Inner city price = $3.50; quantity = 120.

c   Profits = $2,000 + $420 – [(800 + 120) × $1] – $100 = $1,400.

9   a,c   The marginal revenues and Magdalena's revenues are given in Table 14.23.

Table 14.23

Price	Quantity	Revenues	Marginal revenue	Magdalena's revenue
$20	20,000	$400,000	—	$100,000
$18	25,000	$450,000	$10	$112,500
$16	30,000	$480,000	$ 6	$120,000
$14	35,000	$490,000	$ 2	$122,500
$12	40,000	$480,000	–$ 2	$120,000
$10	48,000	$480,000	$ 0	$120,000

b,d   The profix-maximizing price is $16 and the quantity is 30,000, but Magdalena's revenues are maximized at a price of $14, where 35,000 CDs are sold.

e   The solution is illustrated in the diagram.

10   *a*   Marginal revenue is given in Table 14.24.

Table 14.24

Price	Quantity	Revenues	Marginal revenue
$1.00	30,000	$30,000	—
$0.95	40,000	$38,000	$0.80
$0.90	50,000	$45,000	$0.70
$0.85	60,000	$51,000	$0.60
$0.80	70,000	$56,000	$0.50
$0.75	80,000	$60,000	$0.40
$0.70	90,000	$63,000	$0.30
$0.65	100,000	$65,000	$0.20
$0.60	110,000	$66,000	$0.10
$0.55	120,000	$66,000	$0

b   Price = $0.60; quantity = 110,000.
c   The tax increases marginal cost to $0.20. The price becomes $0.65 and the quantity, 100,000.
d   Consumers pay $.05 of the tax.
e   The solution is illustrated in the diagram.

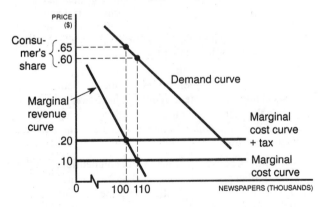

11   *a*   Marginal revenue is given in Table 14.25.

Table 14.25

Price	Quantity	Revenues	Marginal revenue
$45	60,000	$2,700,000	—
$40	80,000	$3,200,000	$25
$35	100,000	$3,500,000	$15
$30	120,000	$3,600,000	$ 5
$25	140,000	$3,500,000	–$ 5

b   Price = $35; quantity = 100,000.
c   Price = $25; quantity = 140,000.
d   The solution is illustrated in the diagram.

12   The elasticity for each point on the demand curve is given in Table 14.26.

Table 14.26

Price	Quantity	Revenues	Marginal revenue	Elasticity
$10	1	$10	—	—
$ 9	2	$18	$8	19/3
$ 8	3	$24	$6	17/5
$ 7	4	$28	$4	15/7
$ 6	5	$30	$2	13/9
$ 5	6	$30	$0	11/11
$ 4	7	$28	–$2	9/11

Along the elastic portion of the demand curve, which is where price exceeds $5, marginal revenue is positive. Marginal revenue equals marginal cost at a price of $9, which is on the elastic portion.

Chapter 15

OLIGOPOLIES

Chapter Review

Chapters 14 and 15 present the three imperfect competitive market structures: monopoly, monopolistic competition, and oligopoly. Chapter 14 dealt with the first two; this chapter rounds out the study with a look at oligopoly.

Oligopolies are industries in which only a few firms dominate. Each firm watches its competitors closely, because each firm's best price, output level, or strategy depends on what its rivals choose. The American automobile industry is a perfect example of an oligopolistic market. Even today, with foreign firms competing in the U.S. market, it is still easy to see how the "big three" (General Motors, Ford, and Chrysler) respond to one another with competing rebate programs, lower prices, or cheap financing. The chapter introduces the Prisoner's Dilemma models to examine the possibilities and motives for collusion. Chapter 16 builds upon the insights of this chapter and Chapter 14 to explore government policy toward imperfect competition.

ESSENTIAL CONCEPTS

1   In **oligopolies**, a few firms dominate the industry. If any one firm changes its price, produces more, or adopts a new strategy, then the other firms in the oligopoly will notice the change and react to it. It is essential, then, that oligopolists pay careful attention and try to anticipate the reactions of rivals. This strategic interaction is the essential feature of oligopolies, and it makes the study of oligopolies both difficult and fascinating.

2   Because total profits are lower when firms compete, oligopolists have the incentive to form a cartel and to collude, fix prices, and share the market. This behavior is not only illegal under U.S. antitrust laws, it is difficult to sustain. First, individual firms are tempted to cheat and take advantage of the higher prices charged by others by undercutting their prices. Further, as demand and costs change over time, oligopolies have trouble renegotiating their tacit agreements. Finally, the pure profits earned by successful colluders attract entry and new competition.

3   The conflict between collusion and competition is at the heart of oligopoly. The combined profits of firms are highest if they collude. Collectively, their incentives are to fix prices and share the market. But each individual firm is tempted by its own self-interest. If the rivals keep their prices high, a firm can undercut and capture the market. The **Prisoner's Dilemma** summarizes this conflict and shows how collusion might work. If the

game is played only once and self-interest quickly takes over, all firms cheat and the equilibrium is competition. If the game is played repeatedly for an indefinite period of time, firms may be able to threaten cheaters with competitive price wars and motivate one another to continue colluding.

4 Certain **restrictive practices** help sustain collusion. These include assigning exclusive territories to individual firms, requiring exclusive dealing at retail outlets, and insisting upon tie-in arrangements that force a customer who buys one product to buy an additional product. These practices can reduce competition by increasing the costs of capturing the customers of rival firms. Firms also facilitate cooperation through such practices as matching low-price offers of rivals.

5 There are three important models of competition in oligopolies.

a If firms are committed to producing a given amount of output, as is the case in industries where fixed costs are high and changing capacity is very expensive, there is quantity or **Cournot competition.** One such example is the steel industry. Setting up a factory to commence or expand production is very expensive, so the firm gets locked in at certain capacities. It tries to select capacities corresponding to a price where profits will be maximized.

b If the costs of increasing capacity are low, then price or **Bertrand competition** reigns. An example of this is the catalog marketing industry. Setting up a mail-order firm is inexpensive, and the firm can vary the size of its orders from suppliers. It selects a price corresponding to a quantity where profits will be maximized.

c The **kinked demand curve** model shows that if firms expect rivals to match a price cut but not price increases, then they are unlikely to change price or quantity.

BEHIND THE ESSENTIAL CONCEPTS

1 The world of perfect competition is simple and precise. The firm cannot affect the market of any competitor; it simply chooses its quantity to maximize profits. The world of oligopoly is rich and varied. Firms try to limit competition and promote collusion. They have a wealth of strategies to choose from: price and quantity, of course, but also such practices as matching offers of rivals and threatening price wars with new entrants or existing firms who cheat on tacit agreements to limit price competition. Oligopoly is an area in which economics has made much progress in the last ten or fifteen years.

2 As a group, firms in an oligopoly want to cooperate, charge high prices, and share monopoly profits, but they always run up against the problem of self-interest. Each individual firm would like to cheat while the others abide by the cooperative strategy. It is this noncooperative behavior by individual firms that promotes eco-

nomic efficiency, because it keeps the oligopolists from cooperating to gouge customers with high prices. It is ironic that if firms were more cooperative, the economy would not work so well.

SELF-TEST

True or False

1 An oligopolist considering lowering its price must anticipate the reactions of its rivals.

2 A cartel is a group of firms engaging in price competition.

3 Antitrust laws allow cartels to negotiate openly to fix prices.

4 Tacit collusion is an implicit understanding among oligopolists that their profits will be higher if they do not compete too vigorously.

5 Offers to match prices charged by rivals result in more price competition.

6 A price leader can help a cartel adjust to changing conditions.

7 One difficulty that cartels have is that when they succeed in raising price, their members are tempted to undercut the cartel price.

8 If the possibility of entry keeps prices competitive, the market is said to be contestible.

9 The Prisoner's Dilemma is a simple game that shows how parties can overcome their self-interest to achieve the benefits of cooperation.

10 Certain restrictive practices such as resale price maintenance and exclusive territories help oligopolies reduce competition and increase profits.

11 Although restrictive practices such as exclusive territories help oligopolists collude, they also promote economic efficiency.

12 In an oligopoly, firms must worry about the reactions of rivals.

13 In Cournot competition, oligopolists choose their quantity expecting that their rivals will produce the same quantity as they.

14 In Bertrand competition, firms choose their price expecting their rivals to keep price constant.

15 If the firm perceives a kinked demand curve, there is a jump in marginal revenue at the current output.

Multiple Choice

1 Unlike firms operating in monopolistically competitive markets, oligopolists

a face downward-sloping demand curves;

b are price takers;

c must worry about how rivals will react to their decisions;

d   set price above marginal cost;

e   a and d.

2   A group of companies that act jointly to divide the industry and maximize profits is called

a   a monopoly;

b   a monopsony;

c   a cartel;

d   an antitrust;

e   none of the above.

3   One difficulty cartels have is that individual firms may cheat and

a   charge less than the agreed-upon price;

b   sell more than the agreed-upon quantity;

c   charge more than the agreed-upon price;

d   a and b;

e   b and c.

4   In the Prisoner's Dilemma,

a   both prisoners act in their own self-interest; this leads to the best alternative from their combined standpoint;

b   both prisoners cooperate to bring about the best alternative;

c   acting in their own self-interest, the prisoners bring about the worst alternative;

d   it is impossible to say what happens because each prisoner must worry about the reactions of the other;

e   none of the above.

5   Collusion is difficult in practice because

a   antitrust laws make explicit price-fixing agreements illegal;

b   individual firms are tempted to cheat and undercut their rivals;

c   as demand and cost conditions change, it is difficult to renegotiate tacit agreements;

d   all of the above;

e   none of the above.

6   When oligopolists publicly offer to match any price charged by any other firm, there will be

a   more price competition;

b   the same amount of price competition;

c   less price competition;

d   trouble because matching offers are illegal;

e   none of the above.

7   In contestable markets,

a   firms can successfully collude to share monopoly profits;

b   firms are unable to collude because cartel members cheat on tacit agreements;

c   potential competition ensures competitive pricing;

d   price returns to the competitive level, but only after entry;

e   firms deter the entry of new competition by carrying excess capacity.

8   A tie-in is

a   a requirement that firms offer the same price as their rivals;

b   an agreement among cartel members to match price cuts but not price increases;

c   a requirement that any customer who buys one product must buy another;

d   a practice whereby the prices of the followers are tied to the leader's price;

e   a threat to meet new entry with resistance.

9   Antitrust laws

a   prohibit collusive behavior;

b   require that firms in an oligopoly charge the same price;

c   punish firms for cheating on collusive agreements;

d   promote collusion by raising rival's costs;

e   bar entry into oligopolies.

10   In an oligopoly the price leader

a   sets the industry's highest price;

b   sets the industry's price and the other firms follow;

c   deters entry by threatening to lower price;

d   ensures cooperation among all firms by threatening to lower price;

e   offers to match the industry's lowest price.

11   In oligopolies firms often share inventories or combine research and development efforts. These practices

a   are illegal under antitrust laws;

b   can facilitate cooperation because firms that cheated on the collusive price agreement may be excluded;

c   are examples of predatory pricing;

d   only exist in contestable markets;

e   are examples of tie-ins.

12   The Prisoner's Dilemma shows

a   the power of antitrust laws;

b   the effectiveness of facilitating practices;

c   the impact of potential competition;

d   the difficulty of sustaining collusive arrangements;

e   the importance of the kinked demand curve.

13   In Cournot competition, the firms

a   compete by choosing quantity, given some conjecture about the quantity that the rival will produce;

b   compete by choosing price, given some conjecture about the price that the rival will charge;

c   match price cuts by rivals but not price increases;

d   collude to fix prices and earn monopoly profits;

e   divide the market in an orderly way.

14   In Bertrand competition, the firms

a   compete by choosing quantity, given some conjecture about the quantity that the rival will produce;

b   compete by choosing price, given some conjecture about the price that the rival will charge;

c   match price cuts by rivals but not price increases;

d   collude to fix prices and earn monopoly profits;

e   divide the market in an orderly way.

15 In laboratory experiments economists have found that

   a participants evolve simple strategies to bring about collusion if the game is repeated a number of times;

   b collusion is nearly impossible;

   c collusion requires the ability to write firm contracts to enforce it;

   d complicated strategies are used by most participants;

   e none of the above.

16 Restrictive practices restrict competition. These include

   a resale price maintenance;

   b exclusive territories;

   c vertical restrictions;

   d horizontal restrictions;

   e all of the above.

17 Marginal revenue for the firm with a kinked demand curve

   a is greater than in monopoly;

   b is less than in monopoly;

   c is the same as in monopoly;

   d has a jump at the level of current output;

   e none of the above.

18 Resale price maintenance is a practice whereby retailers are required to

   a compete vigorously with other retailers;

   b sell only within their exclusive territory;

   c also sell a specific tie-in product;

   d carry no competing products;

   e sell at the list price.

19 Restrictive practices, such as exclusive dealing and exclusive territories, may

   a reduce economic efficiency;

   b restrict competition;

   c raise costs for rivals;

   d lead to duplication of distribution systems;

   e all of the above.

20 If rivals match price cuts but do not match price increases, the demand curve facing the firm

   a is kinked at the current output level;

   b has a jump at the current output level;

   c is horizontal at the current price;

   d is vertical at the current output level;

   e either c or d.

Completion

1 In an oligopoly, there are so few firms that each must consider how its rival will _____ to any change in strategy.

2 A group of companies operating jointly as if they were a monopoly is called a _____.

3 Collusive behavior is prohibited by _____ laws.

4 The _____ is a game that illustrates the problem cartels have in enforcing collusive behavior.

5 Markets in which the threat of competition impels firms to charge the competitive price are called _____.

6 A firm that insists that any other firm selling its products refrain from selling those of its rivals is engaging in _____.

7 _____ is an arrangement whereby retailers agree to sell at the list price.

8 Restrictive practices aimed at wholesalers and retailers selling a producer's goods are called _____.

9 If a firm believes that its rivals will match its price cuts but not its price increases, then it will perceive its demand curve to be _____ at the current price.

10 Firms that conjecture that rival's quantity is fixed are engaging in _____.

Answers to Self-Test

True or False

1	t	6	t	11	f
2	f	7	t	12	t
3	f	8	t	13	f
4	t	9	f	14	t
5	f	10	t	15	t

Multiple Choice

1	c	6	c	11	b	16	e
2	c	7	c	12	d	17	d
3	a	8	c	13	a	18	e
4	c	9	a	14	b	19	e
5	d	10	b	15	a	20	a

Completion

1 react
2 cartel
3 antitrust laws
4 Prisoner's Dilemma
5 contestable
6 exclusive dealing
7 Resale price maintenance
8 vertical restrictions
9 kinked
10 Cournot competition

Doing Economics: Tools and Practice Problems

This section looks at three issues pertaining to oligopoly. First, we consider collusion and the difficulty that cartels have in enforcing their tacit agreements. We see not only how two firms can divide a market and share monopoly profits, but also how difficult it is to maintain a cartel. The cartel's success in restricting output and raising prices tempts each of the cartel members to cheat by producing more than their assigned amounts and undercutting the cartel's price. One way to lessen the incentives to cheat is to assign exclusive territories. We look at collusion and cheating in several problems before turning to some simple game theory problems, using the Prisoner's Dilemma framework to investigate collusion.

CARTELS, COLLUSION, AND CHEATING

Many firms can secretly organize and agree to cooperate to share monopoly profits. Tool Kit 15.1 shows how they might do this. The following problems use this insight to show how individual firms have incentives to cheat and produce more than they agreed. Tool Kit 15.2 shows that when there is quantity competition (Cournot), the same incentive problem arises. This is developed and extended to price competition in the problems.

Tool Kit 15.1: Organizing a Cartel of
Many Price-Taking Firms

To organize a cartel of many firms, one must find the monopoly output and price. Then each firm must be assigned its quota. The following steps show how to proceed.

Step one: Identify and add up the supply curves of the individual firms. The result is the cartel's marginal cost curve.

Step two: Identify the market demand curve, and find its marginal revenue.

Step three: Find the profit-maximizing price and quantity for the cartel by setting marginal revenue equal to marginal cost.

Step four: Determine each firm's output by evenly dividing the cartel's output among its members.

---

1   (Worked problem: collusion and cheating) The Quebec Maple Syrup Board is a cartel of 1,000 maple syrup producers. The demand for maple syrup and the supply curve of one typical producer are given in Table 15.1. The quantity represents gallons.

Table 15.1

Market demand		Firm's supply	
Price	Quantity	Price	Quantity
$10	10,000	$10	60
$ 9	15,000	$ 9	55
$ 8	20,000	$ 8	50
$ 7	25,000	$ 7	45
$ 6	30,000	$ 6	40
$ 5	35,000	$ 5	35
		$ 4	30
		$ 3	25
		$ 2	20

a   Find the profit-maximizing price for the cartel as a whole. How many litres will be sold at this price: How many must each firm produce to sustain this price?

b   If the cartel charges the price computed in part a, how many units would the individual firm like to produce?

c   Now suppose that all firms cheat and the market becomes competitive. Find the equilibrium price and quantity.

Step-by-step solution

Step one (a): Add up the individual supplies. Since there are 1,000 firms, the market supply is simply the quantity supplied by the firm multiplied by 1,000. The market supply is given in Table 15.2.

Table 15.2

Firm's supply		Market supply	
Price	Quantity	Price	Quantity
$10	60	$10	60,000
$ 9	55	$ 9	55,000
$ 8	50	$ 8	50,000
$ 7	45	$ 7	45,000
$ 6	40	$ 6	40,000
$ 5	35	$ 5	35,000
$ 4	30	$ 4	30,000
$ 3	25	$ 3	25,000
$ 2	20	$ 2	20,000

Step two: Derive the marginal revenue curve. First find total revenue, and enter it in the appropriate column. Marginal revenue is the change in total revenue divided by the change in quantity. The answer is given in Table 15.3.

Table 15.3

Market demand		Total	Marginal
Price	Quantity	revenue	revenue
$10	10,000	$100,000	
$ 9	15,000	$135,000	$7
$ 8	20,000	$160,000	$5
$ 7	25,000	$175,000	$3
$ 6	30,000	$180,000	$1
$ 5	35,000	$175,000	–$1

Step three: Find the profit-maximizing price for the cartel. The market supply curve is the cartel's marginal cost. Marginal cost equals marginal revenue when the quantity is 25,000. The corresponding price is $7. Each firm produces 25 gallons.

Step four (b): Find how much the firm would like to supply at the cartel price. At a price of $7, the firm would like to produce 45 units (this number is read off the firm's supply curve), which is 20 more than it is assigned.

Step five (c): If all firms cheat, then the market will become a competitive market and will clear at a price of $5, where each firm produces 35 gallons.

2   (Practice problem: collusion and cheating) The 500 mail-order computer equipment suppliers are (discreetly) forming a cartel. The market demand curve and the supply curve of a typical equipment supplier are given in Table 15.4. The quantity represents the number of computers.

Table 15.4

Market demand		Total revenue	Marginal revenue
Price	Quantity		
$1,000	300,000		
$ 900	400,000		
$ 800	500,000		
$ 700	600,000		
$ 600	700,000		
$ 500	800,000		
$ 400	900,000		
$ 300	1,000,000		

Firm's supply		Market supply	
Price	Quantity	Price	Quantity
$1,000	4,000		
$ 900	3,500		
$ 800	3,000		
$ 700	2,400		
$ 600	2,000		
$ 500	1,600		
$ 400	1,000		
$ 300	500		
$ 200	100		

a   Derive the marginal revenue for the computer equipment supplier market.
b   Add up the 500 individual firm supplies to derive the market supply.
c   Find the profit-maximizing price for the cartel as a whole. How many computers will be sold at this price? How many must each firm sell to sustain this price?
d   If the cartel charges the price computed in part c, how many units would the individual firm like to sell?
e   Now suppose that all firms cheat, and the market becomes competitive. Find the equilibrium price and quantity.

Tool Kit 15.2: Finding the Profit-Maximizing Output in Quantity Competition between Duopolists

In some industries, such as steel or aluminum, the fixed costs of plant and equipment are such a large share of total costs that firms have little discretion in changing output once the machinery is in place. In this case, the competition is over quantity, and the price will be whatever clears the market of the quantities that firms have collectively decided to produce.

Step one: Identify the market demand, marginal cost, and output of the opponent firm.

Step two: Subtract the output of the opponent firm from the market demand. The difference is called the **residual demand curve**:

residual demand = market demand – opponent's output.

Step three: Find the marginal revenue for the residual demand curve.

Step four: Choose the output for which marginal revenue equals marginal cost.

---

3   (Worked problem: quantity competition) The New Chairs for Old Company shares the furniture-refinishing market in Southpoint with the Like New Company. Each uses enormous vats of chemicals, which are expensive to set up but cheap to operate. One vat will permit the refinishing of 10 pieces of furniture per day. The marginal cost for each firm is constant and equal to $4. Table 15.5 gives the market demand.

Table 15.5

Price	Quantity
$7.50	0
$7.00	10
$6.50	20
$6.00	30
$5.50	40
$5.00	50
$4.50	60
$4.00	70

a   Suppose that the two firms try to operate as a cartel and share the market equally. Find the profit-maximizing quantity for each.
b   Now look at the problem from the point of view of the owner of New Chairs for Old. She conjectures that her rival commit to the quantity solved for in part a. Find the profit-maximizing quantity.

Step-by-step solution

Step one (a): We follow the usual procedure for the monopolist: find the marginal revenue and set marginal revenue equal to marginal cost. Table 15.6 gives the marginal revenue.

Table 15.6

Price	Quantity	Total revenue	Marginal revenue
$7.50	0	$ 0	—
$7.00	10	$ 70	$7
$6.50	20	$130	$6
$6.00	30	$180	$5
$5.50	40	$220	$4
$5.00	50	$250	$3
$4.50	60	$270	$2
$4.00	70	$280	$1

Marginal revenue equals marginal cost when the total quantity is 40. Each firm then buys two vats and refinishes 20 pieces of furniture.

Step two (b): Identify the market demand, marginal cost, and output of the opponent firm. The market demand is given in Table 15.5, the marginal cost is $4, and Like New is expected to produce 20.

Step three: Subtract the output of the opponent firm from the market demand, as shown in Table 15.7.

Table 15.7

Price	Quantity
$7.00	0
$6.50	20 – 20 = 0
$6.00	30 – 20 = 10
$5.50	40 – 20 = 20
$5.00	50 – 20 = 30
$4.50	60 – 20 = 40
$4.00	70 – 20 = 50

Step four: Find the marginal revenue for the residual demand curve, as given in Table 15.8.

Step five: Choose the output for which marginal revenue equals marginal cost. When output is 30, marginal revenue and marginal cost both equal $4.

Table 15.8

Price	Quantity	Total revenue	Marginal revenue
$7.00	0	0	—
$6.50	0	0	—
$6.00	10	$ 60	$6
$5.50	20	$110	$5
$5.00	30	$150	$4
$4.50	40	$180	$3
$4.00	50	$200	$2

4   (Practice problem: quantity competition) The Davis Lead Company competes with its rival Anderson Lead. Because the plant and equipment are so expensive and because marginal production costs are so low (only $5 per ton) until capacity is reached, the two firms compete by choosing quantity. The market demand is given in Table 15.9.

Table 15.9

Price	Quantity (tons)
$22.50	0
$20.00	100
$17.50	200
$15.00	300
$12.50	400
$10.00	500
$ 7.50	600

a   Suppose that the two firms try to operate as a cartel and share the market equally. Find the profit-maximizing quantity for each.
b   Now look at the problem from the point of view of the owner of Davis. The owner conjectures that the rival firm will commit to the quantity solved for in part a. Find the profit-maximizing quantity.

5   (Worked problem: price competition) There are two dry-cleaning establishments in Mudville: Jay's Cleaners and Fay's Cleaners. Although they hate each other personally, the two owners have decided to form a cartel. This is illegal, of course, but they meet discreetly. Each faces a marginal cost of $1 per item. Consumers always patronize the lower-price establishment; therefore, either Jay or Fay can capture the entire market by pricing below the other. One additional fact is that in Mudville people only carry half dollars, so the price must be a multiple of $0.50. Table 15.10 gives the market demand.

Table 15.10

Price	Quantity
$3.00	1,500
$2.50	3,000
$2.00	4,500
$1.50	6,000
$1.00	7,500

a   Derive marginal revenue curve, and enter in the table.
b   Find the profit-maximizing price. If they divide the market equally, how many items will each clean?
c   Compute the profits for each firm.
d   Suppose that Fay decides to undercut Jay and capture the market. What price will Fay charge? How many will Fay sell? Compute Fay's profits.

Step-by-step solution

Step one (a): Derive marginal revenue. Follow the usual procedure, as in Table 15.11.

Table 15.11

Price	Quantity	Total revenue	Marginal revenue
$3.00	1,500	$4,500	$3
$2.50	3,000	$7,500	$2
$2.00	4,500	$9,000	$1
$1.50	6,000	$9,000	$0
$1.00	7,500	$7,500	–$1

Step two (b): Find the profit-maximizing price. Marginal cost equals marginal revenue at a price of $2.

Step three (c): At a price of $2, there are 4,500 items cleaned. If each does one-half, then each cleans 2,250. The profits for each are $2 – $1 = $1 per unit, so each earns $2,250.

Step four (d): Fay can capture the market by charging the next-lower price, which is $1.50. Fay will sell 6,000 units. Fay's profit will be $1.50 – $1.00 = $0.50 per unit for a total of $3,000. Fay gains $750 by cheating on their agreement.

6 (Practice problem: price competition) Yuppie Company and its rival Buppie Company sell dark green and gray rag wool sweaters through catalogs. They buy the sweaters from supplier firms for $10 each. The market demand is given in Table 15.12.

Table 15.12

Quantity (sweaters)	Price
0	$27.50
100	$25.00
200	$22.50
300	$20.00
400	$17.50
500	$15.00
600	$12.50

a Derive marginal revenue, and enter in the table.
b Find the profit-maximizing price. If the companies divide the market equally, how many items will each clean?
c Compute the profits for each firm.
d Suppose that Yuppie decides to undercut Buppie and capture the market. What price will it charge? How many will it sell? Compute its profits.

PRISONER'S DILEMMA

The Prisoner's Dilemma is one of the most important models in social science. It shows why groups may have difficulty inducing their members to cooperate and act in the group interest. In this section our interest is in the ability of oligopolists to collude. Tool Kit 15.3 shows how to use this model.

Tool Kit 15.3: Using the Prisoner's Dilemma

The Prisoner's Dilemma highlights the conflict between what is good for the cartel as a whole and what is best for the individual firm. Follow these steps to represent this conflict as a game.

Step one: Draw a box with four cells, and label it as shown.

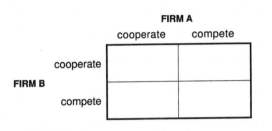

Step two: Identify the payoffs for each party if both cooperate, and enter in the appropriate cell.

Step three: Identify the payoffs for each party if both compete, and enter in the appropriate cell.

Step four: Identify the payoffs for each party if one competes while the other cooperates, and enter in the corresponding cells.

Step five: In the classic Prisoner's Dilemma, competing is always the best strategy, whatever the opponent chooses. Show that competition is the equilibrium.

7   (Worked problem: Prisoner's Dilemma) Chiaravelli
     and Fiegenshau are the only two dentists in Plainville.
     They have been colluding, sharing the market and
     earning monopoly profits of $100,000 each for several
     years. Fiegenshau is considering reducing his price. He
     estimates that if Chiaravelli keeps his price at current
     levels, Fiegenshau would earn $150,000, although
     Chiaravelli's earnings would fall to $25,000. There is
     also the possibility that Chiaravelli would compete
     against Fiegenshau. The resulting price war would re-
     duce the earnings of each to $40,000.

     a   Represent this market as a Prisoner's Dilemma
          game.
     b   Explain why the equilibrium might be achieved
          when both dentists compete.

Step-by-step solution

Step one (a): Draw a box with four cells, and label it as
shown.

CHIARAVELLI

	cooperate	compete
cooperate		
compete		

FIEGENSHAU

Step two: Identify the payoffs for each party if both cooperate, and enter in the appropriate cell. If both cooperate, they
each earn $100,000.

CHIARAVELLI

	cooperate	compete
cooperate	C = $100,000 F = $100,000	
compete		

FIEGENSHAU

Step three: Identify the payoffs for each party if both compete, and enter in the appropriate cell. If both compete, they
each earn $40,000.

CHIARAVELLI

	cooperate	compete
cooperate	C = $100,000 F = $100,000	
compete		C = $40,000 F = $40,000

FIEGENSHAU

Step four: Identify the payoffs for each party if one competes while the other cooperates, and enter in the corresponding cell. In this case, the dentist who competes earns
$150,000, and the other is left with $25,000.

CHIARAVELLI

	cooperate	compete
cooperate	C = $100,000 F = $100,000	C = $150,000 F = $ 25,000
compete	C = $ 25,000 F = $150,000	C = $40,000 F = $40,000

FIEGENSHAU

Step five (b): Show that competition is the equilibrium. For
each party, competition is always the best alternative. If Chiavarelli cooperates, then Fiegenshau can earn more by competing ($150,000 > $100,000). If Chiavarelli competes,
again Fiegenshau earns more by competing ($40,000 >
$25,000). The same is true for Chiavarelli, and both choose
to be competitive.

8   (Practice problem: Prisoner's Dilemma) Upper Penin-
     sula Airlines and Northern Airways share the market
     from Chicago to the winter resorts in the North. If they
     cooperate, they can extract enough monopoly profits
     to earn $400,000 each, but unbridled competition
     would reduce profits to $50,000 each. If one is foolish
     enough to cooperate in its pricing policy while the oth-
     er undercuts it, the cooperating firm would earn $0,
     and the competing firm would earn $800,000.

     a   Represent this market as a Prisoner's Dilemma
          game.
     b   Explain why the equilibrium might be that both
          firms choose a competitive strategy.

9   (Practice problem: Prisoner's Dilemma) Rosewood
     College and Elmwood College are the best private
     schools in the state. Each also prides itself on its
     lacrosse team. If neither offers scholarships for promis-
     ing players, then obviously the cost of scholarships will
     be zero. For $20,000 in scholarships, either could at-
     tract the best players (if the other did not offer scholar-
     ships), win the conference championship, and attract at
     least $50,000 in new donations. In this case, however,
     donations at the losing school would fall by $30,000.
     On the other hand, if both offered scholarships, there
     would be no advantage, no extra donations, and each
     would have spent the $20,000 for nothing.

     a   Represent this market as a Prisoner's Dilemma
          game.
     b   Explain why the equilibrium might be achieved
          when both schools compete.

FACILITATING AND RESTRICTIVE PRACTICES

Oligopolists can use certain practices to facilitate collusion
and restrict competition. These practices may enable them to
get around the incentive to cheat on collusive arrangements.
These problems illustrate how dividing the market into exclusive territories and promising to match competitors' low
prices can promote collusion.

10   (Worked problem: facilitating and restrictive practices)
     This problem builds upon problem 3. Having accumu-
     lated several years of experience with the unpleasant

results of competition, the owners of Southpoint's two furniture-refinishing firms decide to try a new method of collusion. Henceforth, the New Chairs for Old Company will specialize in refinishing chairs, and the Like New Company will take care of the table share of the market. It so happens in Southpoint that exactly half of the business involves tables and half involves chairs. Their marginal costs remain at $4.

a   Compute the profit-maximizing quantity of chairs and tables and the corresponding prices for both companies.
b   Compare the answer to the answer to part a of problem 3.

Step-by-step solution

Step one (a): Divide the market into chair and table markets. The result is given in Table 15.13.

Table 15.13

Price	Quantity of chairs	Quantity of tables
$7.50	0	0
$7.00	5	5
$6.50	10	10
$6.00	15	15
$5.50	20	20
$5.00	25	25
$4.50	30	30
$4.00	35	35

Step two: Compute the marginal revenue for each firm. These are shown in Table 15.14. Note that since the demands are exactly the same, so are the marginal revenue curves. Only one is shown.

Table 15.14

Price	Quantity of chairs	Quantity of tables	Total revenue	Marginal revenue
$7.50	0	0	$ 0	—
$7.00	5	5	$ 35	$7
$6.50	10	10	$ 65	$6
$6.00	15	15	$ 90	$5
$5.50	20	20	$110	$4
$5.00	25	25	$125	$3
$4.50	30	30	$135	$2
$4.00	35	35	$140	$1

Step three (b): Marginal revenue equals marginal cost at a quantity of 20 for each. The market price will be $5.50, which is exactly the outcome that was solved for in part a of problem 3. Dividing the market promotes collusion.

11   (Practice problem: facilitating and restrictive practices) This problem builds upon problem 4. The Davis and Anderson companies have come up with a scheme to promote collusion. From now on, Davis will advertise

and take orders from customers in the West, leaving the eastern half of the market to Anderson. They divide the territories so that exactly half of the customers will go to each firm. The marginal cost remains at $5 per ton, and the market demand is as given in Table 15.9.

a   Compute the profit-maximizing quantity and price for each firm.
b   Compare with the collusive price and quantity solved for in part a of problem 4.

12   (Worked problem: facilitating and restrictive practices) Let's return to Mudville and problem 5, where Fay is considering undercutting Jay.

a   Compute profits if she reduces her price by $50 below the collusive price and Jay matches the price cut. Assume that customers divide themselves equally between the firms charging the same price.
b   Derive Fay's demand curve under the assumption that Jay will match any price cuts but not price increases. Draw a diagram illustrating your answer.

Step-by-step solution

Step one (a): The collusive price is $2.00, and Fay's profits are $2,250. If she cuts price to $1.50 and Jay matches the cut, then the quantity demanded is 6,000, and Fay will serve 3,000 of them.

Step two: Fay earns ($1.50 − $1.00) × 3,000 = $1,500. Because this number is less than collusive profits, the offer to match price cuts by Jay will deter Fay from undercutting him.

Step three (b): To find the demand if Jay matches price cuts (below $2) but not price increases, simply divide the market evenly at prices of $2 or below, and give all the customers to Jay for higher prices. Table 15.15 gives the result. Notice the kink at a price of $2.

Table 15.15

Price	Quantity
$3.00	0
$2.50	0
$2.00	2,250
$1.50	3,000
$1.00	3,750

13   (Practice problem: facilitating and restrictive practices) Return to problem 6 and the competition between Yuppie and Buppie. Suppose that each agree to match price offers of the other.

a   Compute Yuppie's profits if it cuts price by $2.50 below the collusive price and its cut is matched by Buppie. Assume that customers divide themselves equally between firms charging the same price.
b   Derive Yuppie's demand curve assuming that Buppie will match price cuts (below the collusive price) but not price increases.

Answers to Problems

2　*a,b* The marginal revenue and the market supply appear in Table 15.16.

Table 15.16

Market demand		Total revenue	Marginal revenue
Price	Quantity		
$1,000	300,000	$300,000,000	—
$ 900	400,000	$360,000,000	$600
$ 800	500,000	$400,000,000	$400
$ 700	600,000	$420,000,000	$200
$ 600	700,000	$420,000,000	$ 0
$ 500	800,000	$400,000,000	−$200
$ 400	900,000	$360,000,000	−$400
$ 300	1,000,000	$300,000,000	−$600

Firm's supply		Market supply	
Price	Quantity	Price	Quantity
$1,000	4,000	$1,000	2,000,000
$ 900	3,500	$ 900	1,750,000
$ 800	3,000	$ 800	1,500,000
$ 700	2,400	$ 700	1,200,000
$ 600	2,000	$ 600	1,000,000
$ 500	1,600	$ 500	800,000
$ 400	1,000	$ 400	500,000
$ 300	500	$ 300	250,000
$ 200	100	$ 200	50,000

　c　Cartel price = $800; market quantity = 500,000; each firm's quantity = 1,000.
　d　3,000.
　e　Price = $500; quantity = 800,000.

4　*a*　Marginal revenue for the market demand is given in Table 15.17.

Table 15.17

Price	Quantity (tons)	Revenues	Marginal revenue
$22.50	0	$ 0	
$20.00	100	$2,000	$20
$17.50	200	$3,500	$15
$15.00	300	$4,500	$10
$12.50	400	$5,000	$ 5
$10.00	500	$5,000	$ 0
$ 7.50	600	$4,500	−$ 5

Price = $12.50; market quantity = 400; each firm sells 200 tons.
　b　The residual demand is found by subtracting 200 from the market demand. This and marginal revenue appear in Table 15.18.

Table 15.18

Price	Quantity (tons)	Revenues	Marginal revenue
$22.50	0	$ 0	
$20.00	0	$ 0	
$17.50	0	$ 0	
$15.00	100	$1,500	$15
$12.50	200	$2,500	$10
$10.00	300	$3,000	$ 5
$ 7.50	400	$3,000	$ 0

Davis will produce 300. The market quantity will be 200 + 300 = 500, and the price will be $10 per ton.

6　*a*　Marginal revenue for the market demand is given in Table 15.19.

Table 15.19

Price	Quantity (sweaters)	Revenues	Marginal revenue
$27.50	0	$ 0	—
$25.00	100	$2,500	$25
$22.50	200	$4,500	$20
$20.00	300	$6,000	$15
$17.50	400	$7,000	$10
$15.00	500	$7,500	$ 5
$12.50	600	$7,500	$ 0

　b　Cartel price = $17.50; market quantity = 400; each firm sells 200.
　c　Profits = (200 × $17.50) − (200 × $10) = $1,500.
　d　Yuppie's price = $15; quantity = 500; profits = ($15 × 500) − ($10 × 500) = $2,500.

8　*a*

		Upper Peninsula (UP)	
		cooperate	compete
Northern	cooperate	UP = $400,000 N = $400,000	UP = $800,000 N = $50
	compete	UP = $0 N = $800,000	UP = $50,000 N = $50,000

　b　If Northern competes, UP prefers to compete ($800,000 > $400,000). If Northern cooperates, UP still prefers to compete ($50,000 > $0). If UP competes, Northern prefers to compete ($800,000 > $400,000). If UP cooperates, Northern still prefers to compete ($50,000 > $0) Since both always prefer competition, the equilibrium is that both compete and profits are $50,000 each.

9　*a*

		Elmwood	
		cooperate	compete
Rosewood	cooperate	E = $0 R = $0	E = $30,000 R = −$30,000
	compete	E = −$30,000 R = $30,000	E = −$20,000 R = −$20,000

b   If Rosewood cooperates and does not offer scholarships, Elmwood prefers to compete and offer them ($30,000 > $0). If Rosewood competes and offers scholarships, Elmwood still prefers to offer them (–$20,000 > –$30,000). If Elmwood cooperates and does not offer scholarships, Rosewood prefers to offer them ($30,000 > $0). If Elmwood competes and offers scholarships, Rosewood still prefers to offer them (–$20,000 > –$30,000). Since both always prefer competition, the equilibrium is that both compete, offer scholarships, and lose $20,000 each.

11   The demand for each firm's share of the market and the corresponding marginal revenue appear in Table 15.20.

Table 15.20

Price	Quantity (tons)	Revenues	Marginal revenue
$22.50	0	$ 0	—
$20.00	50	$1,000	$20
$17.50	100	$1,750	$15
$15.00	150	$2,250	$10
$12.50	200	$2,500	$ 5
$10.00	250	$2,500	$ 0
$ 7.50	300	$2,250	–$ 5

a   Each firm charges $12.50 and sells 200.
b   The price and quantity are the same as under monopoly.

13   a   If both reduce price by $2.50 to $15.00, the market quantity will equal 500, which implies that each will sell 250. Profits will equal ($15 × 250) – ($10 × 250) = $1,250, which is less than the $1,500 they earn by charging $17.50.
b   Yuppie's demand curve if price cuts below $17.50 are matched but price increases are not is given in Table 15.21.

Table 15.21

Price	Quantity (sweaters)
$27.50	0
$25.00	0
$22.50	0
$20.00	0
$17.50	200
$15.00	250
$12.50	300

Chapter 16

GOVERNMENT POLICIES TOWARD COMPETITION

Chapter Review

Monopolies and oligopolies, explored in Chapters 14 and 15, produce too little output and charge inefficiently high prices. This chapter of the text returns to the role government plays in the economy, this time examining government policies to promote competition. Another important topic is government responses to natural monopolies. Natural monopolies occur in markets like home electric service, where a single firm can produce the good more cheaply than multiple firms can. In Chapter 17, the focus shifts to how firms compete to introduce new products and discover better ways of producing.

ESSENTIAL CONCEPTS

1   Competitive industries allocate resources efficiently. Monopolies and other imperfectly competitive industries, however, often operate inefficiently. Economists study four types of inefficiency.

    a   Monopolies restrict output below what it would be if the industry were competitive. The lower output results in higher prices and a transfer of wealth from consumers to the monopoly. There is an additional loss in consumer surplus, because output is below the level at which all gains from trade are realized. This loss is called the deadweight loss of monopoly.

    b   Although monopoly profits are higher when their costs are lower, monopolies are not forced to produce at the lowest cost. There is some room for **managerial slack**, which allows monopolies to be inefficient.

    c   Although there are examples of monopolies that engage in effective **research and development**, the incentives are less under monopoly.

    d   Because monopolies earn rents (profits above the level necessary to compensate investors), resources are expended to acquire and retain these existing rents. This type of activity is called **rent seeking** and is socially wasteful.

2   In some industries, where there are high fixed and low marginal costs, the lowest cost of production occurs when there is only one firm. Such an industry is called a **natural monopoly**. Figure 16.1 shows that the average cost curve for a natural monopoly is falling and that marginal cost always lies below average cost. Governments sometimes nationalize and operate natural mo-

Figure 16.1

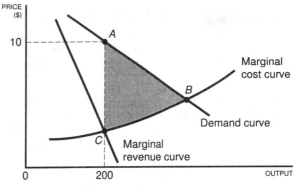

Figure 16.2

nopolies, but more often governments regulate them. A regulatory agency sets prices designed to limit the firm to a normal rate of return. This policy in turn motivates firms to overinvest. Also, because in both the nationalized and regulated cases the pricing decisions are made politically, products may be sold below cost in some markets and above cost in others. This practice is called **cross subsidization.**

3   A final way of dealing with natural monopolies is to increase competition. Examples in the United States include the deregulation of long-distance telephone service and of the trucking and airline industries. Competition provides firms with incentives to innovate and reduce costs, and it eliminates cross subsidization. On the other hand, with more firms in the industry, each firm produces less, that is, chooses a point higher up on the average cost curve.

4   The various ways in which the government attempts to promote competition are called **antitrust policy.** Important pieces of legislation such as the Sherman Act, the Clayton Act, and the establishment of the Federal Trade Commission have outlawed monopolizing, authorized opposition to mergers, and forbidden such types of anticompetitive practices as tying, price discrimination, and exclusive dealing.

BEHIND THE ESSENTIAL CONCEPTS

1   The problem of deadweight loss lies at the heart of economic arguments about making exchange efficient. As an example, look at Figure 16.2, which shows a monopoly output equal to 200. The firm sets the price at $10 and maximizes its profits. Notice, however, that at this point the marginal benefit to consumers of one or more unit (measured, as usual, by the price they're willing to pay) is greater than the marginal cost. This means that producing and selling additional units would create value—there would be gains from trade. The total possible additional gains equal the area of the triangle *ABC*. But these gains are not realized, and therefore they are called the deadweight loss of monopoly.

The idea that exchange creates value and that any reduction in the amount of exchange below the competitive level leads to a deadweight loss (as seen in Figure 16.2) is very important in economics.

2   Firms desiring greater profits seek them in two different ways. First, they offer better products or devise better ways of producing and doing business. These activities do make profits, and they create value and enhance efficiency as well. Firms can also try to convince government to protect them against competition or devise strategies to deter entry. Practices of this type do not create anything, they only redistribute money and reduce economic efficiency. The latter behavior is called rent seeking.

3   In competitive industries, firms are forced to produce at the lowest possible cost. If they do not, new firms will enter the market, undercut the price, and drive existing firms out. In a monopoly, however, whether it is private, nationalized, or regulated, the firm can get away with some slack. It can pay its workers a little more than the going wage, it can postpone adopting the most efficient production techniques, or it can overlook the low-cost suppliers. You can probably see how this could happen in an unregulated monopoly, where there are extra profits, or in a nationalized industry, where the government makes up any losses, but it is also possible in a regulated monopoly because regulators do not always know the lowest cost. The firm has an incentive and the ability to make the regulators believe that it is more costly to do business than it really is. Regulators can prevent fraud, but it is very difficult to find and eliminate waste.

4   In order to determine whether a merger will inhibit competition, the number of firms in an industry and their size relative to the market need to be determined. The geographical size of the market should be considered, as some industries are local, while many have become international. For example, the gold market is a world market. The cement industry, on the other hand, is local. The product is very expensive to transport, and only nearby firms could merge. The similarity of the products also needs to be considered. Is plastic wrap in the same industry as aluminum foil? If so,

does a single producer of plastic wrap have a monopoly, or is it simply another firm in the food-wrapping industry? Economists look at the cross-price effect to determine the extent to which firms are competing. How much does a price decrease by one firm reduce another's demand?

5   Antritrust policy is concerned with prohibiting market domination. This brings up the question of what it means to dominate a market. First, there is the issue of the bounds of the market. What products belong in the market? Economists look at the effect of one good's increase in price on the demand for another. If demand rises significantly, then the goods are part of the same market. The second issue is how different are the products. Here, we look at how much business is lost when price rises. In each case, how prices affect demands is the central idea.

SELF-TEST

True or False

1   Monopolies produce less output than would be produced if the industry were competitive.

2   Monopolies must produce at the lowest cost.

3   Rent seeking refers to anything done in pursuit of monopoly profits.

4   Monopolies have stronger incentives to undertake research and development than do competitive firms.

5   In a natural monopoly, the cost of production is higher because of the lack of competition.

6   Cross subsidization refers to the practice of selling below cost in one market and above cost in another.

7   Regulated natural monopolies are usually forced to charge a price equal to marginal cost.

8   Subjecting a natural monopolist to competition can be an effective strategy if the average cost curve is not too steep.

9   In a horizontal merger, a firm acquires an upstream supplier.

10   Vertical mergers are illegal *per se* in the United States.

11   Enforcement of antitrust laws is the exclusive domain of the U.S. government.

12   One important goal of antitrust policy is to limit the absolute size of firms.

13   Under the rule of reason, a business practice is not illegal if it can be shown to enhance economic efficiency.

14   The Clayton Act outlawed some specific monopoly practices, such as price discrimination.

15   Most current antitrust efforts involve attempting to break up excessively large firms.

Multiple Choice

1   Monopolists set the price

  a   equal to marginal cost;
  b   equal to average cost;
  c   above marginal cost;
  d   below marginal cost;
  e   below average cost.

2   Monopoly output is

  a   the same as the competitive output;
  b   less than the competitive output;
  c   more than the competitive output;
  d   sometimes more and sometimes less than the competitive output;
  e   determined by setting marginal revenue equal to price.

3   The deadweight loss caused by monopoly is

  a   the difference between consumer surplus under the monopoly and what consumer surplus would have been if the industry were competitive;
  b   the amount of monopoly profits;
  c   the increase in cost brought about by managerial slack;
  d   the total of rent-seeking expenditures;
  e   the difference between consumer surplus under the monopoly and what consumer surplus would have been if the industry were competitive minus the transfer from consumers to the monopolist.

4   Managerial slack refers to

  a   the lack of efficiency in some monopolies;
  b   activities designed to protect a monopoly position;
  c   the loss in consumer surplus as a result of restricted output;
  d   the lessened incentives for research and development under monopoly;
  e   the failure of antitrust policies.

5   Among the problems of monopolies are

  a   restricted output;
  b   managerial slack;
  c   reduced incentives for research and development;
  d   rent seeking to protect the monopoly position;
  e   all of the above.

6   Which of the following is not a type of rent seeking?

  a   research aimed at reducing the cost of production;
  b   lobbying the legislature for protection against foreign competition;
  c   contributions to political campaigns for candidates who support regulations favored by the monopoly;
  d   entry-deterring activities;
  e   designing the product to be incompatible with competitors' products.

7   If the cost of production is lowest when there is only one firm, then the industry is a

  a   trust;
  b   natural oligopoly;
  c   natural monopoly;

d   horizontal merger;

e   vertical merger.

8   In a natural monopoly, marginal cost

    a   equals price;

    b   equals average cost;

    c   is less than average cost;

    d   is greater than average cost;

    e   is greater than price.

9   Cross subsidization involves

    a   selling at below cost in some markets and above cost in others;

    b   selling at cost in all markets;

    c   selling above cost in each market;

    d   selling below cost in each market;

    e   a and b.

10   Cross subsidization

    a   occurs in nationalized monopolies but not in regulated monopolies;

    b   occurs in regulated monopolies but not in nationalized monopolies;

    c   occurs in neither regulated nor nationalized monopolies;

    d   occurs in both regulated and nationalized monopolies;

    e   never occurs.

11   Natural monopoly regulation usually sets price equal to

    a   marginal revenue;

    b   marginal cost;

    c   average revenue;

    d   average cost;

    e   average variable cost.

12   Regulated natural monopolies often

    a   invest too much;

    b   invest too little;

    c   hire too much labor;

    d   hire too few workers;

    e   sell too much output.

13   Government policies to promote competition are called

    a   antitrust;

    b   rent seeking;

    c   managerial slack;

    d   natural monopoly;

    e   horizontal mergers.

14   Which of the following is an example of a horizontal merger?

    a   One steel producer buys another steel producer.

    b   A meat-packing firm buys a large cattle ranch.

    c   A maker of chalk buys a pizza delivery firm.

    d   A foreign company buys an American company.

    e   A U.S. company buys a foreign company.

15   Which of the following is an example of a vertical merger?

    a   One steel producer buys another steel producer.

    b   A meat-packing firm buys a large cattle ranch.

c   A maker of chalk buys a pizza delivery firm.

d   A foreign company buys an American company.

e   A U.S. company buys a foreign company.

16   Which of the following is not a goal of antitrust policy?

    a   limit anticompetitive practices;

    b   prevent market domination;

    c   limit the absolute size of firms;

    d   make use of private incentive to sue under antitrust law.

    e   All of the above are goals of antitrust policy.

17   The Federal Trade Commission

    a   issues the regulation that made monopolies illegal;

    b   investigates unfairly competitive practices;

    c   issues orders to cease and desist from unfair practices;

    d   determines whether foreign firms engage in unfair trade practices, such as dumping;

    e   b and c.

18   The act that made monopolizing an industry illegal was the

    a   Sherman Act;

    b   Federal Trade Commission Act;

    c   Robinson-Patman Act;

    d   Celler-Kefauver Act;

    e   Taft-Hartley Act.

19   The hypothesis that regulators eventually serve the interests of the industry that they regulate and not the customers is called the

    a   antitrust hypothesis;

    b   rent-seeking hypothesis;

    c   regulatory capture hypothesis;

    d   natural monopoly hypothesis;

    e   none of the above.

20   A business practice is anticompetitive under the rule of reason if

    a   it is illegal *per se*;

    b   it is in violation of the Clayton Act;

    c   it cannot be shown to be a sensible business practice that promotes efficiency;

    d   it leads to vertical mergers;

    e   it leads to horizontal mergers.

Completion

1   Monopolies restrict output and cause a loss in consumer surplus, part of which is a transfer to the monopolist, and the remainder is called the _____.

2   The fact that, shielded from competition, monopolists may not produce for the lowest costs is called _____.

3   Political contributions and lobbying expenses for the purpose of winning regulations to restrict competition are examples of _____.

4   Regulated or nationalized firms may sell below cost in some markets and above cost in others, a practice known as _____.

5   In a _____, the cost of production is lowest if there is only one firm in the industry.

6   Government efforts to promote competition by restricting anticompetitive tactics or opposing mergers are called _____.

7   When a firm buys a competitor that was producing a competing product, it is called a _____.

8   The purchase by one firm of an upstream supplier or downstream distributor is called a _____.

9   The monopolization of an industry was made illegal by the _____.

10 The _____ investigates and proscribes unfair trade practices.

Answers to Self-Test

True or False

1	t	6	t	11	f
2	f	7	f	12	f
3	f	8	t	13	t
4	f	9	f	14	t
5	f	10	f	15	f

Multiple Choice

1	c	6	a	11	d	16	c
2	b	7	c	12	a	17	e
3	e	8	c	13	a	18	a
4	a	9	a	14	a	19	c
5	e	10	d	15	b	20	c

Completion

1   deadweight loss
2   managerial slack
3   rent seeking
4   cross subsidization
5   natural monopoly
6   antitrust
7   horizontal merger
8   vertical merger
9   Sherman Act
10 Federal Trade Commission

Doing Economics: Tools and Practice Problems

One of the important costs that monopolies impose on the economy is the deadweight loss, which reflects the losses resulting from the fact that monopolies restrict output. Here, we study how to compute the deadweight loss and then move on to consider the regulation of natural monopolies.

DEADWEIGHT LOSS

When a monopoly controls an industry, it can increase its profits by restricting output below the level where price equals marginal cost. By doing so, the monopoly reduces the number of mutually beneficial trades. Because these trades do not occur, there is a loss in consumer surplus, and this loss is called the deadweight burden. (Consumer sur-

plus falls still further because of the higher price that the monopoly charges, but this loss in consumer surplus is only a transfer from consumers to the monopolist and is not part of the deadweight loss.) Tool Kit 16.1 shows how to compute deadweigt loss.

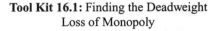

Tool Kit 16.1: Finding the Deadweight Loss of Monopoly

When price is set above marginal cost, the market contracts and there is a deadweight loss. Follow these five steps to compute it.

Step one: Identify the demand and marginal cost curves.

Step two: Calculate marginal revenue.

Step three: Find the monopoly output (Q_m) and price (p_m) by choosing the quantity for which marginal revenue equals marginal cost (MC_m).

Step four: Find the "competitive" quantity (Q_c) by choosing the quantity for which demand equals marginal cost.

Step five: Compute the deadweight loss as the area between the demand and marginal cost curves:

$$\text{deadweight loss} = \tfrac{1}{2}(Q_c - Q_m) \times (p_m - MC_m).$$

(This formula exactly measures the area only when demand is a straight line.)

1 (Worked problem: deadweight loss) The West India Tea Company has been granted the sole franchise to sell green tea in Greenville. Its marginal cost is $5 per box. Demand is given in Table 16.1. Solve for its output and price and the deadweight loss.

Table 16.1

Price	Quantity
$10	10,000
$ 9	15,000
$ 8	20,000
$ 7	25,000
$ 6	30,000
$ 5	35,000

Step-by-step solution

Step one: Identify the demand and marginal cost curves. The demand curve is given in Table 16.1; marginal cost is constant and equal to $5.

Step two: Calculate marginal revenue. Follow the usual procedure outlined in Tool Kit 14.1. The marginal revenue for the West India Tea Company is given in Table 16.2.

Table 16.2

Price	Quantity	Total revenue	Marginal revenue
$10	10,000	$100,000	—
$ 9	15,000	$135,000	$7
$ 8	20,000	$160,000	$5
$ 7	25,000	$175,000	$3
$ 6	30,000	$180,000	$1
$ 5	35,000	$175,000	–$1

Step three: Find the monopoly output by choosing the quantity for which marginal revenue equals marginal cost. Mar-

ginal revenue equals marginal cost when price is $8 and 20,000 boxes are sold.

Step four: Find the competitive quantity by choosing the quantity for which demand equals marginal cost. The competitive price is $5, and the quantity is 35,000.

Step five: Compute the deadweight loss as the area between the demand and marginal cost curves.

$$\begin{aligned}\text{Deadweight loss} &= \tfrac{1}{2}(Q_c - Q_m) \times (p_m - MC_m)\\ &= \tfrac{1}{2}(35,000 - 20,000) \times (\$8 - \$5)\\ &= \$22,500.\end{aligned}$$

2 (Practice problem: deadweight loss) Although its marginal cost is only $4 for each ride, the Calloway Cab Company has bribed the city council in Venal City to grant it monopoly status at the local airport. The demand for rides is given in Table 16.3.

Table 16.3

Price	Quantity
$7.50	0
$7.00	10
$6.50	20
$6.00	30
$5.50	40
$5.00	50
$4.50	60
$4.00	70

Solve for the company's output and price and the deadweight loss.

3 (Practice problem: deadweight loss) As all baseball fans know, there is only one team in Mudville. The marginal cost of another fan in the park is $1, and the demand is given in Table 16.4.

Table 16.4

Price	Quantity
$3.00	1,500
$2.50	3,000
$2.00	4,500
$1.50	6,000
$1.00	7,500

Solve for the team's output and price and the deadweight loss.

NATURAL MONOPOLY

Natural monopolies are industries with high fixed and low marginal costs. Costs in these industries are lowest when there is only one firm. Many so-called natural monopolies, such as public utilities, cable television companies, and phone companies, are regulated by a public commission that prevents the entry of competitors and sets prices just high enough to allow the firms to earn a normal rate of return. This practice mandates that price equal average cost. Tool Kit 16.2 shows how to set price in a regulated monopoly.

Tool Kit 16.2: Finding the Price for a Regulated Natural Monopoly

Public utility commissions often regulate natural monopolies so that they make a normal rate of return. To this end price must equal average cost. Follow these steps.

Step one: Identify the demand curve, marginal cost, and fixed costs.

Step two: Compute the average cost by dividing total cost by quantity:

average cost = total cost/quantity.

Step three: Find the price for which average cost crosses the demand curve. This is the price for a regulated natural monopoly.

---

4   (Worked problem: natural monopoly) Cutthroat Cable Company is the only provider of cable television services in Kings. Most of its costs are access fees and maintenance expenses, and these fixed costs, which do not vary with the number of customers, total $760,000 monthly. The marginal cost of another subscriber is only $1 per month. The company's demand curve is given in Table 16.5.

Table 16.5

Price (per month)	Number of subscribers
$50	10,000
$40	20,000
$30	30,000
$20	40,000
$10	50,000
$ 1	100,000

The Kings Borough Utility Commission regulates the price of cable service and wants to set the price so that

Cutthroat makes a normal rate of return. What price should it mandate?

Step-by-step solution

Step one: Identify the demand curve, marginal cost, and fixed costs. Demand is given in Table 16.5; marginal cost is $1, and fixed costs are $760,000.

Step two: Compute average cost. When price is $50, there are 10,000 subscribers, and total costs are $760,000 + (10,000 × $1) = $770,000. Average cost is $770,000/10,000 = $77. Continuing this procedure, we derive Table 16.6.

Table 16.6

Price	Number of subscribers	Total cost	Average cost
$50	10,000	$770,000	$77.00
$40	20,000	$780,000	$39.00
$30	30,000	$790,000	$26.33
$20	40,000	$800,000	$20.00
$10	50,000	$810,000	$16.20
$ 1	100,000	$860,000	$ 8.60

Step three: Find the price for which average cost crosses the demand curve. This price is $20, and it is the price that the public utility commission will choose.

5   (Practice problem: natural monopoly) The new big-cat exhibit at the Potter Park Zoo is bringing in the public. Demand is given in Table 16.7. The zoo costs the park service only $1 per visitor, but its fixed costs equal $12,000. Governor Scissorhands has declared that no public funds will be used to support zoos, so Potter Park must charge a price just high enough to cover its costs. What price will solve this problem?

Table 16.7

Price	Number of visitors
$8	1,000
$7	2,000
$6	3,000
$5	4,000
$4	5,000
$3	6,000
$2	7,000
$1	8,000

6   (Practice problem: natural monopoly) Country Line Commuter Service runs from rural areas into the city. It has fixed costs of $20,400 and a marginal cost of $10 per commuter. Demand is given in Table 16.8. The Metropolitan Transportation Commission sets the monthly price for a pass on Country Line, and it wants to allow the firm to earn a normal rate of return. Find the price that allows the service to cover its costs.

Table 16.8

Price (per month)	Number of commuters
$200	100
$180	120
$160	140
$140	160
$120	180
$100	200

Answers to Problems

2   The marginal revenue is given in Table 16.9.

Table 16.9

Price	Quantity	Revenues	Marginal revenue
$7.50	0	$ 0	—
$7.00	10	$ 70	$7
$6.50	20	$130	$6
$6.00	30	$180	$5
$5.50	40	$220	$4
$5.00	50	$250	$3
$4.50	60	$270	$2
$4.00	70	$280	$1

The monopoly output and price are 40 and $5.50, respectively. The competitive output and price would be 70 and $4, respectively. The deadweight loss is

$$\tfrac{1}{2} (70 - 40) \times (\$5.50 - \$4.00) = \$22.50.$$

3   The marginal revenue is given in Table 16.10.

Table 16.10

Price	Quantity	Revenues	Marginal revenue
$3.00	1,500	$4,500	$3
$2.50	3,000	$7,500	$2
$2.00	4,500	$9,000	$1
$1.50	6,000	$9,000	$0
$1.00	7,500	$7,500	−$1

The monopoly price and output are $2 and 4,500, respectively. The competitive price and output would be $1 and 7,500, respectively. The deadweight loss is

$$\tfrac{1}{2} \times (7,500 - 4,500) \times (\$2 - \$1) = \$1,500.$$

5   Average cost is given in Table 16.11.

Table 16.11

Price	Number of visitors	Total cost	Average cost
$8	1,000	$13,000	$13.00
$7	2,000	$14,000	$ 7.00
$6	3,000	$15,000	$ 5.00
$5	4,000	$16,000	$ 4.00
$4	5,000	$17,000	$ 3.40
$3	6,000	$18,000	$ 3.00
$2	7,000	$19,000	$ 2.70
$1	8,000	$20,000	$ 2.50

The price that allows Potter Park to cover its costs is $3.

6   Average cost is given in Table 16.12.

Table 16.12

Price	Number of commuters	Total cost	Average cost
$200	100	$21,400	$214.00
$180	120	$21,600	$180.00
$160	140	$21,800	$156.00
$140	160	$22,000	$138.00
$120	180	$22,200	$123.00
$100	200	$22,400	$112.00

Average cost equals price when price is $180. The commission should choose this price.

Chapter 17

TECHNOLOGICAL CHANGE

Chapter Review

Think back once again to the history of the automobile in Chapter 1. At the beginning of this century, the automobile had not been invented, much less produced in any quantity or in the form we know it today. The enormous technological change in the automobile industry during this century is astounding. Yet the basic model of perfect competition assumes that the goods produced and the technology used to produce them do not change. In this chapter, the emphasis shifts to firms as they actively compete to discover new products and new ways of producing. Although many firms may be involved, the race for new ideas brings with it many of the aspects of imperfect competition covered in Chapters 14–16.

The most important point made in this chapter is that imperfect competition is not all bad. It brings with it the positive benefits of technological advance. Government policy to promote technological change includes granting patents, subsidizing research and development (R & D), and occasionally protecting infant industries.

ESSENTIAL CONCEPTS

1   In the basic competitive model, there is one lowest-cost way of producing, and all firms adopt this technology.

The entry of new firms into the market soon drives away any profits, and all firms settle down to produce at the minimum of the average cost curve. The world of **technological change**, however, is vastly different. Firms compete aggressively to develop new products or production processes so that they can earn monopoly profits, at least for a while. For various reasons, the study of technological change must focus on imperfect competition.

2   A **patent** is a property right to an idea, and it gives the owner monopoly status and the opportunity to earn monopoly profits for the duration of the patent. Firms compete in **patent races**, a winner-take-all system in which the first firm with a discovery is awarded that patent, and its competitors get nothing. Because not all ideas are patentable and because to obtain a patent the firm must disclose details of the idea, firms sometimes forgo applying for one and keep the idea a **trade secret.** In this case, the firm earns monopoly profits until its competitors discover the idea or a better one.

3   Patent policy involves two types of trade-offs:

a   The first issue is the **life** of the patent. Longer patents offer greater rewards for winning the race, and at the same time they promote research and development. On the other hand, for the duration of the patent, the firm sells at the monopoly price, which is above marginal cost, and so causes short-run inefficiencies; i.e., deadweight losses.

b The second issue is the **breadth** of the patent. Should patents be given for the narrowly defined idea or something more general? More broadly defined patents increase the rewards for R & D; however, access to the idea is restricted, and this restriction inhibits any subsequent innovative activity that might build on the patented idea.

4 Several features of research and development encourage large-sized firms.

a First, R & D is a *fixed cost*, in the sense that once discovered, an idea can be used many times without additional cost. Fixed costs increase the efficient scale of the firm.

b Second, the **learning curve** shows that costs fall with experience. The more the firm learns, the more it produces, and thus learning by doing encourages firms to increase their size.

c Third, firms have difficulty borrowing to finance R & D. Larger firms with more retained earnings can finance more of their own research.

5 **Basic research** on the nature of fundamental ideas generates such widespread external benefits that it has the two characteristics of **public goods:** Basic research produces knowledge, and it is difficult (not to mention undesirable) to exclude others from learning and taking advantage of new knowledge. Also, the marginal cost of giving another user access to new knowledge is certainly zero. Because basic research has the characteristic features of public goods, the government has an important role to play in providing funding for such work.

6 Because R & D creates external benefits not captured through patents, most economists advocate additional government policies to encourage it. Tax credits for increased R & D spending are one form of subsidy used in the United States. Also, the **infant industry argument for protection** says that new industries require protection against foreign competition until they move down the learning curve and acquire sufficient expertise to compete effectively. Further, antitrust laws can be relaxed to allow for joint ventures.

BEHIND THE ESSENTIAL CONCEPTS

1 Most of microeconomics sings the praises of perfect competition, especially to the extent that it allocates resources efficiently given the existing production technology. But does a perfectly competitive economy always find the best way to generate more advanced technologies of production, better products, and new ways of doing things? This chapter suggests that the answer is no. In order to encourage R & D, the government set up the patent system to motivate firms toward innovation by rewarding the winner with a period of freedom from competition. Perhaps paradoxically, government creates monopoly to encourage competition.

2 Technological advance is a vital engine of economic growth. Because it is so important, government promotes it with a wide range of complementary policies. Longer-lived and more broadly defined patents increase the rewards for R & D, while tax subsidies reduce the cost. Government also provides direct funding for basic research.

3 Economists consider the infant industry argument for protection to be valid but dangerous. Sometimes the protected industry gains expertise through experience and becomes a world-class competitor; other times the industry becomes inefficient and requires constant government support to survive. The difficulty is determining which industries will thrive and which will not.

4 You learned the basic logic of externalities in Chapter 7: whenever costs or benefits of some decision are not borne entirely by the decision maker, there is inefficiency. Most important to note in this chapter are the external benefits not captured by the firm that invests in R & D. These positive externalities include the fruits of subsequent R & D following an initial discovery, the gains after the expiration of the patent, and the consumer surplus arising from the application of the new idea. The firm ignores these externalities and thus undervalues the true social benefit of the R & D. Government policy can improve matters by promoting additional research efforts.

SELF-TEST

True or False

1 Firms engage in R & D expenditures so that they can participate in competitive markets.

2 A patent confers the exclusive right to produce and market an innovation for a limited period of time.

3 Patents and copyrights are forms of intellectual property.

4 The firm that finishes second in a patent race wins nothing.

5 Holders of patents set the price of their goods equal to marginal cost.

6 Patents promote dynamic efficiency at the expense of short-run inefficiency.

7 The length of patents is set to balance the costs of monopoly pricing by patent holders against the incentives to innovate.

8 Defining a patent more broadly might reduce the rate of innovation by denying access to previous innovations.

9 Any firm eligible for a patent will surely apply for one.

10 R & D is a variable cost of production.

11 The learning curve shows how fixed costs decline with experience.

12 One advantage that smaller firms have in R & D is their better access to capital markets.

13 Venture capital firms specialize in assessing the prospects of R & D ventures and providing capital to innovating firms.

14 The market is unlikely to provide enough basic research because basic research is a public good.

15 The antitrust laws inhibit firms from engaging in joint ventures.

Multiple Choice

1 Capitalism is a process of

   a steady and smooth growth in the living standards of every individual;

   b stagnation, in which the same goods are produced in the same way and distributed to the same people;

   c creative destruction, in which new products and technologies continually destroy existing jobs, firms, and even entire industries;

   d efficient allocation of resources in the short run, without any incentives for technological advance;

   e b and d.

2 Firms engage in research and development expenditures in order to

   a destroy their rivals;

   b provide beneficial externalities to society;

   c advance knowledge, which is a public good;

   d gain market power and charge prices above costs;

   e promote perfect competition.

3 Research and development refers to expenditures intended to

   a discover new ideas and products;

   b discover new technologies;

   c develop products and bring them to market;

   d all of the above;

   e a and b.

4 A patent is

   a a property right to an idea;

   b the right to produce and sell an invention or innovation for all time;

   c the right to produce and sell an invention or innovation for a limited time;

   d a and b;

   e a and c.

5 Patents

   a promote short-run efficiency by encouraging firms to set price equal to marginal cost;

   b stimulate research and innovation and promote dynamic efficiency;

   c are awarded to the firm that has devoted the most resources to researching and developing the idea;

   d are given for advances in basic knowledge;

   e all of the above.

6 In the United States, the typical patent life is 17 years. The length involves a trade-off between

   a short-run inefficiency and incentives to innovate;

   b greater incentives to innovate and stimulation of subsequent innovation through greater access to past innovations;

   c promoting research and fostering new product development;

   d the profits of innovators and those of rivals;

   e all of the above.

7 The breadth of patent coverage involves a trade-off between

   a short-run inefficiency and incentives to innovate;

   b greater incentives to innovate and stimulation of subsequent innovation through greater access to past innovations;

   c promoting research and fostering new product development;

   d the profits of innovators and those of rivals;

   e all of the above.

8 Direct rewards from R & D are given

   a in proportion to R & D expenditures;

   b in proportion to market share;

   c based on how many positive externalities are generated;

   d on a winner-take-all basis;

   e equally to all who entered the race.

9 A patent might not be awarded for an innovation if

   a the innovator chose not to apply for the patent, preferring to hide the advance as a trade secret;

   b the idea was too broad to be patentable;

   c other firms had tried harder to find this particular innovation;

   d too many jobs would be destroyed if the patent were awarded;

   e a and b.

10 When patent holders raise price above marginal cost, there is a sacrifice of

   a trade secrets;

   b dynamic efficiency;

   c infant industries;

   d public goods;

   e short-run efficiency.

11 R & D expenditures are

   a variable costs;

   b fixed costs;

   c marginal costs;

   d U-shaped average costs;

   e none of the above.

12 Which of the following is true?

   a Large firms have advantages in R & D because they may have better access to capital markets.

   b Large firms have advantages in R & D because they can reap the cost savings on sales of more units.

c   Small firms have advantages in R & D because of the bureaucratic environment in large corporations.

d   All of the above.

e   a and b.

13 Learning by doing refers to

a   the fact that education only signals higher productivity; it does not increase productivity;

b   the idea that as firms gain experience from production, their costs fall;

c   the fact that R & D is wasteful because firms must produce products before they can innovate;

d   the fact that R & D is the only way to lower costs;

e   none of the above.

14 The learning curve

a   shows the trade-off between short-run and dynamic efficiency;

b   shows the trade-off between providing incentives to innovate and allowing access to previous innovations;

c   shows that patents lead to monopoly profits;

d   shows how marginal cost declines as cumulative experience increases;

e   disproves the infant industry argument.

15 According to the infant industry argument,

a   firms that have higher costs than their foreign rivals should be protected in order to save jobs;

b   firms should be protected if foreign labor costs are so low that the domestic firm cannot compete;

c   firms that have higher costs than their foreign rivals should be protected until they move down the learning curve;

d   free trade is efficient;

e   a, b, and c.

16 Which of the following is not true?

a   Competition drives firms that do not innovate from the market.

b   Competition inhibits innovation by eliminating profits that could be used to finance R & D.

c   Competition leads firms to imitate innovations, eroding returns.

d   Competition spurs R & D by making it clear that the principal way to earn profits is to innovate and capture market power.

e   All of the above.

17 The market will not supply enough R & D because

a   firms that win patent races do not have to pay for the patents;

b   the benefits of R & D spill over to others not directly involved;

c   firms that lose patent races cannot market the innovation;

d   firms that win patent races set price higher than marginal cost;

e   all of the above.

18 Which of the following is not a property of public goods?

a   It is difficult to exclude anyone from the benefits.

b   The marginal cost of an additional user is close to zero.

c   The market is likely to supply too few public goods.

d   All of the above are properties of public goods.

e   a and b.

19 Which of the following types of R & D is most likely to be a public good?

a   basic research;

b   product development;

c   applied research;

d   the costs of marketing new goods and services;

e   all of the above.

20 When firms share research and development efforts,

a   they are in violation of antitrust law;

b   they forgo the right to patent their innovations;

c   they may restrict access to their discoveries, thereby creating an entry barrier;

d   they forgo the right to ask for government subsidies;

e   they undermine dynamic efficiency.

Completion

1   As new products and technologies drive older jobs, technologies, and industries from the market, capitalism, in the words of Joseph Schumpeter, is a process of _____.

2   Expenditures designed to discover new ideas, products, and technologies and bring them to market are called _____.

3   The exclusive right to produce and sell an invention or innovation is a _____.

4   The fact that the rewards of research and development are given on a winner-take-all basis makes R & D a _____.

5   Rather than seek a patent, an innovator may try to hide the new knowledge as a _____.

6   _____ refers to the idea that as firms gain experience, their costs fall.

7   The curve showing how marginal costs of production decline as total experience increases is called the _____.

8   The benefits of research and development spill over to others not directly involved and generate positive _____.

9   Basic research produces knowledge from which it is difficult to exclude potential users and which can be used by others at no cost to the producers; therefore, it is an example of a _____.

10 The hope that an industry not currently able to com-

pete with foreign firms may in time acquire the experience to move down the learning curve is called the _____ argument for protection.

Answers to Self-Test

True or False

1	f	6	t	11	f
2	t	7	t	12	f
3	t	8	t	13	t
4	t	9	f	14	t
5	f	10	f	15	t

Multiple Choice

1	c	6	a	11	b	16	e
2	d	7	b	12	d	17	b
3	d	8	d	13	b	18	d
4	e	9	e	14	d	19	a
5	b	10	e	15	c	20	c

Completion

1 creative destruction
2 research and development
3 patent
4 patent race
5 trade secret
6 Learning by doing
7 learning curve
8 externalities
9 public good
10 infant industry

Doing Economics: Tools and Practice Problems

Firms undertake research and development in order to market new products or to find new and less costly ways of producing. They compete to win patents or secure trade secrets that will allow them to enjoy some protection against competition and to earn above-normal profits. In this section we study the rewards that motivate R & D. First, several problems explore the value of new product patents and trade secrets. Next, we study innovations that result in lower production costs and consider whether incumbent monopolies have as much incentive to innovate as do potential entrants.

PATENTS

The incentive to undertake research and development is the expectation of future profits. Patents allow firms to earn these profits by conferring monopoly status for the duration of the patent. Tool Kit 17.1 shows how to compute the value of a patent and thus the reward for successful innovation.

> **Tool Kit 17.1:** Calculating the Value of a Patent
>
> The developer of a new product may be able to win a patent, which grants the exclusive right to market the product for 17 years. The value of the patent is then the present discounted value of monopoly profits for the duration of the patent. Follow these steps to compute the value of a patent.
>
> *Step one*: Compute monopoly profits resulting from the patent.
>
> *Step two*: Find the present discounted value of 17 years of profits. This number is the value of the patent:
>
> $$\text{value of the patent} = \text{profits} + [(\text{profits})] \times 1(1 + r)^1]$$
> $$+ [(\text{profits}) \times 1/(1 + r)^2] + \ldots$$
> $$+ [(\text{profits}) \times 1/(1 + r)^{16}].$$
>
> (The variable r stands for the real rate of interest. In the problems below, we will set r equal to 3 percent. A shortcut for step two is to multiply profits by 13.47.)

1 (Worked problem: patents) Nu Products, Inc., has come up with another winning idea—a rubberized surface for premium, no-injury waterslide parks. The company wins the patent. Demand for resurfacings is given in Table 17.1, and costs are $20,000 per park. Calculate the value of the patent.

Table 17.1

Price	Parks resurfaced
$60,000	10
$50,000	20
$40,000	30
$30,000	40
$20,000	50

Step-by-step solution

Step one: Compute the monopoly profits resulting from the patent. Table 17.2 gives the marginal revenue for resurfacings.

Table 17.2

Price	Park resurfaced	Revenues	Marginal revenue
$60,000	10	$ 600,000	$60,000
$50,000	20	$1,000,000	$40,000
$40,000	30	$1,200,000	$20,000
$30,000	40	$1,200,000	$ 0
$20,000	50	$1,000,000	–$20,000

Marginal cost equals marginal revenue when price is $40,000 and 30 parks are resurfaced. Profits then equal ($40,000 × 30) – ($20,000 × 30) = $600,000.

Step two: Find the present discounted value of 17 years of profits. This number is the value of the patent.

Value of the patent $= \$600,000 + [(\$600,000) \times 1/(1 + r)^1]$
$+ [(\$600,000) \times 1/(1 + r)^2] +$
$+ \dots [(\$600,000) \times 1/(1 + r)^{16}]$
$= \$600,000 \times 13.47 = \$8,082,000.$

2 (Practice problem: patents) Bugout Pesticide has discovered a new product that kills potato bugs. It wins the patent. The firm's economics department computes that it can expect to earn $100,000 for the length of the patent. Compute the value of the patent.

3 (Practice problem: patents) Nip and Tuck Bodyshapers have developed a new procedure for smoothing those wrinkles that trouble the after-40 generation. They have decided not to apply for a patent, but rather to keep the technique secret. They expect that others will be able to duplicate the procedure in 4 years and that the resulting competition will allow only a normal rate of return thereafter. Their costs are $5,000 per face, and they estimate that the demand curve is as given in Table 17.3.

Table 17.3

Price	Quantity
$30,000	20
$25,000	30
$20,000	40
$15,000	50
$10,000	60
$ 5,000	70

The real interest rate is expected to remain at 5 percent over the period. Find the value of the trade secret.

THE ENTRANT VS. THE INCUMBENT

A firm that discovers and patents a new, lower-cost production technique will be able to earn above-normal profits for the duration of the patent. If the firm is already a monopoly, then it merely takes advantage of the lower costs. If the firm is a potential entrant, it can undercut the existing firm, drive it from the market, and take its place as the incumbent monopolist. Here, we compare the incentives that incumbent and entrant firms have to innovate, and demonstrate that monopolists do have lower incentives to innovate, as we learned in Chapter 16. Tool Kit 17.2 shows how to predict the outcome of competition between a new entrant and the incumbent monopolist. The following problems use this idea to compare incentives to innovate.

Tool Kit 17.2: Finding Equilibrium with an Incumbent Monopolist and a Potential Entrant

When a firm discovers how to produce for less, it is in position to take over an industry. It can set price just below the average cost of its rival and capture all sales. Follow these steps.

Step one: Identify the incumbent's costs, the potential entrant's costs, and the demand curve.

Step two: Find the equilibrium. The incumbent sets price equal to the entrant's average cost and captures the entire market. (Actually, the price must be 1 cent less than the average cost of the entrant, but we will round up in the problems below.)

---

4 (Worked problem: monopolist and potential entrant) Dentalcomp has had the monopoly in the market for computerizing dental offices in Roseville. While other firms could set up a computer system for $20,000, Dentalcomp's costs are only $15,000. Demand is given in Table 17.4.

Table 17.4

Price	Offices computerized
$30,000	20
$25,000	30
$20,000	40
$15,000	50
$10,000	60

a Find the equilibrium.
b Suppose that a new innovation in programming would lower costs to $10,000. Assume that the incumbent, Dentalcomp, discovers and patents the innovation first. Find the new equilibrium and the incumbent's profits. How much is the innovation worth to Dentalcomp?
c Now assume that a potential entrant discovers and patents the innovation first. Find the new equilibrium and the entrant's profits.
d Who has stronger incentives to innovate?

Step-by-step solution

Step one (a): Identify the incumbent's costs, the potential entrant's costs, and the demand curve. The incumbent, Dentalcomp, has an average cost of $15,000; the entrant has an average cost of $20,000. The demand appears in Table 17.4.

Step two: Find the equilibrium. The incumbent sets price equal to the entrant's average cost, which is $20,000, and captures the entire market of 40 offices. Its profits are $(\$20,000 \times 40) - (\$15,000 \times 40) = \$200,000$.

Step three (b): If it discovers the innovation and wins the patent, Dentalcomp is still the low-cost firm. It captures the entire market with the same price of $20,000 and earns profits of $(\$20,000 \times 40) - (\$10,000 \times 40) = \$400,000$.

Step four (c): If a potential entrant discovers the patent first, it becomes the low-price firm. It sets price equal to Dentalcomp's average cost, which is $15,000, and captures the entire market of 50 offices. Its profits are $(\$15,000 \times 50) - (\$10,000 \times 50) = \$250,000$.

Step five (d): The gain to innovation for Dentalcomp is the difference between its profits before and after the innovation, which equals $400,000 − $200,000 = $200,000. The entrant gains $250,000 by innovating and thus has stronger incentives.

5   (Practice problem: monopolist and potential entrant) Blackdare has patented its unique process for extinguishing oil fires. It can put out a typical well fire for $150,000, but its competitors, without access to the patented process, have average costs equal to $200,000. The demand for extinguishing oil fires is given in Table 17.5.

Table 17.5

Price	Fires
$400,000	10
$350,000	12
$300,000	14
$250,000	16
$200,000	18
$150,000	20
$100,000	22

a   Find the equilibrium price and quantity and profits.
b   Suppose that a new innovation in firefighting would lower costs to $100,000. Assume that the incumbent, Blackdare, discovers and patents the innovation first. Find the new equilibrium and the incumbent's profits. How much is the innovation worth to Blackdare?
c   Now assume that a potential entrant discovers and patents the innovation first. Find the new equilibrium and the entrant's profits.
d   Who has the stronger incentives to innovate?

6   (Practice problem: monopolist and potential entrant) PhXXX Pharmaceuticals has a monopoly on the treatment of Rubinksi's Trauma, an obscure ailment of the saliva glands. The average cost of curing a patient is $2,000 for PhXXX. The only other treatment available costs $5,000. Demand for the treatment of Rubinski's Trauma is given in Table 17.6.

Table 17.6

Price	Treatments
$8,000	100
$7,000	200
$6,000	300
$5,000	400
$4,000	500
$3,000	600
$2,000	700
$1,000	800

a   Find the equilibrium price and quantity.
b   Suppose that a new genetically engineered drug would lower treatment costs to $1,000. Assume that the incumbent, PhXXX, discovers and patents the new drug first. Find the new equilibrium and the incumbent's profits. How much is the innovation worth to PhXXX?
c   Now assume that a potential entrant discovers and patents the innovation first. Find the new equilibrium and the entrant's profits.
d   Who has the stronger incentives to innovate?

Answers to Problems

2   Value of patent = $100,000 × 13.47 = $1,347,000.

3   Marginal revenue is given in Table 17.7.

Table 17.7

Price	Quantity	Revenues	Marginal revenue
$30,000	20	$600,000	—
$25,000	30	$750,000	$15,000
$20,000	40	$800,000	$ 5,000
$15,000	50	$750,000	−$ 5,000
$10,000	60	$600,000	−$15,000
$ 5,000	70	$350,000	−$25,000

Marginal revenue equals marginal cost at a price of $20,000, where 40 faces are smoothed. Profits = ($20,000 × 40) − ($5,000 × 40) = $600,000. The value of the trade secret is $600,000 + [($600,000) × 1/(1.05)] + [($600,000) × 1/(1.05)²] + [($600,000) × 1/(1.05)³] = $2,209,380.

5   a   Price = $200,000; quantity = 18; profits = $900,000.
    b   Price = $200,000; quantity = 18; profits = $1,800,000.
    c   Price = $150,000; quantity = 20; profits = $1,000,000.
    d   The entrant would gain $1,000,000, while Blackdare would only gain $1,800,000 − $900,000 = $900,000. The entrant has stronger incentives.

6   a   Price = $5,000; quantity = 400; profits = $1,200,000;
    b   Price = $5,000; quantity = 400; profits = $1,600,000;
    c   Price = $2,000; quantity = 700; profits = $700,000.
    d   The entrant would gain $700,000, while PhXXX would only gain $1,600,000 − $1,200,000 = $400,000. The entrant has stronger incentives.

IMPERFECT INFORMATION IN THE PRODUCT MARKET

Chapter Review

Chapter 18 begins the exploration of the economics of information with a look at information problems in the product market. Why can't customers always be sure of the quality of a good? Why do customers sometimes pay a higher price for a good than the good is worth? This chapter explains the various ways in which the economy attempts to solve these problems. In doing so, the chapter deviates from the basic competitive model to introduce a fascinating world of signaling, reputation, search, and advertising. Imperfect information causes markets to look a lot like the imperfect competition models discussed in Chapters 14–16 (on monopoly and oligopoly). Chapters 19 and 20 will take up imperfect information as well, in the labor and capital markets.

ESSENTIAL CONCEPTS

1   The basic competitive model assumes that information is perfect, that households are well-informed about the prices, quality, and availability of goods and services, and that firms know all input and output prices and the best available technology. Economists now believe that there are important aspects of the economy's performance that are the result of **imperfect information.** For instance, mutually beneficial trades may not occur if customers cannot judge accurately a product's quality.

   If there were such a thing as a market for information, it would not solve the problem. There would be no way for a customer to evaluate information before buying it, and if she already had the information, she would have no need to buy it.

2   **Asymmetric information** exists when one side of the market knows something that the other does not. For example, the seller of a used car may know more about its reliability than the buyer. Asymmetric information can cause the demand curve to be upward sloping, because buyers reason that only low-quality cars would be sold at low prices and that quality increases with price. This odd situation can lead to more than one possible equilibrium, and can cause markets to be thin or nonexistent in spite of potential gains from trade.

3   One way to send buyers a message in a market with asymmetric information is called **signaling.** For example, a seller of quality used cars can distinguish his product by offering warranties or by building expensive showrooms. Buyers will reason that a seller of lemons

could not afford the expenses of honoring the warranty and will conclude that this seller's used cars are reliable. The seller can also charge higher prices, another potentially informative signal. Buyers understand that only lemons would be sold at low prices, and thus they judge the quality according to the price.

4   If buyers can observe the quality of what is sold, then they can provide sellers with good incentives by basing pay on quality. For example, an employer can pay a typist according to the number of errors made. When buyers do not know the quality of goods before purchasing them, markets do not provide built-in incentives for firms to produce high-quality merchandise. Two possible solutions to this incentive problem are **contracts** and **reputations.**

    a   Contracts typically include **contingency clauses**, which make payment depend on the quality of the service. For example, a contract might specify that the service must be performed by a certain date unless there is a strike or bad weather. Spelling out contingencies provides incentives and shares the risk, but it makes contracts complicated. When the terms of a contract are violated, one party is said to be in breach, but if the reasons for the breach are ambiguous, contract enforcement becomes an issue. Certainly, contracts help, but they provide only an imperfect solution to the incentive problems accompanying trade in the presence of asymmetric information.

    b   By repeatedly providing quality goods and service, a firm establishes a reputation, which enables it to earn extra profits. To preserve its valuable reputation, the firm must continue to provide quality. Reputations thus provide firms with incentives to perform well.

5   Because quality is uncertain and also because the same good may be sold at different prices in different locations (**price dispersion**), customers spend time and money in **search**. Rational search balances the benefits (finding better goods at lower prices) against the costs. Customers usually stop searching even though there is more to learn. **Information intermediaries** are firms that gather information to make customer search easier and more effective. Department stores and travel agents are examples of information intermediaries.

6   Firms try to influence customers' purchasing decisions through **informative** and **persuasive advertising.** The goal of advertising is to shift the demand curve to the right, enabling the firm to raise prices and sell more goods. Advertising may also serve as a signal. Customers may reason that only a high-quality product with good sales would justify a large expenditure on advertising.

7   Concern for poorly informed consumers and deceptive advertising has led to **consumer protection legislation**, which attempts to stop false advertising. Such legislation includes truth-in-lending regulations, which require lenders to disclose the true interest rate. Even so, distinguishing between illegal, false advertising and its legal counterparts (confusing and persuasive advertising) is difficult.

BEHIND THE ESSENTIAL CONCEPTS

1   Markets do not necessarily fail when information is imperfect. The market for assets is an example of a very efficient market. Uncertainty in these markets exists, but the uncertainty is symmetric. Neither side knows the ultimate value of the assets they are trading. Efficiency problems arise, however, when information is asymmetric, that is, when one side of the market knows something that the other does not. Many mutually beneficial exchanges do not take place because buyers cannot be sure about quality, and they fear that sellers may exploit their informational advantage and sell lemons.

2   In the basic competitive model, customers ask simple questions such as, "Is the good worth its price?" In the presence of asymmetric information, and, especially signaling, customers must be more sophisticated. The seller of a quality item wants to signal that his goods have value. He could just say, "My goods are great!" but few customers would believe him. If he provides a guarantee and builds an expensive shop, customers may be more confident that he would be there to honor his word should the product fail. The customer infers from the warranty and the shop that the seller's goods are quality goods.

3   The information problems discussed in this chapter lead the market structure away from perfect competition, creating two possible situations: **barriers to entry** and firms with **downward-sloping demand curves.**

    a   Customers who cannot know the quality of goods buy from businesses with good reputations. Because a reputation is built up over time, firms that would otherwise enter an industry will not be able to justify the investment necessary to establish a good reputation. In this scenario, reputation becomes a barrier to entry and results in less competition.

    b   Because customers must search to learn about price and quality, it becomes cheaper for them to shop at familiar stores. Although the goods themselves may be identical, the stores are different in the eyes of the customer because he knows about some stores and is ignorant of others. Thus, a firm faces a downward-sloping demand curve, where high demanders are those who have information about the firm and lower demanders do not as yet.

4   Information problems in the product market run parallel to the problems in the insurance market discussed in Chapter 6. Again, there are two types of information problems.

    a   In the insurance market, when the price of insurance

is high, only the risky customers buy insurance. The mix of customers is adversely selected when the price rises. Adverse selection also appears in the market for lemons. Customers reason that as the price rises, more quality cars are offered for sale, and the fraction of lemons declines. In other words, there is *adverse selection* in the average quality of used cars when the price falls.

    b   *Moral hazard* troubles the insurance market because people who have insurance tend to be less cautious. They lose their incentives to be careful when they are protected against loss. Similarly, in this chapter, we see that suppliers must be given incentives to live up to the terms of their contracts. There is a moral hazard that the other party may not fulfill his promise and instead give some excuse that cannot be verified.

5   Although this chapter is about information problems, you should also keep in mind that markets do economize on the need for gathering information. In deciding what to produce and in what quantities and the method of production, firms do not need to know the preferences or incomes of households, the production techniques of other firms, or the overall quantities of inputs available. They only need to know the price. Similarly, households do not need to know others' tastes or anything about firms. Price conveys all relevant information, a great advantage of markets.

SELF-TEST

True or False

1   In the basic competitive model, individuals know their opportunity sets.

2   In the basic competitive model, firms know the opportunity sets of individuals.

3   Markets for information do not work well because once the consumer has enough information to evaluate the worth of the information, she no longer has the incentive to pay for it.

4   In the lemons model, demand may slope upward if average quality increases as price increases.

5   Supply and demand may cross more than once if customers do not know the quality of the goods they are asked to buy.

6   Lemons markets have adverse selection in that as the price falls, the mix of goods offered for sale contains more low-quality goods.

7   Customers may believe that a product that carries a warranty is reliable because if the product were not reliable, the firm would incur costs honoring the warranty.

8   Even if customers judge the quality of goods by their price, the market always clears in equilibrium.

9   In the rental car market, there is an incentive problem because customers have less reason to drive carefully.

10   Contracts attempt to provide incentives through contingency clauses that specify what each party agrees to do in different situations.

11   Problems of specifying and enforcing quality make it difficult to overcome the incentive problems with contracts.

12   The reputation of a firm may persuade customers that its goods are of high quality because if the firm were to lose its reputation, its profits would fall.

13   The reputations of existing firms attract new competitors to the market because these firms earn higher profits.

14   Markets where customers must search to learn price are characterized by perfect competition.

15   Information intermediaries reduce the search costs of firms and customers.

Multiple Choice

1   In the basic competitive model, households are assumed to know

   a   their opportunity set;
   b   the prices of all goods and services offered for sale;
   c   the characteristics of all goods and services;
   d   their preferences;
   e   all of the above.

2   In the basic competitive model, firms are assumed to know

   a   the best available technology;
   b   the productivity of each job applicant;
   c   all input prices from every possible supplier;
   d   the present and future prices for their outputs;
   e   all of the above.

3   In the basic competitive model, firms are assumed to know

   a   the preferences of individual consumers;
   b   the costs of production for their suppliers;
   c   the overall quantities of available inputs;
   d   all of the above;
   e   none of the above.

4   Markets for information do not work well because

   a   no firm would be willing to sell information;
   b   consumers are not willing to pay for information;
   c   consumers cannot know what they are buying before they actually buy the information;
   d   markets only work to allocate material goods;
   e   all of the above.

5   In the lemons model,

   a   customers know the quality of the goods, but sellers do not;
   b   sellers know the quality of the goods, but customers do not;

c   neither customers nor sellers know the quality of the goods;

d   both customers and sellers know that the quality of the goods is low;

e   none of the above.

6   In the lemons model,

a   average quality rises as price falls;

b   average quality falls as price falls because sellers know the quality, and owners of lower-quality goods are willing to sell at lower prices;

c   average quality does not change as price falls because consumers know quality and will not buy lower-quality goods;

d   average quality may rise or fall as price falls;

e   none of the above.

7   In the lemons model,

a   demand is downward sloping;

b   supply is upward sloping;

c   demand may slope up or down;

d   supply may slope up or down;

e   b and c.

8   Which of the following involve(s) adverse selection?

a   Consumers sometimes make mistakes and select inferior products.

b   Consumers may not be able to find the lowest-price supplier.

c   As the price falls, the fraction of used cars that are lemons increases.

d   As the automobile insurance premium is increased, those least likely to have an accident drop out of the market.

e   c and d.

9   In markets with imperfect information,

a   firms are price takers;

b   firms set prices, taking into account the effect that price has as a signal of quality;

c   price plays no role because consumers are uncertain about quality;

d   markets clear for the usual reasons;

e   there is a uniform market price per unit of quality, but the goods of different firms sell for different prices.

10   Which of the following are examples of informative signals?

a   The seller claims that her goods are high quality.

b   The seller offers a warranty.

c   The seller constructs an expensive showroom.

d   All of the above.

e   b and c.

11   In markets with imperfect information, the incentive problem arises because

a   firms have no incentive to pay lower prices because they do not know the quality;

b   firms have limited incentive to produce good-

quality items if they cannot convince consumers;

c   firms can raise price above the consumer's willingness to pay;

d   firms have no incentive to produce quality items unless they can be patented;

e   firms have no incentive to build reputations.

12   Contracts with provisions that specify what each of the parties must do in certain situations are called

a   signals;

b   adverse selection;

c   contingency clauses;

d   reputations;

e   none of the above.

13   When a party to contract violates its terms, he

a   is in adverse selection;

b   writes a contingency clause;

c   creates price dispersion;

d   is an information intermediary;

e   is in breach.

14   In some markets, the reputations of firms help persuade customers that their products are high quality. In these markets,

a   price remains above the cost of production;

b   firms earn reputation rents;

c   the reputations of existing firms act as a barrier to the entry of new competitors;

d   all of the above;

e   a and b.

15   A firm with a reputation for high-quality goods might not cut its price because

a   cutting price would attract more customers;

b   customers might infer that at the low price, the firm will not have enough incentive to maintain its reputation;

c   lower prices would attract new competitors;

d   the firm cannot set its price—it must be a price taker;

e   a and b.

16   When customers do not have perfect information about price, there may be price dispersion, which means

a   the same good is sold at different prices;

b   the expenses of searching eliminate the gains from trade;

c   customers will search for the best value;

d   all of the above;

e   a and c.

17   When search is costly for customers,

a   the demand curves for a firm's products will be downward sloping;

b   firms will be price takers;

c   the firm will lose all its customers if it raises its price above the prices of its competitor;

d the firm will gain all its competitors' business if it charges lower prices;

e c and d.

18 Markets in which customers must search to learn prices and qualities are best described by the

a competitive model;

b pure monopoly model;

c monopolistic competition model;

d a or b;

e none of the above.

19 An information intermediary

a helps bring together buyers and sellers;

b cannot make money because markets for information do not work well;

c writes contracts for buyers and sellers;

d eliminates the need for advertising;

e c and d.

20 Advertising

a provides price information to potential customers;

b informs customers about which products are available;

c attempts to persuade customers to buy certain products;

d all of the above;

e a and b.

Completion

1 In the market for _____, customers do not know the quality of the goods being sold.

2 Actions taken by sellers to convince buyers of the high quality of their goods are called _____.

3 The _____ arises when the individual is not rewarded for what she does or when she does not have to pay the full costs of what she does.

4 Clauses in contracts that make the payment depend on precisely how the service is performed are called _____.

5 Someone who brings buyers and sellers together is called an _____.

6 The reputations of existing firms act as a _____ against new competition.

7 When the same good is sold at different prices, there is _____.

8 When customers must search for price and quality information, competition is _____.

9 Advertising that conveys information about price, product availability, and quality is called _____ advertising.

10 Advertising may _____ to customers that the product is of high quality because if the quality were poor, the firm would soon lose its new customers and would have wasted its advertising expenses.

Answers to Self-Test

True or False

1	t	6	t	11	t
2	f	7	t	12	t
3	t	8	f	13	f
4	t	9	t	14	f
5	t	10	t	15	t

Multiple Choice

1	e	6	b	11	b	16	e
2	e	7	e	12	c	17	a
3	e	8	e	13	e	18	c
4	c	9	b	14	d	19	a
5	b	10	e	15	b	20	d

Completion

1 lemons
2 signals
3 incentive problem
4 contingency clauses
5 information intermediary
6 barrier to entry
7 price dispersion
8 imperfect
9 informative
10 signal

Doing Economics: Tools and Practice Problems

Three topics are discussed in this section. First, we look at the important **lemons model**, where average quality is higher as price increases. In this situation, we may see upward-sloping demand curves, which may cause markets to fail to exist or may create the possibility of more than one equilibrium. Also, when firms are able to set prices in this model, there is the possibility of excess supply. Second, we turn to price dispersion and search. We explore the benefits and costs of searching and see why the consumer will likely stop searching before the lowest price is found. Finally, we study how advertising increases profits.

LEMONS

When consumers do not know the quality of a good until after they make the purchase, there is asymmetric information in the product market. Firms that produce low-quality goods (lemons) can sell their goods in the high-quality market. If information were perfect, there would be two markets; now there is one. In figuring out their own demand, consumers must estimate how average quality changes as the market expands. Tool Kit 18.1 shows how to derive the demand curve under these circumstances and that it may slope upwards, and some problems explore the consequences.

Tool Kit 18.1: Deriving the Demand Curve When Consumers Do Not Know the Quality of the Good

If they cannot observe the quality of a good at the time of purchase, customers must estimate and base their demand on the average quality available on the market. Follow this four-step procedure.

Step one: Add the supplies of low- and high-quality goods to find the market supply curve.

Price	Quantity supplied
p_1	$Q_{low} + Q_{high}$
p_2	$Q_{low} + Q_{high}$
etc.	

Step two: Find the fractions of high- and low-quality goods at each point on the supply curve.

Fraction of high-quality goods = $Q_{high}/(Q_{low} + Q_{high})$.

Fraction of low-quality goods = $Q_{low}/(Q_{low} + Q_{high})$.

Step three: Find the average value at each point. This number is what consumers are willing to pay; therefore, it is the demand price.

Average value = demand price
= (fraction of high quality × value of high quality)
+ (fraction of low quality × value of low quality).

Step four: Construct the demand curve.

Price = average value	Quantity demanded
p_1	$Q_{low} + Q_{high}$
p_2	$Q_{low} + Q_{high}$
etc.	

1   (Worked problem: lemons) Many firms sell 50-pound packages of meat at the local farmers' market. Customers place a value of $20 on fatty, low-quality beef, and they place a value of $50 on lean, good-quality beef. The beef is wrapped and frozen, so at the time of purchase, customers cannot distinguish the quality of beef they are buying. The supply curves for low- and high-quality beef appear in Table 18.1.

Table 18.1

Low quality		High quality	
Price	Quantity	Price	Quantity
$15	1,000	$15	0
$20	2,000	$20	0
$25	3,000	$25	1,000
$30	4,000	$30	4,000
$35	5,000	$35	10,000
$40	6,000	$40	12,000
$45	7,000	$45	14,000
$50	8,000	$50	16,000

a   Derive the demand curve for beef.
b   Find the market-clearing price (or prices) and quantity (or quantities).
c   For purposes of comparison, suppose that consumers could tell the difference and that there were separate markets for the two types of beef. Find the equilibrium price and quantity for each type of beef. How does the asymmetric information about quality affect the market for high-quality beef?

Step-by-step solution

Step one (a): Add the supplies to find the market supply. For example, if the price is $325, there will be 5,000 low-quality packages of beef and 10,000 high-quality packages for a total of 15,000. Proceeding in this way gives the market supply as shown in Table 18.2.

Table 18.2

	Market supply
Price	Quantity both high (and low quality)
$15	1,000
$20	2,000
$25	4,000
$30	8,000
$35	15,000
$40	18,000
$45	21,000
$50	24,000

Step two: Find the fractions of the total that are high and low quality at each point. For example, if the price is $35, there are 10,000 high-quality packages. The total number of packages is 15,000. The fraction is $(10,000/15,000) \times 100 = 2/3$. Enter the number and continue. The corresponding fraction of low-quality goods is then 1/3. The complete information appears in Table 18.3.

Table 18.3

Price	Low-quality quantity	High-quality quantity	Fraction high	Fraction low
$15	1,000	0	0	1
$20	2,000	0	0	1
$25	3,000	1,000	1/4	3/4
$30	4,000	4,000	1/2	1/2
$35	5,000	10,000	2/3	1/3
$40	6,000	12,000	2/3	1/3
$45	7,000	14,000	2/3	1/3
$50	8,000	16,000	2/3	1/3

Step three: Compute the average value for each price. For example, when the price is $35, there are 5,000 packages valued at $20 and 10,000 valued at $50. The average value is $[(\$20 \times 5,000) + (\$50 \times 10,000)]/15,000 = \$40$. Continue and complete the table as shown in Table 18.4. Note that average value increases with price. This is because at a higher price, the percentage of packages that are high quality is greater.

Table 18.4

Price	Low-quality quantity	High-quality quantity	Fraction high	Average value
$15	1,000	0	0	$20.00
$20	2,000	0	0	$20.00
$25	3,000	1,000	1/4	$27.50
$30	4,000	4,000	1/2	$35.00
$35	5,000	10,000	2/3	$40.00
$40	6,000	12,000	2/3	$40.00
$45	7,000	14,000	2/3	$40.00
$50	8,000	16,000	2/3	$40.00

Step four: Construct the demand curve. It is given in Table 18.5 and drawn in the diagram. The price column is the average value, and the quantity column is the sum of the low- and high-quality quantities.

Table 18.5

Market demand	
Price	Quantity
$20.00	1,000
$20.00	2,000
$27.50	4,000
$35.00	8,000
$40.00	15,000
$40.00	18,000
$40.00	21,000
$40.00	24,000

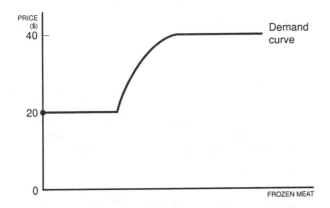

Step five (b): Find the market-clearing prices and quantities. The market clears at a price of $20, where the quantity demanded equals the quantity supplied at 2,000. At this equilibrium, there are no high-quality packages sold. Also, the market clears at a price of $40, where the quantity demanded and the quantity supplied equal 18,000. At this equilibrium, there are 6,000 low-quality and 12,000 high-quality packages. The two equilibria are shown in the diagram.

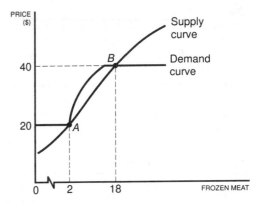

Step six (c): If consumers had perfect information about quality, then there would be a separate low-quality market with 2,000 sold at a price of $20 and a high-quality market with a price of $50 and 16,000 units sold. The asymmetric information destroys the high-quality market in equilibrium *A*. In equilibrium *B*, the high-quality market survives, but the quantity is smaller than it would be with perfect information.

2   (Practice problem: lemons) Trying to appear better educated, many Americans are buying abbreviated guides to culture—lists of novels, operas, and works of art an educated person should know. The guides also include a paragraph or two of witty things to say. The consumers of these books, obviously, cannot judge the quality until they say the wrong thing at the next important social function. The supply curves of low- and high-quality guides are given in Table 18.6. The value of a high-quality guide (complete with video tapes and workbooks) is $300. Low-quality guides are worthless.

Table 18.6

Price	Low-quality guides	High-quality guides
$ 50	1,000	0
$100	2,000	1,000
$150	4,000	6,000
$200	8,000	16,000
$250	12,000	36,000
$300	16,000	48,000

a   Derive the demand curve for guides.
b   Find the market-clearing price (or prices) and quantity (or quantities).
c   For the purposes of comparison, suppose that consumers could tell the difference and that there were separate markets for the two types of guides. Find the equilibrium price and quantity for each type of guide. How does the asymmetric information about quality affect the market for high-quality guides?

3   (Practice problem: lemons) Several new varieties of tomatoes are coming on to the market. Each promises tasty tomatoes with long shelf lives, and a tomato plant that fulfilled this promise would be worth $4. Consumers cannot observe the quality until the end of the growing season, but they suspect that the new hybrids are no better or worse than existing ones valued at $1 per plant. The supply curves of low- and high-quality tomato plants are given in Table 18.7.

Table 18.7

Price	Low-quality tomato plants	High-quality tomato plants
$1.00	10,000	0
$1.50	20,000	5,000
$2.00	30,000	20,000
$2.50	40,000	60,000
$3.00	50,000	100,000
$3.50	60,000	300,000
$4.00	70,000	500,000

a   Derive the demand curve for tomato plants.
b   Find the market-clearing price (or prices) and quantity (or quantities).
c   For the purposes of comparison, suppose that consumers could tell the difference and that there were separate markets for each of the two types of plants. Find the equilibrium price and quantity for each type of plant. How does the asymmetric information about quality affect the market for high-quality plants?

Judging Quality by Price

Because it is more expensive to produce high-quality goods than low, consumers may reason that at low prices only the poor-quality items are offered for sale, and that as price increases, so does average quality. If firms understand this sort of reasoning, they will set price so that quality per dollar is as high as possible, even though this price may not be the market-clearing price. It is possible that shortages will occur, and yet no firm will reduce its price because it knows that it will not gain customers, who believe that lower prices imply lower quality. This is a profound result. In normal competitive markets, the role of prices is only to clear the market. In markets where customers do not know quality, however, price acts as a signal of quality. The price that does the best job of signaling quality may not clear the market. Tool Kit 18.2 shows how price is set in this case.

Tool Kit 18.2: Finding the Price That Maximizes Quality per Dollar

If customers judge quality by price, firms will set price to maximize quality per dollar. Follow these steps to find the right price.

Step one: Identify and plot the relationship between quality and price.

Step two: For each price, find the quality-price ratio: quality-price ratio = quality/price.

Step three: Choose the highest quality-price ratio. Label this point *A*.

Step four: Draw a line from the origin to point *A*. It should be tangent to the quality-price curve, and its slope equals the maximum quality-price ratio.

4   (Worked problem: quality and price) Consumers of 12-gallon fire extinguishers care deeply about the quality of the item, but they cannot distinguish effective and ineffective goods at the time of purchase. The quality of the fire extinguisher only matters if and when it is used. Consumers may reason that at low prices, firms could not afford the quality-control procedures necessary to ensure effective operation. Suppose consumers believe that the relationship between quality and price is as given in Table 18.8.

Table 18.8

Price	Quality (gallons of fire retardant released)
$ 5	0
$10	1.0
$15	4.5
$20	7.0
$25	10.0
$30	11.0
$35	12.0
$40	12.0

a   Find the price that maximizes quality per dollar.

b   Suppose that demand and supply are as given in Table 18.9. Find the equilibrium price. Does it clear the market? Why or why not?

Table 18.9

Price	Demand	Supply
$40	10,000	28,000
$35	12,000	25,000
$30	14,000	21,000
$25	16,000	20,000
$20	17,000	19,000
$15	19,000	17,000
$10	21,000	11,000

Step-by-step solution

Step one (a): Identify and plot the relationship between quality and price. It is given in Table 18.8 and drawn in the diagram.

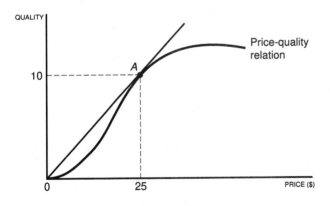

Step two: For each price, find the quality-price ratio. When the price is $40, the quality-price ratio is 12/$40 = 0.30. Continuing, we derive Table 18.10.

Table 18.10

Price	Quality	Quality-price ratio
$ 5	0	—
$10	1.0	0.10
$15	4.5	0.30
$20	7.0	0.35
$25	10.0	0.40
$30	11.0	0.37
$35	12.0	0.34
$40	12.0	0.30

Step three: Choose the highest quality-price ratio. It is 0.40, which occurs at a price of $25.

Step four: Draw a line from the origin to point *A*. It should be tangent to the quality-price curve, and its slope should equal the maximum quality-price ratio, as shown in the diagram.

Step five (b): At a price of $25, the quantity demanded is 16,000, and the quantity supplied is 20,000. Even though there is a surplus of 4,000, firms do not reduce the price. They know that customers would interpret the lower price as a signal of lower quality.

5   (Practice problem: quality and price) Tourists come to San Gordo for the shrimp. Dozens of small establishments offer shrimp, but tourists have little ability to judge the quality before eating. They reason, however, that at low prices the firms cannot afford to ensure that the shrimp are tasty. Suppose consumers believe that the relationship between quality and price is as given in Table 18.11.

Table 18.11

Price (dozen shrimp)	Quality (percentage of tasty shrimp)
$1	10
$2	30
$3	60
$4	70
$5	80
$6	85

a   Find the price that maximizes quality per dollar.

b   Suppose that demand and supply are as given in Table 18.12. Find the equilibrium price. Does it clear the market? Why or why not?

Table 18.12

Price	Demand	Supply
$6	2,000	6,000
$5	2,500	5,500
$4	3,000	5,000
$3	3,500	4,500
$2	4,000	4,000
$1	6,000	3,000

6 (Practice problem: quality and price) The boom in home exercise equipment continues, but there are many purchasers who have given up the quest for the perfect body. These purchasers offer their used equipment for sale. The market also includes those who are selling used lemons, worthless devices that do not perform as advertised. Consumers of used exercise equipment judge that the relationship between price and quality is as given in Table 18.13.

Table 18.13

Price	Quality (calories burned per hour)
$100	100
$200	500
$300	1,100
$400	1,600
$500	1,750

Find the price that maximizes quality per dollar.

SEARCH

In imperfectly competitive markets, different firms may offer the same good for sale at different prices. This situation, called price dispersion, means that consumers must not only decide which goods to purchase, they also must expend time and effort to locate lower price offers and decide which offer to accept. The optimal amount to search is the subject of these problems. As usual, the solution involves carefully balancing benefits and costs. Tool Kit 18.3 shows how.

Tool Kit 18.3: Searching for Lower Prices

When there is price dispersion, customers must search. These steps show how to balance the benefits and costs of searching for lower prices.

Step one: Identify the marginal cost of search and the relationship between search effort and price.

Step two: Calculate the marginal benefits of search: marginal benefit = (change in lowest price)/change in search effort.

Step three: Find the amount of search for which the marginal benefits equal the marginal cost.

Step four: Draw a diagram illustrating the solution.

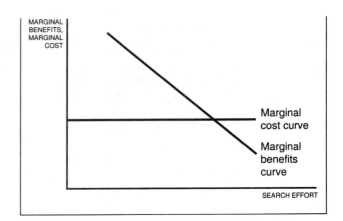

7 (Worked problem: search) Jennifer would like to build a deck behind her new condominium. She has in mind the type she would like and is considering sending away for catalogs offering deck kits. Each catalogue costs $5. The relationship between the lowest appropriate deck kit price and the number of catalogs is given in Table 18.14.

Table 18.14

Number of catalogs ordered	Lowest price found	Marginal benefit
1	$250	
2	$225	
3	$210	
4	$205	
5	$202	
6	$200	

a What is the optimal number of catalogs for Jennifer to order?
b What price does she expect to pay for a deck kit?
c Draw a diagram illustrating your solution.

Step-by-step solution

Step one (a): Identify the marginal cost of search and the relationship between search effort and price. The marginal cost is $5, and the relationship appears in Table 18.14.

Step two: Calculate the marginal benefit of search. The expected price is $250 from the first catalog and $225 from the second. The marginal benefit is thus $25. Continuing, we derive the marginal benefits as shown in Table 18.15.

Table 18.15

Number of catalogs ordered	Lowest price found	Marginal benefit
1	$250	—
2	$225	$25
3	$210	$15
4	$205	$ 5
5	$202	$ 3
6	$200	$ 2

Step three: Find the amount of search for which the marginal benefit equals the marginal cost. This is 4 catalogs, which is the answer to part a.

Step four (b): The expected lowest price is $205, when she buys 4 catalogs.

Step five (c): The solution appears in the diagram.

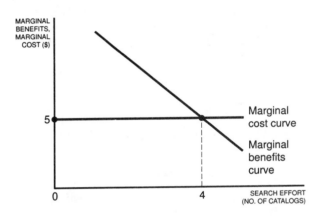

8 (Practice problem: search) Raul wants to refinish his floors. This type of home improvement project is very popular in his neighborhood, and appointments for estimates must be made and paid for weeks in advance. Estimates cost $25, and Raul guesses that the relationship between the number of estimates and the lowest price is as given in Table 18.16.

Table 18.16

Number of estimates	Expected lowest price
1	$800
2	$650
3	$550
4	$500
5	$475
6	$465
7	$460

a What is the optimal number of estimates for Raul to schedule?
b What price does he expect to pay for refinishing his floors?
c Draw a diagram illustrating your solution.

9 (Practice problem: search) The Melling Forging Company needs a new robotic lathe. Several companies offer the lathes, but Melling's management feels there is enough variety that an on-site inspection is needed for each. Time is short, so the company plans to send engineers simultaneously to the plants of some of the firms that sell robotic lathes. The company would like to visit all robotic lathe producers, but a plant visit costs the company $1,000. The relationship between the number of visits and the profits that the new system will earn is given in Table 18.17.

Table 18.17

Number of visits	Expected maximum profitability
1	$18,000
2	$23,000
3	$26,000
4	$27,000
5	$27,500

How many engineers should Melling send?

10 (Practice problem: advertising) Advertising is designed to shift the demand curve to the right. This allows a firm to charge higher prices on the goods that it sells and to adjust the quantity to the profit-maximizing level along the new demand curve. To see how profits change with a successful advertising program, simply follow the procedure outlined in Chapter 14 for deriving marginal revenue and finding the monopoly price and quantity.

Fay's Cleaners has been advertising its new service, which offers customers the opportunity to leave and pick up their dry cleaning at the commuter train station. The demand curves before and after the advertising campaign are given in Table 18.18. Quantity measures suits cleaned and pressed. The marginal cost of each item is $1. Fixed costs equal $1,000.

Table 18.18

Before		After	
Price	Quantity	Price	Quantity
$5.00	100	$5.00	500
$4.50	200	$4.50	1,000
$4.00	300	$4.00	1,500
$3.50	400	$3.50	2,000
$3.00	500	$3.00	2,500
$2.50	600	$2.50	3,000
$2.00	700	$2.00	3,500

a Find the profit-maximizing price and quantity and level of profits before the advertising campaign.

b Find the profit-maximizing price and quantity and level of profits after the advertising campaign.

c How much is the advertising campaign worth to Fay's Cleaners?

11 (Practice problem: advertising) The Gainesville Gekkos, a minor league franchise in the A league, is evaluating its advertising program. The demand curves before and after the advertising campaign are given in Table 18.19. Quantity measures the attendance. The marginal cost of another customer in the park is $0.50. Fixed costs are $50,000.

Table 18.19

Low quality		High quality	
Price	Quantity	Price	Quantity
$10.00	15,000	$10.00	20,000
$ 9.50	17,500	$ 9.50	30,000
$ 9.00	20,000	$ 9.00	40,000
$ 8.50	22,500	$ 8.50	50,000
$ 8.00	25,000	$ 8.00	60,000
$ 7.50	27,500	$ 7.50	70,000
$ 7.00	30,000	$ 7.00	80,000
$ 6.50	32,500	$ 6.50	90,000
$ 6.00	35,000	$ 6.00	100,000
$ 5.50	37,500	$ 5.50	110,000

a Find the profit-maximizing price and quantity and level of profits before the advertising campaign.

b Find the profit-maximizing price and quantity and level of profits after the advertising campaign.

c How much is the advertising campaign worth to the Gainesville Gekkos?

Answers to Problems

2 *a* The market demand and supply curves appear in Table 18.20.

Table 18.20

Price	Low-quality guides	High-quality guides	Total market quantity	Demand price
$ 50	1,000	0	1,000	$ 0
$100	2,000	1,000	3,000	$100
$150	4,000	6,000	10,000	$180
$200	8,000	16,000	24,000	$200
$250	12,000	36,000	48,000	$225
$300	16,000	48,000	64,000	$225

b The market clears at a price of $100, with 1,000 high- and 2,000 low-quality guides. Another market-clearing price is $200, where high-quality guides number 16,000 and low-quality, 8,000.

c If there were perfect information, there would be no low-quality guides, 48,000 high-quality guides, and an equilibrium price equal to $300.

3 *a* The market demand and supply curves appear in Table 18.21.

Table 18.21

Price	Low-quality tomato plants	High-quality tomato plants	Total market quantity	Demand price
$1.00	10,000	0	10,000	$1.00
$1.50	20,000	5,000	25,000	$1.60
$2.00	30,000	20,000	50,000	$2.20
$2.50	40,000	60,000	100,000	$2.80
$3.00	50,000	100,000	150,000	$3.00
$3.50	60,000	300,000	360,000	$3.50
$4.00	70,000	500,000	570,000	$3.63

a The market clears at a price of $1.00 where 10,000 low-quality plants are sold and also at a price of $3.00 where 50,000 low-quality and 100,000 high-quality plants are sold.

c The equilibrium price of low-quality plants would be $1.00 with 10,000 sold. In the high-quality market, the price would equal $4.00, and 500,000 would be sold.

5 *a* The quality-price ratio appears in Table 18.22.

Table 18.22

Price	Quality	Quality-price ratio
$1	10	10.0
$2	30	15.0
$3	60	20.0
$4	70	17.5
$5	80	16.0
$6	85	14.2

Firms choose a price of $3.

b This results in a surplus of 4,500 − 3,500 = 1,000.

6 The quality-price ratio appears in Table 18.23.

Table 18.23

Price	Quality	Quality-price ratio
$100	100	1.00
$200	500	2.50
$300	1,100	3.67
$400	1,600	4.00
$500	1,750	3.50

8 The marginal benefits of searching appear in Table 18.24.

Table 18.24

Number of estimates	Expected lowest price	Marginal benefits
1	$800	—
2	$650	$150
3	$550	$100
4	$500	$ 50
5	$475	$ 25
6	$465	$ 10
7	$460	$ 5

a Raul should get 5 estimates.
b He expects to pay $475.
c

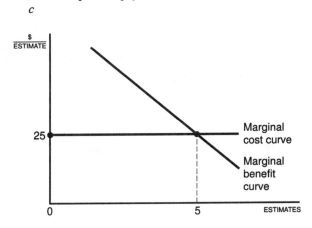

9 The marginal benefits of search appear in Table 18.25.

Table 18.25

Number of visits	Expected maximum profitability	Marginal benefits
1	$18,000	—
2	$23,000	$5,000
3	$26,000	$3,000
4	$27,000	$1,000
5	$27,500	$ 500

The company should send 4 engineers and expect to earn $27,000.

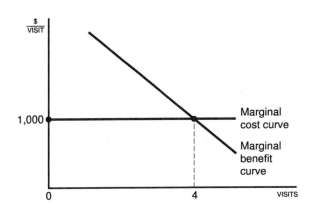

10 *a* Price = $3; quantity = 500; profits = ($3 × 500) − ($1 × 500) − $1,000 − $0.
   b Price = $3; quantity = 2,500; profits = ($3 × 2,500) − ($1 × 2,500) − $1,000 = $4,000.
   c The advertising campaign increases profits by $4,000 −$0 = $4,000.

11 *a* Price = $6; quantity = 32,500; profits = ($7 × 30,000) − ($0.50 × 30,000) − $50,000 = $145,000.
   b Price = $5.50; quantity = 110,000; profits = ($5.50 × 110,000) − ($0.50 × 110,000) − $50,000 = $500,000.
   c The advertising campaign increases profits by $500,000 − $145,000 = $355,000.

Chapter 19

IMPERFECTIONS IN THE LABOR MARKET

Chapter Review

This chapter of the text returns to the labor market and applies the lessons of imperfect competition from Chapter 14 and imperfect information from Chapter 18. The chapter first explores labor unions and compares them to monopolies in the context of the labor they supply to the firm. Next the chapter examines reasons for wage differences. Finally, it takes up the problems of motivating and selecting employees. Particular attention is paid to how different compensation schemes affect incentives. Chapter 20 moves on to explore the capital market from the perspective of imperfect information and the management of the firm.

ESSENTIAL CONCEPTS

1   Employees band together in **unions** to negotiate better working conditions and higher wages. After increasing for decades, the unionized share of the work force has declined since the mid-1950s. Reasons for the decline include an overall improvement in working conditions, relative declines in the sectors of the economy with more unionization, more competitive product markets,

and unfavorable government policy, expecially the Taft-Hartley Act.

2   Unions can be thought of as *monopolies* in the supply of labor to the firm. As such, they raise the wage and allow employment to fall. When the employer firm makes monopoly profits in its own product market, however, it is possible for unions to secure higher wages without reduced employment, at least for a while. Overall, higher union wages probably result in somewhat lower wages for nonunion workers and lower union employment in the long run. Unions also promote job security and have advocated job safety regulations, minimum wages, and immigration restrictions through the political process.

3   Because of imperfect information and other factors, labor is somewhat immobile, and wage differentials exist. Wage differentials may be caused by factors:

   a   **Compensating differentials** are wage differences that reflect characteristics of the job. For example, a police officer may earn more than a firefighter, reflecting the greater danger of police work.

   b   **Information-based differentials** reflect a worker's imperfect information. Workers must search for job offers. A worker currently receiving a low wage may not be able to convince another employer to offer a higher wage because the prospective employer will not know the quality of the worker. This is the lemons model from Chapter 18 applied to the labor market. The difficulty that workers have in moving from job to job gives firms some market power and leads to lower wages.

  c **Productivity wage differentials** simply account for differences in abilities to produce output.

4 **Discrimination** reduces the wages of certain groups. This may involve outright prejudice or just **statistical discrimination**, which results from the use of screening devices (such as degrees from well-established schools) that unintentionally sort out certain classes of workers from the hiring pool. **Affirmative action** requires that firms must actively seek out minorities and women and include them in the applicant pool.

5 Employers must **motivate** workers to perform the task for which they were hired. When the marginal product of a worker is observable, a firm can base pay on output. Thus, **piece-rate systems** provide strong incentives to workers but can subject them to substantial risk. Again, there is a risk-incentive trade-off. When there is concern for the quality, piece-rate systems may fail to give good incentives.

6 Especially when a worker's output is difficult for the employer to observe, the employer may want to **monitor** workers. Also, paying relatively high **efficiency wages** gives workers incentives to work hard and be more productive. Employers can reduce turnover (and training costs) by letting pay and fringe benefits increase with seniority.

7 Sometimes the employer may not know whether output is high because the employees are working hard and well or because the demand for the product is high. In this case, one option is to set up **contests** where workers are paid according to how well they do relative to their peers. Also, basing pay on team performance can encourage workers to monitor and help each other.

BEHIND THE ESSENTIAL CONCEPTS

1 The most important idea to keep in mind when thinking about the labor market is that it is a market. Many of the same models that explained aspects of imperfect product markets appear here in the labor market. Consider the following.

  a Just as the firm may be a monopoly in the product market, a union has monopoly power over the labor supply to the firm. In each case, the price (wage) is set above marginal cost (supply curve of labor), and the quantity (employment) is less.

  b Consumers must search for price and quality information, while workers must search for job offers. In the product market, there is price dispersion; in the labor market, there are information-based wage differentials.

  c Firms need incentives to produce quality products

just as workers need incentives to be productive. There is always the risk-incentive trade-off. Contracts and reputations create incentives in product markets. Monitoring, efficiency wages, seniority benefits, contests, and team rewards create incentives in labor markets.

2 Not only is information imperfect, but exactly what the employer does not know is important. Based upon what she does not know, the employer must choose a means of selecting and motivating her workers. For example:

  a If the employer does not know the productivity of a job applicant, she may rely on signals. A low wage in the current job may indicate low productivity. A college degree may indicate innate abilities.

  b If the employer can observe the marginal productivity of his workers, then he may offer a piece-rate schedule of wages, but this scheme may expose the employee to substantial risk.

  c If the employer cannot observe the effort of her workers, she can monitor them and pay above-market efficiency wages. High wages make the job valuable and make losing the job something to motivate the worker.

  d If the employer thinks that the worker might have other employment opportunities, the employer may offer higher wages and better working conditions to discourage more senior workers from quitting. This becomes especially important if the employer must pay to train new workers.

  e If the employer does not know whether the output of her workers is due to their productivity or due to market conditions, she may set up contests, paying more to workers who do relatively better.

  f If the employer cannot observe the productivity of his employees but if he thinks that the employees are aware of one another's productivity, he can reward good performance by a team, which serves to induces employees to motivate one another.

SELF-TEST

True or False

1 The Wagner Act set up the National Labor Relations Board, which provided procedures for the certification of unions and the prevention of unfair labor practices.

2 The Taft-Hartley Act allowed states to pass right-to-work laws and authorized the president to temporarily suspend strikes.

3 One reason for the decline in the percent of the work force in the private sector that belongs to unions is that consumers have shifted their demand toward more manufacturing and fewer services.

4 Unions act like monopolies in the supply of labor to the firm.

5 Unions power is limited by threats of replacing striking workers and also by unemployment.

6 Wage differentials resulting from differences in job characteristics are called compensating differentials.

7 Imperfect information will not lead to wage differentials if workers search for job opportunities.

8 Employers may be reluctant to offer jobs to workers who currently earn low wages, if they believe that current wages signal low productivity.

9 Statistical discrimination results from overt prejudice.

10 Affirmative action is designed to eliminate union shops.

11 Under a piece-rate system, workers are insured against any risk related to the overall success of the business.

12 Piece-rate systems do not work well if the firm cannot easily and accurately measure the marginal product of workers.

13 Paying higher efficiency wages may motivate workers to be more productive because they perceive that the high-wage job is worth keeping.

14 Firms that are unsure about a task's difficulty can motivate workers by using contests.

15 When pay depends on team performance, workers have incentives to cooperate, work together, and monitor each other's effort.

Multiple Choice

1 In 1935, Congress passed the Wagner Act, which

    a gave legal status to unions;
    b outlawed right-to-work laws;
    c set up the National Labor Relations Board, which provided procedures for the certification of labor unions and for the prevention of unfair labor practices;
    d all of the above;
    e a and c.

2 The Taft-Hartley Act of 1947

    a allowed individual states to pass right-to-work laws;
    b gave the president the power to declare an 80-day cooling off period during which striking workers must return to work;
    c eliminated the National Labor Relations Board;
    d all of the above;
    e a and b.

3 Reasons for the decline in the percentage of the work force that belongs to unions include the following.

    a An overall improvement in working conditions has reduced the demand of workers for unions.
    b Consumer demand has shifted toward the relatively less unionized sectors, such as services.
    c Increasingly competitive markets have limited the power of unions to negotiate increased wages.
    d All of the above.
    e None of the above.

4 In negotiating wages with firms, unions are most like

    a monopolies;
    b monopsonies;
    c competitive firms;
    d individual consumers;
    e none of the above.

5 Unless the firm is making monopoly profits in its product market, the higher wages negotiated by a union must

    a increase the level of employment at the firm;
    b have no effect on the level of employment at the firm;
    c reduce the level of employment at the firm;
    d lead the firm to substitute labor for capital;
    e a and d.

6 Higher wages for union labor

    a increase the supply of nonunion labor;
    b decrease the supply of nonunion labor;
    c reduce wages received by nonunion labor;
    d a and c;
    e b and c.

7 In a labor-management negotiation, the bargaining surplus refers to

    a the fact that although the firm can hire other workers and workers can find other jobs, both sides can gain by reaching agreement;
    b the costs of negotiation in lawyers' and arbitrators' salaries;
    c the strike funds built up by the firms and unions in anticipation of possible work stoppages;
    d the extra workers that union force management to hire;
    e b and d.

8 Compensating differentials are wage differences resulting from

    a the fact that workers must search to find job offers and learn of alternative wages;
    b the fact that employers are unlikely to make offers to workers who currently earn low wages, inferring that these workers may be less productive;
    c differences in job characteristics;
    d wage differences that compensate for differences in productivity;
    e a and b.

9 Jobs that are similar in all respects

    a must pay the same wage, because no worker would take the lower-paying job when higher-paying ones are available;
    b can have different wages according to the theory of compensating differentials;
    c may pay different wages if it takes time and effort for workers to learn about the alternative job possibilities;
    d may pay different wages because employers can pay whatever they want and workers must accept;
    e none of the above.

10 Wage differences that are due to differences in ability to produce output are called

　a　compensating differentials;
　b　information-based differentials;
　c　statistical discrimination;
　d　productivity differentials;
　e　affirmative action.

11 When workers are not aware of alternative job possibilities,

　a　firms may take advantage of their information-based market power and raise wages;
　b　information-based wage differentials may occur;
　c　workers can earn compensating differentials;
　d　all similar workers must earn the same wage for jobs with the same characteristics;
　e　none of the above.

12 Statistical discrimination refers to

　a　wage differences based on statistical measures of productivity differentials;
　b　requirements that firms keep statistics on the numbers of employees in each ethnic group;
　c　requirements that firms actively seek out women and minorities for hiring and promotion;
　d　the use of screening devices that unintentionally sort out members of certain groups;
　e　paying lower wages to workers who have little statistical information about the labor market and alternative job possibilities.

13 Affirmative action refers to

　a　wage differences based on statistical measures of productivity differentials;
　b　requirements that firms keep statistics on the numbers of employees in each ethnic group;
　c　requirements that firms actively seek out women and minorities for hiring and promotion;
　d　the use of screening devices that unintentionally sort out members of certain groups;
　e　paying lower wages to workers who have little statistical information about the labor market and alternative job possibilities.

14 The system of payment in which a worker is paid for each item produced is called

　a　a compensating differential system;
　b　an adverse selection system;
　c　a signaling system;
　d　monopsony;
　e　a piece-rate system.

15 One difficulty with basing workers' pay on their output is that

　a　although workers are given appropriate incentives to work hard, they bear considerable risk;
　b　although they bear the appropriate amount of risk, workers are given little incentive to work hard;
　c　piece-rate schemes are illegal under the Wagner Act;
　d　a and c;
　e　none of the above.

16 Most workers are not paid on a piece-rate basis, because

　a　piece-rate pay is illegal under the Wagner Act;
　b　workers are risk lovers;
　c　it is often difficult to measure the quantity and quality of an individual worker's output;
　d　all of the above;
　e　none of the above.

17 If the employer cannot observe the contribution to output of each worker, she can

　a　monitor a worker's effort;
　b　pay higher wages to increase the cost to the worker of being fired;
　c　set up a piece-work system;
　d　all of the above;
　e　a and b.

18 Efficiency wages

　a　reduce job turnover;
　b　attract more productive job applicants;
　c　motivate workers to put forth more effort;
　d　increase payments to workers;
　e　all of the above.

19 When workers are paid on the basis of relative performance, as in contests,

　a　they are given incentives to be productive, even though management does not know their job's difficulty;
　b　workers are better off because they bear less risk;
　c　workers receive efficiency wages and thus work hard;
　d　turnover is reduced;
　e　all of the above.

20 When pay is based on team performance,

　a　workers are motivated to monitor each other's efforts;
　b　worker are motivated to help each other;
　c　promotions go the those workers who have been more productive;
　d　a and b;
　e　all of the above.

Completion

1 Under _____ legislation, all laborers at unionized establishments must join the union.

2 Unions can raise wages because they have a _____ on the supply of labor to the firm.

3 _____ outlaw union shops.

4 _____ are differences in wages that reflect different job characteristics, such as working conditions or advancement possibilities.

5 _____ results from firms using screening devices that unintentionally sort out members of certain groups from the applicant pool.

6   The system of payment in which a worker is paid for each item produced or each task performed is called a _____ system.

7   The theory that paying higher wages leads to a more productive work force is called _____ theory.

8   Some compensation schemes, such as bonuses for the top sales representatives, base pay on _____ performance.

9   The safety of working conditions is regulated by the _____.

10 The "glass ceiling" that prevents the promotion of women to higher management is an example of _____ discrimination.

Answers to Self-Test

True or False

1	t	6	t	11	f
2	t	7	f	12	t
3	f	8	t	13	t
4	t	9	f	14	t
5	t	10	f	15	t

Multiple Choice

1	e	6	d	11	b	16	c
2	e	7	a	12	d	17	e
3	d	8	c	13	c	18	e
4	a	9	c	14	e	19	a
5	c	10	d	15	a	20	d

Completion

1   union shops
2   monopoly
3   Right to work laws
4   Compensating differentials
5   Statistical discrimination
6   piece-work
7   efficiency wage
8   relative
9   Occupational Safety and Health Administration
10 job

Doing Economics: Tools and Practice Problems

A successful union forms a monopoly in the supply of labor to a firm or industry. We apply the tools of monopoly to study the behavior of unions in several problems in this section. Then we move to compensating differentials, an important source of wage differences among workers. In accepting a job offer, a worker also buys a list of job characteristics, such as safety, advancement potential, training, and the aesthetics of the workplace. We use the budget constraint to show how the labor market offers a choice among job characteristics and establishes an implicit market price for them.

THE WAGE-EMPLOYMENT TRADE-OFF

If a union is able to force the signing of a contract, guaranteeing that only union members will be hired, it is in the position of a monopolist in the supply of labor. Unions may control the supply of labor to an industry, a craft, or an individual firm. The problems here focus on the latter case. Usually unions set wages and let management choose the quantity of labor to hire. In this case, the firm's demand for labor, which is the marginal revenue product, includes all the combinations of wages and employment that the union can achieve. These combinations, in turn, show the trade-off faced by the union. Tool Kit 19.1 shows how to construct the demand for labor and some possible choices that a union might make.

Tool Kit 19.1: Constructing the Union's Trade-off between Wages and Employment

Higher wages usually bring about reduced employment. Follow this procedure to construct the trade-off.

Step one: Identify the production function and the price of the product, and set up a table as follows.

Workers	Output	Revenues	Marginal revenue product

Step two: Find the revenue corresponding to each level of labor use by multiplying the output level by price, and enter the results in the table:

revenues = output × price.

Step three: Compute the marginal revenue product, which is the change in revenue divided by the change in labor, and enter the results in the table:

marginal revenue product
  = change in revenues/change in output.

Step four: Plot the marginal revenue product. This curve is the schedule of possible wage and employment levels.

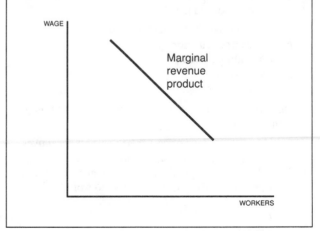

1 (Worked problem: unions) The miners of Davis Lead are represented by the Lead Workers Union, which is considering its stance for the upcoming contract negotiations. The union's economist has estimated a production function for lead, as given in Table 19.1. Its current price is $10 per ton.

Table 19.1

Workers	Output (tons per month)
10	20,000
20	40,000
30	60,000
40	75,000
50	85,000
60	90,000
70	90,000

a Calculate the marginal revenue product, plot it, and interpret it as a schedule of wage and employment possibilities.
b What is the maximum wage? How much employment would result at this wage?
c Workers can earn $5,000 elsewhere. What is the maximum level of employment?

Step-by-step solution

Step one (a): Identify the production function and the price of the product. The production function is given in Table 19.1, and the price of lead is $10 per ton.

Step two: Find the revenue corresponding to each level of labor use. We multiply output by $10, which is the price of lead. When there are 10 workers, output is 20,000, and revenue is 20,000 × $10 = $200,000. Continuing, we derive Table 19.2.

Table 19.2

Workers	Output	Revenues
10	20,000	$200,000
20	40,000	$400,000
30	60,000	$600,000
40	75,000	$750,000
50	85,000	$850,000
60	90,000	$900,000
70	90,000	$900,000

Step three: Compute the marginal revenue product, which is the change in revenue divided by the change in labor. The marginal revenue product for the first 10 workers is $200,000/10 = $20,000. Continuing, we derive Table 19.3.

Table 19.3

Workers	Output	Revenues	Marginal revenue product
10	20,000	$200,000	$20,000
20	40,000	$400,000	$20,000
30	60,000	$600,000	$20,000
40	75,000	$750,000	$15,000
50	85,000	$850,000	$10,000
60	90,000	$900,000	$ 5,000
70	90,000	$900,000	$ 0

Step four: Plot the marginal revenue product.

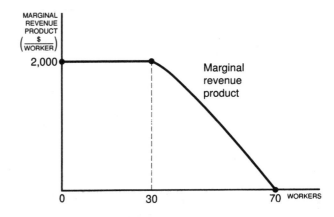

Step five (b): The maximum possible wage is $20,000 per month, and 30 workers will have jobs at this wage.

Step six (c): If the company pays $5,000, which is the alternative wage, there will be 60 workers hired.

2 (Practice problem: unions) Rosewood College's faculty has voted to join the United Professorial Workers Union to win high wages from the administration. Its economics department has estimated the production function, which is given in Table 19.4. Tuition nets Rosewood a profit of $1,000 per student after all expenses (except salaries for professors) are deducted.

Table 19.4

Faculty	Students
20	100
30	600
40	1,000
50	1,300
60	1,500
70	1,600
80	1,600

a Calculate and plot the marginal revenue product schedule. Interpret it as a schedule of salary and employment possibilities.

b   What is the maximum salary that the union could negotiate? Keep in mind that with its enormous endowment, Rosewood would not shut down even if it lost money.

c   The alternative salary for a typical Rosewood professor is $20,000. What is the maximum level of employment?

3   (Practice problem: unions) The cherry pickers at Bingo's Cherry Orchard have won an agreement that the owner will only hire union workers. The production function is given in Table 19.5, and cherries sell for $2 per bushel.

Table 19.5

Pickers	Cherries (bushels per day)
1	24
2	64
3	96
4	120
5	136
6	144
7	148
8	150

a   Calculate and plot the marginal revenue product. Interpret it as a schedule of wage and employment possibilities.

b   What is the maximum wage? Will the orchard shut down if labor is its only nonsunk cost?

c   The workers have an alternative wage of $16 per day. What is the maximum level of employment?

COMPENSATING DIFFERENTIALS

A job offer brings with it a promised wage and a bundle of job characteristics. Workers may not accept the highest-paying job, preferring a lower wage alternative if it offers more attractive nonwage benefits. The additional wage that accompanies a job with some undesirable nonwage aspect is called the compensating differential. The budget constraint allows us to identify and study the trade-off between wages and job characteristics. Tool Kit 19.2 shows the technique.

Tool Kit 19.2: Using Budget Constraints to Analyze Compensating Differentials

When an individual has several job offers, she faces a trade-off between higher wages and other desirable job characteristics. These steps show how to illustrate the trade-off with a budget constraint.

Step one: Draw a set of axes with the wage measured on the vertical axis and the nonwage characteristic on the horizontal.

Step two: Plot a point corresponding to each job offer.

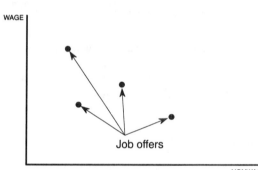

Step three: Cancel the "dominated" offers. The dominated offers represent jobs with both lower wages and less-attractive job characteristics.

Step four: Draw a smooth curve through the undominated job offers. These are the ones that include higher wages and/or more attractive job characteristics. This curve is the budget constraint, reflecting the alternative combinations of wages and job characteristics available to the worker.

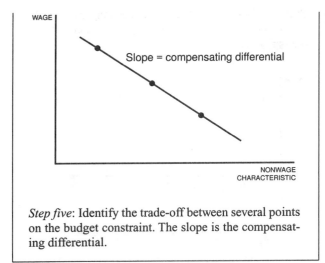

Step five: Identify the trade-off between several points on the budget constraint. The slope is the compensating differential.

4   (Worked problem: compensating differentials) Many parents in two-earner families worry about day care for infants. Recognizing this concern, some progressive companies offer on-site day care, although the facilities vary greatly in quality. Table 19.6 lists some local firms, the entry-level salaries for management trainees, and the expenditure per child for the day care facility.

Table 19.6

Firm	Salary	Expenditure per child
ALX Corp.	$30,000	$5,000
ABX Corp.	$35,000	$3,000
PBX Corp.	$37,000	$4,000
APX Corp.	$46,000	$ 0
AXX Corp.	$40,000	$1,000

a Represent the salaries and day care expenditures as an opportunity set.
b Are there any dominated offers?
c What is the compensating differential for reducing day care expenditures from $5,000 to $4,000? from $1,000 to $0?

Step-by-step solution

Step one (a): Draw a set of axes.

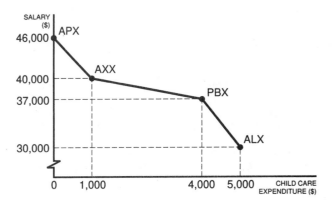

Step two: Plot a point corresponding to each job offer.

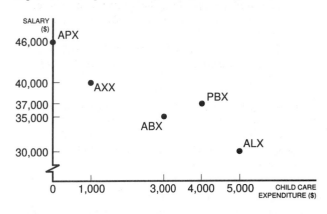

Step three (b): Cancel the dominated offers. The ABX offer, which entails less money and child care expenditure, is dominated by the PBX offer.

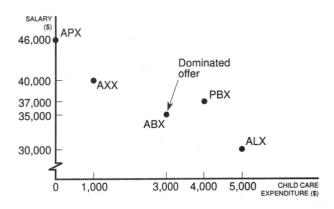

Step four: Draw a smooth curve through the undominated job offers.

Step five (c): Identify the trade-offs between several points on the budget constraint. As the day care expenditure falls from $5,000 to $4,000, salary rises by $37,000 − $30,000 = $7,000. The compensating differential for a decrease from $1,000 to $0 is $46,000 − $40,000 = $6,000.

5   (Practice problem: compensating differentials) Sylvester Stallion is looking for a job. The alternatives, the corresponding annual salaries, and some data on accidental deaths are given in Table 19.7. Sylvester has offers for

each type of job, he is qualified for each, and he considers them equally satisfying except for the risk of death.

Table 19.7

Job	Salary	Deaths per 100,000
Night watchman	$16,000	2
Shoe salesman	$15,000	1 (irate customer)
Clerk in convenience store	$24,000	5
Cab driver	$19,000	6
Armed guard	$22,000	3

a   Represent the job offers as an opportunity set.
b   Without knowing anything about Stallion's willingness to risk death, can you say if there is a job offer he will definitely refuse? Explain.
c   What is the compensating differential for increasing the annual death risk from 1 to 2 deaths per 100,000 workers? What is the compensating differential for increasing the annual death risk from 3 to 5 deaths per 100,000 workers?

6   (Practice problem: compensating differentials) The banking industry in Gotham offers a wide variety of salaries and vacation days. Table 19.8 gives entry salaries and vacation time offered to new hires.

Table 19.8

Bank	Salary	Vacation days
First One	$20,000	5
Bank One	$25,000	8
First Bank	$32,000	5
Premier Bank	$30,000	6
Second Bank	$28,000	7

a   Represent the salaries and vacation days as an opportunity set.
b   Are there any dominated offers?
c   What is the compensating differential for reducing vacation days from 8 to 7? From 6 to 5?

Answers to Problems

2   a   The marginal revenue product schedule is given in Table 19.9.

Table 19.9

Faculty	Students	Revenues	Marginal revenue product
20	100	$ 100,000	—
30	600	$ 600,000	$50,000
40	1,000	$1,000,000	$40,000
50	1,300	$1,300,000	$30,000
60	1,500	$1,500,000	$20,000
70	1,600	$1,600,000	$10,000
80	1,600	$1,600,000	$ 0

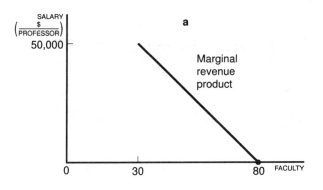

b   The maximum wage is $50,000, at which 30 faculty will be hired.
c   The maximum employment occurs at a wage of $20,000, with 60 faculty.

3   a   The marginal revenue product schedule is given in Table 19.10.

Table 19.10

Pickers	Cherries	Revenues	Marginal revenue product
1	24	$ 48	$48
2	64	$128	$80
3	96	$192	$64
4	120	$240	$48
5	136	$272	$32
6	144	$288	$16
7	148	$296	$ 8
8	150	$300	$ 4

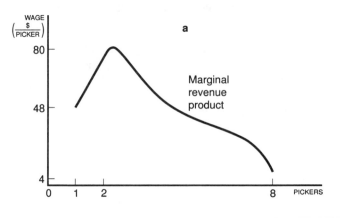

b   The maximum wage is $80, at which there will be 2 pickers.
c   The maximum employment is 6, where the wage equals $16.

5 *a*

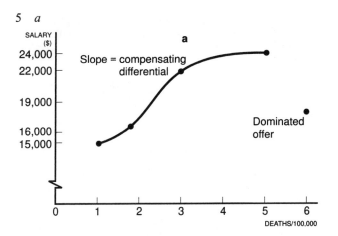

b Stallion will refuse the cab driver offer, which is dominated by the job of clerk in a convenience store.

c $1,000, $2,000.

6 *a*

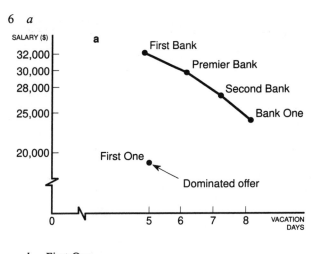

b First One.

c $3,000, $2,000.

FINANCING, CONTROLLING, AND MANAGING THE FIRM

Chapter Review

Information problems pervade the entire economy. This chapter continues the discussion of information problems in markets by turning to the market for financial capital. The same problems caused by asymmetric information in product markets (Chapter 18) and labor markets (Chapter 19) reappear in this chapter, when we consider how the firm is financed, how it is managed, and who owns it.

ESSENTIAL CONCEPTS

1   There are three legal forms for businesses in the United States. A single-owner firm is called a **proprietorship.** A firm with two or more owners is a **partnership.** Ownership of **corporations** is divided into shares, and each owner of a share has voting rights in management elections. The most important feature of the corporate form, however, is **limited liability**. Each owner can lose no more than his or her original investment. In contrast, if a partnership incurs large losses, each partner is fully liable for all the debts.

2   Corporations can finance their investments by borrowing, either from banks or by selling bonds, by issuing new shares of stock (equity finance), or from retained earnings, which are accounting profits not paid out as dividends to owners. If corporate managers act in the interest of the owners, they will maximize the market value of the firm. Surprisingly, the mix of debt and equity finance makes no difference to the market value of the firm.

3   The result that debt does not affect a corporation's market value is the starting point for the analysis of the financial structure of corporations. Nevertheless, there are certain features of real-world corporations that make the level of debt important.

   a   A heavy debt load raises the probability of a costly **bankruptcy.** Banks are reluctant to let a firm's indebtedness grow too large without charging higher interest rates as a risk premium in case of default.

   b   The **tax code** encourages debt because interest is deductible. The fact that capital gains are also treated favorably, however, offsets some of the tilt toward debt finance.

   c   Higher debt loads force managers to keep costs

low and profits high to stave off bankruptcy. Equity finance, on the other hand, may allow managers some freedom to pursue goals other than maximizing the market value.

d   Markets may perceive a firm's issuing debt as a *signal* that managers have confidence in the prospects for the profitability of the firm. This perception will drive up the market value of the firm.

e   Firms that borrow may have to cede substantial *control* to banks or bondholders. This can provide management with different incentives, because shareholders lack information about what management is doing and why.

4   If lenders had perfect information about the default risk of borrowers, then the interest rate would adjust to clear the market for loans. In the real world, however, lenders do not know how risky each borrower is; thus, they give each borrower incentives to pay the loans back. Furthermore, charging higher interest rates attracts especially risky borrowers and motivates borrowers to take on extra risks to earn enough to repay the interest. Rather than raise the interest rate, lenders may ration loans. This phenomenon is known as **credit rationing.**

5   Issuing new shares is one way firms can raise new capital, but this practice may also pose problems. Prospective buyers of shares may reason that managers believe that the firm is overvalued or that it has been turned down on previous loan applications. Such expectations will cause the stock price to fall when new shares are issued. When the price of a stock falls significantly in response to the issuing of new shares, economists say that the firm is **equity rationed.** Few firms raise capital through equity finance in modern economies.

6   Inefficient management lowers the market value of a firm, but shareholders often do not have good enough information to monitor the managers. Other investors may buy up a majority voting share, replace the inefficient managers, and make profits. In this way, the **market for takeovers** can promote efficient management. Some economists have reservations about the effects of hostile takeovers, noting that takeovers are usually financed with additional debt and that the increased indebtedness injures other bondholders. Another important criticism is that the takeover firm may be managed inefficiently itself and may be pursuing the takeover for reasons other than the well-being of its shareholders. These criticisms have led to proposals to limit takeovers, but most economists favor leaving the control of firms to markets.

7   **The principal-agent problem** summarizes the difficulty of providing good incentives to employees. One important example is the case in which the owners of a firm are the principal and the managers are their agents. The owners (the stockholders) want managers to act in the best interest of the firm. The managers, however, may have other interests, and it is difficult for the owners to judge whether a manager takes appropriate actions. The problem for the principal is to design incentives to motivate the managers to work hard and to take the appropriate risks in order to further its own interests.

8   One approach to solving the principal-agent problem is for the manager to buy her share of the enterprise. As an *owner*, she has the appropriate incentives. Another approach to solving the principal-agent problem involves **incentive pay,** such as sales commissions or stock options, which give the manager the right to buy a number of shares at a given price. If she can increase the market value of the firm, she can profit. Finally, the principal can monitor the agent's performance.

9   A fundamental issue in the structure of a large organization is the degree of **centralization.** A centralized, top-down structure has many layers of decision making and review. Its advantages include the approval of fewer bad projects, coordination to account for interdependencies and externalitites within the organization, and a lack of duplication. Decentralized structures grant more autonomy to subunits; they usually approve more good projects and act more quickly with more diversity and experimentation; and they allow management to compare the performance of subunits and decide how to allocate resources within the firm.

10   The issue of how large the firm should be involves how many activites it will do in-house, how many it will contract out, and whether it should **vertically** integrate with its suppliers or its customer firms. If **transactions costs,** which are the extra costs over and above the price of purchasing an item on the market, are high, it may be less costly to do the activities within the firm. One problem with outside contracting may occur if the outside firm must make specialized investments and thereby risk becoming dependent. This is known as a "hold-up problem." Usually the threat of dependency results in higher costs. Generally, it is more efficient to produce some services in-house and purchase others outside.

BEHIND THE ESSENTIAL CONCEPTS

1   Over and over again, economists approach a problem by first understanding a simple situation and then moving on to more realistic complications. When studying corporate finance, the simple starting point is the idea that the method of corporate finance makes no difference to the market value of the firm. It is important for you to understand both the logic of this and why the real world of corporate finance is different.

a   How does the market adjust when the firm uses borrowing rather than new shares to finance new investment? First, what the firm does with the money is unaffected by the means of raising it. Second, a higher debt load makes the stock riskier and lowers its price. The lower price is just enough to keep the market value of the firm the same under debt and equity finance.

b   What is missing from this story? In the real world of corporate finance, firms must worry about the high costs of bankruptcy, and they must consider the tax consequences of debt and equity. Managerial incentives, market perceptions of value based on these incentives, and the ultimate control of the firm's decisions may all be affected by the financial structure of the firm.

2   If a firm raises money by borrowing, the lenders receive interest payments. If it raises money through new equity, then the investors receive dividends and capital gains as the stock price rises. The U.S. tax system affects the firm's decision in the following way: the system encourages borrowing because interest is tax deductible, while it discourages equity finance because dividends are not tax deductible. Offsetting this to some extent is the more favorable treatment capital gains receive in the tax code. The net effect is that the U.S. tax system encourages borrowing to some extent.

3   Whenever one side of the market knows something that the other side does not, there is asymmetric information. In the corporate world, an important example of this is that the owners of the firms (shareholders) will not know everything that management is doing and will not be able to judge whether management's decisions are the right ones. Management may be able to get away with activities that lower profits without the owners knowing. Here is where the market for corporate control comes in with the threat of takeovers. Inefficient management risks being discovered not so much by owners as by other investors, who can purchase the outstanding stock, acquire majority voting status, and replace the laggards.

4   Asymmetric information is also important when the firm goes to the market for loanable funds in search of capital to finance investments. Suppose you are thinking of providing some of this capital by purchasing a corporate bond. You do not know as much about the default risk as the firm issuing the bond, and you should therefore be suspicious about bonds that pay very high interest rates. After all, why would a firm pay high interest rates unless it is selling a risky bond? Other investors reason as you do, and therefore the interest rate does not rise to clear the market for bonds. Firms are credit rationed because of asymmetric information in credit markets.

5   Chapter 10 focused on the efficiency of capital markets. Because each investor seeks the highest rate of return, it will be impossible to beat the market consistently. The credit market problems discussed in this chapter (credit and equity rationing) pertain to the inability of borrowers to obtain loans or raise capital even though they are willing to pay the going rate of return. The conclusion is that capital markets are efficient in valuing different assets, but not efficient in that the market for loanable funds does not clear.

6   This chapter goes a long way beyond the firm in the basic competitive model. The competitive firm has two simple problems to solve: how much should it produce and by what means. Competitive firms hardly need managers. The firms in this chapter are much more realistic and, naturally, more complicated. In addition to the problem of competitive firms, these firms must select employees for tasks, motivate them, monitor their efforts, and account for their outputs. Further, they must deal with uncertainty, determine the degree of centralization, and decide on the number of activities to produce in-house and contract out. It is in solving these problems that real-world managers earn their salaries.

7   As an organization grows, the level of direct control owners exercise diminishes and the problem of providing incentives crops out. When incentives are the issue, the usual suspects appear: asymmetric information in that the principal (the owner) cannot observe and evaluate the activities of her employees (the agents), and moral hazard in that the agents may pursue their own interests and not those of the principal. Solutions to the problem involve the risk-incentive trade-off. For example, basing pay on performance or tying pay to profitability provides stronger incentives but also subjects the agents to more risk. These are fundamental problems within any organization. An understanding of their source and nature, however, may enable you to manage better in any organization that you work for or join.

8   Centralization versus decentralization is a question raised in organizations such as business firms, nonprofit organizations, and government. It is also a fundamental question about the economic system itself. Socialism can be seen as a more centralized system, in which the state makes more economic decisions. Market economies are more decentralized, leaving more decisions to individuals and firms. The debate between socialists and advocates of markets has taken place over the same issues that are discussed in this chapter. Adherents of socialism claim that fewer bad projects are adopted, activities are coordinated better, and there is less duplication. Advocates of market economies point to the abundance of good projects and the diversity, experimentation, and incentives that market economies provide.

9   Transaction costs do not include the purchase price, but rather all those costs in addition to the price. Transactions costs are the costs of using the market: the time, effort, and expense involved in searching the market to find high quality at a good price. Contracts must then be drawn up (at least implicitly) to specify the terms. If it were always easy, reliable, and cheap to use the market, then firms could be quite small and simply buy and sell what they needed among themselves. Often transactions costs are high, and it is cheaper to integrate an activity within the firm even though the added size brings about the problems discussed above.

SELF-TEST

True or False

1 A proprietorship is a firm owned by two or more proprietors.

2 Partnerships offer each partner limited liability in case of bankruptcy.

3 One risk of owning shares of a corporation is that should the firm go out of business, each shareholder is liable for all the debts.

4 If a firm has a heavy debt load, it is said to be highly leveraged.

5 Dividends are tax deductible for firms, because individuals must pay income tax on their dividend earnings.

6 If a firm cannot afford the interest rate charged by banks for loans, then it is credit rationed.

7 Credit rationing occurs because banks and other lenders do not have as much information about default risks as borrowers.

8 Because of credit rationing, the supply of loans exceeds the demand.

9 Investors may infer that the managers of a firm issuing new shares feel that the firm is overvalued by the market.

10 When issuing new shares causes the price of shares to fall substantially, there is credit rationing.

11 The market for takeovers may motivate managers to work hard to increase profits.

12 The principal-agent problem refers to the difficulty in providing incentives within organizations.

13 Centralized decision making provides strong incentives because the directives come from the top.

14 Decentralized decision making leads to the acceptance of more good projects and more bad projects.

15 When transaction costs are high, firms usually will decide to contract out for the service.

Multiple Choice

1 A business with two or more owners, each fully responsible for the liabilities, is called a

a proprietorship;
b partnership;
c limited partnership;
d corporation;
e none of the above.

2 Under the partnership form of business,

a each partner is liable for no more than the amount invested;
b each partner is liable for her share of the debts;
c each partner is fully responsible for all the liabilities of the business;
d neither partner has any liability;
e none of the above.

3 If there is a single owner, the business is called a

a monopsony;
b monopoly;
c partnership;
d proprietorship;
e corporation.

4 Because of limited liability, the owners of corporations

a are exempt from taxes on capital gains that are due to inflation;
b are not taxed on their share of the retained earnings of the firm;
c have only a limited say in the operation of the corporation;
d can lose no more than the amount they invest;
e a and b.

5 Retained earnings equal

a revenues minus expenses minus debt payments minus dividend distributions;
b revenues minus expenses;
c revenues minus debt and dividend distributions;
d revenues minus expenses and interest;
e revenues.

6 A firm is highly leveraged if

a the company union has a representative on the board;
b its outstanding debt is large relative to the value of the firm;
c its equity is large relative to the value of the firm;
d its retained earnings are large relative to the value of the firm;
e c or d.

7 The result that debt does not affect the market value of a firm

a is an accurate description of corporate finance;
b would be true if corporate managers understood economics;
c does not accurately describe the world of corporate finance;
d is true only in monopolistic product markets;
e would be true in the absence of government involvement in capital markets.

8 Because increased debt imposes a greater risk of bankruptcy on the corporation,

a lenders limit the amount they are willing to lend and monitor closely their borrowers;
b banks that are willing to lend require higher interest rates to compensate them for the risk of bankruptcy;
c there is no effect on borrowing and lending incentives because the value of the firm does not depend upon the debt-to-equity ratio;
d there is no effect on borrowing and lending because the financial capital market always clears, and any firm seeking a loan at the going rate can secure one;
e a and b.

9   Overall, the tax code

 a   treats debt and equity finance equally;
 b   favors debt finance because interest is deductible but dividends are not;
 c   favors debt finance because stockholders must pay taxes on dividend income, and this affects their willingness to supply capital;
 d   favors debt because capital gains receive some tax advantages;
 e   b and c.

10   Markets may perceive that a heavy debt position

 a   indicates that managers have confidence in the prospects of the firm;
 b   has no effect on managerial incentives;
 c   indicates that managers have little confidence in the prospects of the firm;
 d   indicates nothing because of the Modigliani-Miller theorem;
 e   b and d.

11   Credit rationing refers to

 a   the means by which prospective borrowers are allocated to banks;
 b   the fact that there is a limited number of seats on the stock exchanges;
 c   the policy that firms must first go to domestic banks before seeking foreign funds;
 d   any situation where individuals or firms cannot obtain funds at the going rate for borrowers of similar risk;
 e   the fact that issuing new shares of stock may cause the stock price to fall.

12   Information in the market for loanable funds is imperfect because

 a   borrowers cannot know the going interest rate;
 b   lenders and borrowers cannot find each other;
 c   good banks are hard to find;
 d   lenders cannot monitor a borrower to ensure that enough care is being taken to prevent default;
 e   a and b.

13   The idea of credit rationing says that if the lender is unsure of the likelihood of default by a certain class of borrowers, he will likely

 a   raise the interest rate to compensate for added risk;
 b   not be willing to raise the interest rate because higher rates may attract a relatively riskier mix of borrowers;
 c   charge an interest rate that leads to excess for funds;
 d   b and c;
 e   none of the above.

14   If a firm issues more shares, the stock price

 a   should not change because the stock market is an example of a competitive market;
 b   should increase because investors will interpret the sale as a signal of confidence in the future;
 c   should decrease because investors will infer that a confident firm would have sought funds from banks;
 d   should not change because of the Modigliani-Miller theorem;
 e   a and d.

15   Takeovers of corporations by others

 a   are never justified because stockholders can oversee the operation of the firm and motivate managers to be efficient;
 b   are never justified because banks and stockholders can oversee the operation of the firm and motivate managers to be efficient;
 c   can be important because other methods of controlling managers are relatively ineffective;
 d   reduce the wealth of shareholders;
 e   a and b.

16   Suppose the owner of the firm wants to motivate the manager to make the decision that he would make in the same situation, but does not have the information necessary to evaluate the decisions made by the manager. This is an example of

 a   comparative advantage;
 b   diminishing returns;
 c   the principal-agent problem;
 d   adverse selection;
 e   none of the above.

17   In the principal-agent problem,

 a   the interests of the principal and agent differ;
 b   the principal cannot judge whether the agent takes the appropriate action by looking at the results;
 c   the agent cannot judge whether the principal takes the appropriate action by looking at the results;
 d   a and c;
 e   a and b.

18   Which of the following is not an advantage of centralized decision making?

 a   Fewer bad projects are accepted.
 b   There is better coordination.
 c   There is less duplication.
 d   There is more experimentation.
 e   Externalities within the organization are accounted for.

19   Which of the following is not an advantage of decentralized decision making?

 a   More good projects are accepted.
 b   There is less duplication.
 c   Decisions are made and implemented more quickly.
 d   There is greater diversity and experimentation.
 e   Incentives are stronger.

20   Which of the following is not a component of transactions costs?

 a   the purchase price;
 b   the time and effort involved in searching the market;
 c   the expense of drawing up contracts;

d   the risk that the supplier will place a low priority on the firm's business.

e   All of the above are transactions costs.

Completion

1   A business with a single owner is called a _____.

2   Two or more individuals owning a business together form a _____.

3   The key distinguishing characteristic of corporations is that their owners have _____.

4   Cash left over after expenses, debt payment, and dividend distributions is called _____.

5   Although it offers some special advantages to equity and debt finance, overall the tax code favors _____.

6   When individuals or firms cannot borrow all they desire at the going interest rate, they are subject to _____.

7   If firms are reluctant to issue new shares of stock because the market may perceive this action as a signal that management does not have enough confidence in the business to borrow, then firms are said to be _____.

8   The difficulty that owners have in motivating managers to act in the interest of ownership is an example of the _____.

9   A firm using _____ decision making usually has a hierarchial structure with a well-defined set of approval layers.

10   Considerable autonomy is granted to subunits of a firm using _____ decision making.

Answers to Self-Test

True or False

1	f	6	f	11	t
2	f	7	t	12	t
3	f	8	f	13	f
4	t	9	t	14	t
5	f	10	f	15	f

Multiple Choice

1	b	6	b	11	d	16	c
2	c	7	c	12	d	17	e
3	d	8	e	13	d	18	d
4	d	9	e	14	c	19	b
5	a	10	a	15	c	20	a

Completion

1   proprietorship
2   partnership
3   limited liability
4   retained earnings
5   debt

6   credit rationing
7   equity rationed
8   principal agent problem
9   centralized
10   decentralized

Doing Economics: Tools and Practice Problems

CREDIT RATIONING

In the basic competitive model, markets clear (supply equals demand) and firms minimize costs. One reason that these outcomes might not occur in the real world is imperfect information. In this section we see how, if banks cannot observe the credit-worthiness of potential borrowers, they may choose to ration credit. Also, we look at incentives issues with some problems concerning the principal-agent relationship. Credit rationing is a reason why firms may not be able to obtain loans even when they are willing to pay the going interest rate. As in the lemon and efficiency wage models, the price (the interest rate in the loanable funds market) has two jobs: it balances supply and demand and influences the riskiness of loan applicants. The latter job refers to the fact that at higher rates of interest, firms may seek funds for riskier projects with greater default rates. Because the interest rate that maximizes the expected rate of return on loans encourages a high percentage of safe loan applicants, it may be too low to clear the market. In this case, supply is less than demand, and there is credit rationing. Tool Kit 20.1 illustrates credit rationing.

Tool Kit 20.1: Credit Rationing

If the mix of applicants grows riskier as the interest rate rises, lenders may choose to ration credit. These steps show how credit rationing brings about a surplus of loanable funds.

Step one: Identify and plot the relationship between the interest rate and the expected rate of return on loans. Also, identify the supply and demand for loans. Note that the demand depends on the interest rate actually charged by banks, but the supply depends on the expected rate of return.

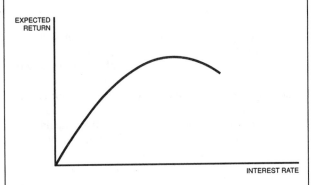

Step two: Find the interest rate that maximizes the expected rate of return. This will be the equilibrium interest rate.

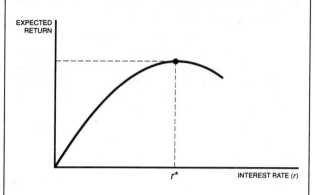

Step three: Find the quantity supplied by substituting the maximum expected rate of return into the supply curve.

Step four: Find the quantity demanded by substituting the equilibrium interest rate (found in step two) into the demand curve.

Step five: Find the amount of credit rationing by subtracting the loans supplied from the loans demanded:

credit rationing = loans demanded – loans supplied.

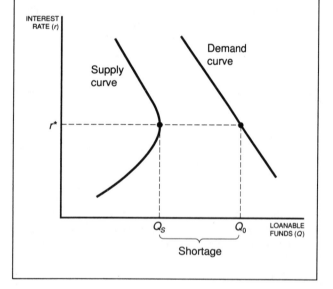

1   (Worked problem: credit rationing) Banks in West Dakota realize that at high interest rates, the pool of loan applicants will include relatively more firms with high default rates. They calculate that the relationship between the interest rate and the expected returns is as given in Table 20.1. The table also gives the supply and demand for new loans. Note that the demand depends on the interest rate actually charged by banks, but the supply depends on the expected rate of return.

Find the equilibrium interest rate and the level of credit rationing.

Table 20.1

Interest rate	Expected rate of return
4.0%	4.0%
4.5%	4.4%
5.0%	4.8%
5.5%	5.2%
6.0%	5.0%
6.5%	4.8%
7.0%	4.0%

Demand for loans		Supply of loans	
Interest rate	Quantity (thousands)	Expected rate of return	Quantity (thousands)
4.0%	$2,500	4.0%	$ 300
4.5%	$1,900	4.4%	$ 400
5.0%	$1,500	4.8%	$ 600
5.5%	$1,200	5.0%	$ 800
6.0%	$1,000	5.2%	$1,000
6.5%	$ 700		
7.0%	$ 400		

Step-by-step solution

Step one: Identify the relationship between the interest rate and the expected rate of return on loans, and the supply and demand for loans. They are given in Table 20.1.

Step two: Find the interest rate that maximizes the expected rate of return. The expected rate of return reaches its maximum of 5.2 percent when the interest rate is 5.5 percent.

Step three: Find the quantity supplied by substituting the maximum expected rate of return into the supply curve; $1,000,000 is supplied when the expected rate of return is 5.2 percent.

Step four: Find the quantity demanded by substituting the equilibrium interest rate into the demand curve; $1,200,000 is supplied when the interest rate is 5.5 percent.

Step five: Find the amount of credit rationing. It is $1,200,000 – $1,000,000 = $200,000. Although there is a shortage, banks will not raise the interest rate because higher interest rates bring about more defaults and a lower expected rate of return.

2   (Practice problem: credit rationing) The relationship between the interest rate and the expected rate of return is given in Table 20.2, which also gives the supply and demand curves for university loans in Gotham. Find the equilibrium interest rate and the amount of credit rationing.

Table 20.2

Interest rate	Expected rate of return
6.0%	5.8%
6.5%	6.0%
7.0%	6.2%
7.5%	6.3%
8.0%	6.2%
8.5%	6.0%
9.0%	5.0%

Demand for loans		Supply of loans	
Interest rate	Quantity (thousands)	Expected rate of return	Quantity (thousands)
6.0%	$8,000	5.0%	$1,000
6.5%	$7,000	5.8%	$1,500
7.0%	$6,000	6.0%	$2,000
7.5%	$5,000	6.2%	$2,500
8.0%	$4,000	6.3%	$3,000
8.5%	$3,000		
9.0%	$2,000		

3   (Practice problem: credit rationing) The relationship between the interest rate and the expected rate of return is given in Table 20.3, which also gives the supply and demand curves for small-business loans in Eastpointe. Find the equilibrium interest rate and the amount of credit rationing.

Table 20.3

Interest rate	Expected rate of return
6.0%	5.0%
6.5%	6.0%
7.0%	6.1%
7.5%	6.0%
8.0%	5.5%
8.5%	5.0%
9.0%	5.0%

Demand for loans		Supply of loans	
Interest rate	Quantity (thousands)	Expected rate of return	Quantity (thousands)
6.0%	$17,000	5.0%	$6,000
6.5%	$15,000	5.5%	$7,000
7.0%	$13,000	6.0%	$8,000
7.5%	$11,000	6.1%	$9,000
8.0%	$ 9,000		
8.5%	$ 7,000		
9.0%	$ 5,000		

INCENTIVES AND THE PRINCIPAL AGENT PROBLEM

Once individuals have been assigned to tasks within an organization, they must be given incentives to perform the tasks in the manner that furthers the goals of the organization. We will look at two aspects of the incentive problem. First, how does the absence of prices within organizations lead to inefficiency? Second, what are the incentive problems associated with sharing the profits?

4   (Worked problem: incentives) The Add advertising agency has several creative teams in its employ, and for years each team has been given a budget of $10,000 for any services that their work requires. The teams hire outside contractors to do layouts and printing. The price of each service is $200 per day.

a   Plot the budget constraint for the typical creative team.

b   The typical team has spent half its budget on each service. Plot the point that corresponds to this choice.

c   Following the recommendation of a consultant, the agency decides to do all its printing in-house. Now the creative teams purchase only layout services from outside the agency. Since they can have their printing services performed at the agency and do not need to purchase printing, their budgets are cut to $5,000. Plot the budget constraint.

d   The agency finds that the print shop is always overcrowded. Why?

Step-by-step solution

Step one (a): Draw coordinate axes, and label the horizontal one "Printing services" and the vertical one "Layout services."

Step two: If the team spends all its budget on printing, it can purchase $10,000/$200 = 50 days. Plot this point along the horizontal axis.

Step three: If the team spends all its budget on layouts, it can purchase $10,000/$200 = 50 days. Plot this point along the vertical axis.

Step four (b): The team spends $5,000 on each service and buys $5,000/$200 = 25 days of each. Plot the point (25, 25) and label it *A*.

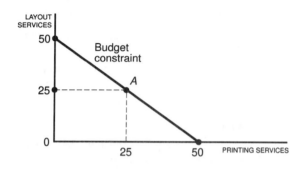

Step five (c): The team has a budget of $5,000. The price of layout service is still $200 per day, but printing is free. The team can still purchase 25 days of layout services, and it can have all of the printing that it wants. The budget constraint is a horizontal line intersecting the vertical axis at 25.

Step six (d): The new way of doing things at the agency allows teams to use printing services without paying for them. In terms of the budget constraint, the teams now can choose all the combinations to the right of point *A*. As long as printing has any value to the team, they will buy more and the shop will be overcrowded.

5   (Practice problem: incentives) Betty and Wilma are copy editors. They pore over manuscripts looking for typographical, grammatical, and other errors. Betty is self-employed and receives $2 per page. Wilma works for Meglith Publishers and receives a straight salary of $800 each week. Each can edit 10 pages an hour, and each has 60 hours available every week. They both like to goof off, and they both like money.

   a   Plot Betty's budget constraint. Put income on the vertical axis and time spent goofing off on the

horizontal. What is the slope of her budget constraint?

   b   Plot Wilma's budget constraint. What is its slope?

   c   Which editor has the greater incentive to goof off? Why?

6   (Worked problem: incentives) Michael and Eliot have part-time jobs as Mexway distributors; they sell soap. The amount that each can sell depends on the time that he puts in knocking on doors. The relationship is given in Table 20.4.

Table 20.4

Time	Revenues
1 hour	$ 40
2 hours	$ 70
3 hours	$ 90
4 hours	$100
5 hours	$105
6 hours	$106

Both Michael and Eliot place a value of $10 on 1 hour of their time.

   a   Complete the marginal benefit column.

   b   How many hours will each work? How much revenue will each earn?

   c   Now suppose that Michael and Eliot form a business to sell soap. They agree to share the revenues. If Michael works 1 hour, he brings in $40, but he gives $20 to Eliot. Michael's personal reward is only $20. Revise the table above to reflect the agreement that revenues are shared.

   d   Complete a marginal benefit column for the revised revenue numbers.

   e   How many hours will each work now?

Step-by-step solution

Step one (a): Complete the marginal benefit column. If Michael works 1 hour, he earns $40, which is the marginal benefit. If he works 2 hours, his revenues rise from $40 to $70, which is a marginal benefit of $30. The results are given in Table 20.5.

Table 20.5

Time	Revenues	Marginal benefit
1 hour	$ 40	$40
2 hours	$ 70	$30
3 hours	$ 90	$20
4 hours	$100	$10
5 hours	$105	$ 5
6 hours	$106	$ 1

Step two (b): The marginal cost of an hour is $10. Setting marginal cost equal to marginal benefit implies 4 hours of work, which brings in $100.

Step three (c): Accounting for the sharing of revenues means that the relationship between time spent selling and the revenues that each gets to keep for himself are in Table 20.6.

Table 20.6

Time	Revenues
1 hour	$20.00
2 hours	$35.00
3 hours	$45.00
4 hours	$50.00
5 hours	$52.50
6 hours	$53.00

Step four (d): Now the marginal benefit is half what it was before, as shown in Table 20.7.

Table 20.7

Time	Revenues	Marginal benefit
1 hour	$20.00	$20.00
2 hours	$35.00	$15.00
3 hours	$45.00	$10.00
4 hours	$50.00	$ 5.00
5 hours	$52.50	$ 2.50
6 hours	$53.00	$ 0.50

Step five (e): Now marginal benefit equals marginal cost at 3 hours worked, which brings in only $45. Sharing the profits means that neither person receives the full benefits of his time and effort. This is the classic incentive problem. Because of bad incentives, each is led to work less.

7   (Practice problem: incentives) Mr. Davis is a sharecropper on a farm owned by Miss Tilly. He gives her one-third of his revenues from farming her 20 acres in rural Mississippi. Table 20.8 gives the relationship between his effort and the revenues from the farm.

Table 20.8

Time	Total revenues	Mr. Davis' revenues	Marginal benefit
1 hour	$18		
2 hours	$33		
3 hours	$45		
4 hours	$54		
5 hours	$60		
6 hours	$63		

Mr. Davis, when not sharecropping, can work in town and make $6 per hour.

a   Complete the table.
b   How much does Mr. Davis choose to work on the farm?
c   If he owned the farm himself and did not share revenues with Miss Tilly, how much would he work on the farm?

Answers to Problems

2   Equilibrium interest rate = 7.5%; expected return = 6.3%; credit rationing = $5,000,000 – $3,000,000 = $2,000,000.

3   Equilibrium interest rate = 7%; expected return = 6.1%; credit rationing = $13,000,000 – $9,000,000 = $4,000,000.

5   *a,b*

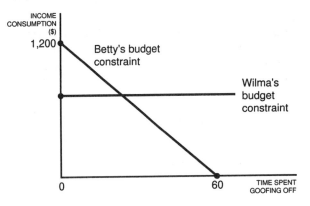

c   Wilma has more opportunities that involve less work; thus, she has more incentive to goof off.

7   a   The completed information is given in Table 20.9.

Table 20.9

Time	Total revenues	Mr. Davis' revenues	Marginal benefit
1 hour	$18	$12	$12
2 hours	$33	$22	$10
3 hours	$45	$30	$ 8
4 hours	$54	$36	$ 6
5 hours	$60	$40	$ 4
6 hours	$63	$42	$ 2

b   He works 4 hours, where the marginal benefit equals marginal cost, which is $6 per hour.
c   If he owned the farm, the marginal benefit would be as given in Table 20.10.

Table 20.10

Time	Revenues	Marginal benefit
1 hour	$18	$18
2 hours	$33	$15
3 hours	$45	$12
4 hours	$54	$ 9
5 hours	$60	$ 6
6 hours	$63	$ 3

Mr. Davis would work 5 hours.

Part Four

Policy Issues

Chapter 21

EXTERNALITIES AND THE ENVIRONMENT

Chapter Review

Of the three major economic players—individuals, firms, and government—the first two have been center stage so far in the text, while the third has mainly stood silently at the side. Government has been the central focus only of Chapters 7 and 16. This is appropriate, because the critical points for you to understand are where markets succeed at answering the main economic questions, where they fail, and how.

Where markets fail, government may have an economic role to play. This chapter wraps up some loose ends with respect to government's role. You have already seen problems of competition, information, and technological change that interfere when private markets are used to answer economic questions. Another major category of market failure is externalities, a concept first introduced in Chapter 7. As you may remember, externalities can be positive or negative. The distinguishing characteristic of externalities is that, positive or negative, they represent benefits or costs that are not captured in the market price. The first example studied in Chapter 21 is pollution. The chapter moves on to natural resources, where the key idea is whether correct incentives exist to conserve.

ESSENTIAL CONCEPTS

1 A market transaction is a voluntary exchange between two parties. Any costs or benefits not captured by market transactions are called **externalities. Positive externalities** are benefits received by others. Markets produce too little activities that generate positive externalities, such as research and development or on-the-job training. Other activities, such as pollution, noise, or congestion, confer costs on others that often do not figure into the market price. Markets create too many of these **negative externalities.**

2 Markets require clearly defined *property rights* in order to allocate resources efficiently. The **Coase's theorem** says that any externality problem could be solved if the government would assign property rights for the externalities. For example, direct pollution of a privately owned lake would not occur unless the owner judged that the benefits exceeded the costs. General environmental pollution is a serious problem because the environment is commonly, not privately, owned.

3 Externalities lead to **market failure** because resources are not allocated efficiently. Individuals consider only their private costs and benefits and ignore the larger so-

cial costs and benefits. Potential governmental solutions to the problems fall into two categories: **command and control regulations** and marketlike devices such as taxes, subsidies, and **marketable permits.** For example, in the case of pollution, governments can issue regulations requiring pollution-control equipment or banning the use of hazardous materials. Alternatively, they can employ more market-oriented policies, such as taxes on pollution emissions, subsidies for pollution abatement, or even creating a market for pollution permits.

4   Private property and the price system enhance the conservation of natural resources. If all is well, current prices reflect the value of natural resources used today and expected future prices equal their expected value in the future. Seeking the highest value for his property, the natural resource owner sells today if the current price exceeds the present discounted value of the future price. If not, he conserves. Thus, private owners make socially efficient decisions.

5   Two problems with private incentive for natural resource conservation exist. First, property rights may not be secure, especially in resource-rich, less-developed countries. If an owner sees a risk of confiscation, she will likely use her resource at a faster than efficient rate. In the same vein, governments often make poor guardians of commonly owned public lands. Second, if capital markets impose borrowing constraints on resource owners, they may substitute faster extraction for borrowing and thereby foil conservation.

BEHIND THE ESSENTIAL CONCEPTS

1   Individuals and firms make efficient decisions when they bear the full costs and benefits of their choice. When externalities are present, some benefit or cost is ignored, and the decision becomes inefficient. The missing ingredient is property rights. Coase's theorem says that if property rights are clearly assigned, decisions will be efficient. The logic can best be understood with an example.

   Suppose that your neighbor likes to play the stereo very loudly each evening while you are reading this book. Clearly, there is an externality. You complain to the building manager, and there are two possible reactions. The manager might say that playing the stereo is a right of all tenants, in effect giving the property right (to make noise) to your neighbor. Or the manager may insist on quiet and give the property right (to silence) to you. According to Coase's theorem, either way of assigning property rights will do. If your neighbor has the right, then you can buy the right to silence by paying your neighbor to be quiet. If you have the right, she must buy your permission to play the music. Of course, you would prefer the latter; nevertheless, in either case, the externality is eliminated and replaced by a market transaction. (Any reader who lives in a college dorm can judge how realistic it is to apply Coase's theorem to externalities.)

2   Pollution is an example of a negative externality. It is a cost ignored by the polluter and borne by others. The inefficiency can be corrected by raising the polluter's private marginal opportunity cost of pollution to the level of the social marginal cost. There are three marketlike ways to do this: taxes on pollution, subsidies for pollution abatement, and marketable pollution permits. Here is how they work.

   a   Suppose that the firm must pay a *tax* of $10 per unit of pollution. Clearly, any pollution now has a private marginal cost of $10, because the tax must be paid.

   b   Suppose that the government pays a *subsidy* of $10 per unit of pollution abatement. Again, the marginal opportunity cost of the pollution is $10, because if the pollution is emitted, it is not abated, and the subsidy is not received.

   c   Under the marketable permits scheme, pollution requires a permit, which must be purchased. The purchase price of the permit is the marginal cost of the pollution. All three marketlike policies put a price on pollution and encourage polluters to find economical ways to reduce emissions.

3   Whether we are using our limited natural resources efficiently and whether we are likely to run out of these resources are important economic questions. The key aspects in the answer to these questions are property rights and markets.

   a   For those resources, such as oil, minerals, and arable farmland, that are *privately owned*, markets provide good incentives for conservation. Future shortages mean high prices in the future. The profit opportunities from future sales motivate owners to conserve resources for the future.

   b   For those resources, such as the ozone layer and endangered species, that are not privately owned, there is no reason for optimism. Since there are *no markets* for these resources, there is no financial incentive to conserve.

SELF-TEST

True or False

1   When there is no government interference, markets will always produce efficient outcomes.

2   The market failures approach assigns to government the task of improving matters when markets allocate resources inefficiently.

3   Markets fail because too many people are motivated by greed.

4   The market will supply too many goods for which there are positive externalities.

5   The social marginal cost is greater than the private marginal cost for a good that generates negative externalities.

6   Coase's theorem contends that externality problems require government intervention.

7 Reassigning property rights can sometimes correct a market failure.

8 Because pollution is an example of a negative externality, economists recommend taxing pollution abatement.

9 Goods for which there are negative externalities should be taxed so that the price captures more of the social costs.

10 The regulation requiring catalytic converters on automobiles is an example of the command and control approach.

11 Marketable permits give no incentive to reduce pollution, because firms that want to pollute can simply buy the permits.

12 Because pollution is a negative externality, it should be eliminated on efficiency grounds.

13 We are using up our limited supply of natural resources because they are sold without concern for the needs of potential future users.

14 Both current and future property rights are essential to provide private owners with incentives to conserve natural resources.

15 If natural resource owners face borrowing constraints, they may conserve more natural resources than is socially efficient.

Multiple Choice

1 The market failures approach to the role of government in the economy says that

a because markets fail, governments must do as much as they can afford;
b governments have a role to play when markets fail to produce efficient outcomes;
c government is less likely to fail than markets;
d the Coase theorem is correct about the role of property rights in producing efficient market outcomes;
e marketable prices will fail to give incentives for natural resource conservation.

2 Examples of market failures include

a externalities;
b a lack of sufficient competition;
c information problems;
d insufficient technological innovation;
e all of the above.

3 The costs of environmental pollution are examples of

a positive externalities;
b public goods;
c negative externalities;
d private costs;
e diminishing returns.

4 Social marginal cost includes

a all marginal costs borne by all individuals in the economy;

b only those marginal costs not included in private marginal cost;
c only those marginal costs included in private marginal cost;
d total revenues minus total private costs;
e marginal revenue minus marginal cost.

5 Coase's theorem claims that

a market outcomes are always efficient;
b when markets fail to produce efficient outcomes, the government should allocate resources;
c negative externalities should be subsidized;
d reassigning property rights can solve externality problems;
e the decisions made by a majority of voters may be inconsistent.

6 Which of the following is not an example of a negative externality?

a Freon gas destroys some of the ozone layer.
b Carbon dioxide emissions bring about global warming.
c Industrial smoke emissions increase lung cancer rates.
d Customers must pay more when the prices of natural resources are increased.
e Runoff of pesticides pollutes streams and rivers.

7 Which of the following is an example of command and control regulations?

a subsidies for the production of goods with positive externalities;
b taxation of goods with negative externalities;
c regulations limiting the allowable level of pollution emissions;
d assigning property rights to victims of environmental pollution;
e nonrivalrous consumption.

8 To reduce emissions of pollution, the government can

a tax pollution abatement;
b subsidize pollution abatement;
c subsidize the sale of polluting goods, such as steel and chemicals;
d reassign to polluters the property rights to pollute;
e take over the production facilities of firms.

9 Under the marketable permits approach to curbing pollution,

a firms purchase permits from the government;
b permits allow firms to emit a certain amount of pollution;
c a market for pollution permits exists for firms to buy and sell the permits;
d firms have strong incentives to reduce pollution;
e all of the above.

10 The market system encourages conservation because

a the price of a natural resource, such as an oil well, equals the present discounted value of potential future uses;

b wasteful exploitation is punished by fines or imprisonment;

c markets always allocate resources efficiently;

d permits from the government are required before natural resources may be sold;

e there is such an abundance of natural resources.

11 Private owners may undervalue future demand for natural resources if

a there are negative externalities associated with the current use of the resource;

b there are positive externalities associated with the current use of the resource;

c property rights are not secure;

d owners may face limited borrowing opportunities;

e b, c, and d.

12 The view that there is a role for government when markets do not produce efficient outcomes is called

a Coase's theorem;

b the market failures approach;

c marketable permits;

d the command and control approach;

e none of the above.

13 How does Coase's theorem recommend that government solve the problem of overgrazing public lands?

a The government should put a tax on beef.

b The government should sell the grazing land to private owners.

c The government should subsidize beef feedlots.

d The government should issue regulations mandating how many cattle can graze per acre in each season.

e Coase's theorem allows no role for government.

14 Which of the following is not an example of a problem with command and control regulations of environmental pollution?

a Firms cannot afford to clean up their pollution.

b Regulations do not allow for variations in circumstances among firms.

c The least cost cleanup technology may not be the mandated one.

d There are limited incentives for technological advance in pollution abatement.

e All of the above are problems with command and control regulations.

15 Which of the following methods can reduce environmental pollution?

a taxes on pollution emissions;

b subsidies for pollution abatement;

c marketable permits;

d command and control regulations;

e all of the above.

16 When the social marginal cost of an activity exceeds its private marginal cost,

a it should be subsidized;

b it should be taxed;

c it should be outlawed;

d a or b;

e a, b, or c.

17 If the government uses the marketable permits policy,

a firms must purchase permits from the government;

b firms may sell their permits to the government but not to other firms;

c firms may buy their permits from the government but not from other firms;

d firms may sell their unused permits, but they may not buy additional permits;

e firms may buy or sell permits as they choose.

18 The marketable permits system specifies that

a firms purchase permits in order to pollute;

b firms may buy permits from other firms;

c firms may sell unused permits to other firms;

d all of the above;

e none of the above.

19 The production of too many goods with negative externalities is an example of

a paternalism;

b consumer sovereignty;

c public failure;

d market failure;

e the voting paradox.

20 In deciding when to extract and sell a mineral deposit, the private owner compares

a the present and expected future prices;

b the present net return and the discounted present value of the future net return;

c the discounted present value of future costs and prices;

d the expected value of future costs and prices;

e present costs and price.

Completion

1 The _____ approach to the role of government calls upon the government when markets fail to produce efficient outcomes.

2 The extra costs and benefits not captured by market transactions are called _____.

3 The _____ cost of pollution is borne entirely by the polluter, while the _____ cost includes all costs borne by individuals in the economy.

4 _____ claims that externality problems can be solved by reassigning property rights.

5 Regulatory measures that set limits on pollution emissions and mandate the use of specific types of pollution-control technologies are examples of the _____ approach.

6 The _____ approach issues to firms permits, which allow them to emit a certain amount of pollution and which can be traded.

7 Government can bring about a reduction in pollution emmissions by subsidizing _____.

8   When social marginal costs exceed private marginal costs there is a _____ externality.

9   High expected future prices motivate private owners to _____ natural resources.

10   When there are negative externalities associated with a good the market will produce too _____.

Answers to Self-Test

True or False

1	f	6	f	11	f
2	t	7	t	12	f
3	f	8	f	13	f
4	f	9	t	14	t
5	t	10	t	15	f

Multiple Choice

1	b	6	d	11	e	16	b
2	e	7	c	12	b	17	e
3	c	8	b	13	b	18	a
4	a	9	e	14	a	19	d
5	d	10	a	15	e	20	b

Completion

1   market failure
2   externalities
3   private, social
4   Coase's theorem
5   command and control
6   marketable permits
7   pollution abatement
8   negative
9   conserve
10   much

Doing Economics: Tools and Practice Problems

The first topic of this section is how taxes and subsidies can be used to encourage an activity for which there are positive externalities. We see how firms can be induced to emit less pollution by engaging in pollution abatement. Next, we turn to markets for goods that generate negative externalities such as noise, congestion, and pollution. A few problems show situations in which market equilibrium levels are too high and investigate how taxes can be used to make the market more efficient. The last topic focuses directly on the market for pollution and the way in which the marketable permits system brings about efficient use of the environment.

POLLUTION ABATEMENT

Like other decisions made by firms, the question of the level of pollution abatement involves marginal benefit and cost reasoning. If the government taxes pollution emissions, then abating pollution saves the tax. If the government subsidizes pollution abatement, then abating pollution earns the subsidy. In each case, the marginal benefit of pollution abatement is determined by the government's policy. Tool Kit 21.1 demonstrates this.

Tool Kit 21.1: Determining the Level of Pollution Abatement

Pollution abatement is encouraged by taxing pollution or subsidizing abatements. Each raises the marginal cost of polluting. Follow these steps to find the resulting level of abatement.

Step one: Identify the cost of pollution emission and abatement.

Step two: Calculate the marginal abatement costs:

marginal abatement cost = change in cost/change in level of pollution abatement.

Step three: Determine the marginal benefit of abatement.

Step four: Set the marginal benefit of pollution abatement equal to its marginal cost.

---

1   (Worked problem: pollution abatement) Runoff from the Lower Indiana Quarta Lead Mine has raised lead levels in the Maumee River. The current level of lead effluent is 10 pounds per month. A filtering technology would enable the company to reduce its effluent. The abatement costs are given in Table 21.1.

Table 21.1

Pollution emitted (pounds/month)	Pollution abated (pounds/month)	Total cost	Marginal cost
10	0	$ 0	—
9	1	$ 10	
8	2	$ 25	
7	3	$ 45	
6	4	$ 70	
5	5	$100	
4	6	$135	
3	7	$175	
2	8	$225	
1	9	$290	
0	10	$400	

a   Suppose that a pollution tax (or fine) of $40 is assessed per kilogram of lead emitted. How much will the company emit? What quantity of pollution will be abated?

b   Suppose that rather than a tax, a subsidy of $40 is given per unit of pollution abated. How much will the company emit? What quantity of pollution will be abated?

c   The firm's profits from the production and sale of lead total $10,000. Compare its profits under the tax and the subsidy plan.

Step-by-step solution

Step one (a): The cost of pollution emission and abatement is given in Table 21.1.

Step two: Calculate the marginal abatement cost. The marginal abatement cost is the extra cost incurred in reducing pollution emissions by 1 more unit. For example, reducing pollution from 10 to 9 units raises costs from $0 to $10; therefore, the marginal abatement cost is $10 for the first unit. The remainder of the schedule is given in Table 21.2.

Table 21.2

Pollution emitted	Pollution abated	Total cost	Marginal cost
10	0	$ 0	—
9	1	$ 10	$ 10
8	2	$ 25	$ 15
7	3	$ 45	$ 20
6	4	$ 70	$ 25
5	5	$100	$ 30
4	6	$135	$ 35
3	7	$175	$ 40
2	8	$225	$ 50
1	9	$290	$ 65
0	10	$400	$110

Step three: Determine the marginal benefit of abatement. Each unit of pollution emitted incurs a tax of $40; thus, the marginal benefit of abatement is $40.

Step four: Set the marginal benefit of pollution abatement equal to its marginal cost. This results in 3 pounds of lead emitted and 7 pounds abated.

Step five (b): When the policy is to subsidize abatement, the marginal benefit is the subsidy, which is $40. Setting $40 equal to the marginal abatement cost again gives 3 pounds of lead emitted and 7 pounds abated. The answer is the same as for part a. Notice that under the subsidy scheme, each unit emitted still costs the firm $40, in the sense that any unit emitted is a unit not abated and a subsidy not received.

Step six (c): Profits under the tax equal $10,000 less the abatement cost and the tax, or

profits = $10,000 − $175 − $40 (3) = $9,705.

Under the subsidy, however,

profits = $10,000 − $175 + $40 (7) = $10,105.

Notice that the difference in profits is $10,105 − $9,705 = $400, which is the magnitude of the tax/subsidy multiplied by the number of units that the firm emits with no regulation. It is the total value of the property right to pollute.

2   (Practice problem: pollution abatement) Avenger of the Sea Tuna kills 20 dolphins during an average harvest. It has various options for reducing the dolphin kill, and the costs are given in Table 21.3.

Table 21.3

Dolphins killed	Dolphins saved	Total cost	Marginal cost
20	0	$ 0	—
18	2	$ 100	
16	4	$ 240	
14	6	$ 400	
12	8	$ 600	
10	10	$ 1,000	
8	12	$ 1,500	
6	14	$ 2,200	
4	16	$ 3,000	
2	18	$ 5,000	
0	20	$10,000	

a   Suppose that a tax (or fine) of $100 is assessed per dolphin killed. How many dolphins will be killed? What number of dolphins will be saved?

b   Suppose that rather than a tax, a subsidy of $100 per dolphin is granted for reductions in the dolphin kill. How many will the company kill? How many will be saved?

c   With no tax or subsidy, the company's profits are $10,000. Compute its profits with the tax and with the subsidy.

3   (Practice problem: pollution abatement) Flying Turkey Air Transport has its hub in Franklin. Dozens of planes land and take off each night causing considerable noise. By muffling engines or other more advanced techniques, the company can reduce its noise. The costs are given in Table 21.4.

Table 21.4

Average level of noise (decibels)	Total cost	Marginal cost
1,000	$ 0	—
900	$ 50	
800	$ 150	
700	$ 300	
600	$ 500	
500	$ 750	
400	$1,100	

a   Suppose that a pollution tax (or fine) of $2.50 is assessed per decibel of noise created. How much will the company create? What quantity of noise will be abated?

b   Suppose that rather than a tax, a subsidy of $2.50 is granted per unit of noise abated. How much will the company create? What quantity of noise will be abated?

c   With no tax or subsidy, the company's profits are $5,000. Compute its profits with the tax and with the subsidy.

MARKETS AND EXTERNALITIES

When there are negative externalities, such as pollution, noise, and congestion, market outcomes will be inefficient. Specifically, there will be more than the socially efficient level. The socially efficient level just balances the social marginal costs with the marginal benefits. But markets ignore the externality and focus only on the private marginal benefits. Tool Kit 21.2 shows how to distinguish private and social benefits and how to compare the market and socially efficient levels.

Tool Kit 21.2: Finding the Efficient Quantity in Markets with Negative Externalities

The production and consumption of many goods causes negative externalities. In these cases, markets bring about too much production and consumption. Follow these steps to compare market and efficient levels.

Step one: Determine the market equilibrium at the intersection of the supply and demand curves.

Step two: Add the marginal external cost to the supply curve, which is the private marginal cost, to determine the social marginal cost curve.

Step three: Find the efficient quantity at the intersection of the demand curve and the social marginal cost curve.

Step four: Compare the market equilibrium and efficient quantities.

---

4   (Worked problem: negative externalities) Runoff from local feedlots is polluting the Red Cedar River. The negative externality per steer is $100. The demand and supply curves for steer are given in Table 21.5.

Table 21.5

Demand		Supply	
Price	Quantity	Price	Quantity
$200	350	$200	1,100
$180	500	$180	1,000
$160	650	$160	900
$140	800	$140	800
$120	950	$120	700
$100	1,100	$100	600
$ 80	1,300	$ 80	500

a   Find the market equilibrium quantity and price.
b   Calculate the social marginal cost, and determine the efficient quantity of steers.

Step-by-step solution

Step one (a): Find the market equilibrium quantity and price. At a price of $140, the market clears with 800 sold.

Step two (b): Find the social marginal cost curve. We add the marginal external cost, which is $100, to the supply curve, which is the private marginal cost. Table 21.6 gives the solution.

Table 21.6

Quantity	Social marginal cost
500	$180
600	$200
700	$220
800	$240
900	$260
1,000	$280
1,100	$300

Step three: Find the efficient quantity at the intersection of the demand curve and the social marginal cost curve. This occurs at a quantity of 500 and a price of $180.

Step four: Compare the market equilibrium and efficient quantities. Notice that the efficient quantity is only 500, while the market produces 800. Incorporating the external cost into the supply curve would raise the price and reduce the quantity to the efficient level.

5   (Practice problem: negative externalities) The private flying lessons at Daredevil Airport cause noise that disturbs local residents. The residents are also uneasy about the periodic crashes. One estimate of the magnitude of the negative externalities is $15 per flight. The market supply and demand curves for flight lessons are given in Table 21.7.

Table 21.7

Demand		Supply	
Price	Quantity	Price	Quantity
$75	10	$75	100
$70	20	$70	80
$65	30	$65	60
$60	40	$60	40
$55	50	$55	20
$50	60	$50	0

a   Find the market equilibrium price and quantity.
b   Calculate the social marginal cost, and find the efficient quantity.

6   (Practice problem: negative externalities) New developments of townhouses are springing up in the ex-urban community of Outland. The supply and demand curves for new townhouses are given in Table 21.8.

Table 21.8

Demand		Supply	
Price	Quantity	Price	Quantity
$140,000	100	$140,000	900
$130,000	200	$130,000	800
$120,000	300	$120,000	700
$110,000	400	$110,000	600
$100,000	500	$100,000	500
$ 90,000	600	$ 90,000	400
$ 80,000	700	$ 80,000	300

a   Find the market equilibrium quantity of townhouses and the corresponding price.

b   The new developments impose costs on other current residents for sewage, transportation, and congestion. An estimate of the magnitude of these negative externalities is $20,000 per townhouse. Find the efficient level of townhouse production and the corresponding price.

MARKETABLE PERMITS

The problem of pollution (and other negative externalities) can be attacked more directly by considering the "market" for pollution itself. The polluters are the demanders for pollution, and their demand curve is just the marginal abatement cost curve. If it costs a firm $40 to clean up a ton of sludge from its emissions, then that firm is willing to pay $40 to be given the right to emit the sludge. The efficient level of pollution occurs where the demand curve intersects the social marginal cost curve, which is the marginal damage done by the pollution. These problems explore the issue of the efficient level of pollution and how a marketable permit scheme can bring about this outcome. Use Tool Kit 21.3.

Tool Kit 21.3: Using Marketable Permits to Bring About the Efficient Level of Pollution

The marketable permit policy sells permits to pollute. The market price for these permits gives firms incentives to reduce pollution. The following procedure shows how to find the number of permits to sell and the market price.

Step one: Identify the demand for pollution (the sum of all the marginal abatement cost curves) and the social marginal cost curve.

Step two: Find the efficient level of pollution, which is at the intersection of the demand for pollution and the marginal abatement cost curve.

Step three: Determine how many permits to sell. This quantity is the efficient level of pollution found in step two.

Step four: Find the market price for the permits. Read this price off the demand curve.

---

7   (Worked problem: marketable permits) Discharges from factories, runoff from farmlands, and many other activities pollute the Metatarsal Lakes. The pollution could be reduced, but any reduction would involve expensive abatement procedures. The marginal abatement cost schedule is given in Table 21.9 along with the social marginal cost of the pollution. (BOD means biochemical oxygen demand.)

Table 21.9

Pollution (millions of pounds/BOD)	Marginal abatement cost	Social marginal cost
100	$1,200	$ 0
200	$1,000	$ 0
300	$ 900	$ 150
400	$ 800	$ 300
500	$ 700	$ 450
600	$ 600	$ 600
700	$ 500	$ 800
800	$ 300	$1,000

Find the efficient level of pollution, and explain how a marketable permits scheme can achieve an efficient outcome.

Step-by-step solution

Step one: Identify the demand for pollution and the social marginal cost curve. The demand is the marginal abatement cost curve given in Table 21.9, which also includes the social marginal cost curve.

Step two: Find the efficient level of pollution. The intersection of the demand for pollution and the marginal abatement cost curve occurs at 600 parts/million.

Step three: Determine how many permits to sell. This number is 600, and each permit entitles the holder to emit 1 part/million of pollution.

Step four: Find the market price for the permits. If 600 permits are offered for sale, their market price will be $600. This price is read off the marginal abatement cost curve at 600 units.

8   (Practice problem: marketable permits) The marginal abatement cost and social marginal cost of pollution in the Northwest Air Shed are given in Table 21.10. Find the efficient level of pollution, and explain how a marketable permits scheme can achieve an efficient outcome. Pollution is measured as metric tons of sulphur oxide.

Table 21.10

Pollution	Marginal abatement cost	Social marginal cost
10	$100	$ 0
20	$ 80	$ 0
30	$ 60	$ 5
40	$ 50	$10
50	$ 40	$20
60	$ 30	$30
70	$ 15	$50

9 (Practice problem: marketable permits) Pesticides, engine oil, chemicals, and other pollutants are finding their way into the groundwater. Abatement is possible but expensive. The marginal abatement cost and social marginal cost of this type of pollution for the Alago Aquifer are given in Table 21.11. Find the efficient level of pollution, and explain how a marketable permits scheme can achieve it.

Table 21.11

Pollution	Marginal abatement cost	Social marginal cost
100	$10,000	$ 10
150	$ 8,000	$ 100
200	$ 6,000	$ 1,000
250	$ 5,000	$ 5,000
300	$ 4,000	$10,000
350	$ 3,000	$20,000

Answers to Problems

2 The marginal abatement cost for reducing the dolphin kill is given in Table 21.12.

Table 21.12

Dolphins killed	Dolphins saved	Total cost	Marginal cost
20	0	$ 0	—
18	2	$ 100	$ 50
16	4	$ 240	$ 70
14	6	$ 400	$ 80
12	8	$ 600	$ 100
10	10	$ 1,000	$ 200
8	12	$ 1,500	$ 250
6	14	$ 2,200	$ 350
4	16	$ 3,000	$ 400
2	18	$ 5,000	$ 1,000
0	20	$10,000	$ 2,500

a The firm reduces its dolphin kill by 8 for a total of 12 killed.
b Again, the firm reduces its dolphin kill by 8 for a total of 12 killed.
c Profits under the tax = $10,000 − (12 × $100) = $8,800; profits under the subsidy = $10,000 + (8 × $100) = $10,800.

3 The marginal abatement cost for noise is given in Table 21.13.

Table 21.13

Average level of noise	Total cost	Marginal cost
1,000	$ 0	—
900	$ 50	$0.50
800	$ 150	$1.00
700	$ 300	$1.50
600	$ 500	$2.00
500	$ 750	$2.50
400	$1,100	$3.50

a The firm will emit 500 decibels (abating 500).
b The firm will abate 500 decibels (emitting 500).
c Profits under tax = $5,000 − (500 × $2.50) = $3,750; profits under subsidy = $5,000 + (500 × $2.50) = $6,250.

5 a Market equilibrium quantity = 40; price = $60;
   b The social marginal cost is given in Table 21.14.

Table 21.14

Quantity	Social marginal cost
0	$65
20	$70
40	$75
60	$80
80	$85
100	$90

Efficient quantity = 20; price = $70.

6 a Market equilibrium quantity = 500; price = $100,000.
   b The social marginal cost is given in Table 21.15.

Table 21.15

Quantity	Social marginal cost
300	$100,000
400	$110,000
500	$120,000
600	$130,000
700	$140,000
800	$150,000
900	$160,000

Efficient quantity = 400; price = $110,000.

8 Efficient level = 60. If 60 permits are sold, the market price will be $30 each, 60 permits will be purchased, and the level of pollution will be 60.

9 Efficient level = 250. If 250 permits are sold, the market price will be $5,000 each, 250 permits will be purchased, and the level of pollution will be 250.

TAXES, TRANSFERS, AND REDISTRIBUTION

Chapter Review

Chapter 22 is about why governments redistribute income and how they do so. It begins with the basic argument of why markets may not provide a satisfactory answer to the question of for whom goods are produced. It looks separately at the tax and transfer system and at social insurance and asks how each promotes a more equitable distribution of the economy's output. The chapter examines the fundamental trade-off between efficiency and equality and discusses various current public-policy controversies.

ESSENTIAL CONCEPTS

1   While the idea of market failure justifies many government policies aimed at improving the efficiency of the economy, the case for **redistribution** of the economy's output depends on overriding social values relating to equality. Markets allocate too small a share of output to those at the lower end of the economic spectrum and too much to those at the upper end, and the distribution has grown more unequal in the last 20 years. Redistribution programs often interfere with economic efficiency, so it is important to pay attention to their design.

2   A good tax system has five important characteristics, the first of which is **fairness**. Economists have emphasized two principles of fairness. **Horizontal equity** says that individuals in the same circumstances should pay the same tax, and **vertical equity** says that taxes should be based on ability to pay. By the standard of vertical equity, the tax system should be **progressive**, which means that the fraction of income paid in taxes should be larger for those with more income.

3   The second characteristic of a good tax system is **efficiency**. The system should change the economy's resource allocation decisions as little as possible and also impose few extra costs on taxpayers. The U.S. tax system often encourages more consumption and production of some goods with special tax provisions called **tax subsidies**. These reduce taxes for those who engage in the favoured activity and result in lower tax revenues for the government. The lost tax revenue is called a **tax expenditure.** Other characteristics of a good tax system include **administrative simplicity, flexibility**, and **transparency**, which means that it should be clear who is paying how much of each tax.

TAXES, TRANSFERS, AND REDISTRIBUTION 245

4 Government transfer programs fall into two categories: income tested, need based programs and social insurance. The former includes AFDC (Aid to Families with Dependent Children), EITC (Earned Income Tax Credit), and public housing. AFDC provides cash assistance to poor families, and the EITC encourages low wage workers to work by making them eligible for a subsidy through the income tax system. AFDC reform proposals center around encouraging work, increasing opportunities, and fostering responsibility.

5 Many social insurance programs, such as Social Security, unemployment insurance, disability insurance, and Medicare, benefit the middle class. They are financed by payroll taxes, but the ultimate burden is in the form of lower wages. Although they are called insurance programs, the provisions of each cause some income to be redistributed.

6 Any program or tax provision that promotes quality inevitably reduces efficiency. This basic **equity-efficiency trade-off** must be faced in making choices about social programs and tax reforms. Overall, income equality in United States, as shown by the **Lorenz curve**, is reduced somewhat by taxation and government programs, but it remains significantly more unequal than in other developed countries.

BEHIND THE ESSENTIAL CONCEPTS

1 You can judge the U.S. tax system on how well it meets the five criteria outlined in the text. The following are some arguments.

   a Fairness: The marginal tax rate, which is the tax paid out of the extra dollar of income, is higher for higher incomes. This aspect and refundable tax credits combine to make the income tax system mildly progressive, although the progressivity is offset somewhat by a variety of special provisions that help higher-income households, such as mortgage interest deductions and capital gains exclusions. Payroll taxes and federal and provincial sales taxes are regressive, however, and in sum, the total tax system is probably fairly flat, slightly progressive at best.

   b Efficiency: Although the 1981 reduction in marginal tax rates and the 1986 tax reform improved the efficiency of the income tax system, many special provisions remain. Further, in 1993 marginal rates rose again.

   c Administrative simplicity: By removing many lower-income individuals from the tax rolls and making tax avoidance less profitable (because marginal tax rates are lower), recent tax reforms have made the U.S. income tax system simpler for some. Overall, the goal remains unmet.

   d Flexibility: In practice, the U.S. income tax system is not flexible because any proposed tax change seems to open up debate on all aspects of the tax code.

   e Transparency: For some taxes, such as the corporation income tax and sales taxes, it is difficult to determine the actual tax burden.

2 The equity-efficiency trade-off is similar to the risk-incentive trade-off you studied in earlier chapters. You learned that an employer who pays commissions, for example, will provide stronger incentives to her sales force than another who pays a straight salary. The result of the strong incentives, however, is risk for the employees. The risk is not only that incomes may be high in some months and low in others, but also that some employees may earn more than others. Just as an employer can have strong incentives at a cost of risk for the employees, an economy can have efficiency at a cost of inequality. Social programs that alleviate poverty also reduce the incentives to earn income. Similarly, progressive income taxation pays for social programs, but discourages effort.

SELF-TEST

True or False

1 Redistribution is necessary to promote a more efficient allocation of resources than the market provides.

2 Horizontal equity says that upper-income individuals should pay a larger fraction of income in taxes.

3 Vertical equity says that people in similar situations should pay the same tax.

4 A tax system is progressive if upper-income individuals pay a larger fraction of income in taxes.

5 The payroll tax is an example of a progressive tax.

6 The U.S. income tax system is quite flexible and able to respond quickly to changes in economic circumstances.

7 The 1986 tax reform reduced administrative complexity somewhat by removing some low-income individuals from the tax rolls and reducing marginal tax rates.

8 The corporate income tax is an example of a transparent tax in that it is easy to see how much each person effectively pays.

9 The earned-income tax credit increases the after-tax income of the working poor.

10 Tax expenditures refer to the lost revenue from tax subsidies, such as the mortgage interest deduction.

11 The Gini coefficient equals twice the area between the Lorenz curve and the 45 degree line.

12 The burden of payroll taxes is the same whether they are paid by workers or their employers.

13 Social Security is an example of a middle-class entitlement program.

14 The Lorenz curve illustrates the efficiency of the economy.

15   The United States has a more equal distribution of economic goods than most other developed economies.

Multiple Choice

1   Which of the following is not an excise tax?

   a   cigarette tax;
   b   tax on alcohol;
   c   gasoline tax;
   d   tax on air travel;
   e   corporate income tax.

2   Horizontal equity means that

   a   people in the same economic situation should pay the same amount in tax;
   b   richer individuals should pay a larger fraction of their income in taxes;
   c   richer individuals should pay a larger monetary amount in taxes;
   d   the marginal tax rate should be higher for higher-income individuals;
   e   the tax schedule should be flat.

3   Vertical equity means that

   a   people in the same economic situation should pay the same amount in taxes;
   b   richer individuals should pay a larger fraction of their income in taxes;
   c   richer individuals should pay a larger monetary amount in taxes;
   d   the marginal tax rate should be higher for higher-income individuals;
   e   the tax schedule should be flat.

4   If lower-income individuals pay a larger fraction of their income in tax, the system is

   a   progressive;
   b   regressive;
   c   transparent;
   d   efficient;
   e   flexible.

5   If the income tax allows a tax credit for any money spent on some item, then there is said to be a

   a   tax subsidy;
   b   tax incidence;
   c   excise tax;
   d   tax burden;
   e   earned-income tax credit.

6   The marginal tax rate is the

   a   extra tax owed on an additional dollar of income;
   b   amount of tax expenditure on an additional dollar of income;
   c   amount of tax subsidy on an additional dollar of income;
   d   ratio of taxes to taxable income;
   e   tax rate at which the earned-income credit no longer applies.

7   The burden of a tax refers to

   a   how many people must pay it;
   b   how difficult it is to determine how much is paid;
   c   who really bears the burden of the tax, taking into account its economic repercussions;
   d   who actually sends the money to the tax authority;
   e   how much the tax distorts economic decisions.

8   An efficient tax system

   a   distorts economic decisions as little as possible;
   b   collects its revenue with as little additional cost to taxpayers as possible;
   c   is flexible;
   d   all of the above;
   e   a and b.

9   Which of the following is not an attribute of a good tax system?

   a   efficiency;
   b   vertical equity;
   c   horizontal equity;
   d   transparency.
   e   All of the above are attributes of good tax systems.

10   Which of the following is not an important issue in welfare reform?

   a   time limited welfare;
   b   job training;
   c   job search training;
   d   fostering responsibility by making parents provide financial support to their children.
   e   All of the above are important issues.

11   Which of the following is not a problem associated with public housing?

   a   reduced labor mobility;
   b   lower quality than that available in the private sector at similar cost;
   c   segregation of the poor;
   d   unequal treatment of families of similar size and income.
   e   all of the above are problems.

12   Assuming that labor supply is inelastic, the effect of the payroll tax is to

   a   reduce wages by the amount that the worker pays;
   b   reduce wages by the amount that the employer pays;
   c   reduce wages by the total amount of the tax regardless of who pays;
   d   leave wage unchanged;
   e   increase wages somewhat.

13   A subsidy that the tax system currently provides to low-wage workers is

   a   unemployment insurance;
   b   the earned-income tax credit;
   c   minimum wage laws;
   d   AFDC;
   e   b and d.

14 The AFDC program

   a is the same as the earned income tax credit;

   b only offers support to those laid off from their last job;

   c is a tax subsidy for low-wage workers;

   d provides support to single parent and other low-income families;

   e all of the above.

15 Social insurance programs in the United States

   a have no redistribution effect;

   b are purely redistributive;

   c provide insurance and also redistribute from higher- to lower-income households;

   d are financed by taxes that have disincentive effects;

   e c and d.

16 Government programs that redistribute income to the poor with money raised by taxes are examples of

   a the equity-efficiency trade-off;

   b middle class entitlements;

   c market failures;

   d consumer sovereignty;

   e none of the above.

17 Economists represent inequality using the

   a Lorenz curve;

   b Stigliz curve;

   c redistribution curve;

   d equity-efficiency trade-off;

   e market failure approach.

18 The Gini coefficient measures inequality by

   a the slope of the Lorenz curve;

   b twice the area between the Lorenz curve and the 45 degree line;

   c the area between the Lorenz curve and the 45 degree line;

   d one half the area between the Lorenz curve and the 45 degree line;

   e the curvature of the Lorenz curve.

19 The incidence of the payroll tax for Social Security almost surely falls

   a evenly between the employer and the employee;

   b entirely on the employee;

   c entirely on the employer;

   d on upper-income salaried workers;

   e on the self-employed.

20 The government's role in redistribution is primarily motivated by

   a market failure;

   b social values concerning those unable to sustain a minimum standard of living;

   c imperfect information;

   d distrust of consumer sovereignty;

   e noncompetitive markets.

Completion

1 The idea that individuals who are in identical situations should pay the same tax is called _____.

2 The idea that people who have more income or wealth should pay more tax is called _____.

3 A tax system in which individuals pay a larger fraction of income as income increases is called _____.

4 The term _____ refers to the revenue lost as a result of tax credits and deductions.

5 A good tax system has the characteristics of _____, which means that it is clear what each person is paying in taxes.

6 The tax owed on an additional dollar of income is the _____.

7 The _____ of a tax refers to who actually bears its economic burden.

8 Under the _____, low wage workers receive tax credits.

9 The _____ measures economic inequality as twice the area between the 45 degree line and the Lorenz curve.

10 The _____ shows the fraction of income earned by the poorest 10 percent, 20 percent, etc.

Answers to Self-Test

True or False

1	f	6	f	11	t
2	f	7	t	12	t
3	f	8	f	13	t
4	t	9	t	14	f
5	f	10	t	15	f

Multiple Choice

1	e	6	a	11	e	16	a
2	a	7	c	12	c	17	a
3	b	8	e	13	b	18	b
4	b	9	e	14	d	19	b
5	a	10	e	15	e	20	b

Completion

1 horizontal equity

2 vertical equity

3 progressive

4 tax expenditure

5 transparency

6 marginal tax rate

7 burden

8 earned-income tax credit

9 Gini coefficient

10 Lorenz curve

Doing Economics: Tools and Practice Problems

One nice way to measure inequality is with the Lorenz curve. It shows how the cumulative percentage of income (or wealth) varies with the population as we move up the income scale. Complete equality implies that the Lorenz curve is a 45 degree line. Tool Kit 22.1 shows how to plot it.

Tool Kit 22.1: Plotting the Lorenz Curve

The Lorenz curve is a convenient way to represent graphically the inequality in income (or any other economic variable). It shows what percentage of income is earned by the lowest 10 percent of the population, the lowest 20 percent, etc. Here is how to plot it.

Step one: Order the groups from lowest income to highest.

Step two: Make a table with headings as follows.

	Cumulative		Cumulative
%	%	%	%
Group population	population	income	income

Step three: Compute the percentage of income for each group, and enter in the table.

Step four: Compute the percentage of the population for each group, and enter in the table.

Step five: Compute the cumulative percentage of income for each group by adding its percentage to all percentages of the lower-income groups, and enter in the table.

Step six: Compute the cumulative percentage of the population for each group by adding its percentage to all percentages of the lower-income groups, and enter in the table.

Step seven: Draw coordinate axes. Label the horizontal one "Cumulative percentage of population" and the vertical one "Cumulative percentage of income."

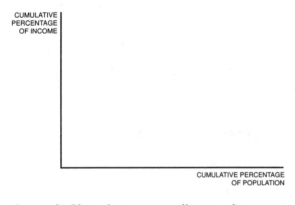

Step eight: Plot points corresponding to each group.

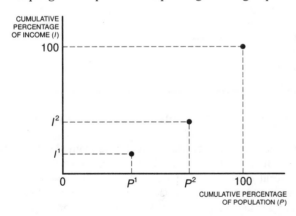

Step nine: Draw a curve connecting the points. This curve is the Lorenz curve.

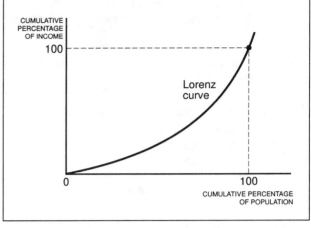

1   (Worked problem: Lorenz curve) In Costa Guano, there are four types of households: peasant farmers, ranchers, shopkeepers, and business owners. The population of each group (in millions) and the income (in U.S. dollar equivalent) of each are given in Table 22.1.

Table 22.1

Income	Population (millions)	
Peasant farmers	$ 5,000	40
Ranchers	$50,000	20
Shopkeepers	$10,000	30
Business owners	$80,000	10

Plot the Lorenz curve.

Step-by-step solution

Step one: Order the groups from lowest income to highest.

Peasant farmers	$ 5,000	40
Shopkeepers	$10,000	30
Ranchers	$50,000	20
Business owners	$80,000	10

Step two: Make a table.

Group	% population	Cumulative % population	% income	Cumulative % income
Peasant farmers				
Shopkeepers				
Ranchers				
Business owners				

Step three: Compute the percentage of income for each group, and enter in the table. For peasant farmers, it is {40 × $5,000/[(40 × $5,000) + (30 × $10,000) + (20 × $50,000) + (10 × $80,000)]} = 14 percent. The completed column is given in Table 22.2.

Step four: Compute the percentage of the population for each group, and enter in the table. For peasant farmers, it is 40/(40 + 30 + 20 + 10) = 40 percent. Continue, and complete the column, which is given in Table 22.2.

Table 22.2

Group	% population	Cumulative % population	% income	Cumulative % income
Peasant farmers	40		14	
Shopkeepers	30		21	
Ranchers	20		7	
Business owners	10		57	

Step five: Compute the cumulative percentage of income for each group by adding its percentages to all percentages of the lower-income groups, and enter in the table. For peasant farmers, it is simply 9 percent. For shopkeepers, it is 14 + 21 = 35 percent. Continue.

Step six: Compute the cumulative percentage of the population for each group by adding its percentage to all percentages of the lower income groups, and enter in the table. For peasant farmers, it is simply 40 percent. For shopkeepers, it is 40 + 30 = 70 percent. Continue. The complete information appears in Table 22.3.

Table 22.3

Group	% population	Cumulative % population	% income	Cumulative % income
Peasant farmers	40	40	14	14
Shopkeepers	30	70	21	35
Ranchers	20	90	7	42
Business owners	10	100	57	100

Step seven: Draw coordinate axes. Label the horizontal one "Cumulative percentage of population" and the vertical one "Cumulative percentage of the income."

Step eight: Plot points corresponding to each group.

Step nine: Draw a curve connecting the points. This curve is the Lorenz curve.

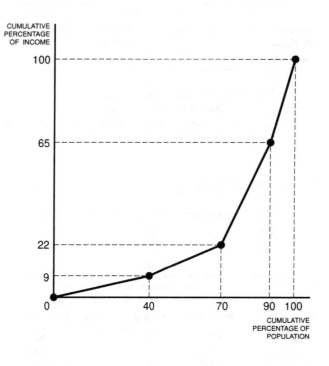

2   (Practice problem: Lorenz curve) Enormous State University is reconsidering the equity of its pay structure. The number of professors in each department and their salaries are given in Table 22.4.

Table 22.4

Department	Number of professors	Salary
Sociology	8	$50,000
Economics	10	$60,000
Marketing	2	$80,000
Literature	16	$30,000
Philosophy	4	$40,000

a   Plot the Lorenz curve.

b   An organization of faculty members proposes paying each professor $50,000. Plot the Lorenz curve for the faculty if this proposal were adopted.

c   What would the Lorenz curve look like if each professor were paid $80,000?

3   (Practice problem: Lorenz curve) Exurbia, a pleasant town outside Gotham City, is populated by factory workers, bureaucrats, professionals, and retirees. The number of each, their income, and wealth of each individual in the group are given in Table 22.5.

Table 22.5

Career	Number	Income	Wealth
Factory workers	100	$30,000	$ 30,000
Bureaucrats	100	$40,000	$ 40,000
Professionals	100	$80,000	$ 80,000
Retirees	100	$50,000	$350,000

a   Plot the Lorenz curve for income.

b   Plot the Lorenz curve for wealth.

c   Compare the two. Is there more inequality in income or in wealth?

Answers to Problems

2   a   The Lorenz curve appears in Table 22.6 and the diagram.

Table 22.6

Department	% population	Cumulative % population	% income	Cumulative % income
Literature	40	40	40	40
Philosophy	10	50	10	50
Sociology	20	70	20	70
Economics	25	95	25	95
Marketing	5	100	5	100

b   The complete information is given in Table 22.7. The Lorenz curve is the 45-degree line if there is equality.

Table 22.7

Department	% population	Cumulative % population	% income	Cumulative % income
Literature	40	40	40	40
Philosophy	10	50	10	50
Sociology	20	70	20	70
Economics	25	95	25	95
Marketing	5	100	5	100

c   The answer does not depend on the magnitude of income, only on its distribution. The answer is the same as for part b.

3   a   The Lorenz curve for income is given in Table 22.8 and the diagram.

Table 22.8

Career	% population	Cumulative % population	% income	Cumulative % income
Factory workers	25	25	15	15
Bureaucrats	25	50	20	35
Retirees	25	75	25	60
Professionals	25	100	40	100

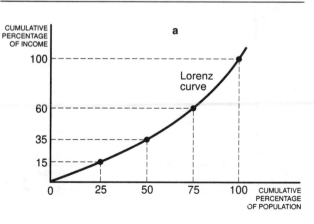

b   The Lorenz curve for wealth is given in Table 22.9 and the diagram.

Table 22.9

Career	% population	Cumulative % population	% income	Cumulative % income
Factory workers	25	25	6	6
Bureaucrats	25	50	8	14
Retirees	25	75	16	30
Professionals	25	100	70	100

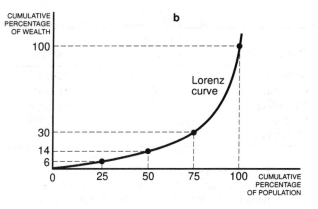

c   Wealth is distributed more unequally than income. The Lorenz curve for wealth is farther from the diagonal (45-degree line) than is the Lorenz curve for income.

Chapter 23

PUBLIC DECISION MAKING

Chapter Review

The economic theory of government, which is called public choice, fills this chapter. In previous chapters we have asked when and how government can improve the economy's resource allocation. Here, the subject concerns how actual governments allocate resources. The focus is on voting, lobbying, and the functioning of bureaucracies. Reasons why governments may fail to work efficiently are explored and decentralization within the federal system is discussed.

ESSENTIAL CONCEPTS

1 According to the economic approach, government is not a coordinated, benign decision-maker, but rather a collection of rational individuals playing a variety of roles. There are voters, candidates, interest groups, and bureaucrats. Economists focus on their choices and on the outcome of the political process.

2 An important way of making public decisions is majority voting. The **voting paradox** illustrates one problem: a majority of the electorate may not hold consistent views as to desirable policies. When it comes to such

matters as deciding how much to spend on fire protection, on the other hand, the median voter model demonstrates that government responds to the preferences of the voter who stands between equal numbers of voters desiring more spending or less spending.

3 The incentives concerning interest groups and bureaucrats may stand in the way of efficient public decisions. The **rent-seeking** activities of interest groups may lead to inefficient policies that benefit their members at the expense of the relatively poorly organized general electorate. Further, once a policy is set, there is the principal agent problem, which inhibits the ability to motivate bureaucrats to act in the public interest.

4 Although there are many examples of efficient government enterprises and helpful programs, government often allocates resources wastefully. Reasons for **public failures** include improper incentives attributable to the constraints of due process, inability to make long-term commitments, and political pressures. Also budgetary and spending problems such as soft budget constraints, the annual appropriations process, and inflexible cost containment restrictions like competitive bidding requirements undermine efficiency. Finally, there is the general problem of unintended consequences and unforeseen incentives and behavior brought about by the

interaction of government policy and the very complex economy.

5   The United States operates a **federal system** of government with functions and responsibilities divided among the various levels of government. The appropriate assignment of task balances the costs and benefits of decentralization. Arguing for a stronger federal government role are the externalities involved in local government decision making, national public goods, and the problem of the national income distribution. On the other side are some factors that argue for allocating functions to state and local government. These include local public goods, the diversity of preferences, and the possibility of experimenting with different solutions to common problems.

BEHIND THE ESSENTIAL CONCEPTS

1   It is important to understand what the voting paradox is and what is is not. It tells us that in certain circumstances majority voting may not be able to make consistent choices or even rank alternatives. This implies that even if all citizens are rational, when they act collectively, they may not be. The voting paradox does not say that every public decision is irrational or inconsistent.

2   One example of a situation where majority voting is consistent is when the decision concerns a single variable for which each individual voter has a preferred level and also favors alternatives closer to this level than others farther away. Examples include funding levels for local public goods such as parks and education. In these cases, the **median voter theory** says that public decisions will reflect the preferences of the median voter. Assuming that the median voter is consistent, public decisions will be consistent. (Nothing in the median voter theory implies that public decisions will be efficient, only that they will be consistent.)

3   The **free rider problem** helps us to understand why special interests may succeed in pushing inefficient programs. People have incentives to free ride when they can draw the benefits of some activity without paying. In smaller groups it is more difficult to avoid paying one's share. Therefore, relatively small groups may be able to lobby more forcefully than larger groups, where people can easily avoid contributing. As an example, consider the sugar quotas that limit the import of foreign sugar. This is surely an inefficient program. Why then do taxpayers not insist that it cease? The reason is that removing sugar quotas would give only a small benefit to any individual.

4   You can understand certain constraints placed on government decision making as imperfect solutions to larger problems. For example, due process constraints prohibit the arbitrary exercise of government power to seize assets. While this is undoubtedly a good thing, due process unfortunately limits the discretion of bureaucrats to tailor decisions to individual circumstances. Similarly, competitive bidding requirements help to minimize corruption in government procurement, but they mandate cumbersome and costly procedures. The government's ability to make long-term commitments does lead to inefficiencies, but it also limits the ability of current legislature from imposing undue burdens on future generations.

5   When you think about the federalism question—which tasks should be assigned to each level of government—you may relate it to the broad issue of decentralized decision making within organizations. As we have seen in other chapters, centralized decision making has the advantage of better coordination. Here, this relates to the ability of the federal government to account for externalities among local governments. On the other hand, decentralization leads to greater experimentation and innovation. Thus we can expect new ways of dealing with policy problems to originate in the U.S. states, which are sometimes called laboratories of democracy.

SELF-TEST

True or False

1   Economists focus on the voting behavior of rational individuals and on the public choices that are the outcome of the political process.

2   The voting paradox shows that majority vote cannot result in a determinate political outcome, and thus it argues for dictatorship.

3   The voting paradox states that political parties will advocate the alternative most preferred by the average voter.

4   Median voter theory shows that when there is a vote over a single issue, individuals have a most-preferred alternative and they vote for alternatives closer to it; the outcome of majority vote reflects the preferences of the median voter.

5   The median voter in a community is the person who earns the average income.

6   Rent seeking refers to activities and expenditures designed to secure special favors from government.

7   Due to the realities of the principal agent problem, public managers may not act in the interest of the electorate.

8   Public enterprises are always less efficient than their private counterparts.

9   Due process is designed to protect against arbitrary use of government's coercive powers.

10   The inability to make long-term commitments can undermine the efficiency of public agencies.

11   Soft budget constraints, the annual appropriations process, and rigid procurement rules constrain government budgetary and spending decisions.

12   Decentralization refers to the provision of government goods and services at the state or local level.

13   When there are externalities in the provision of state and local services, more decentralized decision-making is appropriate.

14   The distribution of income is an example of a local public good.

15   Decentralization allows for experimentation with different solutions to common problems.

Multiple Choice

1   In their study of public decision-making, economists focus on

   a   coalition formation;
   b   the media;
   c   voting behavior and the outcomes of the political process;
   d   biographies of great political leaders;
   e   all of the above.

2   The voting paradox refers to

   a   the tendency of democratic governments to make inconsistent choices;
   b   the reasons for market failure;
   c   the reasons for public failure;
   d   the principle that political parties gravitate toward the political center;
   e   the principal agent problem as applied to motivating bureaucrats.

3   Which of the following voting systems did Kenneth Arrow show to be troubled by potential inconsistencies?

   a   simple majority voting;
   b   weighted majority voting;
   c   two-thirds majority voting;
   d   three-fourths majority voting;
   e   all of the above.

4   Which of the following is not a characteristic of a public choice described by the median voter theory?

   a   The vote concerns a single variable.
   b   Individual voters have a most-preferred outcome.
   c   Voters vote for an alternative based on how close it is to their most-preferred outcome.
   d   Only two alternatives are considered.
   e   All of the above are characteristics of public choices described by the median voter theory.

5   On issues such as school finance, where people have different views about the desirable level of public support, the median voter theory predicts that the majority vote will result in

   a   inconsistent decisions;
   b   no money allocated to schools because everyone cannot agree;
   c   the preferences of the median voter determining the level of funding;
   d   property rights being reassigned;
   e   inefficient public decisions as a result of imperfect information.

6   Consider a majority vote to decide how much land to set aside for a local park. The median voter

   a   earns the average level of income;
   b   desires less park land than half of the voters, but also desires more park land than half of the voters;
   c   lives an average distance from the park;
   d   neither likes nor dislikes parks;
   e   is governed by the voting paradox.

7   Which of the following best describes the relationship between the voting paradox and the median voter theory?

   a   Political scientists believe in the voting paradox, but economists argue that median voter theory more closely describes public decision-making in a democracy.
   b   The median voter theory resolves the voting paradox.
   c   Inconsistencies in democratic decision-making are inevitable; therefore the median voter is an interesting, but incorrect description.
   d   Inconsistencies in democratic decision-making are not inevitable. The median voter theory explains one type of situation where choices are consistent.
   e   While economists once believed in the voting paradox, now they only use the median voter model to study public choices in a democracy.

8   Rents are

   a   moneys paid to landlords;
   b   returns enjoyed by a factor of production that go beyond those required to elicit its supply;
   c   political contributions;
   d   inefficient public decisions resulting from lobbying for special favors from government;
   e   activities, such as lobbying and political contributions, designed to promote the agenda of special interests.

9   Rent seeking refers to

   a   advertising by landlords;
   b   returns enjoyed by a factor of production that go beyond those required to elicit its supply;
   c   special favors from government, such as subsidies and protection from foreign competition;
   d   inefficient public decisions resulting from lobbying for special favors from government;
   e   activities, such as lobbying and political contributions, designed to promote the agenda of special interests.

10   Public managers may not actively pursue the agenda of the electorate because of the

   a   voting paradox;
   b   principal agent problem;
   c   free rider problem;
   d   race to the bottom;
   e   public choice theory.

11   Which of the following is not an example of the principal agent problem as it applies to the administration of government programs?

a   Bureaucrats may act in a risk-averse manner.
b   Public managers may seek to advance their careers by expanding their spheres of influence.
c   Special interests lobby politicians for favors, such as subsidies and protection from competition.
d   Performance of public administrators may be judged by how they conform to procedures.
e   All of the above are examples of the principal agent problem.

12   U.S. government farm policy

a   raises, but does not stabilize, prices of agricultural commodities;
b   stabilizes, but does not raise, prices of agricultural commodities;
c   both raises and stabilizes prices of agricultural commodities;
d   eliminates income risk for farmers;
e   leaves farming decisions to the market.

13   Which of the following contributes to the explanation of United States farm policy?

a   effective rent seeking by farm groups;
b   the ability of relatively small special interests to advance their agenda at the expense of the taxpayer and food consumer;
c   ineffective lobbying by groups representing consumers and taxpayers, due to the free rider problem;
d   all of the above;
e   none of the above.

14   Procedures developed to protect the public against arbitrary use of government power are called

a   due process;
b   soft budget constraints;
c   the law of unintended consequences;
d   rent seeking;
e   federalism.

15   The idea that public enterprises can make losses that are funded by taxpayer moneys is called

a   due process;
b   soft budget constraints;
c   the law of unintended consequences;
d   rent seeking;
e   the principal agent problem.

16   The concept of public failures refers to

a   inefficient decisions by government;
b   inefficient allocations of resources by market;
c   a socially unacceptable distribution of income;
d   the voting paradox;
e   the free rider problem.

17   When government subsidies increase demand and raise costs, it is an example of

a   soft budget constraints;
b   unintended consequences;
c   due process;
d   externalities;
e   market failure.

18   Which of the following are sources of government failure?

a   Due process regulations limit flexibility.
b   Governments have limited ability to make long-term commitments.
c   Expenditures are appropriated on an annual basis.
d   Rigid procurement rules impose excessive costs.
e   All of the above are sources of government failure.

19   Which of the following concerns argues for provision of government goods and services at the state or local level?

a   Some government activities are national public goods.
b   Some government activities generate externalities on neighboring jurisdictions.
c   States and localities can experiment with alternative solutions to common problems.
d   Left to itself, the market may not yield a socially acceptable distribution of income.
e   All of the above argue against provision at the local level.

20   Which of the following concerns argues against provision of government goods and services at the state or local level?

a   Some government activities are local public goods.
b   Left to itself, the market may not yield a socially acceptable distribution of income.
c   States and localities can experiment with alternative solutions to common problems.
d   Preferences and needs of communities may vary.
e   All of the above argue against provision at the local level.

Completion

1   The _____ illustrates the tendency for public decisions to be inconsistent.

2   _____ predicts that in certain cases public decisions will reflect the preferences of the voters whose most-preferred alternative lies in the middle of the distribution of voters, with an equal number of voters desiring more or less of the public good.

3   Activities, such as lobbying and political contributions, designed to secure tax breaks or subsidies are called _____.

4   The notion that the self-interest of public managers may not coincide with the will of the electorate is an example of the _____.

5   Procedures designed to limit the arbitrary use of government power are called _____.

6   Due to _____, government enterprises can suffer financial losses with the deficit funded out of government revenues.

7   Government education loan programs that gave strong incentives to declare bankruptcy are examples of

_____.

8 _____ refers to inefficient decisions by governments.

9 When local government programs create benefits and costs that extend to nonresidents, there are _____.

10 The _____ refers to the incentives that states and localities have to lower benefits to the poor and reduce their population of low-income people.

Answers to Self-Test

True or False

1	t	6	t	11	t
2	f	7	t	12	t
3	f	8	t	13	f
4	t	9	t	14	f
5	f	10	t	15	t

Multiple Choice

1	c	6	b	11	c	16	a
2	a	7	d	12	c	17	b
3	e	8	b	13	d	18	e
4	d	9	e	14	a	19	c
5	c	10	b	15	b	20	b

Completion

1 voting paradox
2 Median voter theory
3 rent seeking
4 principal agent problem
5 due process
6 soft budget constraints
7 unintended consequences
8 Public failures
9 externalities
10 race to the bottom

Doing Economics: Tools and Practice Problems

Public choice theory analyzes the voting behavior of rational individuals and the collective choices that result from the political process. Two important models are the voting paradox and the median voter theory. Together they show that majority voting sometimes, but not always, leads to a determinate outcome. Some problems explore these ideas.

VOTING PARADOX

The voting paradox can arise when people vote to choose among at least three alternatives. If the outcome of majority voting cannot provide a ranking or even pick out unambiguously the best alternative, it reveals a voting paradox. Of course, this may not always occur. Tool Kit 23.1 shows how to use the majority voting model to discover inconsistencies arising from the voting paradox.

Tool Kit 23.1: Finding the Voting Paradox

When at least three individuals must choose among at least three alternatives, the outcome of their majority vote may lead to inconsistencies. Follow this procedure to discover voting paradoxes.

Step one: Identify the alternatives, the voters, and their preferences.

Step two: Choose two alternatives and hold a majority election. Conclude that the winner is chosen over the loser.

Step three: Conduct similar majority votes for each pair of alternatives. (For three alternatives there will be three elections; four alternatives require six.)

Step four: Rank the alternatives on the basis of the outcome of the elections. If the alternative cannot be ranked unambiguously, there is a voting paradox.

---

1 (Worked problem: voting paradox) Alice, Bob, and Colleen are considering lunch at one of three local restaurants: Xerxes, Yellowfoot, and Zeke's. Their preferences are given in Table 23.1.

Table 23.1

Voter	Most preferred	Alternatives	
		Second best	Worst
Alice	Xerxes	Yellowfoot	Zeke's
Bob	Yellowfoot	Zeke's	Xerxes
Colleen	Zeke's	Xerxes	Yellowfoot

a Suppose that they decide by majority vote. Can they rank the three alternatives?

b Is there a most preferred alternative?

Step-by-step solution

Step one: Identify the alternatives (Xerxes, Yellowfoot, and Zeke's), the voters (Alice, Bob, and Colleen), and their preferences (given in the table).

Step two: Choose two alternatives and hold a majority vote election. Let's vote on Xerxes versus Yellowfoot. Alice votes for Xerxes. Bob votes for Yellowfoot. Colleen votes for Xerxes. Xerxes wins two to one; therefore Xerxes is preferred to Yellowfoot.

Step three: Conduct similar majority votes for every pair. Continuing as in step two, Yellowfoot is preferred to Zeke's (Alice and Bob vote for Yellowfoot, defeating Colleen, who votes for Zeke's). Finally, Zeke's wins a majority vote over Xerxes.

Step four: Rank the alternatives. The outcome of the vote is as follows. Xerxes is preferred to Yellowfoot. Yellowfoot is preferred to Zeke's. But Zeke's is preferred to Xerxes. There is an inconsistency, and there is no single most-preferred alternative. This is an example of the voting paradox.

2   (Practice problem: voting paradox) Representatives of the three dormitories at Enormous State University are meeting to vote on how to allocate the Trustee's Grant. There are three alternatives: library expansion, football scholarships, and campus beautification. The preferences are given in Table 23.2.

Table 23.2

Dormatory	Most preferred	Second best	Worst
North Towers	football	library	beautification
Shady Acres	library	football	beautification
Cement Block	library	beautification	football

a   Does majority voting give an unambiguous ranking of the three alternatives?

b   Does majority voting select a single best alternative?

3   (Practice problem: voting paradox) The city council consists of three voting members, who must decide among four alternative sources of funds to make up the budget shortfall. The alternatives are property tax increase, sales tax increase, a cut in recreation funding, and reduced payments into the retirement fund for retired city council members. Their preferences are given in Table 23.3.

Table 23.3

Member	First choice	Second	Third	Fourth
Hammer-mesh	property	sales	recreation	retirement
Menchik	sales	recreation	property	retirement
Davidson	recreation	property	sales	retirement

a   Does majority voting give an unambiguous ranking of the four alternatives?

b   Does majority voting select a single best alternative?

MEDIAN VOTER THEORY

Many elections, such as school bond issues, sales tax referenda, and funding for parks and recreation, involve the choice of a single variable: how much to spend or tax. Usually, voters will have a most-preferred alternative and will vote for the proposal closest to their liking. In this case median voter theory predicts that the outcome will reflect the preferences of the median voter, who is the one preferring the level in the middle of the distribution of voters. Half of the voters prefer more and half prefer less. This theory has been used extensively to analyze funding for local public goods and many other issues decided by local elections. Tool Kit 23.2 shows how to find the median voter and predict the outcome of majority voting.

Tool Kit 23.2: Using Median Voter Theory

When the vote concerns the magnitude of a single variable about which people have a most preferred level and always vote for alternatives closer to that level, the preferences of the median voter will determine the outcome. That is the majority vote will choose the level most preferred by the median voter.

Step one: Identify the variable subject to vote, the voters, and their most-preferred level.

Step two: Order the voters from highest to lowest according to their most-preferred level of the variable.

Step three: Find the median voter. This is the voter in the middle of the list constructed in step two. If there is an odd number of voters, there will be an equal number of voters preferring more than the median voter and an equal number preferring less.

Step four: Predict the outcome of the vote. According to median voter theory, it is the level preferred by the median voter found in step three. (If there is an even number of voters, then take an average of the two in the middle.)

---

4   (Worked problem: median voter theory) Grove City's school board is planning to ask the voters for a new bond issue. The voters and their preferred (per student) level of school funding are given in Table 23.4.

Table 23.4

Voter	Preferred funding
Kowalski	$5,000
Stokowski	$4,000
Litovsk	$3,500
Stanislav	$6,200
Jones	$8,000

a   Who is the median voter?

b   Find the outcome of the election according to the median voter theory.

Step-by-step solution

Step one: Identify the variable subject to vote, the voters, and their most preferred level. The variable is per student school funding. The voters and their preferred level are given above in Table 23.4.

Step two: Order the voters. From high to low, the ordering appears in Table 23.5.

Table 23.5

Voter	Preferred funding
Jones	$8,000
Stanislav	$6,200
Kowalski	$5,000
Stokowski	$4,000
Litovsk	$3,500

Step three: Find the median voter. He is Kowalski. Jones and Stanislav want more; an equal number of voters, Stokowski and Litovsk, want less.

Step four: Predict the outcome. Kowalski, the median voter, desires $5,000 per student. According to median voter theory the outcome will be $5,000 per student.

5   Suppose that four new voters move into Grove City. Their names and preferences are given in Table 23.6.

Table 23.6

Voter	Preferred funding
Cheong	$7,500
Davis	$8,000
Samuels	$7,000
Biddle	$8,000

a   Who is the median voter?
b   Find the outcome of the election according to the median voter theory.

6   Frightened of the recent surge in crime, voters in Pleasantville vow to increase the size of the police department. There are five voters, and their preferences and names are given in Table 23.7.

Table 23.7

Voter	Preferred number of police officers
Davis	1
Lee	1
Gaudin	2
Stevens	1
Mathews	4

a   Who is the median voter?
b   Find the outcome of the election according to the median voter theory.

Answers to Problems

2   *a*   Yes. Football is preferred to beautification. The library is preferred to football. The library is preferred to beautification. There is a ranking: library, football scholarships, campus beautification. In this case there is no voter's paradox.
    b   Yes. Library expansion is the most preferred alternative.

3   *a*   No. Property tax increase defeats sales tax increase; sales defeats recreation cut; recreation cut defeats property tax.
    b   No, there is no single best alternative.

5   *a*   Samuels is the median voter.
    b   The preferred funding is $7,000.

6   *a*   Davis, Lee, or Stevens is the median voter.
    b   The preferred number of officers is 1.

Part Five

Full-Employment Macroeconomics

Chapter 24

MACROECONOMIC GOALS AND MEASURES

Chapter Review

Macroeconomics is concerned with the characteristics of the economy as a whole. This chapter of the text introduces three central macroeconomic variables: the unemployment rate, the inflation rate, and gross domestic product, which is the standard measure of the economy's output. We learn how to measure each variable and discover how each is related to the major goals for the performance of the economy: full employment, price stability, and a high rate of economic growth.

ESSENTIAL CONCEPTS

1 Macroeconomics is concerned with the performance of the economy as a whole. The three important indicators—the level of **unemployment**, the **inflation rate**, and the rate of **economic growth**—are related to the three major markets. High unemployment occurs when demand does not equal supply in the labor market. When demand and supply in product markets are not consistent with a stable price level, there is inflation. Low growth results, in part, when the capital market does not allocate enough funds for investments.

2 The **gross domestic product**, or GDP, measures the output of the economy. It is the money value of the goods and services produced within a country in a year. Adjusting the number for inflation gives real GDP. The rate of increase in the real GDP is the primary measure of economic growth. Although the rate averaged around 3 percent per year from 1950 to 1973, it has fallen to about 1 percent per year since.

3 **Potential GDP** measures what the economy could produce if labor and machines were fully employed. The economy fluctuates, producing below potential GDP in the trough of recession and sometimes exceeding it during the peaks of booms. The ups and downs of the economy are sometimes called the **business cycle**, but the actual path of the economy is not regular.

4 GDP can be measured in three equivalent ways. The **final goods approach** computes the market value of goods sold to their ultimate consumers. The **value-added approach** adds up the additional market value created at each step in the process from production to market. The **income approach** adds the total income received by all individuals and profits retained by firms. Another important measure is **net domestic product**, which subtracts depreciation from the GDP.

5   The **labor force** includes those individuals who are either employed or actively seeking employment. The fraction of the labor force that is without work is called the **unemployment rate.** Unemployment is a persistent phenomenon in the United States: from 5.5 to 7.4 percent of the labor force was unemployed in the early 1990s. This represents an enormous waste of resources, and it can be devastating personally for the unemployed and also for communities with high unemployment.

6   Economists distinguish among four types of unemployment. **Seasonal unemployment** occurs when the jobs are available for only part of the year. People who are between jobs make up **frictional unemployment.** **Structural unemployment**, which is more long-term, arises because the skills of the current labor force do not match the skills required by the available jobs. Finally, **cyclical unemployment** is due to a slowdown in the overall level of economic activity. One of the important tasks of macroeconomics is to understand and reduce cyclical unemployment.

7   The **inflation rate** is the rate of increase in the general level of prices. It is measured using **price indices** such as the consumer price index, or CPI. The annual percentage change in the CPI indicates the increase in the cost of living from one year to the next. Inflation ranged from 3 to 6 percent in the 1980s. Inflation hurts people on fixed incomes because it erodes their purchasing power. When variable, inflation makes borrowing and lending riskier, and it is generally disruptive of the economy.

BEHIND THE ESSENTIAL CONCEPTS

1   If you have a job or are looking for one, then economists count you as a member of the labor force. The unemployment rate is the fraction of the labor force that does not have a job. But the unemployment rate may not measure how hard it is to find work, for several reasons. First, you would be counted as unemployed even if you were only claiming to look for work in order to be eligible for unemployment insurance, or if you were holding out for an unrealistic offer. On the other hand, if, during a recession, you realistically gave up hope of finding a job and stopped looking, you would not be counted as unemployed, but rather as out of the labor force. A **discouraged worker** would be part of the usual decline in the **labor force participation rate** during recessions.

2   Economists use the price index, which is constructed by comparing the cost of a particular basket of goods in different years, to measure inflation. The consumer price index measures your cost of living only if you consume exactly what is in the market basket. It also gives an inexact measure of quality changes and sometimes underestimates the importance of sale items.

3   Similarly, GDP does not quite measure all the output in the economy. It ignores nonmarketed goods, such as the services of unpaid spouses, and it can only be adjusted imperfectly to capture changes in the quality of goods and the value of nonmarketed government services.

SELF-TEST

True or False

1   Productivity refers to output per capita.

2   The gross domestic product measures the money value of goods and services produced within a country during a specific time period.

3   Nominal GDP is real GDP adjusted for inflation.

4   Gross domestic product is the sum of comsumption, investment, government expenditures, and net exports.

5   There are three equally valid ways to compute gross domestic product: final goods, value added, and income.

6   Value added is computed by subtracting a firm's purchases of inputs from its revenues.

7   The unemployment rate measures the percentage of the working-age population that is unemployed.

8   The labor force includes the entire working-age population.

9   Structural unemployment includes those unemployed who have skills that do not match the skills required for currently available jobs.

10 When the economy is on an upswing, cyclical unemployment declines.

11 The price index for the base year equals 100.

12 The wholesale price index is based upon a market basket of goods sold by wholesalers to retailers.

13 The producer price index is based upon a market basket of goods sold by wholesalers to producers.

14 Inflation reduces the purchasing power of people living on fixed incomes.

15 Variable rates of inflation increase the riskiness of borrowing and lending.

Multiple Choice

1   Which of the following is *not* an important macroeconomic goal?

   a   price stability;
   b   full employment;
   c   perfect competition;
   d   rapid growth;
   e   All of the above are important macroeconomic goals.

2   The money value of all goods and services produced within a country in a year is the

   a   gross national product;
   b   gross domestic product;

c   net domestic product;

d   depreciation index;

e   producer price index.

3   Inflation-adjusted gross domestic product is called

a   gross nation product;

b   net domestic product;

c   nominal gross domestic product;

d   real gross domestic product;

e   nominal gross national product.

4   If the price level has risen recently, then the real GDP is

a   greater than the nominal GDP;

b   less than the nominal GDP;

c   equal to the nominal GDP;

d   greater than the GNP;

e   less than the GNP.

5   During recessions, the GDP

a   is less than potential GDP;

b   is greater than potential GDP;

c   is equal to potential GDP;

d   bears no predictable relationship to potential GDP;

e   rises at a decreasing rate.

6   The final goods approach to GDP

a   adds the differences between the revenues and costs of intermediate goods;

b   adds all income received by individuals and governments in the economy;

c   subtracts the inflation rate from the nominal GDP;

d   adds the value of goods, services, and the environment;

e   adds the total money value of goods and services purchased by their ultimate users.

7   The value-added approach to GDP

a   adds the differences between the revenues and costs of intermediate goods;

b   adds all income received by individuals and governments in the economy;

c   substracts the inflation rate from the nominal GDP;

d   adds the value of goods, services, and the environment;

e   adds the total money value of goods and services purchased by their ultimate users.

8   Gross domestic product divided by the number of hours worked equals

a   net domestic product;

b   real GNP;

c   real GDP;

d   productivity;

e   NDP.

9   The total labor force comprises

a   all individuals of working age who are employed;

b   all individuals of working age who are unemployed;

c   all individuals of working age;

d   all heads of households;

e   all individuals of working age who are either employed or unemployed.

10   The costs of unemployment include

a   underutilization of the economy's resources;

b   personal difficulties for unemployed individuals;

c   financial troubles for communities with high unemployment;

d   exacerbated racial and ethnic divisions;

e   all of the above.

11   The unemployment rate is the ratio of the number of unemployed to the

a   number of employed;

b   total labor force;

c   inflation rate;

d   gross domestic product;

e   adult working-age population.

12   The Department of Labor survey probably

a   underestimates the true unemployment rate in that some discouraged workers have given up hope of finding a job;

b   overestimates the true unemployment rate in that some discouraged workers have given up hope of finding a job;

c   underestimates the true unemployment rate in that some individuals who respond that they are actively seeking work are not;

d   overestimates the true unemployment rate in that some individuals who respond that they are actively seeking work are not;

e   a and d.

13   Those individuals who are unemployed because they work in seasonal jobs comprise

a   seasonal unemployment;

b   frictional unemployment;

c   structural unemployment;

d   cyclical unemployment;

e   discouraged-worker unemployment.

14   Those individuals who are temporarily between jobs make up

a   seasonal unemployment;

b   frictional unemployment;

c   structural unemployment;

d   cyclical unemployment;

e   discouraged-worker unemployment.

15   When the skills required by available jobs are not the same as the skills of the unemployed, there is

a   seasonal unemployment;

b   frictional unemployment;

c   structural unemployment;

d   cyclical unemployment;

e   discouraged-worker unemployment.

16   In recessions, the level of economic activity declines and there is an increase in

a   seasonal unemployment;

b   frictional unemployment;

c   structural unemployment;
d   cyclical unemployment;
e   discouraged-worker unemployment.

17   If prices and wages rise at the same rate, the purchasing power of typical workers

a   increases;
b   decreases;
c   remains the same;
d   doubles;
e   falls to zero.

18   When the inflation rate rises and falls unpredictably,

a   lenders gain at the expense of borrowers;
b   borrowers gain at the expense of lenders;
c   there is no appreciable impact on borrowing and lending;
d   borrowing and lending become riskier;
e   lending increases, but borrowing falls.

19   The producer price index includes in its market basket a representative bundle of goods

a   purchased by consumers;
b   sold by wholesalers to retailers;
c   sold by producers to wholesalers;
d   purchased by government;
e   sold by wholesalers to consumers.

20   The price index used to calculate the real gross domestic product is

a   the consumer price index;
b   the producer price index;
c   the weighted average of the producer and consumer price indices;
d   the GDP deflator;
e   an index of raw material prices.

Completion

1   The money value of all final goods and services produced within the country in a year is called the

_____.

2   Dividing nominal GDP by the price level gives

_____.

3   The measure of what the economy could produce given normal levels of frictional unemployment and idle productive capacity is called _____.

4   A firm's revenues minus the cost of intermediate goods equal its _____.

5   _____ is calculated by dividing GDP by the number of hours worked.

6   The unemployment rate is the ratio of the number of unemployed to the _____.

7   People who are temporarily between jobs comprise part of _____ unemployment.

8   _____ unemployment is due to a mismatch between the skills of those without jobs and the skills needed to perform the available jobs.

9   _____ unemployment rises in recession and falls in booms.

10   The percentage increase in the price level from one year to the next is called the _____.

Answers to Self-Test

True or False

1	t	6	t	11	t
2	t	7	f	12	t
3	f	8	f	13	f
4	t	9	t	14	t
5	t	10	t	15	t

Multiple Choice

1	c	6	e	11	b	16	d
2	b	7	a	12	e	17	c
3	d	8	d	13	a	18	d
4	b	9	e	14	b	19	b
5	a	10	e	15	c	20	d

Completion

1   gross domestic product
2   real GDP
3   potential GDP
4   value added
5   Productivity
6   labor force
7   frictional
8   Structural
9   Cyclical
10   inflation rate

Doing Economics: Tools and Practice Problems

In this section, we will explore how economists measure economic performance. After learning how to calculate the rate of inflation, we use this technique to construct the price index and to distinguish real and nominal GDP. Finally, we calculate GDP by the final goods, value-added, and income approaches, verifying that the three techniques give equivalent answers. Although the examples are simplified, you should realize that the government agencies responsible for computing inflation and GDP perform their calculations in the same way.

Inflation

Inflation refers to a general increase in the price level. It is calculated by computing the increase in the cost of purchasing a fixed market basket of goods. The United States government has several inflation measures, including the consumer price index, the producer price index, and the GDP deflator. In these problems we focus on the computation of the consumer price index (CPI). Tool Kit 24.1 shows how it is done.

Tool Kit 24.1: Calculating the Inflation Rate

The inflation rate is the percentage increase in the cost of purchasing a predetermined basket of goods. Follow this procedure to calculate the inflation rate.

Step one: Identify the quantities of each good in the market basket:

quantity of good 1 =

quantity of good 2 =

quantity of good 3 =

Step two: Calculate the cost of purchasing the quantities in the market basket at year 1 prices:

(quantity of good 1 × price in year 1)

+ (quantity of good 2 × price in year 1)

+ (quantity of good 3 × price in year 1)

= cost of living at year 1 prices.

Step three: Calculate the cost of purchasing the quantities in the market basket at year 2 prices:

(quantity of good 1 × price in year 2)

+ (quantity of good 2 × price in year 2)

+ (quantity of good 3 × price in year 2)

= cost of living at year 2 prices.

Step Four: Find the percentage change in the two costs of living by using the following formula:

$$\left[\left(\frac{\text{cost of living at year 2 prices}}{\text{cost of living at year 1 prices}} \right) - 1 \right] \times 100 = \text{inflation rate}.$$

1 (Worked problem: inflation rate) There are three goods consumed in Euthanasia: fast cars, parachute jumps, and hang gliders. The prices and quantities for each in 1990 and the prices in 1991 are given below.

Goods	1990 Prices	Quantities	1991 Prices
Fast cars	$20,000	20	$30,000
Parachute jumps	$ 100	2,500	$ 80
Hang gliders	$ 500	400	$ 800

The market basket comprises the 1990 quantities. Calculate the inflation rate.

Step-by-step solution:

Step one: Identify the quantities in the market basket. There are 20 fast cars, 2,500 parachute jumps, and 400 hang gliders.

Step two: Calculate the cost of purchasing the market basket at 1990 prices:

($20,000 × 20) + ($100 × 2,500) + ($500 × 400) = $850,000.

Step three: Calculate the cost of purchasing the market basket at 1991 prices:

($30,000 × 20) × ($80 × 2,500) + ($800 × 400) = $1,120,000.

Step four: Find the percentage change:

($1,120,000/$850,000 – 1) × 100 = 32 percent.

The inflation rate is 32 percent.

2 (Practice problem: inflation rate) In order to determine how to adjust stipends for disabled workers, the Paper Profits Company wants to compute the inflation rate. It has identified a market basket for stipend recipients. This is given below, along with the prices in 1980 (the year of the last adjustment) and in 1990.

Good or service	Quantity	1980 Prices	1990 Prices
Prepared meals	7	$ 5	$ 6
Housecleaning	1	$25	$30
Physical therapy	3	$50	$75
Compact discs	4	$10	$10

Compute the inflation rate.

3 (Practice problem: inflation rate) A recent graduate of Enormous State University, Lamont has dozens of job offers. He has narrowed his search to jobs in two cities: Gotham and Smallville. In order to compare the offers, he must compute the relative cost of living in the two cities. His market basket and prices are given below.

Good or service	Quantity	Gotham price	Smallville price
2-bedroom apartment	1	$1,500	$300
Pickup truck	1	$ 600	$400
Meals	90	$ 10	$ 5

How much more expensive (in percent) is the cost of living in Gotham than in Smallville?

Inflation Adjustment

The distinction between real and nominal values is essential in macroeconomics. Real values are adjusted for inflation; that is, they measure what would have occurred if the dollar maintained its purchasing power. While the technique is appropriate for any dollar value, in these problems we focus on adjusting nominal GDP. Tool Kit 24.2 shows how to adjust for inflation.

Tool Kit 24.2: Adjusting for Inflation

The money value of all goods and services purchased during a year is the nominal GDP. To get a better idea of how actual output changes from year to year, it is important to adjust this number for inflation. Real GDP is nominal GDP adjusted for inflation, and it gives the value of output measured in base year dollars. Follow this procedure to calculate real GDP.

Step one: Calculate this year's price index. Multiply last year's price index by 1 plus the inflation rate:

last year's price index × (1 + inflation rate)
= current year's price index.

Step two: Calculate this year's real GDP. Divide current nominal GDP by the price index and multiply by 100. The result is current real GDP expressed in base year dollars. (To express real GDP in any other year's dollars, simply multiply by the price index in the desired year and divide by 100.)

(nominal GDP/price index) × 100 = real GDP.

---

4   (Worked problem: adjusting for inflation) The nominal GDP in Monrovia was $2 billion during 1992. The price index for 1991 was 210, and 1992 saw an inflation rate of 30 percent.

  a   Calculate the price index in 1992.
  b   Calculate real GDP for 1992. Express it in base year dollars.
  c   Express real GDP in 1991 dollars.

Step-by-step solution

Step one (a): Calculate the price index for the current year (1992). The price index for 1991 was 210. The inflation rate was 30 percent. The price index for 1992 is

210 × 1.30 = 273.

Step two (b): Calculate this year's real GDP. The current nominal GDP is $2 billion. The 1992 real GDP is

($2 billion/273) × 100 = $732.6 million.

Step three (c): Real GDP in 1991 dollars is

($732.6 × 210)/100 = $1,538 million.

5   (Practice problem: adjusting for inflation) Suppose that the nominal GDP in 1992 is $4 trillion, the 1991 price index is 352, and the 1992 inflation rate is 95 percent.

  a   Calculate the price index in 1992.
  b   Calculate real GDP for 1992. Express it in base year dollars.
  c   Express real GDP in 1991 dollars.

6   (Practice problem: adjusting for inflation) Suppose that sales of new homes total $30 billion in 1992. The 1992 price index is 222. Express the total sales of new homes in base year dollars.

Gross Domestic Product

The market value of all goods and services produced in a year is the gross domestic product. In the macroeconomics section of this book, when we measure the economy's output we will be looking at GDP. It is very important to realize that GDP equals national income; thus it can also be measured by adding all income earned in the economy. Finally, the value added at each step along the production chain gives another equivalent approach to calculating GDP. Tool Kit 24.3 shows how to calculate GDP.

Tool Kit 24.3: Calculating GDP

Gross domestic product is the money value of all goods and services as purchased by their ultimate users. It can be calculated by adding the money value of all final products, by summing the values added by all firms, or by adding the incomes received by all individuals.

Final goods approach

Step one: Determine which goods are purchased by their ultimate users.

Step two: Add the money values (price × quantity) of these goods:

GDP = money value of good 1 +
    money value of good 2 + . . .

Value-added approach

Step one: For each firm, compute the value added by subtracting any payments to other firms from its receipts:

value added = receipts − purchases from other firms.

Step two: Sum the values added of each firm:

GDP = value added at firm 1 +
    value added at firm 2 + . . .

Income approach

Step one: Find the total wages, total dividends, total interest, and any other form of income for all individuals in the economy.

Step two: Add the totals of each kind of income:

GDP = wages + dividends + interest.

---

7   (Worked problem: calculating GDP) Suppose that the economy produces three goods: wheat, flour, and bread. All of the wheat is sold to millers. All of the flour is sold to bakers. Consumers buy the bread from the bakers. The income and expenditure accounts for each of the three industries are given in Table 24.1.

Table 24.1

	Expenditures (billions)	Receipts (billions)
Wheat industry		
Wages	$ 40	$ 50
Dividends	$ 0	
Interest	$ 10	
Flour industry		
Wages	$ 30	$110
Purchases of wheat	$ 50	
Dividends	$ 15	
Interest	$ 15	
Bread industry		
Wages	$ 60	$200
Purchases of flour	$110	
Dividends	$ 30	
Interest	$ 0	

a Calculate (nominal) GDP using the final goods approach.

b Calculate (nominal) GDP using the value-added approach.

c Calculate (nominal) GDP using the income approach.

d Compare the three answers.

Step-by-step solution

Step one (a): Determine which goods are purchased by their ultimate users. Only bread is a final output.

Step two: Add the money value of these goods. The value of bread is $200. The GDP thus equals $200.

Step three (b): Find the value added for each firm or industry.

Value added in wheat = $50 – $0 = $50;
value added in flour = $110 – $50 = $60;
value added in bread = $200 – $110 = $90.

Step four: Sum the value-added numbers.

GDP = $50 + $60 + $90 = $200.

Step five (c): Find the total wages, dividends, and interest.

Total wages = $40 + $30 + $60 = $130;
total dividends = $0 + $15 + $30 = $45;
total interest = $10 + $15 + $0 = $25.

Step six: Add the totals of each income type.

GDP = $130 + $45 + $25 = $200.

Step seven (d): Compare. Note that the GDP equals $200 billion according to each method.

8 (Practice problem: calculating GDP) The economy of Literaria cuts down trees in order to make paper and uses all its paper for books. The expenditure and income accounts for each of the three industries are given in Table 24.2.

Table 24.2

	Expenditures (billions)	Receipts (billions)
Tree industry		
Wages	$ 80	$100
Dividends	$ 20	
Interest	$ 0	
Paper industry		
Wages	$100	$250
Purchases of trees	$100	
Dividends	$ 40	
Interest	$ 10	
Book industry		
Wages	$150	$500
Purchases of paper	$250	
Dividends	$ 50	
Interest	$ 50	

a Calculate (nominal) GDP using the final goods approach.

b Calculate (nominal) GDP using the value-added approach.

c Calculate (nominal) GDP using the income approach.

d Compare the three answers.

9 (Practice problem: calculating GDP) in Computavia, they produce chips, all of which are used in the production of computer hardware. Half of the hardware is purchased by consumers, and half is sold to the software industry. Consumers purchase all of the software. The expenditure and income accounts for each of the three industries are given in Table 24.3.

Table 24.3

	Expenditures (billions)	Receipts (billions)
Chip industry		
Wages	$ 600	$1,000
Dividends	$ 400	
Interest	$ 0	
Hardware industry		
Wages	$ 600	$2,000
Purchases of chips	$1,000	
Dividends	$ 200	
Interest	$ 200	
Software industry		
Wages	$ 600	$2,000
Purchases of hardware	$1,000	
Dividends	$ 0	
Interest	$ 400	

a Calculate (nominal) GDP using the final goods approach.

b Calculate (nominal) GDP using the value-added approach.

c Calculate (nominal) GDP using the income approach.

d Compare the three answers.

Answers to Problems

2 [(42 + 30 + 225 + 40)/(35 + 25 + 150 + 40)] – 1] × 100 = 30 percent.

3 [(1,500 + 600 + 900)/(300 + 400 + 450)] – 1] × 100 = 161 percent.

5 *a* 1992 price index = 352 × 1.95 = 686.4.

   b 1992 real GDP (base year dollars) = (4/686.4) × 100 = $0.58 trillion.

   c 1992 real GDP (1991 dollars) = (0.58 × 352)/100 = $2.042 trillion.

6 (30/222) × 100 = $14 billion.

8 *a* $500 (books).

   b Value added in tree industry = $100 – 0 = $100;

       value added in paper industry = $250 – $100 = $150;

       value added in book industry = $500 – $250 = $250;

       total value added = $100 + $150 + $250 = $500.

   c Wages = $80 + $100 + $150 = $330;

       dividends = $20 + $40 + $50 = $110;

       interest = $0 + $10 + $50 = $60;

       total income = $330 + $110 + $60 = $500.

   d Each answer is $500, which is the GDP.

9 *a* Hardware purchased by consumers = $2,000/2 = $1,000;

       software purchased by consumers = $2,000;

       total final goods = $1,000 + $2,000 = $3,000.

   b Value added in chip industry = $1,000 – $0 = $1,000;

       value added in hardware industry = $2,000 – $1,000 = $1,000;

       value added in software industry = $2,000 – $1,000 = $1,000;

       total value added = $1,000 + $1,000 + $1,000 = $3,000.

   c Wages = $600 + $600 + $600 = $1,800;

       dividends = $400 + $200 + $0 = $600;

       interest = $0 + $200 + $400 = $600;

       total income = $1,800 + $600 + $600 = $3,000.

   d Each answer is $3,000, which is the GDP.

Chapter 25

THE FULL-EMPLOYMENT MODEL

Chapter Review

The full-employment model describes the performance of the economy in the long run, after prices and wages have had time to adjust. Equilibrium in the product, labor, and capital markets combines with a balance in international transactions to bring the economy to full-employment production at the level of its productive capacity or potential GDP. This chapter lays out the essentials of the model, and the following one delves into several of its uses.

ESSENTIAL CONCEPTS

1   This chapter's model is the basic competitive model in which households and firms interact in product, labor, and capital markets. Households supply labor to firms for use in producing goods, and they provide savings that finance firms' investments in plant and equipment. Receiving their wages, interest, and dividends, households purchase the goods in the product market. Wages, interest rates, and product prices adjust to equate supply and demand in each market. The markets are interdependent in the sense that what occurs in any one market affects each of the others.

2   The labor market governs job creation and employment. The demand for labor depends on the productivity of workers, and it slopes downward because as the real wage falls, firms hire labor to substitute for capital and to produce additional output. Households determine their supply of labor, which is assumed to be inelastic. As shown in Figure 25.1, the real wage adjusts to the level at which demand and supply are equal. An in-

Figure 25.1

crease in labor supply shifts the supply curve to the right, increasing employment and reducing the real wage. An increase in the demand for labor (due to improved technology or additional investment) shifts demand to the right, bidding up wages.

3 The capacity of the economy, also called its **potential gross domestic product** or **full-employment output**, depends upon the available technology, its stock of capital, and the supply of labor. With a given capital stock and technology, the **short-run production function** shows how potential output varies with different quantities of labor. Figure 25.2 illustrates the short-run production function and its property of diminishing returns. It is related to the aggregate supply curve shown in Figure 25.3. Notice that aggregate supply does not depend upon product price. An increase in labor supply represents a movement along the short-run production function and a rightward shift in aggregate supply. An increase in the capital stock or a technological advance also shifts aggregate supply to the right.

4 **Aggregate demand** includes consumption, investment, government expenditures, and net exports. It slopes downward as shown in Figure 25.3, chiefly because as the price level falls, the real value of money and other dollar denominated assets rises and people consume more. In equilibrium the price level adjusts to the inter-

section of aggregate demand and aggregate supply, and output equals its full-employment level.

5 The savings of households depend upon their disposable income and interest rates. Panel A of Figure 25.4 shows the supply of funds sloping slightly upward; Panel B shows it as vertical. The demand for funds, also called the investment function, results from firms' intentions to invest in plant and capital equipment. It depends upon their expectations of future profitability and the real interest rate. In equilibrium savings equals investment. A rightward shift in investment raises the interest rate. It increases investment only if the supply of funds is elastic (Panel A).

Figure 25.4

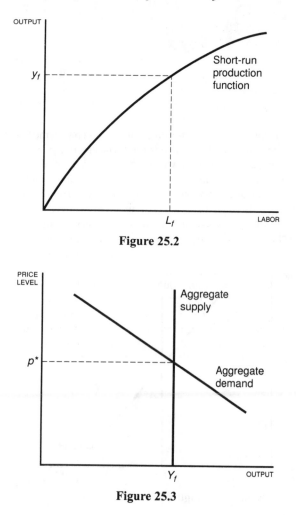

Figure 25.2

Figure 25.3

6 In the economy's general equilibrium all markets clear. There is full employment because the real wage adjusts to bring the demand for labor equal to the supply. At the equilibrium price level aggregate demand equals aggregate supply in the product market, and the economy produces its potential GDP. Finally, the real interest rate finds its equilibrium level where savings equal investment.

7 The general equilibrium model provides a coherent way to view the effects of various changes as they work their way through the three markets. Here are some examples.

a The introduction of personal computers raises the productivity of workers, shifting demand for labor to the right and increasing real wages. In the product market this new technology manifests itself as a rightward shift in aggregate supply. A look at the capital market shows an increase in savings (because households have more income) and an increase in investment.

b   Government expenditures and taxation affect the composition of output. An equal increase in spending and taxes reduces savings and drives up the interest rate. The economy's aggregate supply will not shift, but it will comprise less consumption and investment, offsetting the extra government spending.

c   When the economy is at full employment, money is neutral. This means that an increase in the supply of money shifts aggregate demand to the right, increasing the price level, but the real wage, real interest rate, real output, and real investment remain unchanged.

8   Trade affects the goods market because net exports is one of the four components of aggregate demand, and affects the capital market because foreign households provide an additional source of funds. In a **small open economy**, such as Switzerland, the real interest rate is fixed (determined on international capital markets); therefore any change in domestic savings cannot affect investment. The United States is a large open economy, and its size means that changes in U.S. savings affect interest rates and investment. Also, the world capital market is not fully integrated, a fact that makes investment quite sensitive to changes in U.S. savings.

BEHIND THE ESSENTIAL CONCEPTS

1   While the basic competitive model employed in this chapter is the same basic competitive model studied in microeconomics, there is a difference in interpretation. In macroeconomics we study the behavior or aggregates: total output, total employment, the price level, and so on. We proceed as if all firms produced a single good and as if there were only one kind of labor. This simplification directs attention away from the complexity of the economy and allows us to see the major forces involved in the movements of broad measures of economic performance.

2   Remember that the real wage refers to the amount of goods that an hour of work will buy. When you decide to take a part time job, you focus on what your earnings will allow you to purchase, not simply on the dollars. Similarly, in the capital market the real interest rate governs savings and investment decisions. Households put aside funds in order to consume additional goods at some future date. It is the real increase in purchasing power that motivates savings. The price level, on the other hand, is the nominal price level. Aggregate demand affects this price level, but because aggregate supply is vertical, the economy's output is not affected by aggregated demand. Shifts in aggregate demand, whether brought about by changes in the money supply or anything else, affect only the price level, leaving real

wages, real interest rates, real investment, and output unchanged. This is an essential feature of the full-employment economy.

3   When the price of pancakes falls, people consume more pancakes. They substitute pancakes for scrambled eggs, cereal, or other breakfast foods. When the price level falls, however, there is no comparable opportunity to substitute. Why then does aggregate demand slope down? The answer has to do with households' wealth. A fall in the price level makes your cash worth more. The same number of dollars now buys more goods. When you experience an increase in wealth, you spend some. The same is true of any asset (such as a government bond) that is not indexed for inflation. A lower price level means greater real wealth and more consumption.

4   When the interest rate rises, you have an incentive to save more. The reason is, of course, that a given amount of savings results in more goods in the future. This idea is called the **substitution effect**: at higher interest rates people save more, in effect substituting future for current consumption. Why is the supply of funds so insensitive to changes in the interest rate? The reason is the other factor, the **income effect**. As the interest rate increases, savers have more lifetime wealth. As we have seen, when people experience an increase in wealth, they increase their consumption. This extra consumption means that savings must fall. This income effect counteracts the substitution effect, leaving the supply of funds almost inelastic.

5   In competitive markets firms are price takers. The usual reason is that they are too small relative to the market to affect the price. Any barley farmer who tried to charge above market prices would find no customers. Charging less simply gives away profits for no gain. It is the same with countries in the international capital market. A small country, such as Belgium, Botswana, or Paraguay, simply does not borrow or lend enough funds to affect world interest rates.

6   Study the structure of the full-employment model with care. The basic division of the economy into the three markets and the channels through which the markets affect each other are constants in macroeconomics. Later in the book, we look at unemployment macroeconomics, where prices are first rigid and then adjust slowly. Although these other models have quite different implications, their basic structures mirror the one studied in this chapter. Furthermore, it is important that you understand them in terms of their difference with the full-employment model. If you think about it, it is "economical" to learn one model well and to use that knowledge as a base for learning the others.

SELF-TEST

True or False

1   In the basic competitive model all markets are interdependent.

2   Macroeconomics focuses on the behavior of aggregate measures such as total employment.

3   An increase in the supply of labor causes the real wage to increase.

4   Like most supply curves, aggregate supply slopes upward.

5   The full-employment level of output is the same as potential GDP.

6   The short-run production function exhibits diminishing returns.

7   When the interest rate rises, the income effect motivates savers to increase their savings.

8   The investment function refers to financial investment.

9   In general equilibrium all markets clear.

10 Computerization in industry will cause the supply of labor to shift to the left.

11 An equal increase in government spending and taxation will reduce private investment and consumption.

12 The neutrality of money in the full-employment economy means that an increase in the supply of money increases the price level but has no real effects on output, employment, or investment.

13 In a small, open economy interest rates are fixed because they are determined on international capital markets.

14 The United States is a small, open economy.

15 Most economists agree that money is neutral when the economy is at full employment.

Multiple Choice

1   In the labor market

   a   households supply labor;
   b   the real wage adjusts to clear the market;
   c   firms use the labor supplied by households to produce output;
   d   labor supply is assumed to be inelastic;
   e   all of the above.

2   An increase in the supply of labor causes

   a   an increase in both the real wage and employment;
   b   a decrease in both the real wage and employment;
   c   an increase in the real wage and a decrease in employment;
   d   a decrease in the real wage and an increase in employment;
   e   no change in the real wage because supply is assumed to be inelastic.

3   An increase in investment most likely will shift

   a   the demand for labor to the right;
   b   the supply of labor to the right;
   c   the demand for labor to the left;
   d   the supply of labor to the left;
   e   both the supply and demand for labor to the right.

4   The real wage

   a   must be greater than the nominal wage;
   b   must be equal to the nominal wage when there is full employment;
   c   must be less than the nominal wage when interest rates are high;
   d   must be less than the nominal wage if there are payroll taxes;
   e   none of the above.

5   In this chapter labor supply is assumed to be perfectly inelastic. This means that an increase in the real wage

   a   increases the quantity of labor supplied;
   b   decreases the quantity of labor supplied;
   c   causes no change in the quantity of labor supplied;
   d   causes the nominal wage to fall;
   e   causes no change in the nominal wage.

6   The relationship between employment and output, holding the technology and capital stock fixed, is called the

   a   short-run production function;
   b   full-employment gross domestic product;
   c   short-run aggregate supply;
   d   investment function;
   e   labor supply curve, which is assumed to be inelastic.

7   The short-run production function exhibits diminishing returns. This means that as more labor is used in production, output

   a   diminishes due to overcrowding;
   b   increases at an increasing rate;
   c   decreases at an increasing rate;
   d   increases at a decreasing rate;
   e   decreases at a decreasing rate.

8   Which of the following is not a synonym?

   a   full-employment level of output;
   b   potential gross domestic product;
   c   productive capacity;
   d   aggregate supply;
   e   aggregate demand.

9   If the labor force grows,

   a   aggregate supply shifts to the right;
   b   aggregate demand shifts to the right;
   c   both aggregate supply and aggregate demand shift to the right;
   d   aggregate supply does not shift because it does not depend upon price;
   e   the real wage rises.

10 Aggregate demand slopes downward because as the price level falls,

   a   households substitute among goods;
   b   the real value of money and other dollar denominated assets rises and households increase consumption;
   c   households fear inflation and stock up on necessities;
   d   firms reduce their quantity supplied.

e Aggregate demand does not slope down; it is assumed to be inelastic.

11 The income effect of an increase in the real interest rate causes savers to

a reduce savings because they are better off and want to consume more now;

b increase savings because consumption in the future is cheaper;

c reduce savings because they can meet their target level with less savings;

d increase savings because they are better off and want to consume more in the future;

e choose no change in the level of savings.

12 The substitution effect of an increase in the real interest rate causes savers to

a reduce savings because they are better off and want to consume more now;

b increase savings because consumption in the future is cheaper;

c reduce savings because they can meet their target level with less savings;

d increase savings because they are better off and want to consume more in the future;

e choose no change in the level of savings.

13 The supply of funds depends upon

a the interest rate;

b expectations about future profitability;

c disposable income;

d a and c;

e all of the above.

14 The demand for funds depends upon

a the interest rate;

b expectations about future profitability;

c disposable income;

d a and b;

e all of the above.

15 The relationship between the real interest rate and the level of investment is called the

a short-run production function;

b investment function;

c aggregate supply;

d potential GDP;

e aggregate demand.

16 An equal increase in government spending and taxes

a increases investment because the government spending adds to aggregate demand;

b decreases investment because the increased taxes reduce aggregate demand;

c decreases investment because the increased taxes reduce disposable income and households save less;

d increases investment because the real interest rate falls;

e increases investment because the price level rises.

17 An increase in the money supply

a increases the price level;

b increases the real wage;

c increases the real interest rate;

d a and c;

e all of the above.

18 The neutrality of money in the full-employment economy refers to the idea that changes in the supply of money do not change

a investment;

b output;

c the real wage;

d the real interest rate;

e all of the above.

19 In a small open economy

a interest rates are determined on international capital markets;

b interest rates adjust to equate the domestic demand and supply of funds;

c the supply of savings is perfectly inelastic;

d the demand for funds is perfectly inelastic;

e savings does not depend upon the interest rate.

20 In the United States economy

a investment does not depend upon domestic savings;

b interest rates are fixed, determined on international capital markets;

c domestic savings affect interest rates and investment;

d domestic savings affect investment but not interest rates;

e savings are perfectly inelastic.

Completion

1 In the labor market the _____ adjusts to equate the supply and demand for labor.

2 For a given technology and capital stock the relationship between employment and output is called the _____.

3 The aggregate supply curve shows how much output the economy can produce when it is at _____.

4 Aggregate demand is composed of consumption, investment, government expenditures, and _____.

5 When the interest rate rises households are motivated to save less because of the _____ effect.

6 When government spending and taxes rise in the same amount, the interest rate _____, crowding out private investment and consumption.

7 When there is full employment, an increase in the money supply will increase the _____, but will have no effect on output or any other real variable.

8 The _____ of money refers to the idea that at full employment increases in the money supply have no real effects.

9 In a _____ interest rates are fixed, determined on international capital markets.

10 The United States is a _____, open economy.

Answers to Self-Test

True or False

1	t	6	t	11	t
2	t	7	f	12	t
3	f	8	f	13	t
4	f	9	t	14	f
5	t	10	f	15	t

Multiple Choice

1	e	6	a	11	a	16	c
2	d	7	d	12	b	17	a
3	a	8	e	13	d	18	e
4	e	9	a	14	d	19	a
5	c	10	b	15	b	20	c

Completion

1 real wage
2 short-run production function
3 full employment
4 net exports
5 income
6 increases
7 price level
8 neutrality
9 small, open
10 large

Doing Economics: Tools and Practice Problems

The full-employment model occupies a central place in modern economics because in many areas the economy behaves according to its predictions. For example, the long-run performance of the economy corresponds quite closely to the full-employment model. In this chapter we study the full-employment model in four steps. First, we look at the relationship between the short-run production function and the demand for labor. Next, we consider the links between the labor and product markets. Third, we study how the capital and product markets interrelate before we put it all together with some applications. The focus here is on the structure of the full-employment model. Master this subject and unemployment macroeconomics will go smoothly. (The chapter also covers the open economy, but we will defer study of that model until Chapter 26.)

The Short-Run Production Function and the Demand for Labor

The short-run production function shows how much output results from using various amounts of labor, holding the level of capital input and the technology fixed. From this function we can compute the marginal product of labor, which is the extra output resulting from one more unit of the input labor. This curve is the demand for labor. Tool Kit 25.1 shows how to make the derivation.

Tool Kit 25.1: Deriving the Demand for Labor from the Short-Run Production Function

Firms hire workers to produce output. The additional output that one more worker produces is called the marginal product of labor. The marginal product schedule is also the demand for labor, in the sense that firms choose the amount of labor to hire by setting the marginal product equal to the real wage. Follow these steps to derive the demand for labor.

Step one: Identify and plot the short-run production function.

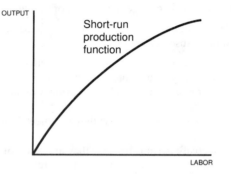

Step two: Compute the marginal product for each level of labor. The marginal product equals the following ratio.

Marginal Product =
$$\text{(Change in Output)/(Change in Labor)}$$

Step three: Plot the marginal product.

Step four: Identify the real wage. To find the quantity demanded of labor, find the quantity for which the real wage equals the marginal product.

1 (Worked problem: demand for labor) This problem looks at Costa Guano, whose currency is the guano. The short-run production function is given in Table 25.1.

a Find the marginal product schedule.
b Suppose, for example, that the real wage is 300 guanos per year. How much labor is demanded?

Table 25.1

Quantity of labor (million person years)	Output (millions of guanos)
0	0
1	600
2	1,100
3	1,500
4	1,800
5	2,000
6	2,100
7	2,150

Step-by-step solution

Step one: Identify and plot the short-run production function. See Table 25.1.

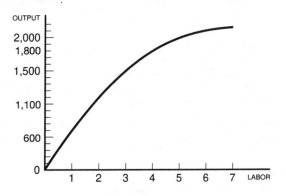

Step two: Compute the marginal product for each level of labor. When the first million workers are used, output rises from 0 to 600 million; therefore the marginal product of this worker is 600. When the second is added, output rises from 600 to 1,100; therefore the second worker's marginal product is 1,100 − 600 = 500. Continuing in the same manner gives the entire marginal product schedule.

Quantity of labor (million person years)	Marginal product of labor
1	600
2	500
3	400
4	300
5	200
6	100
7	50

Step three: Plot the marginal product curve.

Step four: Find the quantity for which the real wage equals the marginal product. The real wage is 300, which equals marginal product when the quantity of labor is 4.

2 (Practice problem: demand for labor) The short-run production function is given in Table 25.2.

a Find the marginal product schedule.
b Suppose that the real wage is 3 thousand dorals. How much labor is demanded?

Table 25.2

Quantity of labor (million person years)	Output (billions of dorals)
0	0
1	25
2	45
3	60
4	70
5	75
6	78
7	80
8	81

3 (Practice problem: demand for labor) In the land of Erehwemos the short-run production function is as given in Table 25.3. The currency is called the wemo.

a Find the marginal product schedule.
b Suppose that the real wage is 3,000 wemos per year. How much labor is demanded?

Table 23.3

Quantity of labor (million person years)	Output (billions of wemos)
0	0
1	5
2	9
3	12
4	14
5	15
6	15.5

The Labor Market and the Product Market

The labor market and product market are linked by the short-run production function. The marginal product of labor, derived from the short-run production function, is the demand for labor, which, together with the supply of labor, determines the real wage. We will assume that the supply of labor is perfectly inelastic, an assumption that is not far from the truth. The short-run production function shows how much output will be produced by the supply of labor, and this quantity of output is the aggregate supply in the product market. Note the direction of influence: from the labor market to the product market. The labor market determines the labor supply and, with the production function, it determines the level of output. Changes in the product market have no impact upon the labor market. Tool Kit 25.2 illustrates this linkage.

Tool Kit 25.2: Deriving Aggregate Supply from the Labor Market and Short-Run Production Function

With the supply of labor and the short-run production function, we can find the economy's aggregate supply, which is also called potential GDP, full-employment output, or capacity. The labor market gives the real wage and the production function gives the aggregate supply. Follow these steps.

Step one: Identify the supply of labor and the short-run production function.

Step two: Find the demand for labor. Follow the steps of Tool Kit 25.1.

Step three: Find the equilibrium real wage. This is the real wage that clears the labor market.

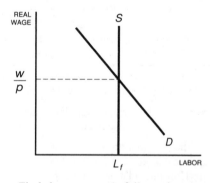

Step four: Find the economy's full employment output. This is the output corresponding to the equilibrium level of labor.

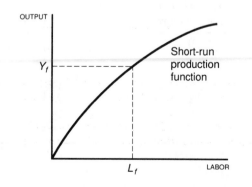

Step five: Plot the aggregate supply curve. This is a vertical line drawn with output equal to its full employment level.

4 (Worked problem: aggregate supply) We continue with Costa Guano, whose production function is given in Table 25.1. The labor supply is inelastic, equal to 5 million.

a   Calculate the marginal product schedule.
b   Find the equilibrium real wage. Draw a diagram of the labor market.
c   Find the economy's potential GDP. Draw the aggregate supply curve.

Step-by-step solution

Step one: Identify the supply of labor and the short-run production function. The production function is given in Table 25.1 and the labor supply equals 5 million.

Step two: Find the demand for labor. The demand for labor is as follows. Notice that it is the same as the marginal product schedule.

Quantity of labor (person years)	Real wage
1	600
2	500
3	400
4	300
5	200
6	100
7	50

Step three: Find the equilibrium real wage. Demand equals supply (5 million) when the wage equals 200.

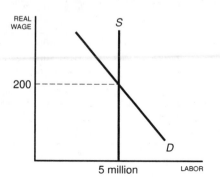

Step four: Find the economy's full-employment output. From the production function, output at 5 million person years equals 2,000 million guanos.

Step five: Plot the aggregate supply curve. Note that output equals 2,000 for each price level.

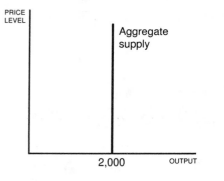

5 (Practice problem: aggregate supply) We continue with the analysis of El Dorado from problem 2. Suppose that the production function is given in Table 25.2 and that the labor supply is inelastic, equal to 3,000 person years.

a Find the demand for labor.
b Find the equilibrium real wage. Draw a diagram of the labor market.

Find the economy's potential GDP. Draw the aggregate supply curve.

6 (Practice problem: aggregate supply) We continue with the country of Erehwemos, where the production function is given in Table 25.3. Suppose that the labor supply is inelastic, equal to 5 million.

a Find the demand for labor.
b Find the equilibrium real wage. Draw a diagram of the labor market.

Find the economy's potential GDP. Draw the aggregate supply curve.

The Product Market and the Capital Market

The capital market determines the quantity of investment. Recall that the real interest rate adjusts to balance the demand and supply of funds. The product market is affected in that investment is one of the four components of aggregate demand. In this case the effects go both ways because the product market affects the capital market through the link between output (which equals income) and savings. For example, an increase in the level of the economy's output will lead households to increase their savings. Tool Kit 25.3 illustrates these linkages.

Tool Kit 25.3: Linking the Product and Capital Markets

The product market determines the economy's output, which equals its income. The capital market is affected because households save a fraction of their income. That fraction is the average propensity to save. The capital market then determines the level of investment, which is one of the components of aggregate demand. Keep straight this two-way influence with the following procedure.

Step one: Identify aggregate supply, aggregate demand (excluding investment), the investment function, and the average propensity to save.

Step two: Find the savings supply (assumed to be inelastic). First, observe that aggregate supply equals output and output equals income. Next, multiply income by the average propensity to save. The product is total savings.

Total savings = income × average propensity to save.

Step three: Find the equilibrum real interest rate and investment level by equating the investment function with total savings.

Step four: Find aggregate demand by adding investment to the aggregate demand (excluding investment).

Step five: Find the equilibrium price level by equating aggregate demand and aggregate supply.

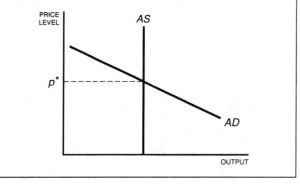

---

7 (Worked problem: product and capital markets) Continuing the analysis of Costa Guano, recall that the short-run production function is given in Table 25.1 and output equals 2,000 million guanos. Costa Guanoans save 10 percent of their income. The invest-

ment function and aggregate demand (excluding investment) are given in Table 25.4.

a Compute total savings.
b Find the equilibrum real interest rate. Draw a diagram of the capital market.
c Find aggregate demand.
d Find the equilibrium price level. Draw a diagram of the product market.

Table 25.4

Investment function		Aggregate demand (excluding investment)	
Investment (millions of guanos)	Real interest rate	Aggregate demand (millions of guanos)	Price level
50	10	1,000	280
75	9	1,200	260
100	8	1,400	240
125	7	1,600	220
150	6	1,800	200
175	5	2,000	180
200	4	2,200	160
225	3	2,400	140

Step one: Identify aggregate supply, aggregate demand (excluding investment), the investment function, and the average propensity to save. See Table 25.4 for the investment function and aggregate demand (excluding investment). Aggregate supply is 2,000 (from problem 4) and the average propensity to save is 0.1.

Step two: Find the savings supply (assumed to be inelastic). Total savings = 2,000 × 0.1 = 200.

Step three: Find the equilibrum real interest rate and investment level by equating the investment function with total savings. The capital market clears when the real interest rate equals 4 percent. Equilibrium investment is then 200.

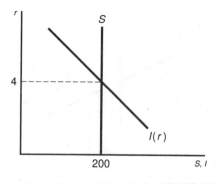

Step four: Find aggregate demand by adding investment to the aggregate demand (excluding investment). Adding investment, which equals 200, to aggregate demand gives the following.

Investment function	Aggregate demand
Aggregate demand (millions of guanos)	Price level
1,200	280
1,400	260
1,600	240
1,800	220
2,000	200
2,200	180
2,400	160
2,600	140

Step five: Find the equilibrium price level by equating aggregate demand and aggregate supply. The product market clears at a price level equal to 200.

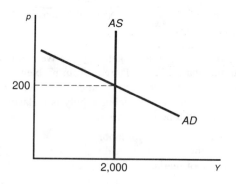

8 (Practice problem: product and capital markets) Continuing the analysis of El Dorado, recall that the short-run production function is given in Table 25.2 and output equals 60 billion dorals. Households save one-sixth of their income in El Dorado. The investment function and the aggregate demand curve (excluding investment) are given in Table 25.5.

a Compute total savings.
b Find the equilibrium real interest rate. Draw a diagram of the capital market.
c Find aggregate demand.
d Find the equilibrium price level. Draw a diagram of the product market.

Table 25.5

Investment function		Aggregate demand (excluding investment)	
Investment (billions of dorals)	Real interest rate	Aggregate demand (billions of dorals)	Price level
3	9	45	200
4	8	50	190
5	7	55	180
6	6	60	170
8	5	65	160
10	4	70	150
15	3	75	140
20	2	80	130

9   Continue with the analysis of Erehwemos, the production function of which is given in Table 25.3. Households save one-third of their income. The investment function and the aggregate demand (excluding investment) are given in Table 25.6. National income equals 15 billion.

a   Compute total savings.
b   Find the equilibrum real interest rate. Draw a diagram of the capital market.
c   Find aggregate demand.
d   Find the equilibrium price level. Draw a diagram of the product market.

Table 25.6

Investment function		Aggregate demand (excluding investment)	
Investment (billions of wemos)	Real interest rate	Aggregate demand (billions of wemos)	Price level
1	10	7	330
2	9	8	320
3	8	9	310
4	7	10	300
5	6	11	290
6	5	12	280
7	4	13	270
8	3	14	260
9	2	15	250

The Labor Market and the Capital Market

The investment function gives the level of investment for each interest rate. It represents firms' judgments about the profitability of potential investments. Since these profits come in the future, the chief determinant of the investment function is business expectations. It also depends upon costs and thus is linked to the labor market through the real wage and to technology. We will not do a separate set of problems here, but keep in mind that the investment function shifts up when technology improves or the real wage falls, and it shifts down in the opposite cases.

The Full-Employment Model

Now we are ready to put the pieces together and use the entire full-employment model to show the effects of various exogenous changes, including shifts in the supply of labor, the short-run production function, the supply of savings, the demand for savings, the money supply, and the size of government. There will be a worked problem and a practice problem for each. As usual, the basic method involves starting with an equilibrium, identifying an exogenous change, shifting curves, finding the new equilibrium, and comparing. This general equilibrium model is complicated because adjustment in one market affects the others, and these effects must be traced through. We will pay special attention to these linkages.

Tool Kit 25.4: Using the Full-Employment Model

The full-employment model is a general equilibrium model. This means that when there is an exogenous change, it starts a process that reverberates through all three markets. To avoid confusion proceed in this step-by-step fashion.

Step one: Start with an equilibrium in the product, labor, and capital markets.

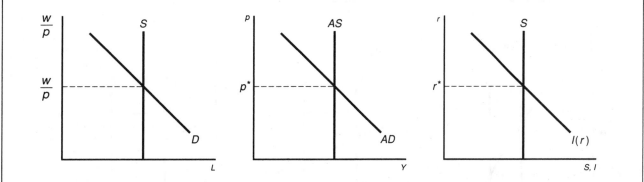

Step two: Identify an exogenous change and determine which curve shifts.

Step three: Shift the curve.

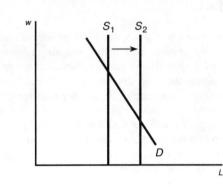

Step four: Find the new (partial) equilibrium in the market where the curve shifted.

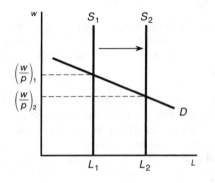

Step five: Trace through the links of the change to the related markets and shift the relevant curves.

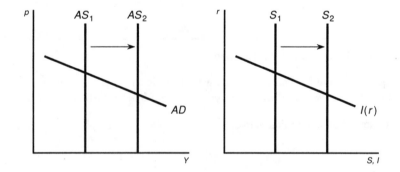

Step six: Find the new general equilibrium and compare.

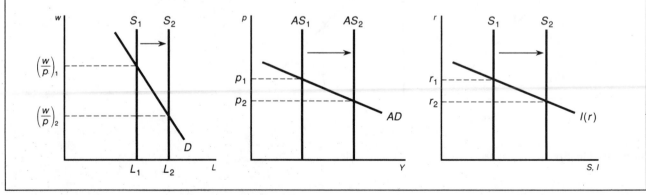

10   (Worked problem: full-employment model) Review problems 1, 4, and 7. This problem continues the analysis of Costa Guano.

a   Draw a diagram illustrating the general equilibrium in the Costa Guano economy as solved for in the answers to problems 1, 4, and 7. In the following always begin with this equilibrium.

b   Suppose that the money supply increases by 10 percent. Trace through the impact of this change in the economy. Show on the diagrams.

c   Now suppose that the demand for investment rises by 50 million guanos at each interest rate. Trace through the impact of this change in the economy. Show on the diagrams.

d   Now suppose that savings falls by 25 million. Of course, consumption will also increase by this same amount. Trace through the impact of this change in the economy. Show on the diagrams.

e   Government expenditures and taxes increase by 50 million. Trace through the impact of this change in the economy. Show on the diagrams.

f   The short-run production function doubles for each level of labor input.

g   The supply of labor decreases to 3 million.

Step-by-step solution

Step one (a): Start with equilibrium in the product, labor, and capital markets.

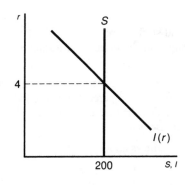

Step two (b): Identify an exogenous change and determine which curve shifts. Aggregate demand shifts up. The new aggregate demand schedule is as follows. Note that the price level has increased 10 percent for each level of output; e.g., $280 + 0.1 (280) = 308$.

Aggregate demand (millions of guanos)	Price level
1,200	308
1,400	296
1,600	264
1,800	242
2,000	220
2,200	198
2,400	176
2,600	154

Step three: Shift the curve.

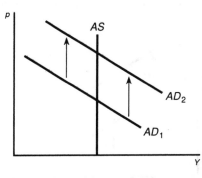

Step four: Find the new (partial) equilibrium in the market where the curve shifted. The new equilibrium price level is 220, which is 10 percent higher.

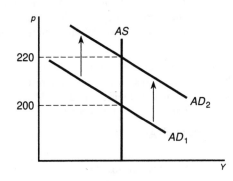

Step five: Trace through the links of the change to the related markets and shift the relevant curves. There are no other effects. Changes in the price level do not affect the capital and labor markets.

Step six: Find the new general equilibrium and compare. The only change is a 10 percent increase in the price level. No real magnitudes change; thus we conclude that the money supply increase is neutral.

Step one (c): Same as above.

Step two: Identify an exogenous change and determine which curve shifts. The investment function shifts up by 50 million at each real interest rate.

Step three: Shift the curve. The new investment function is given below.

Investment function

Investment (millions of guanos)	Real interest rate
100	10
125	9
150	8
175	7
200	6
225	5
250	4
275	3

Step four: Find the new (partial) equilibrium in the market where the curve shifted. The real interest rate rises to 6 percent. Because in this example the supply of savings is inelastic, there is no change in the level of investment.

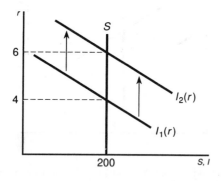

Step five: Trace through the links of the change to the related markets and shift the relevant curves. There are no other real effects. Aggregate demand may shift down because of the interest rate increase, but this would only lead to a fall in the price level.

Step six: Find the new general equilibrium and compare. The only change is the increase in the real interest rate. (If savings supply were upward sloping, there would be an increase in investment at the higher interest rate.)

Step one (d): Same as above.

Step two: Identify an exogenous change and determine which curve shifts. Savings falls to 175 million, and savings supply shifts to the left in the capital market. But the accom-

panying increase in consumption shifts aggregate demand to the right in the product market.

Step three: Shift the curves. The new aggregate demand is below.

Aggregate demand

Aggregate demand (millions of guanos)	Price level
1,175	280
1,375	260
1,575	240
1,775	220
1,975	200
2,175	180
2,375	160
2,575	140

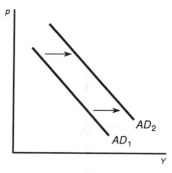

Step four: Find the new (partial) equilibrium in the market where the curve shifted. The real interest rate rises to 5 percent, and investment falls to 175 million. In the product market the price level increases.

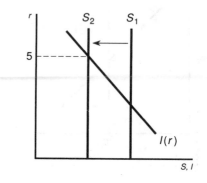

Step five: Trace through the links of the change to the related markets and shift the relevant curves. Aggregate demand must fall by the amount of the decrease in investment. This exactly offsets the increase in consumption; thus the price level returns to its original 200.

Step six: Find the new general equilibrium and compare. The new equilibrium has the same total output, although its composition is different. There is less investment (now only 175) and more consumption. Note how capital market changes do not affect current output. Of course, as time passes the changes in investment will affect the economy's growth rate.

Step one (e): Same as above.

Step two: Identify an exogenous change and determine which curve shifts. The increase in taxes reduces consumption. This shifts aggregate demand to the left. Because households save 10 percent of their income and consume 90 percent, consumption must fall by 45 million. The increase in government expenditures shifts aggregate demand to the right by 50 million. The net effect is a 5 million increase. In the capital market the supply shifts to the left by 5 million.

Step three: Shift the curves.

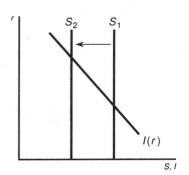

Step four: Find the new (partial) equilibrium in the market where the curve shifted. The real interest rate rises by less than 1 percent, and investment falls by the reduction in savings, which is 5 million. In the product market the price level increases slightly.

Step five: Trace through the links of the change to the related markets and shift the relevant curves. Aggregate demand must fall by the amount of the decrease in investment. This exactly offsets the 5 million increase in step three; thus the price level returns to its original 200.

Step six: Find the new general equilibrium and compare. The new equilibrium has the same total output, although its composition is different. There is less investment (now only 195), less consumption, and more government expenditures.

Step one (f): Same as above.

Step two: Identify an exogenous change and determine which curve shifts. The technological advance shifts the short-run production function up. Usually, this will shift the demands for both capital and labor to the right. In this case, we can calculate the new demand for labor by following the steps sketched in Tool Kit 25.1. Also, because the same amount of labor now produces more output, aggregate supply will shift to the right.

Step three: Shift the curves. The new production function and demand for labor are as follows.

Quantity of labor (million person years)	Output (millions of guanos)	Real wage (same as marginal product)
0	0	
1	1,200	1,200
2	2,200	1,000
3	3,000	800
4	3,600	600
5	4,000	400
6	4,200	200
7	4,300	100

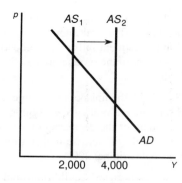

Step four: Find the new (partial) equilibrium in the market where the curve shifted. Labor supply, which equals 5 million, equals labor demand at a real wage of 400. Output increases to 4,000.

Step five: Trace through the links of the change to the related markets and shift the relevant curves. The shift to the right in aggregate supply reduces the price level.

Step six: Find the new general equilibrium and compare. Both output and the real wage double. Also, as firms anticipate higher returns from the better technology, the investment function will shift out, increasing the real interest rate.

Step one (g): Same as above.

Step two: Identify an exogenous change and determine which curve shifts. Labor supply shifts to the left to 3 million.

Step three: Shift the curve.

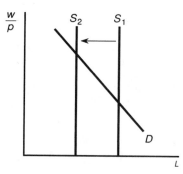

Step four: Find the new (partial) equilibrium in the market where the curve shifted. Note that the real wage increases to 400.

Step five: Trace through the links of the change to the related markets and shift the relevant curves. The reduction in labor reduces output to 1,500 million; thus aggregate supply shifts to the left, increasing the price level. In the capital market, the demand for investment probably falls as firms anticipate higher labor costs.

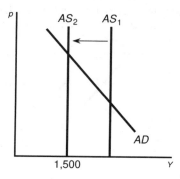

Step six: Find the new general equilibrium and compare.

11   (Practice problem: full-employment model) Review problems 2, 5, and 8. This problem continues the analysis of El Dorado.

  a   Draw a diagram illustrating the general equilibrium in the El Dorado economy as solved for in the answer to problems 2, 5, and 8. In the following always begin with this equilibrium.

  b   Suppose that the money supply increases by 20 percent. Trace through the impact of this change in the economy. Show on the diagrams.

  c   Now suppose that the demand for investment rises by 5 billion dorals at each interest rate. Trace through the impact of this change in the economy. Show on the diagrams.

  d   Now suppose that savings falls by 5 billion. Of course, consumption will also increase by this same amount. Trace through the impact of this change in the economy. Show on the diagrams.

  e   Government expenditures and taxes increase by 30 billion. Trace through the impact of this change in the economy. Show on the diagrams.

  f   The short-run production function doubles for each level of labor input.

  g   The supply of labor increases to 5 million.

12   (Practice problem: full-employment model) Review problems 3, 6, and 9. This problem continues the analysis of Erewhemos.

  a   Draw a diagram illustrating the general equilibrium in the Erewhemos economy as solved for in the answer to problems 3, 6, and 9. In the following always begin with this equilibrium.

  b   Suppose that the money supply increases by 10 percent. Trace through the impact of this change in the economy. Show on the diagrams.

  c   Now suppose that the demand for investment rises by 3 billion wemos at each interest rate. Trace through the impact of this change in the economy. Show on the diagrams.

d   Now suppose that savings falls by 1 billion. Of course, consumption will also increase by this same amount. Trace through the impact of this change in the economy. Show on the diagrams.

e   Government expenditure and taxes fall by 3 billion. Trace through the impact of this change in the economy.

f   The short-run production function doubles for each level of output.

g   The supply of labor decreases to 4 million.

Answers to Problems

2   a   The marginal product schedule is as follows.

Quantity of labor (million person years)	Marginal product
1	25
2	20
3	15
4	10
5	5
6	3
7	2
8	1

b   The quantity of labor demanded is 6 thousand person years of labor.

3   a   The marginal product schedule is as follows.

Quantity of labor (million person years)	Marginal product
1	5,000
2	4,000
3	3,000
4	2,000
5	1,000
6	500

b   The quantity of labor demanded is 3 million person years.

5   a   The demand for labor is as follows.

Quantity of labor (million person years)	Real wage (dorals per year)
1	25
2	20
3	15
4	10
5	5
6	3
7	2
8	1

b   Real wage = 15; output = 60.

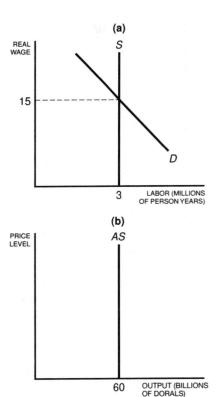

6   a   The demand for labor is as follows.

Quantity of labor (million person years)	Real wage (wemos per year)
1	5,000
2	4,000
3	3,000
4	2,000
5	1,000
6	500

b   Real wage = 1,000 per month; output = 15,000.

8 a   Total savings = 10 billion dorals.

   b   Real interest rate = 4 percent. Investment = 10 billion dorals.

   c   Aggregate demand is shown below.

Aggregate demand (millions of dorals)	Price level
55	200
60	190
65	180
70	170
75	160
80	150
85	140
90	130

   d   Equilibrium price level = 190.

9 a   Total savings = 1/3 × 15 = 5 billion.

   b   Real interest rate = 6 percent. Investment = 5 billion.

   c   Aggregate demand is as follows.

Aggregate demand (billion of wemos)	Price level
12	330
13	320
14	310
15	300
16	290
17	280
18	270
19	260
20	250

   d   Price level = 300.

11 a   General equilibrium is shown below.

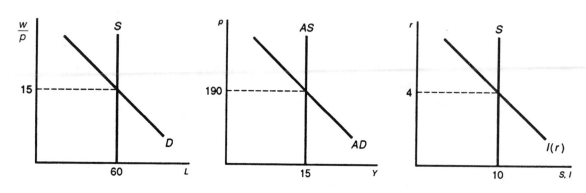

b   Aggregate demand shifts up by 20 percent. The new price level equals 228, but there are no other changes. Money is neutral in the full-employment model.

c   The real interest rate rises to 7 percent. Because the supply of funds is inelastic, the level of investment remains at 10 billion. There are no other changes. If the supply of funds sloped upward, investment would increase and aggregate demand would shift out, driving up the price level. This would result in less consumption to offset the increase in investment.

d   The real interest rate rises to 7 percent. Investment falls to 5 billion. In the product market the increase in consumption shifts aggregate demand to the right by 5 billion, but this is offset by the decrease in investment. The price level remains constant. There are no other changes.

e   The increase in taxes reduces disposable income by 30 billion. Since the average propensity to save is one-sixth, savings falls by 5 billion and consumption falls by 25 billion. The supply of savings shifts left and the real interest rate rises to 7 percent. Investment falls by 5 billion. Aggregate demand shifts right by the 30 billion increase in government expenditures, but it shifts left by the 5 billion fall in investment plus the 25 billion fall in consumption. The net effect is no shift in aggregate demand. The price level remains the same and there are no other changes.

f   The real wage doubles to 30, and output increases to 120. Aggregate supply shifts right to 120 and the price level falls. Savings increases because national income doubles. Also, the demand for investment would increase.

g   The supply of labor shifts to the right, driving the real wage down to 5. Output increases to 75; therefore aggregate supply shifts to the right. The increase in national income increases savings and the supply of funds shifts to the right.

12 *a*   General equilibrium is shown below.

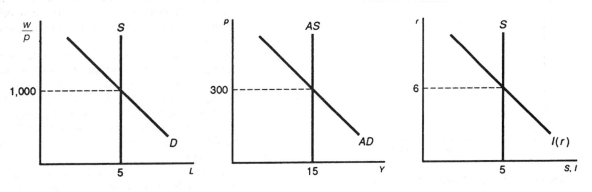

b   Aggregate demand shifts up by 10 percent. The new price level equals 330, but there are no other changes. Money is neutral in the full-employment model.

c   The real interest rate rises to 9 percent. Because the supply of funds is inelastic, the level of investment remains at 5 billion. There are no other changes. If the supply of funds sloped upward, investment would increase and aggregate demand would shift out, driving up the price level. This would result in less consumption to offset the increase in investment.

d   The real interest rate rises to 7 percent. Investment falls by 1 billion. In the product market the increase in consumption shifts aggregate demand to the right by 1 billion, but this is offset by the decrease in investment. The price level remains constant. There are no other changes.

e   The decrease in taxes increases disposable income by 3 billion. Since the average propensity to save

is one-third, savings rises by 1 billion and consumption rises by 2 billion. The supply of savings shifts right and the real interest rate falls to 5 percent. Investment rises by 1 billion. Aggregate demand shifts left by the 3 billion decrease in government expenditures, but it shifts right by the 1 billion rise in investment plus the 2 billion rise in consumption. The net effect is no shift in aggregate demand. The price level remains the same and there are no other changes.

f   The real wage doubles to 2,000, and output increases to 30. Aggregate supply shifts right to 30 and the price level falls. Savings increases because national income doubles. Also, the demand for investment would increase.

g   The supply of labor shifts to the left, driving the real wage up to 2,000. Output decreases to 14 billion; therefore aggregate supply shifts to the left. The decrease in national income decreases savings and the supply of funds shifts to the left.

Chapter 26

USING THE FULL-EMPLOYMENT MODEL

Chapter Review

The full-employment model, developed in Chapter 25, is put to use analyzing the budget deficit, the trade deficit, and the causes of economic growth. The center of attention is the capital market and the openness of the economy to international trade and investment. Considerable use is made of two identities: the basic trade identity and the savings-investment identity. With this chapter the discussion of full-employment macroeconomics draws to a close. The next chapter begins the analysis of unemployment macroeconomics.

ESSENTIAL CONCEPTS

1   The **budget deficit** is the difference between what the government receives in taxes and its expenditures. The United States ran especially large deficits during the 1980s. The debt is the total amount owed by the government accumulated over years of deficit and surplus. Although not large based on international comparisons, it rose substantially during the 1980s.

2   National savings is the sum of private savings and government savings. When the government runs a deficit,

government savings is a negative number. Thus, an increase in the deficit reduces national savings and shifts the supply of funds in the capital market to the left. In a closed economy this shift must raise interest rates and reduce investment. In a small open economy interest rates are set on international capital markets. Because interest rates are fixed, investment will not change. The reduction in national savings will lead to increased borrowing from abroad.

3   The difference between imports and exports in a given year is the **trade deficit** which, according to the basic trade identity, must equal the inflows of foreign capital. The exchange of currencies for imports, exports, and capital flows is governed by the exchange rate, which is the relative price of two currencies. The **exchange rate** adjusts to bring into balance the demands and supplies of all currencies.

4   In an open economy the **savings-investment identity** says that investment equals total savings, which comprises private savings, government savings (the budget deficit), and foreign inflows of capital. Thus if the budget deficit is increased and private savings and investment remain unchanged, capital flows from abroad (which equals the trade deficit) must also increase. Trade deficits are a problem because the foreign bor-

rowing that finances them accumulates into foreign indebtedness, which reduces the future standard of living. Policies to reduce the trade deficit focus on increasing private savings or reducing the budget deficit. Either would shift the supply of savings to the right.

5   Growth requires a more productive labor force, more and better capital, and technological advances. Investments in human capital, plant and equipment, and research and development enhance economic growth. These investments can be stimulated through the use of investment tax credits or accelerated depreciation. Another approach is to increase savings through individual retirement accounts or tax breaks on investment income. The net effect of these policies must balance the gain in private savings with the increased budget deficit caused by the loss in tax revenue. Finally, reduced government expenditures narrow the budget deficit, but reduced government investment may counteract the increased private investment.

BEHIND THE ESSENTIAL CONCEPTS

1   The connection between budget and trade deficits can be seen by examining two identities: the **basic trade identity** and the **savings-investment identity** for an open economy.

a   The basic trade identity is

trade deficit = imports – exports = capital inflows.

This means that if foreign capital flows into the United States (in greater amounts than U.S. capital flows abroad), then the U.S. must run a trade deficit.

b   The savings-investment identity for an open economy is

private savings + capital inflows
= investment + federal budget deficit.

This identity says that unless investment falls and savings rise by enough to finance the budget deficit, the deficit results in capital inflows, which the basic trade identity says must equal the trade deficit.

2   **Federal budget deficits** rose dramatically during the 1980s, increasing the nation's debt to record levels even though the 1980s were a time of peace and relative prosperity. The high deficits can be linked to four causes. Taxes were reduced, defense spending increased, Social Security and Medicare payments grew, and the accumulated debt required higher interest payments. At the same time, the U.S. **trade deficit** reached record levels, causing the United States to slip from creditor to debtor nation status.

3   Government borrowing can affect future generations in three ways. First, the burden can be shifted directly to the future generation by increasing taxes after the current generation has retired. Second, borrowing drives up interest rates and crowds out private investment. Finally, since much of the borrowing comes from abroad and

foreign investors are attracted by higher U.S. interest rates, current borrowing increases foreign indebtedness. Repayment of foreign debt then requires reduced future living standards.

4   *The federal budget deficit caused the trade deficit* in the following way. Government borrowing to finance the budget deficit drove up interest rates and attracted capital flows from abroad. The increased foreign demand for dollars to lend and invest in the United States led to an appreciation of the dollar. The higher exchange rate made U.S. imports cheaper and U.S. exports more expensive. Foreigners bought fewer of the relatively expensive U.S. exports, while Americans bought more of the relatively cheaper imports, and the trade deficit skyrocketed.

5   The currency market is where different currencies are traded in order to make international transactions. Its price is called the exchange rate, and it is governed by supply and demand in a manner similar to other markets. There is a special language to this market, however. When the price of a country's currency rises, we say that its exchange rate *appreciates*; when it falls, we say that the currency *depreciates*. When the price is high, we say that the currency is strong. A weak currency simply means that the price is low.

SELF-TEST

True or False

1   The federal debt is the difference between what the government receives in taxes and what it spends.

2   Both the budget deficit and the federal debt are much larger for the United States than for most European countries.

3   In a closed economy investment equals private savings.

4   Increased budget deficits reduce national savings.

5   In a small open economy increasing the budget deficit shifts supply to the left, increasing the interest rate and reducing investment.

6   The trade deficit always equals capital inflows from abroad.

7   The exchange rate is the relative price of two currencies.

8   When the price of a country's currency rises, it is said to appreciate.

9   According to the savings-investment identity, investment equals the sum of private savings, government savings, and capital flows from abroad.

10   Although it has run large trade deficits for more than a decade, the United States is still a creditor nation.

11   The trade deficit can be reduced by reducing investment or increasing savings.

12   The main keys to increased growth are improving the

productivity of labor, adding capital, and advancing technology.

13 Human capital is the result of investment in education and training the labor force.

14 The interest elasticity of savings is quite high, indicating that an increase in the after tax rate of return will increase savings substantially.

15 In a large open economy like the United States savings and investment tend to move together.

Multiple Choice

1 During much of the 1980s, the United States ran

   a federal budget deficits and trade surpluses;
   b federal budget surpluses and trade deficits;
   c federal budget and trade surpluses;
   d federal budget and trade deficits;
   e balanced federal budgets and trade accounts.

2 Which of the following is true of the relative size of United Stated budget deficits and the federal debt?

   a Neither the deficits nor the debt are as large as those of many European countries and Canada.
   b The deficits are larger than those of European countries and Canada, but the debt has not yet grown as large.
   c The deficits are smaller than those of European countries and Canada, but the debt is greater.
   d Both the deficits and debt are larger than those of European countries and Canada.
   e Neither the deficits nor the debt are as large as those of Japan.

3 The debt/GDP ratio in the United States is about

   a 14;
   b 20;
   c 25;
   d 35;
   e 50.

4 In a closed economy investment equals

   a private savings;
   b private savings minus government savings;
   c government savings;
   d private savings minus government savings minus the budget deficit;
   e the trade deficit.

5 In a closed economy an increase in the budget deficit

   a reduces the interest rate and investment;
   b does not change the interest rate or investment;
   c increases the interest rate and investment;
   d increases the interest rate but reduces investment;
   e decreases the interest rate but increases investment.

6 In a small open economy an increase in the budget deficit

   a reduces the interest rate and investment;
   b does not change the interest rate or investment;

   c increases the interest rate and investment;
   d increases the interest rate but reduces investment;
   e decreases the interest rate but increases investment.

7 When a German buys a United States government bond, the transaction is an example of

   a imports;
   b exports;
   c capital inflows;
   d capital outflows;
   e currency exchange.

8 The basic trade identity says that

   a imports must equal exports;
   b imports must equal capital flows from abroad;
   c exports must equal capital flows from abroad;
   d the trade deficit must equal capital flows from abroad;
   e capital flows from abroad must equal capital flows to overseas economies.

9 If a country invests more overseas than foreign countries invest in it, then

   a its trade account must be in balance;
   b it must run a trade surplus;
   c it must run a trade deficit;
   d it must balance its government budget;
   e its government deficit must equal the net flow of capital to other countries.

10 The exchange rate is

   a the trade deficit between two nations;
   b a country's net inflow of capital;
   c the relative price of two currencies;
   d the rate of appreciation of a country's currency;
   e the rate of depreciation of a country's currency.

11 In an open economy, the savings-investment identity says that

   a private savings must equal private investment;
   b private savings plus capital flows from abroad must equal investment;
   c private savings plus capital flows from abroad must equal investment plus the government deficit;
   d private savings plus capital flows from abroad must equal the government deficits plus the trade deficit;
   e private savings plus capital flows from abroad must equal the government deficit plus the trade deficit plus investment;

12 According to the savings-investment identity for an open economy, investment may be financed from

   a private savings;
   b government savings;
   c capital flows from abroad;
   d all of the above;
   e a and c.

13 Typically, developing economies

   a borrow less than mature economies;

b   borrow while mature economies lend;

c   lend while mature economies borrow;

d   neither borrow nor lend;

e   borrow or lend at the same rates as mature economies.

14   In the mid-1980s, the United States

a   changed status from a creditor to a debtor nation;

b   changed status from a debtor to a creditor nation;

c   remained a creditor nation, while running trade deficits;

d   remained a debtor nation, increasing foreign indebtedness;

e   saw no change in its foreign indebtedness.

15   To reduce the trade deficit, a country can

a   shift the investment function to the left or the savings curve to the right;

b   shift the investment function to the right or the savings curve to the left;

c   shift either the investment function or the savings curve to the right;

d   shift either the investment function or the savings curve to the left;

e   restrict the importation of foreign goods.

16   To increase investment in a closed economy,

a   shift the investment function to the left or the savings curve to the right;

b   shift the investment function to the right or the savings curve to the left;

c   shift either the investment function or the savings curve to the right;

d   shift either the investment function or the savings curve to the left;

e   negotiate with foreign counties to reduce world interest rates.

17   Policies to enhance growth include

a   investment in human capital;

b   investment in plant and equipment;

c   investment in research and development;

d   public investments;

e   all of the above.

18   A 10 percent investment tax credit

a   allows firms to deduct 10 percent of the cost of investment from the tax base;

b   reduces the firms' tax payments by 10 percent;

c   allows firms to subtract 10 percent of the cost of the investment from their tax payment;

d   waives taxes on 10 percent of a firm's investments;

e   offers the opportunity to borrow funds at a 10 percent discount off the market interest rate.

19   Individual retirement accounts and other tax breaks for savers

a   increase savings because households have greater incentive to save;

b   decrease savings because smaller tax collection increases the budget deficit;

c   may increase or decrease savings depending upon the relative magnitude of increased household savings and increased budget deficits;

d   reduce savings because households have greater incentive to save;

e   increase savings because smaller tax collection increases the budget deficit.

20   For the United States increased private savings will likely

a   increase the budget deficit;

b   reduce the budget deficit;

c   increase investment;

d   leave interest rates and investment unchanged;

e   cause the dollar to appreciate.

Completion

1   The _____ is the cumulative amount that the government owes.

2   The difference between government expenditures and revenues is the _____.

3   The basic trade identity says that the trade deficit must equal _____.

4   In an open economy, private savings plus capital flows from abroad must equal investment plus the _____.

5   The relative price of two currencies is called the _____.

6   When the price of a country's currency rises, it is said to _____.

7   The United States is currently a _____ nation.

8   Investments in education and training produce _____.

9   An _____ allows firms to subtract a fraction of the cost of an investment from their taxes.

10   The measure of how much private savings increase when the after tax interest rate falls is called the _____.

Answers to Self-Test

True or False

1	f	6	t	11	t
2	f	7	t	12	t
3	t	8	t	13	t
4	t	9	t	14	f
5	f	10	f	15	t

Multiple Choice

1	d	6	b	11	c	16	c
2	a	7	c	12	d	17	e
3	d	8	d	13	b	18	c
4	a	9	b	14	a	19	c
5	d	10	c	15	a	20	c

Completion

1 federal debt
2 budget deficit
3 capital inflows from abroad
4 budget deficit
5 exchange rate
6 appreciate
7 debtor
8 human capital
9 investment tax credit
10 interest elasticity of savings

Doing Economics: Tools and Practice Problems

The discussion of the three major topics of this chapter—budget deficits, trade deficits, and growth—centers on the capital market. Government finances budget deficits by borrowing funds on the capital market. Trade deficits, through the basic trade identity, result in flows of foreign capital to the capital market. The engine of growth is investment in research, human capital, and capital equipment, and this investment must be financed with capital obtained on the capital market. An essential aspect of the capital market is its openness to international borrowing and savings. We first look at the model of the small open economy and then study the model most appropriate to the United States, the large open economy. Throughout the discussion, the trade and savings investment identities will play an important role.

The Small Open Economy

The international capital market is so huge that a small country's borrowing and lending have no effect on interest rates. Thus, a small open economy can borrow and lend on international markets at a fixed interest rate. Because its investment equals its quantity demanded at that fixed interest rate, domestic savings have no effect on investment. This separation of savings and investment implies that the most important effects of budget deficits concern flows of foreign capital. Another implication identifies trade deficits as a result of domestic savings and investment decisions. Tool Kit 26.1 shows how the small open economy model works.

Took Kit 26.1: Using the Small Open Economy Model

For a small open economy the interest rate is fixed, determined on international capital markets that are large relative to the size of the economy. If the interest rate clears the domestic market, the trade account is balanced. Higher interest rates imply a trade surplus; lower interest rates imply a trade deficit. Follow these steps to analyze the working of the capital market for a small open economy.

Step one: Identify the world interest rate, the demand, and the supply of funds.

Step two: Find the level of investment. This is quantity demanded, and it is read off the demand curve at the world interest rate.

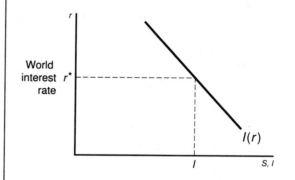

Step three: Find the level of savings. This is the quantity supplied, and it is read off the supply curve at the world interest rate.

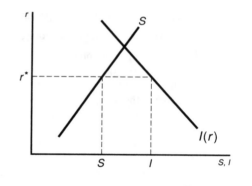

Step four: Find the level of capital inflows or outflows. If the quantity demanded exceeds the quantity supplied, then the country imports capital. Otherwise capital is exported.

Capital inflows from abroad = quantity demanded – quantity supplied (if positive).

Capital outflows to abroad = quantity supplied – quantity demanded (if positive).

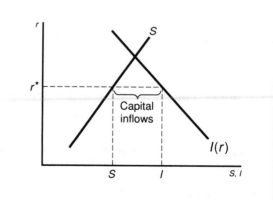

Step five: Find the trade deficit or surplus. If there are capital inflows, the country runs a trade deficit. If there are capital outflows, the country runs a trade surplus.

Trade deficit = inflows of foreign capital.

Trade surplus = outflows of foreign capital.

1 (Worked problem: small open economy) Costa Guano is a small open economy facing a world interest rate equal to 10 percent. Its domestic demand and supply of funds are given in Table 26.1.

a Find the level of investment.
b Find the level of savings.
c Find the level of capital inflows or outflows.
d Does the country run a trade deficit or surplus? How much is it?

Table 26.1

Interest rate (percent)	Demand for funds (millions of guanos)	Supply of funds (millions of guanos)
15	100	100
14	110	90
13	120	80
12	130	70
11	140	60
10	150	50
9	160	40
8	170	30

Step-by-step solution

Step one: Identify the world interest rate, the demand, and the supply of funds. The world interest rate is 10 percent and the demand and supply of funds are given in Table 26.1.

Step two: Find the level of investment. When the interest rate is 10 percent, the demand for funds (investment) equals 150 million.

Step three: Find the level of savings. At an interest rate equal to 10 percent, savings (supply of funds) equals 50 million.

Step four: Find the level of capital inflows or outflows. The quantity demanded exceeds the quantity supplied, so the country imports capital.

Capital inflows from abroad = quantity demanded – quantity supplied = 150 – 50 = 100 million.

Step five: Find the trade deficit or surplus. If there are capital inflows, the country runs a trade deficit.

Trade deficit = inflows of foreign capital = 100 million.

2 (Practice problem: small open economy) El Dorado is a small open economy facing a world interest rate equal to 9 percent. Its domestic demand and supply of funds are given in Table 26.2.

a Find the level of investment.
b Find the level of savings.
c Find the level of capital inflows or outflows.
d Does the country run a trade deficit or surplus? How much is it?

Table 26.2

Interest rate (percent)	Demand for funds (millions of dorals)	Supply of funds (millions of dorals)
11	200	400
10	225	350
9	250	300
8	275	250
7	300	200
6	325	150
5	350	100

3 (Practice problem: small open economy) Erehwemos is a small open economy facing a world interest rate equal to 15 percent. Its domestic demand and supply of funds are given in Table 26.3.

a Find the level of investment.
b Find the level of savings.
c Find the level of capital inflows or outflows.
d Does the country run a trade deficit or surplus? How much is it?

Table 26.3

Interest rate (percent)	Demand for funds (millions of wemos)	Supply of funds (millions of wemos)
20	50	50
19	60	45
18	70	40
17	80	35
16	90	30
15	100	25
14	110	20

Large Open Economy

The United States is a large open economy. This means that domestic savings affects interest rates and the level of investment. Approximately 80 percent of additional savings is invested in the United States. The remaining savings flows abroad. We can analyze large open economies by distinguishing between the domestic and total supply of funds. Tool Kit 26.2 shows how this is done.

Tool Kit 26.2: Using the Large Open Economy Model

Unlike the small open economy model, where foreign savings is perfectly elastic, for the large open economy foreign savings is upward sloping. The interest rate is determined where the total savings supply intersects the domestic demand for funds. Follow these steps.

Step one: Identify the foreign supply of savings, the domestic supply of savings, and the domestic demand for funds (investment function).

Step two: Calculate the total savings supply curve. For each interest rate add the quantity of foreign and domestic savings.

Total savings = foreign savings + domestic savings.

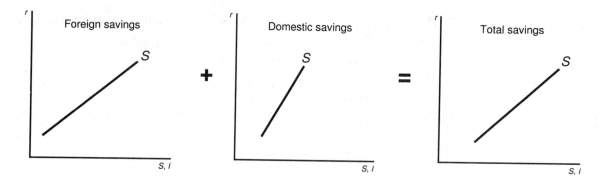

Step three: Find the interest rate that clears the market.

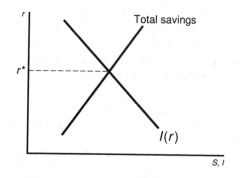

Step four: Find the level of investment. This is the quantity demanded at the equilibrium interest rate.

Step five: Find the level of domestic savings. This is read off the domestic supply of funds at the equilibrium interest rate.

Step six: Calculate the level of capital flows. Recall that this is also the level of the trade deficit.

Capital inflows from abroad = trade deficit = quantity demanded – quantity supplied (if positive).

Capital outflows to abroad = trade surplus = quantity supplied – quantity demanded (if positive).

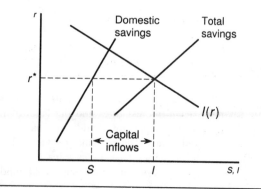

4   (Worked problem: large open economy) Table 26.4 gives the foreign supply of funds, the domestic supply of funds, and the demand for funds (investment function) for a large open economy.

a   Calculate the total supply of funds.
b   Find the equilibrium interest rate.
c   Does this country import or export capital? How much?
d   What is the size of the trade deficit or surplus?

Table 26.4

Interest rate (percent)	Foreign supply (billions of dollars)	Domestic supply (billions of dollars)	Domestic demand (billions of dollars)
12	10,000	15,000	13,000
11	9,000	13,000	16,000
10	8,000	11,000	19,000
9	7,000	9,000	22,000
8	6,000	7,000	25,000
7	5,000	5,000	30,000

Step-by-step solution

Step one: Identify the foreign supply of savings, the domestic supply of savings, and the domestic demand for funds. They are given in Table 26.4.

Step two: Calculate the total savings supply curve. For each interest rate add the quantity of foreign and domestic savings.

Total savings = foreign savings + domestic savings.

At 12 percent total savings = 10,000 + 15,000 = 25,000. At 11 percent total savings = 9,000 + 13,000 = 22,000. Continuing, we get the total supply.

Interest rate (percent)	Total supply (billions of dollars)
12	10,000 + 15,000 = 25,000
11	9,000 + 13,000 = 22,000
10	8,000 + 11,000 = 19,000
9	7,000 + 9,000 = 16,000
8	6,000 + 7,000 = 13,000
7	5,000 + 5,000 = 10,000

Step three: Find the interest rate that clears the market. Supply and demand are equal at $19,000 million when the interest rate is 10 percent.

Step four: Find the level of investment. This is the quantity demanded at the equilibrium interest rate, and it equals $19,000 million.

Step five: Find the level of domestic savings. This is read off the domestic supply of funds at the equilibrium interest rate. At 10 percent the domestic supply is $11,000 million.

Step six: Calculate the level of capital flows. Recall that this is also the level of the trade deficit. Since demand exceeds supply, there will be inflows of capital.

Capital inflows from abroad = trade deficit
= quantity demanded − quantity supplied
= 19,000 − 11,000 = $8,000 million.

5   (Practice problem: large open economy) Table 26.5 gives the foreign supply of funds, the domestic supply of funds, and the demand for funds (investment function) for a large open economy.

a   Calculate the total supply of funds.
b   Find the equilibrium interest rate.
c   Does this country import or export capital? How much?
d   What is the size of the trade deficit or surplus?

Table 26.5

Interest rate (percent)	Foreign supply (billions of dollars)	Domestic supply (billions of dollars)	Domestic demand (billions of dollars)
15	1,000	500	900
14	800	400	1,200
13	600	300	1,500
12	400	200	1,800
11	200	100	2,100
10	100	50	2,500

6   (Practice problem: large open economy) Table 26.6 gives the foreign supply of funds, the domestic supply of funds, and the demand for funds (investment function) for a large open economy.

a   Calculate the total supply of funds.
b   Find the equilibrium interest rate.
c   Does this country import or export capital? How much?
d   What is the size of the trade deficit or surplus?

Table 26.6

Interest rate (percent)	Foreign supply (billions of dollars)	Domestic supply (billions of dollars)	Domestic demand (billions of dollars)
8	200	50	100
7	180	45	110
6	160	40	130
5	140	35	140
4	120	30	150
3	100	25	160
2	80	20	170

Answers to Problems

2   a   Investment = 250.
    b   Savings = 300.
    c   Capital outflows = 50.
    d   Trade surplus = 50.

3   a   Investment = 100.
    b   Savings = 25.

c   Capital inflows = 75.
d   Trade surplus = 75.

5   a

Interest rate (percent)	Total supply (billions of dollars)
15	1,000 + 500 = 1,500
14	800 + 400 = 1,200
13	600 + 300 = 900
12	400 + 200 = 600
11	200 + 100 = 300
10	100 + 50 = 150

b   Interest rate = 14 percent.
c   Capital inflows = 1,200 − 400 = 800.
d   Trade deficit = 800.

6   a

Interest rate (percent)	Total supply (billions of dollars)
8	200 + 50 = 250
7	180 + 45 = 225
6	160 + 40 = 200
5	140 + 35 = 175
4	120 + 30 = 150
3	100 + 25 = 125
2	80 + 20 = 100

b   Interest rate = 4 percent.
c   Capital inflows = 150 − 30 = 120.
d   Trade deficit = 120.

Part Six

Unemployment Macroeconomics

Chapter 27

OVERVIEW OF UNEMPLOYMENT MACROECONOMICS

Chapter Review

Beginning the unemployment part of the course, this chapter sketches how the full-employment model is modified to study downturns in the economy when there is excess capacity and unemployment persists at a high rate. The discussion of the consequences of fixed wages and price for the labor, product, and capital markets provides the framework for the remainder of this part. (In Part Seven we see how wages and prices adjust slowly, leading to the investigation of dynamics.) The chapter concludes by applying this framework to recent macroeconomic history.

ESSENTIAL CONCEPTS

1   Slow adjustment of wages to changes in the supply and demand for labor is the basic explanation for the high levels of unemployment that periodically trouble the economy. This chapter and the others in Part Three develop the model of the economy under the assumptions that wages and prices are rigid and that there is no net change in the capital stock. While this is a simplification, it does expose the basic structure of the economy

and gives results that mirror the behavior of labor and product markets in the short run.

2   The aggregate labor market includes all of the workers and jobs in the economy. If the wages settle at the market-clearing level, the economy would be at full employment. Anyone willing to work at the going wage could find a job. In reality, this is not the case, because wages are somewhat inflexible. When the demand for labor shifts to the left and the wage fails to adjust downward, unemployment exists. The key to understanding unemployment lies in three issues: what causes shifts in the demand for labor; why do wages fail to adjust; and why does the shortage take the form of unemployment rather than a shared reduction in hours among workers. The latter issues are postponed until Part Four; the issue of shifts in labor demand is the focus here.

3   In the product market the vertical aggregate supply intersects with the downward-sloping aggregate demand. If prices settle at the market-clearing level, the economy would produce its potential GDP. Prices are costly to change, however, and in the short run may be rigid. In this case, if demand shifts to the left, for example, the economy's output will fall to the quantity demanded, which is less than aggregate supply. There is excess capacity.

4　Any **demand shock**, such as economic downturns abroad or a loss in business confidence, can bring about a demand shock and production level below the economy's capacity. When there is excess capacity, government may use fiscal policy to shift aggregate demand to the right, restoring full employment without waiting for the slow adjustment of wages and prices. On the other hand, supply shifts have no impact on output when there is excess capacity.

5　The **Federal Reserve Board** uses monetary policy to affect interest rates. This can also shift aggregate demand in that lower interest rates may stimulate investment. The Federal Reserve is also interested in controlling inflation by limiting aggregate demand. It may be too aggressive in raising interest rates, pushing the economy into recession.

6　Examples of the effects of fiscal and monetary policy include the Kennedy tax cut in 1963, a fiscal stimulus that brought the economy out of stagnation into a period of low unemployment, sustained growth, and stable prices, and Federal Reserve chairman Paul Volcker's tight monetary policy, which led to the deep recession of the early 1980s. The most recent recession in 1991 also may have resulted from overaggressive monetary policy, and the reasons for the recovery remain controversial.

BEHIND THE ESSENTIAL CONCEPTS

1　The supply of labor is quite inelastic, but not perfectly so. If the wage rises, more people are willing to work. If the wage that you could currently earn rose high enough, you might get a part-time job, increase the hours at the part-time job you already have, or even drop out of college to get a full-time job. It follows that if the wage falls, individuals voluntarily leave the labor force. Involuntary unemployment, however, differs from voluntary unemployment. If the wage is stuck above the market-clearing level, there is an excess supply of workers, each of whom would like a job at the going wage. Because there is a shortage of jobs, these individuals are involuntarily unemployed.

2　The basic structure of the model developed in this chapter is the same as the full-employment model studied in Chapters 25 and 26. The economy divides into three markets: product, labor, and capital. Further, the various supplies and demands have essentially the same interpretation, and the markets are interdependent. The key difference is that here we assume that price and wages are rigid, whereas in the full-employment version, prices adjust to clear the markets. The reason for the two approaches is that the economy behaves in the long run as the full-employment model predicts. This is natural because prices and wages have time to adjust in the long run. However, in the short run, before there is time for adjustment, the fixed price approach works better.

3　While aggregate demand plays a minor role in full-employment macroeconomics, it takes center stage in unemployment macroeconomics. With fixed prices the short side of the product market determines the output level. When demand exceeds supply, supply is the short side, output is at full employment, but there is upward pressure on prices. When demand falls short of supply, demand is the short side, and output is set at the intersection of demand and the price level. According to this model economic downturns result from insufficient demand.

4　In microeconomics we often look at one market at a time. Macroeconomics, however, is a general equilibrium discipline. We must keep an eye on product, labor, and capital markets. The fundamental lesson from general equilibrium analysis is that markets are linked. The key link between the product and labor market is that shifts in output bring about shifts in the demand for labor. The key link between the capital and product market is that interest rates affect investment and consumption, the two chief components of aggregate demand.

SELF-TEST

True or False

1　The basic explanation for unemployment is that wages do not adjust quickly to their market clearing levels.

2　The focus of this chapter is the short run, when prices and wages are rigid and the net change in the capital stock is small.

3　Involuntary unemployment results when the demand for labor shifts to the right and wages fail to adjust.

4　If reductions in the demand for labor were shared equally among workers, there would not be unemployment, but rather underemployment.

5　The supply curve for labor is quite elastic.

6　If the labor supply curve is upward sloping and wages adjust, then any reduction in the number of jobs represents involuntary unemployment.

7　Most economists agree that the primary causes of disturbance in the labor market are shifts in the demand curve.

8　In the model of the product market prices are assumed to be rigid.

9　A rightward shift in aggregate demand leads to excess capacity and involuntary unemployment.

10　When the economy experiences excess capacity, a rightward shift in aggregate supply increases output.

11　When the economy experiences excess capacity, a rightward shift in aggregate demand increases output.

12　Lower interest rates encourage investment, shifting aggregate demand to the right.

13　The Federal Reserve Board controls monetary policy.

14　The Kennedy tax cut shifted aggregate supply to the right, avoiding a recession.

15 Paul Volcker's restrictive monetary policies shifted aggregate demand to the left, causing the recession of the early 1980s.

Multiple Choice

1 Unemployment macroeconomics deals with the short run, a period of time when

   a product prices are rigid;
   b nominal wages are rigid;
   c real wages are rigid;
   d the net change in the capital stock is small;
   e all of the above.

2 The basic model of the labor market in this chapter is based on the assumption that

   a wages are fixed;
   b product prices are fixed;
   c interest rates and product prices are fixed;
   d wages and product prices are fixed;
   e wages, interest rates, and product prices are fixed.

3 In modern economies, the labor supply curve is

   a perfectly elastic;
   b relatively flat;
   c horizontal;
   d relatively inelastic;
   e downward sloping.

4 Suppose that the demand for labor increases. If the supply of labor is perfectly inelastic, then

   a wages increase;
   b employment increases;
   c both wages and employment increase;
   d wages decrease;
   e both wages and employment decrease.

5 If the wage is the market-clearing wage, then

   a any unemployment is involuntary;
   b any unemployment is voluntary;
   c unemployment is voluntary at low wages and voluntary at high wages;
   d the supply of labor is relatively elastic;
   e none of the above.

6 If every worker who wants a job at prevailing wages has one, then there is

   a full employment;
   b no voluntary unemployment;
   c no inflation;
   d b and c;
   e all of the above.

7 Suppose the demand curve for labor shifts to the left. Then

   a there is full employment if wages are flexible;
   b if wages are inflexible, there is involuntary unemployment;
   c there is unemployment if the supply of labor is relatively inelastic;
   d the supply of labor will also shift to the left;
   e a and b.

8 Suppose the demand curve for labor shifts to the left. If wages are rigid, then

   a most workers work fewer hours;
   b wages rise;
   c most workers work more hours;
   d most workers work the same number of hours, but some individuals will not be able to find employment;
   e most workers work more hours, but some job vacancies will not be filled.

9 The aggregate supply curve is

   a vertical;
   b relatively flat at low levels of output but relatively steep at higher levels of output;
   c relatively steep at low levels of output but relatively flat at higher levels of output;
   d relatively inelastic;
   e horizontal.

10 The aggregate demand and supply model of the product market presented in this chapter is based on the assumption that

   a wages are fixed;
   b product prices are fixed;
   c interest rates and product prices are fixed;
   d wages and product prices are fixed;
   e wages, interest rates, and product prices are fixed.

11 There is excess capacity when

   a aggregate supply is to the left of aggregate demand at the fixed price level;
   b aggregate demand is to the left of aggregate supply at the fixed price level;
   c the price level is fixed above its market clearing level;
   d the demand for labor is elastic;
   e interest rates are set on international capital markets.

12 When there is excess capacity

   a an increase in aggregate demand has no effect on output;
   b an increase in aggregate supply puts upward pressure on prices;
   c a decrease in aggregate supply puts upward pressure on prices;
   d an increase in aggregate demand increases output with little effect on prices;
   e an increase in aggregate supply increases output and reduces the price level.

13 When there is excess demand

   a output is below the economy's potential GDP;
   b output is above the economy's potential GDP;
   c output equals the economy's potential GDP;
   d there is downward pressure on prices;
   e a and d.

14 When there is excess demand

   a an increase in aggregate demand has no effect on output;

b an increase in aggregate supply puts upward pressure on prices;

c a decrease in aggregate supply puts upward pressure on prices;

d an increase in aggregate demand increases output with little effect on prices;

e none of the above.

15 When the government increases defense spending in order to shift aggregate demand to the right it is engaging in

a monetary policy;
b fiscal policy;
c supply restrictions;
d protectionism;
e monetary stimulus.

16 Monetary policy is controlled by the

a U.S. Treasury Department;
b Congress;
c President;
d Federal Reserve;
e b and c.

17 Monetary policy affects aggregate demand through its effect on

a capacity;
b unemployment;
c interest rates;
d real wages;
e the price level.

18 The Kennedy administration's 1963 tax cut caused

a aggregate demand to shift to the left;
b aggregate supply to shift to the left;
c aggregate demand to shift to the right;
d aggregate supply to shift to the right;
e no change in either aggregate supply or demand.

19 The oil price shocks of the early 1970s caused

a aggregate demand to shift to the left;
b aggregate supply to shift to the left;
c aggregate demand to shift to the right;
d aggregate supply to shift to the right;
e no change in either aggregate supply or demand.

20 The onset of the 1991 recession was due in part to

a overaggressive monetary policy;
b the Gulf War inspired oil price shock;
c a weak banking system in the aftermath of the savings and loan crisis;
d all of the above;
e none of the above.

Completion

1 When employers pay the market-clearing wage, any unemployment is _____.

2 If the demand for labor shifts to the left and there is no adjustment in wages, unemployment _____.

3 If the price level is greater than the level at which aggregate demand equals aggregate supply, then there is an excess _____ of goods.

4 Leftward shifts in aggregate demand that lead to downturns in the economy are called _____.

5 When the government increases its expenditures in order to shift aggregate demand to the right and eliminate excess capacity it is performing _____.

6 The _____ controls monetary policy.

7 During a period of excess capacity, a rightward shift in _____ leaves output unchanged.

8 When there is full employment, a rightward shift in _____ puts upward pressure on prices.

9 The Kennedy tax cut shifted the aggregate _____ curve to the _____.

10 In the early 1980s, the Federal Reserve Board took actions that caused the aggregate _____ curve to shift to the _____, leading to both a recession and a reduction in inflation.

Answers to Self-Test

True or False

1	t	6	f	11	t
2	t	7	t	12	t
3	t	8	t	13	t
4	t	9	f	14	f
5	f	10	f	15	t

Multiple Choice

1	e	6	a	11	b	16	d
2	e	7	e	12	d	17	c
3	d	8	d	13	c	18	c
4	a	9	a	14	a	19	b
5	b	10	d	15	b	20	d

Completion

1 voluntary
2 increases
3 supply
4 demand shocks
5 fiscal policy
6 Federal Reserve
7 aggregate supply
8 aggregate demand
9 demand, right
10 demand, left

Doing Economics: Tools and Practice Problems

In the aggregate labor market, the economy's levels of employment, unemployment, and real wages are determined. Unemployment results from the failure of wages to adjust to the market-clearing level, and several problems explore this relationship between sticky wages and unemployment. The output of the economy is determined in the product market, but with rigid prices it may not be clear. The key to analyzing how low output is affected by changes in the economy is to find out whether the initial equilibrium is at the intersection of aggregate demand and supply or one of excess demand or supply. Several problems study this issue.

Unemployment and Rigid Wages

When real wages remain stuck above market-clearing levels, the number of workers willing to work at the going wage exceeds the number of jobs available. This excess supply of labor is involuntary unemployment and is part of the overall unemployment rate. In this section we calculate the real wage by adjusting the nominal wage for inflation and then determine the level of unemployment. Tool Kit 27.1 shows how to proceed.

Tool Kit 27.1: Determining the Unemployment Rate

Above market-clearing real wages lead to unemployment. The level of unemployment is the amount of excess supply in the labor market. Follow these steps to see this relationship.

Step one: Identify the demand curve, the supply curve, and the nominal wage and price level.

Step two: Find the real wage by adjusting the nominal wage for inflation:

real wage = (nominal wage/price index) × 100.

Step three: Substitute the real wage into the demand curve and find the quantity demanded. This is the number of jobs available.

Step four: Substitute the real wage into the supply curve and find the quantity supplied. This is the number of workers willing to work at the going wage.

Step five: Find the quantity of unemployment by subtracting the quantity demanded from the quantity supplied:

unemployment =
quantity supplied – quantity demanded.

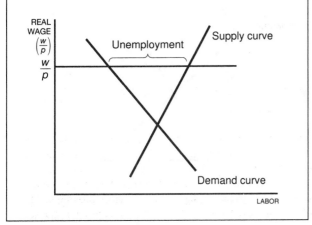

---

1 (Worked problem: unemployment rate) The nominal wage level equals $2,400 per month, and the price index equals 120. Table 27.1 gives the demand and supply of labor. Find the level of unemployment.

Table 27.1

Real wage	Demand	Supply
$2,400	6,000	18,000
$2,200	7,000	16,000
$2,000	8,000	14,000
$1,800	9,000	12,000
$1,600	10,000	10,000
$1,400	11,000	8,000
$1,200	12,000	6,000

Step-by-step solution

Step one: Identify the demand curve, the supply curve, and the nominal wage and price level. The demand and supply are given in Table 27.1, the nominal wage is $2,400, and the price index equals 120.

Step two: Find the real wage by adjusting the nominal wage for inflation:

real wage = ($2,400/120) × 100 = $2,000.

Step three: Substitute the real wage into the demand curve, and find the quantity demanded. It is 8,000.

Step four: Substitute the real wage into the supply curve, and find the quantity supplied. It is 14,000.

Step five: Find the quantity of unemployment by subtracting the quantity demanded from the quantity supplied:

unemployment = 14,000 – 8,000 = 6,000.

2 (Practice problem: unemployment rate) Suppose that the nominal wage level remains at $2,400, as in problem 1, and the demand and supply curves remain as in Table 27.1 but the price level increases to 150. Find the new level of unemployment.

3 (Practice problem: unemployment rate) Suppose that the nominal wage is $3,300, the price index is 150, and the demand and supply curves are as given in Table 27.1. Find the level of unemployment.

4 (Practice problem: unemployment rate) For each of the following, find the level of unemployment given the demand and supply of labor shown in Table 27.2.

a   Nominal wage = $50,000; price level = 100.
b   Nominal wage = $50,000; price level = 125.
c   Nominal wage = $50,000; price level = 167.
d   Nominal wage = $60,000; price level = 120.

Table 27.2

Real wage	Demand	Supply
$60,000	8,000	26,000
$55,000	10,000	25,000
$50,000	12,000	24,000
$45,000	14,000	23,000
$40,000	16,000	22,000
$35,000	18,000	21,000
$30,000	20,000	20,000
$25,000	22,000	19,000

The Labor Market with Rigid Wages

When either the demand or supply of labor shifts and wages fail to adjust to the market-clearing level, there is unemployment. In modern economies, wages exhibit downward rigidity, although they do adjust upward when conditions warrant. In the following problems real wages are assumed to be inflexible downward, but flexible upward. Tool Kit 27.2 shows how to analyze labor markets under these conditions.

Tool Kit 27.2: Analyzing the Labor Market with Rigid Real Wages and Unemployment

If the labor market is at its market-clearing equilibrium and demand or supply shifts, it may not move to the new market-clearing equilibrium if the real wage does not adjust. Follow these steps to analyze a labor market in which the real wage is rigid when market conditions call for it to fall.

Step one: Start with a market-clearing equilibrium in the labor market.

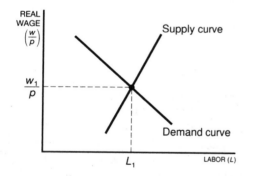

Step two: Identify a cause, and determine which curve shifts.

Step three: Shift the supply or demand curve.

Step four: Find the new equilibrium. If there is excess demand, increase the real wage to the market-clearing level. If there is excess supply, keep the real wage constant.

Step five: Show the level of unemployment as the difference between quantity demanded and quantity supplied.

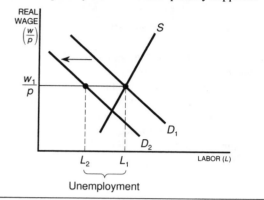

---

5 (Worked problem: rigid wages) Suppose a deep recession strikes the economy. Show the effect on real wages, unemployment, and the labor market.

Step-by-step solution

Step one: Start with an equilibrium.

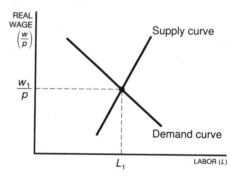

Step two: Identify a cause, and determine which curve shifts. The economy's output falls in a recession, and this reduces the demand for labor.

Step three: Shift the demand curve. It shifts left.

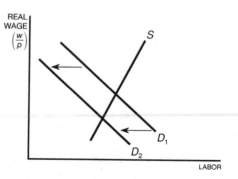

Step four: Find the new equilibrium. Although there is an excess supply of labor, wages do not adjust downward, because they are assumed rigid.

Step five: Show the level of unemployment.

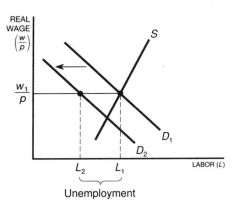

6   (Practice problem: rigid wages) Strife abroad leads to a wave of new immigration. Show the effect on real wages, unemployment, and the labor market.

7   (Practice problem: rigid wages) For each of the following, show the effect on real wages, unemployment, and the labor market.

   a   The economy booms, and its output increases.
   b   As barriers fall, millions of women enter the labor market.
   c   The demand for U.S. exports soars, and the economy's output expands to meet the demand.
   d   The baby bust generation reaches working age, and the number of new entrants declines.
   e   Recession overseas reduces the demand for U.S. exports, and the economy falls into a recession.

The Product Market with Rigid Prices

When prices are rigid, the economy may not reach equilibrium at full employment. In this case the short-run equilibrium will occur where the rigid price level meets the short side of the market. If aggregate demand is less than aggregate supply, the economy will have excess capacity. If aggregate demand at this price level exceeds aggregate supply, the economy will produce at capacity, but the price level will remain below the intersection. In these two cases the economy responds differently to shifts in aggregate demand or supply. Tool Kit 27.3 shows how to analyze the product market with rigid prices.

Tool Kit 27.3: Using Aggregate Demand and Supply When Prices are Rigid

When prices are rigid, aggregate demand and supply shift for the same reasons they shift when prices are flexible. Table 27.3 lists some important causes of these shifts. The difference is that output must adjust to the short side of the market. These steps show how to find the short-run equilibrium when prices are rigid.

Table 27.3

Shifts in aggregate demand: changes in consumption, investment, government spending, or net exports.

Shifts in aggregate supply: increases in capacity (aggregate supply shifts right) or changes in import prices (aggregate supply shifts up or down).

Step one: Start with an equilibrium. This may be at the intersection of aggregate supply and demand or not.

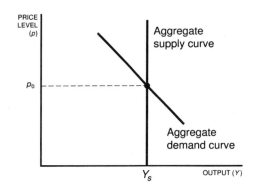

Step two: Identify an exogenous cause and determine which curve shifts and in what direction.

Step three: Shift the curve.

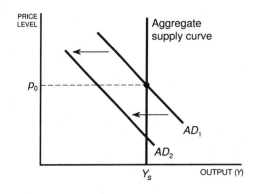

Step four: Find the new equilibrium level of output. This will occur at the intersection of the rigid price level and the short side of the market; that is the lesser of aggregate demand or supply.

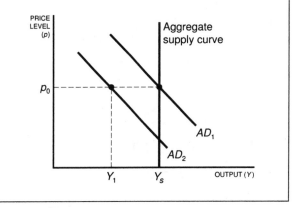

8 (Worked problem: aggregate demand and supply) The economy is in deep recession with high unemployment and a great deal of excess capacity. The government grants an investment tax credit, and firms respond with larger levels of private investment. Show the effect on equilibrium output.

Step-by-step solution

Step one: Start with an equilibrium. Because the economy is in deep recession, this will be on the flat portion of the aggregate supply curve.

Step two: Identify a cause, and determine which curve shifts and in what direction. The increase in investment shifts aggregate demand to the right.

Step three: Shift the curve.

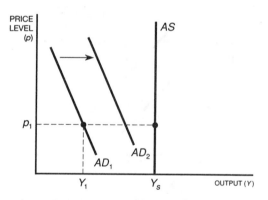

Step four: Find the new equilibrium, and compare the output and price levels. Output increases with little or no change in the price level.

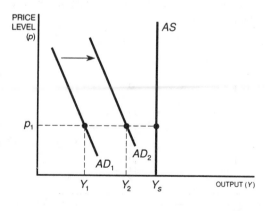

9 (Practice problem: aggregate demand and supply) The economy is brimming with activity. Although unemployment and idle production capacity are at 10-year lows, foreign demand for U.S. exports surges still higher. Show the effect on equilibrium output.

10 (Practice problem: aggregate demand and supply) For each of the following, show the effect on equilibrium output.

  a The economy is in equilibrium at the intersection of aggregate demand and aggregate supply. Tight monetary policy raises interest rates, and this causes a dramatic decline in new investment.

  b The economy is in deep recession, and the government stimulates private consumption with a tax cut.

  c The economy is at maximum capacity, and the government increases its spending.

  d The economy is in equilibrium at the intersection of aggregate demand and aggregate supply. The government increases income taxes.

  e The economy is in deep recession, and foreign demand for exports falls still further.

  f The economy is in equilibrium at the intersection of aggregate demand and aggregate supply. The price of imported oil rises by 50 percent.

  g The economy is in deep recession, and the price of imported oil rises by 50 percent.

  h The economy is at maximum capacity. There is excess demand. Capacity expands.

Answers to Problems

2 Real wage = ($2,400/150) × 100 = $1,600; unemployment = 10,000 – 10,000 = 0.

3 Real wage = ($3,300/150) × 100 = $2,200; unemployment = 16,000 – 7,000 = 9,000.

4 a Real wage = ($50,000/100) × 100 = $50,000; unemployment = 24,000 – 12,000 = 12,000.

  b Real wage = ($50,000/125) × 100 = $40,000; unemployment = 22,000 – 16,000 = 6,000.

  c Real wage = ($50,000/167) × 100 = $30,000; unemployment = 20,000 – 20,000 = 0.

  d Real wage = ($60,000/120) × 100 = $50,000; unemployment = 24,000 – 12,000 = 12,000.

6 The supply curve shifts to the right, and the wage fails to adjust downward; this results in unemployment equal to $L_s - L_1$.

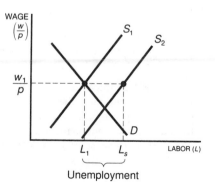

7 *a* The demand curve shifts to the right, and wages adjust upward to clear the market.

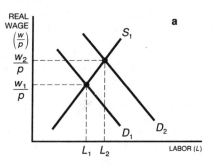

b The supply curve shifts to the right, and the wage fails to adjust downward; this results in unemployment equal to $L_s - L_1$.

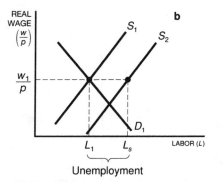

c The demand curve shifts to the right, and wage adjusts upward to clear the market.

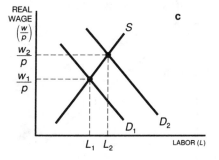

d The supply curve shifts to the left, and the wage adjusts upward to clear the market.

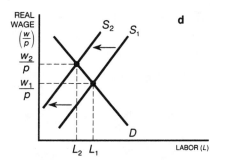

e The demand curve shifts to the left, and the wage fails to adjust downward; this results in unemployment equal to $L1 - L_s$.

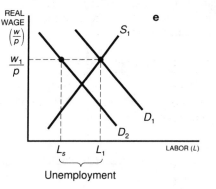

9 Aggregate demand shifts to the right; this leaves output unchanged.

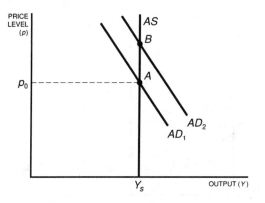

10 *a* Aggregate demand shifts to the left and decreases output.

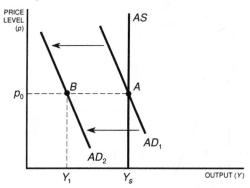

b Aggregate demand shifts to the right; this increases output.

c Aggregate demand shifts to the right; this leaves output unchanged.

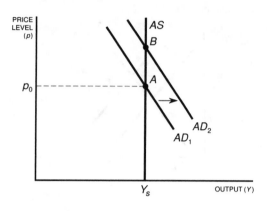

d Aggregate demand shifts to the left and decreases output.

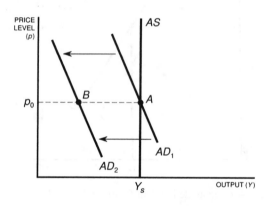

e Aggregate demand shifts to the left; this decreases output.

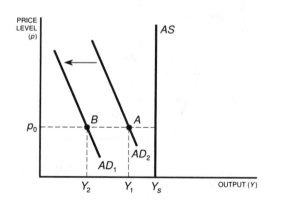

f Aggregate supply shifts to the left; this decreases output.

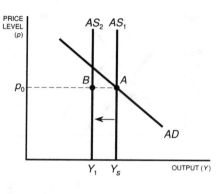

g Aggregate supply shifts to the left; this leaves output unchanged.

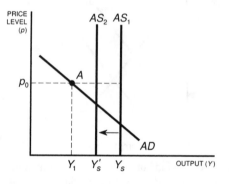

h Aggregate supply shifts to the right; this increases output.

Chapter 28

AGGREGATE DEMAND

Chapter Review

Chapter 27 showed how in the short run the economy's level of output is governed by aggregate demand. This chapter takes a look behind aggregate demand and explains what it is composed of and how it is determined. Income-expenditure analysis is used to show how the economy reaches an equilibrium on the demand side and why the equilibrium changes. The multiplier process, by which changes in spending ripple through the economy, is explained.

ESSENTIAL CONCEPTS

1   **Income-expenditure analysis** starts with the assumption that the price level is fixed. Aggregate expenditures then depend upon national income, and the **aggregate expenditures schedule,** drawn in Figure 28.1, shows how aggregate expenditures increase as national income increases. Because national income equals national output (GDP), the horizontal axis also measures output. Aggregate expenditures equal output where the aggregate expenditures schedule crosses the 45-degree line. This is the equilibrium, and at this point all of the economy's output is purchased.

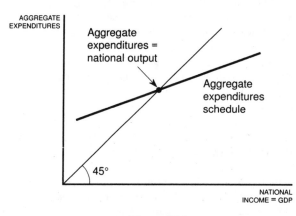

Figure 28.1

2   Aggregate expenditures comprise consumption, investment, government purchases, and net exports, as shown by the equation

$$AE = C + I + G + E.$$

Changes in any of the components of expenditure shift the aggregate expenditures schedule up or down and cause equilibrium output to change. In Figure 28.2 *AE* shifts up and output increases.

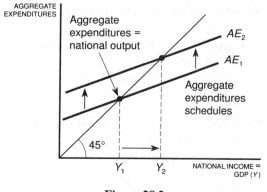

Figure 28.2

3   The **consumption function** describes the relationship between income and consumption. The additional consumption resulting from a one-dollar increase in income is the **marginal propensity to consume** (*MPC*), which is the slope of the consumption function. The **marginal propensity to save** (*MPS*) is the additional amount saved out of a one-dollar increase in income.

4   The **investment multiplier** shows that when aggregate expenditures shift, the change in output is greater than the change in spending. It works as follows. Suppose investment increases. This investment causes incomes to rise and, through the marginal propensity to consume, causes a second round of extra consumption spending. This extra round of consumption further increases incomes and generates a third round of spending. The process continues, and the ultimate increase in output equals the multiplier times the initial change in spending. The formula for the multiplier is $1/(1 - MPC)$.

5   Income taxation makes the consumption function flatter because some of the extra income is taken in taxes, rather than spent. Similarly, in an open economy, some spending leaves the economy for imported goods, further flattening the aggregate expenditures schedule. Both taxes and imports cause the multiplier to be smaller.

BEHIND THE ESSENTIAL CONCEPTS

1   You might wonder why we need an entire chapter on aggregate demand. Although it appears simple (just another downward-sloping demand), the aggregate demand curve masks some complexity. Income-expenditure analysis shows that the amount of aggregate demand at any given price level is an equilibrium, where desired spending is brought into equality with output. Like most equilibria in the economy, this one requires some adjustment time as inventories rise or fall toward their appropriate level and as successive rounds of spending work their way through the economy. For some purposes we may be satisfied with limiting our attention to the aggregate demand curve. Other purposes require the deeper look given by the income-expenditure approach.

2   You might wonder what role prices play in income-expenditure analysis. Prices are determined by supply and demand, but here we are concerned only with the demand side. At this level of analysis, prices are fixed; one way of thinking about this is that the economy is operating on the flat portion of the aggregate supply curve.

3   How does the economy reach equilibrium without price adjustment? **Inventories** play the key role.

   a   If GDP is below equilibrium, then households and firms want to buy more than the economy produces. Firms notice this when they sell the goods they have on inventory. Firms produce more to restore inventories, and GDP increases.

   b   If GDP is above equilibrium, the story is reversed. Households and firms buy less than the economy produces, inventories of unsold goods accumulate, and firms cut back on production. GDP falls.

4   A helpful way to understand the multiplier process and why the multiplier is smaller when there are taxes and trade is to think in terms of injections and leakages. Suppose that the economy gets an injection of new spending, say an increase in exports. Some people will receive this money, and they will save some and spend some. We say that the money that is saved "leaks" out of the system. The money that is spent becomes other people's income; they in turn save some and spend some, and the process continues. The total amount of spending generated is a multiple of the initial injection. But any leakage reduces the total amount of spending. Clearly, taxes go to the government. That is a leakage. Money spent on imports goes abroad—another leakage. More leakages means less spending and a smaller multiplier.

SELF-TEST

True or False

1   Aggregate expenditures include what households, firms, and government spend on goods and services produced in the United States.

2   As income increases by one dollar, aggregate expenditures increase by less than one dollar.

3   The statement that national income equals national output is an example of an equilibrium relationship.

4   The statement that aggregate expenditures equal national output is an example of an equilibrium relationship.

5   Unplanned inventories equal zero in equilibrium.

6   The aggregate expenditures schedule gives total desired spending at each price level.

7   Aggregate expenditures equal consumption plus investment plus government purchases plus net exports.

8   Net exports equal imports minus exports.

9 The relationship between a household's income and its consumption is called its consumption function.

10 Disposable income equals national income plus taxes.

11 The marginal propensity to consume equals the marginal propensity to save.

12 The multiplier equals 1 divided by the marginal propensity to consume.

13 An increase in investment causes equilibrium output to increase by more than the change in investment.

14 A higher tax rate on income means that the multiplier is larger.

15 Imports increase as income increases.

Multiple Choice

1 This chapter focuses on the case where
a aggregate demand equals aggregate supply;
b aggregate demand is greater than aggregate supply;
c aggregate demand is less than aggregate supply;
d prices are fully flexible;
e the economy's capacity is fully utilized.

2 The aggregate expendures schedule traces out the relationship between the economy's total expenditures and national income.
a keeping output fixed;
b at a given price level;
c as price changes to clear the product market;
d holding consumption fixed;
e holding net exports fixed.

3 As income increases, aggregate expenditures
a increase;.
b decrease;
c remain the same;
d increase or decrease depending on how product prices change;
e increase or decrease depending on events in the capital market.

4 The marginal propensity to consume gives
a the fraction of extra income that will be consumed;
b the ratio of consumption to income;
c the fraction of extra consumption that comes from wage income;
d the fraction of extra consumption that comes from interest and dividends;
e the ratio of consumption out of wage income to consumption out of interest and dividend income.

5 The aggregate expenditures schedule
a is horizontal;
b is horizontal for low levels of output, upward sloping for intermediate levels of output, and steep at high levels of output;
c is upward sloping;
d is downward sloping;
e is a 45-degree line.

6 If national income were zero, consumption would
a be zero;
b be positive because people would borrow or consume out of savings;
c equal autonomous consumption;
d b and c;
e none of the above.

7 The statement that national income is equal to national output is an example of
a an equilibrium relationship;
b an identity;
c a behavioral relationship;
d a hypothesis;
e an assumption.

8 The statement that aggregate expenditures equal aggregate output is an example of
a an equilibrium relationship;
b an identity;
c a behavioral relationship;
d a hypothesis;
e an assumption.

9 In equilibrium, it is true that
a the output of the economy must be purchased;
b aggregate expenditures equal national output;
c aggregate expenditures equal what households, firms, and government want to spend at the equilibrium level of national income;
d unplanned inventories equal zero;
e all of the above.

10 An upward shift in the aggregate expenditures schedule occurs when
a households, firms, and government decide to spend more at each level of income;
b households, firms, and government decide to spend less at each level of income;
c households, firms, and government decide to spend less at each price level;
d households, firms, and government decide to spend more at each price level;
e the economy is in recession.

11 Which of the following is not a component of aggregate expenditures?
a consumption;
b investment;
c government purchases;
d net exports;
e taxes.

12 The household's consumption function traces out the relationship between its consumption and its
a investment;
b income;
c taxes;
d inflation rate;
e total expenditure.

13 The slope of the aggregate expenditures schedule equals

a zero;

b the average propensity to save;

c the marginal propensity to save;

d the average propensity to consume;

e the marginal propensity to consume.

14 The marginal propensity to save equals

a the marginal propensity to consume;

b 1 plus the marginal propensity to consume;

c 1 minus the marginal propensity to consume;

d the reciprocal of the marginal propensity to consume;

e none of the above.

15 Autonomous consumption is

a the extra consumption out of an additional dollar of income;

b the ratio of consumption to disposable income;

c that part of consumption that does not depend on disposable income;

d the extra savings out of an additional dollar of income;

e the level of consumption when desired inventories equal zero.

16 When investment increases, equilibrium output

a increases by more than the change in investment;

b increases by less than the change in investment;

c increases by the same amount as the change in investment;

d decreases by less than the change in investment;

e decreases by more than the change in investment.

17 In the simple model without taxes, the multiplier equals

a 1 divided by the marginal propensity to save;

b the marginal propensity to save;

c the marginal propensity to consume;

d 1 divided by the marginal propensity to consume;

e zero.

18 Adding taxes to the income-expenditure model causes

a disposable income to be less than national income;

b the aggregate expenditures schedule to be flatter;

c the multiplier to be smaller;

d the aggregate consumption function to be flatter;

e all of the above.

19 The amount of each extra dollar of disposable income spent on imports is the

a marginal propensity to import;

b marginal propensity to consume;

c marginal propensity to save;

d marginal propensity to export;

e marginal propensity to invest.

20 Adding international trade to the income-expenditure model causes

a the multiplier to be larger;

b the aggregate expenditures schedule to be flatter;

c the aggregate expenditures schedule to be steeper;

d the equilibrium level of output to be lower;

e a and c.

Completion

1 The relationship between the economy's total expenditures and national income is summarized by the _____.

2 The _____ traces the relationship between consumption and disposable income.

3 The portion of consumption that does not depend upon income is called _____.

4 The fraction of additional income that is consumed is called the _____.

5 National output increases by more than the amount of a given increase in investment by a factor called the _____.

6 When firms cannot sell all that they produce, they experience an increase in _____.

7 The relationship between national income and imports is summarized by the _____.

8 The additional imports purchased as a result of a one-dollar increase in income is called the _____. .

9 An economy actively engaged in international trade and investment is called an _____.

10 The difference between imports and exports equals a _____.

Answers to Self-Test

True or False

1	t	6	f	11	f
2	t	7	t	12	f
3	f	8	f	13	t
4	t	9	t	14	f
5	t	10	f	15	t

Multiple Choice

1	c	6	d	11	e	16	a
2	b	7	b	12	b	17	a
3	a	8	a	13	e	18	e
4	a	9	e	14	c	19	a
5	c	10	a	15	c	20	b

Completion

1 aggregate expenditures schedule
2 consumption function
3 autonomous consumption
4 marginal propensity to consume
5 multiplier
6 unplanned inventories
7 import function
8 marginal propensity to import
9 open economy
10 trade deficit

Doing Economics: Tools and Practice Problems

The topic of this section is income-expenditure analysis. We begin with an explanation of the tools needed and follow with problems involving economies with no taxes or imports. For each, we find the consumption function, calculate the aggregate expenditures schedule, and solve for the economy's equilibrium output. We then study the multiplier process, which shows how a change in spending brings about a larger change in equilibrium output. Finally, we consider progressively more complicated problems with income taxes and imports, where the net export function must be calculated. An important lesson of these latter problems concerns how taxes and imports affect the multiplier and the stability of the economy.

Tool Kit 28.1: Finding the Aggregate Consumption Function

Aggregate expenditures equal the sum of consumption, investment, government spending, and net exports. The first step is to find the aggregate consumption function, which shows the level of consumption that corresponds to each level of national income.

Step one: Identify the marginal propensity to consume (*MPC*), autonomous consumption, and the income tax rate.

Step two: Calculate the aggregate consumption function by substituting various values of national income into the following formula:

aggregate consumption = autonomous consumption + [national income (1 − tax rate)] × MPC.

(Note that the term in brackets is disposable income, which equals national income when the tax rate is zero.)

Tool Kit 28.2: Finding the Net Export Function

In an open economy, net exports must be included in aggregate expenditures. The **net export function** shows the level of net exports that corresponds to each level of national income.

Step one: Identify the marginal propensity to import (*MPI*), the tax rate, and the level of exports.

Step two: Calculate the import function by substituting various levels of national income into the following formula:

imports = [national income (1 − tax rate)] *MPI*.

Step three: Find the net export function by subtracting imports from exports for every level of national income:

net exports = exports − imports.

Tool Kit 28.3: Finding the Aggregate Expenditures Schedule

With the aggregate consumption and net export functions in place, the aggregate expenditures schedule can be calculated. The aggregate expenditures schedule shows the level of aggregate spending corresponding to each level of national income.

Step one: Identify the aggregate consumption function, the level of investment spending, the level of government spending, and the net export function.

Step two: Calculate the aggregate expenditures schedule by summing consumption, investment, government spending, and net exports for each level of national income:

$$AE = C + I + G + X.$$

Tool Kit 28.4: Using Income-Expenditure Analysis to Determine the Equilibrium

We find the equilibrium level of output and national income (which are always equal), where the aggregate expenditures schedule crosses the 45-degree line. At this point, consumers, firms, government, and foreigners spend just enough to purchase the economy's output.

Step one: Identify the aggregate expenditures schedule.

Step two: Choose a level of national income, and find the corresponding level of aggregate expenditures. If they are equal, stop. This is the equilibrium level of output.

Step three: If aggregate expenditures exceed national income, then inventories will fall, firms will increase production, and output will expand. Choose a greater level of national income, and repeat step one. If aggregate expenditures are less than national income, then inventories will rise, firms will cut back production, and output will decrease. Choose a lower level of national income, and repeat step one.

Step four: Continue until the equilibrium is found.

Tool Kit 28.5: Using Multiplier Analysis to Find the Ultimate Change in Output Caused by an Initial Change in Spending

The great lesson of income-expenditure analysis is that an initial change in spending ripples through the economy and ultimately results in a larger change in output. The process by which this happens is the multiplier process, and the multiplier itself shows how much larger than the initial change in spending is the ultimate change in output.

Step one: Identify the marginal propensity to consume, the tax rate, the marginal propensity to import, and the initial change in spending.

Step two: Calculate the multiplier. Use the appropriate formula:

no taxes or imports:	$1/(1 - MPC)$
income taxes:	$1/[1 - MPC\,(1 - \text{tax rate})]$
open economy (no taxes):	$1/[1 - (MPC + MPI)]$
open economy with taxes:	$1/[1 - (MPC - MPI)\,(1 - \text{tax rate})]$.

Step three: Calculate the ultimate change in output by multiplying the initial change in spending by the multiplier:

change in output = (change in spending) × multiplier.

Step four: Verify the result in step three by adding the change in spending to the original aggregate expenditures schedule and solving for the new equilibrium level of output.

---

1 (Worked problem: income-expenditure analysis) For years, Costa Guano has remained closed to foreign trade and investment. The government of the isolated nation spends no money and collects none in taxes. Autonomous consumption is 300 million guanos (the currency of Costa Guano), and the marginal propensity to consume equals 0.8. Finally, domestic private investment equals 100 million guanos.

a Find the aggregate consumption function.
b Find the aggregate expenditures schedule.
c Calculate equilibrium output and national income.
d Brimming with confidence, Costa Guano's firms increase their investment spending by 100 million (for a total of 200 million). Calculate the multiplier and the ultimate change in output brought about by this increase in investment.

Step-by-step solution

Step one (a): Find the aggregate consumption function. Identify the *MPC,* autonomous consumption, and the tax rate. The *MPC* is 0.8, autonomous consumption is 300 million, but the tax rate is zero.

Step two: Calculate the aggregate consumption function. When national income equals zero, aggregate consumption equals autonomous consumption (300 million). At 500 million in national income, consumption equals 300 + 0.8 (500) = 700 million. Continuing, we derive Table 28.1.

Table 28.1

National income (millions of guanos)	Aggregate consumption
0	300
500	700
1,000	1,100
1,500	1,500
2,000	1,900
2,500	2,300
3,000	2,700

Step one (b): Find the aggregate expenditures schedule. Identify the aggregate consumption function, investment, government spending, and the net export function. The aggregate consumption function is given in Table 28.1, and investment equals 100 million. Government spending and net exports equal zero.

Step two: Calculate the aggregate expenditures schedule adding investment and consumption, as shown in Table 28.2.

Table 28.2

National income	Aggregate consumption	Investment	Aggregate expenditures
0	300	100	400
500	700	100	800
1,000	1,100	100	1,200
1,500	1,500	100	1,600
2,000	1,900	100	2,000
2,500	2,300	100	2,400
3,000	2,700	100	2,800

Step one (c): Calculate equilibrium output and national income. Identify the aggregate expenditures schedule. It appears in Table 28.2.

Step two: Choose a level of national income. When national income is 2,000 million, aggregate expenditures equal 2,000 million. Consumers and firms purchase exactly the economy's output of 2,000 million.

Step one (d): Calculate the multiplier and the ultimate change in output brought about by this increase in investment of 100 million (from 100 to 200). Identify the marginal propensity to consume, the tax rate, the marginal propensity to import, and the initial change in spending. The *MPC* is 0.8, the initial change in spending is 100 million. There are no taxes or imports.

Step two: Calculate the multiplier. Because there are no taxes or imports, the multiplier equals

$1/(1 - MPC) = 1/(1 - 0.8) = 1/0.2 = 5.$

Step three: Calculate the ultimate change in output:

change in output = 100 × 5 = 500 million.

Step four: Verify the result in step three by adding the change in spending to the original aggregate expenditures schedule and solving for the new equilibrium level of output. The new aggregate expenditures schedule is given in Table 28.3.

Table 28.3

National income	Aggregate consumption	Investment	Aggregate expenditures
0	300	200	500
500	700	200	900
1,000	1,100	200	1,300
1,500	1,500	200	1,700
2,000	1,900	200	2,100
2,500	2,300	200	2,500
3,000	2,700	200	2,900

The new equilibrium level of output is 2,500 million, which is 500 million more than originally. It checks!

2 (Practice problem: income-expenditure analysis) El Dorado, an insular economy closed to foreign trade and investment, has no income-based taxes, and its government spends nothing. The marginal propensity to consume is 0.9, autonomous consumption is 5 billion dorals (the currency of El Dorado), and private investment totals 1 billion. (Hint: Choose national income in intervals of 10 billion; that is, 0, 10, 20, etc.)

    a   Find the aggregate consumption function.

    b   Find the aggregate expenditures schedule.

    c   Calculate equilibrium output and national income.

    d   After a period of stability, investment in El Dorado jumps to 2 billion dorals. Calculate the multiplier and the ultimate change in output brought about by this increase in investment.

3 (Practice problem: income-expenditure analysis) In Erehwemos, there is no taxation and also no government spending. The economy is closed to the outside world. All investment is undertaken by private domestic firms, and the total is 2 billion wemos (the Erehwemosian currency). The marginal propensity to consume is 0.75, and autonomous consumption is 2 billion. (Hint: Choose national income levels in intervals of 4 billion; that is, 0, 4, 8, 12, etc.)

    a   Find the aggregate consumption function.

    b   Find the aggregate expenditures schedule.

    c   Calculate equilibrium output and national income.

    d   Investment climbs to 4 billion. Calculate the multiplier and the ultimate change in output brought about by this increase in investment.

4 (Worked problem: income-expenditure analysis) This problem builds on problem 1. Recognizing the need for infrastructure investment, the government of Costa Guano institutes an income tax with a flat rate of 25 percent and spends 300 million. Private investment continues at 200 million, the marginal propensity to consume is 0.8, and autonomous consumption equals 300 million. The economy remains closed to foreign trade.

    a   Find the consumption function.

    b   Find the aggregate expenditures schedule.

    c   Find the equilibrium level of output.

    d   Suppose that the government raises its spending by 200 million (for a total of 500 million). Calculate the multiplier, and solve for the ultimate change in output brought about by the increase in government spending.

Step-by-step solution

Step one (a): Identify the marginal propensity to consume, autonomous consumption, and the income tax rate. The *MPC* is 0.8, autonomous consumption equals 300 million, and the income tax rate is 25 percent.

Step two: Calculate the aggregate consumption function. When national income equals zero, aggregate consumption equals autonomous consumption (300 million). At 500 million in national income, aggregate consumption = 300 + [500 (1 − 0.25)] × 0.8 = 600. Continuing, we derive Table 28.4.

Table 28.4

National income (millions of guanos)	Aggregate consumption
0	300
500	600
1,000	900
1,500	1,200
2,000	1,500
2,500	1,800
3,000	2,100

Step one (b): Identify the aggregate consumption function, investment, government spending, and the net export function. The aggregate consumption function is given in Table 28.4, investment equals 200 million, and government spending equals 300 million. Net exports remain zero.

Step two: Calculate the aggregate expenditures schedule by adding consumption, investment, and government spending, as shown in Table 9.5.

Table 28.5

National income	Aggregate consumption	Investment	Government spending	Aggregate expenditures
0	300	200	300	800
500	600	200	300	1,100
1,000	900	200	300	1,400
1,500	1,200	200	300	1,700
2,000	1,500	200	300	2,000
2,500	1,800	200	300	2,300
3,000	2,100	200	300	2,600

Step one (c): Identify the aggregate expenditures schedule. It appears in Table 28.5.

Step two: Choose a level of national income. When national income is 2,000 million, aggregate expenditures equal 2,000 million. Consumers and firms purchase exactly the economy's output of 2,000 million.

Step one (d): Identify the marginal propensity to consume, the tax rate, the marginal propensity to import, and the initial change in spending. The *MPC* is 0.8, and the initial change in spending is 200 million. The tax rate is 25 percent, but there are no imports.

Step two: Calculate the multiplier. Because there is an income tax but no imports, the multiplier equals

$$1/[1 - MPC\,(1 - \text{tax rate})] = 1/[1 - 0.8\,(1 - 0.25)]$$
$$= 1/(1 - 0.6) = 1/0.4 = 2.5.$$

(In problem 1, there was no income tax and the multiplier equalled 5. Here, the income tax reduces the multiplier to 2.5.)

Step three: Calculate the ultimate change in output:

change in output = 200 × 2.5 = 500 million.

Step four: Verify the result in step three by adding the change in spending to the original aggregate expenditures schedule and solving for the new equilibrium level of output. The new aggregate expenditures schedule is given in Table 28.6.

Table 28.6

National income	Aggregate consumption	Investment	Government spending	Aggregate expenditures
0	300	200	500	1,000
500	600	200	500	1,300
1,000	900	200	500	1,600
1,500	1,200	200	500	1,900
2,000	1,500	200	500	2,200
2,500	1,800	200	500	2,500
3,000	2,100	200	500	2,800

The new equilibrium level of output is 2,500 million, which is 500 million more than originally. It checks. The economy is more stable with the income tax, for it took a 200-million change in spending to change output by 500 million in problem 1, where there was no tax.

5   (Practice problem: income-expenditure analysis) This problem builds on problem 2. An income tax system is passed by El Dorado's Council of Ministers. The flat tax rate is 1/9 on all income, and the government plans to spend 3 billion. The marginal propensity to consume remains at 0.9, autonomous consumption is 5 billion, and private investment continues at 2 billion.

  a   Find the consumption function.
  b   Find the aggregate expenditures schedule.
  c   Find the equilibrium level of output.
  d   Suppose that the government raises its spending by 4 billion (for a total of 7 billion). Calculate the multiplier, and solve for the ultimate change in output brought about by the increase in government spending.

6   (Practice problem: income-expenditure analysis) This problem builds on problem 3. Erehwemos institutes an income tax with a flat rate of 1/3. The government

spends 2 billion wemos. The marginal propensity to consume remains at 0.75, autonomous consumption equals 2 billion, and private investment equals 4 billion.

  a   Find the aggregate consumption function.
  b   Find the aggregate expenditures schedule.
  c   Calculate equilibrium output and national income.
  d   Responding to the war threat from neighboring Erehwon, the government doubles spending. The increase in government spending is 2 billion (for a total of 4 billion). Calculate the multiplier and the ultimate change in output brought about by this increase in government spending.

7   (Worked problem: income-expenditure analysis) This problem builds on problems 1 and 4. Costa Guano has opened its economy to foreign trade. It exports 500 million in world markets. Its citizens have developed tastes for foreign goods, however, and their marginal propensity to import is 1/3. Autonomous consumption remains at 300 million, investment equals 200 million, government spending has returned to 300 million, the marginal propensity to consume is 0.8, and the tax rate is 25 percent.

  a   Find the aggregate consumption function.
  b   Find the net export function.
  c   Find the aggregate expenditures schedule.
  d   Find the equilibrium level of output.
  e   Suppose that exports increase by 325 million (for a total of 825 million). Calculate the multiplier, and solve for the ultimate change in output brought about by the increase in exports.

Step-by-step solution

Step one (a and b): The aggregate consumption function is the same as in problem 4 and is given in Table 28.4. Identify the marginal propensity to import, the tax rate, and the level of exports. The *MPI* equals 1/3, the tax rate is 25 percent, and the level of exports equals 500 million guanos.

Step two: Calculate the import function. When national income is zero, so are imports. When national income is 500 million, imports = [500 × (1 − 0.25)] × 1/3 = 125 million. Continuing, we derive the import function in Table 28.7.

Table 28.7

National income	Imports
0	0
500	125
1,000	250
1,500	375
2,000	500
2,500	625
3,000	750

Step three: Find the net export function. When national income is zero, net exports are 500 − 0 = 500 million. When national income is 500, net exports are 500 − 125 = 375. Continuing, we derive the net export function in Table 28.8.

Table 28.8

National income	Exports	Imports	Net exports
0	500	0	500
500	500	125	375
1,000	500	250	250
1,500	500	375	125
2,000	500	500	0
2,500	500	625	–125
3,000	500	750	–250

Step one (c): Identify the aggregate consumption function, investment, government spending, and the net export function. The aggregate consumption function is given in Table 28.4, investment equals 200 million, government spending is 300 million, and the net export function appears in Table 28.8.

Step two: Calculate the aggregate expenditures schedule by adding consumption, investment, government spending, and net exports. Table 28.9 gives the results.

Table 28.9

National income	Aggregate consumption	Investment	Government spending	Net exports	Aggregate expenditures
0	300	200	300	500	1,300
500	600	200	300	375	1,475
1,000	900	200	300	250	1,650
1,500	1,200	200	300	125	1,825
2,000	1,500	200	300	0	2,000
2,500	1,800	200	300	–125	2,175
3,000	2,100	200	300	–250	2,350

Step one (d): Identify the aggregate expenditures schedule. It is given in Table 28.9.

Step two: Choose a level of national income. When national income equals 2,000 million, aggregate expenditures equal 2,000 million, and this is the equilibrium level of output.

Step one (e): Identify the marginal propensity to consume, the tax rate, the marginal propensity to import, and the initial change in spending. The *MPC* is 0.8, the tax rate is 25 percent, the *MPI* equals 1/3, and exports increase by 325 million.

Step two: Calculate the multiplier. The multiplier

$$= 1/[1 - (MPC - MPI)(1 - \text{tax rate})]$$

$$= 1/[1 - (0.8 - 1/3)(1 - 0.25)] = 20/13 = 1.54.$$

Note that in the open economy, the multiplier is smaller than in the closed economy of problem 4.

Step three: Calculate the ultimate change in output:

change in output = 325 × 20/13 = 500.

Step four: Verify the result in step three by adding the change in exports to the original aggregate expenditures

schedule (Table 28.9) and solving for the new equilibrium level of output. The new aggregate expenditures schedule is given in Table 28.10. (Note that the increase in exports increases net exports by 325 million.)

Table 28.10

National income	Aggregate consumption	Investment	Government spending	Net exports	Aggregate expenditures
0	300	200	300	825	1,625
500	600	200	300	700	1,800
1,000	900	200	300	575	1,975
1,500	1,200	200	300	450	2,150
2,000	1,500	200	300	325	2,325
2,500	1,800	200	300	200	2,500
3,000	2,100	200	300	75	2,825

The new equilibrium level of output is 2,500 million, which is 500 million more than originally. It checks. The open economy is yet more stable because it took a 325 million change in spending to change output by 500 million.

8 (Practice problem: income-expenditure analysis) This problem builds on problems 2 and 5. The new economics minister wins the day with a brilliant argument against protectionism, and El Dorado opens its economy. Its exports surge to 14 billion. The marginal propensity to import is 9/40, the marginal propensity to consume remains at 0.9, autonomous consumption is 5 billion, private investment is 2 billion, and the government spends 3 billion.

a Find the consumption function.
b Find the net export function.
c Find the aggregate expenditures schedule.
d Find the equilibrium level of output.
e Suppose that exports increase by 4 billion (for a total of 18 billion). Calculate the multiplier, and solve for the ultimate change in output brought about by the increase in exports.

9 (Practice problem: income-expenditure analysis) This problem builds on problems 3 and 6. With peace at hand, the Erehwemos economy is opened to foreign trade and investment. Exports equal 8/3 (2.67) billion, and the marginal propensity to import is 0.25. Government spending has returned to 2 billion, but private investment remains at 4 billion. Autonomous consumption is also 2 billion, and the marginal propensity to consume remains at 0.75. Finally, the tax rate is 1/3.

a Find the aggregate consumption function.
b Find the net export function.
c Find the aggregate expenditures schedule.
d Calculate the equilibrium output and national income.
e Exports increase to 16/3 (5.33) billion. Calculate the multiplier and the ultimate change in output brought about by this increase in exports.

Answers to Problems

2   Table 28.11 gives

   a   the aggregate consumption function and
   b   the aggregate expenditures schedule.

Table 28.11

National income (billions of dorals)	Aggregate consumption	Investment	Aggregate expenditures
0	5	1	6
10	14	1	15
20	23	1	24
30	32	1	33
40	41	1	42
50	50	1	51
60	59	1	60
70	68	1	69
80	77	1	78
90	86	1	87
100	95	1	96

   c   Equilibrium output is 60 billion.
   d   The multiplier is $1/(1 - 0.9) = 10$. The change in output is $1 \times 10 = 10$. Table 28.12 shows that when investment increases to 2 billion, equilibrium output grows to 70 billion. It verifies that equilibrium output increases by 10 (from 60 to 70 billion), as indicated above.

Table 28.12

National income	Aggregate consumption	Investment	Aggregate expenditures
0	5	2	7
10	14	2	16
20	23	2	25
30	32	2	34
40	41	2	43
50	50	2	52
60	59	2	61
70	68	2	70
80	77	2	79
90	86	2	88
100	95	2	97

3   Table 28.13 gives

   a   the aggregate consumption function and
   b   the aggregate expenditures schedule.

Table 28.13

National income (billions of wemos)	Aggregate consumption	Investment	Aggregate expenditures
0	2	2	4
4	5	2	7
8	8	2	10
12	11	2	13
16	14	2	16
20	17	2	19
24	20	2	22
28	23	2	25

   c   Equilibrium output is 16 billion.
   d   The multiplier is $1/(1 - MPC) = 1/(1 - 0.75) = 4$. The change in output is $2 \times 4 = 8$. This is verified by Table 28.14, which shows that the new equilibrium output is 24 billion.

Table 28.14

National income	Aggregate consumption	Investment	Aggregate expenditures
0	2	4	6
4	5	4	9
8	8	4	12
12	11	4	15
16	14	4	18
20	17	4	21
24	20	4	24
28	23	4	27

5   Table 28.15 shows

   a   the aggregate consumption function and
   b   the aggregate expenditures schedule.

Table 28.15

National income (billions of dorals)	Aggregate consumption	Investment	Government spending	Aggregate expenditures
0	5	2	3	10
10	13	2	3	18
20	21	2	3	26
30	29	2	3	34
40	37	2	3	42
50	45	2	3	50
60	53	2	3	58
70	61	2	3	66
80	69	2	3	74
90	77	2	3	82
100	85	2	3	90

   c   The equilibrium level of output is 50 billion.
   d   The multiplier is $1/[1 - MPC(1 - t)] = 1/[1 - 0.9(1 - 1/9)] = 5$. The change in output is $4 \times 5 = 20$

billion. Table 28.16 shows that when government spending is 7 billion, the new equilibrium output is 70 billion, which represents an increase of 20 billion.

Table 28.16

National income	Aggregate consumption	Investment	Government spending	Aggregate expenditures
0	5	2	7	14
10	13	2	7	22
20	21	2	7	30
30	29	2	7	38
40	37	2	7	46
50	45	2	7	54
60	53	2	7	62
70	61	2	7	70
80	69	2	7	78
90	77	2	7	86
100	85	2	7	94

6   Table 28.17 gives

   a   the aggregate consumption function and

   b   the aggregate expenditures schedule.

Table 28.17

National income (billions of wemos)	Aggregate consumption	Investment	Government spending	Aggregate expenditures
0	2	4	2	8
4	4	4	2	10
8	6	4	2	12
12	8	4	2	14
16	10	4	2	16
20	12	4	2	18
24	14	4	2	20
28	16	4	2	22

   c   Equilibrium output is 16 billion.

   d   The multiplier is $1/[1 - MPC(1 - t)] = 1/[1 - 0.75 (1 - 1/3)] = 2$. The change in equilibrium output is $2 \times 2 = 4$ billion, as is verified by Table 28.18, which shows that the new equilibrium output is 20 billion.

Table 28.18

National income	Aggregate consumption	Investment	Government spending	Aggregate expenditures
0	2	4	4	10
4	4	4	4	12
8	6	4	4	14
12	8	4	4	16
16	10	4	4	18
20	12	4	4	20
24	14	4	4	22
28	16	4	4	24

8   Table 28.19 shows

   a   the aggregate consumption function,

   b   the net export function, and

   c   the aggregate expenditures schedule.

Table 28.19

National income (billions of dorals)	Aggregate consumption	Investment	Government spending	Net exports	Aggregate expenditures
0	5	2	3	14	24
10	13	2	3	12	30
20	21	2	3	10	26
30	29	2	3	8	42
40	37	2	3	6	48
50	45	2	3	4	54
60	53	2	3	2	60
70	61	2	3	0	66
80	69	2	3	-2	72
90	77	2	3	-4	78
100	85	2	3	-6	84

   d   Equilibrium output is 60 billion.

   e   The multiplier is $1/[1 - (MPC - MPI)(1 - t)] = 1/[1 - (0.9 - 9/40)(1 - 1/9)] = 2.5$. The change in output is $4 \times 2.5 = 10$. Table 28.20 shows that the new equilibrium output is 70 billion, which indicates an increase of 10 billion.

Table 28.20

National income	Aggregate consumption	Investment	Government spending	Net exports	Aggregate expenditures
0	5	2	3	18	28
10	13	2	3	16	34
20	21	2	3	14	40
30	29	2	3	12	46
40	37	2	3	10	52
50	45	2	3	8	58
60	53	2	3	6	64
70	61	2	3	4	70
80	69	2	3	2	76
90	77	2	3	0	82
100	85	2	3	-6	84

9   Table 28.21 shows

   a   the aggregate consumption function,

   b   the net export function, and

   c   the aggregate expenditures schedule.

Table 28.21

National income (billions of dorals)	Aggregate consumption	Invest-ment	Govern-ment spending	Net exports	Aggregate expenditures
0	2	4	2	2⅔	10⅔
4	4	4	2	2	12
8	6	4	2	1⅓	13⅓
12	8	4	2	⅔	14⅔
16	10	4	2	0	16
20	12	4	2	−⅔	17⅓
24	14	4	2	−1⅓	18⅔
28	16	4	2	−2	20

Table 28.22

National income (billions of dorals)	Aggregate consumption	Invest-ment	Govern-ment spending	Net exports	Aggregate expenditures
0	2	4	2	5⅓	13⅓
4	4	4	2	4⅔	14⅔
8	6	4	2	4	16
12	8	4	2	3⅓	17⅓
16	10	4	2	2⅔	18⅔
20	12	4	2	2	20
24	14	4	2	1⅓	21⅓
28	16	4	2	⅔	22⅔

d   Equilibrium output equals 16 billion.

e   The multiplier is $1/[1 - (MPC - MPI)(1 - t)] = 1/[1 - (0.75 - 0.25)(1 - ⅓)] = 1.5$. The change in output is $(8/3) \times 1.5 = 4$ billion. Table 28.22 shows that the new equilibrium output equals 20 billion, which is an increase of 4 billion.

Chapter 29

CONSUMPTION AND INVESTMENT

Chapter Review

This chapter moves behind aggregate expenditures and gives a deeper look at two of its components—consumption and investment. The important issues involve how consumption and investment are determined and the causes of shifts in the consumption and investment functions. This chapter concludes the discussion of income-expenditure analysis. The next three chapters move on to the topics of money and monetary policy.

ESSENTIAL CONCEPTS

1   What determines **consumption** expenditures? The basic building block is the **Keynesian consumption function,** which gives the relationship between consumption and current income. Figure 29.1 shows that as current income increases by one dollar, consumption increases by the marginal propensity to consume. Other, more future-oriented theories of consumption are the **life-cycle hypothesis** and the **permanent income hypothesis.** These hypotheses shift the focus away from current in-

Figure 29.1

come to expected future income, interest rates, and prices.

2   The life-cycle hypothesis asserts that individuals plan their consumption over their entire lifetime. Thus, people save during their working years when income is high in order to provide for consumption during retirement. Because savings play such an important role, cur-

rent and expected future interest rates as well as expected future income have significant effects on the level of consumption. The life-cycle hypothesis is a future-oriented explanation. It implies that the relationship between consumption and current income would be quite flat, as shown in Figure 29.2.

Figure 29.2

3   The permanent income hypothesis also argues that people rationally plan their present and future consumption, saving in good years to provide extra consumption in bad years. Again, the focus is on both current and future income, interest rates, and prices. The permanent income hypothesis reconciles the discrepancy between the aggregate and the individual: over time, aggregate consumption increases in the same proportion as income, while for individuals consumption increases by a smaller proportion than income.

4   In reality, the relationship between current income and consumption is not as flat as the future-oriented theories suggest. Two explanations of why consumption seems to be more dependent on current income involve **durable goods consumption** and **credit rationing.** When incomes fall during recessions, individuals postpone purchases of durable goods. Because they are uncertain when and if good times will return, they take the safer alternative of making do with old durable goods. Further, when incomes fall, individuals find borrowing more difficult than the permanent income hypothesis asserts. Banks also are unsure of the future incomes of borrowers and are reluctant to lend money to the unemployed. It is safer for banks to lend money to those who do not need it!

5   **Investment** includes firms' purchases of new plant and equipment and inventories, and households' purchases of new houses, which are durable goods. Business investment in plant and equipment is based on the expectation that future profits from the investment will more than outweigh the current investment expenditure. Of course, the firm must discount future revenues and costs; therefore, the interest rate is important. The investment schedule gives the total value of investment at each rate of interest. Lower interest rates increase the present value of profits and lead to more investment.

6   Firms face technological risks and market risks and they demand compensation, the size of which depends upon the size of the risks, their ability to share the risks, and their willingness to bear the risks themselves. The other important factor is the availability of funds. During recessions the investment schedule shifts to the left because expectations of profits decrease, risks appear larger, risk-sharing opportunities diminish, firms grow less willing to bear risks, and available funds dry up.

7   Firms hold inventories of inputs in order to **facilitate production;** a firm can be sure that the inputs will be there when needed. Firms may hold inventories of output in order to **smooth production;** that is, the firm can produce at a steady rate and always have enough to meet a highly variable consumer demand. Nonetheless, inventories are much more variable than output and contribute to the instability of the economy. During downturns, for example, it is less risky for firms to cut production and sell off inventories than to continue to produce in the hope that good times will return.

BEHIND THE ESSENTIAL CONCEPTS

1   The marginal propensity to consume out of current income is quite high, and thus the consumption function slopes up rather steeply. Why, then, do we study the future-oriented theories of consumption, which stress the future and predict a flat consumption function? The answer is that the life-cycle and permanent income hypotheses provide a deeper understanding of consumption, especially of what factors might cause the Keynesian consumption function to shift and the stability of the relationship. For example, in recessions, people become pessimistic about future incomes and postpone durable goods purchases, shifting the consumption function and aggregate expenditures down. Remember that the central questions in macroeconomics involve the fluctuations in the economy; therefore, it is vital to understand the causes of the changes.

2   The life-cycle and permanent income hypotheses involve borrowing and savings; thus, they teach us the importance of capital markets. If you were always able to obtain credit, your consumption would not vary much. You could borrow in low-income years (such as during college), live well, and repay during high-income years. But capital markets are not perfect; credit rationing suggests that banks are reluctant to let you borrow against future earnings. When your income is less during recessions and you need money, the best available option is to postpone major purchases. Imperfect capital markets make consumption more variable, and thus they are at the center of the discussion about economic ups and downs.

3   To see why business investment is volatile and why it fluctuates over the business cycle, put yourself in the shoes of a business owner. The economy is in recession, and customers are not buying your products. Profits are

down, and you have little retained earnings to spend on investment. The bank will not lend to you because it perceives your precarious financial position. Even if you could obtain funds, a recession is not the time to take risks. During good times, a failed investment may only mean lower profits; during bad times, it may mean bankruptcy. The safest option is to postpone purchases of new plant and equipment, cut production, and sell off inventories.

4   While modern macroeconomists of every school think that a firm microeconomic foundation for their theories is essential, the differences between microeconomics and macroeconomics are interesting. Microeconomics focuses largely on prices. In the basic competitive model, prices always adjust and clear the market. Even when imperfect competition is the subject, economists focus on the failure of prices to capture all costs and benefits or to find the right level. In macroeconomics, especially the new Keynesian approach, prices do not do their job, and markets do not always clear. Consumption is driven by income, not so much by prices. There is still an equilibrium, but it is one in which income, not price, adjusts until desired aggregate spending equals output.

SELF-TEST

True or False

1   The Keynesian consumption function describes the relationship between consumption and permanent disposable income.

2   According to the life-cycle hypothesis, people save during working years to provide for consumption during retirement.

3   According to the permanent income hypothesis, people save during good years to offset low income during bad years.

4   The future-oriented theories of consumption imply that the consumption function is relatively flat.

5   The future-oriented theories of consumption imply that the multiplier is large.

6   Future-oriented theories of consumption imply that current income is relatively less important than wealth.

7   Spending on durable goods is less variable than spending on nondurable goods.

8   A borrower is credit rationed if she cannot afford the interest rate at which banks are willing to lend.

9   Consumption depends more on current disposable income than the future-oriented theories of consumption imply.

10   The investment spending relevant for aggregate expenditures includes purchases of capital equipment by firms and purchases of shares by individuals.

11   Almost all of the volatility in investment is explained by variations in real interest rates.

12   Firms finance most investment out of retained earnings.

13   Firms usually perceive that investment is riskier during recessions.

14   Opportunities to share risk increase during recessions.

15   In the United States economy, inventories fluctuate less than output because firms try to smooth production and produce at a steady rate.

Multiple Choice

1   The view that current disposable income determines current consumption is consistent with the

a   Keynesian consumption function;
b   life-cycle hypothesis;
c   permanent income hypothesis;
d   all of the above;
e   b and c.

2   The idea that individuals save during working years in order to provide for consumption during retirement is called the

a   Keynesian consumption function;
b   life-cycle hypothesis;
c   permanent income hypothesis;
d   all of the above;
e   b and c.

3   The theory that people save in good years to provide for extra consumption in bad years is called the

a   Keynesian consumption function;
b   life-cycle hypothesis;
c   permanent income hypothesis;
d   b and c;
e   all of the above.

4   Which of the following emphasize(s) that expected future income affects current consumption?

a   Keynesian consumption function;
b   life-cycle hypothesis;
c   permanent income hypothesis;
d   all of the above;
e   b and c.

5   Which of the following imply(ies) that a temporary tax cut will significantly increase current consumption?

a   Keynesian consumption function;
b   life-cycle hypothesis;
c   permanent income hypothesis;
d   all of the above;
e   b and c.

6   According to the future-oriented consumption theories, the multiplier is

a   quite small;
b   zero;
c   large;
d   small in recessions but large in booms;
e   large in recessions but small in booms.

7 If the price of an asset that an individual owns rises, then that individual is said to receive

   a human capital;
   b capital gains;
   c retained earnings;
   d temporary income;
   e disposable income.

8 Which of the following are reasons why consumption depends more on current income than the future-oriented theories might suggest?

   a Individuals can postpone purchases of durable goods when current income falls.
   b Banks are reluctant to lend money to people whose current income is low.
   c Individuals can see through the corporate veil, reducing their consumption when profits fall.
   d Government tax and spending policies do not affect individual consumption.
   e a and b.

9 An individual is credit rationed if

   a he cannot afford the interest charged on a loan;
   b banks charge a higher rate of interest to reflect their perception of the risk that he will not repay on schedule;
   c he is unable to borrow even though he is willing to pay the interest, and the interest rate reflects the risk of lending to him;
   d he has no savings;
   e he has no current income.

10 The component of aggregate expenditures that is most variable is probably

   a investment;
   b consumption;
   c government expenditures;
   d net exports;
   e They are equally variable.

11 For aggregate expenditure calculation, which of the following is not included in investment spending?

   a purchases of new capital goods;
   b inventories accumulated in anticipation of sales;
   c purchases of used capital goods;
   d purchases of new homes;
   e none of the above.

12 Before investing, businesses must

   a predict future revenues;
   b predict future costs;
   c adjust future revenues and costs for inflation;
   d compute the present value of profits using the real interest rate;
   e all of the above.

13 The investment function describes the total value of investment at each

   a price level;
   b level of disposable income;
   c level of national income;
   d level of GDP;
   e rate of interest.

14 Real interest rates

   a are quite volatile, reflecting instability in the capital market;
   b vary enough to provide a good explanation of short-term variations in investment;
   c vary little;
   d are irrelevant to the investment decision;
   e change very little but lead to large changes in the level of investment because investment demand is quite elastic.

15 The compensation that firms require to justify the risk of investment depends upon

   a their ability to share the risks;
   b their willingness to bear the risks;
   c the magnitude of the risks;
   d all of the above;
   e none of the above.

16 Most investment is financed

   a out of retained earnings;
   b by borrowing at the real interest rate;
   c by issuing new shares;
   d by selling bonds;
   e by raising product prices.

17 Firms invest less during recessions because

   a retained earnings fall as revenues decline faster than expenses;
   b as individual firms cut back on investment and inventories, national output falls owing to the multiplier effect, further reducing the profitability of investment;
   c banks are less willing to lend because they foresee a greater risk that the loans will not be repaid;
   d firms' forecasts of the profitability of investment become more pessimistic;
   e all of the above.

18 The theory that investment is more volatile than output because firms try to keep a constant ratio of their capital stock to output is called

   a the investment accelerator;
   b Tobin's *q*;
   c the investment multiplier;
   d the production-facilitating theory;
   e the production-smoothing theory.

19 Which of the following correctly states the correlation between inventories and output according to the two theories of inventory investment?

   a Both production smoothing and production facilitating imply that output and inventories are negatively correlated.
   b Both production smoothing and production facilitating imply that output and inventories are positively correlated.
   c Production smoothing implies that output and in-

CONSUMPTION AND INVESTMENT

ventories are negatively correlated, but production facilitating implies that they are positively correlated.

d Production smoothing implies that output and inventories are negatively correlated, but production facilitating implies that they are positively correlated.

e Neither theory implies anything about the correlation.

20 Ways of stimulating investment include

a increasing business confidence by maintaining high output and full employment;

b tax breaks for investment, such as the investment tax credit;

c increasing the availability of credit through monetary policy;

d direct government lending programs;

e all of the above.

Completion

1 The present discounted value of expected future wages is called _____.

2 According to the _____ hypothesis, people save during their working years in order to increase consumption after retirement.

3 The _____ hypothesis argues that people save during good earning years to provide extra consumption during bad years.

4 The Keynesian consumption function stresses the relationship between consumption and _____.

5 Future-oriented theories of consumption, such as the permanent income and life-cycle hypotheses, imply that the aggregate expenditures schedule is _____.

6 The ability to postpone purchases of durable goods and the fact that it is difficult to borrow against future earnings make consumption _____ dependent on current income.

7 Changes in the level of _____ are the principal reason for the economy's instability.

8 Most firms finance most of their investment through _____.

9 Inventories generally _____ during recessions.

10 The _____ theory explains why inventories would decrease during recessions.

Answers to Self-Test

True or False

1	f	6	t	11	f
2	t	7	f	12	t
3	t	8	f	13	t
4	t	9	t	14	f
5	f	10	f	15	f

Multiple Choice

1	a	6	a	11	c	16	a
2	b	7	b	12	e	17	e
3	c	8	e	13	e	18	a
4	e	9	c	14	c	19	c
5	a	10	a	15	d	20	e

Completion

1 human capital
2 life-cycle
3 permanent income
4 current income
5 relatively flat
6 more
7 investment
8 retained earnings
9 increase
10 production facilitating

Doing Economics: Tools and Practice Problems

Using income-expenditure analysis is the first subject in this section. We see how factors that cause changes in consumption and investment bring about shifts in the aggregate expenditures schedule and new equilibrium levels of output. Next, we look carefully at the notion of Ricardian equivalence and study how government fiscal policies might be offset by private savings and borrowing, leaving consumption unchanged. In the real world, consumption is affected by government tax and spending policies. One important explanation involves the cost and availability of credit. Several problems show how imperfect capital markets lead to the failure of Ricardian equivalence.

INCOME-EXPENDITURE ANALYSIS

Income-expenditure analysis can be used to answer such questions as "What is the effect on output of a change in interest rates?" In general, when some economic event causes a change in consumption or investment, the aggregate expenditures schedule will shift and bring about a change in the equilibrium level of output. Table 29.1 lists some important factors that change consumption and investment.

Tool Kit 29.1: Using Income-Expenditure Analysis

Changes in consumption or investment will shift the aggregate expenditures curve and bring about a change in output. The change in output will be a multiple of the initial change in spending. Follow these steps.

Table 29.1

Shifts in Aggregate Expenditures

Changes in consumption, which are related to changes in wealth, real interest rates, credit availability, or estimates of future earnings.

Changes in investment, which are related to changes in real interest rates, stock prices, credit availability, retained earnings, expectations of profitability, perceptions of risk, or willingness to bear risk.

Step one: Start with an equilibrium.

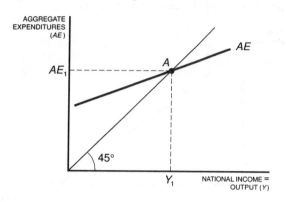

Step two: Identify a cause, and determine its effect on consumption, investment, or both.

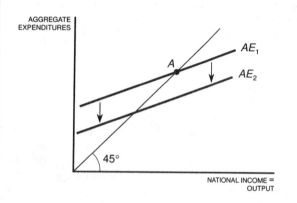

Step three: If consumption or investment increases, shift the aggregate expenditures schedule up; if either decreases, shift the schedule down.

Step four: Find the new equilibrium level of output, and compare.

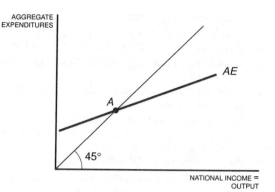

Step two: Identify a cause, and determine its effect on consumption, investment, or both. The increase in stock prices makes individuals wealthier, inducing them to increase consumption. Firms can finance more investment by issuing new shares; thus, investment increases.

Step three: Shift the aggregate expenditures schedule. Because both consumption and investment increase, it shifts up.

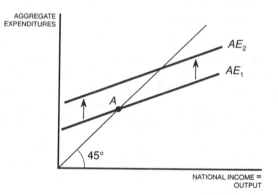

Step four: Find the new equilibrium, and compare. In the new equilibrium, output is greater. The increase in stock prices has brought about an increase in the economy's output.

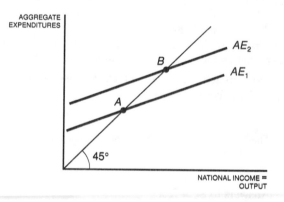

1   (Worked problem: income-expenditure analysis) Use income-expenditure analysis to explain the impact of a boom in the stock market.

Step-by-step solution

Step one: Start with an equilibrium.

2   (Practice problem: income-expenditure analysis) Use income-expenditure analysis to determine the impact of an increase in real interest rates.

3   (Practice problem: income-expenditure analysis) Use income-expenditure analysis to determine the impact of each of the following.

a Firms anticipate an economic downturn accompanied by lower profits.

b The economy has fallen into recession, and because bankruptcies threaten, firms are less willing to bear risk.

c Believing that the defence budget will be cut, consumers fear layoffs.

d Retained earnings reach a four-year high.

e Tight monetary policy has limited the availability of credit for households and firms.

f Real interest rates fall by 2 percent.

g Uncertain about the consequences of the free-trade agreement with Mexico, firms perceive a risky future.

h Loose monetary policy increases the availability of credit.

THE BARRO-RICARDO ARGUMENT

When the government increases spending without a tax increase, it finances its deficit by selling bonds. Today's bonds must be repaid, however. This means that future taxpayers are liable for the debts incurred to finance current spending. The notion of Barro and Ricardo says that households will save now in order to be able to pay the future tax liability, and these savings will completely offset the effects of government deficit finance. In this section, we see how this might be true if capital markets were perfect, and several reasons why private savings do not offset government deficits in the real world: credit constraints and different interest rates for borrowing and lending. The lesson is that imperfect capital markets are an important reason why fiscal policy can be effective.

Tool Kit 29.2: Exploring the Barro-Ricardo Argument

The household's budget constraint shows what combinations of current and future consumption are possible given expectations of current and future income and interest rates. We can use it to analyze the Barro-Ricardo argument that private savings offset budget deficits and thus fiscal policy is ineffective. Follow this procedure.

Step one: Draw the two-period budget constraint for the typical household.

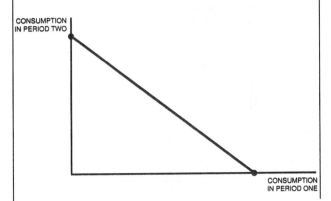

Step two: Choose a point that reflects the household's consumption and savings decisions. Label it *A*.

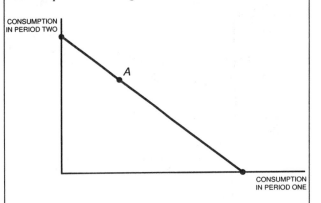

Step three: Show the effect of government borrowing by adding the extra spending to current consumption (the horizontal coordinate of *A*) and subtracting the future tax liability from future consumption (the vertical coordinate of *A*). Label the new point *B*.

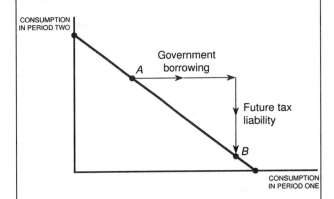

Step four: Determine if point *B* lies on or above the original budget constraint.

Step five: If *B* is on the original budget constraint, then Ricardian equivalence holds, and the household will save to return to point *A* because *A* indicates their preferred decision. If *B* is above the original budget constraint, Ricardian equivalence is not true, and the household may choose to consume more today.

---

4 (Worked problem: Barro-Ricardo) Doctor Campbell and her husband make $210,000 per year and expect that their real earnings will continue for at least 10 years. Although they expect a 50 percent real interest rate over the 10-year period, they neither borrow nor save. The government passes a college subsidy program that will give the Campbells an extra $10,000 this year. It finances this program by issuing 10-year bonds that pay a 50 percent real rate of return over the period. The Campbells expect that they will pay their share of the tax liability when the bonds come due in 10 years. Analyze how the program will affect the Campbells' savings decision and whether Ricardian equivalence would hold.

Step-by-step solution

Step one: Draw the two-period budget constraint. The present discounted value of their income equals $210,000 + [$210,000 × (1/1 + .50)] = $350,000, which is the horizontal intercept. The future equivalent is [$210,000 × (1 + .50)] + $210,000 = $525,000, which is the vertical intercept. The slope is 525,000/350,000 = 1.50, which is 1 plus the interest rate.

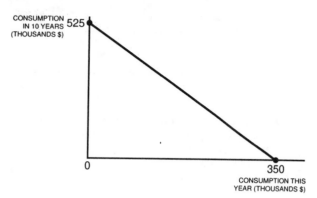

Step two: Choose a point that reflects the household's consumption and savings decisions. The Campbells neither save nor borrow, so they choose to consume $210,000 in each year.

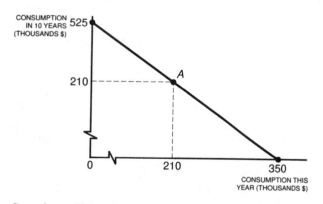

Step three: Show the effect of the program. It gives the Campbells $10,000 now, but it takes away $10,000 × (1 + .50) = $15,000 in 10 years. This moves their chosen point from *A* to *B*.

Step four: Determine if point *B* lies on or above the original budget constraint. Clearly, *B* is on the same budget constraint.

Step five: If B is on the original budget constraint, then Ricardian equivalence holds, and the household will save to return to point *A* because *A* indicates their preferred decision. The Campbells merely increase their savings to $10,000. The principal and interest will be just enough to pay the tax increase that they expect in 10 years. The government borrowing is exactly offset by private savings.

5 (Practice problem: Barro-Ricardo) The typical person in Ricardania earns 20,000 ricks (the local currency) annually. The real interest rate is 5 percent per year, and the typical person borrows 2,000 ricks. The government decides to stimulate the economy by giving each person 5,000 ricks. To finance this grant, the government sells one-year bonds that also pay 5 percent. Taxes will be increased next year to pay off the bonds. Analyze how the grant will affect the typical person's borrowing and savings decisions and also whether Ricardian equivalence would hold in Ricardania.

6 (Worked problem: Barro-Ricardo) Return to the Campbells of problem 4. All information is the same except the real interest rate for borrowing, which is now 100 percent over the 10-year period. Analyze how the program will affect the Campbells' savings decision and whether Ricardian equivalence would hold.

Step-by-step solution

Step one: Draw the two-period budget constraint. The vertical intercept remains as in problem 4, but the horizontal intercept now equals the present value of income discounted at 100 percent = $210,000 + [$210,000 × 1/(1 + 1.00)] = $315,000.

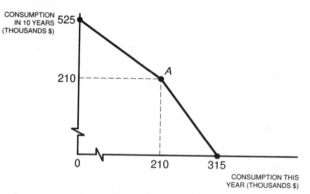

Step two: Choose a point that reflects the household's consumption and savings decisions. The Campbells continue to choose to consume $210,000 in each period.

Step three: Show the effect of the government program. As in problem 4, it increases current consumption by $10,000 and reduces future consumption by $15,000, as shown by point *B*.

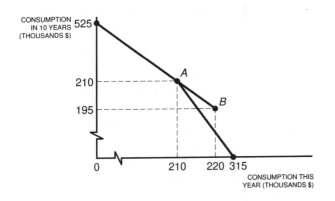

Step four: Determine if point *B* lies on or above the original budget constraint. It is now above.

Step five: If *B* is above the original constraint, Ricardian equivalence is not true, and the household may choose to consume more today. The deficit finance allows the Campbells to consume more today than it would if they had to borrow the money from a bank. They may choose any point on the line segment between *B* and *A*, and their choice will indicate more consumption. In this case, the government deficit increases consumption.

7 (Practice problem: Ricardian equivalence) Return to problem 5, and suppose that all information is the same except that the borrowing interest rate is 20 percent. Analyze how the grant will affect the typical person's borrowing and savings decisions and also whether Ricardian equivalence would hold in Ricardania.

8 (Practice problem: Ricardian equivalence) Although the Johnsons earn $50,000 per year after taxes and expect to continue to earn the same in real terms for the next 5 years, they have a bad credit history and cannot borrow. They could earn 25 percent on their savings, but they do not have any. Analyze the effect on the Johnsons' budget constraint of a current tax cut of $10,000 financed by a five-year bond paying 25 percent over the period. The bond will be repaid with tax increases, and the Johnsons expect that their share of the tax increase will pay off the bonds issued to finance their share of the current tax cut.

Answers to Problems

2 The increase in real interest rates reduces consumption (durable goods purchases fall) and investment, shifts aggregate expenditures down, and reduces output.

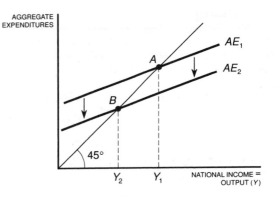

3 *a* Investment falls, shifting aggregate expenditures down and reducing output.

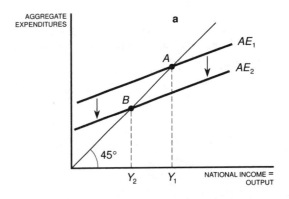

b Investment falls, shifting aggregate expenditures down and reducing output.

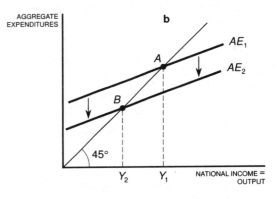

c Consumption falls, shifting aggregate expenditures down and reducing output.

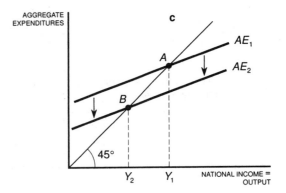

d   Investment increases, shifting aggregate expenditures up and increasing output.

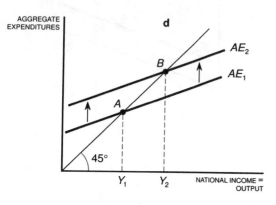

e   Investment and purchases of durable goods fall, shifting aggregate expenditures down and reducing output.

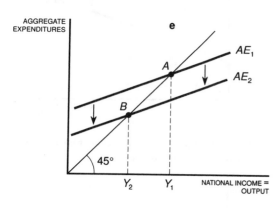

f   Investment and purchases of durable goods rise, shifting aggregate expenditures up and increasing output.

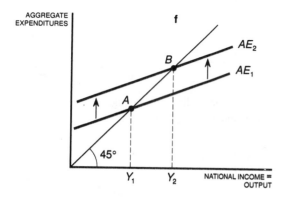

g   Investment falls, shifting aggregate expenditures down and reducing output.

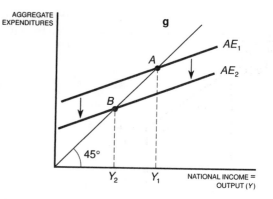

h   Investment increases, shifting aggregate expenditures up and increasing output.

5

7

8

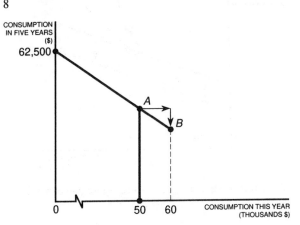

MONEY, BANKING, AND CREDIT

Chapter Review

This chapter begins the study of money. What money is and the purposes it serves in the economy are the first two topics. The discussion then introduces the concept of the money supply and explains how the banking system creates money. The chapter also discusses the Federal Reserve, the institution of government responsible for regulating the money supply, ensuring the availability of credit, and promoting the stability of the banking system. This material on money, banking, and credit is complemented by the next chapter's study of how money affects the real economy in the short run. This part concludes with Chapter 32, the analysis of monetary and fiscal policy.

ESSENTIAL CONCEPTS

1 Economists define **money** by what it does. Money serves three functions. It is a **medium of exchange,** facilitating trades between firms and households. It is a **store of value,** permitting individuals to buy and sell at different times. Finally, it is a **unit of account,** helping people measure the relative value of different goods.

2 Since there are many financial assets that perform money's three functions to some degree, the **money supply** is measured in several ways. The most important measure is **M1,** which includes currency, traveler's checks, and demand deposits (checking accounts). Other measures, such as **M2** and **M3,** include progressively less liquid assets. The liquidity of an asset refers to how easy it is to convert into M1. The now rather common practice of buying on credit using credit cards or home equity loans makes specifying the size of the money supply more difficult.

3 The **financial system** includes all the institutions that help savers and borrowers transact. **Financial intermediaries,** such as banks and savings and loan associations, are the firms that stand between savers and borrowers. The **Federal Reserve** is the central bank of the United States. It regulates banks to ensure their financial health and also controls the money supply and availability of credit to promote and stabilize overall economic activity.

4 While the Federal Reserve (or Fed) controls the money supply, money itself is created by the banking system. Banks operate on the **fractional reserve system,** which means that they keep only a fraction of deposits on hand as reserves. Thus, an intitial deposit (or other increase in

reserves) results in additional loans, which ultimately return to the banking system as more deposits. The process of deposit expansion continues until total deposits have grown by a multiple of the initial deposit. The **money multiplier** is the relationship between the initial deposit and the ultimate change in total deposits.

5   The Federal Reserve has three instruments for controlling the money supply. Most important, it buys and sells government bonds. This activity is called **open market operations.** The Fed also specifies the level of **required reserves** that banks must keep on hand or on deposit at the Fed. Finally, the Fed Sets the **discount rate,** which is the interest rate charged to banks when borrowing from the Fed.

6   Ensuring the stability of the United States banking system and reducing the threat of bank runs are important responsibilities of the Federal Reserve and other government agencies. The Fed acts as a lender of last resort, providing liquidity to troubled banks, and it sets reserve requirements. Government-mandated capital requirements add to the incentives that bank owners have to manage risks carefully. The Federal Deposit Insurance Corporation insures depositors against bank failure.

BEHIND THE ESSENTIAL CONCEPTS

1   How do the Fed's instruments affect the money supply? Each works by increasing or decreasing banks' reserves, affecting the money available for loans.

   a   When the Fed engages in open market operations, it buys and sells bonds. If it buys a bond, for example, the money that it pays is deposited in a bank. The bank's reserves increase, and it in turn can grant new loans.

   b   When the Fed decreases reserve requirements, banks can reduce their reserves and again make new loans.

   c   When the Fed increases the discount rate, banks know that borrowing from the Fed will be more expensive. They guard against having to borrow by keeping more reserves and making fewer loans.

2   Figure 30.1 will help you keep straight how open market operations affect the money supply. On the left is the Fed's vault, where it keeps stacks of bonds and currency.

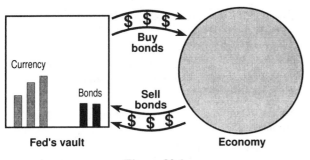

Figure 30.1

The currency in the vault is not money, because it is not in the economy. On the right is the economy. If the Fed buys bonds, currency flows from the vault into the economy and increases the money supply. If the Fed sells bonds, the money it receives leaves the economy and goes into the vault, where it is no longer money.

3   Both the Federal Reserve and the U.S. Treasury sell government bonds. You can keep the two straight if you remember why the bonds are sold. The Treasury sells bonds to borrow money to finance government spending. When the Treasury sells bonds, the money is spent, and it stays in the economy. The Fed sells bonds to reduce the money supply. When the Fed sells bonds, the money it receives goes into the Fed's vault and leaves the economy.

4   You should not confuse the money multiplier in this chapter with the fiscal multiplier introduced in Chapter 28. They are two different concepts. The fiscal multiplier shows that an increase in aggregate expenditures—for example, in investment—brings about a larger increase in output. The money multiplier shows that an increase in reserves leads to a larger increase in total deposits.

5   The *workings* of the fiscal and money multipliers, however, are similar. With the fiscal multiplier, an initial increase in spending creates additional income, which leads to a second round of spending when some of the income is consumed. The sequence is spending—income—additional spending, etc. Each successive round of spending is smaller, and the process ultimately settles down.

   With the money multiplier, an initial increase in deposits leads to new loans, which ultimately are deposited back in the banking system. The sequence here is deposits—loans—deposits—additional loans, etc. Each successive round of deposits is smaller, and again the process ultimately settles down.

6   The *formulas* for the multipliers are also similar. The fiscal multiplier equals 1 divided by the marginal propensity to save. You can think of savings as a leakage, which makes the next round of spending smaller than the last one. The formula for the money multiplier is 1 divided by the reserve ratio. Again, in that they are not loaned out, reserves are like a leakage, and making the next round of deposits smaller than the previous round.

7   One of the fundamental trade-offs in economic life is risk and incentives. We have seen this notion many times, and it appears again in this chapter on the subject of deposit insurance. The Federal Deposit Insurance Corporation (FDIC) protects your money against loss in case of bank failure. Because you know that your money is safe, you seek the highest rate of interest and have little incentive to worry about the financial health of the bank. Banks know how you think and are motivated to grant risky loans, seeking high average returns so that they can afford to pay high rates of interest. Thus, deposit insurance reduces the risk for depositors, but it creates incentives that lead to reckless lending. This problem led to the savings and loan crisis in the 1980s,

and it is the motivation for regulations such as capital requirements that promote bank safety.

SELF-TEST

True or False

1 The term "money" refers only to currency and coins in circulation.

2 The store of value function of money refers to its use as a measure of the relative value of goods.

3 The money supply is an example of a flow variable.

4 M1 includes currency, traveler's checks, and demand deposits.

5 An asset is liquid if it is easily converted into money (M1).

6 Financial intermediaries are firms that provide a link between savers and borrowers.

7 The Federal Reserve is the central bank of the United States.

8 The Federal Reserve is an independent agency funded out of the profits of its operations.

9 A bank's net worth equals its liabilities minus its assets.

10 Banks operate on the fractional reserve system, which means that they hold only a fraction of the amount of deposits in reserve.

11 The money multiplier implies that total deposits increase by a multiple of an initial deposit.

12 The Federal Reserve controls the money supply by mandating maximum interest rates that banks can charge their best customers.

13 The discount rate is the interest rate that the Fed charges on loans to banks.

14 Open market operations refer to the buying and selling of government bonds by the Federal Reserve.

15 Federal deposit insurance lessens the risk faced by depositors but also reduces their incentives to monitor the performance of banks.

Multiple Choice

1 Trade without the use of money is called

 a double coincidence of wants;
 b medium of exchange;
 c barter;
 d unit of account;
 e multiple deposit.

2 Double coincidence of wants refers to

 a the fact that in order for two individuals to barter, each must have what the other wants and want what the other has;
 b the fact that money must be both a store of value and a medium of exchange;
 c the unlikely possibility that two individuals will have exactly the same tastes;
 d the fact that dividends are taxed twice;
 e the fact that the Federal Reserve engages in open market operations and sets the discount rate.

3 The use of money to facilitate exchange is its

 a medium of exchange function;
 b store of value function;
 c unit of account function;
 d double coincidence of wants function;
 e fractional reserve function.

4 The use of money to measure the relative value of goods and services is its

 a medium of exchange function;
 b store of value function;
 c unit of account function;
 d double coincidence of wants function;
 e fractional reserve function.

5 The use of money as a means of preserving purchasing power for a time period is its

 a medium of exchange function;
 b store of value function;
 c unit of account function;
 d double coincidence of wants function;
 e fractional reserve function.

6 The economic definition of money is

 a currency, traveler's checks, and demand deposits;
 b M1;
 c anything that acts as a medium of exchange, store of value, and unit of account;
 d anything that avoids the double coincidence of wants problem;
 e a and b.

7 Which of the following is not included in M1?

 a currency;
 b demand deposits (checking accounts);
 c traveler's checks;
 d certificates of deposit.
 e All of the above are included.

8 Which of the following is not included in M2?

 a M1;
 b certificates of deposit;
 c Eurodollar accounts;
 d savings accounts up to $100,000;
 e All of the above are included.

9 Which of the following is not included in M3?

 a M1;
 b M2;
 c savings accounts over $100,000;
 d institutional money-market mutual funds;
 e corporate retained earnings.

10 An agreement by a bank to lend up to some specified amount is a

 a money market mutal fund;
 b certificate of deposit;

c line of credit;
d unit of account;
e savings account.

11 Which of the following are not financial intermediaries?

a banks;
b savings and loans;
c mutual funds;
d life insurance companies;
e All of the above are financial intermediaries.

12 The objectives of government involvement in the financial system include

a protecting consumers;
b stabilizing the level of economic activity;
c protecting banks from unfair competition;
d creating jobs in the financial sector;
e a and b.

13 The central bank of the United States is

a the Bank of America;
b Chase Manhattan Bank;
c the Federal Reserve;
d the U.S. Treasury;
e the Comptroller of the Currency.

14 The Federal Reserve is

a an agency of the executive branch, subject to presidential control;
b an agency funded by Congress and subject to congressional oversight;
c an independent agency funded out of the profits of its operations;
d an agency funded and overseen by the major U.S. banks;
e an agency funded and overseen by the major Wall Street brokerage houses.

15 The fractional reserve system in banking means that banks

a lend a fraction of their money to consumers and a fraction to businesses;
b hold a fraction of the amount on deposit in reserves;
c hold a fraction of the amount on loan in reserves;
d lend a fraction of their money to foreign businesses and a fraction to domestic businesses;
e may or may not belong to the Federal Reserve system.

16 The discount rate is

a the interest rate charged by the Fed on loans to banks;
b the interest rate paid by the Fed on deposits;
c the difference between the interest rate charged by the Fed and that charged in the market;
d the maximum allowable difference between interest charged on loans to consumers and loans to banks;
e the interest rate ceiling on credit card balances.

17 Which of the following is not a way in which the Federal Reserve can increase the money supply?

a Lower the discount rate.
b Reduce the reserve requirement.
c Buy Treasury bills.
d Sell Treasury bills.
e All of the above are ways to increase the money supply.

18 The money multiplier shows that

a the rich get richer;
b an increase in aggregate expenditures brings about a larger increase in national income;
c an increase in reserves leads to a larger increase in total deposits;
d a multiple of deposits must be held as reserves;
e deregulation leads to instability in the banking system.

19 Open market operations, the most important means by which the Fed controls the money supply, involve

a changing the discount rate;
b setting interest rates;
c changing the reserve requirement;
d buying and selling government bonds;
e placing varying restrictions on foreign borrowing and lending.

20 The Federal Deposit Insurance Corporation

a acts as the central bank of United States;
b ensures that banks will not fail;
c insures deposits (of up to $100,000) in case of bank collapse;
d protects banks against unfair foreign competition;
e sets the reserve requirement for bank deposits.

Completion

1 For a trade to take place in a barter economy, each individual must have what the other wants and want what the other has; that is, there must be a _____.

2 Money facilitates exchange; it is performing its _____ function.

3 Money holds on to its purchasing power; it is performing its _____ function.

4 People use money as a measuring rod, taking advantage of the _____ function of money.

5 Currency, traveler's checks, and checking accounts are included in the _____ measure of money.

6 Firms that act as go-betweens for savers and borrowers are called _____.

7 The central bank in United States is called the _____.

8 When the Federal Reserve buys and sells bonds, it is engaging in _____.

9 The minimum level of reserves that banks must keep on hand is its _____.

10 The interest rate charged to banks by the Federal Reserve is called the _____.

Answers to Self-Test

True or False

1	f	6	t	11	t
2	f	7	t	12	f
3	f	8	t	13	t
4	t	9	f	14	t
5	t	10	t	15	t

Multiple Choice

1	c	6	c	11	e	16	a
2	a	7	d	12	e	17	d
3	a	8	e	13	c	18	c
4	c	9	e	14	c	19	d
5	b	10	c	15	b	20	c

Completion

1 double coincidence of wants
2 medium of exchange
3 store of value
4 unit of account
5 M1
6 financial intermediaries
7 Federal Reserve
8 open market operations
9 required reserves
10 discount rate

Doing Economics: Tools and Practice Problems

In this section, we learn about the balance sheet of banks, where assets, liabilities, and net worth are recorded, and use this tool to see how open market operations lead to changes in deposits, to trace through the deposit expansion process, and to compute the money multiplier.

THE BALANCE SHEET

Before we can understand how banks create money, we must master the balance sheet. This keeps track of assets and liabilities as they change when money is deposited and loaned. Tool Kit 30.1 shows how to construct the bank's balance sheet and to compute its net worth.

Tool Kit 30.1: Constructing the Balance Sheet

The balance sheet is a "T-account," with assets listed on the left and liabilities and net worth on the right. When anything changes, net worth must adjust to keep the right and left sides in balance. To create a balance sheet, follow this procedure.

Step one: Make a T-account. Label the left column "Assets" and the right column "Liabilities and net worth."

Assets	Liabilities and net worth

Step two: Enter each of the assets (outstanding loans, bond holdings, reserves) in the left column, and sum the assets.

Assets	Liabilities and net worth
Loans	
Bonds	
Deposits	
Total assets	

Step three: Enter each of the liabilities (deposits) in the right column, and sum the liabilities.

Assets	Liabilities and net worth
Loans	Deposits
Bonds	
Deposits	
Total assets	

Step four: Compute net worth by subtracting liabilities from assets:

$$\text{net worth} = \text{assets} - \text{liabilities}.$$

Enter net worth in the right column.

Assets	Liabilities and net worth
Loans	Deposits
Bonds	
Deposits	Net worth
Total assets	

Step five: Sum the right and left columns, and check that the balance sheet is in balance.

Assets	Liabilities and net worth
Loans	Deposits
Bonds	
Deposits	
Total assets = total liabilities + net worth.	

---

1 (Worked problem: balance sheet) President Bank has $18 million in outstanding loans, $3 million in government bonds, reserves of $4 million, and deposits equal to $20 million. Compute its net worth, and construct the balance sheet.

Step-by-step solution

Step one: Make a T-account.

President Bank's Balance Sheet

Assets	Liabilities and net worth

Step two: Enter each of the assets (outstanding loans, bond holdings, reserves) in the left column, and sum the assets.

President Bank's Balance Sheet

Assets	Liabilities and net worth
Loans outstanding = $18 million Government bonds = $3 million Reserves = $4 million Total assets = $25 million	

Step three: Enter each of the liabilities (deposits) in the right-hand column, and sum the liabilities.

President Bank's Balance Sheet

Assets	Liabilities and net worth
Loans outstanding = $18 million Government bonds = $3 million Reserves = $4 million Total assets = $25 million	Deposits = $20 million

Step four: Compute net worth:

$$\text{net worth} = 18 + 3 + 4 - 20 = \$5 \text{ million}.$$

Enter net worth in the right-hand column.

President Bank's Balance Sheet

Assets	Liabilities and net worth
Loans outstanding = $18 million Government bonds = $3 million Reserves = $4 million Total assets = $25 million	Deposits = $20 million Net worth = $5 million

Step five: Sum the right and left columns, and check that the balance sheet is in balance.

President Bank's Balance Sheet

Assets	Liabilities and net worth
Loans outstanding = $18 million Government bonds = $3 million Reserves = $4 million Total assets = $25 million	Deposits = $20 million Net worth = $5 million Total liabilities plus net worth = $25 million

2 (Practice problem: balance sheet) First Bank has $220 million in outstanding loans, $10 million in government bonds, $25 million in reserves, and $240 million in deposits. Compute its net worth, and construct its balance sheet.

3 (Practice problem: balance sheet) Second Bank has $400 million in outstanding loans, $25 million in government bonds, $50 million in reserves, and $450 million in deposits. Compute its net worth, and construct its balance sheet.

MONEY CREATION

Using the fractional reserve system, banks create money. When banks receive a new deposit, they keep only a fraction on hand in reserve and loan out the remainder. But the loans find their way back into the banking system, increasing deposits further and setting off a new round of loans. When the process settles down, total deposits in the banking system have increased by a multiple of the initial deposit.

Tool Kit 30.2: Understanding Deposit Expansion and the Money Multiplier

Banks create money. Through the fractional reserve system deposits result in additional loans and further deposits. Follow these steps to see how the money creation process works through the banking system.

Step one: Construct a combined balance sheet for the banking system.

Step two: Identify the initial deposit, and add it to the banking system's deposits.

Step three: Identify the reserve ratio. Calculate the required increase in reserves made necessary by the initial deposit, and add it to the banking system's reserves:

new required reserves = reserve ratio × initial deposit.

Step four: Calculate the new loans that the deposit allows, and add the amount to the banking system's loans:

new loans = initial deposit – new required reserves.

This completes round one of the deposit expansion process. (Remember to recompute the total assets and liabilities and net worth.)

Step five: Trace through a few more rounds by repeating steps two through four. The initial deposit for round two is the amount of new loans from round one.

Step six: Compute the final expansion in deposits. This will be the increase in the money supply:

final deposit expansion = initial deposit/reserve ratio.

Because there are no other leakages in this example, the money multiplier equals 1/reserve ratio.

---

4 (Worked problem: deposit expansion and money multiplier) The banking system in Costa Guano has $4 billion in outstanding loans, $1 billion in government bonds, $1 billion in reserves, and deposits of $5 billion. Its reserve ratio is 0.20. (Monetary magnitudes are converted to U.S. dollar equivalents.)

a Construct the combined balance sheet.
b A new deposit of $1 billion arrives from abroad. Trace through three rounds of the deposit expansion process, and compute the final deposit expansion.

Step-by-step solution

Step one (a): Construct a combined balance sheet for the banking system.

Costa Guano's Combined Balance Sheet

Assets	Liabilities and net worth
Loans outstanding = $4 billion Government bonds = $1 billion Reserves = $1 billion Total assets = $6 billion	Deposits = $5 billion Net worth = $1 billion Total liabilities plus net worth = $6 billion

Step two (b): Identify the initial deposit, and add it to the banking system's deposits. The deposit is $1 billion.

Step three: Identify the reserve ratio. Calculate the required increase in reserves made necessary by the initial deposit, and add it to the banking system's reserves:

new required reserves = 0.20×1 = $0.2 billion.

Step four: Calculate the new loans that the deposit allows, and add the amount to the banking system's loans:

new loans = $1 - 0.2$ = $0.8 billion.

Costa Guano's Combined Balance Sheet (round one)

Assets	Liabilities and net worth
Loans outstanding = $4.8 billion Government bonds = $1 billion Reserves = $1.2 billion Total assets = $7 billion	Deposits = $6 billion Net worth = $1 billion Total liabilities plus net worth = $7 billion

This completes round one of the deposit expansion process. (Note the new totals.)

Step five: Trace through a few more rounds by repeating steps two through four. The initial deposit for round two is the amount of new loans from round one.

Costa Guano's Combined Balance Sheet (round two)

Assets	Liabilities and net worth
Loans outstanding = $5.44 billion Government bonds = $1 billion Reserves = $1.36 billion Total assets = $7.8 billion	Deposits = $6.8 billion Net worth = $1 billion Total liabilities plus net worth = $7.8 billion

Costa Guano's Combined Balance Sheet (round three)

Assets	Liabilities and net worth
Loans outstanding = $5.95 billion Government bonds = $1 billion Reserves = $1.49 billion Total assets = $8.44 billion	Deposits = $7.44 billion Net worth = $1 billion Total liabilities plus net worth = $8.44 billion

Step six: Compute the final expansion in deposits. This will be the increase in the money supply:

final deposit expansion = $1/(0.2)$ = $5 billion.

5 (Practice problem: deposit expansion and money multiplier) In El Dorado, the banking system has outstanding loans of $200 million, government bonds of $10 million, reserves of $30 million, and deposits of $210 million. Its reserve ratio is 1/7. (Monetary magnitudes are converted to dollar equivalents.)

  a Construct the combined balance sheet.
  b A new deposit of $49 million arrives from abroad. Trace through two rounds of the deposit expansion process, and compute the final deposit expansion.

6 (Practice problem: deposit expansion and money multiplier) The Erehwemos banking system has outstanding loans of $45 billion, government bonds of $2 billion,

reserves of $5 billion, and deposits of $50 billion. Its reserve ratio is 0.10. (Monetary magnitudes are converted to U.S. dollar equivalents.)

  a Construct the combined balance sheet.
  b A new deposit of $5 billion arrives from abroad. Trace through three rounds of the deposit expansion process, and compute the final deposit expansion.

Answers to Problems

2

First Bank's Balance Sheet

Assets	Liabilities and net worth
Loans outstanding = $220 million Government bonds = $10 million Reserves = $25 million Total assets = $255 million	Deposits = $240 million Net worth = $15 million Total liabilities plus net worth = $255 million

3

Second Bank's Balance Sheet

Assets	Liabilities and net worth
Loans outstanding = $400 million Government bonds = $25 million Reserves = $50 million Total assets = $475 million	Deposits = $450 million Net worth = $25 million Total liabilities plus net worth = $475 million

5 *a*

El Dorado's Combined Balance Sheet

Assets	Liabilities and net worth
Loans outstanding = $200 million Government bonds = $10 million Reserves = $30 million Total assets = $240 million	Deposits = $210 million Net worth = $30 million Total liabilities plus net worth = $240 million

b

El Dorado's Combined Balance Sheet (round one)

Assets	Liabilities and net worth
Loans outstanding = $242 million Government bonds = $10 million Reserves = $37 million Total assets = $289 million	Deposits = $259 million Net worth = $30 million Total liabilities plus net worth = $289 million

El Dorado's Combined Balance Sheet (round two)

Assets	Liabilities and net worth
Loans outstanding = $278 million	Deposits = $301 million
Government bonds = $10 million	
Reserves = $43 million	Net worth = $30 million
Total assets = $331 million	Total liabilities plus net worth = $331 million

Final deposit expansion = 49/(1/7) = $343 million.

6   a

Erehwemos's Combined Balance Sheet (round one)

Assets	Liabilities and net worth
Loans outstanding = $45 billion	Deposits = $50 billion
Government bonds = $2 billion	
Reserves = $5 billion	Net worth = $2 billion
Total assets = $52 billion	Total liabilities plus net worth = $52 billion

b

Erehwemos's Combined Balance Sheet (round two)

Assets	Liabilities and net worth
Loans outstanding = $49.5 billion	Deposits = $55 billion
Government bonds = $2 billion	
Reserves = $5.5 billion	Net worth = $2 billion
Total assets = $57 billion	Total liabilities plus net worth = $57 billion

Erehwemos's Combined Balance Sheet (round three)

Assets	Liabilities and net worth
Loans outstanding = $53.55 billion	Deposits = $59.5 billion
Government bonds = $2 billion	
Reserves = $5.95 billion	Net worth = $2 billion
Total assets = $61.5 billion	Total liabilities plus net worth = $61.5 billion

Final deposit expansion = 5/(0.1) = $50 billion.

Chapter 31

MONETARY THEORY

Chapter Review

Chapter 30 showed how the Federal Reserve can use its instruments to bring about changes in the money supply and the availability of credit. This chapter discusses how these changes affect the economy. The most important issues involve changes in the money supply that affect output, prices, or both, and the channels through which these changes operate. There is some disagreement among economists concerning the latter issue, and the chapter outlines the sources of contention and the consequences for monetary policy. The concluding section explains how monetary policy works in the international monetary system of the world's interdependent economies.

ESSENTIAL CONCEPTS

1   With fixed prices, if the money supply is increased, people may either hold onto the money or spend it. If they hold it, aggregate demand will remain unchanged. If they spend it, aggregate demand will shift to the right, and output will increase. This can be seen from the definition of **velocity:**

$$V = pQ/M,$$

where p is the fixed price index, Q is output, and M is the money supply. An increase in M must result in a decrease in V or an increase in Q. The big question in this chapter is how a change in M can affect output.

2   **Traditional monetary theory** starts with the demand for money to facilitate transactions. The opportunity cost of holding money is the **nominal interest rate,** which is determined by the intersection of supply and demand for money. An increase in the money supply lowers interest rates, stimulates investment, and shifts aggregate demand. The resulting increases in output and income shift the demand for money to the right, mitigating the fall in the interest rate.

3   The effectiveness of monetary policy depends upon three factors. First, there is the elasticity of money demand, which indicates how much the interest rate will fall for a given increase in money supply. The next issue is how much additional investment will result from the fall in the interest rate—i.e., sensitivity of investment to the interest rate. Finally there is the size of the multiplier, which measures how much output will increase for a given change in investment. In deep recessions each of these factors is likely to be small, and most economists agree that at these times monetary policy is unlikely to provide much stimulus.

4 Another view, held by monetarists, rearranges the definition of velocity as $M = pQ/V$ and interprets this equation as the demand for money. They assume that velocity is constant and that output is at its full employment level; therefore, an increase in money supply must increase Q by shifting aggregate demand to the right. The assumption about velocity implies that money demand does not depend on the interest rate.

5 Criticism of traditional monetary theory centers around two relationships. First, there is the relationship between money and income. Even if the supply of money affects the volume of transactions, most transactions involve exchanges of financial assets, which have no direct bearing on output. Also, the rise of credit card use and money market checking make traditional forms of money unnecessary. Second, the assumed relationship between interest rates and the demand for money may be undermined by interest-bearing checking accounts. If the checking account pays market interest rates, then the opportunity cost of holding money is zero. At any rate, the fact that real interest rates vary little casts doubt on the traditional view.

6 Monetary policy does work, however. Some recent theories stress alternative mechanisms. A likely channel through which money can affect output is through credit availability. Tight monetary policy may reduce the supply of loans. In addition, there may be portfolio effects whereby, for example, changes in nominal interest rates alter the value of bonds and stocks, affecting the incentives to raise new capital.

7 In the open economy monetary policy also works through exchange rates. For example, lower interest rates reduce the demand for dollars and lower the U.S. exchange rate. This depreciation makes exports attractive to foreign buyers and the resulting increase in net exports shifts aggregate demand. The open economy does limit the ability of the Fed to restrict credit, however, because U.S. borrowers can go elsewhere for funds.

BEHIND THE ESSENTIAL CONCEPTS

1 There are areas of disagreement about monetary theory and policy, but there is also a good deal of common ground. Concerning monetary theory, most economists recognize that the Federal Reserve controls the money supply through the use of its three instruments: open market operations, reserve requirements, and the discount rate. Most economists also agree that the demand for money depends upon income. In the area of monetary policy, economists believe that in deep recessions increases in the money supply will likely be ineffective, in mild recessions increases will shift aggregate demand and help the economy recover, and when the economy is operating at capacity, they will result only in higher prices. Severely restricting the money supply and credit availability, on the other hand, will cause a recession. Also, most economists agree that in the long run, money affects only the price level.

2 There is no consensus about how credit availability and the money supply work their way through the economy, but there are four possibilities.
  a A larger money supply lowers interest rates and increases investment.
  b A larger money supply directly shifts aggregate demand because velocity is constant.
  c A larger money supply brings about higher stock and bond prices, which lead to more consumption and investment.
  d Looser credit motivates more lending.

3 The logic of credit rationing is as follows. Banks ration credit because they fear that raising the interest rate would attract low-quality (risky) borrowers, many of whom would default. Because the interest rate remains below market clearing, there is an excess demand for loans.

SELF-TEST

True or False

1 The velocity of money is the ratio of nominal GDP to the price level.
2 The demand for money arising from its use as a unit of account is called the transactions demand for money.
3 The transactions demand for money increases as nominal income increases.
4 The opportunity cost of holding money is the nominal interest rate.
5 According to traditional monetary theory, the nominal interest rate is determined by the intersection of the supply and demand for money.
6 According to traditional monetary theory, an increase in the money supply will lower interest rates and increase investment except during deep recessions.
7 Monetary policy is more effective when the multiplier is large.
8 The theory that the velocity is constant and thus increases in the money supply bring about equal proportional increases in income is called the quantity theory of money.
9 Monetarists believe that money is important and that the government should use active monetary policy to influence the fluctuations in the economy.
10 Until recently, the velocity of money has increased steadily, although the upward trend slowed during recessions.
11 Federal Reserve policies may affect the ability of banks to make loans, but they cannot force banks to lend.
12 Because of credit rationing, interest rates may not rise even though there is an excess demand for money.

13 If the interest rate falls and banks are willing to lend, investment will increase unless firms have an elastic demand for loans.

14 In an open economy an increase in the money supply appreciates the currency and increases net exports.

15 In an open economy the Fed's attempt to restrict the availability of credit may be undermined if borrowers look abroad for funds.

Multiple Choice

1 When the Federal Reserve increases the supply of money,

   a   individuals may hold the additional money, decreasing velocity;
   b   individuals may spend the money, leading to more output;
   c   individuals may spend the money, shifting aggregate demand to the left;
   d   all of the above.
   e   a and b.

2 Which definition of money is used in this chapter?

   a   M1;
   b   M2;
   c   M3;
   d   Eurodollars, money market mutual funds, and deposits in excess of $100,000;
   e   all of the above.

3 Velocity is defined as the ratio of

   a   GDP to the price level;
   b   the price level to GDP;
   c   GDP to the money supply;
   d   the money supply to GDP;
   e   M2 to M1.

4 According to traditional monetary theory, changes in the money supply affect the economy through

   a   the interest rates;
   b   the velocity;
   c   the foreign exchange market;
   d   the quantity theory of money;
   e   credit availability.

5 The transactions demand for money refers to money held

   a   as a medium of exchange;
   b   as a store of value;
   c   as a unit of account;
   d   as a precaution against unexpected need such as illness or job loss;
   e   as a hedge against deflation.

6 Which of the following will cause an increase in the demand for money?

   a   an increase in real income;
   b   an increase in nominal income;
   c   an increase in velocity;
   d   an increase in the nominal interest rate;
   e   an increase in the real interest rate.

7 The opportunity cost of holding money is

   a   the exchange rate;
   b   the velocity;
   c   the real interest rate;
   d   the nominal interest rate;
   e   none of the above.

8 Which of the following is not a principle of traditional monetary theory?

   a   The nominal interest rate is the opportunity cost of holding money.
   b   The demand for money decreases as the interest rate rises.
   c   The interest rate is determined by the intersection of money demand and money supply.
   d   The velocity of money is stable.
   e   All of the above are principles of traditional monetary theory.

9 Which of the following is a tenet of the traditional theory of monetary policy?

   a   Monetary policy is ineffective because it cannot affect the interest rate.
   b   Monetary policy is especially effective in deep recessions when money is scarce.
   c   Monetary policy is ineffective in deep recessions.
   d   Monetary policy is ineffective because investment is not affected by changes in interest rates.
   e   Monetary policy is effective but is too dangerous to use.

10 Monetary policy is more effective when

   a   the elasticity of money demand is low;
   b   investment is sensitive to changes in the interest rate;
   c   the multiplier is low;
   d   prices are flexible;
   e   the economy is in deep recession.

11 According to traditional monetary theory, monetary policy affects output by

   a   altering the availability of credit;
   b   changing the exchange rate and thus net exports;
   c   affecting stock prices and thus firms' incentives to raise funds for investment on the stock market;
   d   changing interest rates and investment;
   e   changing the size of the government deficit.

12 One criticism of traditional monetary theory is

   a   real interest rates are too variable to explain the variation in investment;
   b   most transactions involve the exchange of assets, not the purchase of goods;
   c   most checking accounts pay no interest;
   d   the velocity is surely not a constant;
   e   there are many definitions of money.

13 Monetarists believe that

   a   the velocity of money is stable over time;
   b   the velocity of money is unpredictable;
   c   the quantity theory of money is no longer a sensible way to look at the economy;
   d   money serves no function as a store of value;

e   the velocity of money increases as the money supply grows.

14   According to credit availability theories, an increase in the money supply will stimulate the economy when

   a   interest rates fall;
   b   stock prices rise;
   c   bond prices rise;
   d   interest rates rise;
   e   banks make more loans on easier terms.

15   According to credit availability theories, Federal Reserve policies

   a   affect the ability of banks to lend, but cannot force them to lend;
   b   affect the willingness of banks to lend, but cannot affect the ability of banks to lend;
   c   affect the ability and willingness of banks to lend by lowering interest rates;
   d   may not stimulate the economy if banks buy fewer Treasury bills;
   e   c and d.

16   Banks may be reluctant to lend even though the return on Treasury bills is lower if

   a   default rates are high;
   b   their net worth is low;
   c   other banks have gone bankrupt;
   d   all of the above;
   e   Banks will always seek the higher returns, and if Treasury bill returns are relatively low, banks will not be reluctant to lend.

17   Even though there is an excess demand for credit, banks may not increase the interest rate if

   a   Treasury bill interest rates are high;
   b   increased interest rates have an adverse selection effect by attracting riskier borrowers;
   c   Treasury bill interest rates are low;
   d   credit rationing is illegal;
   e   borrowers cannot afford higher interest rates.

18   Portfolio theories of how monetary policy affects the economy focus on the role of money

   a   as a medium of exchange;
   b   as a store of value;
   c   as a unit of account;
   d   as a precaution against unexpected need such as illness or job loss;
   e   as a hedge against deflation.

19   According to portfolio theories, the Federal Reserve can increase the money supply, lower interest rates, and shift aggregate demand because

   a   when interest rates fall, stock prices rise and firms invest more when stock prices are high;
   b   when interest rates fall, stock prices rise and people increase consumption because they are wealthier;
   c   open market operations increase banks' reserves, and their response leads to higher stock prices;
   d   all of the above;
   e   none of the above.

20   In the open economy an increase in the money supply

   a   depreciates the exchange rate;
   b   increases exports;
   c   reduces imports;
   d   increases net exports;
   e   all of the above.

Completion

1   Gross domestic product divided by the money supply equals the _____.

2   Money held for use as a medium of exchange forms the _____.

3   The opportunity cost of holding money is the _____.

4   The view that money affects the economy through changes in interest rates and investment is the _____ monetary theory.

5   According to _____, velocity is constant and increases in the money supply bring about proportionate increases in national income.

6   _____ believe that there is a stable and predictable relationship between the money supply and national income.

7   _____ occurs when there is an excess demand for credit but banks do not raise interest rates for fear of attracting less credit-worthy borrowers.

8   According to _____ theories, changes in the money supply may lead to different levels of investment without changing interest rates.

9   A decrease in the supply of money leads to an _____ of the exchange rate.

10   The open economy _____ the ability of the Fed to limit credit.

Answers to Self-Test

True or False

1	f	6	t	11	t
2	f	7	t	12	t
3	t	8	t	13	f
4	t	9	f	14	f
5	t	10	t	15	t

Multiple Choice

1	e	6	b	11	d	16	d
2	a	7	d	12	b	17	b
3	c	8	d	13	a	18	b
4	a	9	c	14	e	19	d
5	a	10	b	15	a	20	e

Completion

1   velocity
2   money supply
3   nominal interest rate
4   traditional
5   monetarism
6   Monetarists
7   Credit rationing
8   portfolio

9   appreciation
10   reduces

Doing Economics: Tools and Practice Problems

The traditional theory of how changes in the money supply affect the economy argues that money supply determines in-terest rates in the money market. Although there are problems associated with this theory, it represents the best starting point for the study of monetary policy. In this section, we work problems that trace the channels through which money moves to shift aggregate demand and alter the equilibrium output of the economy. Tool Kit 31.1 explores traditional monetary theory.

Tool Kit 31.1: Using Traditional Monetary Theory

According to this view of money and the economy, the nominal interest rate, which is the opportunity cost of holding money, is determined by the intersection of the supply and demand curves for money. An increase in the supply of money shifts the supply curve to the right and lowers the interest rate. Finally, lower interest rates induce more investment and shift aggregate demand to the right.

Step one: Identify the demand curve for money, the supply curve for money, and the investment function.

Step two: Start with an equilibrium in which the supply and demand curves for money intersect at the nominal interest rate. The level of investment is read off the investment function at this interest rate.

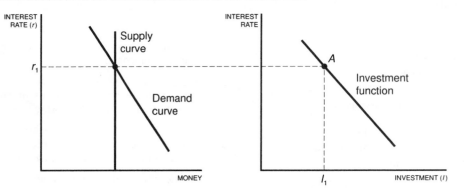

Step three: Shift the money supply curve to reflect the change in the money supply.

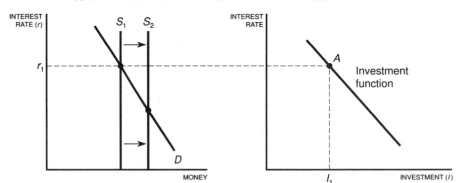

Step four: Find the new equilibrium interest rate.

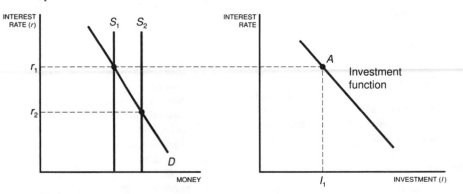

Step five: Determine the change in investment by reading the new level of investment off the investment function.

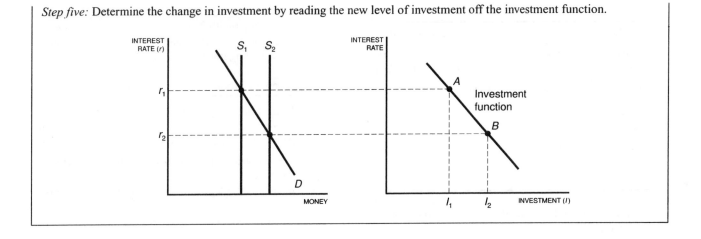

1 (Worked problem: traditional monetary theory) The money demand and investment function are given in Table 31.1. The initial money supply is $1.8 billion.

Table 31.1

Money demand		Investment function	
Nominal interest rate	Money demand (billions $)	Real interest rate	Investment ($100 million)
10%	1.0	10%	2
9%	1.2	9%	3
8%	1.4	8%	4
7%	1.6	7%	5
6%	1.8	6%	6
5%	2.0	5%	7
4%	2.2	4%	8

a   Find the equilibrium interest rate and level of investment.
b   Suppose the Federal Reserve lowers required reserves, and the money supply increases to $2 billion. Determine the new interest rate and level of investment.
c   How does aggregate demand shift?

Step-by-step solution

Step one (a): Identify the demand curve for money, the money supply, and the investment function. See Table 31.1 for the money demand and the investment function. The money supply is $1.8 billion.

Step two: Start with an equilibrium in which the supply and demand curves for money intersect at the nominal interest rate. The level of investment is read off the investment function at this interest rate. The initial equilibrium interest rate is 6 percent, which induces firms to invest $600 million.

Step three (b): Shift the money supply curve to reflect the change in the money supply.

Step four: Find the new equilibrium interest rate. It is 5 percent.

Step five: Determine the change in investment by reading the new level of investment off the investment function. Firms increase their investment levels to $700 million, which represents an increase of $100 million.

Step six (c): Aggregate demand shifts to the right.

2 (Practice problem: traditional monetary theory) The money demand and investment function are given in Table 31.2. The initial money supply is $4.2 billion.

Table 31.2

Money demand		Investment function	
Nominal interest rate	Money demand (billions $)	Real interest rate	Investment ($100 million)
10%	2.5	10%	2.0
9%	3.0	9%	4.0
8%	3.3	8%	5.0
7%	3.6	7%	6.0
6%	3.9	6%	7.0
5%	4.2	5%	7.5
4%	4.5	4%	8.0

a   Find the equilibrium interest rate and level of investment.
b   Suppose the Federal Reserve sells bonds, causing the money supply to decrease to $3.6 billion. Determine the new interest rate and level of investment.
c   How does aggregate demand shift?

3 (Practice problem: traditional monetary theory) The money demand and investment function are given in Table 31.3. The initial money supply is $5.5 billion.

Table 31.3

Money demand		Investment function	
Nominal interest rate	Money demand (billions $)	Real interest rate	Investment ($100 million)
10%	4.5	10%	12.0
9%	5.0	9%	14.0
8%	5.5	8%	15.0
7%	6.0	7%	16.0
6%	6.5	6%	17.0
5%	7.0	5%	17.5
4%	7.5	4%	18.0

a   Find the equilibrium interest rate and level of investment.

b   Suppose the Federal Reserve buys bonds, causing the money supply to increase to $7 billion. Determine the new interest rate and level of investment.

c   How does aggregate demand shift?

Answers to Problems

2   *a*   Interest rate = 5 percent; investment = $750 million.

    b   Interest rate = 7 percent; investment = $600 million.

    c   Aggregate demand shifts to the left.

3   *a*   Interest rate = 8 percent; investment = $1,500 million.

    b   Interest rate = 5 percent; investment = $1,750 million.

    c   Aggregate demand shifts to the right.

Chapter 32

FISCAL AND MONETARY POLICY

Chapter Review

The basic model of unemployment macroeconomics is completed in this chapter, which pulls together the material on the real economy from Chapters 28 and 29 with that on the monetary system in Chapters 30 and 31. The chapter compares the effects of fiscal and monetary policy and analyzes some issues concerning their use in the current economy. The next chapter begins the section on dynamics.

ESSENTIAL CONCEPTS

1   **Fiscal policy** is the use of government tax and expenditure policies to improve the performance of the economy. When there is excess capacity an increase in government expenditures or a tax cut shifts aggregate demand to the right, moving the economy toward full employment. Whether the gain in current output is worth the increased indebtedness depends upon how much private investment is crowded out, whether government spending is for consumption or investment, and how much of the deficit is financed by borrowing from abroad.

2   The government can still use fiscal policy even if it is constrained to keep a balanced budget. Although the required tax increase offsets somewhat the effect of higher government expenditures, some stimulus remains. The **balanced budget multiplier** equals one, which means that aggregate demand shifts to the right by exactly the amount of the extra government spending.

3   Monetary policy can also be used. A larger money supply lowers interest rates and makes credit available, increasing private investment. Also, the exchange rate falls, stimulating a rise in net exports. Both combine to shift aggregate demand to the right. Monetary policy is also important as it interacts with fiscal policy. In response to a fiscal stimulus the Fed may pursue an **accommodative monetary policy**. This stance keeps interest rates from rising, which would limit the fiscal stimulus.

4   Monetary and fiscal policy differ in how they affect the composition of output. Monetary policy's lower interest rates bring about more investment. The impact of fiscal policy depends upon the mix of additional expenditures and tax cuts and also upon how government expenditures are divided between consumption and investment.

5   Monetary policy is certainly ineffective in deep recessions. Fiscal policy's power may be limited if consumers anticipate future tax increases to pay off the deficit, if government borrowing increases interest rates (crowding out investment), or if changes in the exchange rate reduce net exports. None of these is likely in deep recessions, however.

6   Monetary policy's impact is delayed by the time it takes lower interest rates to stimulate investment. Government spending in principle can work immediately. It does take time for government to pass laws and administer the spending. Certain programs, such as unemployment insurance and progressive income taxes, act as **automatic stabilizers**, quickly causing greater spending and reduced taxes during recessions.

7   A **balanced budget amendment** requiring the government to avoid deficit would probably destabilize the economy because it would prevent the automatic stabilizers from doing their job. In this case all of the responsibility for stabilization would rest with monetary policy. One compromise would keep the **full-employment deficit** at zero. This is what the deficit would be if the economy were operating at full employment, and it is a measure of fiscal responsibility.

BEHIND THE ESSENTIAL CONCEPTS

1   Government can use fiscal policy in two ways. First, it can stimulate the economy during recessions. Here government takes an active role, making up for the shortfall in private spending. Another approach works automatically. Taxes, such as personal or corporate income taxes, which decrease as income decreases, and programs such as welfare and unemployment insurance act as automatic stabilizers. These programs provide additional spending during downturns without explicit government action.

2   The instruments of government policy include fiscal policy measures such as tax rates and levels of expenditures, and monetary instruments such as open market operations, reserve requirements, and the discount rate. In different circumstances some form of each policy may be appropriate. They differ in their effectiveness, how they change the mix of output, and the speed of implementation.

3   The actual budget deficit computes the difference between government expenditures and tax revenues. When the economy falls into recession, however, tax collections diminish. Households earn less income and pay less income tax. Business profits fall and so do corporate tax collections. Spending increases on unemployment insurance and welfare programs. All of these combine to bring about a deficit without any change in policy. The full-employment deficit measures what the deficit would be at full employment. Tax and expenditure policies that result in no full-employment deficit will nevertheless lead to actual budget deficits when the economy is operating below capacity.

SELF-TEST

True or False

1   Fiscal policy aims to improve macroeconomic performance by promoting fiscal responsibility among banks and other financial intermediaries.

2   When the government increases expenditures or cuts taxes to provide a fiscal stimulus, there is an increase in the federal debt.

3   Government borrowing to finance the deficit may crowd out private investment.

4   If government spending and taxes increase by the same amount, then aggregate demand will not change.

5   The balanced budget multiplier equals one.

6   In a closed economy monetary policy works by changing interest rates and investment.

7   In an open economy monetary policy changes exchange rates and net exports.

8   If the Fed pursues accommodative monetary policy, it will cut the money supply when government spending increases.

9   While monetary policy stimulates investment, fiscal policy may crowd it out.

10   Most economists agree that fiscal policy is ineffective in deep recessions.

11   One problem with fiscal policy is the time it takes for government to take action.

12   The impact of monetary policy is delayed while firms take time to respond to lower interest rates with new investment.

13   Unemployment insurance helps stabilize the economy by increasing government expenditures during recessions.

14   Amending the Constitution to require a balanced budget would place all of the responsibility for stabilizing the economy on the Federal Reserve.

15   The full-employment deficit is what the actual budget deficit would be if the economy were operating at full employment.

Multiple Choice

1   Fiscal policy includes
   a   maintaining a stable money supply;
   b   using consumer product safety regulation to promote consumer confidence;
   c   regulating the banking and securities industries to encourage sound investment;
   d   using government expenditures and taxation to improve macroeconomic performance;
   e   funding oversight agencies, such as the General Accounting Office, to ensure that government carries out its fiduciary responsibilities.

2   Providing fiscal stimulus with a current budget deficit affects future generations by

a accumulating a federal debt for which they are responsible;

b reducing current private investment by driving up current interest rates;

c incurring foreign indebtedness by financing the deficit with bonds sold abroad;

d a and b;

e all of the above.

3 An increase in government spending holding the level of taxes constant will

a shift the aggregate expenditures schedule up;

b leave the aggregate expenditures schedule unchanged;

c shift the aggregate expenditures schedule down;

d rotate the aggregate expenditures schedule to the left;

e rotate the aggregate expenditures schedule to the right.

4 An increase in taxes holding the level of government spending constant will

a shift the aggregate expenditures schedule up;

b leave the aggregate expenditures schedule unchanged;

c shift the aggregate expenditures schedule down;

d rotate the aggregate expenditures schedule to the left;

e rotate the aggregate expenditures schedule to the right.

5 An increase in both government spending and taxes, keeping the overall budget balanced, will

a shift the aggregate expenditures schedule up;

b leave the aggregate expenditures schedule unchanged;

c shift the aggregate expenditures schedule down;

d rotate the aggregate expenditures schedule to the left;

e rotate the aggregate expenditures schedule to the right.

6 Deficit spending is financed by

a taxes;

b spending cuts;

c borrowing throught the sale of Treasury bills and bonds to investors;

d printing money;

e the multiplier.

7 Increased government expenditures

a reduce total investment;

b reduce private investment but may increase total investment if the additional government expenditures include public investment, such as roads or research and development;

c increase private investment;

d reduce foreign indebtedness;

e may reduce total investment if the Federal Reserve pursues accommodative monetary policy.

8 The balanced budget multiplier equals

a one;

b zero, because the stimulus provided by increased government spending is offset by the fiscal drag of the tax increase;

c one divided by the marginal propensity to consume;

d one divided by the reserve ratio;

e two.

9 When there is excess capacity, an increase in the money supply leads to

a lower interest rates;

b increased investment;

c greater credit availability;

d exchange rate depreciation;

e all of the above.

10 Accommodative monetary policy refers to

a keeping a strong currency to accommodate importers;

b driving down the exchange rate to promote exports;

c complementing the objectives of fiscal policy by adjusting the money supply to keep interest rates from rising;

d maintaining a stable money supply;

e letting the money supply grow at a rate equal to the growth in output.

11 Crowding out refers to

a the possibility that taxes reduce private investment;

b the effect of inflation on the real value of the accumulated government debt;

c the possibility that government borrowing may reduce private investment;

d the effect of protectionism on the trade balance;

e the effect of imports on the market share of domestic firms.

12 Which of the following illustrates problems with the effectiveness of a policy instrument?

a Even though the Federal Reserve undertakes policies that increase bank reserves, it may not be able to motivate banks to make new loans.

b Looser monetary policy, even though it was designed to increase investment, might instead cause the dollar to depreciate and increase net exports.

c Monetary policy often concentrates its effects on particular sectors, such as export-competing industries or consumer durables.

d There are lags in the government's ability to recognize and implement fiscal programs.

e Individuals may treat tax cuts as temporary and increase consumption.

13 Which of the following illustrates a concern with the effect of a policy instrument on the composition of output?

a Even though the Federal Reserve undertakes policies that increase bank reserves, it may not be able to motivate banks to make new loans.

b Looser monetary policy, even though it was designed to increase investment, might instead cause the dollar to depreciate and increase net exports.

c Monetary policy often concentrates its effects on particular sectors, such as export-competing industries or consumer durables.

d There are lags in the government's ability to recognize and implement fiscal programs.

e Individuals may treat tax cuts as temporary and increase consumption.

14 Mechanisms that increase the government deficit during recessions and decrease it during economic booms are called

a balanced budget multipliers;
b full-employment deficits;
c automatic stabilizers;
d political business cycles;
e none of the above.

15 Automatic stabilizers are

a programs, such as unemployment insurance or progressive taxation, that increase spending during recessions and reduce it during economic booms;
b policy rules that restrain the use of discretionary fiscal and monetary policy;
c the adjustments that individuals with rational expectations make to offset fiscal and monetary policies;
d market responses, such as increased interest rates, that limit the ability of government to stimulate the economy;
e a and c.

16 Which of the following is not an automatic stabilizer?

a income taxes;
b unemployment insurance;
c food stamps;
d Social Security benefits;
e All of the above are automatic stabilizers.

17 Which of the following relates to the issue of lags in monetary and fiscal policy?

a Monetary policy's effectiveness is delayed while businesses wait to undertake new investments.
b Governments take time to make decisions about tax and expenditure changes.
c Exchange rates adjust slowly.
d a and b.
e All of the above.

18 State and local government spending tends to

a increase in booms and decrease in recessions, thus reducing the volatility of the economy;
b increase in booms and decrease in recessions, thus increasing the volatility of the economy;
c decrease in booms and increase in recessions, thus reducing the volatility of the economy;
d decrease in booms and increase in recessions, thus increasing the volatility of the economy;
e be stable over the business cycle and neither increase nor reduce the volatility.

19 A Balanced Budget Amendment to the U.S. Constitution would

a eliminate the ability of the government to provide fiscal stimulus;
b place most of the burden of stabilization on monetary policy;
c probably destabilize the economy by limiting the impact of automatic stabilizers;
d b and c;
e all of the above.

20 The deficit that would occur if the economy were at full employment under current spending and tax policies is called the

a balanced budget multiplier;
b full-employment deficit;
c trade deficit;
d total accumulated government debt;
e real budget deficit.

Completion

1 _____ involves the use of taxation and government spending to improve macroeconomic performance.

2 The balanced budget multiplier equals _____.

3 If the government spends more than it raises in taxes, the deficit is financed by _____.

4 _____ includes infrastructure and spending for education and research.

5 _____ monetary policy furthers the goals of fiscal policy by adjusting the money supply to keep interest rates from rising and crowding out private investment.

6 _____ refers to the possibility that government borrowing may reduce private investment.

7 Mechanisms that reduce government spending or raise taxes in recessions are called _____.

8 State and local government expenditures vary _____ than GDP.

9 The _____ would preclude the use of deficit financed fiscal policy.

10 The _____ equals the deficit that would have occurred if government revenues and spending were at their full-employment levels.

Answers to Self-Test

True or False

1	f	6	t	11	t
2	t	7	t	12	t
3	t	8	f	13	t
4	f	9	t	14	t
5	t	10	f	15	t

Multiple Choice

1	d	6	c	11	c	16	c
2	e	7	b	12	a	17	d
3	a	8	a	13	b	18	b
4	c	9	e	14	c	19	d
5	a	10	c	15	a	20	b

Completion

1 Fiscal policy
2 one
3 borrowing
4 Government investment
5 Accommodative
6 Crowding out
7 automatic stabilizers
8 more
9 balanced budget amendment
10 full-employment deficit

Doing Economics: Tools and Practice Problems

Fiscal policy involves the use of government expenditures and taxation to influence the macroeconomic performance of the economy. It works by shifting aggregate demand: up in the cases of tax cuts or expenditure increases; down when taxes are raised or expenditures decreased. The multiplier plays a crucial role, determining the magnitude of the change in aggregate demand that results from an initial fiscal policy measure. In this section we use income-expenditure analysis to study balanced budget changes in fiscal policy. Tool Kit 32.1 shows how to analyze the impact of changes in government spending accompanied by tax changes of equal size.

1 (Worked problem: balanced budget fiscal policy) In Isle de Guano (a neighbor of Costa Guano) the marginal propensity to consume is 0.75 and the tax rate is a rather high 50 percent. Autonomous consumption is 10 million, investment is zero, and government spending is 40 million guanos.

   a Compute the aggregate consumption function.
   b Compute the aggregate expenditures schedule.
   c Find the equilibrium level of output.
   d Is the budget balanced?

Suppose that government spending is increased to 60 million and the tax rate is increased to 60 percent.

   d Compute the new aggregate consumption function.
   e Compute the new aggregate expenditures schedule.
   f Find the new equilibrium level of output.
   g Compute the change in tax revenues. Is this a balanced budget change in fiscal policy?
   h Verify that the change in output equals the change in government spending, i.e., that the multiplier equals one.

Step-by-step solution

Step one: Identify the marginal propensity to consume, the initial tax rate, autonomous consumption, investment, and

---

Tool Kit 32.1: Analyzing Government Spending with Tax Changes

When there are equal changes in government spending and taxes, output will change by an equivalent amount. Economists say that the balanced budget multiplier is one. Follow these steps.

Step one: Identify the marginal propensity to consume, the initial tax rate, investment, and the level of government spending.

Step two: Compute the consumption function.

Step three: Compute the aggregate expenditures schedule and find the equilibrium level of output.

Step four: Identify the new tax rate and use this information to calculate the new aggregate consumption function.

Step five: Identify the new level of government spending and compute the new aggregate expenditures schedule.

Step six: Find the new equilibrium level of output.

Step seven: Verify that the change in tax revenue equals the change in government spending:

Change in tax revenues = new tax rate × new output
− original tax rate × original output.

Step eight: Verify that the balanced budget multiplier equals one:

Multiplier =
(Change in output)/(change in government spending).

---

the level of government spending. The marginal propensity to consume is 0.75 and the tax rate is 50 percent. Autonomous consumption is 10 million, investment is zero, and government spending is 40 million.

Step two: Compute the consumption function. When national income is zero, consumption is 10 million. When national income is 20 million, consumption equals 0.75 × (1 − 0.5) × 20 + 10 = 17.5. Continuing, we derive the consumption function.

National income	Consumption
0	10
20	17.5
40	25
60	32.5
80	40
100	47.5
120	55

Step three: Compute the aggregate expenditures schedule and find the equilibrium level of output. Since investment equals zero and there is no trade, aggregate expenditures equal consumption plus government.

National income	Consumption	Government expenditures	Aggregate expenditures
0	10	40	50
20	17.5	40	57.5
40	25	40	65
60	32.5	40	72.5
80	40	40	80
100	47.5	40	87.5
120	55	40	95

Equilibrium output is 80. The budget is balanced; taxes = $0.5 \times 80 = 40$ = government expenditures.

Step four: Identify the new tax rate and use this information to calculate the new aggregate consumption function. The new tax rate is 60 percent. When national income is 20 million, consumption equals $0.75 \times (1 - 0.6) \times 20 + 10 = 16$. Continuing, we derive the consumption function.

National income	Consumption
0	10
20	16
40	22
60	28
80	34
100	40
120	46

Step five: Identify the new level of government spending and compute the new aggregate expenditures schedule. Government now spends 60 million. The new aggregate expenditures schedule is as follows.

National income	Consumption	Government expenditures	Aggregate expenditures
0	10	60	70
20	16	60	76
40	22	60	82
60	28	60	88
80	34	60	94
100	40	60	100
120	46	60	106

Step six: Find the new equilibrium level of output. It equals 100.

Step seven: Verify that the change in tax revenue equals the change in government spending.

Change in tax revenues = new tax rate × new output
− original tax rate × original output;
$= 0.60 \times 100 - 0.50 \times 80 = 20$ million.

Step eight: Verify that the balanced budget multiplier equals one.

Multiplier = (change in output)/
(change in government spending);
$= (100 - 80)/(60 - 40) = 1$.

2   (Practice problem: balanced budget fiscal policy) In Silverado (a neighbor of El Dorado) the marginal propensity to consume is 0.8 and the tax rate is one-third. Both

autonomous consumption and investment are 100 billion, and government spending is 500 billion dorals.

a   Compute the aggregate consumption function.
b   Compute the aggregate expenditures schedule.
c   Find the equilibrium level of output.
d   Is the budget balanced?

Suppose that government spending is decreased to 200 million and the tax rate is decreased to one-sixth.

e   Compute the new aggregate consumption function.
f   Compute the new aggregate expenditures schedule.
g   Find the new equilibrium level of output.
h   Compute the change in tax revenues. Is this a balanced budget change in fiscal policy?
i   Verify that the change in output equals the change in government spending, i.e., that the multiplier equals one.

3   (Practice problem: balanced budget fiscal policy) In Wohon (a neighbor of Erehwemos) the marginal propensity to consume is 0.9 and the tax rate is one-sixth. Autonomous consumption equals 5 billion and investment is 15 billion, and government spending is 40 billion hons.

a   Compute the aggregate consumption function.
b   Compute the aggregate expenditures schedule.
c   Find the equilibrium level of output.
d   Is its budget balanced?

Suppose that government spending is increased to 120 million and the tax rate is increased to three-eighths (0.375).

e   Compute the new aggregate consumption function.
f   Compute the new aggregate expenditures schedule.
g   Find the new equilibrium level of output.
h   Compute the change in tax revenues. Is this a balanced budget change in fiscal policy?
i   Verify that the change in output equals the change in government spending, i.e., that the multiplier equals one.

Answers to Problems

2   *a* and *b*

National income	Consumption	Investment	Government expenditures	Aggregate expenditures
0	100	100	500	700
300	260	100	500	860
600	420	100	500	1,020
900	580	100	500	1,180
1,200	740	100	500	1,340
1,500	900	100	500	1,500
1,800	1060	100	500	1,660

c   Equilibrium output is 1,500.
d   Tax revenues = $1/3 \times 1,500 = 500$ = government expenditures.
e   and *f*

National income	Consumption	Investment	Government expenditures	Aggregate expenditures
0	100	100	200	400
300	300	100	200	600
600	500	100	200	800
900	700	100	200	1,000
1,200	900	100	200	1,200
1,500	1,200	100	200	1,400
1,800	1,500	100	200	1,600

g   Equilibrium output is 1,200.
h   Tax revenues = $1/6 \times 1{,}200 = 200$ = government revenues. The budget is still balanced.
i   Multiplier = $(1{,}500 - 1{,}200)/(500 - 200) = 1$.

3   a and b

National income	Consumption	Investment	Government expenditures	Aggregate expenditures
0	5	15	40	60
40	35	15	40	90
80	65	15	40	120
120	95	15	40	150
160	125	15	40	180
200	155	15	40	210
240	185	15	40	240
280	215	15	40	270
320	245	15	40	300

c   Equilibrium output is 240.
d   Tax revenues = $1/6 \times 240 = 40$ = government expenditures.
e and f

National income	Consumption	Investment	Government expenditures	Aggregate expenditures
0	5	15	120	140
40	27.5	15	120	162.5
80	50	15	120	185
120	72.5	15	120	207.5
160	95	15	120	230
200	117.5	15	120	252.5
240	140	15	120	275
280	162.5	15	120	297.5
320	185	15	120	320

g   Equilibrium output is 320.
h   Tax revenues = $0.375 \times 320 = 120$ = government revenues. The budget is still balanced.
i   Multiplier = $(320 - 240)/(120 - 40) = 1$.

Part Seven

Dynamics and Macro Policy

Chapter 33

INFLATION: WAGE AND PRICE DYNAMICS

Chapter Review

This chapter begins the study of dynamics, i.e., how things change. The focus is on inflation, its costs, and, in particular, its relationship with unemployment. The Phillips curve summarizes this relationship, and the chapter explains how the Phillips curve relates to the aggregate demand and supply framework. The role of monetary policy receives attention both in its closed and open economy varieties. A more microeconomic discussion of price rigidities closes the chapter.

ESSENTIAL CONCEPTS

1 **Inflation** is a general rise in the price level over time. If anticipated, it causes little disruption because households and firms can plan for and offset any troublesome effects. Inflation hurts lenders because they are repaid with cheaper dollars. It hurts investors because they are taxed on returns from their investments that barely compensate for the higher price level. Holders of currency see inflation erode its purchasing power. Inflation causes further trouble because it distorts relative prices and, when variable, contributes to the riskiness of borrowing and lending. The costs of inflation can be softened

somewhat by **indexing,** which means linking future payments to some measure of inflation.

2 When at the current price level aggregate demand exceeds aggregate supply, there is full employment but upward pressure on prices. The opposite is the case when aggregate demand is less than aggregate supply and unemployment is high. The **Phillips curve,** shown in Figure 33.1, illustrates the trade-off between unemployment and inflation. Decreases in inflation increase un-

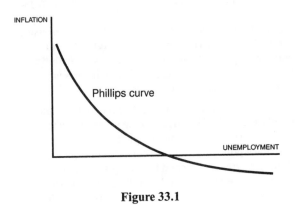

Figure 33.1

employment (at least in the short run) until unemployment reaches its so-called **natural rate,** when the price level is constant.

3   When workers and firms expect inflation, the Phillips curve shifts up. This higher curve is called the **expectations-augmented Phillips curve.** When inflation equals the expected rate, the economy is at its natural rate. If government tries to keep unemployment below this level, inflation will continue to rise, even accelerate. Thus, the natural rate equals the **NAIRU** (non-accelerating inflation rate of unemployment), and it is the unemployment rate consistent with constant inflation. The NAIRU itself varies over time with factors such as the entry of women in the labor force. Currently, it is probably around 5.5 percent in the United States.

4   In the long run firms and workers use all available current and past information and adjust their expectations of inflation. Economists say that they have **rational expectations.** The unemployment rate returns to the NAIRU, which implies that the **long-run Phillips curve** is vertical. This fact means that a country experiencing high inflation may be able to put in place a credible program that convinces firms and workers of its resolve to lower inflation. As they expect lower inflation, the Phillips curve would shift down rapidly, allowing inflation to fall without a rise in unemployment. In other circumstances a long recession may be required.

5   In the long run, when prices and wages have time to adjust, the long-run aggregate supply curve is vertical. The **short-run aggregate supply curve** shows the levels of output at different price levels, holding wages fixed. It is horizontal at low levels of output, then upward sloping and nearly vertical at high price levels. Because machines and workers temporarily can be worked overtime, the vertical portion of the short-run aggregate supply curve lies to the right of the long-run aggregate supply. Finally, equilibrium in the short run depends upon the price level. If the price level is above the intersection of short-run aggregate supply and demand, then output is determined by aggregate demand, the short side of the market. A price level below the intersection implies that output equals short-run aggregate supply.

6   Increases in aggregate demand do not increase the price level when there is excess capacity; otherwise, they put upward pressure on prices. Similarly, when short-run aggregate supply shifts to the left, inflationary pressures form. The former is called **demand-pull inflation;** the latter, **cost-push inflation.** Once underway, **inflation inertia** sets in as expectations of price increases lead workers to demand wage increases.

7   In the long-run full-employment economy more money simply means higher prices. In the short run, when prices are fixed, the money supply affects only output. Monetary policy can set off demand-pull inflation by shifting aggregate demand to the right when the economy is at full employment. Regardless of the reason for the start of inflation, monetary policy has a role in its continuation. Restrictive monetary policy dampens inflation, but accommodative monetary policy may accelerate it if the money supply is allowed to grow faster than the sum of the real growth rate and the existing inflation rate.

8   Relatively high inflation depreciates a country's currency because investors realize that if they hold assets in that currency, inflation will erode its value. Thus, monetary policy affects exchange rates. Investors, of course, form expectations about future monetary policy and inflation rates, and these expectations get built into exchange rates in much the same way that expectations of inflation affect the price level. Investors' expectations can reinforce or counteract the intentions of the monetary authorities.

9   Firms may be reluctant to change prices for three reasons. First, changing prices is expensive. Economists refer to this reason as **menu costs,** analogous to the expense restaurants incur when printing new menus. Second, the uncertainties associated with changing prices may be greater than those associated with changing output. Customers may revise their expectations about prices and postpone purchases if they see prices falling. Finally, in oligopolies, firms may face *kinked demand curves.* Firms can facilitate cooperation by offering to match price cuts. This strategy puts a kink in each firm's demand curve at the current price. Cutting prices gains few extra customers, and firms may prefer to postpone price decreases.

BEHIND THE ESSENTIAL CONCEPTS

1   When inflation is anticipated, its effects are limited. To understand this better, imagine that you are borrowing $10,000 from your uncle for this year's tuition. To compensate him for living without his money for a year, he wants a 3 percent real rate of return. If there is no inflation, you simply agree to pay him 3 percent interest. If inflation is expected to be 7 percent, you pay him 10 percent interest, which gives him 7 percent to make up for the increase in prices and leaves a 3 percent real return. All contracts can be indexed in this way; therefore a mild, steady rate of inflation does not impose serious costs on the economy.

2   An unpredictable rate of inflation is very costly. Suppose that inflation is uncertain, that it might be 14 percent or 0 percent with equal probability. The average inflation rate is still 7 percent, but now when you borrow from your uncle, there is risk. If you pay the same 10 percent and inflation is zero, your uncle earns a 10 percent real return—a bonanza! On the other hand, if inflation turns out to be 14 percent, he nets negative 4 percent, and receives back less in real terms than he lent. You can see how a variable and unpredictable rate of inflation imposes risks on capital markets.

3   Another of the important costs of inflation involves the tax code. Most economists favor indexing. The tax code

is indexed to some extent; for example, income tax brackets are adjusted each year for inflation. Investment earnings, however, are not indexed. If you start a business for $100,000 and sell it for $150,000 in 5 years and if the inflation rate is 50 percent over those years, then your real return is zero. Nevertheless, you would be liable for taxes on your nominal gains of $50,000. A sensible reform would exempt nominal gains from taxes.

4   When the price is stuck at somewhere other than its market-clearing level, the quantity of output is determined by the short side of the market. If the price is too high to clear the market, then demand is the short side. Although suppliers would like to produce more, there is not enough demand, and thus the output equals the quantity demanded. On the other hand, when the price is too low to clear the market, supply is the short side. Demanders would like to purchase more goods, but only what suppliers can profitably produce is made available. In this case, the output equals the quantity supplied.

5   Inflation in the long run is a simple issue: money growth determines inflation. In the time before relative prices have adjusted to their market clearing levels, however, inflation is a complex issue, involving shocks to aggregate demand and supply, accommodating or restrictive monetary policy, the credibility of the monetary authorities, and expectations. Inflation can arise for nonmonetary reasons and if it is expected to continue, it can persist for a period. Eventually, it will adjust to a rate determined by the growth in the money supply, but the time of adjustment depends upon what investors think the monetary authorities will do. Expectation formation is not an exact science.

SELF-TEST

True or False

1   The U.S. tax system is fully indexed for inflation.

2   Inflation makes it expensive to hold money, because as the price level rises, money becomes less valuable.

3   The Phillips curve shows the relationship between unemployment and inflation.

4   The natural rate of unemployment is the rate that would occur if inflation were zero.

5   When workers and firms expect inflation to increase, the expectations-augmented Phillips curve shifts up.

6   If the government tries to keep the unemployment rate below the NAIRU, the result will be increased inflation.

7   The long-run Phillips curve is downward sloping.

8   The short-run aggregate supply curve can never lie to the right of the long-run aggregate supply.

9   When the price is stuck above the level at which ag-

gregate demand and aggregate supply intersect, output equals aggregate supply.

10   When the price is stuck below the level at which aggregate demand and aggregate supply intersect, output equals aggregate supply.

11   Because inflation is always a monetary phenomenon, demand-pull inflation must start with an increase in the money supply.

12   If international investors expect a restrictive monetary policy, the currency will appreciate.

13   Menu costs refer to the expense of changing prices.

14   Firms perceive greater risk during economic downturns and may choose the safer path of reducing output rather than reducing price.

15   Firms facing a kinked demand curve are unlikely to change price when their costs decrease.

Multiple Choice

1   Cost-of-living adjustments, or COLAs, are a type of

   a   wage and price control;
   b   indexation;
   c   monetary target;
   d   discretionary monetary policy;
   e   inflation tax.

2   If not anticipated, an increase in inflation will

   a   hurt both borrowers and lenders;
   b   help both borrowers and lenders;
   c   hurt borrowers but help lenders;
   d   hurt lenders but help borrowers;
   e   have no effect on either borrowers or lenders.

3   Inflation

   a   does not affect taxpayers, because the tax system is fully indexed;
   b   does not affect taxpayers, because only real income is taxed;
   c   does not affect taxpayers, because only nominal income is taxed;
   d   frequently injures investors, who are taxed on high nominal incomes, even though inflation makes their real income small or even negative;
   e   hurts wage earners but not investors.

4   The inflation tax refers to

   a   the fact that inflation makes it expensive to hold money;
   b   the fact that the earnings of investors are not adjusted for inflation;
   c   the fact that wages are not adjusted for inflation;
   d   the injury suffered by borrowers in inflationary times;
   e   the injury suffered by lenders in inflationary times.

5   Inflation often distorts

   a   nominal prices;
   b   relative prices;

c absolute prices;
d average prices;
e none of the above.

6 The trade-off between inflation and unemployment is illustrated by the

a aggregate demand curve;
b aggregate supply curve;
c Phillips curve;
d aggregate expenditures schedule;
e money demand curve.

7 The natural rate of unemployment is the rate that prevails

a when there is no inflation;
b during hyperinflation;
c when inflation equals its natural rate;
d when there are no wage and price controls;
e in inflationary spirals.

8 If people expect inflation to be higher, then the

a Phillips curve is vertical in the short run;
b Phillips curve shifts to the right;
c Phillips curve shifts to the left;
d Phillips curve does not shift, because it assumes that expectations are always rational;
e Phillips curve is horizontal in the long run.

9 If the government tries to keep unemployment below the NAIRU,

a inflation will decrease;
b there will be no effect on inflation;
c inflation will increase;
d there will be stagflation;
e the Phillips curve will shift to the left.

10 In the long run the Phillips curve is

a downward sloping;
b upward sloping;
c horizontal;
d vertical;
e increasing at a decreasing rate.

11 When people form expectations based on the structure of the economy, their expectations are said to be

a irrational;
b rational;
c adaptive;
d unrealistic;
e myopic.

12 If the price level is stuck above the level at which aggregate demand and aggregate supply intersect, then

a output is less than firms are willing to supply;
b output is more than firms are willing to supply;
c output is less than the economy is willing to purchase;
d output is more than the economy is willing to purchase;
e a and d.

13 When the price level is stuck above the intersection of aggregate demand and long-run aggregate supply,

a output equals the level at which aggregate demand and long-run aggregate supply intersect;
b output equals aggregate demand at the current price level;
c output equals short-run aggregate supply at the current price level;
d output is greater than it is at the intersection of aggregate demand and aggregate supply;
e c and d.

14 When the price level is stuck below the intersection of aggregate demand and short-run aggregate supply,

a output equals the level at which aggregate demand and aggregate supply intersect;
b output equals short-run aggregate supply at the current price level;
c output equals aggregate demand at the current price level;
d output is less than it is at the intersection of aggregate demand and short-run aggregate supply;
e b and d.

15 Which of the following can cause inflation to begin?

a demand shocks;
b supply shocks;
c monetary shocks;
d wage and price controls;
e a, b, and c.

16 If investors expect restrictive monetary policy,

a the exchange rate will appreciate;
b the exchange rate will depreciate;
c there will be no change in the exchange rate;
d the exchange rate may move up or down depending upon whether these expectations are rational;
e the exchange rate will rise if there is excess capacity but fall if the economy is operating at full employment.

17 The costs of changing prices are called

a variable costs;
b sunk costs;
c fixed costs;
d pricing costs;
e menu costs.

18 During recessions, firms perceive that

a cutting prices is riskier than cutting production;
b increasing prices is riskier than increasing production;
c cutting production is riskier than cutting prices;
d increasing prices is riskier than increasing production;
e none of the above.

19 Which of the following is not true of the beliefs of firms facing a kinked demand curve?

a Their customers will quickly learn of price increases, and they will lose business.

b Other firms' customers will be slow to learn of any price cuts, gaining the firm little new business.

c Rivals may match price cuts.

d Rivals will not match price increases.

e All of the above are true.

20 For a firm facing a kinked demand curve, when its marginal cost increases slightly,

a the price will rise;

b the price will stay the same;

c the price will fall;

d output will increase;

e output will decrease.

Completion

1 Formally linking any payment, such as wages or taxes, to inflation is called _____.

2 The trade-off between unemployment and inflation is represented by the _____.

3 The rate of unemployment that would result if there were no inflation is the _____.

4 If the government tries to maintain the unemployment rate below the _____, inflation will increase.

5 Inflation perpetuated by increases in government or investment spending is _____ inflation.

6 Inflation perpetuated by wage increases is an example of _____ inflation.

7 When both the unemployment rate and inflation rate are high there is _____.

8 If investors expect increased inflation, the exchange rate will _____.

9 The costs of changing prices are called _____.

10 Firms that believe that rivals will match price cuts but not price increases face a _____ demand curve.

Answers to Self-Test

True or False

1	f	6	t	11	f
2	t	7	f	12	t
3	t	8	f	13	t
4	t	9	f	14	t
5	t	10	t	15	t

Multiple Choice

1	b	6	c	11	b	16	a
2	d	7	a	12	e	17	e
3	d	8	b	13	c	18	a
4	a	9	c	14	e	19	e
5	b	10	d	15	e	20	b

Completion

1 indexing

2 Phillips curve

3 natural rate

4 NAIRU

5 demand-pull

6 cost-push

7 stagflation

8 depreciate

9 menu costs

10 kinked

Doing Economics: Tools and Practice Problems

In Chapter 24, we learned how to measure inflation and construct the price index. In this chapter, we use those tools to study cost-of-living provisions in contracts and to make comparisons between prices at different times. The goals are to understand how the economy deals with steady and predictable inflation and to develop a feel for the difference between real and nominal values.

Tool Kit 33.1: Using Cost-of-Living Provisions to Adjust Wages and Prices

Wage agreements between employer and employees, contracts between firms and their suppliers, government entitlement programs, and even the income tax system are indexed for inflation with cost-of-living provisions. These provisions specify that wages, prices, or other important economic variables must be adjusted to reflect inflation. The problems in this section show how to do this using the consumer price index. Table 33.1 gives the consumer price index for every year since 1954. (You can look up these numbers and a wealth of other economic data in the *Economic Report of the President*.)

Step one: Identify the dollar amount to be adjusted, that year's price index, and the current price index.

Step two: Convert the amount to current dollars:

current dollar equivalent = amount × (current price index/past price index).

---

1 (Worked problem: cost-of-living provisions) Dan's Steel Company offered a wage of $15 per hour in 1980. A cost-of-living provision in the contrast guaranteed that the nominal wage would be increased to compensate for inflation. Use the consumer price index given in Table 33.1 to calculate the wage in each year since 1980.

Step-by-step solution

Step one: The wage in 1980 was $15. To find the inflation-adjusted wage in 1981, we need the price index in 1980, which is 82.4, and in 1981, which is 90.9.

Step two: Convert the wage to 1981 dollars:

wage in 1981 = $15 × (90.9/82.4) = $16.55.

Table 33.1

Year or month	All items	Food and beverages		Housing				Apparel and upkeep	Transportation	Medical care	Entertainment	Other goods and services	Energy
		Total	Food	Total	Shelter	Fuel and other utilities	Household furnishings and operation						
1954	26.9		28.2		22.5	22.6		43.1	26.1	17.8			
1955	26.8		27.8		22.7	23.0		42.9	25.8	18.2			
1956	27.2		28.0		23.1	23.6		43.7	26.2	18.9			
1957	28.1		28.9		24.0	24.3		44.5	27.7	19.7			
1958	28.9		30.2		24.5	24.8		44.6	28.6	20.6			21.5
1959	29.1		29.7		24.7	25.4		45.0	29.8	21.5			21.5
1960	29.6		30.0		25.2	26.0		45.7	29.8	22.3			21.9
1961	29.9		30.4		25.4	26.3		46.1	30.1	22.9			22.4
1962	30.2		30.6		25.8	26.3		46.3	30.8	23.5			22.5
1963	30.6		31.1		26.1	26.6		46.9	30.9	24.1			22.6
1964	31.0		31.5		26.5	26.6		47.3	31.4	24.6			22.6
1965	31.5		32.2		27.0	26.6		47.8	31.9	25.2			22.5
1966	32.4		33.8		27.8	26.7		49.0	32.3	25.3			22.9
1967	33.4	35.0	34.1	30.8	28.8	27.1	42.0	51.0	33.3	28.2	40.7	35.1	23.3
1968	34.8	36.2	35.3	32.0	30.1	27.4	43.6	53.7	34.3	29.9	43.0	36.9	23.8
1969	36.7	38.1	37.1	34.0	32.6	28.0	45.2	56.8	35.7	31.9	45.2	38.7	24.2
1970	38.8	40.1	39.2	36.4	35.5	29.1	46.8	59.2	37.5	34.0	47.5	40.9	24.8
1971	40.5	41.4	40.4	38.0	37.0	31.1	48.6	61.1	39.5	36.1	50.0	42.9	25.5
1972	41.8	43.1	42.1	39.4	38.7	32.5	49.7	62.3	39.9	37.3	51.5	44.7	26.5
1973	44.4	48.8	48.2	41.2	40.5	34.3	51.1	64.6	41.2	38.8	52.9	46.4	27.2
1974	49.3	55.5	55.1	45.8	44.4	40.7	56.8	69.4	45.8	42.4	56.9	49.8	29.4
1975	53.8	60.2	59.8	50.7	48.8	45.4	63.4	72.5	50.1	47.5	62.0	53.9	38.1
1976	56.9	62.1	61.6	53.8	51.5	49.4	67.3	75.2	55.1	52.0	65.1	57.0	42.1
1977	60.6	65.8	65.5	57.4	54.9	54.7	70.4	78.6	59.0	57.0	68.3	60.4	45.1
1978	65.2	72.2	72.0	62.4	60.5	58.5	74.7	81.4	61.7	61.8	71.9	64.3	49.4
1979	72.6	79.9	79.9	70.1	68.9	64.8	79.9	84.9	70.5	67.5	76.5	68.9	52.5
1980	82.4	86.7	86.8	81.1	81.0	75.4	86.3	90.9	83.1	74.9	83.6	75.2	65.7
1981	90.9	93.5	93.6	90.4	90.5	86.4	93.0	95.3	93.2	82.9	90.1	82.6	86.0
1982	96.5	97.3	97.4	96.9	96.9	94.9	98.0	97.8	97.0	92.5	96.0	91.1	97.7
1983	99.6	99.5	99.4	99.5	99.1	100.2	100.2	100.2	99.3	100.6	100.1	101.1	99.2
1984	103.9	103.2	103.2	103.6	104.0	104.8	101.9	102.1	103.7	106.8	103.8	107.9	99.9
1985	107.6	105.6	105.6	107.7	109.8	106.5	103.8	105.0	106.4	113.5	107.9	114.5	100.9
1986	109.6	109.1	109.0	110.9	115.8	104.1	105.2	105.9	102.3	120.0	111.6	121.4	101.6
1987	113.6	113.5	113.5	114.2	121.3	103.0	107.1	110.6	105.4	130.1	115.3	128.5	88.2
1988	118.3	118.2	118.2	118.5	127.1	104.4	109.4	115.4	108.7	138.6	120.3	137.0	88.6
1989	124.0	124.9	125.1	123.0	132.8	107.8	111.2	118.6	114.1	149.3	126.5	147.7	89.3
1990	130.7	132.1	132.4	128.5	140.0	111.6	113.3	124.1	120.5	162.8	132.4	159.0	94.3
1991	136.2	136.8	136.3	133.6	146.3	115.3	116.0	128.7	123.8	177.0	138.4	171.6	102.1
1992	140.3	138.7	137.9	137.5	151.2	117.8	118.0	131.9	126.5	190.1	142.3	183.3	102.5
1993	144.5	141.6	140.9	141.2	155.7	121.3	119.3	133.7	130.4	201.4	145.8	192.9	103.0
1994	148.2	144.9	144.3	144.8	160.5	122.8	121.0	133.4	134.3	211.0	150.1	198.5	104.2
1995	152.4	148.9	148.4	148.5	165.7	123.7	123.0	132.0	139.1	220.5	153.9	206.9	104.6
1994: Jan	146.2	144.3	143.7	142.9	158.1	121.6	120.5	130.4	131.6	206.4	148.5	195.1	105.2
Feb	146.7	143.6	142.9	143.7	159.1	122.4	120.4	132.4	131.9	207.7	149.1	195.2	101.3
Mar	147.2	143.9	143.2	144.1	159.8	122.4	120.6	136.1	132.2	208.3	149.6	195.5	102.0
Apr	147.4	144.0	143.4	143.9	159.6	121.6	120.6	136.4	132.6	209.2	149.7	196.4	101.9
May	147.5	144.1	143.5	144.1	159.6	122.2	121.1	135.6	132.8	209.7	149.9	197.1	102.0
June	148.0	144.2	143.5	144.9	160.1	124.2	121.4	133.8	133.8	210.4	149.8	197.6	102.9
July	148.4	144.8	144.2	145.4	160.8	124.3	121.5	130.9	134.6	211.5	150.2	198.0	105.7
Aug	149.0	145.3	144.8	145.9	161.7	124.3	121.4	131.1	135.9	212.2	150.2	199.4	106.8
Sept	149.4	145.6	145.0	145.8	161.6	124.2	121.4	134.2	135.9	212.8	150.7	201.4	108.5
Oct	149.5	145.6	145.0	145.7	162.0	122.4	121.4	135.2	136.1	214.0	151.0	201.9	108.2
Nov	149.7	145.9	145.3	145.5	162.1	121.8	121.1	134.2	137.1	214.7	151.6	202.3	105.8
Dec	149.7	147.2	146.8	145.4	161.8	122.0	120.8	130.5	137.1	215.3	151.2	202.4	105.7
1995: Jan	150.3	147.9	147.5	146.4	162.9	122.9	121.8	129.4	137.3	216.6	152.1	203.0	104.7
Feb	150.9	147.8	147.4	147.0	163.8	122.6	122.4	131.1	137.5	217.9	152.5	204.1	104.2
Mar	151.4	147.9	147.4	147.4	164.5	122.3	122.6	134.4	138.0	218.4	152.6	204.0	103.7
Apr	151.9	148.9	148.4	147.4	164.7	122.1	122.6	134.8	139.1	218.9	153.3	204.3	103.2
May	152.2	148.7	148.3	147.6	164.8	122.5	122.7	133.4	140.3	219.3	153.6	204.9	103.9
June	152.5	148.4	147.9	148.5	165.5	125.0	122.5	130.5	141.1	219.8	153.2	205.3	106.3
July	152.5	148.6	148.1	149.2	166.4	125.1	123.0	128.3	140.1	220.8	153.6	205.7	109.3
Aug	152.9	148.9	148.4	149.6	166.8	125.7	123.4	130.1	139.2	221.6	154.1	207.7	108.1
Sept	153.2	149.4	148.9	149.5	166.8	124.9	123.8	132.7	138.8	222.1	154.9	210.2	107.4
Oct	153.7	149.8	149.4	149.7	167.3	123.9	123.9	134.5	139.4	222.9	155.2	210.7	106.2
Nov	153.6	149.8	149.4	149.4	167.3	123.1	123.6	133.7	139.4	223.5	156.0	211.2	104.5
Dec	153.5	150.3	149.9	149.7	167.4	123.7	123.8	130.6	139.1	223.8	156.2	211.1	102.8

Source: Department of Labor, Bureau of Labor Statistics

The wage in 1982 is $15 × (96.5/82.4) = $17.57. Proceeding similarly, we derive the information in Table 33.2.

Table 33.2

Year	Wage
1980	$15.00
1981	$16.55
1982	$17.57
1983	$18.13
1984	$18.91
1985	$19.59
1986	$19.95
1987	$20.68
1988	$21.54
1989	$22.57
1990	$23.79
1991	$24.79
1992	$25.54
1993	$26.30
1994	$26.98
1995	$27.74

2   (Practice problem: cost-of-living provisions) The Social Security tax is applied to earnings up to a statutory maximum. Any earnings above this limit are taxed. Table 33.3 gives the maximum earnings for selected years.

Table 33.3

Year	Maximum taxable annual earnings
1950	$ 3,000
1960	$ 4,800
1970	$ 7,800
1980	$25,900
1990	$51,300

The maximum was $3,000 in 1950. Adjust this number for inflation for 1960, 1970, 1980, and 1990, and compare the result with the actual numbers in Table 33.1. Has the maximum taxable earning limit kept up with or outpaced inflation?

3   (Practice problem: cost-of-living provisions) The Tax Reform Act of 1986 set the rates at 15 percent for the first $17,850 of income for single persons and 28 percent for any income above that amount. To avoid "bracket creep," the income level at which the rates change is supposed to be indexed for inflation. Use the consumer price index numbers in Table 33.1 to adjust for inflation.

Answers to Problems

2   Adjusted limit in 1960 = $3,000 × (29.6/24.1) = $3,684.65; adjusted limit in 1970 = $3,000 × (38.8/24.1) = $4,829.88; adjusted limit in 1980 = $3,000 × (82.4/24.1) = $10,257.26; adjusted limit in 1990 = $3,000 × (130.7/24.1) = $16,269.71.

3   Adjusted level in 1987 = $17,850 × (113.6/109.6) = $18,501; adjusted level in 1988 = $17,850 × (118.3/109.6) = $19,267; adjusted level in 1989 = $17,850 × (124.0/109.6) = $20,195; adjusted level in 1990 = $17,850 × (130.7/109.6) = $21,286; adjusted level in 1991 = $17,850 × (136.2\109.6) = $22,182; adjusted level in 1992 = $17,850 × (140.3/109.6) = $22,850; adjusted level in 1993 = $17,850 × (144.5/109.6) = $23,534; adjusted level in 1994 = $17,850 × (148.2/109.6) = $24,137; adjusted level in 1995 = $17,850 × 152.4/109.6 = $24,821.

Chapter 34

UNEMPLOYMENT: UNDERSTANDING WAGE RIGIDITIES

Chapter Review

The last chapter focused on inflation. This chapter zeroes in on the labor market to examine the causes of unemployment more closely. The key issue is why wages fail to adjust to clear the market and bring about full employment. In recent years economists have put forward several new ideas about this problem, and these ideas are discussed and evaluated here. The next chapter completes Part Four on dynamics with some analysis of the policy issues involved in the unemployment–inflation trade-off.

ESSENTIAL CONCEPTS

1   While unemployment fluctuates substantially in the United States, there is little variation in real wages. Why not? We know that changes in product demand cause the labor demand to shift. Unless supply shifts to match the shifts in demand or supply is perfectly elastic (two propositions that are surely wrong), the explanation must lie in a microeconomic analysis of sticky real wages.

2   Wages may not adjust to bring about full employment for several reasons.

a   **Union contracts** may specify wages above the market-clearing level. If the demand for labor falls, the union may not agree to accept lower wages.

b   Firms may have informal agreements, or **implicit contracts**, with their risk-averse workers to provide fixed wages as a kind of insurance against economic downturns.

c   **Insider-outsider theory** observes that because existing workers must train new hires, the current work force may not be willing to provide training to newly hired workers unless they are paid the same wage.

d   **Minimum wage laws** mandate a price floor in the labor market.

e   **Efficiency wage theory** shows how firms may make higher profits by paying wages that are above the market-clearing level, because workers have incentives to work harder and be more productive.

3   There are three reasons why firms can increase the productivity of their workers by paying the higher efficiency wage rather than the market wage.

a   When a firm cuts its wage, some workers leave. These workers are likely to be the firm's most productive workers who will have good alternatives elsewhere. The pool of the firm's new hires will be of lower quality when the wage offer is less. Thus, the overall quality of the work force is poorer at lower wages. This phenomenon is called adverse selection.

b   Workers may put forth greater effort on a job that pays more than alternative jobs. In effect, the higher wage makes the job more valuable to the worker and motivates her to work harder for fear of losing the high-paying job.

c   By paying higher wages, firms can reduce the rate at which workers quit—the labor turnover rate. Because it is costly to hire and train new workers, a firm's profits may be higher than they would if it paid lower wages.

4   **Okun's law** says that a 2 percent increase in output is needed to bring about a 1 percent decrease in unemployment. One explanation for this is **labor hoarding,** where firms retain workers during downturns in order to have them available when demand returns. This is a form of disguised unemployment.

5   One policy option is to attempt to increase wage flexibility through profit sharing or substituting bonuses for some percentage of the wage bill. Another recommends reducing the costs of unemployment with a more generous unemployment insurance system. Both proposals run into the risk-incentive trade-off, which shows that when workers are protected from risk, they lose incentives to put forth effort.

a   If workers receive more of their wages in the form of profit sharing, their earnings become more flexible, rising in booms and falling in recessions. Such a policy reduces the risk of unemployment, yet increases the risk of income loss during economic downturns.

b   Unemployment insurance protects workers against income loss if they are laid off, yet it reduces their incentives to find and accept new jobs.

BEHIND THE ESSENTIAL CONCEPTS

1   While each of the reasons for wage rigidity listed above has some validity, the efficiency wage theory is the most satisfactory explanation. Economists favor efficiency wage theory because it explains three important facts about the labor market: the failure of wages to adjust to market-clearing levels, the fact that firms lay off excess workers during downturns rather than share the available work equally among the firm's total labor demand, and the fact that wages adjust slowly when economic conditions change.

2   The efficiency wage theory explains rigid wages in the following way. Suppose you are an employer. You need quality workers who put forth a lot of effort and remain loyal to your firm. Your problem is how to keep and motivate your good workers. If you pay the market-clearing wage, jobs with your firm will be worth no more than those of other firms. Your workers will know that they can quickly find work elsewhere at the going wage. The efficiency wage solves the problem in a very clever way. It is part carrot and part stick. You offer the carrot of higher wages, and gain influence over your workers with the stick, which is the threat to take away the job. Your workers have good incentives to stay, because the job is now worth more than their alternatives.

3   Once you understand why one firm gains by paying its workers wages above market-clearing levels, you can then see that other firms will do the same. It might seem to you that if all firms pay higher wages, then no firm offers anything special. But because all wages are higher than the market-clearing level, there remains a surplus of unemployed workers and not enough jobs to go around. Losing a valuable job represents a substantial cost to your workers, not because other jobs pay less, but because workers without jobs face a considerable time of unemployment.

4   Unemployment is a surplus of labor, or workers. You might ask, "Why don't the unemployed offer to work for less?" After all, the usual explanation for why the price of anything adjusts down to the market-clearing level is that the suppliers who cannot find buyers offer to sell at lower prices. In the efficiency wage world, however, if the unemployed offer to work at lower wages, the manager of the firm will conclude that they are either low-quality workers who will not make the required effort or that they will soon look for other employment. Remember that the efficiency wage is just high enough to attract, motivate, and keep quality workers. Any offer to do quality work for less is simply not credible.

5   When the demand for labor falls during economic downturns, firms use layoffs to reduce the size of the work force rather than share the available work among their workers. Why? According to the efficiency wage view, sharing work lowers average earnings in the same way that cutting wages does. If you let your employees share the work, you will lose your high-quality workers and have difficulty motivating those who stay. It is better to use layoffs.

6   A final implication of the efficiency wage theory is that wages adjust slowly. Put yourself again in the shoes of an employer. If business falls off, you may want to cut wages, but first you must see whether your competitors will reduce *their* wages. If you move too soon, you may lose your best workers. Efficiency wage theory counsels waiting, perhaps spending a few dollars more in labor costs.

SELF-TEST

True or False

1   The real wage is the nominal wage adjusted for inflation.

2   If supply is perfectly elastic, then when demand shifts, real wages will not change.

3   Whether they actually cause an increase in wages for

their members, unions slow the pace of wage adjustment.

4 Employment levels fluctuate quite dramatically; nevertheless, real wages are rather stable.

5 Most union contracts contain provisions for adjusting wages downward when the firm's demand for labor shifts.

6 Cost of living adjustment provisions (COLAs) allow real wages to remain stable even though inflation increases.

7 An implicit contract is an informal arrangement between workers and firms, often involving the firm's paying constant wages even as the wages its workers could receive elsewhere change.

8 Implicit contract theory also explains why real wages of job seekers do not decline significantly during recessions.

9 According to insider-outsider theory, a firm's current workers refuse to train new hires unless the new hires receive similar wages.

10 The minimum wage is a price ceiling in the market for unskilled labor.

11 According to efficiency wage theory, the firm can make more profits by paying higher wages.

12 One reason firms may not wish to pay lower wages is the adverse selection effect, whereby the average quality of the pool of workers willing to accept a job with a firm depends upon the wage offered.

13 As a general rule, the efficiency wage is less than the market-clearing wage.

14 Efficiency wage theory implies that wages will adjust slowly because firms are reluctant to change wages before their competitors do.

15 Unemployment affects most demographic groups equally.

Multiple Choice

1 The demand curve for labor studied in this chapter

   a shows the total amount of labor demanded by all firms in the economy at each wage;
   b is drawn assuming that product prices are fixed;
   c may shift to the right but never shifts to the left;
   d is upward sloping, according to efficiency wage theory;
   e a and b.

2 The real wage

   a equals the efficiency wage;
   b equals the nominal wage when expectations have adjusted to the actual rate of inflation;
   c equals the nominal wage adjusted for errors in forming expectations;
   d equals the nominal wage adjusted for inflation;
   e equals the wage negotiated in the union contract and modified by the COLA.

3 Which of the following is not a possible explanation for wage rigidity?

   a The supply curve of labor is horizontal (perfectly elastic).
   b The labor supply curve shifts along with the demand curve for labor.
   c The demand curve for labor is perfectly inelastic.
   d Union contracts restrict wage adjustment.
   e Some firms have implicit contracts with their risk-averse workers to provide insurance by paying the same wage even as the market wage varies.

4 Unemployment results if

   a the demand for labor shifts to the left, and wages fail to adjust;
   b the supply of labor shifts to the left, and wages fail to adjust;
   c the demand for labor shifts to the right, and wages fail to adjust;
   d the supply of labor shifts to the right, and wages fail to adjust;
   e a and d.

5 If the supply of labor is upward sloping and demand shifts to the right, then

   a if wages adjust to the market-clearing level, anyone willing to work at the going wage can eventually find a job;
   b if wages adjust to the market-clearing level, any unemployment will be involuntary;
   c if wages adjust to the market-clearing level, employment will decrease;
   d if wages do not adjust to the market-clearing level, any unemployment will be involuntary;
   e if wages do not adjust to the market-clearing level, the supply of labor will shift to the right.

6 In modern economies, when the demand for labor falls,

   a the real wage always falls to clear the market;
   b the real wage does not change, but workers share the available jobs by each working fewer hours;
   c the real wage does not change, but workers share the available jobs by rotating between full time and unemployment;
   d the real wage does not change, and some workers are laid off while others retain employment;
   e b and c.

7 Which of the following is an explanation of the failure of real wages to adjust to changes in the demand and supply of labor?

   a union contracts;
   b implicit contracts;
   c insider-outsider theory;
   d efficiency wage theory;
   e all of the above.

8 The minimum wage is a

   a price floor in the labor market, causing the quantity of workers demanded to exceed the quantity supplied;
   b price floor in the labor market, causing the quanti-

ty of workers demanded to be less than the quantity supplied;

   c price ceiling in the labor market, causing the quantity of workers demanded to exceed the quantity supplied;

   d price ceiling in the labor market, causing the quantity of workers demanded to be less than the quantity supplied;

   e a and d.

9 The theory that argues that firms have an informal agreement to protect risk-averse workers from variations in their incomes by paying the same wage even though their alternative wage changes is called

   a efficiency wage theory;
   b implicit contract theory;
   c insider-outsider theory;
   d minimum wage theory;
   e none of the above.

10 The theory that points out that it is not in the interests of the firm's workers to train newcomers if the new hires receive lower wages is

   a efficiency wage theory;
   b implicit contract theory;
   c insider-outsider theory;
   d minimum wage theory;
   e none of the above.

11 The theory that says that wages above market-clearing wages motivate workers to put forth effort and remain with the high-paying firm is

   a efficiency wage theory;
   b implicit contract theory;
   c insider-outsider theory;
   d minimum wage theory;
   e none of the above.

12 Typically, when the firm's demand for labor falls, it

   a immediately cuts wages for all workers;
   b shares the available work among all its workers;
   c reduces the size of its labor force through layoffs;
   d idles some of its capital stock in order to keep its workers busy;
   e retains its entire work force at current wages, hoping that business will return.

13 Efficiency wage theory emphasizes that higher wages are important to

   a motivate workers;
   b retain high-quality workers;
   c attract high-quality job applicants;
   d reduce turnover;
   e all of the above.

14 Unemployment typically

   a affects different groups in the economy equally;
   b affects high-skilled, high-wage workers more because employers can save more in labor costs by laying them off;
   c affects lower-skilled and part-time workers more;
   d affects only those paid on a piece-work basis;
   e none of the above.

15 The system under which workers are paid on the basis of what they produce is called

   a efficiency wages;
   b implicit contracts;
   c the insider-outsider system;
   d minimum wages;
   e piece work.

16 If wages and prices fall in the same proportion, then real wages

   a increase;
   b decrease;
   c stay the same;
   d may increase or decrease depending on the absolute level of the real wage;
   e may increase or decrease depending on the absolute level of the nominal wage.

17 Firms that keep their best workers on the payroll hoping that business will pick up are engaging in

   a piece work;
   b labor hoarding;
   c profit sharing;
   d layoffs;
   e union busting.

18 Okun's law asserts that

   a for every 1 percent decrease in output, unemployment increases by 1 percent;
   b for every 1 percent decrease in unemployment, output increases by 2 percent;
   c for every 1 percent decrease in unemployment, output increases by less than 1 percent;
   d for every 1 percent decrease in output, unemployment increases 2 percent;
   e for every 1 percent decrease in output, unemployment increases by less than 1 percent.

19 If workers received some of their compensation in the form of bonuses tied to the profit level, then

   a wages would be more flexible;
   b unemployment would fall;
   c workers would be exposed to a greater risk of income fluctuations;
   d all of the above;
   e none of the above.

20 Unemployment compensation

   a increases the risk of income fluctuations for workers;
   b reduces unemployment;
   c gives unemployed workers more incentive to look for and accept job offers;
   d increases both risk and incentives to look for work;
   e decreases both risk and incentives to look for work.

Completion

1 Wage _____ refers to the failure of wages to adjust sufficiently to changes in the demand or supply curve of labor.

2 An understanding between a firm and its workers that

requires the payment of constant wages is called an
_____.

3   According to _____ theory, the current employees of a firm refuse to train new hires unless their wages are comparable.

4   The minimum wage is a government-mandated price _____ in the labor market.

5   Paying higher wages can increase _____ by attracting more qualified workers, increasing effort, and reducing turnover.

6   The wage that minimizes total labor costs is called the _____ wage.

7   Because it is expensive to hire and fire workers, firms may _____ employees during recessions.

8   _____ says that if output increases by 2 percent, unemployment falls by 1 percent.

9   Making wages more flexible by substituting some form of profit sharing may be unattractive to workers who are relatively _____.

10 Unemployment insurance reduces the risk associated with unemployment, but it also reduces the _____ of the unemployed to search for work.

Answers to Self-Test

True or False

1	t	6	t	11	t
2	t	7	t	12	t
3	t	8	f	13	f
4	t	9	t	14	t
5	f	10	f	15	f

Multiple Choice

1	e	6	d	11	a	16	c
2	d	7	e	12	c	17	b
3	c	8	b	13	e	18	b
4	e	9	b	14	c	19	d
5	a	10	c	15	e	20	e

Completion

1   rigidity
2   implicit contract
3   insider-outsider
4   floor
5   productivity
6   efficiency
7   hoard
8   Okun's law
9   risk averse
10 incentives

Doing Economics: Tools and Practice Problems

Involuntary unemployment results when the wage does not adjust to clear the market. Efficiency wage theory explains the failure of wages to bring about full employment. It also implies that firms will use layoffs (rather than job sharing)

Tool Kit 34.1: Determining the Efficiency Wage

Firms perceive that the productivity of their workers depends upon the wage. Higher wages motivate workers to put forth effort, attract a high-quality pool of applicants, and reduce turnover. When productivity depends on the wage, the profit-maximizing strategy for the firm is to set the wage at the level that attains the highest output per dollar. This level is achieved when the ratio of productivity (output per hour) to the wage rate is maximized.

Step one: Identify and graph the productivity-wage relationship.

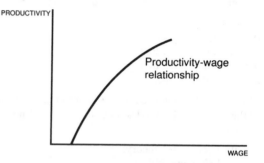

Step two: Calculate the ratio of productivity to the wage for each wage level. This ratio gives output per dollar spent on labor:

$$\text{output per dollar} = \text{productivity/wage}.$$

Step three: Choose the wage for which the corresponding productivity-wage ratio is the highest. Label this point *A* on the graph of the productivity-wage relationship.

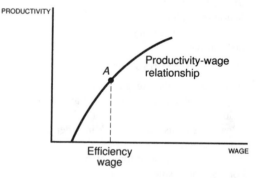

Step four: Draw a line from the origin to *A*. The slope of this line is the productivity-wage ratio. The line should be tangent, and so indicates that output per dollar is maximized.

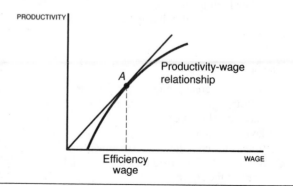

to reduce the work force when the demand for labor is low, and wages will adjust slowly as conditions change. In this section, we learn how to determine the efficiency wage.

1 (Worked problem: efficiency wage) Murray's Auto Parts has had trouble with labor turnover. Once its workers are trained, they leave. A consultant points out that productivity would be higher if the firm could keep its workers and that one way to discourage quitting is to pay higher wages. The consultant estimates that the relationship between productivity and wages is as shown in Table 34.1.

Table 34.1

Wage (per hour)	Productivity ($ sales per hour)
$4	8.00
$5	12.50
$6	18.00
$7	24.50
$8	26.00
$9	27.00

Determine the efficiency wage for Murray's.

Step-by-step solution

Step one: Identify and graph the productivity-wage relation-

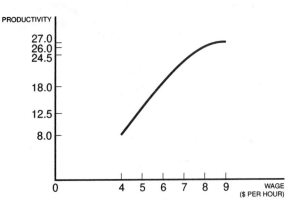

ship.
Step two: Calculate the ratio of productivity to the wage for each wage level. This ratio is shown in Table 34.2.

Table 34.2

Wage ($ per hour)	Productivity ($ sales per hour)	Productivity/wage
$4	8.00	2.00
$5	12.50	2.50
$6	18.00	3.00
$7	24.50	3.50
$8	26.00	3.25
$9	27.00	3.00

Step three: Choose the wage for which the corresponding productivity-wage ratio is the highest. The efficiency wage is $7 per hour and is shown as point A.

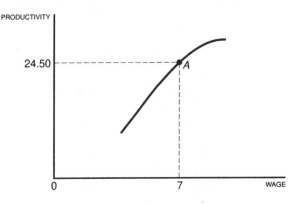

Step four: Draw a line from the origin to A. The slope of this line is the productivity-wage ratio, which is 3.5. The line is tangent, indicating that output per dollar is maximized.

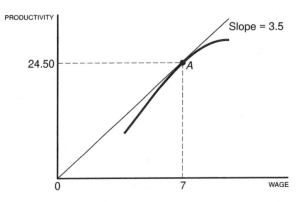

2 (Practice problem: efficiency wage) Moe's Lawn Care has plenty of customers, but Moe is having difficulty getting his mowers to work hard. He cannot monitor each worker all the time and suspects that there is considerable shirking on the job. His brother-in-law, always ready with helpful advice, suggests that if wages were higher, his workers would put forth more effort for fear of losing a well-paying job. Moe considers this and estimates that the relationship between wages and productivity is as appears in Table 34.3.

Table 34.3

Wage (per month)	Productivity (acres mowed per month)
$ 900	800
$1,000	1,000
$1,100	1,320
$1,200	1,680
$1,300	1,950
$1,400	1,960

Determine the efficiency wage for Moe's business.

3   (Practice problem: efficiency wage) Luke's Warm and Now food delivery business needs good drivers. He thinks that he may get a better pool of applicants if he offers higher wages. Table 34.4 shows the relationship between the wage and productivity.

Table 34.4

Wage (per hour)	Productivity (deliveries per week)
$200	110
$220	114
$240	130
$260	146
$280	160
$300	168

Determine the efficiency wage.

Answers to Problems

2   Table 34.5 shows the productivity-wage ratio. The efficiency wage is $1,300 per month, as shown in the diagram.

Table 34.5

Wage	Productivity	Productivity/wage
$ 900	800	0.89
$1,000	1,000	1.00
$1,000	1,320	1.20
$1,200	1,680	1.40
$1,300	1,950	1.50
$1,400	1,960	1.40

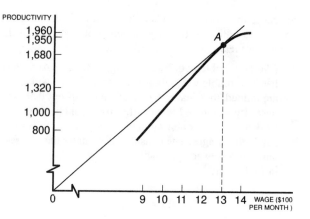

3   Table 34.6 shows the productivity-wage ratio.

Table 34.6

Wage	Productivity	Productivity/wage
$200	100	0.50
$220	114	0.52
$240	130	0.54
$260	146	0.56
$280	160	0.57
$300	168	0.56

The efficiency wage is $280 per week, as shown in the diagram.

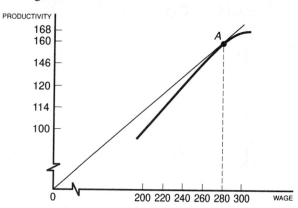

Chapter 35

INFLATION VS. UNEMPLOYMENT: APPROACHES TO POLICY

CHAPTER REVIEW

In closing the discussion of dynamics this chapter brings together the insights of Chapter 33, on the trade-off between inflation and unemployment, and Chapter 34, on the reasons for slow adjustment of real wages. Here the emphasis is on policy alternatives: what can be done to stabilize the economy, control inflation, and reduce the rate of unemployment. The book returns to the other major macroeconomic goal—growth—in the next chapter.

ESSENTIAL CONCEPTS

1   Attempting to push the unemployment rate below the NAIRU only results in increased inflation. There is always some uncertainty about the exact level of the NAIRU, however, and thus there is some room for disagreement. The main policy question is how aggressive should the government be in lowering unemployment or fighting inflation. The answer depends on how one values the relative costs of inflation and unemployment.

2   Facing the problem of the business cycle with its varying levels of output and occasional episodes of high unemployment, economists split into two camps. **Inter-**ventionists believe that government has an important role to play in fostering a more stable economy. **Non-interventionists** see little prospect that government can succeed and much risk that government actions will exacerbate the economy's fluctuations.

3   Among the alternative schools of thought, there are the following.

   a   **Real business cycle theory** places the blame for fluctuations on exogenous shocks, such as the oil price increases of the 1970s. They recommend that government leave hands off, letting the money supply increase at the rate of growth of real GDP.

   b   **New classical macroeconomics** stresses the concept of rational expectations, whereby households and firms recognize and offset the effects of government actions. For example, current deficits motivate households to rationally anticipate future tax increases. They save more and that counteracts the fiscal stimulus of the deficit.

   c   **Monetarism** stresses the inability of government to effectively carry out an interventionist program. Monetarists emphasize the lags in determining the need for and completing the interventionist policies and also the perverse incentives that the political environment gives to governments.

4   Non-interventionists recommend tying the hands of government with **fixed rules,** such as balanced budgets and stable monetary growth. They stress that this policy would remove one source of instability, namely uncertainty surrounding future government policy. Fixing government policy mitigates the problem of **dynamic consistency** by giving households and firms confidence that government will not reverse direction when conditions change.

5   Interventionists counter with arguments that downturns can persist for a long time and that government can reduce their duration both with automatic and discretionary policies. The leading school, new Keynesianism, emphasizes the endogenous forces in the economy that amplify shocks and cause their effects to persist. These include the **multiplier-accelerator,** according to which as firms try to keep a constant inventory to sales ratio, output varies much more than sales. These variations are further amplified by the multiplier process. The economy expands rapidly, only to bump against capacity constraints at full employment, and then it slumps into recession.

6   Interventionists call for policies, such as automatic stabilizers, that alter the structure of the economy and strengthen its ability to dampen shocks. They also support the use of discretionary fiscal and monetary policy. In recessions, government should increase the budget deficit to stimulate the economy. Also, the Fed should use active monetary policy to counteract economic fluctuations. Finally, interventionists advocate labor market policies that lower the NAIRU, including promoting labor mobility, reducing some types of business regulation, and opening the economy to free trade.

7   Recent macroeconomic history illustrates the ideas of this chapter. In the early 1960s a tax cut forestalled an impending recession and brought about an extended period of growth with stable prices. Late in the decade expenditures on the Vietnam War and Great Society programs overheated the economy. The increasing inflation was magnified by oil price increases in the 1970s. In the early 1980s the Fed tightened money growth to reduce inflation at the cost of a long and deep recession. With fiscal policy constrained by a decade of large budget deficits, debate in the early 1990s centered around the aggressiveness of monetary policy.

BEHIND THE ESSENTIAL CONCEPTS

1   Economists use the term business cycle to refer to the ups and downs of the economy. Although there are certain regularities (in recessions output falls, unemployment rises, the work week shortens, and inflation slows), the length of the cycle is quite unpredictable. For example, expansions can persist from 12 to more than 100 months, but their post World War II average is 50. The end of an expansion is difficult to predict, because the probability of its continuing hardly falls as it ages. All of this makes predicting the path of the economy a hazardous and uncertain endeavor.

2   When the economy is hit with a shock, such as an increase in oil prices, households and firms take actions. Some of these actions offset the impact of the shock and dampen its effects. For example, while you would reduce your demand for gasoline, you and others might buy high-mileage cars. Similarly, firms invest in energy-saving equipment, leading to increased production and employment in that sector. All of these responses to changes in relative prices keep aggregate demand, output, and employment high. On the other hand, there are mechanisms in the economy that amplify the shock. High energy use industries contract, firms go out of business, and their workers are laid off. Income and consumption fall and the multiplier process worsens the decline. Sometimes the dampening activities dominate; for example, when the stock market crashed in 1987, the economy continued its expansion. Other times the shock is amplified and the economy is thrown into recession.

3   If inflation is undesirable, why not simply outlaw it with **wage and price controls**? Although they have been used in wartime and were tried during the Nixon administration in the early 1970s, wage and price controls do not have much support among economists. Suppose that the government mandated that no price rise more than 1 percent per year. In some markets where relative prices were stable or falling, this regulation would make no difference. But in others where relative prices were rising, market prices would bump against the ceiling and shortages would appear. An alternative policy with a lighter touch is **moral suasion**, where the government tries to persuade firms to keep prices in check.

4   The discussion of this chapter draws a clear distinction in order to emphasize the differences among economists and explore the logic of their arguments. For example, the non-interventionists forswear discretionary policy and argue for fixed rules, such as a steady growth rate for the money supply. Interventionists point out that some discretion must be used in the choice of **monetary aggregate** and in the timing of open market operations. Once room for some discretion is admitted, they recommend a more active use of monetary policy.

SELF-TEST

True or False

1   If the government attempts to keep the inflation rate below the NAIRU, unemployment will accelerate.

2   Bondholders generally advocate an aggressive anti-inflation program.

3   Interventionists favor fixed policy rules such as balanced budgets and steady money growth.

4   There is little variation in the length of expansions in the United States since World War II.

5   The probability that an expansion will end rises rapidly with the length of the expansion.

6   The probability that a contraction will end rises rapidly with the length of the contraction.

7   A 1 percent reduction in the unemployment rate requires a 2 percent reduction in the economy's output.

8   Real business cycle theory attributes the variability of output to exogenous shocks.

9   The dynamic consistency problem refers to the difficulty of maintaining full employment when wages and prices change.

10 New classical economists such as Robert Lucas have emphasized the importance of rational expectations.

11 New Keynesians differ from older Keynesian economists in their emphasis on microeconomics.

12 The effectiveness of fiscal policy may be undermined by the lags in the time it takes government to make decisions.

13 If the economy slips slightly below the NAIRU, rapid inflation results.

14 The multiplier accelerator is an example of an endogenous cause of economic downturns.

15 The NAIRU is probably around 8 percent.

Multiple Choice

1   Lowering the unemployment rate by 1 percent increases output by

a   1 percent;
b   2 percent;
c   3 percent;
d   4 percent;
e   5 percent.

2   The probability that an expansion will end in the next month

a   rises rapidly as the expansion ages;
b   is constant;
c   falls rapidly as the expansion ages;
d   rises only slightly as the expansion ages;
e   falls slightly as the expansion ages.

3   The probability that a contraction will end in the next month

a   rises rapidly as the contraction ages;
b   is constant;
c   falls rapidly as the contraction ages;
d   rises only slightly as the contraction ages;
e   falls slightly as the contraction ages.

4   The idea variations in output are due to exogenous shocks to which the market reacts quickly to restore full employment is a tenet of

a   real business cycle theory;
b   new classical macroeconomics;
c   monetarism;
d   New Keynesianism;
e   supply-side economics.

5   The idea that actions of rational individuals offset the impact of government actions is associated with

a   real business cycle theory;
b   new classical macroeconomics;
c   monetarism;
d   New Keynesianism;
e   supply-side economics.

6   Doubts about the government's ability to carry out discretionary fiscal and monetary policy are stressed by believers in

a   real business cycle theory;
b   new classical macroeconomics;
c   monetarism;
d   New Keynesianism;
e   supply-side economics.

7   The belief that government can be effective with discretionary fiscal and monetary policy is part of

a   real business cycle theory;
b   new classical macroeconomics;
b   monetarism;
d   New Keynesianism;
e   supply-side economics.

8   Non-interventionist economists view government as a source of instability and advocate

a   binding fiscal and monetary policy with fixed policy rules;
b   using fiscal and monetary policies with discretion;
c   returning oversight of the money supply to the private sector;
d   dynamic inconsistency;
e   repealing the accelerator.

9   Which of the following is not an example of a policy rule advocated by non-interventionists?

a   The money supply should increase at a fixed rate each year.
b   The money supply should be adjusted to stimulate aggregate demand in recessions and constrain aggregate demand in inflationary times.
c   The budget deficit should be zero.
d   Government expenditures should be a fixed percentage of GDP.
e   The money supply should increase with the rate of output.

10 Dynamic consistency refers to

a   the fact that most business cycles follow the same pattern;
b   the recommendation that government policy follow certain fixed rules;
c   the issue of whether the government will carry out its promises;
d   the political business-cycle explanation for economic fluctuations;
e   the need to harmonize fiscal and monetary policy.

11 The New Keynesian view is that economic fluctuations are

a   due to endogenous forces and predictable;

b   due to random, exogenous shocks and unpredictable;

c   chiefly due to misguided monetary and fiscal policy;

d   due to exogenous shocks but are amplified and made persistent by the economic system;

e   none of the above.

12   The accelerator model of the economy assumes that firms want to keep the

a   ratio of output to labor constant;

b   ratio of investment to sales constant;

c   level of unemployment constant;

d   rate of growth in the money supply constant;

e   level of full-employment GDP constant.

13   New Keynesians advocate

a   policies to lower the NAIRU, such as reducing business regulation;

b   discretionary monetary policy;

c   discretionary fiscal policy;

d   automatic stabilizers;

e   all of the above.

14   Most economists agree that in the long run the Phillips curve is

a   vertical;

b   horizontal;

c   upward sloping;

d   downward sloping;

e   inelastic.

15   The idea that the economy expands rapidly until it hits capacity constraints and then plunges in recessions argues that the causes of fluctuations are

a   exogenous shocks;

b   endogenous;

c   uncertainty over government policy;

d   rational expectations;

e   dynamic consistency.

16   Which of the following represents a mechanism that amplifies shock to the economy?

a   The multiplier.

b   Changes in relative prices lead household and firms to change their consumption and production patterns.

c   Changes in interest rates affect the demand for investment.

d   Households and firms with rational expectations anticipate the effects of shocks.

e   Government uses discretionary monetary and fiscal policy.

17   Which of the following might reduce the NAIRU by shifting aggregate supply to the right?

a   moral suasion;

b   wage and price controls;

c   a fixed rule mandating steady money growth;

d   unemployment insurance;

e   policies that promote labor mobility.

18   Which policy likely promotes labor mobility?

a   training programs for displaced workers;

b   moral suasion;

c   regulations requiring notification in anticipation of layoffs;

d   reducing business regulation;

e   automatic stabilizers.

19   A period of high inflation occurred during the

a   1950s;

b   1960s;

c   1970s;

d   1980s;

e   1990s.

20   The high deficits of the 1980s precluded the use of

a   discretionary monetary policy;

b   discretionary fiscal policy;

c   automatic stabilizers;

d   fixed rules for steady money growth;

e   policies to reduce the NAIRU.

Completion

1   _____ shocks such as wars or monetary restrictions start outside the economy.

2   _____ holds that prices and wages are quite flexible and recommends that the government not try to smooth economic fluctuations.

3   Households and firms that understand the structure of the economy are said to have _____.

4   The _____ refers to the inability of government to credibly promise not to change policy.

5   _____ advocate discretionary fiscal and monetary policy, automatic stabilizers, and policies to reduce the NAIRU.

6   New Keynesians stress that although externally generated shocks may hit the economy, the system can _____ them and cause the effects to _____.

7   Regulations that prohibit rapid increases in wages and prices are called _____.

8   When the government attempts to persuade firms to keep prices and wages low, it uses _____.

9   Targets, such as M1 and M2, are called _____.

10   Unemployment insurance and income taxes are examples of _____.

Answers to Self-Test

True or False

1	t	6	t	11	t
2	t	7	f	12	t
3	f	8	t	13	f
4	f	9	f	14	t
5	f	10	t	15	f

Multiple Choice

1	b	6	c	11	c	16	a
2	b	7	d	12	b	17	e
3	a	8	c	13	e	18	a
4	a	9	b	14	a	19	c
5	b	10	d	15	b	20	b

Completion

1 Exogenous
2 Real business cycle theory
3 rational expectations
4 dynamic consistency problem
5 New Keynesian economists
6 amplify, persist
7 wage and price controls
8 moral suasion
9 monetary aggregates
10 automatic stabilizers

Doing Economics: Tools and Practice Problems

The economy is continually buffeted by shocks. Consumer tastes change, new technologies are discovered, bad weather appears, or import prices surge. There are mechanisms within the economy that dampen the impact of shocks. These include flexible prices, rational expectations, labor mobility, and government policies, such as automatic stabilizers. On the other hand, there are factors such as the multiplier and accelerator that amplify shocks. Tool Kit 35.1 illustrates how these mechanisms can exacerbate instability.

Tool Kit 35.1: The Multiplier-Accelerator Process

The accelerator is the capital-output ratio. Firms in many industries try to keep this constant. The multiplier determines how much aggregate demand shifts when there is a change in spending, such as an increase in investment. These mechanisms can combine to amplify shocks. Follow these steps.

Step one: Identify the accelerator, the multiplier, and the change in spending.

Step two: Multiply the change in spending by the accelerator. This gives the extra investment needed to keep the capital-output ratio constant.

Required investment = change in spending × accelerator.

Step three: Multiply the product in step two by the multiplier. This gives the change in output resulting from the extra investment.

Change in output = new investment × multiplier.

Step four: Multiply the product in step three by the accelerator. This gives the second round of additional investment needed to keep the capital-output ratio constant.

Required investment = change in output × accelerator.

---

1 (Worked problem: multiplier-accelerator) Output is $5 trillion and the capital stock equals $15 trillion. The multiplier is 2. Suppose that a new investment project of $10 billion is undertaken.

   a Trace through the impact of this using the multiplier-accelerator.

   b Do you think the process can continue unabated? Why or why not?

Step-by-step solution

Step one: Identify the accelerator, the multiplier, and the change in spending. The accelerator is 15/5 = 3 and the multiplier is 2. The initial change in spending is $10 billion.

Step two: Multiply the change in spending by the accelerator. This gives the extra investment needed to keep the capital-output ratio constant.

Required investment = change in spending × accelerator
= $10 billion × 3 = $30 billion.

Step three: Multiply the product in step two by the multiplier. This gives the change in output resulting from the extra investment.

Change in output = new investment × multiplier
= $30 billion × 2 = $60 billion.

Step four: Multiply the product in step three by the accelerator. This gives the second round of additional investment needed to keep the capital-output ratio constant.

Required investment = change in output × accelerator
= $60 billion × 3 = $180 billion.

Of course, the process cannot continue too long, because the economy has capacity constraints.

2 (Practice problem: multiplier-accelerator) Output is $2 trillion and the capital stock equals $4 trillion. The multiplier is 2.5. Suppose that a new investment project of $30 billion is undertaken.

   a Trace through the impact of this using the multiplier-accelerator.

   b Do you think the process can continue unabated? Why or why not?

3 (Practice problem: multiplier-accelerator) Output is $7 trillion and the capital stock equals $14 trillion. The multiplier is 1.5. Suppose that a new investment project of $15 billion is undertaken.

   a Trace through the impact of this using the multiplier-accelerator.

   b Do you think the process can continue unabated? Why or why not?

Answers to Problems

2   *a*   Required investment = $30 billion × 4/2 = $60 billion; change in output = $60 billion × 2.5 = $150 billion; additional investment = $150 billion × 2 = $300 billion.

   b   No. The economy will eventually run into capacity constraints.

3   *a*   Required investment = $15 billion × 14/7 = $30 billion; change in output = $30 billion × 1.5 = $45 billion; additional investment = $45 billion × 2 = $90 billion.

   b   No. The economy will eventually run into capacity constraints.

Issues in Macroeconomic Policy

Chapter 36

GROWTH AND PRODUCTIVITY

Chapter Review

This chapter of the text begins Part Eight, which builds on the lessons of the previous four parts and takes a detailed look at some major macroeconomic problems. The chapter focuses on the causes of growth and the potential for continued expansion. The key concept is productivity, defined as output per worker. The next two chapters turn to problems associated with recent U.S. history: budget deficits and trade policy.

ESSENTIAL CONCEPTS

1   Although the U.S. economy has grown enormously in this century, the rate of growth in **productivity** (output per hour worked) has slowed in the past two decades. This slowdown has led to a loss of confidence in U.S. technological leadership, caused real wages (although not family incomes) to decline, and exacerbated inequality in living standards.

2   The four causes of growth in productivity are the accumulation of capital goods, an improvement in the

quality of the labor force, an increase in the efficiency of resource allocation, and technological advance. Concerns about productivity slowdown have led economists to propose policies designed to restore rapid growth.

3   Figure 36.1 represents the production function, which shows the relationship between inputs and outputs. It il-

Figure 36.1

lustrates that the accumulation of capital goods per worker brings about an increase in output per worker; however, the increase is subject to the **law of diminishing returns.** Economists call the increase in captial per worker **capital deepening.**

4   Although today's world capital market allows international borrowing, **capital accumulation** clearly requires more domestic savings and investment. U.S. savings rates have fallen because more generous Social Security benefits have reduced incentives to save for retirement, while improved capital markets have made borrowing easier. In addition, savings rates have suffered because the fraction of the population in the prime savings years (45–65) has declined. Promoting savings through tax policy is likely to be ineffective because savings are relatively unresponsive to changes in after-tax returns, and investment is subject to diminishing returns. U.S. investment has fallen because of high real interest rates, an uncertain investment climate, and some unwise government regulations.

5   Investment in skills and education improves the quality of the labor force. Economists call this **human capital.** Although the U.S. educational system has considerable strengths, especially in higher education, there is concern about the level of funding, quality of teachers, and other problems.

6   The economy expanded during this century as resources moved from traditional agriculture to higher productivity employment in manufacturing. Presently, the movement is toward the service sector, where some economists think the potential for productivity gains is more limited.

7   **Technological change** shifts the production function up and can outstrip diminishing returns. Although not everyone benefits from every innovation, technological change increases productivity, employment, and living standards overall. **Learning by doing** and **research and development** are important sources of technological progress. Sound macroeconomic policies that encourage full employment, R & D funding and tax subsidies, more science and technology education, and better government regulation all promote technological advance.

8   Total factor productivity analysis helps quantify the role of different factors in increasing productivity. After accounting for the increase due to more physical and human capital, economists attribute the residual increase to improvements in technology. This analysis shows that most productivity increases are due to technological change.

9   Economic growth both creates and destroys jobs. As new techniques of producing drive old ways from the market, displaced workers see declining standards of living. The difficulty involved in transition to new lines of employment may call for government programs to finance retraining and ease the transition.

BEHIND THE ESSENTIAL CONCEPTS

1   You should be clear about the distinction between factors that lead to movements along the production function and those that cause shifts. Capital accumulation moves the economy along its production function, as shown in Figure 36.1. An improvement in technology, on the other hand, shifts the production function. In Figure 36.2, the technological advance increases output without increasing the capital stock.

Figure 36.2

2   Productivity equals output per worker. As population grows, capital goods must be accumulated for the new workers to use. Because output per worker depends on how much capital each has to work with, this extra capital only keeps productivity constant. Additional capital goods must be accumulated to increase the amount of capital per worker, so that productivity can grow.

3   To see why U.S. savings rates are low, you need to understand the **life-cycle theory of savings.** According to this view, you save in order to consume in the future. Thus, the trade-off is current vs. future consumption. You will probably save during your working years to build up funds for retirement. Because the fraction of the population in the working years has declined, so has overall national savings. As Social Security and Medicare became more generous and individuals accumulated unexpected wealth through the increase in housing prices, the need to save for retirement declined. As private and public insurance improved, there has been less need to save for future emergencies. Many of these developments are good, but an unfortunate side effect is the accompanying disincentive to save.

4   Giving workers more capital to work with—capital deepening—accounts for only one-eighth of the growth in productivity. How do economists know this? One reason is that until recently productivity grew at a steady rate, a fact that cannot be explained by capital accumulation. If it were capital deepening, then the movement along the production function would run into diminish-

ing returns. Therefore it must be a shift in the production function, probably brought about by human capital accumulation or technological advance.

5   Some have argued that the available natural resources set up limits to growth. Certain natural resources, such as petroleum and agricultural land, are privately owned and traded in well-organized markets. These markets provide good incentives for conservation and preservation. If oil becomes scarce, for example, its price will rise, and world oil stocks will be conserved. This type of natural resource will probably not limit the world's growth. The ozone, oceans, and the genetic diversity in threatened natural habitats, on the other hand, are natural resources that are commonly owned and not traded in markets. The world's economy provides no incentive to conserve or preserve these resources. Their destruction is an external cost, not captured by prices. These global environmental problems may pose threats to increased living standards. Their solution requires cooperation among the world's governments.

SELF-TEST

True or False

1   Productivity measures output per unit of capital goods.

2   U.S. productivity growth slowed in the early 1980s.

3   Productivity in the United States is the highest among developed economies.

4   The law of diminishing returns says that technological advance must bring about slower growth in the future.

5   Capital deepening refers to increases in the number of workers per unit of capital.

6   During the 1980s taxes on capital income rose.

7   One reason for low U.S. savings rates during the 1980s is that the fraction of the population in the prime savings years declined.

8   A country's infrastructure includes its roads, bridges, sewer systems, and airports.

9   Investment in infrastructure has increased substantially during recent years.

10   Human capital refers to the plant and equipment that workers use on the job.

11   A great strength of the American educational system is its junior colleges and state universities.

12   Increased international trade raises U.S. productivity by shifting workers to export sectors where productivity is higher.

13   Everyone benefits from each technological advance through higher productivity and growth.

14   Total factor productivity analysis is used to distinguish between growth due to increases in labor and capital from that due to technological advance.

15   Market incentives ensure that such natural resources as rain forests and the global environment will be preserved.

Multiple Choice

1   Productivity is

  a   the extra output from the marginal worker;
  b   hours worked divided by output;
  c   output per hour worked;
  d   the number of workers required to produce the next unit of output;
  e   output divided by the total number of inputs.

2   The U.S. rate of growth in productivity

  a   sped up in the late 1960s and 1970s;
  b   has been nearly constant throughout the twentieth century;
  c   slowed significantly in the 1970s and early 1980s;
  d   increased steadily through the twentieth century;
  e   fell dramatically in the 1980s.

3   Over the business cycle productivity

  a   grows at approximately the same rate;
  b   falls as the economy enters a downturn, but rises faster than output as the economy commences recovery;
  c   rises as the economy enters a downturn, but falls as the economy recovers;
  d   grows faster during recessions because output falls less than employment;
  e   may grow at a faster or slower rate, depending upon monetary and fiscal policy.

4   The causes of growth include

  a   the accumulation of capital goods;
  b   improvement in the quality of the labor force;
  c   more efficient allocation of resources;
  d   technological advance;
  e   all of the above.

5   Capital deepening refers to

  a   increased numbers of workers per unit of capital;
  b   increases in capital per worker;
  c   decreases in capital per worker;
  d   reallocation of capital from less productive to more productive sectors;
  e   government investment in infrastructure.

6   According to the law of diminishing returns, as the economy accumulates more capital, output increases

  a   at the same rate as capital grows;
  b   at a slower rate than capital grows;
  c   at a faster rate than capital grows;
  d   only if new workers enter the labor force;
  e   only if the new capital equipment takes advantage of new and better technologies.

7   Savings accumulated for retirement are called

  a   life-cycle savings;
  b   target savings;
  c   precautionary savings;

   d   bequest savings;

   e   permanent income savings;

8   Savings accumulated for use in emergencies are called

   a   life-cycle savings;

   b   target savings;

   c   precautionary savings;

   d   bequest savings;

   e   permanent income savings.

9   According to the life-cycle theory, savings in the United States were low in the 1980s because

   a   the fraction of the population that is retired decreased;

   b   the fraction of the population in the prime savings years (45–65) increased;

   c   the fraction of the population in the prime savings years (45–65) decreased;

   d   the population as a whole increased;

   e   the fraction of the population in the prime savings years (21–44) decreased.

10   During the 1980s, tax changes

   a   encouraged savings by increasing the real after-tax rate of return to savings;

   b   encouraged savings by decreasing the real after-tax rate of return to savings;

   c   discouraged savings by increasing the real after-tax rate of return to savings;

   d   discouraged savings by decreasing the real after-tax rate of return to savings;

   e   had no impact on savings.

11   When the economy is at full employment, which of the following will not increase investment?

   a   reducing the fiscal deficit;

   b   shifting government spending toward infrastructure investment;

   c   subsidizing investment;

   d   using tax policies such as IRAs;

   e   All of the above increase investment.

12   The production function shows the relationship between

   a   the levels of inputs and the level of output;

   b   technology and growth;

   c   productivity and real wages;

   d   learning and experience;

   e   productivity and output.

13   During the 1980s, investment in infrastructure

   a   was adequate, but the level of business investment was low;

   b   was inadequate but was offset by a high level of business investment;

   c   was inadequate and exacerbated the effects of the low level of business investment;

   d   was low because tax changes made it more expensive;

   e   was adequate, as was the level of business investment.

14   Human capital refers to

   a   the capital goods that individuals own;

   b   education and skills that increase the productivity of individuals;

   c   fertility;

   d   output per hour worked;

   e   the capital goods that workers use on the job.

15   Which of the following is not a strength of the U.S. educational system?

   a   the absence of early tracking of students in lower grades;

   b   the relatively open system of junior colleges and state universitites;

   c   the research universities;

   d   the high percentage of students choosing majors in science and technology;

   e   All of the above are strengths.

16   Telecommunications deregulation and expanded international trade will

   a   raise overall productivity because productivity is higher than average in these sectors;

   b   raise overall productivity because productivity is lower than average in these sectors;

   c   reduce overall productivity because productivity is higher than average in these sectors;

   d   reduce overall productivity because productivity is lower than average in these sectors;

   e   leave overall productivity unchanged.

17   Technological change

   a   shifts the production function so that the same number of inputs produce more output;

   b   shifts the production function so that more output is produced but only if additional capital goods are used;

   c   shifts the production function so that more output is produced but only if additional workers are hired;

   d   increases productivity for capital but not for workers;

   e   increases productivity but does not shift the production function.

18   The method that attributes that part of the growth in productivity that cannot be explained by increases in labor and capital to technological advance is called

   a   total factor productivity analysis;

   b   partial productivity analysis;

   c   capital deepening;

   d   capital widening;

   e   sustainable development.

19   The economy's growth in output is equal to

   a   its growth in productivity;

   b   the sum of its growth in the labor force and its capital accumulation;

   c   the sum of its growth in hours worked and its growth in productivity;

   d   the marginal product of labor times the number of

hours worked plus the marginal product of capital times the capital stock;

e   the sum of private savings, government savings, and net inflows of capital from abroad.

20   Sustainable development refers to growth without

a   excessive technological advance;

b   excessive population increase;

c   excessive capital investment;

d   excessive natural resource exploitation;

e   all of the above.

Completion

1   _____ is defined as output per hour worked.

2   The _____ relates the levels of inputs to the level of output.

3   A country's roads, airports, bridges, sewer lines, and railroads make up its _____.

4   Economists refer to education and skills as _____.

5   Increases in capital per worker are called _____.

6   Savings for a specific purpose, such as college tuition, are called _____.

7   According to the _____, successive increments in capital lead to smaller increases in output per worker.

8   The savings that a household sets aside in case of emergency or illness are called _____.

9   Economists use _____ to discover the magnitude of technological advance.

10   Advocates of _____ seek policies to preserve the environment and natural resources while increasing living standards.

Answers to Self-Test

True or False

1	f	6	f	11	t
2	f	7	t	12	t
3	t	8	t	13	f
4	f	9	f	14	t
5	f	10	f	15	f

Multiple Choice

1	c	6	b	11	c	16	a
2	c	7	a	12	a	17	a
3	b	8	c	13	c	18	a
4	e	9	c	14	b	19	c
5	b	10	a	15	d	20	d

Completion

1   Productivity
2   production function
3   infrastructure
4   human capital
5   capital deepening

6   target savings
7   law of diminishing returns
8   precautionary savings
9   total factor productivity analysis
10   sustainable growth

Doing Economics: Tools and Practice Problems

Two important factors in the U.S. productivity slowdown are low savings and misallocated investment. In this section, we study some reasons for low savings rates: demographic changes, improved opportunities for consumer borrowing, and more generous Social Security benefits. Also, we see how favorable tax treatment of certain types of projects misallocates investment.

REASONS FOR LOW SAVINGS RATES: DEMOGRAPHIC CHANGES

One important fact about the current population of the United States is that generations, or cohorts, are of different sizes. The so-called baby boom generation, now around 35 to 50, is significantly larger than its parents' generation and also its children's generation. This fact has important implications for national savings because, as the life-cycle model predicts, individuals save at different rates during their lifetimes. Generally, people will save little in their early years, a great deal in middle age, and less when retired. When generations are of different sizes, then the national savings rate will fluctuate as the relatively large generation moves through the high-savings years.

1   (Worked problem: low savings rates) There was zero population growth in the state of Steady for centuries until now. People in Steady behave exactly as the life-cycle model predicts, saving at different rates during the successive periods of their lives. The savings supply curves for three age classes of equal size are given in Table 36.1.

Table 36.1

Interest rate	Savings		
	Young	*Middle*	*Old*
4%	$1,000	$20,000	$5,000
6%	$1,100	$25,000	$5,000
8%	$1,200	$30,000	$5,000
10%	$1,200	$35,000	$5,000

a   Suppose the generation that is now young is twice as large as the other generations, which are of equal size. Calculate the supply of savings for the economy.

b   Twenty years from now, the large generation will be middle-aged. The currently old will die and be replaced by the cohort that is now middle-aged. Calculate the supply of savings for the economy in 20 years.

c   Forty years from now, the large generation will be old. The young and middle generations will be half the size of the large generation. Calculate the supply of savings in 40 years.

d   Plot the three savings supplies, and notice the fluctuations in savings supply caused by the demographic transition.

Step-by-step solution

Step one (a): We find the market supply of savings by summing the total amount of savings at each interest rate. If the interest rate is 4 percent, then total savings will be

$$(2 \times \$1,000) + (1 \times \$20,000) + (1 \times \$5,000) = \$27,000.$$

We multiply the $1,000, which is the savings of the young, by 2 because there are twice as many young people.

Step two: At a 6 percent interest rate, the supply of savings is

$$(2 \times \$1,100) + \$25,000 + \$5,000 = \$32,200.$$

Continuing the process derives the entire supply of savings, which is as follows.

Interest rate	Savings
4%	$27,000
6%	$32,200
8%	$37,400
10%	$42,400

Step three (b): To find the total supply of savings 20 years from now when the large generation will be middle-aged, multiply the supply of savings in the middle-aged generation by 2 and add it to the others. For example, at a 4 percent interest rate, total savings are

$$\$1,000 + (2 \times \$20,000) + \$5,000 = \$46,000.$$

Continuing gives the supply of savings in 20 years.

Interest rate	Savings
4%	$46,000
6%	$56,100
8%	$66,200
10%	$76,200

Step four (c): Total savings 40 years from now are found by multiplying the savings of the old by 2 and adding them to the savings of the others. The supply curve is

Interest rate	Savings
4%	$31,000
6%	$36,100
8%	$41,200
10%	$46,200

Step five (d): Plot the curves. Clearly, supply shifts to the right as the large generation moves into the high-savings years and shifts to the left when they retire.

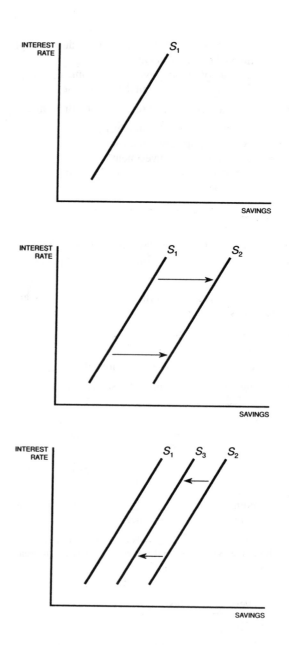

2   (Practice problem: low savings rates) Using the same data as in problem 1, suppose that a baby boomlet generation follows 40 years behind the large generation. In other words, every other generation will be twice as large as the generations were in Steady for centuries. Derive the supply of savings for the economy for 20-year intervals. Begin with a small young generation.

REASONS FOR LOW SAVINGS RATES: LOWER INTEREST RATES FOR BORROWING

One of the great strengths of the U.S. economy is its efficient capital market. Recently a combination of factors, for example credit cards, home equity loans, and bank deregulation, have increased access for borrowers. Lower interest rates for borrowers rotate part of the budget constraint out, giving the household more opportunities to consume more today.

3   (Worked problem: low savings rates) Harold and Myla take home $60,000 each year. They can earn 4 percent on any savings, but they must borrow at 14 percent.

   a   Plot their two-period budget constraint.

   b   A preapproved application for a new credit card arrives. The interest rate on the unpaid balance will be 8 percent. Plot their new two-period budget constraint, and compare it with the answer to part a.

Step-by-step solution

Step one (a): Plot the budget constraint with the 4 percent interest rate. The slope is 1.04, and it passes through the point $60,000 now and $60,000 next year.

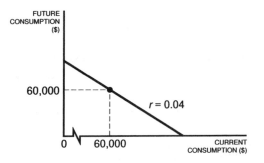

Step two: Plot the budget constraint with the 14 percent interest rate. The slope is 1.14, and it passes through the point $60,000 now and $60,000 next year.

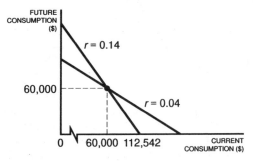

Step three: Darken the portion of each budget constraint that lies under the other constraint. This is the answer to part a.

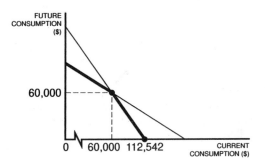

Step four (b): Again, plot the budget constraint with the 4 percent interest rate as in step one.

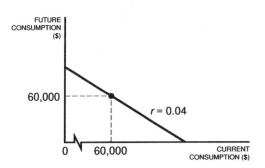

Step five: Plot the budget constraint with the 8 percent interest rate. The slope is 1.08, and it passes through the point $60,000 now and $60,000 next year.

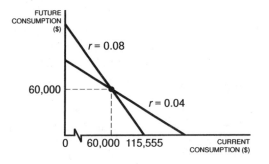

Step six: Darken the portion of each budget constraint that lies under the other constraint. This is the answer to part b.

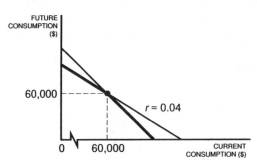

Step seven: Compare the two budget constraints. The lower interest rate gives Harold and Myla more opportunities, but the extra opportunities all involve borrowing.

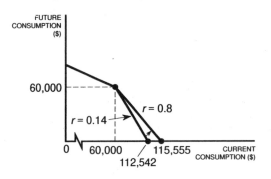

4   (Practice problem: low savings rates) Bill takes home $10,000 this year, but he anticipates taking home $30,000 next year. He can earn 8 percent on savings, but he has a poor credit rating and must pay 19 percent to borrow.

   a   Plot his two-period budget constraint.
   b   Through his credit union at his new job, Bill can obtain loans for 10 percent. Plot his new two-period budget constraint, and compare.

REASONS FOR LOW SAVINGS RATES: INCREASED SOCIAL SECURITY BENEFITS

Social Security certainly reduce people's incentives to save for retirement, and because it is financed on a pay-as-you-go basis, it reduces national savings. Increases in Social Security benefits during the 1970s further reduced savings incentives. The next two problems use the two-period budget constraint to illustrate this idea.

5   (Worked problem: low savings rates) Juwan has 10 years until retirement. He earns $40,000 after taxes and expects to receive $20,000 in Social Security benefits when he retires. He expects that over the 10-year interval until retirement he can earn a 100 percent rate of return, and he currently saves $5,000 per year.

   a   Calculate the present discounted value of his Social Security benefits.
   b   Draw his two-period budget constraint, and plot his chosen point.
   c   Suppose that his Social Security benefits are increased to $30,000. His Social Security taxes are also increased by $5,000, which reduces his current net income to $35,000. Draw his two-period budget constraint.
   d   How much does Juwan now save?

   Step-by-step solution

Step one (a): The present discounted value of his benefit payment is $20,000/(1 + r) = $20,000/(1 + 1) = $10,000.

Step two (b): Draw his two-period budget constraint. Label the axes "Current consumption" and "Retirement consumption." The slope is $1 + r$, and the interest rate for the 10-year period is 100 percent. The horizontal intercept is the present discounted value of all income, which is $40,000 + $10,000 = $50,000.

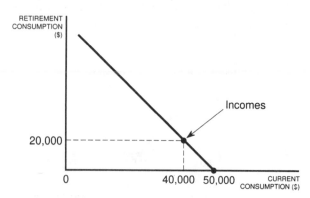

Step three: Plot his chosen point. Juwan chooses to save $5,000; thus, he consumes $40,000 – $5,000 = $35,000 now. The $5,000 grows to $10,000 in 10 years, which enables consumption of $20,000 + $10,000 = $30,000.

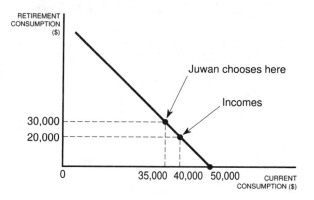

Step four (c): Plot his new budget constraint. The present discounted value of his benefits is now $30,000/2 = $15,000. The horizontal intercept is $15,000 + $35,000 = $50,000, which is unchanged. Because neither the present discounted value of his two-period income nor the interest rate changes, the budget constraint remains the same.

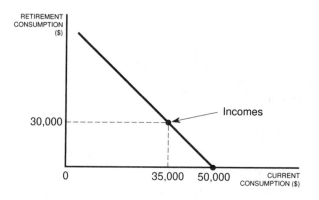

Step five (d): Because he has the same budget constraint, he chooses the same point. But he achieves this combination of current and retirement consumption by reducing his savings to zero. The increase in Social Security benefits has reduced Juwan's savings by exactly $5,000.

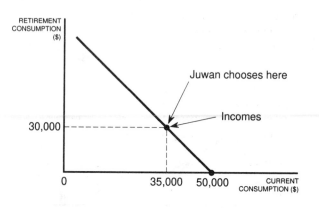

6 (Practice problem: low savings rates) Mai Lin is only 10 years from retirement. She can expect to receive $2 in interest for every $1 saved for retirement. She takes home $60,000 annually, saves $10,000 each year, and expects Social Security benefits of $30,000 when she retires.

a   Plot her two-period budget constraint.
b   Suppose the American Association of Retired Persons has a banner year lobbying Congress and wins a 50 percent increase in benefits. Taxes also rise so that the budget constraint does not change. How will Mai Lin's consumption now and during retirement change? How will her savings change?

Subsidies and the Allocation of Investment

Preferential tax treatment of certain types of investment can reallocate an economy's capital stock. A subsidy to a particular type of investment will raise its return, and since investors always seek the highest rate of return, they will reallocate their portfolio to take advantage of the subsidy. Tool Kit 36.1 shows the link between subsidies and reallocation.

Tool Kit 36.1: Showing How Subsidies Can Reallocate Investment

Subsidies shift up the demand for investment in the subsidized sector. This reallocates investment. These steps outline the procedure for analyzing the impact of a subsidy in one sector.

Step one: Add up the demands of each sector for capital.

Step two: Find the market-clearing rate of interest.

Step three: Substitute the market-clearing rate of interest into each demand to determine the allocation of investment that occurs without subsidy.

Step four: Add the subsidy to the demand for capital in the subsidized sector.

Step five: Repeat steps one through three.

Step six: Compare the allocation found in step five with that found in step three.

---

7 (Worked problem: allocation of investment) The 1986 Tax Reform Act eliminated certain provisions that gave preferential tax treatment to real estate. To see the effect that these tax subsidies have, consider Table 36.2, which gives the demands for capital by the real estate and manufacturing sectors in billions of U.S. dollars. The supply of financial capital for the two sectors is $3,900 billion.

Table 36.2

Interest rate	Demand in the real estate sector (billions)	Demand in the manufacturing sector (billions)
10%	$1,000	$2,000
9%	$1,100	$2,200
8%	$1,200	$2,400
7%	$1,300	$2,600
6%	$1,400	$2,800
5%	$1,500	$3,000
4%	$1,600	$3,200

a   Find the market allocation.
b   Suppose the tax subsidy amounts to an extra 3 percent annual earnings for a real estate investment. Find the allocation.
c   How does the tax subsidy alter the equilibrium allocation of capital?

Step-by-step solution

Step one (a): Add the demands of each sector for capital. We choose an interest rate, and sum the quantity demanded in each sector. When the interest rate is 10 percent, the total quantity demanded is $1,000 + $2,000 = $3,000 billion. Continuing, we derive Table 36.3.

Table 36.3

Interest rate	Real estate	Manufacturing	Total
10%	$1,000	$2,000	$3,000
9%	$1,100	$2,200	$3,300
8%	$1,200	$2,400	$3,600
7%	$1,300	$2,600	$3,900
6%	$1,400	$2,800	$4,200
5%	$1,500	$3,000	$4,500
4%	$1,600	$3,200	$4,800

Step two: Find the market-clearing rate of interest. Quantity supplied, which is $3,900 billion, equals quantity demanded when the interest rate is 7 percent.

Step three: Substitute the market-clearing rate of interest into each demand to determine the allocation of investment. The 7 percent rate of interest brings about an allocation of $1,300 billion in real estate and $2,600 billion in manufacturing.

Step four (b): Add the subsidy to the demand for capital in the subsidized sector. Simply add 3 percent to the interest rate column for the real estate sector. Table 36.4 gives the result.

Table 36.4

Interest rate	Real estate
13%	$1,000
12%	$1,100
11%	$1,200
10%	$1,300
9%	$1,400
8%	$1,500
7%	$1,600

Step five: Repeat steps one through three. Table 36.5 gives the new total demand.

Table 36.5

Interest rate	Real estate	Manufacturing	Total
13%	$1,000	$2,000	$3,000
12%	$1,100	$2,000	$3,100
11%	$1,200	$2,000	$3,200
10%	$1,300	$2,000	$3,300
9%	$1,400	$2,200	$3,600
8%	$1,500	$2,400	$3,900
7%	$1,600	$2,600	$4,200
6%	$1,600	$2,800	$4,400
5%	$1,700	$3,000	$4,700
4%	$1,800	$3,200	$5,000

The market clears at an 8 percent interest rate with an allocation of $1,500 billion to real estate and $2,400 billion to manufacturing.

Step six (c): Compare the allocation found in step five with that found in step three. The tax subsidy increases the real estate sector's allocation from $1,300 to $1,500 billion, reducing the manufacturing sector's allocation from $2,600 billion to $2,400. In effect, $200 billion is reallocated from manufacturing to real estate.

8 (Practice problem: allocation of investment) Table 36.6 gives the demands for financial capital in the sector that produces goods for export and the sector that produces goods that compete with imports. The available supply of capital is $200 billion.

Table 36.6

Interest rate	Demand in the import-competing sector (billions)	Demand in the export sector (billions)
12%	$ 30	$ 40
11%	$ 50	$ 50
10%	$ 60	$ 60
9%	$ 70	$ 80
8%	$ 80	$ 90
7%	$100	$100
6%	$120	$110
5%	$140	$120

a Find the market allocation.
b Worried about lost market share to imports, a protectionist Congress passes a series of tax subsidies and trade barriers. Suppose that the tax subsidies and import controls amount to an extra 5 percent annual earnings for import-competing investment. Find the new allocation.
c How does the tax policy alter the equilibrium allocation of capital?

9 (Practice problem: allocation of investment) Preferential tax treatment can reallocate investment capital across regions. The enterprise zone idea offers tax breaks to firms that locate in specified areas such as impoverished inner cities. To see how this policy might work,

consider Table 36.7, which gives demands for capital in enterprise zones and elsewhere. Assume that the tax breaks are worth 6 percent and the total quantity supplied equals $10 billion.

Table 36.7

Interest rate	Demand in the the enterprise zones (billions)	Demand elsewhere (billions)
9%	$0.6	$ 8.2
8%	$0.8	$ 8.6
7%	$1.0	$ 9.0
6%	$1.2	$ 9.8
5%	$1.4	$10.8
4%	$1.6	$12.0
3%	$1.8	$15.0
2%	$2.0	$20.0

a Find the market allocation without the tax breaks and the corresponding interest rate.
b Find the demand curves with the tax breaks.
c Find the new allocation brought about by the tax breaks. How does the tax policy alter the equilibrium allocation of capital?

Answers to Problems

2 With a small young generation, a large middle-aged generation, and a small old generation, the supply of savings is as follows.

Interest rate	Savings
4%	$46,000
6%	$56,100
8%	$66,200
10%	$76,200

When the young generation is large, the middle-aged generation small, and the old generation large, the supply of savings is as follows.

Interest rate	Savings
4%	$46,000
6%	$56,100
8%	$66,200
10%	$76,200

4 a

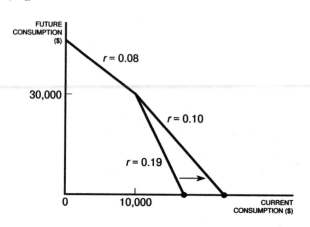

b   With the lower interest rate for borrowing, Bill's budget constraint rotates out, giving him new opportunities, all of which involve borrowing more.

6   a

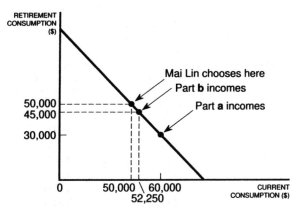

b   The budget constraint does not change, so neither do her current and retirement consumptions. The increase in Social Security benefits reduces her savings by $7,500.

8   a   The equilibrium interest rate is 7 percent, and the allocation is $100 billion to each sector.

b   Table 36.8 gives the demands with the tax subsidy and trade protection policies.

Table 36.8

Interest rate	Imports	Exports	Total
17%	$ 30	$40	$ 70
16%	$ 50	$40	$ 90
15%	$ 60	$40	$100
14%	$ 70	$40	$110
13%	$ 80	$40	$120
12%	$100	$40	$140
11%	$120	$50	$170
10%	$140	$60	$200
9%	$140	$80	$220
8%	$140	$90	$220

c   The market clears at an interest rate of 10 percent with an allocation of $140 billion to the import-competing sector and $60 billion to the export sector. The policies shift $40 billion from the export to the import-competing sector.

9   a   The market allocation without the enterprise zone tax breaks is $1 billion in the zones and $9 billion elsewhere and the interest rate is 7 percent.

b   Table 36.9 gives the demands with the tax breaks.

Table 36.9

Interest rate	Demand in the enterprise zones	Demand elsewhere	Total
15%	$0.6	$ 8.2	$ 8.8
14%	$0.8	$ 8.2	$ 9.0
13%	$1.0	$ 8.2	$ 9.2
12%	$1.2	$ 8.2	$ 9.4
11%	$1.4	$ 8.2	$ 9.6
10%	$1.6	$ 8.2	$ 9.8
9%	$1.8	$ 8.2	$10.0
8%	$2.0	$ 8.6	$10.6
7%	$2.0	$ 9.0	$11.0
6%	$2.0	$ 9.8	$11.8
5%	$2.0	$10.8	$12.8

c   The new equilibrium allocation is $1.8 billion to the enterprise zones and $8.2 billion elsewhere at an equilibrium interest rate of 9 percent. The tax breaks shift $0.8 billion to the zones from elsewhere in the economy.

Chapter 37

DEFICITS AND DEFICIT REDUCTION

Chapter Review

The U.S. budget deficit exploded during the 1980s. This chapter discusses some of the causes and consequences and also looks into proposals to solve the deficit problem. How the deficit affects the economy, especially its future, is a key topic. There is also discussion of the long-term fiscal problems facing the United States.

ESSENTIAL CONCEPTS

1 **Federal budget deficits** rose dramatically during the 1980s, increasing the nation's debt to record levels, even though the 1980s were a time of peace and relative prosperity. The high deficits can be linked to five causes. Taxes were reduced, defense spending increased, Social Security and Medicare payments grew, more was spent on health care, and the accumulated debt required higher interest payments.

2 Government borrowing can affect future generations in three ways. First, the burden can be shifted directly to the future generation by increasing taxes after the current generation has retired. Second, borrowing drives up

interest rates and crowds out private investment. Finally, since much of the borrowing comes from abroad and foreign investors are attracted by higher U.S. interest rates, current borrowing increases foreign indebtedness. Repayment of foreign debt then requires reduced future living standards. The Barro-Ricardo argument that private savings will offset the future effects of current deficits has not proven true.

3 Reducing the budget deficit requires either cutting expenditures or increasing taxes. Federal government expenditures fall into two categories. **Discretionary spending** is authorized on an annual basis and it includes defense, education, training, and the funds necessary to run the government. **Nondiscretionary spending** comprises interest on the debt and **entitlements,** which are automatic payments to individuals who meet certain legal requirements. These programs include Social Security, Medicare, Medicaid, food stamps, and unemployment insurance.

4 Another approach is to deal with the budgetary process itself. The Budget Enforcement Act mandates that the Congressional Budget Office calculate the cost of each new program. The line item veto gives the President the power to veto any particular line item of the budget. Finally, many advocate keeping a capital budget for the

government. Parallel with business accounting practices, this reform would distinguish between government investments and government consumption expenditures.

5 The long-term budgetary problem in the United States is entitlement spending for Social Security and Medicare, because of anticipated increases in both the size of the elderly population and health care costs. Proposed reforms in Social Security include reducing benefits by increasing the retirement age, means testing for benefits, and investing Social Security Trust Fund assets in equities. On the Medicare issue one set of reforms, including Medical Savings Accounts, focuses on patient incentives. Managed care moves in another direction, seeking to give doctors incentives to reduce the use and expense of medical care. Ultimately, the problem rests on the question of how much of society's resources should be allocated to health care for the elderly, especially for expensive technological innovations.

BEHIND THE ESSENTIAL CONCEPTS

1 If you are the age of the typical college student, say 19 or 20, you will pay for some of the current federal budget deficit. Government borrowing is sopping up private savings and crowding out private investment. Currently capital goods are not purchased, research and development is not undertaken, and businesses are not started. Furthermore, the trade deficit caused by the budget deficits is financed by selling off U.S. assets. Reduced investment and the sale of assets will result in lower living standards in the future.

2 The distinction between stocks and flows is important in this chapter. The annual federal buget deficit is a flow, and the corresponding stock is the federal debt, which is the sum of past accumulated deficits. The trade deficit is also a flow variable. It is the difference between what U.S. households and firms import and export. The basic trade identity makes it clear that the trade deficit is financed by capital flows. Now capital flows into the United States when foreign nationals buy U.S. assets and when U.S. firms borrow from abroad. Both of these activities affect the credit position of the United States. The relationship between these trade deficits and the U.S. status as a debtor nation is that the accumulated trade deficits have led to a stock of foreign indebtedness.

3 The Barro-Ricardo argument claims that current budget deficits have no impact. Specifically, whether government expenditures are financed by taxes or borrowing makes no difference in either the present or the future. If the spending is paid for with taxes, then current disposable income and consumption fall. If the government borrows, then rational individuals anticipate future taxes and put aside the money now. This increase in savings is just enough to pay for the future tax liability. In either case, the impact on the economy is the same.

4 There is an important distinction between solving the current budget deficit problem and setting up incentives to ensure that future deficit problems will not arise. Our current deficit problem came about, in part, because of unrealistic tax and entitlement decisions. Social Security and Medicare increases and tax cuts were made without adequate consideration of their budgetary consequences. The Budget Enforcement Act addresses this problem by forcing Congress to face the costs of any new program. Congress can choose to go ahead with the programs, but at least there is a scoring of the costs.

5 The main worry about budget deficits is how they affect the future standard of living. Of course, we want the current Congress to have incentives to recognize this. According to current procedures, however, there is little reason to recognize the future benefits of current government investments, because a dollar of current spending counts the same whether it is for investment or consumption. This is why many economists advocate capital budgeting. It would require computing the change in the value of government assets, giving incentives to create and maintain the infrastructure.

SELF-TEST

True or False

1 During the 1980s the U.S. budget deficit was high, but there have been other episodes of equally high peacetime deficits.

2 Early in the Reagan administration, taxes were cut well below their 1970s levels.

3 As a fraction of GDP, defense spending is higher today than it was during the Vietnam War.

4 Government borrowing does not matter because the bonds sold to finance the deficit are purchased by Americans.

5 Government borrowing drives up the interest rate and crowds out private investment.

6 The largest single component of government spending is national defense.

7 Welfare payments other than Medicaid account for slightly more than 25 percent of federal government expenditures.

8 The Barro-Ricardo argument claims that when the government runs a deficit, private savings increase to offset the government dissaving.

9 Defense spending is an example of a nondiscretionary expenditure.

10 The Budget Enforcement Act effectively outlaws budget deficits.

11 The United States government computes and publishes a capital budget each year.

12   Over the next few decades the proportion of the population that is elderly will remain about what it is today.

13   While health care costs have been rising, the rate of increase is no faster than the rate of inflation.

14   The Social Security Trust Fund currently is not invested in equities.

15   Managed care refers to reforms designed to give health care providers incentives to economize on health care.

Multiple Choice

1   During the 1980s, the United States ran

  a   very high federal budget deficits;
  b   very high federal budget surpluses;
  c   typical peacetime federal budget surpluses;
  d   typical peacetime federal budget deficits;
  e   balanced federal budgets.

2   The tax cuts enacted early in the Reagan presidency reduced the percentage of GDP taken in taxes

  a   to historically low levels;
  b   well below the levels taken in the 1970s;
  c   to about the level of the 1970s;
  d   to levels somewhat higher than in the 1970s;
  e   none of the above.

3   Which federal expenditures increased during the 1980s?

  a   defense;
  b   Social Security;
  c   Medicare;
  d   interest on the debt;
  e   all of the above.

4   Federal budget deficits

  a   increase private investment by reducing the interest rate;
  b   crowd out private investment by increasing the interest rate;
  c   may not reduce future output if the borrowing finances government investments such as roads or research and development;
  d   always reduce future consumption because future generations must pay taxes to repay the debt;
  e   b and c.

5   Government borrowing to finance the deficit

  a   crowds out both foreign and U.S. private investment;
  b   crowds out U.S. private investment by raising the interest rate but causes increased foreign investment;
  c   crowds out foreign investment by increasing the exchange rate but has no effect on U.S. private investment;
  d   attracts foreign investment, and the extra competition leads to increased U.S. private investment;
  e   causes the exchange rate to depreciate.

6   Which of the following is not true?

  a   The burden of current govenment deficits necessarily falls on the current generation.
  b   The burden of current government deficits may be shifted to future generations if taxes are increased after the current generation retires.
  c   The burden of current government deficits may be shifted to future generations if current borrowing replaces private investment.
  d   The burden of current government deficits may be shifted to future generations if current borrowing increases foreign indebtedness.
  e   All of the above are true.

7   The largest single component of government expenditure is

  a   defense;
  b   interest on the debt;
  c   Social Security;
  d   education;
  e   welfare.

8   The Barro-Ricardo argument states that

  a   government deficits crowd out private investment and consumption;
  b   the burden of government deficits falls on future generations;
  c   private savings increase to offset government deficits;
  d   increases in interest rates crowd out private investment;
  e   the deficit does not matter because we owe it to ourselves.

9   Which of the following is an example of discretionary spending?

  a   Medicare;
  b   Medicaid;
  c   Social Security;
  d   interest on the national debt;
  e   none of the above.

10   Which of the following is an example of nondiscretionary spending?

  a   defense expenditures;
  b   most education and training expenditures;
  c   money for roads and bridges;
  d   Medicare;
  e   money to run the government.

11   Which of the following is an example of an entitlement?

  a   Medicare;
  b   Medicaid;
  c   Social Security;
  d   Aid to Families with Dependent Children (welfare);
  e   all of the above.

12   The Budget Enforcement Act requires that

  a   the federal government budget is balanced each year;
  b   the federal government budget is balanced on average over each business cycle;

c the Congressional Budget Office calculate the cost of any new government program;

d the federal government must compute and balance its capital budget;

e the President be given the line item veto.

13 A capital budget

a keeps track of government investment expenditures;

b does not distinguish between government investments and government consumption expenditures;

c must equal the trade deficit, according to the basic trade identity;

d must always balance, according to the Budget Enforcement Act;

e gives the President the line item veto.

14 The line item veto

a keeps track of government investment expenditures;

b gives the President power to veto appropriations bills;

c repeals Congress's authority to override presidential vetoes;

d gives the Congressional Budget Office the power to veto new programs;

e gives the President the power to veto particular spending items in large appropriations bills.

15 Because of the increase in life expectancy,

a the proportion of elderly in the population will increase;

b the number of workers per retired person will decrease;

c Medicare payments will increase;

d Social Security payments will increase;

e all of the above.

16 The fraction of the Social Security Trust Fund currently invested in equities is about

a 0;

b one-fourth;

c one-half;

d three-fourths;

e 1.

17 During the 1980s and 1990s health care costs

a have increased on a pace with inflation;

b have increased less rapidly than inflation;

c have increased more rapidly than inflation;

d have fallen;

e have remained constant.

18 Means testing of Social Security and Medicare benefits refers to

a requiring all recipients to produce documents verifying their eligibility;

b charging beneficiaries a copayment for medical tests;

c ensuring that the trust funds have sufficient means to pay all current bills;

d limiting payments to doctors and hospitals;

e requiring higher payments from those with more income.

19 Programs that give health care providers greater incentive to economize on costs are called

a means testing;

b entitlements;

c managed care;

d capital budgeting;

e fee-for-service.

20 The proposal for Medical Savings Accounts would

a reduce payments to health care providers;

b limit payments for costly new technologies;

c give greater incentives to health care providers;

d allow individuals to set aside money in a tax-exempt account to meet medical expenses;

e invest the Social Security Trust Fund money in equities.

Completion

1 The difference between government expenditures and revenues is the _____.

2 The total accumulated sum of past deficits is the _____.

3 The _____ equals what the budget deficit would be if the economy were at full employment.

4 The _____ subtracts interest payments from the budget deficit.

5 The program that pays health costs for the elderly is called _____.

6 The _____ says that private savings rise to offset government deficits.

7 Interest on the government debt is an example of _____.

8 _____ gives incentives to health care providers to economize on health care.

9 _____ allow households to put aside money in tax-free accounts to pay for medical expenses.

10 _____ refers to requiring upper income recipients to pay more for Medicare.

Answers to Self-Test

True or False

1	f	6	f	11	f
2	f	7	f	12	f
3	f	8	t	13	f
4	f	9	f	14	t
5	t	10	f	15	t

Multiple Choice

1	a	6	a	11	e	16	a
2	c	7	c	12	c	17	c
3	e	8	c	13	a	18	e
4	e	9	e	14	e	19	c
5	b	10	d	15	e	20	d

Completion

1 budget deficit

2 government debt

3   structural deficit
4   primary deficit
5   Medicare
6   Barro-Ricardo argument
7   nondiscretionary spending
8   Managed care
9   Medical Savings Accounts
10   Means testing

Doing Economics: Tools and Practice Problems

The budget deficit may seem like a simple calculation: government spending minus government revenues. For different purposes, however, economists argue for different measures. We know that automatic stabilizers, such as unemployment insurance, bring about an increase in the budget deficit during recessions, even though there is no change in law. The structural deficit corrects for the effects of economic downturns by calculating what the budget deficit would be if the economy were at full employment. Another measure, the inflation-adjusted deficit, looks at the change in the real value of the outstanding government debt. Finally, the primary deficit ignores interest on the current debt. Tool Kit 37.1 shows how to keep all of this straight.

Tool Kit 37.1: Calculating the Deficits

The various deficit measures are explained. Follow the steps.

Step one: Identify the average tax rate, national income, full-employment national income, government expenditures, the outstanding debt, the nominal interest rate, and the inflation rate.

Step two: Calculate the budget deficit. This is just government revenues less its expenditures.

Budget deficit = government expenditures
– average tax rate × national income.

Step three: Calculate the structural deficit. Here we use what revenues would be if the economy were at full employment.

Structural deficit = government expenditures
– average tax rate × full employment income.

Step four: Calculate the inflation-adjusted deficit. This measure takes into account the change in the real value of the outstanding debt.

Inflation-adjusted deficit = government expenditures
– average tax rate × national income
– inflation rate × outstanding debt.

Step five: Calculate the primary deficit. This measure ignores interest on the debt.

Primary deficit = government expenditures
– average tax rate × national income
– nominal interest rate × outstanding debt.

---

1   (Worked problem: deficits) The Costa Guanoan Economic Report of the Dictator gives the following information.

Table 37.1

National income	$60 million
Average tax rate	20 percent
Full-employment national income	$80 million
Government expenditures	$25 million
Outstanding debt	$80 million
Inflation rate	10 percent
Nominal interest rate	15 percent

a   Calculate the budget deficit.
b   Calculate the structural deficit.
c   Calculate the inflation-adjusted deficit.
d   Calculate the primary deficit.

Step-by-step solution

Step one: Identify the average tax rate, national income, full-employment national income, government expenditures, the outstanding debt, the nominal interest rate, and the inflation rate. All are given in Table 37.1.

Step two: Calculate the budget deficit.

Budget deficit = government expenditures
– average tax rate × national income
= 25 – 0.20 × 60 = $13 million.

Step three: Calculate the structural deficit.

Structural deficit = government expenditures
– average tax rate × full employment income
= 25 – 0.20 × 80 = $9 million.

Step four: Calculate the inflation-adjusted deficit.

Inflation-adjusted deficit = government expenditures
– average tax rate × national income
– inflation rate × outstanding debt
= 25 – 0.20 × 60 – 0.10 × 80 = $5 million.

Step five: Calculate the primary deficit.

Primary deficit = government expenditures
– average tax rate × national income
– nominal interest rate × outstanding debt
= 25 – 0.20 × 60 – 0.15 × 80 = $1 million.

2   (Practice problem: deficits) The El Dorado Economic Report of the Government gives the following information.

Table 37.2

National income	$8 billion
Average tax rate	25 percent
Full-employment national income	$8 billion
Government expenditures	$4 billion
Outstanding debt	$6 billion
Inflation rate	20 percent
Nominal interest rate	30 percent

a   Calculate the budget deficit.
b   Calculate the structural deficit.
c   Calculate the inflation-adjusted deficit.
d   Calculate the primary deficit.

3   (Practice problem: deficits) The Erehwemos Economic Report of the Oligarchy gives the following information.

Table 37.3

National income	$80 billion
Average tax rate	40 percent
Full-employment national income	$100 billion
Government expenditures	$50 billion
Outstanding debt	$500 billion
Inflation rate	5 percent
Nominal interest rate	10 percent

a   Calculate the budget deficit.
b   Calculate the structural deficit.
c   Calculate the inflation-adjusted deficit.
d   Calculate the primary deficit.

Answers to Problems

2   a   Budget deficit = $4 - 0.25 \times 8 = \$2$ billion.
    b   Structural deficit = $4 - 0.25 \times 8 = \$2$ billion.
    c   Inflation-adjusted deficit = $4 - 0.25 \times 8 - 0.20 \times 6 = \$0.8$ billion.
    d   Primary deficit = $4 - 0.25 \times 8 - 0.30 \times 6 = \$0.2$ billion.

3   a   Budget deficit = $50 - 0.40 \times 80 = \$18$ billion.
    b   Structural deficit = $50 - 0.40 \times 100 = \$10$ billion.
    c   Inflation-adjusted deficit = $50 - 0.40 \times 80 - 0.05 \times 500 = \$7$ billion surplus.
    d   Primary deficit = $50 - 0.40 \times 80 - 0.10 \times 500 = \$32$ billion surplus.

Chapter 38

TRADE POLICY

Chapter Review

Governments affect the flows of traded goods through tariffs, quotas, other nontariff barriers, and a series of fair trade laws. This chapter discusses how these measures affect markets, who wins, who loses, and their political rationale. There is also discussion of the major international institutions governing trade.

ESSENTIAL CONCEPTS

1   Countries practicing protection use commercial policies to restrict imports. These trade barriers include tariffs, quotas, other nontariff barriers, and fair trade laws. Tariffs, which are taxes on imported goods, raise domestic prices, injuring consumers while providing some benefit to producers. Overall the economy suffers, losing consumer surplus and wasting resources producing goods that could be imported more cheaply.

2   Quotas are limits on the quantity of imports. By restricting supply they force up prices and lead to the same types of deadweight burdens as do tariffs. Rather than collecting tariff revenues, the government confers on certain firms extra profits from importing, called quota rents. Other nontariff barriers, such as voluntary export restraints (VERs), have similar effects. In the case of VERs the quota rent accrues to foreign exporters.

3   While ostensibly designed to promote competition, fair trade laws are protectionist. These include anti-dumping laws that prohibit the sale of imports below the cost of production and subsidies to domestic producers, usually justified to offset the impact of foreign subsidies.

4   The political rationale for trade lies in the fact that certain groups lose from trade. Competition from imports may lead firms to close plants or even cease operations. Their displaced workers suffer large losses. Also, foreign competition may drive down wages in certain sectors or erode market power. Lost profits and laid-off unionized workers create a demand for protectionist relief.

5   Other arguments for protection may have some limited validity. The **infant industry argument** claims that import barriers may allow a young industry time to acquire the experience necessary to be competitive on the world market. Usually, however, direct assistance is a better policy. There is also the strategic trade argument,

whereby protected domestic firms exploit economies of scale to undercut their foreign competitors.

6 After World War II the **General Agreement on Tariffs and Trade (GATT)** was founded to reduce trade barriers. Its three basic principles were reciprocity, nondiscrimination, and transparency, and it succeeded in greatly reducing tariffs. In 1995 it was replaced by the **World Trade Organization (WTO)** as attention turned to nontariff barriers and intellectual property. The WTO has procedures for adjudicating trade disputes.

7 Regional trading blocs, such as the **European Union** and the **North American Free Trade Agreement (NAFTA),** remove trading barriers for member countries, and this brings about the benefits of trade creation, expanded trade within the bloc. On the other hand, the discrimination against those outside the bloc causes trade diversion. Goods that may be less costly from outsiders are produced within the bloc.

BEHIND THE ESSENTIAL CONCEPTS

1 A tariff is just a tax on imports, and we analyze its effects in the same way that we analyze a tax on a domestic good. If the suppliers must pay the tax, it shifts the supply curve up by the amount of the tax and the price rises to the intersection of the demand and the new supply. In the case of a tariff the price is set on the world market. This price simply shifts up by the amount of the tariff, and the new equilibrium is read off the demand and supply curves. There is more on how to do this in Tool Kit 38.1.

2 Tariffs, quotas, and voluntary export restraints are equivalent in one sense. Each raises prices to consumers, reduces the quantity demanded, reduces imports, and increases domestic supply. In another way, however, they are quite different. Tariff revenue is collected by the government. In the case of quotas there is an equivalent amount of money collected by importers. They can earn excess profits because the quota protects them from competition. In the case of voluntary export restraints, the two governments force the foreign suppliers to restrict output. But we know from monopoly theory that this results in higher prices and monopoly profits. In each case there are extra revenues collected: tariff revenue to the government, quota rents to the licensed importer, and VER excess profits to foreign firms.

3 When a country enters a regional trading bloc, it eliminates trade barriers with the other members, while keeping barriers up against nonmembers. This discrimination favors production within the bloc. Trade that otherwise would have occurred with nonmember countries is diverted to member countries. Since this likely goes against the principle of comparative advantage, there is a waste. Balanced against this inefficiency are the benefits of expanded trade among member countries. When trade agreements are global, however, there is no downside. It is all trade creation.

4 Why do we care about dumping? After all, if foreign producers want to sell us goods below cost, then should we not just accept their generosity? One fear is that after driving domestic producers from the market, the foreign firms will take advantage of their monopoly position and raise prices. This practice is called predatory pricing and it is illegal in the United States. In theory, anti-dumping laws make the practice illegal for foreign firms. In practice, however, these laws are used to protect domestic firms from low-cost foreign competition.

5 The infant industry argument claims that temporary protection may allow firms to grow more efficient and ultimately to prosper. The policy is like an investment, sacrificing the current gains from importing cheaper goods for long-run profitability. Of course, it should only be applied if the present value of the future profits exceeds the current costs. But in that case firms in the industry should be able to raise capital to stay in business while they are gaining experience. Governments are in no better position to evaluate the prospects of infant industries than the capital market.

SELF-TEST

True or False

1 Policies that restrict the import of foreign goods are examples of protection.

2 Tariffs are taxes on exports.

3 Tariffs reduce the quantity supplied domestically.

4 Although they also result in higher prices, quotas differ from tariffs in that firms licensed to import earn quota rents.

5 Voluntary export restraints allow foreign firms to collude and raise prices.

6 Anti-dumping laws make it illegal to sell goods abroad below the cost of production.

7 Predatory pricing refers to selling below cost in order to drive rivals from the markets.

8 Strategic trade theory points out the possibility of protecting domestic firms so that they can exploit economies of scale to undercut their foreign rivals.

9 When there is free trade between two countries, the net benefits are positive in each country.

10 When there is free trade between two countries, all individuals gain.

11 Most of the recent decline in wages in the United States is due to international trade.

12 Regional trading blocs can divert trade from nonmember to member countries.

13 Regional trading blocs expand trade both among member and nonmember countries.

14 The GATT successfully reduced tariffs among most of the world's countries.

15   The WTO adjudicates trade disputes among the United States, Canada, and Mexico.

Multiple Choice

1   Which of the following are trade barriers?

   a   tariffs;
   b   quotas;
   c   voluntary export restraints;
   d   fair trade laws;
   e   all of the above.

2   Policies that affect imports or exports are called

   a   commercial policies;
   b   protection;
   c   free trade;
   d   nontariff barriers;
   e   fair trade laws.

3   Tariffs are

   a   taxes on exports;
   b   subsidies on exports;
   c   taxes on imports;
   d   subsidies on imports;
   e   voluntary export restraints.

4   When a small country imposes a tariff, the domestic price

   a   rises by more than the amount of the tariff;
   b   rises by an amount equal to the tariff;
   c   rises by less than the amount of the tariff;
   d   stays the same because only imported goods pay the tariff;
   e   falls.

5   Tariffs, quotas, and voluntary exports restraints are similar in that each

   a   raises domestic prices;
   b   reduces domestic prices;
   c   reduces domestic consumption;
   d   increases domestic output;
   e   a, c, and d.

6   When a tariff is imposed the net loss to the United States includes

   a   tariff revenues;
   b   lost consumer surplus due to less consumption of the good;
   c   higher costs of producing the good domestically;
   d   b and c;
   e   all of the above.

7   When a quota is imposed, the net loss to the United States includes

   a   quota rents;
   b   lost consumer surplus due to less consumption of the good;
   c   higher costs of producing the good domestically;
   d   b and c;
   e   all of the above.

8   When a voluntary exports restraint is imposed, the net loss to the United States includes

   a   excess profits;
   b   lost consumer surplus due to less consumption of the good;
   c   higher costs of producing the good domestically;
   d   b and c;
   e   all of the above.

9   Dumping refers to

   a   selling goods abroad for less than the going price;
   b   selling goods abroad without paying tariffs;
   c   selling goods abroad below the cost of production;
   d   selling goods abroad above the cost of production;
   e   selling excess inventories abroad.

10   Predatory pricing refers to

   a   pricing above cost to reap excess profits;
   b   pricing below cost to drive rivals from the market;
   c   bribing politicians to receive licenses to import;
   d   not reducing price when the firm is subsidized;
   e   using intellectual property without paying for it.

11   Which of the following groups generally favors free trade?

   a   exporters;
   b   unions;
   c   firms earning monopoly profits;
   d   workers in import industries;
   e   low-wage workers.

12   Economists estimate that the percentage of the recent fall in wages that is due to trade is

   a   10;
   b   20;
   c   30;
   d   50;
   e   100.

13   Beggar-thy-neighbor policies attempt to

   a   increase national consumption by reducing exports;
   b   increase national savings by reducing foreign aid;
   c   increase national output by reducing imports;
   d   decrease national savings by reducing imports;
   e   decrease the budget deficit by exporting taxes.

14   During the Great Depression, the Hawley-Smoot tariffs

   a   raised tariffs on imported goods;
   b   drastically reduced imports;
   c   led to foreign retaliation;
   d   contributed to the economic downturn;
   e   all of the above.

15   During the first years of the Great Depression

   a   U.S. imports fell;
   b   U.S. exports fell;
   c   U.S. GDP fell;
   d   all of the above;
   e   none of the above.

16   Which of the following is not a result of international trade in the United States?

   a   lower wages for skilled workers;

b lower wages for unskilled workers;

c lower profits in industries where competition is limited;

d lower wages in industries where competition is limited;

e none of the above.

17 The infant industry argument advocates

    a temporary protection while firms gain experience needed to compete with foreign rivals;

    b lowering prices to drive foreign rivals out of business;

    c protection so that domestic firms can take advantage of economies of scale;

    d subsidizing firms that face competition from foreign firms subsidized by their governments;

    e quotas rather than tariffs.

18 Strategic trade theory can be used to argue for

    a temporary protection while firms gain experience needed to compete with foreign rivals;

    b lowering prices to drive foreign rivals out of business;

    c protection so that domestic firms can take advantage of economies of scale;

    d subsidizing firms that face competition from foreign firms subsidized by their governments;

    e quotas rather than tariffs.

19 The organization established after World War II for the purpose of reducing trade barriers is called

    a WTO;

    b GATT;

    c NAFTA;

    d European Union;

    e OECD.

20 Regional trading blocs can lead to

    a the diversion of trade from member to nonmember countries;

    b the diversion of trade from nonmember to member countries;

    c the creation of trade among member countries;

    d the creation of trade between member and nonmember countries;

    e b and c.

Completion

1 _____ involves restricting the import of foreign goods.

2 Policies that affect imports or exports are called _____.

3 Taxes on imports are called _____.

4 When the government imposes quotas, firms licensed to import may earn extra profits, called _____.

5 An agreement whereby foreign firms limit sales of their good in domestic markets is called a _____.

6 Selling products abroad at prices below the cost of production is called _____.

7 The _____ proposes temporary protection while firms gain experience to become competitive.

8 Formed after World War II, the _____ promoted free trade among most of the world's countries.

9 The global trading organization that directed attention toward nontariff barriers, agricultural subsidies, and intellectual property is called _____.

10 Regional trading blocs, such as NAFTA or the European Union, expand trade within the bloc but the net benefits may not be positive if there is too much

_____.

Answers to Self-Test

True or False

1	t	6	t	11	f
2	f	7	t	12	t
3	f	8	t	13	f
4	t	9	t	14	t
5	t	10	f	15	f

Multiple Choice

1	e	6	d	11	a	16	a
2	a	7	d	12	b	17	a
3	c	8	e	13	c	18	c
4	b	9	c	14	e	19	b
5	e	10	b	15	d	20	e

Completion

1 Protection

2 commercial policies

3 tariffs

4 quota rents

5 voluntary export restraint

6 dumping

7 infant industry argument

8 General Agreement on Tariffs and Trade

9 World Trade Organization

10 trade diversion

Doing Economics: Tools and Practice Problems

We use the small open economy model introduced in Chapter 26 to study the effects of three commercial policies: tariffs, quotas, and voluntary export restraints. This model starts with the idea that price is determined on world markets and that relative to that world market the country's output is too small to affect price. The country, in other words, is a price taker. For each of the policies we will determine the effects upon the market equilibrium and also the deadweight burdens. Tool Kit 38.1 shows how to get started.

Tool Kit 38.1: Finding the Free Trade Equilibrium in a Small Open Economy

In a small open economy the quantity demanded is what consumers demand at the fixed world price, and the quantity supplied is what producers offer for sale at that price. These quantities need not be equal. The difference is the level of imports or exports. Follow these steps.

Step one: Identify the world price, the demand curve, and the supply curve.

Step two: Find the quantity demanded. This is read off the demand curve at the world price.

Step three: Find the quantity supplied. This is read off the supply curve at the world price.

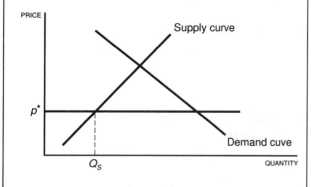

Step four: Find the level of imports or exports. If the quantity demanded exceeds the quantity supplied, then the country imports the goods. Otherwise the good is exported.

Imports = quantity demanded – quantity supplied (if positive).

Exports = quantity supplied – quantity demanded (if positive).

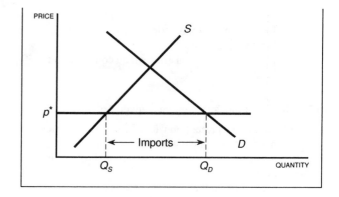

1   (Worked problem: small open economy) The world price of high-grade aluminum is $1,200 per metric ton. The United States demands and supplies are given below in Table 38.1.

   a   Find the quantity demanded and the quantity supplied.
   b   Is high-grade aluminum exported or imported? What is the amount?

Table 38.1

Demand		Supply	
Price	*Quantity (metric tons)*	*Price*	*Quantity (metric tons)*
$2,000	100,000	$2,000	400,000
$1,800	150,000	$1,800	300,000
$1,600	200,000	$1,600	200,000
$1,400	250,000	$1,400	100,000
$1,200	300,000	$1,200	50,000
$1,000	350,000	$1,000	25,000

Step-by-step solution

Step one: Identify the world price, the demand curve, and the supply curve. The world price is $1,400 and the demand and supply curves are given in Table 38.1.

Step two: Find the quantity demanded. When the price is $1,200, the quantity demanded is 300,000 metric tons.

Step three: Find the quantity supplied. When the price is $1,400, the quantity supplied is 50,000 metric tons.

Step four: Find the level of imports or exports. The quantity demanded exceeds the quantity supplied, so the country imports the good.

Imports = quantity demanded – quantity supplied
= 300,000 – 50,000 = 250,000.

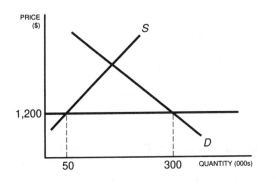

PRICE ($)

S

1,200

D

50   300   QUANTITY (000s)

2 (Practice problem: small open economy) The world price of coffee is 4 cents per pound. The United States demands and supplies are given in Table 38.2.

  a Find the quantity demanded and the quantity supplied.

  b Is coffee exported or imported? What is the amount?

Table 38.2

Demand		Supply	
Price (cents per pound)	Quantity (million pounds)	Price (cents per pound	Quantity (million pounds)
8	14,000	8	20,000
7	16,000	7	18,000
6	18,000	6	16,000
5	20,000	5	14,000
4	22,000	4	12,000
3	24,000	3	10,000
2	26,000	2	8,000
1	28,000	1	6,000

3 (Practice problem: small open economy) The world price of sugar is 1 cent per pound. The United States demand and supply curves are given in Table 38.3.

  a Find the quantity demanded and the quantity supplied.

  b Is sugar exported or imported? What is the amount?

Table 38.3

Demand		Supply	
Price (cents per pound)	Quantity (million pounds)	Price (cents per pound)	Quantity (million pounds)
4.0	1,000	4.0	900
3.5	1,100	3.5	850
3.0	1,200	3.0	800
2.5	1,300	2.5	750
2.0	1,400	2.0	700
1.5	1,500	1.5	650
1.0	1,600	1.0	600

Tariffs

Tariffs are taxes on imported goods. Economists analyze their impact by looking at how markets adjust. Like other taxes, they change market outcomes and bring about deadweight burdens. Fewer goods are sold and consumers lose surplus. Also, the economy wastes resources by producing goods that are more cheaply obtained abroad. We follow the usual procedure of starting with an equilibrium, shifting curves, finding the new equilibrium, and comparing. Tool Kit 38.2 shows how to find the deadweight burden of tariffs.

Tool Kit 38.2: Determining the Effects of Tariffs

Tariffs raise domestic prices above world price. This increase reduces consumption and increases production and creates deadweight burdens. These steps show how to analyze tariffs.

Step one: Identify the world price, the demand curve, the supply curve, and the tariff.

Step two: Find the new world price. The new world price increases by exactly the amount of the tariff.

New world price = old world price + tariff.

Step three: Find the new equilibrium quantity demanded, quantity supplied, and level of imports. Follow the steps of Tool Kit 38.1.

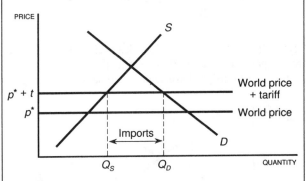

Step four: Calculate tariff revenue.

Tariff revenue = tariff × imports.

Step five: Show the area of the deadweight burden. There are two parts. Triangle DEF represents the loss in consumer surplus due to reduced consumption. Triangle ABC represents the waste of resources brought about by producing domestically when it is less expensive to import.

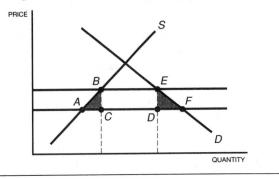

4   (Worked problem: tariffs) This problem continues with the market for high-grade aluminum. The demand and supply data are given in Table 38.1. The world price is $1,400 and the tariff rate is $200 per metric ton.

   a   Find the new equilibrium.
   b   Calculate tariff revenue.
   c   Show the deadweight burden.

Step-by-step solution

Step one: Identify the world price, the demand curve, the supply curve, and the tariff. The world price is $1,200, the demand and supply curves are in Table 38.1, and the tariff rate is $200 per metric ton.

Step two: Find the new world price. The new world price increases by exactly the amount of the tariff.

New world price = old world price + tariff
= $1,200 + $200 = $1,400.

Step three (a): Find the new equilibrium quantity demanded, quantity supplied, and level of imports. When the price is $1,400, the quantity demanded is 250,000, the quantity supplied is 100,000, and the level of imports is 250,000 – 100,000 = 150,000.

Step four (b): Calculate tariff revenue.

Tariff revenue = tariff × imports
= $200 × 150,000
= $30,000,000.

Step five (c): Show the area of the deadweight burden. There are two parts. Triangle DEF represents the loss in consumer surplus due to reduced consumption. Triangle ABC repre-

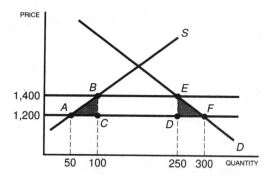

sents the waste of resources brought about by producing domestically when it is less expensive to import.

5   (Practice problem: tariffs) This problem continues with the market for coffee. The demand and supply curves are given in Table 38.2. The world price is 6 cents per pound and the tariff rate is 2 cents per pound.

   a   Find the new equilibrium.
   b   Calculate tariff revenue.
   c   Show the deadweight burden.

6   (Practice problem: tariffs) This problem continues with the market for sugar. The demand and supply

curves are given in Table 38.3. The world price is 1 cent per pound and the tariff rate is 1/2 cent per pound.

   a   Find the new equilibrium.
   b   Calculate tariff revenue.
   c   Show the deadweight burden.

Quotas and Voluntary Export Restraints

Both quotas and VERs reduce imports. Quotas are imposed by the importing country, and VERs are "voluntarily" agreed to by the exporting country. Both raise prices, reduce consumption, and increase domestic production. Accordingly, both lead to deadweight burdens of exactly the same type as do tariffs. Follow along with Tool Kit 38.3.

Tool Kit 38.3: Quotas

Quotas, whether imposed or voluntary, raise prices, reduce consumption, increase production, and cause deadweight burdens. Follow these steps.

Step one: Identify the world price, the demand curve, the supply curve, and the quota.

Step two: Find the total supply curve. This is just the domestic supply curve added to the quota.

Total supply = domestic supply + quota.

Step three: Find the equilibrium price. Simply equate the total supply with the demand.

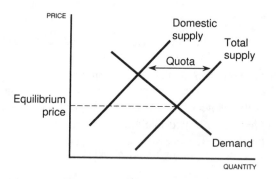

Step four: Find the domestic quantity supplied. This is read off the domestic supply curve.

Step five: Calculate the quota rents. This is the extra money earned by licensed importers.

Quota rents = (new price – world price) × imports.

Step six: Show the area of the deadweight burden. There are two parts. Triangle DEF represents the loss in consumer surplus due to reduced consumption. Triangle ABC represents the waste of resources brought about by producing domestically when it is less expensive to import.

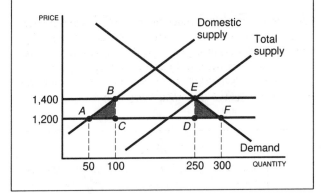

7   (Worked problem: tariffs) This problem continues with the market for high-grade aluminum. The demand and supply curves are given in Table 38.1. The world price is $1,200 and the import quota is 150,000 metric tons.

a   Find the new equilibrium.
b   Calculate quota rents.
c   Show the deadweight burden.

Step-by-step solution

Step one: Identify the world price, the demand curve, the supply curve, and the quota. The world price is $1,200, demand and supply are given in Table 38.1, and the quota is 150,000.

Step two: Find the total supply curve. This is just the domestic supply curve added to the quota.

Total supply = domestic supply + quota.

Supply

Price	Quantity (metric tons)
$2,000	400,000 + 150,000 = 550,000
$1,800	300,000 + 150,000 = 450,000
$1,600	200,000 + 150,000 = 350,000
$1,400	100,000 + 150,000 = 250,000
$1,200	50,000 + 150,000 = 200,000
$1,000	25,000 + 150,000 = 175,000

Step three: Find the equilibrium price. Total supply equals demand when the price is $1,400. The equilibrium quantity is 250,000.

Step four: Find the domestic quantity supplied. When the price is $1,400, domestic supply equals 100,000.

Step five: Calculate the quota rents. This is the extra money earned by licensed importers.

Quota rents = (new price – world price) × imports
= ($1,400 – $1,200) × 150,000.

Step six: Show the area of the deadweight burden. There are two parts. Triangle DEF represents the loss in consumer surplus due to reduced consumption. Triangle ABC represents the waste of resources brought about by producing domestically when it is less expensive to import.

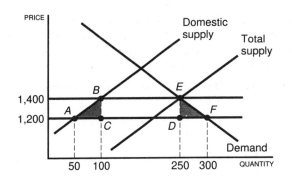

8   (Practice problem: quotas) This problem continues with the market for coffee. The demand and supply curves are given in Table 38.2. The world price is 6 cents and the import quota is 10,000 million pounds.

a   Find the new equilibrium.
b   Calculate quota rents.
c   Show the deadweight burden.

9   (Practice problem: quotas) This problem continues with the market for sugar. The demand and supply curves are given in Table 38.3. The world price is 1 cent and the import quota is 1,000 million pounds.

a   Find the new equilibrium.
b   Calculate quota rents.
c   Show the deadweight burden.

Answers to Problems

2   *a*   Quantity demanded = 22,000; quantity supplied = 12,000.
b   Imports = 22,000 – 12,000 = 10,000.

3   *a*   Quantity demanded = 1,600; quantity supplied = 600.
b   Imports = 1,600 – 600 = 1,000.

5   *a*   Quantity demanded = 18,000; quantity supplied = 16,000; imports = 18,000 – 16,000 = 2,000.
b   Tariff revenue = 2 × 2,000 = 4,000 million cents = $40,000,000.

c

c

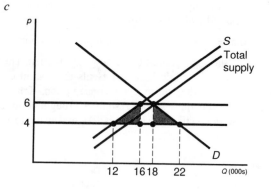

6   *a*   Quantity demanded = 1,500; quantity supplied =
650; imports = 1,500 − 650 = 850.

   b   Tariff revenue = 0.5 × 850 = 425 million cents =
$4,250,000.

   c

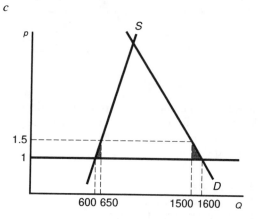

8   *a*   New price = 6 cents per pound; quantity demanded
= 18,000; quantity supplied = 16,000; imports =
18,000 − 16,000 = 2,000.

   b   Quota rents = 2 × 2,000 = 4,000 million cents =
$40,000,000.

9   *a*   New price = 1.5 cents per pound; quantity demanded = 1,500; quantity supplied = 650; imports =
1,500 − 650 = 850.

   b   Quota rents = 0.5 × 850 = 425 million cents =
$4,250,000.

   c

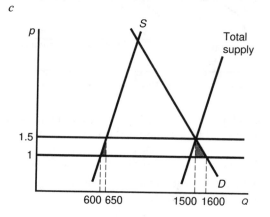

Chapter 39

ALTERNATIVE ECONOMIC SYSTEMS

Chapter Review

This chapter compares the nature and performance of the system we have studied throughout this book, the mixed economy, with some alternatives, namely the economic systems that evolved in the former Soviet Union and Eastern Europe in this century. The chapter includes some discussion of the worker-managed firms found in what used to be Yugoslavia as well as the incorporation of markets into the socialist economies of Hungary and Communist China. The book concludes in the next chapter with the topic of developing economies.

ESSENTIAL CONCEPTS

1 In **socialist** economies, the government owns the means of production; in **Communist** countries, it owns all property. Both systems have a high degree of government control of economic decisions, or **central planning,** which stands in contrast to the market system prevalent in the **market economies** (also called capitalist because of the prominent role played by private capital). The economies of Western Europe, Japan, and the United States rely on private property and markets for most economic decisions.

2 Appalled by the extreme economic inequality that accompanied the industrial revolution, Karl Marx predicted the downfall of capitalism and its replacement by a communist state. His ideas were implemented to some extent by Vladmir Lenin and Joseph Stalin in the Soviet Union from 1917 until recently.

3 **Soviet-style socialism** coordinated economic activity through a series of centrally administered plans that answered the basic economic questions of what is to be produced, how it is to be produced, and for whom. A system of political controls and rewards backed up by force replaced market incentives. In the labor market, this system assigned workers to jobs and limited labor mobility. The capital market was replaced by central directions that pursued a low-consumption, high-investment strategy emphasizing heavy industry. Goods were produced according to the plan and sold at prices controlled below market-clearing levels, leading to shortages and long lines at stores. Despite the ideology of "to each according to his needs," much inequality remained.

4 Soviet-style socialism failed for at least two reasons. It provided no *incentives* to managers; they could not keep

any profits, nor were they responsible for losses. Furthermore, the planning mechanism was unable to gather the needed *information* to allocate resources efficiently or to monitor workers and firms in order to ensure that the plan was carried through effectively. Prices, which were set arbitrarily, did not convey information about relative scarcity and value, as do market prices.

5   Under **market socialism** as in Hungary, the central planners set prices and order managers to maximize profits. This revision of the system performs only a little better than Soviet-style socialism; prices are set without good information, and managers, still without property rights, have no incentives to pursue profits. Some success was achieved with the "responsibility system" in China, where farmers were allowed to sell their produce and keep some of the proceeds. Yugoslavia instituted worker-managed firms as a partial step towards markets.

6   The transition from Soviet-style socialism to market economies is difficult and fraught with problems. The transition begins with a period of disruption, falling living standards, and high unemployment as old, inefficient factories are closed and resources are reallocated. Inflation rises as price controls are relaxed. Limiting budget deficits, controlling credit, and privatization of government-owned assets, including land, are difficult in countries making the transition. Finally, it will take a long time for all of the various institutions that support market economies to evolve. Nearly all of the former communist countries are moving toward the market economy, although the pace of transition varies widely.

BEHIND THE ESSENTIAL CONCEPTS

1   The main disadvantages of central government control are gathering the information needed to determine the optimal decisions, and giving incentives to managers and workers. Every organization, whether it operates within a market or a socialist economy, faces these problems. The difficulty with the socialist system is that the economy is simply too large an organization to control from the center.

2   The experiment with worker-managed firms in Yugoslavia showed interesting results. Since workers shared the profits, their goal was not to maximize total profits but rather to maximize profits per worker. This reduced the incentive to hire additional workers, because any new worker would cause the profit pie to be sliced more thinly. Further, the incentives to invest and increase the value of the enterprise were limited because it could not be sold.

3   The Soviet-style socialist economies bottled up inflation by controlling prices below the market-clearing levels and by providing fewer goods than people wanted to buy. Because there were so few goods to spend money on, savings rates were especially high, a phenomenon known as monetary overhang. As prices are freed from government control, they rise to market-clearing levels, but inflation grows even more as people spend their monetary overhang.

4   Despite claims of eliminating unemployment, the Soviet-style socialist economies did have disguised unemployment. Workers were assigned to firms, and layoffs were banned. Plants with excess workers simply kept them on the payroll. Because they were subject to the **soft budget constraint**, any losses resulting from the excess payroll were covered by the central government.

SELF-TEST

True or False

1   Under socialism, the state owns the means of production.

2   In mixed economies, there is a reliance on markets for most decisions, but government also plays a substantial role.

3   Karl Marx led the Russian revolution of 1917, establishing a Marxist state.

4   Under central planning, important decisions are made at the plant level.

5   In Soviet-style economies, incentives were provided by force.

6   In Soviet-style economies, there was little job mobility but some disguised unemployment.

7   The Soviet Union pursued a high-investment, low-consumption economic plan.

8   Soviet-style socialist economies nearly eliminated economic inequality.

9   Although socialist economies lost the competition for efficient production, they were able to protect their environment.

10   Most economists believe that the experiment in Soviet-style socialism was a failure.

11   Bureaucrats lacked the information to make efficient decisions under Soviet-style socialism.

12   Under market socialism, prices replace planning in determining investment decisions.

13   Worker-managed firms have little incentive to hire more workers.

14   The movement from socialism to a more market-oriented economy has caused prices to increase.

15   Privatization refers to the process of eliminating price controls and returning the function of setting prices to private firms.

Multiple Choice

1   Socialism is the system under which

   a   the state owns all property, including the means of production and all land;

   b   the state owns the means of production;

   c   there is a heavy reliance on firms and households interacting in markets;

   d   there is a heavy reliance on markets and a considerable role for government;

   e   workers own and manage the firms.

2   Under communism,

   a   the state owns all property, including the means of production and all land;

   b   the state owns the means of production;

   c   there is a heavy reliance on firms and households interacting in markets;

   d   there is a heavy reliance on markets and a considerable role for government;

   e   workers own and manage the firms.

3   In a mixed economy,

   a   the state owns all property, including the means of production and all land;

   b   the state owns the means of production;

   c   there is a heavy reliance on firms and households interacting in markets;

   d   there is a heavy reliance on markets and a considerable role for government;

   e   workers own and manage the firms.

4   The Russian revolution of 1917, which installed communism, was led by

   a   Marx;

   b   Oscar Lange;

   c   Lenin;

   d   Stalin;

   e   Mises.

5   The forced collectivization of agriculture was ordered by

   a   Marx;

   b   Oscar Lange;

   c   Lenin;

   d   Stalin;

   e   Mises.

6   Under Stalin the Soviet Union increased investment by

   a   maintaining high rates of return for savings;

   b   keeping wages low;

   c   limiting the supply of consumer goods;

   d   attracting foreign investment;

   e   b and c.

7   Under central planning,

   a   the government makes all significant economic decisions;

   b   government-owned property is sold or given to individuals;

   c   workers own and manage their firms;

   d   prices are set by the interplay of supply and demand;

   e   land is redistributed to those who have worked it.

8   Under socialism, in the labor market,

   a   wages adjust to clear the market;

   b   firms pay above market-clearing efficiency wages to keep and motivate their best workers;

   c   workers are assigned jobs, and there is very little labor mobility;

   d   unions set wages through collective bargaining;

   e   workers own and manage their own firms.

9   In Soviet-style socialist economies, the allocation of investment capital is determined by

   a   workers who own and manage their own firms;

   b   the capital market;

   c   the government;

   d   majority vote;

   e   none of the above.

10   In Soviet-style socialist economies, prices

   a   were outlawed;

   b   were set equal to market-clearing levels;

   c   were set above market-clearing levels;

   d   were set below market-clearing levels;

   e   were determined by the forces of supply and demand.

11   The Soviet Union pursued a policy of

   a   high investment and low consumption;

   b   high consumption and low investment;

   c   high investment and high consumption;

   d   low investment and low consumption;

   e   none of the above.

12   Socialist enterprises often face soft budget constraints, which means that

   a   workers share the profits equally;

   b   firms that continue to make losses are absorbed by larger firms;

   c   the government makes up any losses;

   d   workers do not have to work unless the firm makes a profit;

   e   workers are assigned jobs and thus are never unemployed.

13   Amomg the problems of central planning are

   a   the lack of incentives that managers have to operate firms efficiently;

   b   the lack of information needed to make efficient decisions;

   c   the fact that prices, not determined by markets, could not provide informative signals;

   d   the difficulty in monitoring the performance of managers and workers;

   e   all of the above.

14   Under market socialism,

   a   government makes the investment decisions;

   b   firms maximize profits at the prices they face;

   c   workers own and manage their own firms;

   d   all of the above;

   e   a and b.

15   In China, farmers were allowed to sell most of what they produced and keep the profits under

   a   collectivized agriculture;

b farmer cooperatives;

c the responsibility system;

d land reform;

e privatization.

16 Worker-managed farms were instituted in

a China;

b the USSR;

c Poland;

d Hungary;

e Yugoslavia.

17 Which of the following was not a problem with worker-owned cooperatives?

a Workers had little incentive to undertake investments that paid off after they left the firm.

b Keeping a share of the profits motivated workers to work hard in smaller firms.

c Cooperatives had little incentive to hire new workers.

d The aging work force diminished investment incentives.

e The reluctance to hire workers contributed to the unemployment problem.

18 Environment policy in the Soviet Union was characterized by

a low energy prices;

b lack of anti-pollution measures;

c intensive farming with high pesticide use and much soil erosion;

d lack of nuclear safety equipment;

e all of the above.

19 Privatization refers to

a the transfer to individuals of property formerly owned by the state;

b the fact that managers under Soviet-style socialism kept information private;

c the consolidation of agriculture into large firms;

d the policy that allowed private farmers in China to sell much of what they produced;

e the attempt to combine the best features of socialism and private enterprise.

20 Which of the following are problems involved in the transition from socialism to market economies?

a inflation;

b unemployment;

c the lack of a safety net;

d falling living standards;

e All of the above are problems.

Completion

1 The government owns and operates the means of production under _____.

2 Under _____, the government owns all property.

3 The system of _____ gives the government and its ministries control over economic decisions.

4 Economies with a heavy reliance on markets but also a considerable role for government are referred to as _____.

5 _____ believed that the capitalist system would eventually collapse and evolve into communism.

6 _____ forced the collectivization of farms, causing a famine in which millions died.

7 According to _____, economies can combine the advantages of market mechanisms with public ownership of the means of production.

8 Worker-owned _____, in which workers hired managers and received the profits, were countenanced in Yugoslavia.

9 Transferring businesses and property from public ownership to individuals is called _____.

10 Among the formerly Communist countries _____ proceeded most quickly in the macroeconomic aspects of the transition to a market economy.

Answers to Self-Test

True or False

1	t	6	t	11	t
2	t	7	t	12	f
3	f	8	f	13	t
4	f	9	f	14	t
5	t	10	t	15	f

Multiple Choice

1	b	6	e	11	a	16	e
2	a	7	a	12	c	17	b
3	d	8	c	13	e	18	e
4	c	9	c	14	e	19	a
5	d	10	d	15	c	20	e

Completion

1 socialism

2 communism

3 central planning

4 mixed economies

5 Karl Marx

6 Stalin

7 market socialism

8 cooperatives

9 privatization

10 Poland

Doing Economics: Tools and Practice Problems

In a planned economy, such as Soviet-style socialism, the state owns and must allocate the means of production. To gain some understanding of the allocation problem the state must solve, we first look at some relatively simple problems involving how to allocate a resource between different plants or regions that produce the same good. The next topic involves a Yugoslavian experiment with firms owned and managed by the workers. We explore the problem of how many workers to hire.

Efficient Resource Allocation

Compared to market economies, socialism allocated resources poorly. This means that resources were not assigned to task efficiently and that the economy produced inside its production possibilities. While markets use prices to guide allocations, socialist managers must gather a great deal of information about productivity in alternative uses, form a coherent plan, direct the allocation, and monitor performance to see that the plan is carried out. The combined information and incentive problems overwhelmed the capacity of planners. Tool Kit 39.1 shows how to solve allocation problems when the information is available.

Tool Kit 39.1: Finding the Efficient Allocation of a Resource

When new productive resources become available, state bureaucrats must decide how to use them. The solution to this problem requires information about production functions. Tool Kit 39.1 looks at how to allocate resources efficiently. Follow the steps.

Step one: Identify the production functions for each possible use.

Step two: Compute the marginal product for each quantity of the resource:

marginal product = change in output/change in input.

Step three: Allocate the first unit of the resource to the activity with the highest marginal product.

Step four: Allocate the second unit of the resource to the activity with the next highest marginal product.

Step five: Continue until the available supply of the resource is exhausted.

---

1 (Worked problem: planning and efficient allocation) The Commissar of Fishing has received eight new trawlers for cod. She must decide how to allocate the new vessels between the Black Sea and Caspian Sea fleets. The production functions for each fleet are given in Table 39.1.

Table 39.1

Number of trawlers	Harvest of Black Sea cod (tons per week)	Harvest of Caspian Sea cod (tons per week)
1	9	20
2	17	36
3	24	50
4	30	62
5	35	72
6	39	80
7	42	86
8	44	90

a Find the efficient allocation of trawlers;
b Suppose the commissar does not know the production functions and simply allocates the trawlers equally between the fleets. How many fewer tons of cod will be harvested?

Step-by-step solution

Step one (a): Identify the production functions for each possible use. They are given in Table 39.1.

Step two: Compute the marginal product for each quantity of the resource. The first trawler in the Black Sea harvests 10 tons. The second one increases the harvest to 19, which is a marginal product of 19 − 10 = 9. Continuing, we derive Table 39.2.

Table 39.2

Number of trawlers	Harvest of Black Sea cod	Marginal product	Harvest of Caspian Sea cod	Marginal product
1	9	9	20	20
2	17	8	36	16
3	24	7	50	14
4	30	6	62	12
5	35	5	72	10
6	39	4	80	8
7	42	3	86	6
8	44	2	90	4

Step three: Allocate the first unit of the resource to the activity with the highest marginal product. The highest marginal product is 20 in the Caspian Sea.

Step four: Allocate the second unit of the resource to the activity with the next highest marginal product. The next highest marginal product is 16, again in the Caspian Sea.

Step five: Continue until the available supply of the resource is exhausted. If 6 trawlers are allocated to the Caspian, where the output is 80, and 2 to the Black Sea, where the output is 17, then the output of cod is 97. The allocation is efficient, and this is the answer to part a.

Step six (b): If 4 trawlers are sent to each region, total output is 30 + 62 = 92, which is 5 less than if the allocation were efficient.

2 (Practice problem: planning and efficient allocation) Nine new tractors roll off the assembly line at the huge state-owned tractor works in Braslov. Many cooperative farms have requested new tractors, and the minister in charge must allocate them. The production functions for three farms are given in Table 39.3. Output is measured as thousands of bushels of wheat.

a Find the efficient allocation of tractors;
b Compute the waste if the tractors are divided equally among the three farms.

Table 39.3

Tractors	Output at farm #1	Output at farm #2	Output at farm #3
0	30	100	50
1	40	150	90
2	49	180	120
3	57	200	140
4	64	210	150
5	70	215	155
6	75	218	160
7	79	220	164
8	82	220	166
9	82	220	167

3   (Practice problem: planning and efficient allocation) Six new locomotives are made available for either the north-south route or the east-west route. The production functions for each route are given in Table 39.4. Output is measured as numbers of standard containers per week.

Table 39.4

Locomotives	East-west route output	North-south route output
1	1,000	1,000
2	1,800	1,600
3	2,500	2,000
4	3,000	2,200
5	3,300	2,300
6	3,500	2,400

a   Find the efficient allocation of locomotives.
b   How much output is wasted if all are allocated to the east-west route?

Worker-Managed Firms

One experiment in market socialism occurred in the former Yugoslavia when the government sanctioned the creation of firms owned and managed by workers. The profits from each firm were shared equally among the workers. Worker-managed firms do seek profits, but they do not maximize total profits; rather, their goal is to make profits per worker as large as possible. Generally, this practice results in fewer workers hired than under a full-fledged market system. Tool Kit 39.2 demonstrates this.

Tool Kit 39.2: Finding the Level of Employment in a Worker-Managed Firm

Because it is run by workers who share in the profits, a worker-managed firm will seek to maximize profits per worker. This differs from the goal of firms in market economies, which maximize profits. Follow these steps to find the level of employment in worker-managed firms.

Step one: Identify the production function and the product price.

Step two: Compute the total revenue at each level of employment by multiplying the output by the product price:

revenues = output × product price.

Step three: Compute profits by subtracting costs from revenue:

profits = revenues − costs.

Step four: Compute profits per worker by dividing profits by the corresponding number of workers. This is the share of profits going to each worker.

profits per worker = profits/number of workers.

Step five: Find the level of employment for which profits per worker is highest. This is the equilibrium level of employment in the worker-managed firm.

---

4   (Worked problem: worker-managed firms) The new branch of the Hair Cuttery is ready to open. It will be owned and managed by the stylists. The price of haircuts is $10, and the production function is given in Table 39.5. Fixed costs equal $50 per day. Find the equilibrium number of stylists.

Table 39.5

Stylists	Haircuts per day
1	6
2	16
3	30
4	42
5	50
6	56
7	60

Step-by-step solution

Step one: Identify the production function and the product price. The production function is given in Table 39.5, and the price is $10.

Step two: Compute the total revenue at each level of employment by multiplying the output by the product price. When the number of stylists is 1, output is 6 and revenues equal 6 × $10 = $60. Continuing, we complete the column as shown in Table 39.6.

Step three: Compute profits by subtracting costs from revenue. We subtract $50 from the revenue column. The completed information is given in Table 39.6.

Table 39.6

Stylists	Haircuts per day	Revenues	Profits
1	6	$ 60	$ 10
2	16	$160	$110
3	30	$300	$250
4	42	$420	$370
5	50	$500	$450
6	56	$560	$510
7	60	$600	$550

Step four: Compute profits per worker by dividing profits by the corresponding number of workers. This is the share of profits going to each worker. For example, profits per worker when there is one stylist equal $10/1 = $10. Continuing, we derive Table 39.7.

Table 39.7

Stylists	Haircuts per day	Revenues	Profits	Profits per stylist
1	6	$ 60	$ 10	$10.00
2	16	$160	$110	$55.00
3	30	$300	$250	$83.33
4	42	$420	$370	$92.50
5	50	$500	$450	$90.00
6	56	$560	$510	$85.00
7	60	$600	$550	$76.57

Step five: Find the level of employment for which profits per worker is highest. The equilibrium level of employment is 4, where profits per worker equal $92.50.

5 (Practice problem: worker-managed firms) Moe's Lite-Brite Charcoal Company soaks charcoal in lighter fluid for $1 per bag. Its production function is given in Table 39.8. Moe is selling his business and all of the equipment to the employees. Their fixed cost including the payment on the loan to finance the sale will be $500 per day. Find the equilibrium level of employment when Moe's becomes worker managed.

Table 39.8

Workers	Output per day
1	100
2	500
3	1,500
4	2,500
5	2,900
6	3,300

6 (Practice problem: worker-managed firms) The Thelonius Thimble Company is to become worker owned and managed next month when the likable Thelonius retires. He is giving the business to the workers, and they will have no fixed cost. Thimbles sell for $.10 each. The production function is given in Table 39.9. Find the equilib-

rium number of employees of the worker-managed thimble company.

Table 39.9

Workers	Thimbles
1	2,000
2	5,000
3	10,000
4	13,000
5	15,000
6	17,000

Answers to Problems

2 Table 39.10 gives the marginal product of tractors at each of the farms.

Table 39.10

	Farm #1		Farm #2		Farm #3	
Tractors	Output	Marginal product	Output	Marginal product	Output	Marginal product
0	30	30	100	100	50	50
1	40	10	150	50	90	40
2	49	9	180	30	120	30
3	57	8	200	20	140	20
4	64	7	210	10	150	10
5	70	6	215	5	155	5
6	75	5	218	3	160	5
7	79	4	220	2	164	4
8	82	3	220	0	166	2
9	82	0	220	0	167	1

a The efficient allocation is 1 tractor to farm #1, 4 tractors to farm #2, and 4 tractors to farm #3.

b The output of the tractors divided equally is 57 + 200 + 140 = 397. The output at the efficient allocation is 40 + 210 + 150 = 400. The waste is 400 – 397 = 3, and since output is measured in thousands of bushels, this represents 3,000 bushels.

3 Table 39.11 gives the marginal product along each route.

Table 39.11

	East-west route		North-south route	
Locomotives	Output	Marginal product	Output	Marginal product
1	1,000	1,000	1,000	1,000
2	1,800	800	1,600	600
3	2,500	700	2,000	400
4	3,000	500	2,200	200
5	3,300	300	2,300	100
6	3,500	200	2,400	100

a The efficient allocation is 4 to the east-west route and 2 to the north-south route.

b Output is 3,500 if all are allocated to the east-west route. Output is 3,000 + 1,600 = 4,600 at the efficient allocation. The waste is 4,600 – 3,500 = 1,100.

5   Table 39.12 gives profits per worker, which are maximized when the firm includes 4 workers.

Table 39.12

Workers	Output per day	Revenues	Profits	Profits per worker
1	100	$ 100	−$ 400	−$400
2	500	$ 500	$ 0	$ 0
3	1,500	$1,500	$1,000	$333
4	2,500	$2,500	$2,000	$500
5	2,900	$2,900	$2,400	$480
6	3,300	$3,300	$2,800	$466

6   Table 39.13 gives profits per worker, which are maximized when the number of workers is 3.

Table 39.13

Workers	Output per day	Revenues	Profits	Profits per worker
1	2,000	$ 200	$ 200	$200
2	5,000	$ 500	$ 500	$250
3	10,000	$1,000	$1,000	$333
4	13,000	$1,300	$1,300	$325
5	15,000	$1,500	$1,500	$300
6	17,000	$1,700	$1,700	$283

Chapter 40

DEVELOPMENT

Chapter Review

This chapter takes up less developed countries. It examines living standards in these countries as well as the causes of underdevelopment and the prospects for bringing the living standards up to those of the developed countries. The chapter closes with a look at the policies some countries have pursued, namely the relative advantages of the export-led and import-competing strategies.

ESSENTIAL CONCEPTS

1   In **less developed countries (LDCs)** GDP per capita was less than $675 in 1992. The per capita income gap among developed countries has narrowed over the past century, while it has widened between the developed and less developed world. Although a few countries have successfully raised their living standards, most of the LDCs remain in grinding poverty. Agricultural gains from the **green revolution**, improvements in health and life expectancy, and the emergence of the **newly industrialized countries** of East Asia are some examples of successful economic development.

2   Although there is considerable variation among LDCs, agriculture dominates the economy in most. In the rural sector, farming takes place on small, labor-intensive farms with poorer techniques and less fertilizer than in the developed world. **Sharecropping** remains a widespread arrangement. Redistribution of land ownership through **land reform** has at times been successful, but dramatic inequality remains. In the urban sector, wages are far higher, and many individuals have migrated to the cities. Such migration has caused massive unemployment and squalor. The term **dual economy** describes the vast difference between the rural and urban sectors.

3   The institutions and structure of the economy in LDCs do not facilitate growth. Although savings rates are high, there is a shortage of capital. The absence of efficient capital markets keeps the limited capital from its most productive use. An inadequate supply of skilled workers accompanies burgeoning population growth, which reduces the ratio of capital to workers and lowers productivity. Also, the lack of developed capital markets and ill-advised government interventions have kept the limited capital from its most productive use. All of this plus extreme inequality characterize LDCs.

4   The failure of markets in their countries has led most

LDCs to adopt *central planning*. Because planners do not have sufficient information to make correct decisions, central planning has not been successful. An overreliance on heavy industry, corruption, and widespread interference in trade and foreign exchange are common problems of actual LDC development efforts. A common policy, import substitution, emphasizes the development of domestic markets by substituting domestic production for imports. The pervasive role of government also motivates wasteful rent seeking. Another clear failure has been in providing needed **infrastructure**, especially a sound legal system.

5   The success of the East Asian economies points to several policy successes. These countries practiced the sound macroeconomic policies of low budget deficits and low inflation. Other policies encouraged high savings rates, literacy, college education, and the explicit promotion of certain export-oriented industries. This export-led strategy protects and encourages certain industries judged to be potentially successful against world competition. Dynamic comparative advantage, based on acquired education and skills, has guided the most successful of these policies, but there have been some failures. One final benefit is the high level of economic equality, suggesting that there is not necessarily a trade-off between growth and equality.

BEHIND THE ESSENTIAL CONCEPTS

1   The case for central planning in LDCs has always rested on the pervasive *market failures*. Clearly, markets do a poor job allocating resources in these countries. Yet the failure of planning provides a salient example of *government failure*. Although the potential for beneficial government intervention exists, governments have made matters worse.

2   Real world markets are complicated, and the institutions that help them work have taken time to evolve. Reputations, repeated business arrangements, implicit contracts, and other institutions help ease the information problems that trouble imperfectly competitive markets. In the LDCs, these institutions are not present, and in their absence, resource allocation is worse.

3   Observing varying levels of success and failure around the world, we can compile a list of good development policies. First, there must be sound macroeconomics, i.e., fiscal responsibility and a stable monetary system. Second, the economies must direct themselves toward the rest of the world by reducing trade barriers, encouraging foreign investment, and promoting exports. This approach helps to transfer more advanced technology from abroad and provides a natural test for success. Government can allocate more of its budget to investment and less to consumption, such as food subsidies. Finally, policies such as land reform and universal education (including women) not only contribute to development, but also promote equality.

4   The term "vicious circle" is often used with respect to LDCs. Poor households cannot afford education and must scratch out a living in labor-intensive activities, such as subsistence farming. They not only lack the education to practice birth control, but also have incentives to raise more children, who are economically useful. The population growth reduces capital per worker, keeping the economy in underdevelopment.

5   The education of women plays an especially important role in development. You can see this in terms of the costs and benefits of children. More educated women understand and practice birth control. Also, as education allows their earnings to increase, they realize that the opportunity cost of having children is high and limit family size. Lower population growth means more capital per worker and higher output.

SELF-TEST

True or False

1   Over the past century, the income gap between the industrialized and less developed economies has narrowed.

2   One success story in the less developed world has been the emergence of the newly industrialized countries, such as Singapore and Taiwan.

3   Increases in life expectancy and improvements in infant mortality have allowed rapid population growth in many LDCs.

4   In poor countries, agriculture plays a more prominent role, often accounting for 80 percent of GNP.

5   The LDCs have much less capital per person than the United States because their savings rates are very low.

6   The absence of capital markets in LDCs prevents the limited supply of capital from finding its most efficient use.

7   Land reform transfers agricultural land to those who work it.

8   Inequality can inhibit development by leading to political instability and a poor climate for foreign investment.

9   Sharecropping gives good incentives for the tenant farmer to work hard and maintain the productivity of the land.

10   Central planning enables developing countries to coordinate all the related activities in a single coherent development strategy.

11   An important element of a country's infrastructure is its legal system.

12   A difficulty with the export-led strategy is that it protects inefficient domestic producers from the competition of foreign firms.

13   One problem with import substitution is that it is difficult to remove trade barriers once they are imposed.

14 The successful East Asian economies have achieved high growth rates, but this has occurred at the cost of extreme inequality.

15 Educating women leads to lower birth rates because as their education brings higher wages, the opportunity cost of devoting time to raise children rises.

Multiple Choice

1 What fraction of the world's population lives in LDCs?

a one-fourth;
b one-half;
c three-fourths;
d one-third;
e one-sixth.

2 Over the past century, the income gap

a has widened among high-income countries;
b has narrowed among high-income countries;
c has grown wider between high- and low-income countries;
d has narrowed between high- and low-income countries;
e b anc c.

3 The green revolution refers to

a the spread of concern for the environment in the LDCs;
b the World Bank's largely successful efforts to aid development by lending money for infrastructure investment;
c the development and spread to LDCs of new agricultural technologies, which brought about huge increases in output;
d improvements in life expectancy and infant mortality statistics in the LDCs;
e none of the above.

4 Agriculture in the developed countries

a uses larger farms than in the LDCs;
b uses fewer workers per acre than in LDCs;
c uses more fertilizer per acre than in LDCs;
d is more mechanized than in LDCs;
e all of the above.

5 Sharecropping refers to

a the fact that much of the agricultural output in the LDCs is taken in taxes;
b the World Bank's policy of matching agricultural gains in LDCs with food shipments;
c the sharing of technological know-how between agricultural research centers in the developed world and the LDCs;
d the system in which the landlord takes a share of the output of a farm;
e the system in which farmers set aside a fraction of their output to support religious institutions.

6 The term dual economies refers to

a the disparity between the developed and underdeveloped economies;

b the disparity between men's and women's earnings in the LDCs;
c the disparity between upper and lower incomes in the LDCs;
d the disparity between rural and urban life in the LDCs;
e the disparity between the efficiency of the market sector and the inefficiency of governments in LDCs.

7 In LDCs, it is generally true that

a savings rates are low;
b because it is in short supply, capital is used very intensively;
c because the capital stock is so low, the marginal return to capital is much higher than in developed countries;
d the lack of effective capital markets keeps capital from its most productive uses;
e the stable political environments attract foreign investment.

8 The debt crises experienced by several LDCs in the 1980s were caused by

a high interest rates;
b the world recession in the early 1980s;
c lack of prudence in lending by banks;
d U.S. government deposit insurance;
e all of the above.

9 In LDCs, the population

a is large and well educated;
b is falling because of the poor medical care and meager diets;
c is growing too rapidly, causing an excess supply of trained workers;
d is growing too rapidly, but includes too few vocationally trained, skilled workers;
e none of the above.

10 The low returns to capital in the LDCs are the result of

a shortages of capital;
b low supplies of capital;
c lack of markets to allocate capital efficiently;
d b and c;
e all of the above.

11 In LDCs,

a both labor and capital markets work well;
b while labor markets work well, capital markets fail to allocate efficiently the scarce capital;
c while capital markets work well, ethnic divisions and language barriers hinder the labor market;
d neither capital nor labor markets work efficiently;
e there are no labor or capital markets.

12 Sir Arthur Lewis argued that the surplus of labor contributes to economic growth by

a supporting strong governments that can provide stability needed to attract foreign investment;
b keeping wages low, which leads to high profits and investment;

c discouraging population growth through high unemployment;

d emigrating and sending earnings home;

e attracting foreign investment with low wages.

13 Export-led growth strategies have promoted

a agriculture, where LDCs have had comparative advantage;

b substitution of domestic production for imported
goods;

c land reform;

d export industries aligned with the principle of dynamic comparative advantage, which is based on
acquired skills, education, and technology;

e government control of production in order to maximize exports.

14 What best describes the relationship between inequality and economic growth?

a The countries that have developed most rapidly
have lower levels of inequality.

b The countries that have developed most rapidly
have higher levels of inequality.

c There is no consistent relationship between inequality and the pace of development.

d Planned economies have developed rapidly with
low inequality, but unplanned ones have only developed when inequality is high.

e Planned economies have developed rapidly with
high inequality, but unplanned ones have only developed when inequality is low.

15 Inequality may inhibit development by

a leading to political instability and a poor investment climate;

b fostering the development of sharecropping;

c leading governments to impose high tax rates;

d forcing governments to spend on food subsidies
rather than investment;

e all of the above.

16 Most economists

a favor central planning by LDCs because planners
can better coordinate all the aspects of major projects;

b favor central planning by LDCs because planners
have better information about whether projects
will be successful;

c are skeptical about central planning because planners lack the needed information;

d see no need for planning of any kind;

e view planning as neither beneficial nor harmful
because of the policy ineffectiveness proposition.

17 Rent seeking refers to

a the payments made by sharecroppers;

b activities by individuals to get special benefits
from governments;

c campaigns to attract foreign investment;

d the failure of sharecroppers to maintain the land;

e none of the above.

18 Which of the following is not part of a country's infrastructure?

a roads;

b bridges;

c ports;

d legal system;

e All of the above are part of the infrastructure.

19 Encouraging the production and export of goods in
which the country has a comparative advantage is the
strategy called

a export-led growth;

b central planning;

c dynamic comparative advantage;

d import substitution;

e laissez-faire.

20 Encouraging the development of a domestic market by
substituting domestically produced goods for imports
is called

a export-led growth;

b central planning;

c dynamic comparative advantage;

d import substitution;

e laissez-faire.

Completion

1 Economists refer to the poorest nations of the world as
_____.

2 Nations that have recently moved from being quite
poor to being middle-income countries, including
South Korea and Hong Kong, are called _____.

3 The development of new seeds, fertilizers, and agricultural practices that brought about increases in agricultural output in the LDCs during the 1960s and 1970s
was called the _____.

4 In many LDCs, there is a _____, which includes
a poor rural sector alongside a relatively more advanced urban sector.

5 A country's roads, ports, bridges, and legal system
compose its _____.

6 _____ is a strategy according to which governments encourage exports to stimulate growth.

7 _____ is a strategy whereby the focus is on substituting domestic goods for imports to develop self-
sufficiency.

8 Countries that have large numbers of unemployed
or underemployed workers are said to have
_____.

9 _____ refers to activities designed to secure
government favors, such as import licenses or access
to foreign exchange.

10 The _____ is the most important of the international agencies that lend funds to LDCs to aid in development.

Answers to Self-Test

True or False

1	f	6	t	11	t
2	t	7	t	12	f
3	t	8	t	13	t
4	t	9	f	14	f
5	f	10	f	15	t

Multiple Choice

1	c	6	d	11	d	16	c
2	e	7	d	12	b	17	b
3	c	8	e	13	d	18	e
4	e	9	d	14	a	19	a
5	d	10	e	15	e	20	d

Completion

1   less developed countries
2   newly industrialized countries
3   green revolution
4   dual economy
5   infrastructure
6   Export-led growth
7   Import substitution
8   labor surplus
9   Rent seeking
10 World Bank

Doing Economics: Tools and Practice Problems

Two important problems that impede growth in underdeveloped countries are the absence of markets to allocate resources efficiently, and the prevalence of institutions, such as sharecropping, that provide weak incentives. We study both of these problems in this section. Underdeveloped economies not only have limited supplies of capital and skilled labor, they also lack good markets to allocate what supplies they have. In this section, we consider the efficient allocation of resources, how markets achieve this allocation, and the losses that result from misallocation.

1   (Worked problem: absence of markets) The World Bank has made $10 million available for development projects in Costa Guano. Two possible uses for the money are building roads and building irrigation systems. The present discounted value of investments in each sector is given in Table 40.1.

Table 40.1

Investment (millions)	Irrigation projects (millions)	Roads (millions)
$ 1	$10	$ 25
$ 2	$18	$ 45
$ 3	$25	$ 60
$ 4	$31	$ 72
$ 5	$36	$ 83
$ 6	$40	$ 93
$ 7	$43	$102
$ 8	$45	$110
$ 9	$46	$116
$10	$46	$120

a   Find the efficient allocation of the $10 million.
b   How would competitive markets allocate the money?
c   The party in power in Costa Guano draws much of its support from agriculture. If it used all of the money for irrigation, how much less would the benefits be?

Step-by-step solution

Step one (a): To find the efficient allocation, we adapt the procedure outlined in Tool Kit 40.1. Identify the production functions for each possible use. Here we are given the relationship between investment and the benefits of investment in Table 40.1.

Step two: Compute the marginal benefit for each quantity of the resource. We compute marginal benefit in the usual way. For example, the marginal benefit of the first $1 million in investment in irrigation is $10 million. Continuing, we derive Table 40.2.

Table 40.2

Investment (millions)	Irrigation projects	Marginal benefit	Roads	Marginal benefit
$ 1	$10	$10	$ 25	$25
$ 2	$18	$ 8	$ 45	$20
$ 3	$25	$ 7	$ 60	$15
$ 4	$31	$ 6	$ 72	$12
$ 5	$36	$ 5	$ 83	$11
$ 6	$40	$ 4	$ 93	$10
$ 7	$43	$ 3	$102	$ 9
$ 8	$45	$ 2	$110	$ 8
$ 9	$46	$ 1	$116	$ 6
$10	$46	$ 0	$120	$ 4

Step three: Allocate the first unit of the resource to the activity with the highest marginal benefit. The first $1 million is allocated to road building, where it has a marginal benefit of $25 million.

Step four: Allocate the second unit of the resource to the activity with the next highest marginal benefit. The second $1 million is allocated to road building, where it has a marginal benefit of $20 million.

Step five: Continue until the available supply of the resource is exhausted. We allocate $8 million to roads and $2 million to irrigation.

Step one (b): To find the competitive market allocation, simply interpret the marginal benefits as the demand for the investment money, and follow the procedure in the first three steps of Tool Kit 36.1. Add each sector's demand for capital. When the price is $25 million, the total quantity demanded is $1 million by the road-building industry. When the price falls to $20 million, the quantity demanded is $2 million. Continuing, we derive the demand in Table 40.3.

Table 40.3

Price (million/million)	Quantity (millions of investment)
$25	$ 1
$20	$ 2
$15	$ 3
$12	$ 4
$11	$ 5
$10	$ 7 ($1 each for roads and irrigation)
$ 9	$ 8
$ 8	$10
$ 7	$11 etc.

Step two: Find the market-clearing price. The market clears at a price of $8 million.

Step three: Substitute the market-clearing price into each demand to determine the allocation of investment. At a price of $8 million, road builders will purchase $8 million, and irrigation firms will purchase $2 million. This is exactly the efficient allocation.

Step four (c): If all the investment money is used in irrigation projects, then the total benefit will be $46 million. The efficient allocation gives benefits equal to $18 million (irrigation) + $110 million (roads) = $128 million. Thus the waste that is due to misallocation is $128 – $46 = $82 million.

2 (Practice problem: absence of markets) Eight engineers return to Zaire with their diplomas from MIT. They can work for the government building bridges or in the mining sector. The (U.S. dollar equivalent) value of output produced in each sector is given in Table 40.4.

Table 40.4

Engineers	Roads	Mining
1	$200,000	$100,000
2	$280,000	$190,000
3	$350,000	$270,000
4	$410,000	$330,000
5	$450,000	$360,000
6	$480,000	$380,000
7	$500,000	$400,000
8	$500,000	$400,000

a Find the efficient allocation of the 8 engineers.
b How would competitive markets allocate the engineers?
c The president for life likes roads. How much is wasted if all 8 engineers are sent to build roads?

3 (Practice problem: absence of markets) The Zambizi River can provide up to 100 million gallons annually for irrigation. Both the cotton and millet crops would benefit from irrigation, and the benefits are given in Table 40.5.

Table 40.5

Water (millions of gallons)	Cotton (millions)	Millet (millions)
1	$ 50	$ 25
2	$ 95	$ 50
3	$135	$ 75
4	$170	$100
5	$200	$125
6	$225	$150
7	$245	$175
8	$260	$190
9	$270	$200
10	$275	$200

a Find the efficient allocation of the water.
b How would competitive markets allocate the water?
c The president for life allocates 80 million to millet and the rest to cotton. How much value is wasted?

Sharecropping

In underdeveloped economies, much farming takes place under conditions of sharecropping, where the landlord receives a fixed percentage of the output of the farm. The landlord's share of output is an externality from the point of view of the tenant, and as in all similar situations, there are incentive problems. Tool Kit 40.1 shows how to analyze sharecropping.

Tool Kit 40.1: Analyzing Sharecropping

Under sharecropping the farmer pays a fraction of the output to the landlord. This creates poor incentives to work hard and maintain the land and equipment. Follow these steps.

Step one: Find the full marginal benefits and costs of the tenant's effort.

Step two: Find the efficient level of effort, which is the level at which marginal benefits equal marginal cost.

Step three: Calculate the tenant's marginal private benefits, multiplying the full marginal benefits by the tenant's share.

Step four: Find the equilibrium level of effort, which is the level at which marginal private benefits equal marginal cost.

Step five: Compare the equilibrium and efficient levels of the activity.

---

4 (Worked problem: analyzing sharecropping) Mahragh grows sorghum on 20 acres in Chad. He gives one-half of his output in rent to the landlord. The current price is $1 per bushel, and Table 40.6 gives the production function. Finally, Mahragh could devote time each day to his wife's bicycle manufacture business, where he could earn $30 for each daily hour.

Table 40.6

Effort (hours per day)	Sorghum (bushels)
1	120
2	210
3	270
4	300
5	315
6	321
7	324

a Find the efficient level of effort.
b Find the equilibrium level of effort.

Step-by-step solution

Step one (a): Find the full marginal benefits and costs of the tenant's effort. We first compute the marginal product in bushels of sorghum and then multiply by the price of sorghum to find the dollar value. The first 2 hours of daily effort increase output to 120 bushels, which sell for $120. Continuing, we derive Table 40.7.

Table 40.7

Effort (hours per day)	Sorghum (bushels)	Marginal product (bushels per daily hour)	Marginal benefits (per daily hour)
1	120	120	$120
2	210	90	$ 90
3	270	60	$ 60
4	300	30	$ 30
5	315	15	$ 15
6	321	6	$ 6
7	324	3	$ 3

Step two: Find the efficient level of effort, which is the level at which marginal benefits equal marginal cost. The marginal cost, which is $30, equals marginal benefits at 4 hours per day.

Step three (b): Calculate the marginal private benefits by multiplying the full marginal benefits by the tenant's share. Mahragh's share is one-half; so if he works 1 hour each day, his marginal private benefits equal $120 × 1/2 = $60. Continuing, we derive Table 40.8.

Table 40.8

Effort	Marginal private benefits (per daily hour)
1	$60.00
2	$45.00
3	$30.00
4	$15.00
5	$ 7.50
6	$ 3.00
7	$ 1.50

Step four: Find the equilibrium level of effort, which is the level at which marginal private benefits equal marginal cost. The marginal private benefits equal marginal cost at 3 hours per day.

Step five: Compare the equilibrium and efficient levels of the activity. Mahragh works 3 hours each day, which is 1 less than the efficient number of hours.

5 (Practice problem: analyzing sharecropping) Mr. Droulig is a sharecropper on a farm owned by the bank. He gives one-third of his revenues from farming 20 acres in rural Mali to the bank. Table 40.9 gives the relationship between his effort and the revenues from the farm.

Table 40.9

Time (hours)	Total revenues
1	$18
2	$33
3	$45
4	$54
5	$60
6	$63

Mr. Droulig, when not sharecropping, can work in town and make $6 per hour.

a If he owned the farm himself and did not share revenues with the bank, how much would he work on the farm?
b How much does Mr. Droulig choose to work on the farm?

6 (Practice problem: analyzing sharecropping) Protecting farms against soil erosion is vital in the Sahel region of sub-Saharan Africa. The benefits of effort (in U.S. dollar equivalent) for a typical farm are given in Table 40.10. Assume that the marginal cost of effort is $100 and that sharecroppers pay one-half their yield in rent.

a Find the level of effort for owners.
b Find the level of effort for sharecroppers.

Table 40.10

Effort (days)	Benefits
1	$ 500
2	$ 900
3	$1,200
4	$1,400
5	$1,500
6	$1,500

Answers to Problems

2 The marginal benefits of the engineers in each sector are given in Table 40.11.

Table 40.11

Engineers	Roads	Marginal benefits	Mining	Marginal benefits
1	$200,000	$200,000	$100,000	$100,000
2	$280,000	$ 90,000	$190,000	$ 90,000
3	$350,000	$ 80,000	$270,000	$ 80,000
4	$410,000	$ 60,000	$330,000	$ 60,000
5	$450,000	$ 40,000	$360,000	$ 30,000
6	$480,000	$ 30,000	$380,000	$ 20,000
7	$500,000	$ 20,000	$400,000	$ 20,000
8	$500,000	$ 0	$400,000	$ 0

a   The efficient allocation is 4 engineers to each sector.

b   The market would allocate 4 to each sector with a wage of $60,000.

c   The total benefits if all are allocated to roads equal $500,000. At the efficient allocation, the total benefits equal $410,000 + $330,000 = $740,000. The waste is $740,000 – $500,000 = $240,000.

3   Table 40.12 gives the marginal benefits of irrigation water for each crop.

Table 40.12

Water	Cotton	Marginal benefit	Millet	Marginal benefit
1	$ 50	$50	$ 25	$25
2	$ 95	$45	$ 50	$25
3	$135	$40	$ 75	$25
4	$170	$35	$100	$25
5	$200	$30	$125	$25
6	$225	$25	$150	$25
7	$245	$20	$175	$25
8	$260	$15	$190	$15
9	$270	$10	$200	$10
10	$275	$ 5	$200	$ 0

a   The efficient allocation is 6 million gallons to cotton and 4 million to millet.

b   The market would allocate 6 million to cotton and 4 million to millet with a price equal to $25.

c   Using 8 million for cotton and 2 million for millet gives benefits equal to $260 + $50 = $310. The efficient allocation gives benefits equal to $225 + $100 = $325 million. The waste is $325 – $310 = $15.

5   Table 40.13 gives the full marginal benefits and the private marginal benefits of time.

Table 40.13

Time	Total revenues	Full marginal benefits	Private marginal benefits
1	$18	$18	$12
2	$33	$15	$10
3	$45	$12	$ 8
4	$54	$ 9	$ 6
5	$60	$ 6	$ 4
6	$63	$ 3	$ 2

a   The efficient amount of time is 5 hours.

b   Mr. Droulig works 4 hours each day.

6   Table 40.14 gives the owner's and sharecropper's marginal benefits of efforts to reduce soil erosion.

Table 40.14

Effort	Benefits	Owner's marginal benefits	Sharecropper's marginal benefits
1	$ 500	$500	$250
2	$ 900	$400	$200
3	$1,200	$300	$150
4	$1,400	$200	$100
5	$1,500	$100	$ 50
6	$1,500	$ 0	$ 0

a   The owner would devote 5 days.

b   The sharecropper would devote 4 days.